D1238470

CULTURE *in the* AMERICAN SOUTHWEST

Number Twelve

TARLETON STATE UNIVERSITY

Southwestern Studies in the Humanities

CULTURE
in the
AMERICAN
SOUTHWEST

The Earth, the Sky, the People

KEITH L. BRYANT, JR.

Texas A&M University Press

College Station

The paper used in this book meets the minimum
requirements of the American National Standard for Permanence
of Paper for Printed Library Materials, z39.48-1984.
Binding materials have been chosen for durability.

Portions of chapters 6 and 8 were previously published:

Copyright by the Western History Association. Reprinted by permission.
"Roman Temples, Glass Boxes, and Babylonian Deco: Art Museum Architecture
and the Cultural Maturation of the Southwest," *Western Historical Quarterly*
(February, 1991): 45–71.

Reprinted by permission of *Great Plains Quarterly,*
"The Art Museum as Personal Statement:
The Southwestern Experience," 9, no. 2
(spring, 1989): 100–117.

Library of Congress Cataloging-in-Publication Data

Bryant, Keith L., 1937–
Culture in the American Southwest : the earth, the sky, the people / Keith L. Bryant, Jr.
p. cm. — (Tarleton State University southwestern studies in the humanities ; no. 12)
Includes bibliographical references and index.
ISBN 0-89096-948-5 (cloth)
1. Indians of North America — Cultural assimilation — Southwest, New.   2.Indians of
North America — Southwest, New — Social life and customs.   3. Whites — Southwest, New —
Social life and customs.   4. Southwest, New — Cultural policy.   5. Southwest, New — Social
life and customs.   I. Title.   II. Series.
E78.S7 B78 2000
306'.0979 — dc21
00-044317

For

Jennifer and Craig and

in memory of "Bob"

They came of age in the Southwest.

CONTENTS

List of Illustrations, *ix*

Acknowledgments, *xi*

Introduction, *3*

Chapter 1. Cultures and Conquests, *13*

Chapter 2. The Importation of Anglo Culture, 1850–1900, *32*

Chapter 3. Cities and Culture, 1900–1920, *67*

Chapter 4. A Regional Culture Is Formulated, 1920–1940, *112*

Chapter 5. Nationalization of a Regional Culture, 1940–1960, *169*

Chapter 6. Institutional Culture/Creating Icons, 1960–1980, *214*

Chapter 7. A Renaissance with Many Voices, 1960–1980, *246*

Chapter 8. The Exportation of a Regional Culture, 1980–1995, *277*

Notes, *309*

Selected Bibliography, *359*

Index, *367*

ILLUSTRATIONS

1. Casa Grande, *15*

2. Mesa Verde, *17*

3. Decorated pipe bag, *18*

4. Taos Pueblo, *19*

5. Mission church, Salinas National Monument, New Mexico, *22*

6. Mission San Xavier del Bac, Arizona, *23*

7. Mission San Jose de Tumacacori, *24*

8. Church at Ranchos de Taos, New Mexico, *25*

9. Potter María Martinez, *28*

10. Bradbury Building, Los Angeles, *45*

11. "Four Horsemen of the Eucalypts," *59*

12. Mary Hunter Austin, *60*

13. Gamble House, Pasadena, California, *74*

14. Walter Dodge House, Los Angeles, *83*

15. "Prairie style" house, *84*

16. Mills Building, El Paso, *86*

17. *The Primitive Sculptor,* by E. I. Couse, *91*

18. *In Cattle Country,* by Herbert "Buck" Dunton, *93*

19. Huntington Library, San Marino, California, *99*

20. Willa Cather at Mesa Verde, 1915, *103*

21. Downtown Phoenix skyscrapers, *115*

22. Lawyers Title Building, Albuquerque, *117*

23. Taliesin West, Arizona, *119*

24. Boston Avenue Methodist Church, Tulsa, *120*

25. *Canon Synchromy (Orange),* by Stanton Macdonald-Wright, *128*

26. Oscar B. Jacobson and Kiowa artists, 1929, *129*

27. Mabel Dodge Luhan and Tony Luhan, *132*

28. D. H. Lawrence, Frieda Lawrence, and Witter Bynner, *134*

29. Alice Corbin Henderson and William Penhallow Henderson, *136*

30. Victor Higgins, *158*

31. *Erosion No. 2: Mother Earth Laid Bare,* by Alexandre Hogue, *164*

32. Lynn Riggs, *166*

33. Price Tower, Bartlesville, Oklahoma, *176*

34. Paul Horgan, *181*

35. Houston Museum of Fine Arts, *190*

36. Millicent Rogers, *192*

37. Marion Koogler McNay, *194*

38. McNay Museum, San Antonio, *195*

39. Philbrook Art Center, *196*

40. Nina Vance, *208*

41. City Hall, Tempe, Arizona, *220*

42. Citizens National Bank, Oklahoma City, *221*

43. Grady Gammage Auditorium, Arizona State University, *225*

44. Sir John Barbirolli and Miss Ima Jane Hogg, *227*

45. Amon Carter Museum of Art, Fort Worth, *235*

46. Kimbell Art Museum, Fort Worth, *236*

47. Velma Kimbell with Mr. and Mrs. Louis Kahn, *237*

48. Contemporary Arts Museum, Houston, *244*

49. *Vaquero,* by Luis Jimenez, *251*

50. *Southwest Pieta,* Luis Jimenez, *252*

51. Larry McMurtry, *269*

52. Skyscrapers in Tulsa, *278*

53. Downtown Austin, Texas, *283*

54. San Antonio Library, *284*

55. United Bank Tower, Tucson, *285*

56. Postmodern house, Albuquerque, *286*

57. The Menil Collection, Houston, *287*

58. Los Angeles Museum of Contemporary Art, *290*

59. Los Angeles County Museum of Art, *292*

60. San Antonio Museum of Art, *293*

61. Mark Medoff and Phyllis Frelich, *303*

62. Beverly Lowry, *306*

ACKNOWLEDGMENTS

As in any project of this magnitude, the author acquired significant debts to institutions and individuals. The University of Akron Research Committee provided travel funds, and the College of Arts and Sciences granted a Faculty Development Leave for 1995–96. At Texas A&M University, the Research Committee and the College of Liberal Arts supported the project with travel grants. Librarians, staff members, and volunteers at many libraries and archives sought fugitive materials and responded cheerfully to requests for arcane books, scrapbooks, clipping files, and manuscript boxes. Particularly helpful were individuals at the following institutions: the American History Center and the Harry Ransom Humanities Research Center at the University of Texas in Austin; the Archives of the Texas A&M University Library; the Western History Collection at the University of Oklahoma; the Oklahoma Historical Society; McFarland Library at the University of Tulsa; the Manuscript Collection of the Zimmermann Library of the University of New Mexico; the University of Arizona Library; the Library of Arizona State University; the Huntington Library; the San Diego Historical Society; and the University of Southern California Library. As usual, the staff of the Interlibrary Loan Department of Bierce Library of the University of Akron proved their skills in locating unusual requests for rare materials to be found only in the strangest repositories. To all of the above, an expression of thanks is due.

A special debt of gratitude is owed Jennifer L. Bryant and my wife, Margaret. The former's keen eye, sense of style, and copyediting skills made this a far better manuscript. Once again the latter demonstrated her ability to read hundreds of scrawled pages and convert them into a printed manuscript. And once again, she did so with grace, good humor, and enormous patience.

CULTURE
in the
AMERICAN
SOUTHWEST

Introduction

You can sense it looking out the car window. On Interstate 40 or 20 or 25, as on old Route 66, you know when you enter the Southwest. It's the sky; it's the land; it's the light. When you stop for gasoline it's the accents, the attire, and the attitudes that tell you the people are different. At 30,000 feet elevation you peer out the airplane window at an earth of vibrant colors—red, orange, yellow, gray, white, and sometimes, green. Landforms are sharp, steeply crested, and open spaces are marked with mesas standing like citadels of loneliness. Ranches and suburbs, reservations and cities—all are unified by a sky seemingly without end. Vast stretches of desert, snow-capped mountains, and canyons like deep gashes carved in the earth delight your emotions. Piñon pine forests, cactus, sagebrush, mesquite, ocotillo, and the short grass of the llano fight for the modest moisture brought by winds from the south and the west. Office workers in skyscrapers in Fort Worth and Oklahoma City observe the flat lands to the west intersecting with a far-distant horizon. A Hispanic family on the West Mesa of Albuquerque sits in its backyard and watches a sunrise over Sandia Peak. A teenage Navajo girl brings her sheep to a clear, cold pool, a spring that her family has visited for a hundred years. All are united by the land, brought together by a shared feeling for a region simultaneously beautiful, threatening, enchanting, stimulating, and hurtful. The Apache youth driving his pickup to a rodeo in Los Angeles County is part of this land. So is the retired military officer, pausing on a Sun City golf course to look at the mountains. The Hispanic children helping harvest chilies bond with the legacy of their ancestors. The earth and the sky form and shape the culture of the society of the region. This is the American Southwest.

The peoples of the Southwest share a regional consciousness, their topophilia. Theirs is a land of limitless expanse of light and color, a land of shapes and mass and volume seemingly in constant change. They have what the novelist Lawrence Durrell has called a "spirit of place." Southwesterners are aware of the land, aware that they have been and are being shaped by it. They respond to the stimuli of sky, light, and geography. The natural world, the environment, produces dreams and visions and transports the consciousness. The visionary landscape dwarfs human scale; it evokes memories and a desire to discover, to explore. Geography adds detail to myths and inspires creativity. The earth and the sky serve to link peoples from distinctly different cultures into a vibrant society in constant flux.[1]

Space and place are the shared components of the world in which we live. The physical environment influences our sense of proportion and generates an affection for the land. As the geographer Yi-Fu Tuan has written, "Space plus culture equals place." For humankind, "place is security, space is freedom: we are attached to one and long for the other."[2] A "place" is a part of the entire environment that has been embraced by human feelings. Concepts of place and space permeate the societies of Native Americans, Hispanics, and Anglos in the Southwest. The memory of the land and one's relationship to it are part of Navajo oral tradition, of Hispanic music, and of Anglo fiction and art. Site transforms humankind just as humans alter the landscape. The culture of the Southwest is the intersection of "spirit," "place," and "vision."[3]

The Southwest is a distinctive place in the minds of those who live there, though they strongly disagree about its precise geographical boundaries. It is the "spirit of place" that produces the sense of belonging, of being part of the region. *Genius loci* affects writers, artists, architects, and other cultural creators, but it also evokes a deep emotional response from West Texas farmers, Zuni jewelry makers, and Tucson barrio residents.[4] A regional domestic sociology emerges from an identity that is self-conscious and sensory driven. Regional symbols and myths unify disparate peoples just as concretely as the sky and the land.[5]

Awe-inspiring vistas and human isolation establish the relationship of the senses to the land. Speaking of the Southwest, the painter Georgia O'Keeffe contended, "One seems to have more sky than earth in one's world."[6] The vast landscape, the open sky, and the textures of the earth inspire the imagination and, in the nineteenth and much of the twentieth centuries, caused southwesterners to develop an overwhelming sense of optimism, to experiment, and to take risks. Opportunities for advancement and for positive change seem possible when the land itself appears unending, open, and challenging. Attachment to and identification with place establish a sense of regionalism.[7]

The southwestern landscape not only enables but also humbles the human spirit, forcing the inhabitants to accept a reduced relationship with the earth. Incredible light, natural grandeur, ancient peoples, romantic myths, and a geography at once beautiful and yet brutal thus molded the southwestern societies. Site effected a sense of participation, a feeling of belonging. In the Southwest, geography, landscape, sky, environment, scale, isolation, and space shaped human characteristics and collective personality, what the writer Paul Horgan called the "unselfconscious." Myth and reality blended to establish traditions that could be shared. That there is no direct relationship between historical facts and popular beliefs and images is a constant in the region.[8]

History, ethnicity, earth, and sky shaped a region and its peoples, producing characteristics identified as "southwestern." But those traits may not be the ones observed by outsiders. The aura of romantic space established a frame of mind, attitudes, and beliefs that permeated the societies. The Southwest became a place of intensive intercultural exchange where three traditions—Hispanic, Native American, and Anglo—reacted to and with each other as well as the environment.[9] Although "cultural regions" cannot be delineated by political boundaries, those who would define the term must approach geographical boundaries "with hat in hand."[10]

Ross Calvin, a thoughtful and sagacious resident of the Southwest, employed the notion of geographical determinism in his 1934 book *Sky Determines*. He emphasized the sky as the life source for the region's unique flora and fauna. By withholding moisture from the earth, the sky forced adaptation by all the inhabitants. The sky provided life but also freedom, silence, and majesty. A health-seeker in Silver City, New Mexico, Calvin echoed the writings of Mary Austin and Walter Prescott Webb on the impact of aridity on the residents of the region. A mixture of romanticism, observations, and impressions, Calvin's theme lacked scientific evidence, but it reflected southwesterners' feelings about their land.[11] The novelist Larry McMurtry's alter ego, Danny Deck, driving east of El Paso while returning to Texas from the literary jungles of California, mused: "It was the sky that was Texas, the sky that welcomed me back. . . . The sky was what I had been missing. . . . It had such depth and such spaciousness and such incredible compass, it took so much in and circled one with such a tremendous generous space that it was impossible not to feel more intensely with it above you."[12] This powerful geographical influence cannot be denied. It molds the regional culture.[13]

But where is the Southwest? If political boundaries are ineffectual in defining cultural parameters, what geographical contours can we use to fix this "sense of place"? The modern Southwest is a vast region located to the west and south of a line drawn from Houston up to Tulsa to Colorado Springs and westward to

Los Angeles. The southern boundary blurs along the political border with Mexico where Mexican, Hispanic, and Anglo cultures mingle, largely without distinction. Like the occupants, the boundaries are in constant flux. Just as the boundaries moved to include Houston after oil was discovered at nearby Spindletop in 1901, so too did petroleum smooth the way for Dallas, Tulsa, and Oklahoma City to enter the Southwest.[14] Defining the region by urban sites is not accidental. The Southwest has been and continues to be an urban society. The ancient Anasazi formed communal societies, as did the later Pueblo peoples. Santa Fe, Tucson, and El Paso predate the cities on the eastern seaboard by one hundred years. Native Americans, Hispanics, and Anglos swelled the populations of southwestern cities, where an institutionalized culture emerged.[15]

The Southwest is a region of increasing commonality, yet diversity continues. For example, Spanish has contributed to the language of all the people. Native American and Hispanic architecture flavor the cityscapes of the towns and urban places. Native American Presbyterian churches stand in the shadows of the bell towers of predominantly Hispanic Roman Catholic churches while glass cathedrals of fundamentalist Protestants dominate suburban southern California. The complexity of the culture alone clearly reveals that the region is not simply "a state of mind."[16]

The Southwest is what its residents perceive, their "mental maps." There is a broadly felt regional self-consciousness. This sense of regionalism has intensified in the twentieth century, reflecting the economic growth and maturation achieved in the past fifty years. Even though the sociologists Howard W. Odum and Harry Estill Moore saw the Southwest as a potential empire at the end of the Great Depression, it was, they contended, "the least American of all regions." The extraordinary diversity of peoples, the rapid urbanization, and the landscape set the Southwest apart.[17] And yet a substantial segment of the migration to the region, especially to parts of Oklahoma, New Mexico, Arizona, western Texas, and southern California, consisted of educated, upper-middle-class Anglo entrepreneurs and professionals with shared beliefs. They brought a sense of optimism, a willingness to experiment, and aggressive economic motivations that regional resources enhanced and the society enthroned. They served as dynamic catalytic agents abetted by German Jewish merchants and Hispanic business leaders.[18] As the writer Erna Fergusson noted in 1940: "The arid Southwest has always been too strong, too indomitable for most people. Those who can stand it have had to learn that man does not modify this country; it transforms him, deeply."[19] Those who came and stayed accepted the travails of the arid climate because of a belief in progress and a hope for eventual economic success. The region became a composite of peoples continually contesting each other for position and place. Fluidity among and between the peoples who occupied the space and shared in its identity led to the creation of a regional culture—a culture that became an ordering principle of the Southwest.[20]

The southwestern culture blends but does not homogenize three predominant societies: Native American, Hispanic, and Anglo. It contains almost 80 percent of the Native American population of the United States, with substantial numbers of Indians living in the cities of the region as well as on the reservations. The Native Americans are as much a part of Dallas as they are of northern Arizona or southwestern Oklahoma. In terms of Mexican population, Los Angeles is now the second-largest city in the world, behind only Mexico City. The traditional barrios of Tucson, San Antonio, and Albuquerque have been replicated in San Diego, Oklahoma City, Phoenix, Fort Worth, and Austin. The mythic view of and the romanticized notions about Native American and Hispanic cultures as pastoral have been transformed by the reality of "low-riders" on urban streets and freeways and "English spoken here" signs in retail shops.

Both Native Americans and Hispanics define the Southwest as their "homeland," a place that was forcibly occupied and is now "shared" with the Anglos. Native American religions, oral traditions, arts, and more recently, written literature emphasize the relationship of the people to their land. For Hispanics, the Southwest is "the lost land," a land conquered by the Anglos as a result of the Mexican Cession.[21] They have a clear geographical image of the Southwest, as well as an emotional sense of place, identity, and history. "Southwest" is an Anglo term, but Hispanics know what the word signifies. A desire to reclaim that space led to an invigorated Chicano movement in the 1960s and to the myth of Aztlán, an ancient Aztec homeland located in the Southwest. The Hispanic culture has made its mark on the regional image in language, architecture, folklore, and diet.[22]

In the twentieth century, even as the Southwest developed the strong characteristics that define the region, the social and economic elites, largely Anglo, sought to win recognition and approval from the East and Midwest for their cultural attainments. They tried to overcome a self-consciousness that suggested they were somehow culturally inferior because of where they lived. Paradoxically, the region sought both integration and separation, without recognition that the goals were contradictory. Although southwesterners wanted to demonstrate the distinctiveness of their region, they also wanted positive notice of their cultural achievements.[23] A dynamic tension emerged between those who sought to re-create a Western European culture of operas, symphonies, and classical theater and those who wanted to create original novels, plays, music, and dances based on regional themes and resources.

A "region" is an entity with distinct natural and cultural traits that distinguish the area from its neighbors. It may be occupied by dissimilar peoples who, though artificially brought together, have over time adapted to a common existence in which they instinctively feel themselves a part. The occupants establish a relationship with a place that sometimes overcomes ethnic, religious, and social differences. Regions are formed by dynamic processes and are continuously shaped by human culture. A shared history has accentuated the southwesterner's sense of belonging to the land. Recent events in the former Soviet Union, former Yugoslavia, and central Africa show that regionalism has not lost its vitality.[24] Certainly that is true of the American Southwest.

The peoples of the Southwest share a memory of personal experiences within the history of the region. Over time a collective past has linked this identity with the land. Navajo and Pueblo storytellers convey to their peoples a history that is at once geographical and religious. Modern Hispanic writers such as Rudolfo Anaya emphasize the relationship of Spanish-surnamed people to the land. Anglo artists, from the Taos romantics to the abstract expressionists of Los Angeles, joined people to place on their canvases. Although the residents of the Southwest have been a part of national history, their memories are deeply entwined in a regional identification that is in fact largely based on a created past.[25]

Nowhere is the regionalism of the Southwest more apparent than in its quest for cultural maturation. Western European cultural institutions and ideas arrived during the first conquest by the Spanish. In October, 1598, on the banks of the Río Bravo del Norte, a group of Spanish actors performed for Don Juan de Oñate and his settlers en route to Santa Fe. The troupe entertained the seven hundred colonists in a performance that predated the settlement of Virginia and Massachusetts.[26] These cultural ideas were strongly reinforced by the Anglo American invasions of the nineteenth century. "High culture" meant civilization, as well as intellectual and social acceptance. Bach fugues were played on stages above saloons; dramas by Shakespeare were performed by itinerant actors whose lines were quietly recited by audiences thoroughly familiar with the plays; chromo reproductions of paintings by Rembrandt and Reubens were hung on adobe walls. Social distinctions were few: the infrequency of artistic performances meant that merchants, doctors, lawyers, and their spouses sat next to miners, farmers, ranchers, laborers, and schoolteachers. Seats in smoky "opera houses" cost fifty cents for a padded chair, but for twenty-five cents or even a dime, you could stand in the back of the hall. Recitations, choral groups, and amateur plays followed the soldiers, surveyors, land agents, and U.S. marshals.[27]

The Anglos thus brought their cultural roots to the Southwest and replanted them immediately. Anglo settlers wanted to reestablish a culture that reflected the highest level of the society they had left. Traditional cultural symbols were enduring and structural and gave a sense of permanence, a feeling of security in a new land.[28] By the turn of the century, Anglos in the region had followed the national trend that redefined "high" culture and distinguished it from "low" as arbiters of taste determined what was to be respected. Definitions of cultural norms have been and continue to be in constant flux. Whereas Shakespeare was part of a common culture throughout most of the nineteenth century, his plays had become part of an elevated "high culture" by 1900. Southwesterners embraced the notion of culture as enrichment and intellectual nourishment and moved quickly to demonstrate their acceptance of these new national norms.[29] Rudimentary symphony orchestras, regional opera companies, and fledgling art museums graced the larger communities; touring theatrical companies slowly disappeared as local "little theaters" emerged.

Replication of a Western European culture might win recognition in the East, but regional authors, musicians, actors, architects, singers, artists, and dancers eventually decided not only to re-create but also to innovate. The new environment unleashed creative powers, and the fusion of elements in a new locale created a regional culture. By the late 1890s the newest arrivals in the Southwest had become creators of culture as well as consumers. Artists applied the techniques of impressionism to a landscape filled with pure light. Local writers produced novels and short stories descriptive of the land and its native populations. Though the result was initially more imitative than innovative, the increasing urbanization, growing economy, and continuing aspirations stimulated the creative juices of Native Americans, Hispanics, and Anglos alike. After World War II, economic maturation produced an environment that nurtured those aspirations. The dynamic forces released in the second half of the twentieth century made the Southwest an exporter as well as an importer of culture.[30]

It should be made clear that "popular culture" in the Southwest also helped shape a regional identification, as other scholars have shown. But the focus of this book is the high culture of music, art, architecture, literature, theater, and ballet. In music, the composer Roy Harris of Oklahoma is included but not the composer-singer Willie Nelson of Texas. The novelists Leslie Marmon Silko and N. Scott Momaday are high culture; Edna Ferber is not. Neither does "high culture" mean "Anglo culture," as the novels and short stories of Silko (Laguna) and Sandra Cisneros (Hispanic) attest. The art of Fritz Scholder (California Mission) and Allan Houser (Apache) found an audience in all three southwestern societies.

Although the leadership of the "highbrow" culture may have been upper or upper-middle class, its audience and patronage came from all parts of the society.

In the Southwest, Hispanics, Native Americans, and Anglos embraced elements of the emerging culture. Hispanic families in the barrios made financial sacrifices so that their children could learn to play the violin, cello, or viola, take private lessons, and attend performances by the symphony orchestra. The family listened to Bach and Mozart as well as Falla. Even the most casual observer at art museums and galleries, theaters, and concert halls in the region today can see audiences representing a broad range of society. Forms of the high arts attained mass popularity in the twentieth century as the exaggerated antithesis between the "worthy" and the "unworthy" blurred. Rigid, class-bound categories that had emerged in the late nineteenth century were abandoned as a shared public culture emerged.[31]

This cultural phenomenon was largely urban. The urban societies established by Native Americans and the patterns of the Spanish and Anglo conquests and settlements meant that there was no rolling frontier or line of settlement in the region but rather widely scattered population concentrations that emerged as towns and cities. Pueblos became missions, presidios, communities, and finally urban places. The pioneers of the Southwest—whether they were herders from Spain, Jewish merchants from Germany, Methodist missionaries from England, or railroad laborers from Italy—reestablished the culture of Western Europe at the same time that they constructed false-front stores and erected barbed-wire fences. There was no generational cultural lag. From the outset, Western Europeans who entered these settlements turned to their cultural roots for sustenance in the Southwest.[32]

Institutions of culture thus emerged with the process of urbanization. They provided the residents with a sense of community even as they gave access to music, theater, and art. Urban places offered a cultural life that was, from the beginning, diverse and colorful. Artists, musicians, and architects settled in towns thirsting for cultural outlets. The residents gave them patronage and applauded their contributions. Magazines brought news of artistic currents, drawings of new designs in architecture, and reviews of contemporary fiction and theater. Subscription libraries and bookstores could be found in places with only a few hundred residents. The coming of the railroad meant performances by touring opera and theatrical companies, often from Europe. When the English writer James Bryce visited the West in the 1880s, he noted the presence of an extended cultural life in what he called "the most American part of America." Bryce saw an urbanized society not unlike that of the eastern seaboard.[33] In less than half a century, the Anglo American southwesterners had transplanted a cultural heritage that flourished.

In this transplantation, women played a crucial, critical role. Again and again, the leaders in forming cultural institutions were women. Colonel Samuel Rosenbaum, a longtime member of the board of the Philadelphia Symphony Orchestra, once declared, "Give me six women and a bag of cookies, and a box of tea, and you will have a symphony orchestra."[34] The quip failed to acknowledge that women did much more than bake cookies and serve tea. In the Southwest they raised funds, hired halls, recruited conductors and musicians, and frequently played in the orchestras. They not only organized art exhibitions and founded museums but also painted and sculpted. Women designed buildings, wrote novels and short stories, and formed dance companies. It has been argued that in the East and Midwest, once women created cultural institutions, men replaced them on the boards of directors and relegated them to lesser roles. The experience of women in the Southwest was and is far different. Their role was often that of the general rather than the spear carrier in the drive to establish cultural institutions. They retained positions of leadership and set the tone for the institutions. Women pioneered in the theater — Margo Jones of Dallas and Nina Vance of Houston, for example. They joined major ballet companies, as did the Osage ballerinas from Oklahoma, and often retired as teachers of dance in the region. The critic John Mason Brown once declared, most inelegantly, "Women are the Typhoid Marys of American culture."[35] Women both recognized the need to create opportunities for artistic and literary expression and exercised their own talents as artists, writers, musicians, and designers. The culture of the modern Southwest is largely their work and their legacy.

From Houston to Los Angeles, from Tulsa to Tucson, the Southwest remains a unique region of the United States. It reflects the distinct contributions of three cultures. Anglos, Hispanics, and Native Americans have demonstrated the significance of interaction with the environment. They share a sense of place, a love for the land. This, then, is the story of the many peoples living across this dramatic landscape, under a vast blue sky, and of the culture they created.

CHAPTER I

Cultures & Conquests

By 200 B.C., settlers of the Basketmaker culture occupied caves in what is today the Four Corners area of northwestern New Mexico, establishing a permanent society based on agriculture. Within five centuries, these peoples had organized villages composed of "pit houses," circular units occupied by one or two families. They gradually moved into unit housing constructed above ground, structures known as *pueblos*. Large housing blocks, religious chambers, irrigated fields, intricate communication systems, and food distribution networks demarked the classical period of the Pueblo peoples, from A.D. 1100 to 1300. In size and construction techniques, both the cliff houses of Mesa Verde in southwestern Colorado and the "Great House" of Chaco Canyon in New Mexico demonstrate the emergence of a vibrant, highly sophisticated culture.[1] From the outset, these Pueblo peoples, known as the Anasazis, believed that their society, the earth, and the sky were one. Native Americans in the Southwest thus established cultures that reflected and interacted with the region, setting a pattern that was continued for over two millennia.

As the Pueblo culture reached a peak in terms of refinement, bands of Athapaskan-speaking Indians from western Canada migrated south into present northern New Mexico and Arizona. These newcomers, the Navajos or Dinehs, were hunters and gatherers but quickly adapted to the patterns of the Pueblos, becoming agriculturalists and settling along the verdant valleys of the Chama River and in the San Juan Basin. Their raids on the Pueblos introduced not only captives but also new food products, woven items, and decorated pottery. As the Navajos extended their raids to the east they contacted Plains tribes, and regular patterns of trade emerged. Game, buffalo hides, colored stones, feathers, and other goods became so highly valued that fighting was suspended during trade days. The Navajos established permanent settlements, began to weave cloth, and started to develop items that could be exchanged in their expanding and increasingly complex world.[2]

In the Mogollon Mountains of New Mexico and Arizona and along the Gila and Salt Rivers, other societies emerged almost simultaneously with the Pueblo peoples. The Mogollon and Hohokam cultures also erected large-scale buildings and created highly sophisticated arts, especially basketry and pottery. The Hohokams established agricultural villages of brush-and-mud huts scattered over a large area of central Arizona. They built more than 600 miles of canals, constructed ball courts, and perfected a distinctive buff-colored pottery with red designs. The Mogollon people expanded to the north and west, and by the thirteenth century many had been absorbed by the Pueblo culture. They left a legacy, however, of extraordinary decorative pottery. The Native American societies in the Southwest thus became diverse within a relatively brief period.[3]

While the Puebloan peoples extended their settlements south along the Rio Grande, other societies entered the region. The Yumas settled along the Colorado River in southwestern Arizona even as the Apaches occupied southern Arizona and New Mexico and then roamed far to the north and east. On the southern plains the Comanches, Arapahoes, and Cheyennes competed for buffalo, water, and trade goods. Hunters and gatherers, wanderers over vast areas, the Plains tribes interacted with the Sioux nations in the far north and later with the Navajos to the west. They too made the earth, the sky, and the environment the sources of their religious beliefs and the subjects of their arts.

Forming hundreds of societies scattered across a land of seemingly infinite geographical variety, the first occupants of the region developed similar attitudes about themselves and their place in the universe. The Pueblo peoples, for example, believed that the earth was square, that there were six sacred directions, and that the sky and the earth were deities. Their spirit world was filled with heroes and villains, but they believed that good triumphed over evil: warm south winds defeated cold north winds. An underlying force united all elements of an external world. Even before humankind arrived on the earth, an order had been established that served as a framework for all existence. The realities of that world consisted of deserts, rivers, lakes, mountains, animals, and plants. Colors and directions merged; east was white, and south was red. Animals and colors formed elements of fetishes and rituals, just as the lakes and mountains held the homes of the gods from which the people drew strength. These beliefs created harmony and order in Pueblo life and supported the integration of these symbols into their decorative arts and oral traditions.[4]

Architecture serves as a primary example of the ways in which Native Americans adapted to their environment and related to their view of the universe. In

FIGURE 1

*The builders of Casa Grande in central Arizona left no clues as to
the purpose of this massive structure. Author's collection.*

New Mexico and Arizona the warm, dry land of strong colors and bright light produced particular needs in terms of shelter. The sun seared rock or adobe walls throughout the day, and with warmth radiating from the earth at night, strong walls, narrow windows, and raised floors were required. The Indians built structures near sources of water and shade in places like Mesa Verde and Chaco Canyon. In central Arizona, around 1350, the Hohokams erected Casa Grande, a four-story earthen structure that possibly served as a ceremonial building or as an astrological observatory but that unquestionably showed their ability to create caliche structures far larger and more complex than simple brush-and-mud huts.

The Navajo and the Apache peoples developed hogans and "wikiups" in response to the climate and weather, turning to the land for materials. The hogan ("home place"), a one-room, six-sided structure heated by a central fireplace, was the core of Navajo mythology, the Blessingway. The hogan was a gift to the Navajos, whose oral traditions and music formed part of the Blessingway. After First Man and First Woman completed a journey through three underworlds, they met Talking God, who gave them the first hogan, shaped like Gobernador Knob Mountain in New Mexico. The hogan had four cornerposts — one made of white shell, one of turquoise, one of abalone, and one of obsidian, the four sacred minerals. The door of the hogan faced east, to meet the rising sun and to avoid the prevailing cold winds of the north and west. Talking God also provided the "female" hogan, a dome-roofed structure that resembled Huerfano Mountain. Hogans had to be purified periodically, since they provided shelter and, more important, harmony and beauty. Many hogan-blessing songs spoke to the relationship of the Navajos with their homes:

> Beauty extends from the surroundings of my hogan,
> it extends from the woman.
> Beauty radiates from it in every
> direction, so it does.[5]

The Papago and Pima peoples of Arizona used earth and water to build mud huts and constructed lodgings along watercourses and under trees as they sought shelter from the sun and the heat. Called the Ki, the houses of these descendants of the Hohokams were far smaller than Casa Grande but often shared the Casa Grande construction technique of stacking hand-shaped loaves of adobe. The Ki provided shelter in the winter, but in the heat of the summer the Pimas moved to arbors, called *ramadas* by the conquering Spanish.[6] Adaptation to the environment and the use of natural materials became constants in Native American architecture.

The residents of Mesa Verde used the topography of that immense monolith to create multistoried houses of stone and timber to shelter them from the sun and protect them from their enemies. Masonry buildings incorporated cool caves and smooth concave mesa walls overlooking steep canyons. Monumental houses, such as Pueblo Bonito, New Mexico, contained hundreds of rooms on several levels and appeared, at a distance, to be part of the rocky spires, canyons, and cliffs. The cliff dwellers constructed practical and efficient buildings that incorporated the concepts of mass and proportion. Within these gigantic structures they created paintings, textiles, and ceremonial arts. They embellished utilitarian objects with designs based on plants, animal life, and geometric shapes. At the height of the Puebloan culture, the decorative pottery of black-on-white

CULTURE *in the* AMERICAN SOUTHWEST

FIGURE 2

*The residents of Mesa Verde built multistoried structures of elaborate design
that reflected their relationship to the land. Author's collection.*

wares included intricate religious symbols. Not only architects and engineers,
the Pueblo peoples were also artists attuned to their environment.[7]

Plains tribes also created an architecture, a portable architecture. Kiowas,
Comanches, Cheyennes, Pawnees, and others used buffalo hides and pine poles
to form tipis. These shelters combined portability, strength, and ease of erection
with artistic enrichment. Bright red or white, the tipis were not perfect cones;
their builders deliberately placed a steeper rear side against the prevailing west
wind. The doorway, like that of the hogan, faced the rising sun. The tanned-
hide walls resisted rain and snow while offering a surface on which to paint
large figures and geometric forms. Dogs pulled the V-shaped travois; later the
introduction of horses led to much larger tipis with more decorative furnishings.[8] The designs on the tipi walls linked the Plains people to their environment.

Anasazi or Pueblo architecture evolved as builders sought to balance the
forces of nature, economic concerns, and a more complex mythology. Like their
Plains counterparts, Pueblos placed the back of the structure to the wind. They
added roofs and terraces of mud to the south to absorb heat in the winter

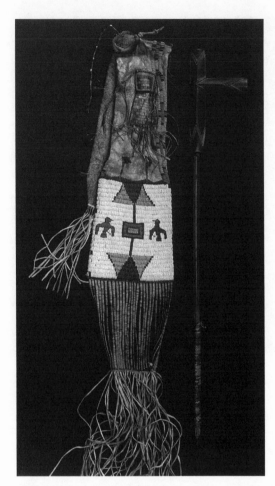

FIGURE 3
*The Plains Indians decorated
their pipes, pipe bags, and
medicine bags with the colors
and symbols of the earth. Courtesy
Woolaroc Museum, Bartlesville,
Oklahoma.*

months. Adobe walls beamed with timber protected the Pueblos from the sun, snow, and their enemies. Population growth led to multistoried buildings with windowless first floors, wooden ladders leading to the terraces, and timbered ceilings. Between the buildings, circular excavations, or kivas, became the center of religious life. Some of the "great kivas," enormous circular rooms, incorporated murals depicting the Pueblos and their religious beliefs. The larger pueblos, such as Montezuma's Castle in Arizona, showed a design skill as advanced as that being used in Europe at a similar time.[9] It is no wonder that the Spanish conquistadors stood in awe of these vast condominiums.

Beyond architecture, Native American culture in the Southwest centered on aspects of the daily lives of a diverse people. Their music, art, dances, and oral traditions drew from nature. Within a changing environment they incorporated the spirit drawn from their relationship with the land. In their oral traditions,

FIGURE 4

The design and building materials of Taos Pueblo linked its people to the land and the vast sky above. Author's collection.

the peoples gave the land meaning; the land became a cultural landscape. The Papagos spoke of an unfinished earth; darkness lay upon the waters, and from that nearly soundless place came life: a child was born. Pueblo high priests preserved the stories and prayers containing morals that doomed evil-doers. Birds, snakes, bears, and deer populated the stories as metaphors for the people. The oral tradition reinforced beliefs in the clan and the family and brought the Pueblos into harmony with the earth from which they sprang.[10]

Graphic arts repeated the tales and myths on kiva walls, sandstone cliffs, buffalo hides, clay pottery, jewelry, and fetishes. From the first appearance of humankind there were artists in the Southwest. Form, color, and design related to beliefs but often were decorative as well as religious and utilitarian. As early as A.D. 900, the Pueblos created pictographs composed of strange beings and imagined objects. Colors applied to rocks, walls, and ceilings — as well as scrape, gouged, or pecked surfaces — used shapes and textures that depicted the other world as well as daily life. Complex symbols evolved into linear constructions that covered walls and the surfaces of pottery and baskets. Mogollon potters, using red or black on white, brought together symbols of animals and plants with abstract geometric patterns in a highly stylized pottery. Carved wood and stone figures became religious objects as artisans incorporated stones, mica, beads, feathers, and hair into fetishes. Elaborate headdresses, tooled leather, and garments of skins carried forward the theme of oneness—the people, the land, and the sky. Paintings at the Jemez Pueblo kiva brought together the sun, the moon, and the stars with the pueblo as the center of the universe.[11] Neither clouds nor lightning could separate the people from the sky.

With the limited resources in the arid deserts of present-day southern California, Native Americans produced a culture that Anglo conquerors believed to be less sophisticated than that of the Pueblos. The tribes located closer to the Pacific Ocean dedicated their wealth to elaborate costumes and highly decorated baskets. In their pictographs, artists produced drawings of complex and decorative mythological figures. The almost total decimation of these peoples and their cultures by the first conquest, that of the Spaniards, left little record of their oral traditions or their graphic arts, however.[12]

The societies of the Native Americans of California, as well as other southwestern tribes, reflected their interrelationship with Mesoamerican peoples to the south. The idea of the village, dietary patterns, pottery and its decoration, and architectural concepts linked the Hohokam, Pueblo, and Mogollon peoples to those who occupied what is now northern Mexico. The Apaches and others moved freely through this area, transferring goods, captives, and ideas from one society to another.[13]

These exchanges led to jewelry that incorporated items from the material cultures of many peoples. The feathers of parrots and macaws became part of lengthy necklaces. Abalone shells, jet beads, and brightly colored stones joined by cordage decorated the necks, wrists, and clothes of the southwestern Indians. Hundreds of beads formed into necklaces ten or twelve feet long demonstrated the wealth and social position of the owner. Turquoise stones, geometric designs, and elements of bones decorated bow guards and religious objects alike. Once limited to carving wood, Plains artists traded for stones and shells that they used to produce a wider variety of objects. They decorated clothes and hides and created ornaments with which they danced. The earth provided artistic materials and inspiration; it was the main subject of the oral tradition, and it was the source of food and shelter.[14] The earth and the people were one. Not even the coming of the conquistadores and the disasters that followed severed that tie.

The Spanish conquests of the sixteenth, seventeenth, and eighteenth centuries first disrupted and then decimated the Native American societies of the Southwest. A new economic system and religion arrived, as did new diseases.

The conquerors also produced a new race as the first generation of mestizos was born. But just as the Spanish altered the lives of the Native Americans, the indigenous peoples challenged and changed the culture of their oppressors. Spanish military expeditions conquered the region for "God and the King" but soon fell under the influence of the land and its peoples. For example, as Francisco Vásquez de Coronado's soldiers, led by Hernando de Alvarado in 1540, passed beneath the Acoma Pueblo perched high on a mesa above the surrounding plain, they were stunned by its majesty and complexity. A troop under Pedro de Tovar roamed the lands of the Hopis and marveled at the size and construction techniques of their buildings. Alvarado also visited the Pecos Pueblo, with its four-story buildings of adobe, an architectural style that Spanish settlers would eventually emulate. The Spanish brought new fruit trees and vegetable crops, but they also discovered and subsequently cultivated the corn, beans, and squash of the Native Americans.[15] The earth and the sky soon dominated the Spanish just as they had the first settlers of the region.

Spanish colonists moved across the Rio Grande into present Texas and New Mexico while priests created missions in southern Arizona and California. The sites of ancient pueblos became Hispanic communities: Santa Fe in 1609, El Paso in 1659, Albuquerque in 1706, and Tucson in 1763. Near watercourses, the settlers established farms and ranches in the wake of Jesuit and Franciscan missionaries, who entered the pueblos preaching about a singular God who, they hoped, would replace the deities of the Indians. The colonists built houses of adobe not unlike those of their rapidly displaced neighbors. They took into account the climate, weather, water supplies, soil fertility, and rainfall in considering not only the structures they built but also the crops and trees they planted.[16] Adaptation and adoption formulated a society far removed from Spain, and even from Mexico City.

Missionaries brought saints, bells, chapels, and cloisters to the Southwest, but they too saw the advantages of adopting aspects of the Native American societies. Saving souls meant organizing agricultural production, of both old and new crops, and restructuring housing near the chapel so that workers could be present to build large churches. Massive edifices made of adobe or stone walls four feet thick rose above the pueblos even as the local populations declined, riddled with diseases and frequently overworked. Adobe, timber, and stone in the churches of New Mexico formed simple, undecorated exterior walls of flat surfaces. In California and Arizona the church fathers produced complex, rectilinear designs with vaults, domes, arches of cut stone, and substantial bell towers. Ornate inside and out, these cathedrals of the desert blended the tradi-

FIGURE 5

Mission churches, such as those at the Salinas National Monument in New Mexico, rose above ancient pueblos, combining European styles and native materials. Author's collection.

tions of Iberia with the architecture of the pueblos.[17] The friars in California converted hunters and gatherers to Catholicism and subsumed the indigenous architectural materials to their own needs.

In the Salinas Valley of central New Mexico, the world of the Pueblos changed dramatically as monumental churches physically overwhelmed the villages. San Gregorio de Abó, with its unusual buttresses, could be seen for miles rising above the plain. At San Buenaventura in Gran Quivira and at Quarai's Nuestra Señora de la Purísima Concepción de Cuaral, priests combined a European heritage with native materials and labor to produce churches that symbolized the presence of God and the might of the Spanish conquerors.[18]

In the Sonoran desert home of the Papago peoples, priests and native laborers collaborated on San Xavier del Bac, a Spanish Renaissance and Churrigueresque confection. Blindingly white under the relentless sun, the burned brick walls covered with lime supported high arches, domes, and bell towers with octagonal and arcaded belfries. Founded in 1692 by Father Eusebio Kino, San Xavier rose above the valley as a monument to the Spanish Baroque and to Byzantine domes. Papago laborers, threatened constantly by Apache raiders, completed the building in 1797, but unknown artisans continued to work in the interior, painting lavish religious scenes on the walls of the church. In silver and gold leaf,

CULTURE *in the* AMERICAN SOUTHWEST

FIGURE 6

*"The White Dove of the Desert," Mission San Xavier del Bac near Tucson, Arizona,
is a symphony of domes, carvings, arches, and flying buttresses. Author's collection.*

vermilion and Prussian blue, the brightly colored frescoes conveyed images of
the Holy Family to Papago and Pima worshipers.[19]

Only a few miles to the south at Tumacacori, Jesuit and later Franciscan
priests directed Pima workers who erected a church more like those of New
Mexico. A plainer facade of painted lime plaster and arches of adobe bricks suggested a simpler God. Ponderosa pine timbers, hauled laboriously from the
Santa Rita Mountains, supported the high ceiling. Unlike its spectacular neighbor to the north, San José de Tumacacori, with its massive adobe walls and
arcaded corridors, merged into the surrounding landscape.[20]

From the Rio Grande to Santa Barbara, the Catholic fathers and native workers and artisans fashioned new architectural styles. The outbuildings used as con-
vents, residences, and storage facilities embraced the one-story adobe of the

FIGURE 7
Though never completed, Mission San Jose de Tumacacori demonstrates the
tenacity of its Catholic priests and Pima workers. Author's collection.

pueblos. Thick walls, narrow windows, patios, and plazas descended directly
from the indigenous style and yet were perfectly compatible with the Iberian
architectural heritage of the priests. The colonists who followed the church fathers copied these models on a simpler scale, as did the secular officials who built
"palaces" for the governors in San Antonio, Tucson, and Santa Fe. Although the
Pueblos of New Mexico resisted their conquerors in a bloody revolution in 1680,
the patterns established before the revolt continued with the reconquest that
followed. New missions rose on the ashes of the old, the Roman Catholic God
and the Sky Gods of the Pueblos coexisted or merged, and the dances of the
Pueblo peoples combined elements of a High Mass with the Rain Dance.[21] A
cultural amalgamation occurred on the dusty plazas in the heart of the pueblos.

Even as the Franciscan fathers directed ever-declining flocks, colonists ex-

CULTURE *in the* AMERICAN SOUTHWEST

FIGURE 8
Georgia O'Keeffe's paintings made the rear of the church at
Ranchos de Taos, New Mexico, famous. Author's collection.

panded their landholdings across the region. Young male Hispanics, seeking
wealth and adventure, found wives and concubines among Native American
women. Mixed-blood children and grandchildren inherited two cultures and
would, within three generations, become the dominant force in the society. They
expanded herds of cows and sheep brought from Spain to Mexico and then to
the Southwest. The horses they traded or lost transformed the lives of the Plains
Indians, who gained mobility and increased their material possessions, now
more easily transported. Trade goods brought or acquired by the Hispanic settlers included metal-working tools, santos, carved vigas and lintels, furniture,
and leather-working equipment. Artisans followed the farmers and ranchers,
painting two-dimensional portraits, decorating plastered walls, and carving saints
for niches around the family altar.[22]

In the province of Texas, the Hispanic settlers built towns of one-story stone
houses and shops around military plazas. *Empresarios* constructed more elaborate
homes on their extensive holdings, sometimes adding red-tile roofs and arched
porches to shade the thick walls. Settlers pushed north and east, clashing with
the Comanches and Kiowas now roaming the province on horseback, attacking
those encroaching on their domain. The colonists named rivers and creeks, la-
beled landforms, and established towns with Hispanic roots. Words such as
mesa, sierra, canyon, and *rio* were followed by terms such as *remuda, rancho, som-*

brero, corral, and *poncho.* Like their counterparts in California and New Mexico, the settlers of Texas gave a patina and language to the region even as they learned to respect their new environment.[23]

The architecture of the Hispanic settlers spread north into present-day Colorado after the Mexican-American War as farmers occupied the river valleys. Small adobe buildings around a plaza appeared as early as 1851 in the village of San Luis. Newly established agricultural villages reproduced the society of the Rio Grande valley. Where the danger of raids by Cheyennes or Comanches existed, largely east of the Sangre de Cristo Mountains, the villages took on the character of military posts, with windows and doors opening only on the plaza and with solid walls facing the exterior. The destruction of earlier settlements in 1833, 1843, and 1846 meant that only the most intrepid occupied the area, but farmers, herders, and traders accepted the risks. They brought to their villages wood carvings, decorated-tin picture frames, and traditional arts and crafts largely religious in subject matter.[24] Hispanic culture expanded across the region, permanently altering the landscape.

The Spanish conquest shattered the lives of the indigenous peoples. Thousands of years of accumulated culture collided with a society that possessed powerful weapons of war and thought. The Spanish introduced metal-working technology that altered the crafting of jewelry; herds of sheep provided wool that revolutionized the production of textiles; and pottery, both as a religious and as a secular object, became a source of income. The Pueblo peoples, and later the Apaches and Navajos, roamed a vast area bartering shells, feathers, and skins for blankets and jewelry. The Pueblo men wove cloth from plant fibers, and the women threw pots and wove baskets. Among the Navajos, women were the weavers, producing a surplus that could be traded. The introduction of sheep, cattle, and new technologies led to expanded and differentiated art forms.[25]

Mogollon and Anasazi peoples had produced jewelry of mica, turquoise, jet, bone, and stone for at least a millennium before the conquest, but new materials transformed indigenous cultures and arts. Spanish soldiers carried weapons of iron and steel and wore crucifixes of silver and gold. The Native Americans marveled at these metals and slowly began to obtain objects ranging from iron pots to coins, axes, and other tools. Navajo iron workers learned to replicate Spanish and later Anglo American tools, but not until the 1850s did silversmithing enter the Indian orbit. In 1850 or 1851 a Navajo iron worker, Atsídí Sani, became the first silversmith of his tribe. He then taught others during the incarceration of the Navajos at Fort Sumner from 1863 to 1868. After their return to the reservation, the smiths produced rings, buttons, earrings, and belts of metal disks strung on leather. These "concho belts" soon incorporated larger silver pieces of

CULTURE *in the* AMERICAN SOUTHWEST

intricate design. The Navajos acquired skills in filing, engraving, and scratching and developed their own methods for stamping and punching. They set the silver with turquoise and other stones, creating medallions, necklaces, pendants, and dress ornaments. The artists produced jewelry that was strong, simple in design, symmetrical, and pure in materials. They also created a market for their work. By 1900 the demand for Navajo and Zuni silver had expanded from a few tourists to shops and stores across the country. The Native Americans exported jewelry based on designs over a thousand years old.[26] Silver squash blossom necklaces worn over silk dresses designed by Worth soon graced the salons of New York City.

The Pueblo potters also found a market for their jars, bowls, and plates. The domestic water containers, ollas, and storage jars were generally too large for use beyond the home, but smaller vessels could be sold to tourists, and a domestic product became a commercial item. The coming of the railroad in the 1880s expanded the market. Initially, this pottery was largely gaudy curio pieces. After 1900, skilled potters such as the Hopis Nampeyo and Lesou and the San Ildefonsans María and Julián Martinez, encouraged by the Fred Harvey Company, perfected techniques that allowed for smooth surfaces and for etched designs based on potsherds of the ancients. Birds, deer, bears, turtles, and mythological figures appeared on bowls and plates. Geometric designs from the Mimbres pottery of the Mogollon region provided yet another motif. As the commercial market expanded, each Pueblo specialized in the use of particular clays or finishes. White clays at Acoma, Laguna, Zuni, and Isleta produced pottery that, with black decorations, recalled Mimbres and Hohokam wares. Blackware from Santa Clara and San Ildefonso, produced with the Martinez techniques, found ready buyers at the Fred Harvey shops and along the platforms of the Santa Fe Railroad station in Albuquerque. Bold geometric scratched designs from Santa Clara and figures from Cochiti, especially storytellers, joined the flow of pottery entering the marketplace.[27]

The transformation of Navajo textiles began with the acquisition of sheep in the seventeenth century. The production of woolen textiles based on ancient designs underwent several significant changes. Some Pueblo weavers joined the Navajos after the revolt of 1680, bringing with them not only their own designs and weaving techniques but also concepts acquired from Hispanic artisans. Thus the Navajos added wool to cotton and other fibers as a medium and were exposed to nontraditional design elements. Navajo artisans invented new looms to weave cloth and blankets much more rapidly. Large herds of sheep produced wool even as the weavers found and developed beautiful and more durable dyes. Simple patterns became more complex with the addition of colors. Each weaver

FIGURE 9

Famed pueblo potter María Martinez helped to create a market for clay vessels with roots in the culture of the Anasazis. Western History Collection, University of Oklahoma Libraries.

developed personal designs, knowing that she was a direct descendant of Spider Woman who had taught weaving on a loom constructed under the direction of Spider Man. Myths and the Blessingway brought inspiration to the weavers.[28]

Responding to the marketplace, the Navajos largely abandoned the weaving of cloth by the 1890s. They could not compete with cheap, machine-produced fabrics. Production shifted almost entirely to blankets, called "rugs" by the tourists, and with the introduction of aniline dyes, the blankets became even more colorful. The long wool of the churro sheep, spun and then woven on upright looms, produced strong, durable blankets. Working without preliminary sketches, the weavers turned to the Yei, rectangular god figures, for inspiration or to the Yeibchei, human dancers dressed as Yei. Borders often incorporated a spirit trail that allowed the good spirits of the blanket to escape; the weaver could then produce yet another quality blanket. The blankets that were traded at posts near the reservations, or sold to Fred Harvey agents, contained designs that Spider Woman had taught the Navajos. She told the people to weave using sky, earth, sun rays, and lightning as raw materials, and they did. Blankets woven from the bottom up grew out of the earth. A blanket draped around the body symbolized all of the earth and its spirits rendered in a physical form.[29] The Navajos wrapped themselves in their beliefs and their land.

Both the Spanish and then the Anglo conquests transformed Indian painting in terms of methods and techniques, but like the Navajo blankets, the subject matter of the artists remained largely unchanged. Painting among southwestern Indians had achieved a high level of sophistication long before the Spanish arrived. It served as a vital element in ceremonies and rituals and helped maintain harmony with nature. The Indian artists borrowed from each other — Navajo sandpainting evolved from contacts with the Pueblos — during the Spanish conquest. Anasazi wall paintings, part of the petroglyphic tradition, differed substantially from those the Navajos produced centuries later. More significantly, by the 1850s and 1860s Anglo teachers, missionaries, and federal agents exposed young painters to the traditions of western European art. Given watercolors and oil paints in a wide range of colors, budding Indian painters altered the idea of art as ceremony and ritual and moved beyond the styles of their ancestors. They also entered the commercial market with work that was three dimensional in concept, brightly colored, and broader in subject matter. By 1900 Indian painters found a market for pictures acceptable to an Anglo aesthetic. Navajo, Hopi, and Pueblo artists, largely males, adjusted to the Anglo culture, but many of their paintings depended on subject matter drawn from the wall and sand painters of old.[30]

Hispanic weavers, tinsmiths, and wood-carvers likewise found a new market for their arts and crafts, but one that required changes in their traditional modes. Weaving played a central economic role among the Hispanic families living in the Rio Grande valley. By 1790, one-third of the heads of households in Albuquerque were weavers. Men and women sheared, carded, spun, and wove at treadle looms. Homespun (sabanilla) for clothes, blankets (fresadas), and carpets (jergas) poured from their looms. The coming of the railroad, which brought cheap, machine-made textiles, doomed the production of cloth, but the weaving of blankets continued, especially in the northern New Mexico villages such as Chimayo. There, banded blankets, some of the Saltillo style of Mexico, continued in production, using both natural and aniline dyes.[31]

Tinsmithing developed after 1840 when the metal arrived in the Santa Fe Trail trade or was brought in by the U.S. Army. Tinplate, pure tin coated on iron or steel, required only simple tools, and the artisans shaped functional objects in a variety of decorative motifs. Picture frames, candleholders, lanterns, chandeliers, and religious articles flowed from workshops in small villages. The coming of kerosene lamps, and later electricity, terminated much of the commercial market, however, leaving only a handful of smiths in remote villages.[32]

The Anglo conquest played havoc with Hispanic folk arts. The demand for carved religious figures *(santos)* and altar screens *(retablos)* declined. *Bultos,* sculptures of saints, found little commercial appeal among the largely Protestant Anglos. *Santerros* ("saint-makers") depended on the faithful of the villages and small parish churches as a market for their output. The traditional wood carving that had developed around Cordova, New Mexico, all but died out, though some carvers turned to secular objects, usually furniture, that could be sold to the Anglos.[33]

The Hispanic people fought to preserve their culture. Grandparents and parents in Hispanic households passed to their grandchildren and children a rich oral tradition that linked the generations and provided needed continuity in the midst of rapid change. The printing press did not arrive in New Mexico until 1834, leaving the settlers little choice but to supplement their meager holdings of books with a strong oral tradition. The *cuentos* — stories, folklore, legends, and myths — gave life to the spirit of the people. Storytellers transmitted historical narratives and tales to delight and to instruct their families. Peninsular *cuentos* came with the Spanish colonists, who then expanded this literature on the frontiers of New Spain. In California, Texas, New Mexico, and Arizona, the storytellers kept the legends and myths alive even as they created entirely new *cuentos.* These stories encompassed colonial experiences and focused on the contours of the earth, plants, animals, and birds. Tales hundreds of years old received new settings and characters, but the emphasis on family, tradition, and the relationship to the land remained constant.[34]

The tales of the storytellers reinforced and influenced Hispanic music and theater. The colonists from Iberia brought a love of music and drama. Folk songs and plays, centuries old, were part of the Hispanic cultural heritage. Roman Catholic fathers introduced music at the missions and, using homemade instruments, formed orchestras. While the mission choirs and musicians sang and played hymns and church music, the orchestras performed fandangos and other secular songs. In 1833, Mexican law secularized mission lands, and the Indians of California abandoned the churches, but they took their musical training back to the villages and pueblos. When the Hispanic settlers arrived, they brought a legacy of music and theater that continued the earlier work of the priests and missionaries.

The colonists performed dances, such as El Jarabe Tapatía, a dance drama, and sang songs about work and play. Much of the music came from the Canary Islands, the former home of many settlers, but their guitars, flutes, and violins produced a wide range of Iberian folk music. Larger villages organized bands to play at dances, and creative musicians adapted Spanish tunes to lyrics about the

CULTURE *in the* AMERICAN SOUTHWEST

Southwest and their daily lives. San Antonio, El Paso, Santa Fe, and Tucson saw a variety of musical performances, ranging from boys' choirs of the church to secular music brought from Iberia.[35]

Hispanic culture before the Anglo conquest embraced an Iberian heritage, but it soon developed new expressions. Festivals and fiestas often included dramatic religious plays, particularly on holy days. The principals in these productions might also perform secular dramas on weekday evenings. As communities grew, more settlers with trained voices arrived, and concerts became part of the culture. Spanish theater of the sixteenth and seventeenth centuries had rivaled that of Elizabethan England, and copies of plays from that era came to the far-flung outposts of New Spain. The colonists performed *Los Cristianos y los Moros,* a drama of the battles between the Christians and the Moors, as well as *Los Pastores* and *Los Tres Reyos Magos,* Christmas folk plays.[36] Native Americans witnessed these dramas, with some even participating in the religious and secular plays, and incorporated these Iberian elements into their own oral traditions.

The Native American and Hispanic cultures converged in the Southwest. The purity of both societies was lost as they mingled. Hispanics brought traditions tempered by contacts with the Moslem world and with other Europeans. The settlers of the eighteenth and nineteenth centuries, coming from Mexico, reflected contacts with Mesoamerican peoples. From the time of Coronado's expedition until the Mexican-American War, Native Americans and Hispanics blended to produce a society largely mestizo in biological and cultural terms. In the second conquest, Anglo Americans expressed shock at this blending, which appeared to them to violate the laws of nature. The depth of this Hispanophobia reinforced racist feelings that overlooked the rich cultural attributes that had resulted.[37] Ironically, some Native Americans withstood the impact of both conquests, maintained their culture, resisted Christianity, and continued their oral traditions, rituals, and ceremonies. The onslaught of the Anglo Americans between the 1840s and the 1890s further transformed the region, but the Native American and Hispanic cultures rejected total amalgamation and assimilation. Life in an often harsh land taught the lesson that preservation of one's culture was a key to the survival of family and self. Thus the peoples endured.

CHAPTER 2

The Importation of Anglo Culture

1850–1900

Between the end of the Mexican-American War and the ushering in of the twentieth century, the Southwest witnessed a rapid transformation. A region with a relatively small population became interlaced by a network of cities. Villages, such as Los Angeles, became major urban centers, as did towns like San Antonio, Houston, and Dallas. Places that had barely existed as settlements became instant cities—Tulsa, Oklahoma City, and Phoenix, for example. Railroads brought economic change and hundreds of thousands of new residents drawn largely from the Midwest. The middle- and upper-middle-class Anglo Americans brought copies of Shakespeare's plays, lines of which they could recite at length. Pianos and sheet music for Mozart, Bach, and Handel went west, as did European and American novels and collections of poetry. Artists brought oils, easels, pastels, sketchbooks, and a wide range of styles. Itinerant architects with plan books and their own ideas found clients ready to construct new homes, commercial buildings, schools, and churches. Drawing from the cultural roots of western Europe, the Anglo Americans sought to re-create a society based on the one they had left behind. Little did they realize how quickly that would occur or how rapidly those cultural attributes would be altered by the people they encountered and the land they occupied.

Although some immigrants moved to the region to establish farms and ranches, most Anglo Americans came from cities and towns and settled in an urban Southwest. Although the region had no major cities in 1850, the vast influx of settlers soon created large urban places.[1] Some of the established communities, such as El Paso, Tucson, and Santa Fe, lagged behind the rise of other towns, but some, such as San Antonio, blossomed. A village of 3,488 in 1850, San Antonio claimed 12,256 people in 1870. The railroad arrived in 1876, and the population rose to 37,673 by 1890 and to 53,321 by the turn of the century.[2] Street signs, largely in Spanish, now included English, German, and French wording. Except for Galveston, Texas boasted nothing more than small towns in 1850: Houston was a village of 2,396 people and Austin a settlement of 629. As late as 1880, none of the major cities of the South could be found in Texas, but by 1900, three of the twelve largest urban centers in that census district were San Antonio, Houston, and Dallas. As early as the 1860s, urban places dominated the Lone Star State economically and socially; they were sources of capital and culture.[3]

The dramatic changes that occurred between 1860 and 1900 can also be seen in California, where an agriculturally centered economy based on the production of wheat and fruit crops, as well as ranching, became an industrially oriented urban economy shortly after 1900. Petroleum, manufacturing, food processing, and the film industry reshaped the economy of southern California. The state, with only 310,000 people in 1860, could boast one of the nation's fastest-growing cities by the end of the century. A farm village of 4,385 in the year before the Civil War began, Los Angeles swelled to 50,395 in 1890 after acquiring its second railroad. Los Angeleños who welcomed the new century numbered 102,000. The census of 1850 said Los Angeles had no newspaper, hospital, college, library, public school, or Protestant church, but by the end of the 1890s it had all those elements of society as well as opera and theatrical performances, a budding symphony, and multistoried buildings of experimental design. Los Angeles came to dominate southern California and much of Arizona and Nevada.[4]

Not all of the urban growth of the period occurred in major centers. Smaller cities and larger towns soon dotted the region. By 1900 El Paso boasted a population of nearly 16,000. Albuquerque with 6,238, Tucson with 7,531, and Phoenix with 5,544 lagged behind the regional growth rate, however.[5] Some communities nearly died in the era, San Diego being a prime example. A massive real estate boom in the 1880s saw the population of San Diego swell from 2,600 at the outset of the decade to an estimated 40,000 by 1886. Then the boom went bust, and San Diego could claim only 16,000 in 1890 and slightly more than 17,000 in 1900. Although San Diego suffered from serious economic travails in these years, the residents continued to frequent the opera and the theater and supported artists, musicians, and architects.[6]

By the 1890s, urban institutions dominated the society of the Southwest. A thirst for a dynamic cultural life reproduced the attributes of midwestern and eastern cities. In their physical manifestations, southwestern urban places resembled their eastern counterparts. Measures of economic success suggested that the gap between the urban and the rural populations in the region was substantially greater than that which existed in the Midwest and the Northeast. But in terms of diversity of peoples, the cities of the Southwest were as much a polyglot as urban centers in the rest of the nation.

Urban places before the Anglo American conquest consisted largely of Hispanics and a few Native Americans. In San Antonio, German immigrants and a few French settlers provided ethnic diversity. German Jews in Galveston, Italian farmers in southern California, and Irish railroad builders added other voices to the regional population. An influx of immigrants after the 1860s brought greater diversity. Czechs, Bohemians, and Moravians settled in central Texas, and some of the younger people drifted to the cities. Galveston needed consuls from a dozen countries to represent the waves of immigrants using that port as an entrepôt. The expanding rail system offered access to interior communities, producing ethnically mixed populations in Dallas, Albuquerque, and Fort Worth. Hispanics continued to migrate north from Mexico, and small numbers of African Americans moved westward into Texas towns and cities.[7] The U.S. Census Bureau could hardly keep up with these demographic changes.

In some communities the foreign born represented 20 to 40 percent of the population, but that proportion began to decline in the 1890s as massive numbers of Anglo Americans entered the region. Whereas earlier migrants tended to be single young men, now families, indeed extended families, came to the Southwest. They entered the mercantile trade, opened banks, established professional practices, bought and sold real estate, promoted tourism and facilities for tourists, and encouraged the farmers and ranchers in the hinterlands. The Anglos pushed aside Hispanic businesspeople in many instances. They exhibited aggressive economic behavior driven by a strong sense of superiority and destiny. Self-confident, optimistic, and ambitious, the Anglos took risks, innovated, and frequently failed, but they soon dominated the economy and the society.[8]

Wherever economic and social momentum failed to follow that pattern, Hispanics maintained a significant presence as community leaders. In Arizona, New Mexico, and the Rio Grande valley of Texas, merchants and professionals kept the Hispanic communities vibrant. The production of cotton, wool, vegetables, meat, and citrus provided economic support. Hispanic business figures maintained strong alliances with Mexican firms in the decades before the revolution in Mexico in 1910. A prosperous minority, the *ricos* represented an elite that successfully competed with the first wave of Anglo settlers. Tucson's bicultural community typified this phase of urban development, but the town soon fell behind a far more aggressive Phoenix. The arrival of a second railroad in 1895 stimulated the development of the Salt River valley, and the largely Anglo Phoenix soon replaced Tucson as the territory's largest urban center. Hispanic communities, under great social and economic pressure, frequently turned to their cultural roots for sustenance, especially for music and the theater.[9] Paradoxically, the threats represented by the Anglo newcomers stimulated cultural activities among Hispanic peoples.

By 1900 the Southwest had acquired cities and towns and the veneer of an imported culture. Las Vegas in New Mexico Territory, Guthrie in Oklahoma Territory, and Phoenix in Arizona Territory each had more than 5,000 people, as well as opera houses, musical organizations, and multistoried buildings of eclectic Victorian styles. Trading centers, seats of government, and homes to cultural institutions, such places attracted swarms of settlers. In larger cities such as Houston, cultural elites emerged among the economically successful.[10] Driven by a sense of noblesse oblige and a desire for both external and local recognition, they formed cultural institutions that emulated those of the East and Midwest. Still, much of the region remained in a raw state well into the Gay Nineties. On March 29, 1882, the *Tombstone Epitaph* of Arizona Territory reported a desperate gunfight in which a "good man" died, as did two cowboy rustlers. However, the newspaper also announced that a dancing school would soon open at Turnverein Hall.[11] Observers who visited the Southwest extolled its cultural achievements.

Writers and journalists, spurred by books and articles about the region, took advantage of the new rail lines and flocked to the Southwest. In the 1890s, the young novelist and short-story writer Stephen Crane found Texas not so different from the rest of the nation; the East had invaded the West.[12] Obviously, the Southwest was catching up with the rest of the nation. In 1830 the intrepid Josiah Gregg had reported, "There is no part of the civilized globe, perhaps, where the arts have been so much neglected."[13] But some fifty years later the critic Charles H. Shinn observed, "There is the surprise of finding a civilization far less crude, a state of society far less wild, than the almost invariable preconception." The settlements in California embodied a purely commercial civilization, Shinn declared, for the state was "in almost every respect an intensification of the American spirit."[14] The English journalist James Bryce echoed that sentiment in 1889: "What America is to Europe, what Western America is to Eastern, that is California to the other Western states."[15] Bryce added, "For the West is the most American part of America, that is to say the part where those features which distinguish America from Europe came out in the strongest relief."[16] Nearly four decades later, in a subsequent edition of his narrative, Bryce left the statement intact. Caught up in an Anglo American sense of destiny and a belief in the superiority of American society, Josiah Strong extolled the West as embodying the virtues of the nation. A minister and propagandist, Strong wrote in 1885: "The time will doubtless come when a majority of the great cities of the country will be west of the Mississippi. This will result naturally from the greater eventual population of the West."[17] Many southwesterners shared that vision in 1900 and saw not only great cities but centers of civilization and culture.

The physical evolution of settled places revealed the impact of the second conquest as Anglo Americans imported new architectural styles and building materials. The Spanish-influenced modes of design and construction were quickly supplanted, but elements of past styles remained, if only because the environment dictated adaptation. Spanish urban designs in New Mexico centered on plazas surrounded by one-story houses of adobe. In California and New Mexico, the adobe homes often had dirt or clay floors, and glass windows were rare. New Mexico women moved the kitchen to a room on the north side of the house in the spring and to a southern room in the fall to minimize the heat in the summer and to maximize the warmth in winter. Hacienda rooms were numerous, but small because of the limited length of ceiling beams. In an effort to keep the houses clean, homemakers stretched muslin across the dirt ceilings. Porticos supported by tree trunks shielded the walls from the sun and provided a place of refuge from the heat. The Spanish had adapted quickly to the environment and had absorbed the principals of Native American architecture.[18]

Anglo Americans initially rejected the "mud towns" they found in the Southwest. They wanted buildings and homes of wood or stone, glass windows, wooden floors, and metal ceilings and roofs. Indeed, there were a few extremists, like Secretary of War Charles M. Conrad, who urged Congress to purchase all the private holdings in New Mexico Territory and give the area back to the Native Americans. General William Tecumseh Sherman suggested in 1864 that diplomatic efforts be made to return parts of the Southwest to Mexico. His perception of the region rested to a great extent on his view of the indigenous architecture. Touring New Mexico Territory with President Rutherford B. Hayes, Sherman told an audience in the Santa Fe plaza: "I hope that ten years hence there won't be an adobe house in the Territory. I want to see you learn to make them of brick, with slanting roofs. Yankees don't like flat roofs or roofs of dirt."[19]

The "Yankees" did modify the prevailing modes in New Mexico and Arizona Territories, creating a "territorial style" that combined adobe walls with sloped, galvanized-metal roofs and Greek Revival details. Anglo Americans established sawmills that produced cut lumber for pedimented lintels, slotted shutters, paneled doors, and window frames of neoclassical styles. The "Yankees" quickly saw the advantages of porticos and arcades, but they replaced tree-trunk columns and adobe arches with wooden posts and decorative moldings. Anglo settlers imported millwork for interiors, brick for cornices and exterior columns, and lime plaster to cover the adobe walls. They painted double-hung, glazed windows and shutters with blue oil paint. A gentle blending of Spanish and Anglo American tastes created a functional and graceful architecture.[20]

The agricultural trading center of Albuquerque, founded as Villa de Alburquerque in 1706, reflected a Renaissance concept of town planning, with its main plaza dominated by San Felipe de Neri Church and surrounded by one-story commercial buildings and houses. The town's 1,600 people, a number swelled by 400 soldiers in 1860, prospered, and some buildings acquired an additional story. When the "iron horse" reached the community, however, the Atchison, Topeka, and Santa Fe Railroad founded a "new," linear-oriented town over a mile away. Anglo Americans simply moved the heart of the community to the tracks and erected structures made of the brick, stone, and lumber brought by the railway. A two-story stone courthouse with a tower built in 1886 and the wealthy merchant Franz Huning's Italianate castle of 1883 symbolized the transformation of the community. Huning may have used dried-sod bricks and wood sheathing painted and carved to look like stone, but the elaborate two-story house represented the future outline of the community's appearance.[21]

For hundreds of years, architecture in the Southwest had rested on the imaginative use of local building materials. Now the railroads and the steamships along the Pacific coast brought not only lumber and bricks but also the machinery to produce those items. Also on board were carpenters, brick masons, and stone cutters and their tools. Passengers carried with them magazines and plan books for Greek Revival, Gothic, Queen Anne, Italianate, and Cape Cod houses, as well as a determination to re-create these designs in the "wilderness." Paying no attention to the fact that these styles were totally inappropriate for the climate and the geography, the Anglo Americans sought to transplant the New England town to southern California, the Georgia plantation house to Texas, and the midwestern farm community to Oklahoma. The immigrants, cultural conservatives, saw architecture as a means to maintain the society and provide stability in a new environment.[22]

Eclectic architecture spread across the region, and in communities like Los Angeles it served to replicate the Midwest. Spanish Governor Felipe de Neve had founded El Pueblo Nuestra Señora la Reina de Los Angeles in 1781, laying out an extensive community with a plaza at the center. By the mid–nineteenth century, the Los Angeles presidio consisted of one- and two-story buildings of adobe with flat roofs, balconies, and porches. Ornamentation, minimal at best, consisted largely of wrought metal or carved wood. Charles Brace visited the town in 1868 and called it "simply a Spanish mud village." But the sleepy "mud village" became Americanized very quickly. A railroad reached the town from the port of San Pedro in 1869, and the Southern Pacific Railroad arrived from

San Francisco in 1876. A boom in agricultural production and tourism soon fueled the local economy. Publicity brought Anglo Americans, swelling the population to over 11,000 by 1880. Locally produced clay bricks replaced adobe, and cut lumber soon augmented the bricks. Frame houses and stores replaced adobe buildings. Hotels of several stories, with decorated gables and mansard roofs, vied with commercial structures for attention from pedestrians. Garishly over-ornamented structures emulated those of the East and Midwest. A polyglot population of Hispanics, Anglo Americans, and German and Irish immigrants watched the construction of banks, land offices, and small-scale manufacturing facilities. They rode the horse-drawn streetcars and drank the local wine. Nearby "colonies" formed the basis of the suburbs that Felipe de Neve had envisioned. Former wheat fields sprouted Victorian houses filled with Anglo Americans imbued with a sense of optimism and a desire for material success.[23]

After the Anglo conquest, Yankees also discovered economic opportunity in El Paso, strategically located on the Rio Grande at the major pass to the north. El Paso's merchants and traders served farmers and ranchers on both sides of the border. A community of adobe, the town was transformed by the arrival of the railroad in 1881. Anglos built two- and three-story commercial structures around Pioneer Plaza, utilizing Second Empire styles to include mansard roofs, spires, turrets, and wrought-iron decorations. By 1887 the town of only 5,000 people included the Merrick Building, a three-story Romanesque structure designed by two local architects, John J. Stewart and William J. Carpenter. Corinthian columns of cast iron, terra-cotta panels, brick, sandstone, and a tin cornice created a variety of textures and colors. Nothing about the Merrick Building hinted of the indigenous architecture of the region. The investors who constructed the building sought that which was acceptable to Eastern taste-makers.[24]

The presidio of San Antonio, consisting largely of adobe houses and stores, entered a period of transition in the 1840s when German craftsmen arrived and began to construct houses and buildings from the local cream-colored limestone. Using Alsatian stone-cutting and erecting techniques, they fashioned buildings with sloping roofs and modest ornamentation. By the time of the outbreak of the Civil War, the community's elite lived in substantial homes with silver fixtures and wood floors of cured cypress. The cosmopolitan population, only 3,488 in 1850, grew with an influx of Mexican, German, and Irish immigrants, as well as troops of soldiers. St. Mary's Academy, and later Incarnate Word College, acquired limestone buildings and students from southern Texas and northern Mexico. Although the Civil War interrupted San Antonio's growth, the cessation of hostilities brought renewed prosperity as the cattle business flourished. On Kaiser Wilhelm Strasse, wealthy German merchants built mansions of Pecos sandstone and cream-colored limestone. Richly detailed with towers, loggias, and hand-stamped shingles, the homes contained billiard rooms, gaslights, ballrooms, fireplaces, and richly painted and paneled walls. These stone houses echoed the hotels, stores, and commercial buildings springing up around the plaza in front of the decaying Alamo. The "new" San Antonio reflected little of its Mexican heritage; its model was Europe.[25]

Similarly, the port of Galveston, which had always looked to the sea, turned to Europe and New York as sources for its architecture. The major entrepôt for the Republic of Texas from 1836 to 1846, Galveston continued to prosper until the Civil War. Massive shipments of cotton created jobs in the compresses and on the wharves. Merchants, traders, factors, and shippers profited from "King Cotton." Along The Strand and on Tremont Street, merchants built stores in the Second Empire style with mansard roofs, dormers, decorative ironwork, and rusticated stone walls. Italianate commercial buildings included Florentine or Venetian brackets, cornices, and pilasters. Cotton factors and merchants imported iron building fronts from New York in a variety of styles, adding to the eclectic appearance of the commercial district. They ordered the fronts from catalogs, buying an array of columns, capitals, bases, brackets, and finials.[26] The Civil War virtually terminated exports, and Galveston languished, but peace brought renewed prosperity.

The character of Galveston changed abruptly with the arrival of the architect Nicholas J. Clayton in 1872. From County Cork, Ireland, via Cincinnati, Clayton had worked as a marble carver and in the building trades. The Lone Star State's major practitioner of High Victorian architecture, Clayton produced buildings of decorative brick and stonework, the most renowned being his medical building for the University of Texas. "Old Red," constructed in 1891, consisted of generous, rounded forms with colossal stone arches, arched windows, a red-tile roof, and decorative brickwork. A well-balanced mass, the building, with its ornate cut stone, epitomized Clayton's designs. Galveston acquired homes, churches, and commercial buildings that reflected Clayton's lavish use of stone and brick in perfect proportions. His attention to detail and concern for pleasing his clients led to commissions from the Roman Catholic Church, cotton brokers, and bankers. When Clayton concluded his work, Galveston no longer evoked a vision of a raw port town; instead it epitomized Victorian civilization and the endurance and determination of the community.[27] Galveston did not look like New Orleans or Savannah or Charleston; to even casual observers, Galveston appeared to be a late-nineteenth-century eastern city. It was but one example in Texas.

Despite the southern ancestry of many Texans, the presence of slavery before

1865, the dominance of King Cotton, and the secession of the Lone Star State, the architectural heritage of Texas was rarely antebellum Dixie. Only in the eastern communities of Jefferson and Beaumont did the Greek Revival plantation home serve as a model. As early as the 1850s, the use of brick rather than wood and the introduction of domes and cornices incorporating classical elements moved builders away from the Greek Revival style. German masons combined stone and bricks to create facades that were drawn from the Renaissance or the Romanesque style. Iron decorations in Gothic motifs and wooden casements and pediments produced European forms. Prosperous farmers and town dwellers eschewed the cabin and the dogtrot house and sought a Victorian cottage, if not a mansion.

The shift from the Greek Revival to the Victorian style from the 1850s to the 1870s was facilitated by the railways, which brought new building materials and craftsmen. The architect Abner Cook came to the frontier town of Austin from Nashville in the late 1830s. He designed homes in the Federal style and in the Greek Revival style, including the governor's mansion. But Cook also adopted Texas limestone and brick, especially for his public and commercial buildings. When the Democratic political leader and businessman "Colonel" Edward H. House constructed a home in Austin in 1891, he hired the architect Frank Freeman of New York to design a Richardson Romanesque structure of red sandstone.[28] Like other Texans, House wanted to be seen as "progressive" and not longing for the antebellum South.

The Texas economy expanded rapidly between 1870 and the depression of 1893, especially in the new urban centers. Trained architects arrived to participate in the urbanization process. Clients constructed larger office buildings, stores, hotels, and industrial facilities. Along the main streets of Houston, Dallas, and Fort Worth and even in the smaller cities, multistoried business blocks symbolized the urbanization of the state. Skylines changed as buildings rose to three or four floors and later five to eight stories with the use of iron framing and elevators. The Hurley Building in Fort Worth (1890) and the Binz Office Building in Houston (1894) served as examples of taller, more ornate commercial structures. The Board of Trade Building in Fort Worth (1888), a Renaissance Revival building, featured polychromatic stone and rich decorations. A mansard roof, dormers, balconies, a corner tower, iron trim at the roof line, and arched windows rose above a blue-and-red sandstone base. The Scanlan Building of Houston (1885) used Parisian street architecture as a motif. Texas architects, seeking to avoid provincialism, turned to styles popular in the Northeast and Europe. They also used sophisticated materials and advanced technology.[29]

Commercial buildings reflected the economies of the cities. The red-and-white Renaissance Revival Cotton Exchange in Houston (1884–85) housed brokers who had replaced the older trading firms in Galveston as the economy of that port began to falter.[30] Although laid out as a town in 1844, Dallas failed to grow substantially until the first railroad arrived in 1872. The population jumped to 7,000 as cotton, lumber, wheat, and livestock began to pass through the community. The small one-story brick buildings of the 1860s fell under the shadows of the two- and three-story commercial structures that spread along the principal streets. High Victorian stores of heavy stone and brick displayed merchandise to ranchers, farmers, and the blue-collar workers who moved to Dallas.[31] After the Texas and Pacific Railway entered Fort Worth in 1876, the city streets soon filled with cattle herds being moved to stock pens along the track. The Ellis Hotel opened in 1885 to serve the cattle buyers and dealers. The four-story hotel, with its mansard roof, stone quoins, and iron front, stretched along an avenue crowded with wagons, buggies, and streetcars. By 1891 Fort Worth boasted of a seven-story "skyscraper." Within two decades, this small "cow town" had become a city with free public schools, two colleges, many churches, and several legitimate theaters.[32] Charles Francis Adams, a political figure, railroad president, and prominent East Coast intellectual, declared in 1889, "From a one-mule town Fort Worth had grown to a city of large proportions and great commercial importance."[33] Members of the chamber of commerce probably stood and cheered.

Architectural embellishments could be found even in smaller communities. Texas architects placed Richardson Romanesque hotels, office buildings, railroad stations, schools, and churches in communities of only a few thousand. The architects A. O. Watson of Austin and Eugene T. Heiner of Houston reproduced, on a small scale, H. H. Richardson's Allegheny County Courthouse in Pittsburgh, Pennsylvania, for the Dewitt County seat in the town of Cuero. Rusticated stone, massive proportions, and balance aped Richardson's triumph.[34] The census of 1870 recorded not one person in the entire Texas panhandle, but by 1908, the town of Dalhart sported the two-story Felton Opera House.[35] The farmers and ranchers who conducted business at the courthouse belonged to the Methodist Church, attended events at the opera house, and sent their children to the town school, emulating their more urban neighbors. They took advantage of cut lumber, mass-produced millwork, and architectural metal details to construct homes in the Queen Anne or Victorian style. In contrast to the drab prairie, the houses were painted in bright colors to highlight the scrollwork, gables, and bays. Rural Texans abandoned adobe and sod and sought the most popular architectural styles for their homes.[36] A large two-story Gothic Revival house in three shades of green with white trim might startle a traveling salesman or a Comanche brave crossing West Texas, but the ranchers took pride in their economic success, and their houses epitomized that achievement.

Ornate Victorian houses in San Diego served the same purposes: providing shelter and a symbol of status. Father Junipero Serra established the first of California's missions on a hill above San Deigo Bay in 1769. Located in a remote coastal area, San Diego grew very slowly under Spanish and then Mexican rule. Not until the mid-1860s did the settlement experience rapid development with the arrival of the promoter Alonzo E. Horton. An entrepreneur from Wisconsin, Horton established a "new" town some four miles south of the mission. He bought almost a thousand acres of pueblo land at auction, laid out streets and lots, and began to promote the region's salubrious climate and economic potential. His community did not become the terminus of a transcontinental railroad as he hoped, however, and the 4,000 residents faced a bleak future. Booms and busts marked San Diego's history in the Gilded Age, but the initiation of the California Southern Railroad in 1881 ushered in a major growth period. The railroad sought to link with the westward extension of the Atchison, Topeka, and Santa Fe Railroad to form a through line to Kansas City and Chicago. With the completion of the connection four years later, the population soared to 40,000. Large commercial buildings appeared, a streetcar system was operating, and arc lights mounted on tall poles illuminated the city at night. New residents flocked in, bringing architectural tastes wholly at variance with San Diego's "Old Town."[37]

Horton's subdivisions looked like midwestern and New England towns transported to a Mediterranean climate. Wooden false fronts gave way to multi-storied commercial buildings and houses decorated with porches, cornices, turrets, and gables. Lumber, glass, bricks, and other construction materials arrived by ship until the railroad brought lower freight charges. A flood of new residents, arriving at a rate of 4,000 to 5,000 per month in 1887, demanded instant housing. Tourists occupied rooms in the lavish "redwood palace," Hotel del Coronado, but many arrivals sought permanent homes. Houses in the Stick, Queen Anne, Italianate, and Eastlake styles sprang up in Horton's "new town." Some were small one-story cottages, but other houses, often built of pre-cut lumber, were enormous in size and elaborate in decoration. The lathe and power saw turned cheap lumber into "gingerbread" for the new residential districts. Villa Montezuma, built in 1887 for the mystic composer and writer Benjamin Jesse Frances Shepard, set the tone for the community. The villa featured towers, gables, wrought iron, tall red-brick chimneys, stained glass, and hardwood in the interior. The villa symbolized the boom, but Shepard stayed only two years.

CULTURE *in the* AMERICAN SOUTHWEST

A collapse in the real estate market caused others to leave as well, and San Diego's population fell to only 16,000 by 1890. The sugar magnate John D. Spreckels picked up the pieces, and by 1900 San Diego had begun to grow again, an outpost of Victorian architecture on the Pacific Ocean.[38]

Inland towns also became small Victorian cities as the newcomers to Albuquerque, Tucson, and Phoenix rejected adobe for good, solid, clay-fired brick and cut white-pine or fir lumber. Steam-powered sawmills and jigsaws provided lumber and wooden trims for Albuquerque's Victorian houses. The railway brought glass, hardware, carpets, and stuffed furniture. L- or T-shaped houses replaced the square adobe structures designed for defense against marauders. Red brick and brightly painted wood altered the character of the city.[39] Phoenix too changed rapidly as small homes with plain facades gave way to wide porches, mansard roofs, cupolas, metal trim, and ornate carved-wood balustrades. As part of an effort to promote tourism, in 1896 the Chicago health-seeker John C. Adams built a four-story, 150-room hotel that included an electric elevator and a roof garden. The architect W. R. Norton came to Phoenix in 1894 to renew his health and found clients for homes costing $8,000 to $10,000. Broad streets lined with trees flanked the new subdivisions.[40] Although still a frontier town as late as 1900, Tucson's adobe presidio gave way as settlers from the Midwest brought Victorian ideals to the desert country. The University of Arizona's "Old Main," a transplanted midwestern college building, anchored one end of town in 1891 while the courthouse dominated the other. Between them rose wooden and brick Victorian houses of many styles and colors. The New York editor-publisher Whitelaw Reid commented in 1896 that the two Arizona towns offered advantages of climate that attracted both tourists and permanent residents.[41] The rise of tourism in the Southwest soon adorned the landscape with massive hotels built like those in the Berkshires or the Adirondacks.

Town promoters, territorial officials, and the railroads mounted campaigns to attract tourists and potential residents to the region. As early as 1881, the Santa Fe Railroad began to develop the Montezuma Hotel six miles north of Las Vegas, New Mexico. A rambling, wood-framed Queen Anne hostelry, the Montezuma contained 270 rooms, gas lights, steam heat, and running water. Over 150 guests of the railroad came from Boston for the opening of the hotel. Consumed by fire in 1884, the structure was replaced by an equally opulent sandstone-and-brick building with enormous towers and ballustraded verandas. The prominent Chicago architectural firm of Brown and Root turned to the Queen Anne style again but selected warm natural colors for the exterior, which was both rustic and sophisticated.[42]

The author Frank Baum used San Diego's Hotel Del Coronado as the model for the Emerald City in his book *The Wizard of Oz*. Built of redwood in 1888, "this great pile of lumber" of red-roofed turrets and white verandas was the world's largest wooden structure when it opened. Thomas Edison personally supervised the installation of the electric lights. Famous guests came from the outset, and they spread the word about San Diego's beauty and climate. Three "bird-cage elevators" conveyed guests to the 379 rooms, where views of the foothills and the Pacific became topics of letters, newspaper articles, book chapters, and real estate puffery.[43]

Los Angeles likewise boomed in the 1880s as Anglo Americans swept aside the old pueblo, erecting businesses and homes. They constructed the ornate Grand Opera House, said to be the finest west of the Mississippi River. After the Atchison, Topeka, and Santa Fe Railroad arrived in 1887, three or four trains came from Chicago each day filled with tourists, investors, health-seekers, and promoters. The boom of the 1880s saw first a cable-car system and then a network of electric interurban railroad lines that joined the outlying communities to Los Angeles. Citrus production soared but became a poor second economically with the discovery of oil in 1892. By 1900 the City of Angels claimed over 100,000 people, having doubled its population in a decade. The port at San Pedro prospered, and small manufacturing facilities emerged. The boulevards linking the communities of Los Angeles County followed the routes of the Los Angeles Railway streetcar lines and the interurbans of the Pacific Electric System.[44] Along these streets, housing developments followed, with homes constructed in a stunning array of Victorian styles. The newcomers wanted houses just like those they had left behind in Dayton and Des Moines.

Architects arrived with the construction boom, and soon commercial structures of four, five, and six stories appeared. Locally produced clay bricks combined with iron-and-steel frames to give downtown Los Angeles the appearance of a midwestern city. The introduction of structural steel in the Homer Laughlin Building (1898) initiated the construction of new office towers in excess of ten floors. Facades with Corinthian columns and Renaissance cornices gave way to unadorned walls in the Chicago style. The initial building boom saw Richardson Romanesque and Second Empire commercial structures, but architects and their clients read journals from the East and Midwest, saw drawings and photographs of the most recently constructed buildings, and determined to emulate the au courant styles. The Los Angeles County Courthouse, a huge red-sandstone pile, opened in 1891. Designed in the Richardson Romanesque style, the rusticated walls, arched windows, and ornate gables were topped by a massive clock tower.[45] It would be among the city's last major buildings designed in that mode.

The Bradbury Building, opened two years later, represented the future, not

FIGURE 10

The Bradbury Building in Los Angeles, with its light-filled center and open elevator cages, represented a major innovation in commercial architecture. Author's collection.

the past. George Herbert Wyman had come to Los Angeles from Dayton, Ohio, in 1891. Only thirty-one years old but weakened by pneumonia, he sought to regain his health in southern California. Although apprenticed to an architect in Ohio only briefly, he joined the Los Angeles designer Sumner P. Hunt. Hired by the Mexican mining millionaire Louis Bradbury to produce an office building, Hunt proposed a conventional plan that was rejected. Bradbury then offered the commission to Wyman, who risked his career by leaving his position with Hunt and accepting the job. Influenced by a description of a futuristic office complex in Edward Bellamy's utopian novel *Looking Backward: 2000–1887*, Wyman produced an influential piece of architecture. Bellamy's fictional building featured a vast central hall filled with sunlight from a glass dome. Walls frescoed in mellow colors softened the light. Thus inspired, Wyman designed a steel-framed building with a central light court. The exterior of the five-story building, brick and sandstone, included modest suggestions of the Romanesque but reflected the incipient Chicago style in its muted decorations. Wyman's interior directly followed Bellamy's description. Art Nouveau wrought-iron staircases and open-bridge crossings allowed light to penetrate each floor. Bird-cage elevators with revealed works linked the balconies on each level. Narrow Corinthian columns and organic imagery added to the sense of light and space. Wyman thus created a courtyard that emphasized movement and rhythm, technology flooded with sunlight. Fantasy became reality.[46] The Bradbury Building influenced Los Angeles architecture for decades and became the subject of numerous articles in architectural journals nationwide.

Entrepreneurs across the Southwest, even in smaller places, risked substantial capital in erecting buildings designed by neophytes such as Wyman and by major, established firms such as Chicago's Sullivan and Adler. Louis Sullivan and Pankmar Adler created the famous Chicago Auditorium Theater in 1886–87, gaining international renown for the massive structure housing an acoustically perfect auditorium that Sullivan decorated in dozens of shades of gold. If that building was good enough for Chicago, status-seeking entrepreneurs in Pueblo, Colorado, wanted a copy. In 1888–89, Sullivan and Adler designed the Pueblo Opera House Block, which included a 1,100-seat theater, offices, stores, a 131-foot observation tower, and a roof garden. Sullivan wrote to the Grand Opera House Association, "A building should be adapted to the climate of the locality." He later added, "Every city should have an architecture distinctly its own." The Romanesque facade of rusticated Manitou stone and granite rose four stories above a gray-granite base. Three arches marked the entrance to the opera house and its interior, where Sullivan designed a gold-leaf proscenium arch and employed brilliant colors. The decorations included clusters of electric lights. The largest Sullivan and Adler building outside of Chicago, the Pueblo Opera House, at a cost of $400,000, symbolized southwesterners' longing for acceptance and approval, their desire for a venue for high culture, and their willingness to run great financial risks to obtain these goals.[47]

The Anglo American settlers of the Southwest zealously engaged in individual and collective efforts to create an instant culture in their instant cities. Incipient towns followed the models of Dallas and Los Angeles in constructing buildings and homes in architectural styles critically acceptable. Frequently they used local materials and modern technology to reproduce designs from the East and Midwest. In Las Vegas, New Mexico Territory, a town established in 1835, the arrival of the railroad in 1879 led to substantial growth. Charles Ilfeld created a mercantile empire in the area, and soon hotels, stores, banks, and other buildings appeared with Italianate, Gothic, and Queen Anne details. Businesspeople placed tin roofs and machine-cut lumber facades over old adobe walls and fronts. A "new" town near the railroad supplanted the old pueblo. Neoclassical and Romanesque structures of locally cut sandstone in yellow ocher, brown, and plum brown lined the main streets, which appeared to be catalogs of architectural styles. Italian stone cutters, itinerant finish carpenters, and local capital produced a Masonic temple (1895) and a city hall (1892) in the Romanesque style, located near vernacular structures with rubble and ashlar masonry, and an Elks Club building in a Tudor Revival motif.[48] Las Vegas, with the Sangre de Cristo Mountains as a backdrop, sought civic grandeur in the 1890s.

Even raw, new communities sought status and recognition through their architecture. On the morning of April 22, 1889, Guthrie, Oklahoma Territory, consisted of a railway siding, a few tents, and several small wooden buildings. The next day, thousands of people roamed over stakes and string lines arguing about street locations, plats, and ownership. The "run" into the "unassigned land" brought 15,000 settlers the first day, and within twenty-four hours, carpenters had erected the framework for homes. The railroad brought pre-cut lumber and even preassembled walls that quickly became homes in many styles. The architect Joseph Foucart arrived shortly thereafter to give the community a sense of style and grace. A native of Belgium who had studied in France, Foucart came to Guthrie only a month after the Run of '89. Opening an office in the raw town, he immediately received commissions. Guthrie soon claimed a permanent population of 12,000 and acquired six railroad lines, six banks, five daily newspapers, and the territorial capital. The city government granted a street railway franchise in June, and the first city directory was published in July. Foucart set to work.[49]

Entrepreneurs in Guthrie directed Foucart to design fireproof masonry buildings to replace the hastily erected frame structures. Using native red sandstone and bricks made of red Oklahoma clay, Foucart turned to Europe for his inspirations. Undoubtedly familiar with the theories of Eugene Villoet-le-Duc, the leading French architectural critic, Foucart followed his dictates requiring rational planning, structural unity, and Gothic styling. The result was buildings that filled their lots, facades that sat flush with the sidewalk, and walls that were penetrated with arched openings. Foucart beveled the corners of buildings at major street intersections, adding towers, decorative entrances, and pilasters. Solid, load-bearing walls were accented with stone and cast-iron columns. Minarets, cupolas, round windows, stone lintels, and intricate patterns of brickwork added to the sense of solidity and opulence. Foucart embraced the Gothic, Romanesque, and High Victorian styles, with gloriously eclectic results. The entrance to the Grey Brothers Block (1890) had an oriel at the second and third floors, and the State Capital Publishing Company building (1895) had an open, three-dimensional tower at its entrance. Foucart's eclecticism also ran rampant in the houses he designed. Red bricks, round windows, stone trim, Romanesque arches, and turreted towers came together in elegant two- and three-story homes. Foucart's designs set the tone for this instant city, and other practitioners in Guthrie followed his lead.[50] As a consequence, this prairie city could have fit quite comfortably in Iowa, Illinois, or Ohio — which is exactly what the Sooners wanted. There was no indigenous architecture.

Only a few miles south of Guthrie, upstart Oklahoma, another railroad siding, became Oklahoma City after April 22, 1889, when 4,000 people established residence. Henry Overholser had ten carloads of lumber for sale, and within hours prefabricated wooden buildings dotted the flat prairie. Masonry structures replaced frame buildings as the city began to grow. By 1907, the year of statehood, over 30,000 people resided in Oklahoma City. Three years later the state capital was moved from Guthrie to Oklahoma City, and the rate of growth accelerated. Overholser prospered as a developer, streetcar-line owner, and land speculator. He built a mansion in 1904 in a modified Victorian Gothic style with leaded-art glass windows, nine fireplaces, and woodwork of mahogany and Antwerp oak. As a civic leader, politician, and booster, Overholser recognized the need for the city to have cultural amenities. On Grand Avenue he built the Overholser Opera House, a spacious, opulently decorated venue for opera, symphony orchestras, and drama. Adjacent to a large streetcar and interurban terminal, the opera house drew patrons from throughout central Oklahoma.[51]

Overholser understood that cultural events helped the community grow. His response was essentially the same as that of entrepreneurs in Los Angeles, merchants in Galveston, and Mexican traders in Tucson. Southwesterners wanted to hear classical music and operas. Although one historian of music in the United States has declared that settlers in the West had "virtually no contact with the developing cultivated tradition in the eastern urban centers" and that musical life was vastly different and inferior on the frontier, that was absolutely not the case in the Southwest.[52] In settlements composed of young male adventurers, traders, and soldiers, violins, guitars, brass instruments, and harmonicas produced ballads and folk music as well as the music of Bach, Mozart, and Handel. As communities grew and women and children arrived in larger numbers, choirs, chamber music groups, and recitals became commonplace. "Opera houses," often no more than open spaces above saloons, served as venues for excerpts of operettas or operas and for touring groups of musicians and actors. Immigrants from Spain, Italy, France, and Germany brought their own particular musical heritages, broadening the offerings and tastes of the Anglo Americans.[53] By the 1870s, many southwestern communities had acquired not only opera houses but also local performers and teachers of classical music.

Isolated Los Angeles, a sleepy farm community, sought to bring musicians to perform publicly as early as the 1860s. Performers came by boat from San Francisco to present concerts and recitals. Pianists, soloists, and small opera companies visited the town. By 1878 the Philharmonic Society promoted musical events, and a few years later a local chamber orchestra performed. Organ concerts at Los Angeles churches included masses composed by Mozart. The German colony formed Teutonia, a society that cultivated singing. Some of its members taught music in the local schools and gave private lessons as well. In November, 1865, the Gerardo López del Castillo Spanish Company from Mexico City presented an interact of Verdi's *Attila* during a performance of *La trenza de sus cabellos* by Tomás Rodríguez Rubí. The guitarist Miguel S. Arévalo moved to Los Angeles in 1871 and became director of the Los Angeles Musical Association. For three decades he performed, composed, and taught, giving the Hispanic community a cultural leader and giving the growing town a trained, professional musician. The gas-lit Turnverein Hall, built in 1875, witnessed music performed in Spanish, Italian, German, and English.[54]

Even the more isolated and smaller settlements shared the longing for classical music. In Arizona Territory, itinerant Mexican musical groups performed before miners, soldiers, and townspeople in Tucson and Bisbee. German Jewish merchants in New Mexico Territory brought violins and pianos to the raw settlements, and sonatas, leider, and études rang out over the desert.[55]

German and French settlers in Texas introduced church and folk music, as well as the classics drawn from their cultural heritages. They brought or imported pianos, musical instruments, sheet music, and opera scores. In 1838, at Houston's first theater, Madam Thielemann (Louise Ehlers) sang with an orchestra. She had previously performed in Germany and New York. The Robert Kleberg family arrived in Texas in 1834, bringing a fine piano. Their neighbors in the "German" towns formed singing societies such as the Singers' Union–Texas Saengerbund in New Braunfels. Composers sent songs about Texas, written in German, back to the homeland. The German-speaking settlers built music halls, organized concerts, and joined choirs and orchestras in the midst of the turmoil over Texas independence, the Mexican-American War, and continuing battles with Native Americans.

In communities such as San Antonio, where Germans composed one-third of the population, Europeans dominated the musical life. The mayor of San Antonio, Mr. Thielepape, also served as president of the Beethoven Club, which hosted the southern poet Sidney Lanier, who played a flute for the members. Casino Hall in San Antonio served as the venue for concerts and choir performances, but the Turnverein, with its large stage and hall, was the most important theater for music in the town. Germans, Hispanics, and Anglo Americans attended operas performed by touring companies from Mexico City, and the arrival of the railroad meant that troupes could come from New York, New Orleans, and California as well. A Sängerfest in San Antonio attracted singing societies from central Texas towns; they performed music by Mendelssohn, Kreutzer, Hayden, and Mozart. By 1874 an orchestra had so matured that it was able to present Bellini's *Norma* overture and music by Rossini. A San Antonio orchestra performed Mendelssohn's Symphony no. 4 ("The Italian") in 1887 to an enthusiastic audience. French settlers from Castroville, Czechs from central Texas towns, and Swedes from Round Rock came to San Antonio to attend the opera, to purchase sheet music and instruments, and frequently to perform. By the 1880s, San Antonio had a lively musical culture.[56]

A crude village of wooden buildings in the 1840s, Houston became a small city by 1900. During that half century of growth, residents demanded music and theatrical productions. From the first musical performance in 1838 to large-scale operas in the 1890s, audiences sought more than popular entertainment. A concert in 1840 included works by Mozart and Rossini, a prelude to opera performances in the 1860s. The audiences were educated, and when the Roncari Opera Troupe with a full orchestra and chorus presented a poor production of Verdi's *La Traviata* and *Il Trovatore,* the response proved cold. Neither the audience nor local critics praised opera badly sung. When Emma Juch introduced Wagner with a production of *Tannhäuser* in 1892, the reaction was far more favorable. The level of sophistication of Houstonians became clear when the Metropolitan Opera arrived in 1901, with Emma Eames and Ernestine Schumann-Heink performing in *Lohengrin.* Houstonians knew quality performances, and they demanded that the classics be respected even when presented in crude halls with poor acoustics.[57]

Until the coming of the railroad, El Paso survived musically with street bands and itinerant performers. Musical societies presented recitals, but the desire for quality classical music grew stronger each year. The opening of Chopin Hall in 1896, an "elegant and plush" theater, provided a venue for a concert with music by Gounod, Beethoven, Chopin, and Schubert. Chopin Hall also hosted members of the Metropolitan Opera, who sang selections by Wagner. The McGinty Club formed a two-hundred-piece marching band that played light classical music; by 1915, it had evolved into the El Paso Symphony Orchestra.[58]

The thirst for operatic and symphonic music could be found across the

Southwest, and where economic resources were available, opera houses appeared hard on the heels of settlement. The opera house and touring opera companies marked the contours of the society emerging in the Southwest. Although the national depression of 1873 reduced the number of "grand opera" performances, the operettas of Offenbach and of Gilbert and Sullivan often played to packed houses in Houston, Dallas, and Los Angeles. By the late 1880s, "grand opera" had returned to the larger cities, and not even the depression in 1893 deterred the companies roving the region on its vastly expanded rail network.[59]

Los Angeles offers an example of the success of large-scale operatic productions in the Southwest. The City of Angels acquired several venues for opera as the community matured. Rail connections to San Francisco gave touring companies an opportunity to expand their territory beyond northern California. The Fabbri-Müller Opera Company performed scenes from Bellini's *Norma* and Weber's *Der Freischütz* in 1880. In 1897 the Del Conti Opera Company offered the U.S. premiere of *La Boheme*. When Emma Abbott brought her troupe to Los Angeles in the 1880s, she, like other stars, took great liberties with the music. Abbott inserted "Nearer My God to Thee" in the middle of *La Traviata,* for example.

Los Angeles audiences rejected such theatrics by the 1890s. They expected and heard "pure" performances. When Theodore Thomas brought the American Opera Company to Los Angeles, the singing was in English, but the famous conductor stuck to the score and the libretto. The entrepreneur O. G. Weyse advanced $20,000 to the company, touring as the National Opera, for five performances. Huge crowds rewarded Weyse financially and Thomas critically. Later, Adelina Patti came, in her private railway car, to sing in *Faust,* the Columbia Opera Company offered *Cavalleria Rusticana,* and Emma Juch performed in *Rigoletto, The Flying Dutchman,* and *L'Africaine.* A cold audience greeted Nellie Melba in April, 1898, when she sang "Rosina" in *The Barber of Seville,* but her radiance and charm won the audience over in the second act with her rendering of "Contro un cor." She rewarded the audience with encores of "Swanee River" and, since it was the middle of the Spanish-American War, "The Star Spangled Banner." Melba knew how to work an American audience, but operagoers in Los Angeles, as in other southwestern cities, expected the best. They knew the music and the stories, especially of Italian operas, and they demanded that *Norma* or *Lucia di Lammermoor* be respected by the orchestras and singers.[60]

When Lynden Ellsworth Behymer arrived in Los Angeles in 1896, he discovered a thriving musical and theatrical world. Coming from Dakota Territory with little capital, he found work selling peanuts and programs at Child's Opera House. Although only twenty-four years old, Behymer quickly recognized the opportunities for a skilled promoter. He located talent for opera houses and printed their programs. Behymer formed a booking agency, importing talent from New York and Chicago, and traveled abroad to contact agents and performers. In 1887 he brought Adelina Patti to Los Angeles, with a guarantee of $3,000, and had to find extra chairs for the overflow crowd. He promoted Theodore Thomas's opera company and other major troupes. By the end of the 1890s, Behymer was the city's leading impresario. He brought the Metropolitan Opera to Los Angeles in 1900 and watched 4,000 people listen to Nellie Melba sing *Mimi*. Audience support was such that in 1905, the Metropolitan brought an elaborate production of *Parsifal* that required a revolving stage. Behymer booked opera companies, Sarah Bernhardt, and Ignacy Paderewski; Los Angeles had achieved musical and theatrical maturity.[61]

The Los Angeles Philharmonic Society, founded in 1878, floundered for a decade, but the population growth brought new musicians and larger audiences. In 1888–89, the Austrian conductor Adolph Willhartitz conducted four concerts. His programs included Beethoven's Fifth Symphony, Haydn's *Creation,* and a Mozart concerto for two pianos. Using amateur players and singers, Willhartitz brought the community a repertoire of classical music. The orchestra struggled through the 1890s, falling on hard times. It was revived once again in 1898, when Harley Hamilton, a violinist, led thirty-five musicians in a program ranging from Beethoven to Strauss. The six concerts that season laid the basis for the Philharmonic that blossomed after 1920.[62] Los Angeles no longer stood in San Francisco's shadow musically, and it now dominated its smaller neighbor to the south, San Diego.

The business boom of the 1880s had provided financial support for San Diego's cultural life. Families from New England and the Midwest brought heritages that included musical performances. While early organizations bringing music to the town included the San Diego Silver Coronet Band formed by Gustav Schroeppel in 1874, within a decade the Philharmonic Society brought performers from New York and Europe. The men and women who belonged to the Philharmonic Society paid dues of twenty-five to fifty cents per month to help sponsor musical events. Local productions of Gilbert and Sullivan's *H.M.S. Pinafore* (1879) and *Patience* (1882) were mounted at Horton Hall only a year after their London premieres. The San Diego Amateur Opera Society offered *The Mikado* (1886) at Leach's Opera House. The end of the real estate boom left the community short of tenors and basses, however. Refusing to admit cultural defeat, Gertrude Gilbert served as president of the Amphion Club for sixteen years after its founding in 1893. Under her leadership, the original twenty members of the club grew to over sixteen hundred in the 1920s. The club encouraged local musicians and artists and brought the Los Angeles Philharmonic Orchestra to San Diego. Its members sponsored and participated in the San Diego Opera Society and the Civic Opera Company. San Diegans heard Paderewski at the Fisher Opera House and attended concerts with musical offerings ranging from Verdi and Donizetti to John Philip Sousa and Stephen Collins Foster.[63] The Anglo American immigrants reproduced a musical culture in the midst of a frantic boom-and-bust economy.

Like Gertrude Gilbert in San Diego, Anna Goodman Hertzberg of San Antonio led her community's efforts to create a musical culture. Hertzberg had come to San Antonio as a teenager in 1832. A pianist and a graduate of the New York Conservatory of Music, she formed the Tuesday Musical Club, which brought Maude Powers, Fritz Kreisler, and Madame Schumann-Heink to the city. The first woman elected to local office (the Board of Education), she used her position to promote musical programs in the schools. Hertzberg and her associates attended the Emma Abbott Opera Company performances in 1886, when the Grand Opera House opened. Abbott and her entourage presented six performances including *Rigoletto, Carmen,* and *Il Trovatore.* The opera house, a three-story brick building that had cost $125,000, served a community of only 40,000 people. Yet the 1,800 seats were filled night after night, and Abbott grossed $10,300.[64] Situated on the major railway line between New Orleans and California, San Antonio, like much of the rest of Texas, benefited from its location when touring companies scheduled performances between the coasts.

Throughout the 1880s and 1890s, opera troupes visited the Lone Star State, often playing in sold-out opera houses. Emma Juch came to San Antonio in December, 1890, performed four operas, including *Faust* and *Lohengrin,* toured for a week, returned, performed *The Flying Dutchman,* and then moved on to El Paso. Large, enthusiastic audiences at San Antonio's Grand Opera House greeted Rosa Palacios, the "Patti of Mexico," when the Mexican Opera Company presented *La Mascotte* and *Martha* in 1888. Palacios sang in *La Traviata* to wild applause. Opera houses in Fort Worth, Dallas, Houston, and El Paso hosted touring companies. Multistoried structures often seating over one thousand people, the theaters offered lavish appointments and an opportunity for road companies to make substantial profits. Opera troupes from Mexico, Germany, Italy, and France, as well as companies from New York and Chicago, appeared in major towns and cities. The small town of Austin hosted *Trompette* by Mellhac and Lecocq and performed by the Geistinger Opera Company. Marie Geistinger and "one hundred artists" sang in French, but the "English libretto of this opera [was] available from ushers." The Millett Opera House had been remodeled with orchestra and box seats to separate genteel patrons from "objectionable characters."[65] Although Adelina Patti decried the Texans, "the natives [who] turned out of their huts to stare" at her railway car, there was genuine longing for classical music and theater in Texas.[66] In 1880, in the settlement of Cuero, the Amateur Club performed *Trial by Jury* with six principals and a chorus. Savoyards would have blanched, no doubt, but music formed a vital part of southwestern society and culture.[67]

Oklahoma City, founded in April, 1889, had organized musical groups by the fall, and that winter a choir of seventy-five performed music by Haydn and Handel. The town had yet to emerge from tents and prefabricated buildings, but as one settler declared, "We were mad about music."[68]

Southwesterners were "mad about" the theater too, especially Shakespeare. Trappers, miners, soldiers, cowboys, and farmers read Shakespeare's plays and flocked to the nearest opera house to see performances. They annoyed actors by reciting the lines as the plays proceeded. At first there were amateur productions, but soon itinerant traveling troupes arrived, by stage or wagon and then by rail. Restless troops of the Fourth Infantry Regiment, stationed at Corpus Christi in 1845, staged a performance of *Othello* with Lieutenant Ulysses S. Grant as Desdemona. But within seven years, this small community of 700 people heard a theatrical company from New Orleans perform with costumes and scenery. This pattern occurred in Texas and across the region.[69]

Houston acquired a theater before the city built a church. Amateurs such as the political leaders Sam Houston and Mirabeau Lamar gave performances, but by the late 1830s, professionals toured the Bayou City and Galveston, coming by boat from New Orleans. The first professional performance, Sheridan Knowles's *The Hunchback,* was followed by *Othello, Romeo and Juliet,* and *Richard III.* A small town of 2,000, Houston longed for the theater. More sophisticated Galveston, with a large immigrant population, in 1867 accepted a production of *Hamlet* that featured a woman, Sophie Miles, in the lead, a role she had played for one hundred nights at Sadler's Wells Theater in London. By the 1890s, with the city's population swollen to 50,000, Houston theatergoers regularly saw Edwin Forrest, Fanny Davenport, Thomas Keene, Edwin Booth, and Otis Skinner in productions of the classics.[70]

Smaller communities such as Austin and El Paso generated audiences for Shakespeare, comedies, and contemporary plays. In 1874, the English actor-playwright Wybert Reeve came to Austin to star in *Woman in White* by Wilkie Collins. He found a crude town and a poorly appointed hotel, but even at rehearsals Reeve was greeted by "Rule Britannia" played by the theater's orchestra. At one performance a shot rang out during the last act. Two patrons settled an argument in the alley behind the theater; the survivor returned to see the conclusion of the play. As the town, and the audiences, matured, the local elite, such as Colonel and Mrs. E. M. House, entertained Maurice Barrymore, Helene Modjeska, and Anna Held when they came to perform.[71] Frequently the companies moved on to San Antonio or El Paso. In the latter city, Myar's Opera House presented and produced classical plays and operas. A performance of *The Count of Monte Cristo* starring James O'Neil opened this splendid venue in 1887. Soon the small city had several theaters for plays, musicals, vaudeville, and repertory players.[72]

San Antonio audiences attended plays performed in English, Spanish, and German in the 1840s. Touring companies and local amateurs played in Casino Hall while Spanish-language theatrical performances often took place in tents. The grounds of the Menger Hotel hosted German theatrical productions, as did Scholz Palm Garden, before they moved to Casino Hall in 1858. Audiences for plays in German came from Fredericksburg and New Braunfels. The latter community mounted its own production of *Wallenstein,* a trilogy by Schiller, in 1850. Plays both idealistic and romantic reflected nineteenth-century German culture. By the 1880s, however, the sophisticated dramas began to give way to comedies and musicals. After the railroad reached San Antonio in 1877, touring companies attracted large audiences, and productions in English soon displaced German theatrical performances. New venues with modern technical facilities hosted stars such as Lillie Langtry, a local favorite. But audiences and local critics refused to accept second- or third-rate productions, and no egos were spared. Displeased playgoers booed or walked out, and newspaper reviews trashed weak performances.[73]

Even relatively isolated communities such as Tombstone and Tucson in Arizona Territory and Las Vegas in New Mexico Territory not only sought plays but also demanded quality drama. The miners of Tombstone went to the Birdcage Variety Theater for Gilbert and Sullivan or vaudeville shows and to Schieffelin Hall for the classics and contemporary plays. The vaudevillian Eddie Foy entertained at the Birdcage, and Nellie Boyd of Chicago brought her drama troupe to Tombstone in 1880–81. Both their performances were well received.[74] Tucson audiences could attend Spanish-language plays performed by companies from Mexico or amateur plays produced by The Thespians, who offered *East Lynne* in 1882.[75] In the 1880s, Las Vegas, New Mexico, boasted five opera houses and eight local theatrical groups. There was also a Drama Society at nearby Fort Union. La Sociedad Dramátic presented plays in Spanish with leading citizens in the casts, such as the future governor Ezequiel C. de Baca. By the turn of the century, Las Vegas offered dramas, operas, operettas, oratorios, and minstrels.[76]

The history of theater in Los Angeles and San Diego paralleled the experiences in Houston and San Antonio. The first dramatic performance in English in Los Angeles took place in the spring of 1848, when the officers and men of a volunteer regiment from New York presented a play in a one-story adobe building. From the time of that performance into the 1860s, amateur productions brought one-act plays, sketches, and an occasional classical drama. By the end of the 1860s, touring companies offered plays in repertory in Los Angeles and San Diego. The coming of the railroad meant larger productions with full sets and elaborate costumes. The spectacular growth of the City of Angels spurred the construction of major theaters such as the Grand Opera House. Erected in 1884 by a local businessman, the theater seated 1,200 in plush surroundings. This venue and others hosted one-week stands by E. H. Sothern, Lillian Russell, Maurice Barrymore, Sarah Bernhardt, and other leading actors. Shakespeare plays, *Camille, Oliver Twist,* and contemporary dramas attracted large audiences. Local stock companies faded as road shows captured the stages of the city's many theaters. An increasingly Anglo, middle-class population flocked to the theater to see American or British plays.[77] A mass entertainment medium organized on a commercial basis, theater appealed to a large segment of the local population.

The Loring Opera House in Riverside and theaters in San Diego emulated the success of theatrical productions in Los Angeles. Frank A. Miller, the founder of the Mission Inn in Riverside, led the group that built the Loring, and he attracted stars to this theater located in a town of only 5,000 people. Horton Hall and the Fisher Opera House in San Diego offered drama, comedies, and light opera. The San Diego Literary and Dramatic Union and the San Diego Amateur Dramatic Association offered plays in the 1870s, but within a decade audiences shifted their allegiance to the touring companies arriving by rail from the East.[78]

Hispanic theatergoers in the Southwest also patronized touring companies, from Mexico or Spain, but indigenous organizations often survived this competition. In many communities, local Hispanic theatrical groups remained vibrant well into the early 1900s. Theater represented a basic element in Hispanic American culture, continuing from that first play presented near the Rio Grande in 1598. Spanish and Mexican settlers continued to produce pastorales and heroic dramas, but by the middle of the nineteenth century, professional actors entered the region and began to perform classic Iberian dramas and comedies. Gerardo López del Castillo took his Compañía Española from Mazatlán by boat to San Diego and Los Angeles and then overland from Baja California to Tucson and towns in northern Mexico. The José Pérez Company toured from Los Angeles to Tucson and into Mexico. Soon circuits developed, sending Spanish theatrical groups along the border from San Antonio to Laredo, El Paso, Tucson, and Los

Angeles. Productions ranged from Victor Hugo's *Tyrant of Padua* to works by Juan de Arizo and Antonio de Leiva. Dramas from Spain's Golden Age or from contemporary Mexican playwrights found receptive audiences. The quality of these productions rose quickly after the Mexican Revolution of 1910. Mexican actors, actresses, writers, and producers fled with thousands of other refugees to the United States. Residential companies gained seasoned thespians, and touring groups enhanced and broadened their repertories. New theaters opened in the border cities, many becoming cultural centers for the expanding Hispanic communities.[79] Southwesterners, whether their language was Spanish or English, longed for theatrical performances, and by the 1860s and 1870s they could applaud quality productions across the region.

Southwesterners also craved literature, and they imported books, magazines, newspapers, and journals. One of the first stores to open in each settlement was a bookshop selling the most recently published novels from Great Britain and the East, copies of journals such as *Blackwood's* and the *Edinburgh Review,* and playbooks from New York and London. Publications in English, Spanish, German, and French lined the shelves of mercantile stores, stationers, and newspaper offices. But southwesterners remained largely consumers of literature.[80] In a lecture delivered to the faculty and students at the University of California in 1875, William C. Bartlett prophesied, "In all that relates to education, literature, and art, it is early spring-time in California."[81] He then lamented: "The little that has been done here in art is rather a sign of better things to come. Art must not only have inspiration, but it needs wealth and the society of a ripe community for its best estate."[82]

Unfortunately, the raw towns of the Southwest rarely provided the nurturing necessary for the creative writer. Literature produced in the region came largely from the pens of authors passing through the Southwest. William Sydney Porter, ("O. Henry") lived in Austin, Texas, from 1884 to 1898. Ranch hand, druggist, bookkeeper, draftsman, bank clerk, and fugitive from justice, Porter wrote over 250 short stories, many about Texas and the region. His stories gained great acclaim after 1900 as he populated narratives with Austin characters he knew from the bank, newspaper, saloons, and dance halls. Years would pass before Austinites realized that the well-known Mr. Porter, a likable drinking partner and card-game enthusiast, was also "O. Henry."[83]

The most widely read novel of the Southwest before 1900 came from the pen of Helen Fiske Hunt Jackson, a Colorado resident from 1873 to 1885. Most of her work was produced in Colorado Springs except for her bestseller, *Ramona,* published in 1884. This novel romanticized the Indians of California in a tale of love and adventure. The Native Americans are derived in character from James

Fenimore Cooper's Mohicans while the Anglo Americans provide the villains in this tale of early California. Lauded for her portrayal of Native Americans, Jackson spent much of her life promoting Indian rights. Though neither an accurate portrait of California Indians nor good literature, *Ramona* introduced millions of readers to the Southwest. They soon sought other books about the region.[84]

Some found what they desired in the publications of Charles Fletcher Lummis. Lummis, or "Don Carlos" as he preferred to be called, defined the Southwest for most Americans between 1884 and 1900. In books, essays, speeches, editorials, and travel literature, Lummis glorified the Hispanic traditions of the region, romanticized the Native Americans, and rhapsodized eloquently about the land and its flora and fauna. More than any other writer, Lummis developed a sense of cultural self-awareness among southwesterners while simultaneously creating a regional image that has lasted for more than a century. He celebrated the region in fact and fancy, never concerned about accuracy but exploiting the mythology of a golden age that never existed. He encouraged others to take up their pens to promote the region, and as editor of *The Land of Sunshine* after 1894, Lummis cultivated a crop of writers who echoed his sentiments. Domineering, energetic, intelligent, and articulate, "Don Carlos" formulated a vision of the land of "Poco Tiempo."[85]

Ironically, Lummis came from New England, graduated from Harvard University, where he was a scholar and athlete, and had deep roots in the Northeast. He married, became ill, and moved to Ohio, where he farmed and edited a newspaper. In 1884–85, on a "romantic impulse," he spent 143 days tramping some 3,500 miles from the Buckeye State to Los Angeles. Along the way he fell in love with New Mexico, Arizona, and California. The dispatches he sent to Harrison Gray Otis of the *Los Angeles Times* won him a job as city editor when he arrived in California. *A Tramp across the Continent* demonstrated his flair for the romantic as he extolled the simplicity and charm of Native Americans and Hispanics in the land of "sun, silence, and adobe."

Following General George H. Crook's campaign against the Apaches in 1886, Lummis came to admire the Indians far more than their pursuers. A paralytic stroke two years later sent Lummis to New Mexico to regain his health. For three years he rode, hunted, fished, and explored, living with Amado Chavez, a member of one of the territory's leading families. He resided briefly at Isleta Pueblo, then became a friend of the Swiss anthropologist Adolph F. Bandelier, with whom he toured the Southwest for several years. His articles for *Harpers's, Youth's Companion, St. Nicholas, Century,* and *Scribners* were published as *A New Mexico David* in 1891. There followed in rapid order nine more books in which Lummis refuted the Anglo American concept of the "evil" Spanish in the South-

FIGURE II

"The Four Horsemen of the Eucalypts" pose at mission San Juan Capistrano. (From left: Will Rogers, Eugene Manlove Rhodes, Vicente Blasco Ibanez, and Charles F. Lummis.) This is one of the churches Lummis labored to preserve. Southwest Museum Collection, Los Angeles.

west and praised the Native Americans and their way of life. His successful romances and inspirational stories sold by the thousands to readers eager to learn about the "real" Southwest.[86]

Returning to Los Angeles in 1893, Lummis built a boulder-and-adobe home, El Alisal, in Arroyo Seco. His house became the center of the cultural life of Los

Angeles. The poets Edwin Markham and Joaquin Miller were frequent guests, as were the writer Mary Austin, the singer Mary Garden, and the actress Helena Modjeska. *The Land of Sunshine* evolved into *Out West,* and Lummis recruited new talent for his journal. In 1905 he was elected City Librarian, serving for six years. He also labored to gather historical materials for his dream, the Southwest Museum, for which he raised over $450,000. Lummis led the fight to preserve the decaying California missions, the center of Hispanic society. In a corduroy suit, white cotton shirt, red sash, and Stetson hat, he conducted tours of the missions with their crumbling walls and dilapidated roofs. Soliciting funds from individuals, historical societies, businesses, and religious groups, Lummis and his supporters in the Landmarks Club mounted a successful preservation effort. He recognized the importance of tourism and the need to create a historical tradition: "The old missions are worth more money . . . than our oil, our oranges, or even our climate."[87]

A significant and influential figure in the southwestern culture, Lummis discovered the region as a source of literary inspiration. A crusader for Native American rights, for the preservation of the Roman Catholic missions, and for a regional literature, Lummis left a major legacy. His friends overlooked his sexual peccadilloes and his unlimited egotism because of his contributions. Lummis formulated a style of writing and a conceptualization of the Southwest that provided George Wharton James, Mary Austin, John Charles Van Dyke, and others with a readership eager to be a part of a recognizable historical tradition.[88]

Van Dyke, an art historian, wrote forty books of criticism in a career that encompassed five decades. A professor of art history, a lawyer, and a librarian, Van Dyke defended the concept of "art for art's sake" and was devoted to the ideas of the British critic John Ruskin. A respiratory ailment brought him to Los Angeles in 1897, where Van Dyke fell victim not to disease but to the land and its vast expanse. With his brother Theodore, a widely recognized ecologist, he roamed the Mojave, Colorado, and Sonoran Deserts, collecting information, making notes, and recording observations. Carrying a rifle and a pistol, wearing cotton clothing, and eating powdered food he prepared himself, Van Dyke meandered across the deserts. Color was the key, he contended, and his book *The Desert,* first published in 1901, emphasized tones of color and shades of light. Geology, flora, fauna, and weather were always described in the phrases of the artist; Van Dyke's word pictures vividly portrayed deserts totally unlike the harsh, deadly concepts held by most of his readers. Color intoxicated him, and Van Dyke's ability to convey that flavor to his readers enhanced the work of Lummis and others.[89]

Like Van Dyke, Lummis believed that Americans needed to see the Southwest, if only in illustrations or paintings. As editor of *Out West,* Lummis sought paintings and sketches from artists in the region, and he pleaded for painters to come west and discover the land. Lummis declared that if an artist bought a train ticket to the Southwest, the painter would discover unlimited subjects: "If he'll get himself kicked off a Santa Fe train anywhere between Trinidad and Los Angeles," Lummis declared, "he can sit down where he lights; and get more 'subjects' than he ever dreamed of before." The atmosphere of Palestine and Egypt, with the Alps thrown in, could be found in the Southwest, Lummis wrote.[90] Artists arrived slowly in the 1880s and 1890s, precursors to a virtual stampede after 1900. The pioneer painters did exactly what Lummis hoped: they painted the subjects about which he wrote, and they used the same romantic tone.

The atmosphere of the Southwest drew artists captivated by the light, a bright clear light, and by an earth of many colors, shapes, and masses. Indigenous peoples, as remote to New Yorkers as the Arabs of North Africa, guaranteed subjects that appealed to artists and viewers alike. From the earliest painters who came with military and exploratory expeditions to the trained Impressionists of the 1890s, artists found the region overwhelming in beauty and an ideal subject for their brushes. The painters moved beyond the camera-like renderings required for the reports of the explorers to romantic realism and then to Impressionistic works. Richard Kern, an expeditionary artist, created a visual history of Native Americans as he painted the ruined pueblos. In galleries and in magazine and book illustrations, Frederic Remington's realistically rendered scenes of Native Americans, Hispanics, soldiers, and cowboys fired the imaginations of viewers. His paintings of the Southwest were often even more romantic and dramatic in subject matter than those of other areas.[91] The grandeur of the Southwest and the diversity of its peoples offered unlimited opportunities for the artist and the illustrator.

As early as 1866, the landscapist Worthington Whittredge painted the towns of Albuquerque and Santa Fe, and the future Impressionist Willard Leroy Metcalf worked among the Zuni people, sending illustrations to *Harper's* and *Century*. This trickle of painters accelerated in the 1890s as the Atchison, Topeka, and Santa Fe Railroad brought artists to the region. Seeking to generate publicity to enhance tourism, the railroad gave the artists free tickets and sponsored expeditions to the Grand Canyon, the Painted Desert, and the pueblos. Thomas Moran, Fernand Lungren, and others painted huge canvases of the Grand Canyon and other natural wonders, paintings that soon graced the pages of national magazines and railroad company publications. The paintings emphasized the land and its peoples, generating substantial traffic for the carrier and publicity for the Southwest.[92]

Whereas most artists before 1900 came to the region only in the spring or summer and packed into the Grand Canyon or northern New Mexico, a few resident artists established permanent roots. Louis Akin lived with the Indians of Arizona Territory and hoped to establish an artist colony there. Encouraged by Lummis, Maynard Dixon resided and painted at several locales, and his efforts found a place in *Out West* and other magazines.[93] Although few painters of national reputation lived permanently in the Southwest, visiting artists continued to encourage their colleagues to depict the region. In 1871 Whittredge found the juxtaposition of the plains and the Rockies to be "more gorgeous and beautiful . . . than anything ever witnessed on the world renowned Campagna of Rome. Those who have claimed so much for atmosphere of Italy, never saw the atmosphere of our plains near the mountains."[94]

While the natural beauty of the Southwest served as a magnet attracting artists, the prosperous residents of the region's booming cities sought to emulate their counterparts in the East and Midwest by acquiring paintings for the walls of their High Victorian homes. A young entrepreneur named Levy brought one hundred oil paintings to Los Angeles in 1874, opened a gallery, and attempted to auction his holdings. Though his sales were meager, there were buyers for

German landscapes, bucolic hunting scenes, and marine paintings. Far more successful was the sale of a large consignment of paintings from London, Paris, Rome, Milan, Madrid, and Florence in 1887. The Ruskin Art Club, founded the next year, sponsored an informal museum and art gallery where etchings and prints by Old Masters could be seen.[95] Los Angeleños wanted to acquire the acceptable in art, for as the *Overland Monthly* declared, California was "in almost every respect an intensification of the American spirit. . . . All this is merely America, 'only more so.'"[96]

Like many other upper-middle-class Americans, art patrons of Los Angeles purchased second- or third-rate European paintings rather than quality work by local artists. By the 1890s, resident artists in southern California were producing paintings that gained critical admiration in the East long before finding buyers in California. Elmer Wachtel visited Los Angeles in 1882, and George Gardner Symons came two years later; both found southern California so attractive that they ultimately became residents. The first permanent artists in the city, William Joseph McCloskey and Alberta Binford McCloskey, had professional training — William with Thomas Eakins at the Pennsylvania Academy of Fine Arts and Alberta with William Merritt Chase in New York. The McCloskeys painted portraits and still lifes featuring flowers and citrus. They encouraged the work of other artists, especially women. Edith White, who had studied at the Art Students League in New York, Fannie Elya Duvall, who had worked with James McNeill Whistler in Europe, and Ellen Farr formed the nucleus of art colonies in Los Angeles and Pasadena. A sense of place and history dominated their works as they painted exotic flowers, still lifes, and genre scenes. They formed a quality-oriented body of artists in the city and its soon-to-be suburbs.[97]

Los Angeles art patrons, not wanting to be viewed as aloof and disinterested, became more receptive to local painters in the 1890s and, at the same time, became increasingly enamored with Impressionism. The artistic controversies in Paris generated great interest in the Impressionists, and the acquisition of works by Claude Monet, Edgar Degas, and Mary Stevenson Cassatt by museums and connoisseurs in the East whetted the tastes of southern Californians. Impressionism also provided an extraordinary means to depict the sunlight of the area, the flowers, and the landscape. Sunny scenes in bright colors were far more congenial to newly built mansions than the dark, somber tones of the Renaissance. Artist colonies at Santa Barbara, Laguna Beach, and San Diego responded to this regional shift and the growing market.[98]

In 1895 the Society of Fine Arts of Southern California exhibited eighty-four paintings that included watercolors by Elmer Wachtel and landscapes in oil by Charles S. Ward and Regina O'Kane. The paintings were vigorous examples of luminous brushwork and rich colors.[99] The exhibition demonstrated the division among regional artists as some painters continued to work in a realistic style while others rushed to embrace Impressionism, a split equally apparent in New York, Boston, and Philadelphia. Los Angeles native son Guy Rose went to Paris in 1888, studied at the Julian Academy with Jules Lefebre and Benjamin Constant, leading art educators, and won the grand prize at the academy's exhibition of 1891. He met Monet in Normandy while on an excursion and soon became a pupil of the moody Impressionist. Rose returned to Los Angeles in 1891 to exhibit twenty paintings, some clearly influenced by Monet. He traveled back and forth between Los Angeles and France for years, and as his style evolved he moved closer to Modernists such as Henri Matisse, Raoul Dufy, and Maurice Utrillo. He found buyers for his paintings in California, though some thought his style was increasingly "decadent."[100]

Other painters in the City of Angels stayed the course with a realism that absorbed the manipulation of light advanced by Impressionism but retained traditional brush strokes and modeling. William Lees Judson, Elmer Wachtel, and Maynard Dixon formed the core of a group of painters who became known as the Arroyo School. The English-born Judson, who had come to California in 1893 as a health-seeker, stayed and became a professor of art at the University of Southern California. He had studied the work of Édouard Manet in Paris, and he applied the French painter's ideas of sun-kissed light and strong color to southern California. Judson painted seascapes, Arroyo Seco, the missions, and the beaches, influencing other artists and his students to do the same. Wachtel and his wife, the painter Marian Kavanagh, lived in Arroyo Seco. They found color everywhere—in the fields of wildflowers, the sunsets along the coast, and the brooks in the canyons.[101] The Arroyo School established a style that would dominate painting in southern California for decades.

At Laguna Beach, forty miles south of Los Angeles, and at San Diego, other artists developed styles not far removed from those of the Arroyo School. George Gardner Symons established a studio at Laguna Beach in the 1890s, and the English watercolorist Norman St. Clair soon followed. After 1900, studios sprang up along two miles of coast, where realists and Impressionists alike painted the beaches and coastal mountains in bright light and vivid colors.[102] San Diego stores offered "chromos" or lithographs for the new homes of the 1870s, and the entrepreneur Alonzo Horton purchased paintings from local artists and commissioned portraits, but the absence of wealthy patrons precluded an active art life until the 1890s. In addition, except for a few painters at La Jolla and Coronado, there were only itinerants in the area. In the 1890s, however, Alice Klauber and Ammi Farnham led a small and dedicated group of artists.

CULTURE *in the* AMERICAN SOUTHWEST

They were joined in 1897 by Charles Fries who, like Farnham, was strongly influenced by the Munich School, with its dark portraits and landscapes. The art life of San Diego changed dramatically with the arrival of Maurice Braun in 1909. Trained at the National Academy of Design and a student of William Merritt Chase, the Hungarian-born Braun joined the Theosophist colony at Point Loma and began to paint Impressionistic landscapes based on space and color relationships. A teacher and founder of the Fine Arts Academy of San Diego, Braun brought Impressionism to the city and reshaped its art.[103]

Artistic endeavors in Texas before 1900 paralleled those of southern California as artists roamed from town to town seeking commissions or came with exploratory expeditions to paint highly detailed, almost scientific works. Galveston served as the port of entry for European artists, largely Germans, who painted portraits of the upper class and then moved on to Houston or San Antonio. For example, Louisa Heuser Wueste, trained at Düsseldorf by artists affiliated with that city's academy, joined her family in San Antonio in 1857. She painted portraits that were strong and unembellished, with flourishes common for the times.[104] In San Antonio she met the French painter Jean Louis Theodore Gentilz, who had accompanied Count Henri Castro's colonists to Texas in 1834. Serving as a surveyor, engineer, and artist, the twenty-four-year old Gentilz helped to settle the frontier town of Castroville on the Medina River. He painted miniature scenes of life on the Texas frontier until returning to France in 1846. After escorting groups of colonists back to Texas, Gentilz settled in San Antonio, where he taught art and painted jewel-like scenes of urban life. He depicted the activities of common people at labor, in commerce, and at entertainment. Gentilz thus created a historical record of the area around San Antonio and Castroville. Hispanic peoples found in Gentilz a sympathetic painter who appreciated their society even as Anglo Americans came to dominate San Antonio and Texas.[105]

Trained, professional artists in San Antonio before 1900 included members of the Onderdonk family, who lavished their talents on landscapes that idealized the flora of south Texas, especially the bluebonnets and Indian paintbrush. Robert Jenkins Onderdonk taught painting in the city, and some of his students formed the Van Dyck Club in 1886 to further art and to sponsor exhibits. This early effort to create an art life led to an artists' organization that became the San Antonio Art League. Onderdonk's daughter Eleanor, a respected miniaturist, played a key role in the art establishment. When Robert Onderdonk moved to Dallas, his son Julian, a budding artist, remained briefly in San Antonio. Julian subsequently moved to New York to study at the Art Students League and with William Merritt Chase at the Shinnecock Hills Summer School of Art. The experience with Chase shaped Julian's career; on returning to San Antonio, he painted shimmering landscapes of cacti, mesquite, and flowers. Referred to as the "Bluebonnet Painter," a label he hated, Onderdonk brought to the vast Texas landscape an aesthetic of light and color drawn from Impressionism.[106] The Onderdonks also helped to create an art appreciation that would lead to the formation of an art museum in the city and to a strong commitment to art education.

Similar developments occurred in Colorado Springs. The English-born artist Walter Paris settled in Colorado Springs in 1872 and for five years produced watercolors of the town, the Garden of the Gods, Manitou Springs, and the Rockies. The majestic scenery attracted other painters such as Harvey Otis Young, who had also been educated in Europe. A native of Vermont, Young painted in Manitou Springs from 1879 until moving to Denver in 1887. The scenes produced by Paris and Young drew other artists to Colorado Springs, and by the end of the 1880s, a colony took root. While some artists, like Paris, were trained in an architectural tradition, others reflected an acquaintance with the Barbizon School and its employment of dark greens and browns. In 1888 a major loan exhibition in Colorado Springs demonstrated the quality of these local artists. This vibrancy continued after 1900 and would lead to the establishment of the Broadmoor Art Academy in 1919.[107] Here, as elsewhere in the region, a critical mass of artists and patrons responded to cultural longings set in a place of earthly grandeur.

From Colorado Springs to San Diego, from Houston to Phoenix, southwesterners had created a region of towns and cities by the end of the 1890s. They longed for classical music, opera, theater, and art for reasons of aesthetic need as well as social acceptance. They imported singers, musicians, actors, and artists to re-create the culture they had left behind. Rising wealth, burgeoning cities, and aspirations for recognition resulted in an imported culture. By the turn of the century, this urbanized society had established institutions fostering creativity, and thus southwesterners had begun to generate as well as import cultural forms. They wrote novels, produced paintings, organized symphonies and opera companies, and established art museums—all attributes of a cultivated urban society. A dynamic tension emerged in the region: at the same time that southwesterners wanted critical acceptance by easterners and Europeans of their replication of cultural institutions, they also sought recognition for their own creative achievements.

CHAPTER 3

Cities & Culture

1900–1920

Urban growth and cultural maturation accelerated in the Southwest between 1900 and 1920. Artists, writers, musicians, and architects flocked to the region from the East, Midwest, and Europe. Substantial immigration shaped regional cultural organizations while the land and the climate had a major impact on the new residents. Investors, business leaders, and young professionals entered the Southwest as risk-takers, eager to reach for the economic "gold ring." As they built, promoted, and boomed their adopted communities, they also pushed for the cultural attainments that signified sophistication and taste.

For the first time, the Southwest began to influence the national culture. Writers ranging from Zane Grey to Mary Austin and Willa Cather introduced the region to millions of readers. The painters in the Taos and Santa Fe art colonies romanticized Native Americans and the geography of northern New Mexico, even as young Georgia O'Keeffe created abstract landscapes in the Texas Panhandle. The cities flourished, producing demands for institutional cultural organizations, especially museums and symphony orchestras. Theatrical entrepreneurs in Los Angeles sent productions to Broadway. National and even international journals praised the Arts and Crafts houses of the Greene brothers of Pasadena and the cubist buildings designed by Irving Gill in San Diego. Buildings in the Mission and Spanish Colonial Revival styles and houses in the California bungalow style soon could be seen in Bismark, North Dakota, and Akron, Ohio. This cultural ferment in the Southwest attracted intellectuals from Europe seeking an escape from urban life and the horrors of World War I. They sought a land of sun and silence in which to write, paint, and compose. Ironically, southwesterners found the cultural trappings of the western European society that they desired to emulate in large urban settings, whereas the European artists and intellectuals sought a society that was rural, simple, and undemanding. These crosscurrents dominated the first two decades of the twentieth century in the Southwest.

The depression of 1893 fatally struck certain portions of the region, especially agriculture and mining, but other economic forces produced substantial expansion by the turn of the century. The discovery of oil east of Houston at Spindletop in 1901 inaugurated a series of major finds in Oklahoma, central and eastern Texas, southern California, and southeastern New Mexico. Vast profits from petroleum generated income for regional firms, which subsequently provided capital for banks, insurance companies, and other endeavors. National firms such as Armour and Swift built large meat-processing facilities in Fort Worth and Oklahoma City. The expansion of wheat and cotton production led to huge elevators, mills, and compresses, as well as the manufacture of food products and clothing. Culturally self-conscious and commercially imperial upper-class and upper-middle-class communities emerged.[1]

A substantial number of the eight million newcomers who crossed the Mississippi River at the turn of the century settled in the Southwest, bringing with them venture capital and a sense of optimism. The region possessed resources and opportunity, and the younger sons of midwestern and eastern families believed they could re-create the fortunes of their parents. Retirees and health-seekers arrived in large numbers, occupying the suburbs of Los Angeles and forming new neighborhoods in Phoenix and Tucson. The region's ethnic diversity became even more evident, and by the 1920s nearly one-third of westerners were foreign-born. Migration from Mexico added to the mix, and by 1920, almost one-fourth of all Texans were of Hispanic origin. City promoters and boomers, hoping to attract the new residents, took steps to expand the urban Southwest.[2]

The U.S. Census Bureau documented the sheer numbers of southwesterners as the population expanded at rates that stunned even typically optimistic chambers of commerce. The 10,000 people in Oklahoma City in 1900 became 91,000 in two decades; Tulsa grew from a settlement of 1,400 to over 72,000 in the same period. By 1920, Arizona, a territory with no major community in 1890, was a state in which over one-third of the people lived in urban areas. Phoenix was a small city of 29,000 by 1920, and Tucson claimed a population of over 20,000. Phoenix already boasted suburbs in Tempe, Glendale, and Mesa. Only Albuquerque lagged behind, its population reaching just 15,000, and New Mexico remained largely rural. This was not so in Texas: by 1920, Houston claimed 138,000 people, Dallas 159,000, and San Antonio over 160,000. Fort Worth had more than 100,000 residents, and El Paso had grown to some 77,000. In Cali-

CULTURE *in the* AMERICAN SOUTHWEST

fornia, Los Angeles exploded from 102,000 people to over 300,000 residents between 1900 and 1910. Los Angeles grew with the discovery of petroleum, the expansion of its port and manufacturing facilities, the arrival of retirees, and the creation of the motion picture industry.[3] The poet Vachel Lindsay hoped that Los Angeles would become "the Boston of Photoplay," and he argued that the City of Angels could emerge as America's new cultural capital.[4] The Los Angeles Board of Realtors could not have said it better.

Architecture served as the primary physical symbol of urban growth, and southwestern cities initially looked not unlike those of the East and Midwest. Public and private buildings became more sophisticated in conception and larger in size. Business and political leaders demanded the most modern structures in terms of design and technology, and home buyers sought the critically acceptable styles. Yet there were those who dared to construct buildings and houses that were in advance of the accepted and the traditional, and there were architects willing to experiment and to innovate.[5]

One of the instant urban centers of the early twentieth century, Oklahoma City soon claimed Romanesque Revival warehouses of red sandstone in its commercial district and a business community of large office buildings of modern design. The investor Charles Colcord constructed an elegant twelve-story office building of steel and reinforced concrete faced with magnificent terra-cotta ornamentation. Colcord had witnessed the destruction caused by earthquake and fire in San Francisco, and he told the architect William A. Wells that he wanted a structure using the best technology available. The year before the Colcord Building opened, the smaller but even more opulent Baum Building was dedicated. For this building, the architect Solomon ("Sol") Andrew Layton brought together terra-cotta, marble slabs, and ornate pinnacles along the parapet while repeating Gothic arches, creating exotic references to the Doge's Palace in Venice. In a frenzy of construction before 1910, the Pioneer Building, the Skirvin Hotel, and Central High School added to the robust downtown of Oklahoma City. The strong vertical lines of William Wells's Pioneer Building of ornamental limestone embraced the theories of Louis Sullivan. For Central High School, Layton used "Collegiate Gothic," a style to be repeated in the forty-six public schools he produced. The dean of Oklahoma City architects, Layton and his associates designed the state capitol, sixteen courthouses, and buildings for the University of Oklahoma. Layton gave his clients solid construction, tasteful ornamentation, and buildings based on the newest concepts from the Northeast. The oilman William B. Skirvin hired Layton to design his six-story hotel, but the rapid growth of the city led them to add two additional floors. Skirvin insisted on marble floors, not carpet, in the lobby, since the guests tracked in oily mud when they arrived from the oil fields and construction sites.[6] The German economist Max Weber visited Oklahoma City in 1904 and noted the boom: "There is fabulous bustle here, and I cannot help but find tremendous fascination in it, despite the stench of petroleum and the fumes."[7]

Petroleum created Tulsa as well. A rough, raw town when incorporated in 1898, the community boomed when drillers struck oil at nearby Red Fork three years later. The Glenn Pool discovery in 1905 brought 5,000 new residents, a five-story Beaux Arts Revival bank building, and a dozen office structures and hotels. The little cowtown soon acquired large, modern, fireproof buildings and a skyline visible for miles around.[8]

The experiences of Oklahoma City and Tulsa were repeated in Texas, where the rising cities of Dallas, Houston, San Antonio, and Fort Worth acquired substantial new buildings in vibrant downtown districts. The skyscraper symbolized modern urban development, and Texas business leaders wanted such buildings for their banks, oil enterprises, and insurance companies. They wanted to be progressive and build "a real city." They demolished older Victorian structures to make room for steel-framed buildings based on the Chicago style and the concepts of Louis Sullivan. The Southwestern Life Building in Dallas (1913) was a Sullivanesque masterpiece, with crisp vertical lines and an ornate cornice. In 1907 the fifteen-story Praetorian Building opened, but its archaic Victorian exterior masked the major engineering advance of its structural steel skeleton. Cass Gilbert's sixty-story, Gothic-inspired Woolworth Building in New York City, the tallest building in the world, influenced the Busch Building in Dallas with a similar motif. The brewery baron Adolphus Busch turned to the high style of the École des Beaux Arts for his Adolphus Hotel (1912). A simple massing terminated in a mansard roof with bronze ornamentation. The heads supporting the cornices reflected Busch's German origins, but the interior received furnishings and decorations in the styles of Louis XIV, XV, and XVI. The hotel, opulent inside and out, served cotton brokers, oil speculators, real estate promoters, and the well-heeled traveling public.[9]

Urban rivalry between Dallas and Houston emerged early, and Houstonians refused to lag their northern neighbors in any area. In 1900, this city of nearly 50,000 had no symphony, no museums, and only a small library. But by 1905, it had buildings of seven and eight stories, and more were under construction. From the outset, builders in Houston turned to major architectural firms in New York, Chicago, and Europe for designs, a pattern repeated throughout the century. Warren and Wetmore of New York, D. H. Burnham of Chicago, Cram, Goodhue, and Ferguson of Boston, and other leading architects came to Houston to produce office buildings, the Rice Institute, hotels, railway stations, and public structures.[10] Houston had to have the best, the most renowned.

The skyscrapers did not reflect urban land values; rather they were a means of advertising and a source of prestige. If D. H. Burnham produced a "Flatiron Building" for lower Manhattan, Fort Worth had to have one also. In 1907–1908, the firm of Sanguinet and Staats designed a seven-story structure, then the tallest in Texas, for a triangularly shaped site. A copy of the New York City original in a Renaissance Revival style, the Fort Worth building of reinforced concrete over steel was crowned with a heavy cornice complete with gargoyles and panthers.[11] The Amicable Insurance Company of Waco built a twenty-story tower in 1911, the tallest building west of the Mississippi River. This rectangular slab used widely spaced columns as a frame and an elaborate cross bracing to deal with wind shear, an advanced concept. The Amicable Building advertised not only the firm but also the boosterism of Waco. These tall buildings shocked the landscape, standing as lonely intrusions above the prairie. They were dramatic; they created a distinct impression.[12]

Texas architects and their clients eschewed Victorian styles after 1900 and turned to the concepts of the École des Beaux Arts of Paris or to the ideas of Louis Sullivan. Courthouses, city halls, schools, and other public buildings appeared with classical porticos, pediments, columns, capitals, and friezes. Domes, pavilions, and balustrades decorated post offices, libraries, and university buildings. The architects of Texas sought historical roots by emulating the designs of the firms of McKim, Meade, and White and Carrére and Hastings. Pennsylvania Station, designed by the former, and the New York Public Library, designed by the latter, served as models for El Paso, Fort Worth, and Houston architects. They studied professional journals, made extensive tours of the East and Midwest, and closely followed national trends. They soon found places in their portfolios for the Prairie School, the Mission Revival, and the Spanish Colonial Revival styles as well. A regional eclecticism emerged by 1920.[13]

Similar patterns evolved in San Diego and Los Angeles. Although the great boom of the 1880s left an overbuilt San Diego, by the early 1900s city residents were revitalizing their community. New commercial buildings and hotels, evidence of the return of prosperity, graced the downtown area as the sugar magnate John D. Spreckels pumped capital into the city. He hired the architect Harrison Albright to design the Union Building, the Golden West Hotel, and the Spreckels Theater Building in the Chicago style. The last structure had a clean, direct exterior and a neo-Baroque theater inside, whereas the hotel was designed for "working men." San Diego business leaders, encouraged by Spreckels and others, began to plan an elaborate celebration to coincide with the opening of the Panama Canal. That festival would subsequently revolutionize southwestern architecture.[14]

Architectural styles in Los Angeles reflected the eclecticism of Texas and Oklahoma as designers abandoned the Victorian modes for nonresidential structures. Gothic churches, neoclassical public buildings, and Chicago-style office complexes served the burgeoning city. Large structures, such as the Pacific Electric Building, borrowed from Louis Sullivan, with plain facades rising to ornate cornices. These reinforced concrete, multistoried buildings had little decoration at the street level. A small town trying to be a city, Los Angeles hired an urban planner in 1907 to identify problems as the downtown area became jammed with traffic. Pacific Electric interurbans and Los Angeles Railway streetcars brought tens of thousands of people to a congested downtown each day. The tallest building in 1902, seven stories in height, had been eclipsed by structures twice as high. Stores, hotels, offices, theaters, and governmental buildings were built without concern for the width of streets, the availability of utilities, or aesthetic values.[15]

Phoenix, Tucson, and Albuquerque also embraced modern currents in architecture after 1900, but their relatively small populations prevented construction of structures as large or as elaborate as those found in other regional centers. The leaders of Phoenix brought in a second railroad, successfully fought to move the state capital to their town, and persuaded the federal government to construct Roosevelt Dam in order to expand agricultural production. Many members of the Phoenix elite had strong ties to Chicago and knew well its skyscraper styles and the impact of its world fair, the Columbian Exposition of 1893. They believed that boosterism and promotion would bring tourists as well as investors. The town grew as three- and four-story business blocks and hotels were constructed of stone and brick. Architects sought to harmonize the buildings and the landscape by employing natural textures and earth colors, but not adobe! In Tucson, the architect David Holmes and his brother Jesse H. Holmes produced classically styled buildings for the University of Arizona campus and a few commercial structures, but despite their knowledge of the work of Sullivan and of Burnham, the buildings they designed were mundane at best. Albuquerque added few buildings of significant style; rather, residents could point to the architect Charles Whittlesey's house, a Norwegian villa, as a symbol of sophistication.[16]

The cityscapes of the Southwest in 1900 thus followed the historic pattern that had evolved during the first conquest. The physical and social environments produced towns and cities with low profiles and horizontal lines. Houses with

CULTURE *in the* AMERICAN SOUTHWEST

flat or shallow- angle roofs spread across broad expanses, with yards usually on all four sides. Grid-patterned streets repeated the regularity established by the housing forms. But commercial and residential architecture in the Southwest was about to be transformed by the currents emanating from southern California, particularly the style known as the California bungalow.[17]

The word *bungalow* derives from the Bengali noun *b'ngl'*, which described a low house with galleries or porches all around, and from the Hindi adjective *bangl'*, which meant things belonging to Bengal. The British military, occupying India, had developed a housing form that employed the concept of a square, wood-frame house with porches on several sides and gently sloping roof lines: the bungalow. The design spread to England in the nineteenth century, and a few examples appeared in the eastern United States after 1876 but made no significant impression. After 1900, the concept emerged in California and soon dominated housing styles from Los Angeles to Houston.

The bungalow design spread in the United States as part of the Arts and Crafts movement. Originating in England during the late Victorian period, the Arts and Crafts idea was soon flourishing in the United States. Drawing on medieval English folk sources, the movement emphasized the use of natural materials with harmonious designs. Craftspeople carved wooden decorative pieces for stairways, mantels, doors, cabinets, and beams. Stone fireplaces, rough brick walls, and flagstone floors emphasized the role of crafts in artful forms.[18]

The leading practitioners of the Arts and Crafts concept in southern California were the Greene brothers. Charles Sumner Greene and Henry Mather Greene, born in Cincinnati, later moved with their parents to St. Louis, where they attended Manual High School. Their teacher Calvin Milton Woodward taught them handwork and the liberal arts, preparing them for college at the Massachusetts Institute of Technology. Graduating from MIT in 1891, the brothers went to Pasadena to visit their parents two years later. The Greene brothers stayed in California and began to design houses in the booming environment. They created a vernacular style using a variety of boards and shingles; their love of wood in all forms permeated the homes. Elements of the bungalow style and the Arts and Crafts movement merged in their plans. Wood in many colors and textures blended with cobblestone chimneys and large windows, deep porches, and heavily landscaped lawns. The Greenes wanted their houses to have an intimate contact with the site and with nature. The colors of the exteriors — brown and several shades of green — blended with extensive gardens and shrubs brought close to the walls. Clean, simple designs brought the Greenes a stream of clients.[19]

As their practice thrived, the Greenes produced houses of seven or eight rooms for $3,000 to $5,000, but they also designed much larger homes, includ-

FIGURE 13
Architects Greene & Greene launched the bungalow "craze" with their classic Gamble House in Pasadena. Author's collection.

ing their masterpiece, the Gamble House. Constructed in Pasadena in 1908 for David B. and Mary Gamble of the Procter & Gamble Company, this home broke with traditional designs and incorporated redwood, pale-colored plaster, built-in furniture, side terraces, and open sleeping porches. The Greenes brought the living spaces outdoors, capturing the cool air from the nearby arroyo. Wood in structural timbers, and in shingles and decorative panels of Japanese designs, celebrated the Greenes' devotion to natural materials. The Gamble House emerged as a symphony in teak, maple, cedar, redwood, and oak, all hand-rubbed to a satin finish. Elements of a medieval Japanese pavilion and the Arts and Crafts movement came together in a classic design.[20]

The Greenes added similar elements to other bungalows, such as a large interior patio for the Arturo Bandini house in 1903, and they later incorporated adobe walls in some designs. Larger gables appeared with horizontal redwood siding and porches across the facade. Even larger gables perpendicular to the facade produced the "airplane" bungalow. As their style evolved, particularly after 1914 when Charles moved to Carmel, the houses became simpler, with less intricate detailing. The Greenes' houses were featured in architectural journals and popular magazines, and plan books soon appeared with standardized homes based on their concepts. Lumber companies saw great potential in these designs

CULTURE *in the* AMERICAN SOUTHWEST

and began to produce pre-cut lumber for the standard plans. The enormous demand for housing in Los Angeles led to miles and miles of streets lined with bungalows. The concept incorporated features that dealt with the climate, the desire for natural materials, and a lifestyle that focused on the out-of-doors.[21]

Population increases in southwestern cities produced demands for affordable middle-class housing, and the bungalow provided the answer. "Craftsman" and "airplane" bungalows spread across the Southwest. The homes had no basements because of the soils, and the exposed foundations were hidden by shrubs and plantings. Lumber companies dictated room sizes with their pre-cut studs and beams, but the interiors received a wide range of trims. Although some bungalow designs used brick, the bungalows of Lubbock, Phoenix, and Tulsa, like those of Pasadena, were largely of wood construction. Some elements of Frank Lloyd Wright's Prairie-style houses merged with the bungalow, such as wide overhanging eaves and low roof lines. Some versions followed the Gamble House concept of a second floor with many windows to allow the heat of the lower floor to rise and create air circulation, a prime need in Houston, Oklahoma City, and Tucson. The Greenes provided inspiration for three generations of builders who produced homes for the masses, a democratic or egalitarian form of housing. The suburb, the automobile, and the bungalow formed the urban setting in the Southwest.[22] The popular songwriter George Devereaux summed up the romance of the style:

I just got off the Sunset Train
I'm from the Angel Town,
The Golden West Los Angeles,
Where the sun shines all year 'round.
I left a girlie back there,
She's the sweetest girl I know,
She said "Good-bye, I'll wait for you"
In the land of the bungalow.

Chorus:
In the Land of the Bungalow,
Away from the ice and snow,
Away from the cold,
To the Land of the Gold,
Away where the poppies grow,
Away to the setting sun,
To the home of the orange blossom
To the land of fruit and honey,

Where it does not take much money
To own a bungalow

I just can't keep my thought away,
from California's shores,
The land of flowers and winter showers,
How I miss you more and more.
As soon as I can get away,
I know that I will go
Back to the girl I love best,
In the land of the Bungalow.[23]

Charles Greene appreciated the adaptability of the bungalow for mass housing, but he moved on to employ other historical elements in his designs, especially architecture in the Mission Revival style: "The old art of California — that of the mission fathers — is old enough to be romantic and mysterious too. Study it and you will find a deeper meaning than books tell of sun-dried bricks and plaster show. Then, too, those old monks came from a climate not unlike this. They built after their own fashion and their knowledge of climate and habits of life, were bred in the bone. Therefore, giving heed to these necessary and effective qualities there is good and just reason why we should study their works."[24]

Greene echoed the views of the writer Charles Lummis, who lived just down the arroyo. He also reflected the ideas of the craftsman Gustav Stickley, who was producing "mission oak" furniture based on designs from the eighteenth century. The Southwest possessed vast expanses of desert, non-Anglo peoples, and ancient ruins of earlier civilizations. It had decaying missions and churches established by Roman Catholic friars and priests. These attributes, plus a desire to establish a regional architecture, led to the "Mission Revival." And like the bungalow, Mission Revival houses soon appeared in the Dakotas, the Carolinas, and the Old Northwest.

The Mission Revival style of architecture also spread to commercial designs. Why should southwestern cities look just like metropolitan centers elsewhere? Why couldn't regional architects use the Southwest's unique elements to forge a new mode?[25] In 1910, Arthur B. Benton, an architect and preservationist, told the First Southwest City Planning Conference in Los Angeles: "The railroads, the hotels, the commercial bodies all use our old Missions to attract tourists and dollars to themselves." Why not use the form to create a "modern architecture"? Benton accurately prophesied the changes of the next eight decades.[26]

The California Building at the World's Columbian Exposition in Chicago stood almost alone in rejecting the classical architecture of the fair as the state

CULTURE *in the* AMERICAN SOUTHWEST

presented itself in the form of a mission. From that time well into the 1930s, the Mission Revival symbolized an effort to establish historical roots through a harmonious architecture. Buildings used extensive stuccoed surfaces, arched portals and loggias, tile roofs, and projecting gables with scalloped edges. Bell towers, round windows, and modest ornamentation over central doors suggested the quaint image of a Golden Age. Hotels, such as the Mission Inn in Riverside and the Potter Hotel in Santa Barbara, and railway stations in San Diego and Santa Ana employed the Mission Revival style as part of a drive to attract tourists. Homes ranging from huge complexes to modest cottages appeared in the Mission Revival mode. Roman Catholic colleges and parochial schools employed the form, as did courthouses, libraries, hospitals, and public schools. Some architects toyed with Mission Revival, adding decorative elements to suggest something Spanish, Moorish, or even Italian.[27] No doubt the Franciscan fathers would have been startled to see bell towers, fountains, and gardens as a motif for stores, railway stations, and Protestant churches. The style was picturesque, historic, and sublime.

Mission Revival and its emerging offshoots provided opportunities for younger architects, especially women. The University of California at Berkeley opened its architectural school in 1904, and half of the class of ten students were women. Many of the school's graduates joined previously all-male firms, but a few struck out on their own. One graduate, Julia Morgan, the first woman licensed in California as an architect, also attended the École des Beaux Arts in Paris. Leading her own firm, Morgan achieved international recognition for the Hearst Castle at San Simeon, but she also worked extensively in the Mission Revival style. Her Hollywood Studio Club with its courtyard, arched openings, and wrought-iron balustrade is but one example. Another was the Los Angeles Examiner Building, also designed for William Randolph Hearst. In San Diego, Lilian Jeannette Rice utilized reinforced concrete and plain geometric surfaces in unique projects. Tile roofs, inner courtyards, and grillwork decorated the homes and apartment houses she designed. In the early 1920s, Rice created an entire Spanish village at Rancho Santa Fe, a large land-development project. Working with the architect Hazel Waterman, Rice achieved a deep sensitivity for the natural contours of the site, and she preserved the trees, shrubs and arroyos. Waterman had become an architect at age thirty-seven, after her husband died. She restored homes built during the Spanish colonial period and worked in an eclectic Mediterranean style. She sought to blend architecture with the landscape. Lutah Maria Riggs at Santa Barbara and Edla Muir in Brentwood, Santa Monica, and Beverly Hills continued these traditions as preservationists and architects. Riggs and Muir practiced until the 1940s and moved forward to the

International Style, but their earlier designs captured the essence of Mission Revival even as the mode spread beyond California.²⁸

The Mission Revival style appealed strongly to Dr. Alexander John Chandler of Detroit, who moved to the Salt River valley of Arizona in 1887 and in 1912 founded the town of Chandler. The community was to be the "Pasadena of Arizona" in the midst of what Chandler called "the realized mirage." At the center of the town stood the San Marcos Hotel surrounded by orange and lemon groves, cactus, bougainvillea, and peach and olive trees. Built of cast-in-place concrete, a very early demonstration of this technique, the San Marcos featured arches, arcades, patios, and deep porches in the Mission Revival style. A luxury hotel in the desert, a caravansary, the San Marcos projected the atmosphere of a Franciscan settlement.²⁹ The impact of the hotel could soon be seen in Tucson and Phoenix.

One of the main proponents of the Mission Revival style, the Atchison, Topeka, and Santa Fe Railway, erected hotels and stations along its routes as part of a quest for tourists. E. P. Ripley, president of the railway, occupied a winter home in Pasadena, and he saw the possibilities presented by this romantic style. In the midst of a major modernization program, the railway joined with the Fred Harvey Company to erect new hotels and tourist facilities. Their architects, such as Charles F. Whittlesey, borrowed from the missions at Acoma and other pueblos to design stations and hotels that were long, low, and strongly horizontal. Lengthy, arched arcades protected travelers from the sun. Adobe walls, simulated in concrete, joined porches, balconies, vigas, and carved wooden door and window frames in the Mission Revival style. The Alvarado Hotel in Albuquerque (1905) epitomized the concept repeated in the Casteñada Hotel at Las Vegas, El Ortiz at Lamy, and El Navajo at Gallup. Giant train stations at San Bernardino, Needles, and Amarillo echoed the style of the Harvey Houses.³⁰

As part of the effort to achieve a high degree of authenticity and create sophisticated appointments, the railway and Harvey hired Mary E. J. Coulter to decorate the interiors. Coulter had trained as an artist in California and then apprenticed as an architect in St. Paul. Hired in 1902 to decorate the Indian Building at the Alvarado Hotel, Coulter studied Native American arts, archeology, and history to create a motif for the hotel. She believed that the architecture and the interiors had to be in harmony with the environment. Coulter hired Indian artisans to decorate the building using ancient designs and artifacts. The railway and Harvey found her work to be excellent, and over the next four decades Coulter completed more than twenty projects for them. At the Grand Canyon she used natural materials and Hopi designs in The Lookout, Hermit's Rest, Phantom Ranch, and other facilities. Coulter produced interiors at hotels, such as El Ortiz, that Owen Wister described as "like a private house of someone who had lavished thought and care upon every nook." Soon Coulter took responsibility for entire projects, and she continued to do so until 1947 when, at age seventy-nine, she completed the Painted Desert Inn. A dogmatic and tough perfectionist, Coulter worked in "a man's world" of construction and design, but builders and artisans respected her and the integrity she brought to the projects.[31] Tourists also responded to her work and to the Santa Fe Railway's efforts. As one proper New Englander wrote: "A very large hotel called the Alvarado adjoins the depot here. These are of the old Moorish architecture, and, with their quaint arches, towers and facades form absolutely the most attractive group of buildings I have seen since I left Boston."[32]

The Santa Rita Hotel in Tucson, banks in Texas, and stores in New Mexico all utilized the Mission Revival motif. When the Italian sculptor Pompeo Coppini journeyed to San Antonio in 1901, he stepped off the train into "real Italian sunshine, with the same gorgeous blue sky," where tropical plants and blooming flowers combined with the architecture to remind him of the Mediterranean and "home."[33] This was precisely the image that the promoters and romanticists sought. The ironies of this historicism were many, but perhaps the most obvious was the fact that middle-class Protestants moved to the Southwest and occupied houses and worshipped in churches designed to resemble miniature Roman Catholic missions.

Mission Revival spawned other styles, the most significant being the Spanish Colonial Revival. The impetus to expand on the mission concept came largely from the Panama-California Exposition held in 1915 at San Diego to celebrate the opening of the Panama Canal. San Diego had only 35,000 residents in 1909, but the chamber of commerce decided to organize a major exposition on fourteen hundred acres of undeveloped park land. The celebration was designed to ignite an economic recovery for the community. Citizens voted to issue $1,750,000 in bonds, and the organizers raised another $1,000,000 in subscriptions. They hired the famous Olmsted brothers to landscape the park, but a dispute over the design led to the brothers' departure. Far more successful was the decision to hire Bertram Grosvenor Goodhue as the chief architect.[34]

The organizers did not want a repeat of the "White City" of the Chicago World's Columbian Exposition in 1893; they wanted a theme that reflected the local heritage. Goodhue, a partner in the firm of Cram, Goodhue, and Ferguson of Boston, had visited Mexico several times and had published a book, *Mexican Memories*. He saw Mexican architecture as an amalgamation of craft, structure, ornamentation, and cultural statement. He traveled by train from New Orleans to San Diego, viewing the indigenous architecture. Lobbying strongly to obtain the San Diego commission, Goodhue decided to employ elements of Mexican architecture as his theme.[35]

Rejecting the Olmsted plan to locate the exposition in the park's canyons, the organizers told Goodhue to place the focus on the site's central mesa. On the mesa, Goodhue grouped buildings into a "village," with ideas drawn from Mexico, Spain, and Italy. He lavished cast-stone decorations on the walls, entries, cornices, and towers. Moorish details included minaret-like towers, reflecting pools, fountains, pergolas, domes, and patios. The five permanent buildings were larger and even more ornate than the many temporary structures. To reach the mesa, Goodhue designed the Cabrillo Bridge of seven graceful arches modeled after the Alcantara Bridge in Toledo, Spain. Goodhue fashioned a Spanish "city" of white walls in what became Balboa Park. The California State Building reminded the three and one-half million visitors of a Spanish cathedral while the New Mexico State Building looked like a Pueblo mission. The *San Diego Union* declared, "This is not an exposition, it is . . . the expression of an idea."[36] It was a fair in a garden setting, "a vision of romance." The critic Eugen Neuhaus proclaimed: "The San Diego Exposition will not have been a mere celebration. It will be considered a milestone in the civilization of the West."[37]

Grafting the decorative elements of the Mexican Churrigueresque to the basic Mission Revival concept, Goodhue launched the Spanish Colonial Revival style, which became a basic mode of southwestern architectural expression. The design proved appropriate to the climate and the geography and created a tradition and a history where none had existed before. Entire communities adopted this style — Santa Barbara, for example — and though the Spanish Colonial Revival lent itself to large buildings such as schools and churches, it soon could be found also in service stations and automobile garages. The architects George Washington Smith in Santa Barbara, Elmer Grey and Myron Hunt in Los Angeles, and Atlee B. Ayres in San Antonio designed exquisite homes in variations of the Spanish Colonial Revival. By the 1920s and 1930s, they had abandoned the more flamboyant aspects of Goodhue's concepts, but the basic elements remained.[38]

One of the structures at the exposition received extravagant praise for its simplicity and "naiveté": the New Mexico State Building. It stood in sharp contrast to Goodhue's heavy ornamentation; its architects, Isaac Hamilton Rapp and William Morris Rapp, had created a revelation. Born in Illinois, Isaac Rapp served as an apprentice to an architect and in 1888 moved to Trinidad, Colorado, where he established a practice. After his brother William joined Isaac in 1892, the two designed buildings in Colorado and New Mexico using historical models. They borrowed from medieval and Romanesque styles before receiving a commission to produce the New Mexico Territorial Building at the World's Fair in St. Louis in 1904. That structure used the Mission Revival mode, as did their Elks Club in Santa Fe, built in 1912. The success of the St. Louis project led to their winning the commission for the New Mexico State Building at San Diego. Earlier architects had used the Pueblo missions and the multistoried Pueblo communities as models, but the results were often clumsy and amateurish. An exception was Coulter's Hopi House at the Grand Canyon, which demonstrated the effects that could be achieved with a concern for detail and authenticity. The Rapps turned to the missions of Acoma, Pecos, Laguna, San Felipe, and Cochiti for their inspiration and produced a building that had simple lines and little ornamentation but won high praise from critics and tourists. Their building followed suggestions made by Dr. Edgar L. Hewett, founder and first director of the Museum of New Mexico.[39]

Hewett and artists such as Carlos Vierra and William Penhallow Henderson, as well as Santa Fe's leaders, sought to preserve the character of that town, and the Rapps were strongly influenced by their effort. The New Mexico Territorial Legislature had designated the Palace of the Governors as a museum in 1909, and Hewett repaired the building and removed the alterations that had been made by the Anglo Americans. He provided artists with studios in the Palace, which soon became overcrowded. The state legislature in 1915 voted to create a new art gallery, using the Rapps' San Diego building for the design, and to place the building on a corner of the plaza. The larger scheme, produced by Hewett and the City Planning Board, called for a comprehensive program to end the use of pitched roofs and sheet metal and to restrict building design in the town. They proposed one- or two-story buildings without gables or arches but with portals, balconies, courtyards, and patios. There was to be no ornamentation. Stepped masses replicating the lines of the pueblos were allowed. The restrictions virtually described the Rapps' San Diego building. The Santa Fe Chamber of Commerce called for the end of the bungalows and for the removal of wood fronts from adobe structures. The new art gallery, designated the Fine Arts Building, set the stage for the emergence of the "Santa Fe style."

Across the street from the Palace, the Rapps reproduced their San Diego building. Business leaders raised funds, and Vierra, Kenneth Chapman, and other artists produced murals, furniture, and carved-wood trim. The "mud village" began to evolve into a picturesque community. Adobe plaster covered the brick walls of the museum building, called "The Cathedral of the Desert" by Charles Lummis.[40] The artist Robert Henri wrote to a friend when the museum opened in 1917: "The museum here looks as though it were a precious child of the Santa Fe sky and the Santa Fe mountains. . . . It seems warmly at home as if it had always been here."[41] He hoped it would shame away the ubiquitous bungalows. Indeed, the restored Palace of 1610 and the museum of 1915 looked like longtime companions. Hewett, in his dedication speech, said: "We feel that our people here in the Southwest do have a life in keeping with the soil, the skies, winds, clouds, spaces — that they have ordered their lives in honest, simple harmonious ways. We are glad that the artists understand them."[42]

Santa Fe and the Southwest embraced the concepts of the Rapps and the city planners. The plaza was redone in the Santa Fe style, with La Fonda Hotel of 1921 as an anchor diagonally across the square from the Fine Arts Building. The Rapps designed the hotel with thick walls, buttresses, stepped masses, balconies, portals, exposed beams, and small windows. As the town grew, artists constructed homes and studios in a style that had no pure historical basis. Indeed, the Rapps, Hewett, Henri, and Henderson were all from the East or Midwest, and as conservative conservationists, they developed an eclectic style that spread across the region. The Fort Worth Livestock Exchange appeared in a form similar to the Santa Fe style, as did the Hotel Galvez in Galveston. The Phelps Dodge Corporation hired Goodhue to design an entire town in southwestern New Mexico, Tyrone, in the Mission and Spanish Colonial Revival styles, but Goodhue's homes, library, department store, railroad station, hospital, and school had much more in common with the emerging eclectic style. Pale-pink stucco, red-tile roofs, and arched colonnades, all without ornamentation, were closer to the ideas of the Rapps than they were to Goodhue's own ideas evident at the San Diego exposition. The vision of the Rapps even crossed the country, including structures such as the Baptist Church of Cape May, New Jersey.

Not all architects embraced these southwestern architectural themes, and one innovator, Irving Gill of San Diego, cautioned, "It is safe to say that more architectural crimes have been committed in their name [the missions] than in any other, unless it be the Grecian temples."[43] One of the most innovative architects in the early twentieth century, Gill abandoned historical references, used new construction technologies, and revolutionized designs for homes in southern California. Born in New York in 1870, Gill had studied architecture as an apprentice in Syracuse. In 1891 he moved to Chicago to work for Adler and Sullivan. There he fell under the influence of a young Frank Lloyd Wright. Health problems led Gill to move to San Diego, where in the late 1890s he designed traditionally styled houses. But Gill sought to escape from the past. "The west has an opportunity unparalleled in the history of the world," he said, "for it is the newest white page turned for registration."[44] The West fed his desire to pioneer: "In California we have the great wide plains, arched blue skies that are fresh chapters yet unwritten. We have noble mountains, lovely little hills and canyons

waiting to hold the record of this generation's history, ideals, imagination, sense
of romance and honesty."[45]

Abandoning his partner in 1906, Gill struck out on his own. There was great
support for him to design the Panama-California Exposition, but Goodhue lobbied hard for the commission and won. Gill worked briefly on the project with
Goodhue but resigned to go his own way. The Spanish Colonial Revival with
all its ornamentation was anathema to his ideals. "If we, the architects of the
West, wish to do great work we must dare to be simple, must have the courage
to fling aside every device that distracts the eye from structural beauty, must
break through convention and get down to fundamental truths."[46]

After 1906, Gill followed his conviction that houses should be plain but as
substantial as boulders. Ornamentation, he argued, should be left to nature. His
houses became simple cubes with creamy walls, rising boldly, unrelieved by a
cornice. These abstract forms borrowed from the missions only arches, colonnades, and gardens, not decorations. Gill achieved the simplicity of a boulder by

FIGURE 15

*Henry Trost brought the "Prairie style" to the Southwest and modified the
concept to adapt to the land and the sky. Author's collection.*

using concrete in an imaginative way. To obtain the cubist shapes, he poured
concrete in forms on the ground and then tilted them into place. He emphasized
the plastic quality of concrete, stressing the geometry as well as the liquidity of
concrete in a series of homes. The Russell C. Allen home (1907) in Bonita received boxlike shapes, and houses for Henry H. Timken (1911) and for the
Scripps family (1915–16) were abstract cubes with large windows. Using the mass
and proportions of the missions, Gill employed reinforced concrete to suggest
the smooth stucco walls of those pioneer churches. Simple doors and windows,
minimalist interiors, beautifully designed gardens, and great care for the site
marked his work. The La Jolla Women's Club (1913–14), with its plain arcaded
porch and flat roof, epitomized his style, but the home he designed for the pat-
ent medicine king Walter Luther Dodge in Los Angeles (1916) was his masterpiece. A series of cubes stepped back from the facade, large rectangular windows
with steel frames, a flat roof, and detailed landscaping produced a home not
unlike those designed by the Austrian Adolf Loos, who was even then launching
a new era in European architecture.[47] Gill stood on the cusp of modernism.

The atelier of Adler and Sullivan and the presence of Frank Lloyd Wright
inspired yet another southwestern architect, Henry Charles Trost. Born in Toledo, Ohio, of German immigrant parents, Trost studied drafting and in 1880

drifted west first to Colorado, then to Texas, and then to Louisiana. He designed buildings in the Second Empire style in Pueblo and Colorado Springs and worked with Nicholas Clayton in Galveston. By the late 1880s, he was in Chicago, observing the work of Adler and Sullivan and becoming a disciple of the latter. Trost abandoned his commitment to Beaux Arts classicism and embraced Sullivan's emphasis on nature and organic architecture. In 1899 Trost moved to Tucson, where he designed homes, schools, and commercial buildings. The church at San Xavier whetted his interest in the Spanish Baroque, as did the growing influence of the Mission Revival. The Owls Club in Tucson (1899) blended Sullivanesque ornamentation with the Mission Revival. Trost had seen the California Building at Chicago in 1893, read the works of Lummis, and shared an enthusiasm for indigenous architecture. Before moving to El Paso in 1904, Trost designed Mission-style homes, the classical Carnegie Library, the Santa Rita Hotel, and many other buildings in this eclectic format.

Forming a partnership with his brother Gustavus Adolphus Trost, Charles Trost became the premier architect in El Paso, and soon buildings by Trost and Trost could be found throughout the Southwest.[48] While Trost worked in many styles, even producing a Southern Colonial mansion, he introduced Frank Lloyd Wright's Prairie-style houses to the region. Trost's own home in Sunset Heights (1908) epitomized the importance of Wright's influence. The Trost house, in cream and brown, adapted the Prairie style to the climate and weather of the Southwest with wide eaves, shaded porches, and large windows. He used Wright's horizontal brick, art glass, and recessed entry formulations. In his houses in El Paso, Trost reproduced Wright's ideas through his own interpretation: "The atmosphere of the Southwest is wonderfully clear. The mountain masses are rugged and their shadows and contrasts are sharply defined. The sunset tints are primary colors, illuminated with wonderful gold and purple. The horizons are infinite — long, distant level lines, broken only by the far-off mountains or the scrubby desert vegetation against the sky."[49]

Trost's architecture incorporated the philosophies of Sullivan and Wright tempered by his own aesthetic that reflected the earth, sky, and people of the Southwest. Like Irving Gill, Trost turned to reinforced concrete to obtain the earth colors and textures of the region. His early concrete commercial buildings employed modest Sullivan-like ornamentation, and his twelve-story Mills Building (1910–11) was "the tallest concrete building in the world." Strong vertical lines, rounded windows, and a wide cornice reminded viewers of Sullivan's Carson-Pirie-Scott Department Store in Chicago. The facade expressed the rhythm of the concrete piers using Sullivan's idea of "base, capital and shaft."

FIGURE 16
Despite "modernization," the Mills Building in El Paso retains its place
as one of the region's pioneer skyscrapers. Author's collection.

The Hotel Paso del Norte followed shortly, as did other commercial buildings in El Paso, Albuquerque, Tucson, and Phoenix. Trost established a reputation for solid designs, concern for the site, and imaginative responses to clients.[50]

Perhaps his most unusual commission came from the Texas State School of Mines and Metallurgy at El Paso. The Main Building was destroyed by fire in 1916, and the campus needed to be redesigned. Kathleen Worrell, wife of the dean of the School of Mines, had read an article in the *National Geographic* of April, 1914, on Buhtan in East Asia and was struck by the similarities between the geography of that country and that of El Paso. She urged that the new school buildings be Bhutanese in style. The school president agreed, and Trost produced buildings with battered or sloping walls, low hipped roofs, deep-set windows, and ornamental friezes. Five buildings on the rugged site created "Lamaseries on the hill."[51]

Trost rejected Wright's dictum against using historical elements in architecture, a philosophy Wright continually violated himself, and Trost's hotels and skyscrapers of the 1920s borrowed from the Mission and Spanish Revival styles. Trost defended his approach as not imitative but rather as responsive to the atmosphere and the climate. Heat, aridity, brilliant colors, lengthy horizons, and mountain masses dictated the parameters of Spanish architecture in the Southwest, Trost believed, and these conditions guided his own work. Thick walls, deep porches, high ceilings, patios, and fountains responded to the undulating land. Trost's Prairie-style houses in El Paso and Albuquerque had double attics under large gables to vent heat from the living quarters. His Franciscan Hotel in Albuquerque (1923) sought to "catch the elusive atmosphere of that most typical of all regional architecture — the Pueblo Indian theme."[52] The seven-story hotel looked like an enormous pueblo, with thick walls, blocklike forms, and stepped masses. Crude details on the cubelike blocks blended the pueblo aesthetic and modernism. Architectural journals and critics praised the Franciscan for its daring and innovative conception.[53] Trost designed many other hotels across the region, as well as skyscrapers. His Luhrs Tower (1920) in Phoenix and Bassett Tower (1929–30) in El Paso were strong, vertical buildings that he embellished with Art Moderne and Art Deco details in Spanish Colonial Revival and Native American motifs. Trost's substantial architectural legacy in the Southwest reflected his imagination interacting with the environment.

Trost's reaction to the region paralleled that of the artists who discovered the Southwest after 1900. Between the turn of the century and 1920, artists in the region responded to international trends in the styles they adopted. The splendor of the unique landscape became a theme of both realists and early modernists, as did portraits of the peoples of the region. The recognition by the rest of the nation of the unique features of the Southwest as seen by these artists helped define the United States and its self-image. That had not seemed possible earlier, when the art of the East was viewed as academic and cultured and that of the West as provincial and incomplete.[54] One critic wrote, "Here is a land made for the artist, — or was the artist made for the land?" Everett C. Maxwell noted, "The Southwest must virtually produce its own interpreters."[55] There were problems of scale, color, and light, as well as the need to capture the sublime in the midst of grandeur. In the aftermath of the epoch battles between the academics and the Impressionists in France, young American painters embraced the techniques of the latter with a vengeance. No sooner had Impressionism become an American artistic canon than members of "The Eight" and other artists led a revolt that emphasized urban life and portraits of common people. The "Ash Can School" offered reality, not romance, and painted the city, not rural America. The public still found much to admire in Frederic Remington and Charles M. Russell and their action-charged paintings and sculpture, but the art world moved rapidly past that romantic interpretation to a post-Impressionist world of Henri Matisse, Paul Cézanne, and Pablo Picasso. The art and artists of the Southwest emerged in the midst of enormous stylistic turbulence and ferment at home and abroad.

Artists of the Southwest tried to cater to audiences both popular and critical. Seeking to earn a living, they worked with magazine editors and writers. Fernand Lungren painted landscapes and Native Americans in the Southwest for decades, often turning to Charles Lummis for guidance. Lummis published Lungren's illustrations in *Out West* and tried to place the artist's work in journals such as *McClure's Magazine*.[56] Owen Wister, author of *The Virginian*, advised Lungren about which paintings to submit to the annual competition of the National Academy of Design and which to send to an exhibition in Rome. Wister described a painting he had seen on Lungren's easel during a visit to the artist's studio. The top of the painting had a cloud that "hovered and glowed[,] a tremendous luminous apparition of rose cloud hanging down from heaven like Genesis, Exodus, the birth of the Ten Commandments and The Day of Judgement. *That* is to *be* Mine."[57] Wister's words suggested the problems of painters like Lungren, who wanted to place illustrations in popular outlets and yet win critical praise in New York and Europe.

One popular painter was the Texan Frank Reaugh, who studied in Paris in the 1880s before returning to the Lone Star State, where he produced paintings of ranches and Longhorn cattle. He would paint Longhorns for almost fifty years while teaching art in Dallas. His opalescent pastels graced many a Texas home. Yet even though he exhibited at the World's Columbian Exposition in Chicago in 1893, Reaugh remained little known outside Texas.[58] His subject matter and style never altered.

The same fate befell the Onderdonks and the Texas sculptor Elisabet Ney. Trained in the East, Robert Jenkins Onderdonk and his son, Robert Julian Onderdonk, painted, taught, and organized art exhibitions in Dallas and San Antonio, earning a regional reputation. Although Robert Julian's Impressionism was mainstream, his choice of subject matter had little appeal for eastern critics and galleries. His landscapes portrayed the atmospheric effects, the wildflowers, and the intense heat of Texas summers, but his enthusiasm and talents were rarely recognized north of the Red River or east of the Sabine.[59]

CULTURE *in the* AMERICAN SOUTHWEST

Elisabet Ney was born in Germany and trained there as a sculptor. In Europe "Miss Ney" sculpted the famous—royalty, composers, and politicians—but in 1871 a tragedy in her personal life brought her to rural Texas, where she lived for nearly two decades in obscurity on a farm. When she won a commission for statues for the new capitol in Austin, she moved there, opened a studio, and launched a second career. Aided by the Texas Women's Commission, she exhibited at the World's Columbian Exposition, but her work remained largely unknown except among Texans. Ney's monumental statues of Texas heroes emulated the classical work she had done in Europe.[60] Did Stephen F. Austin really look like Count Otto von Bismarck? Ney's work satisfied the needs of Texans seeking to view the heroes of the Texas Republic in terms of ancient Greek gods and Roman generals, but her talents received little critical recognition.

Similarly, the artists of Arizona's plateau country fared well in terms of popular acclaim, but their landscapes and portraits of Native Americans were rarely selected for exhibition at the National Academy of Design or the international competition at the Carnegie Institute in Pittsburgh. Arizona artists fell victim to the romance of place. The painter William R. Leigh visited Arizona's First Mesa in 1912 and recalled, "I was eager to waste no time whatever; I saw that I needed studies of everything—the vegetation, the rocks, the plains, the mesas, the sky, the Indians and their dwellings."[61] Leigh's illustrations for books and magazines demonstrated his abilities, especially the manipulation of light in night scenes, but his romantic view of the West mirrored Remington and Russell.

Leigh's contemporary Maynard Dixon did progress as an artist, but his stylized mesas and clouds were castigated as "art deco cumulus." Born in Fresno, California, and trained as an illustrator in San Francisco, Dixon went to New York in 1907 to seek magazine commissions. Encouraged by Lummis, who published his work, Dixon decided to return to the Southwest. "I am being paid to lie about the west," he wrote. "I am going back home where I can do honest work."[62] He spent time on the Hopi and Navajo reservations, where his palette matured and brightened as he painted portraits of the native peoples. His goal was to interpret the poetry and pathos in the lives of western people as seen amid the grandeur, sternness, and loneliness of the land. Dixon's huge murals and large canvases expressed concepts of freedom and space in an increasingly stylized manner.

The land also stunned the painter Kate T. Cory when she stepped off the train at Canyon Diablo in northern Arizona in 1905. Educated as an artist in New York, she came to join Louis Akin's "art colony," only to discover she *was* the colony. The train porter called her an "unfortunate pilgrim," but Cory adjusted. "It took one half a minute to reinstate myself mentally in the ranks of the sound in body and another to be quite sure I had not been dropped at some prehistoric ruin."[63] For the next seven years she painted and took photographs at Oraibi and Walpi in the Hopi country. She made her home at First Mesa, which "you reached . . . by ladders and little stone steps, and made your peace with the growling dogs on the ascent; but oh! the view when you got there."[64] Cory's paintings moved beyond the romanticism of Akin, and in 1913 her work was included in that most significant statement about modern art, the Armory Show in New York. Her paintings presaged the artistic trends that developed in the region before World War I.

Another artist, Joseph Henry Sharp, produced traditional portraits of Indians throughout the West and in his travels visited Santa Fe in 1883 and Taos in 1893. Fascinated with northern New Mexico, he shared his enthusiasm with two artists studying at the Academie Julian in Paris: Ernest L. Blumenschein and Bert Phillips. While visiting in Europe, he met the two young painters, who wanted "fresh material." Sharp told them to go to the Rockies, to go home, and to paint at Taos.[65] The greenhorns traveled to Denver in 1898 and departed in a wagon headed south. A broken wagon wheel sent them on foot to the Taos Plateau. Blumenschein stood mesmerized: "Never shall I forget the first powerful impressions; my own impressions direct from a new land through my own eyes. Not another man's picture this, not another's adventure. The great naked anatomy of a majestic landscape once tortured, now calm; the fitness of adobe houses to their tawny surroundings; the vastness and overwhelming beauty of skies; terrible drama of storms; peace of night — all in beauty of color, vigorous form, everchanging light."[66]

A small village located in a lush valley of the Sangre de Cristo Mountains, Taos sat at an elevation of 7,000 feet, providing crystal-clear skies that stretched over a landscape of vivid colors. Aspen groves, piñon pine forests, and stands of cottonwoods contrasted sharply with eroded arroyos, mesas, canyons, and buttes in yellow, red, orange, and brown earth colors. The sky offered deep blue, azure, purple, red, and rose horizons, often filled with clouds of fleece or puffs of smoke. The mountains curled in a crescent around the valley on the east, and a desert extended west to the canyon of the Rio Grande. Blumenschein recalled: "When I came into this valley — for the first time in my life, I saw whole paintings right before my eyes. Everywhere I looked I saw paintings perfectly organized ready for paint."[67]

Sharp had provided sound advice, and Blumenschein and Phillips moved into an adobe house and began to paint. Phillips became a permanent resident. Blumenschein returned to Paris, where he persuaded E. Irving Couse to try Taos. Couse arrived in 1902 and found the St. Louis artist Oscar E. Berninghaus paint-

CULTURE *in the* AMERICAN SOUTHWEST

FIGURE 17

*E. I. Couse's formulaic and historically inaccurate paintings of Pueblo Indians won acceptance
from the public. The* Primitive Sculptor, *courtesy Woolaroc Museum, Bartlesville, Oklahoma.*

ing there as well. Sharp returned to Taos in the summers, joining his friends.
The foundation of the Taos art colony had been laid.

The artists recorded a "dying race" of Native Americans at the Taos Pueblo
as well as the grandeur of the landscape. They admired the quiet dignity of the
Indians and the romantic Hispanic community. The semi-wilderness captured
their imaginations, for as Herbert Dunton, another member of the colony,
wrote, "There was no other place which lent to them so enduring an appeal—
remote from commercialism and the sordid, restful in its peaceful isolation,
quiet along its crooked valley, in the soft shadows of adobe walls."[68] Sharp,
Phillips, Blumenschein, and Couse had studied at the Academie Julian, the leading art school in Europe, where they had followed a rigidly conventional salon
style of art. They were joined in Taos by E. Martin Hennings, who had studied
at the Munich Royal Academy, and by Walter Ufer, who had been a student at
the Royal Academy in Dresden. Although they all had very conservative training, the Taos painters generally rejected salon-style studio art and took their
canvases and paints outdoors. But they also rejected the pastel pinks, soft greens,

and purple shadows of the Impressionists. In remote northern New Mexico, their art moved closer in style—though not in subject matter—to that of the urban paintings of John Sloan, William Glackens, and Robert Henri.[69]

The Taos Society of Artists, formed in 1912, found great success. Victor Higgins joined the society two years later, and the eight members discovered a ready market for their work. They exhibited in the East and Midwest, but greater fame came through their work for the Santa Fe Railway and Fred Harvey. Hundreds of thousands of calendars, menus, matchbook covers, advertisements, and brochures reproduced their work. The railway purchased paintings for depots and ticket offices. Fred Harvey placed their paintings in hotels and restaurants. Their "marketable" art gained acceptance because of the humanistic orientation and romantic vision. The geography and the subject matter transformed their style of painting as they placed greater emphasis on color, light, and broad brush strokes. The vast sky and the terrain lent themselves to huge canvases.[70] Ufer moved toward extreme realism while Higgins and others became more lyrical.

All the Taos artists owed a debt to Native American art. They not only painted portraits of Native Americans and genre scenes of the Taos Pueblo and of Indians practicing their arts and crafts, but also borrowed from Native American artistic elements for their own work. Ufer's portraits included arrangements of pottery, jewelry, and weavings, and he incorporated a balance in his designs that drew from the symmetry of Native American crafts. Couse's formulaic portraits often depicted the creation of jewelry, pottery, and baskets. The Taos artists found the colors and compositions of Native American paintings and blankets to be key to their own work. Music, dances, and ceremonials provided more than subject matter. The artists wanted to capture the mental and spiritual life of the Indians, and their canvases often reflected the abstract nature of Native American painting.[71]

Higgins made clear the Indians' influence on his art: "The Taoseños are living in a natural state, entirely independent of the world. They have dignity in spite of their lack of riches, and nobility in spite of their humble mode of living. Coupled with this impressive simplicity, the country makes its inhabitants daring and lovers of the 'chance.'"[72] Dunton found the Native American festivals irresistible and sought to portray the basic elements of the Fiesta of San Geronimo. The beauty of the scene was the essence of spirit, "and over all is that marvelous blue canopy of the sky before which the great cumulus clouds are still passing in majestic review."[73] The fame of Taos brought dozens of artists; a few became permanent residents, but others came only for the summer.

The artist colony that formed in Santa Fe followed this pattern. Carlos Vierra arrived in 1904 and found the artist Warren Rollins in residence. They were

FIGURE 18

In Cattle Country *by Herbert "Buck" Dunton was part of the genre that created the popular image of the Southwest. Courtesy Cushing Memorial Library, Special Collections, Texas A&M University.*

joined by Kenneth Chapman and Gerald Cassidy, and soon numerous artists were to be found in the capital. Encouraged by the open society and by Edgar Hewett and the School of American Archaeology, these artists produced portraits, genre scenes, and landscapes not unlike those of their colleagues in Taos. Their subject matter, however, emphasized the Hispanic community.[74] By the mid-1920s, the Santa Fe art colony had acquired an international reputation, primarily as a consequence of the presence of painters who broke away from representational art.

The Swedish artist Birgir Sandzen wrote in 1915 that the Southwest could contribute to the rise of a national school of painting, and indeed that process had begun in New Mexico. Robert Henri came to New Mexico in 1914 and painted in a style that reflected his rebellion against Impressionism and its canon. Henri urged his students and colleagues to go to Santa Fe. John Sloan came in 1919 and would return nearly every summer until his death. Marsden Harley and other modernists joined him. Bringing the stylistic seeds planted at the Armory Show of 1913, they reflected the rise of abstraction and precisionism in American art.[75]

As the forces of post-Impressionism began to be felt in Santa Fe, a young schoolteacher in Canyon, Texas, also embraced the land and made it her art. "I am loving the plains more than ever it seems—and the sky—Anita you have never seen SKY—it is wonderful."[76] So wrote Georgia O'Keeffe to her friend Anita Pollitzer on September 11, 1916. O'Keeffe taught art for the Amarillo Public Schools from 1912 to 1914 before returning to the Texas Panhandle to teach at the West Texas Normal College at Canyon in 1916–18. Those years shaped her life and her art: "I lived on the plains of north Texas for four years. It is the only place I ever felt that I really belonged—that I really felt at home. That was my country—terrible winds and a wonderful emptiness."[77]

She found the Llano Estacado totally removed from her childhood in Wisconsin and her art-school days with William Merritt Chase in New York. Between the years at Amarillo and Canyon she studied at Columbia Teachers College with Arthur Wesley Dow, who encouraged O'Keeffe to abandon her Art Students League training and to use her world as an inspiration. Employing watercolors and paper, she painted abstract landscapes and flowers. Her paintings conveyed power and expressed the vast sweep of the plains. In *Train Coming in—Canyon, Texas,* she took a Santa Fe Railway train and created clouds of smoke and steam in biomorphic shapes across the prairie. The Evening Star, the rising and falling terrain, even the dried grasses provoked paintings ethereal and yet dynamic.[78]

> Tonight I walked into the sunset. . . . The whole sky . . . was just blazing—and grey-blue clouds were rioting all through the hotness of it.
>
> The eastern sky was all grey-blue—bunches of clouds—different kinds of clouds—sticking around everywhere and the whole thing—lit up—first in one place—then in another with flashes of lightning—sometimes just sheet lightning—and sometimes sheet lightning with a sharp bright zigzag flashing across it.[79]

O'Keeffe fretted that she liked the plains too much, but she added, "I'm so glad I'm out here."[80] Then a friend took her to Palo Duro Canyon, and a whole new world opened for O'Keeffe. There she painted the canyon walls of red, orange, yellow, and white. Outcroppings, arroyos, patterns of light across the rocks, and the sparse vegetation sharply etched in shades of green filled her paper. The canyon became her spiritual home: "Like a small Grand Canyon . . . wonderful . . . and not like anything I had known before."[81] Standing in the bottom of the crevice was "like standing in a bowl of red light."[82] O'Keeffe painted and drew, employing curves, circles, and angles in abstract forms and colors at once bright and hazy. She had discovered the Southwest and her artistic voice.

A western trip with her sister Claudia in 1917 led to a detour through Albuquerque and northern New Mexico. In Santa Fe, O'Keeffe told her sister, "In

CULTURE *in the* AMERICAN SOUTHWEST

my mind, I was always on my way back to New Mexico."[83] She went on to Denver and the Rockies, but Texas and New Mexico proved irresistible. The following year she visited a ranch owned by a friend at Waring, Texas, near San Antonio. She found freedom and isolation on the ranch and wrote to the gallery owner Alfred Stieglitz for her paintbox and brushes. "It's a wonderful place — I wonder why everyone doesn't live here."[84] Stieglitz exhibited her paintings at 291, his famous New York gallery, and O'Keeffe quickly became a nationally known artist. She formulated her own style, but O'Keeffe's abstractions were part of the rise of modernism. Her work for the next sixty years reflected the light and color that she had discovered in the Southwest. The region became her space.

The impact of the Armory Show and the rise of modernism brought acceptance and acclaim to painters like Georgia O'Keeffe, but in southern California, orthodox Impressionism continued to prevail, remaining virtually unchallenged until the 1930s. Elmer Wachtel, Marion Kavanagh, William Wendt, Guy Rose, George Gardner Symons, and other Impressionists produced large, brilliantly colored canvases. They were joined by Donna Schuster and Edgar A. Payne, who strengthened the "Eucalyptus School of Art." That derogatory appellation was undeserved, since there was no "school," but these painters were left behind by the artistic tide sweeping the country. Claude Monet remained their model, not Matisse. They employed plein air painting to capture the beauty and magic of a special time and place.[85] The Pasadena tilemaker Ernest A. Batchelder commented, "There is something inspiring in the ample hills, the blue sky, the bigness of the out-of-doors that calls forth latent forces."[86] In 1909 the art critic Marian Seares expressed the hope that California artists would reach the front rank of contemporary painters, but that was not to be.[87]

The conservatism of art in southern California gained reinforcements as older realists and Impressionists moved to Los Angeles, Santa Barbara, Pasadena, and San Diego as retirees or part-time residents. The Swedish artist Carl Oscar Borg became the center of the art colony in Santa Barbara while continuing to paint landscapes of Arizona and portraits of Native Americans in a realistic, colorful manner. Thomas Moran and Edward Borein joined him, producing giant landscapes and genre paintings of vaqueros. Together with Fernand Lungren, they maintained the stylistic status quo. The art colonies at Laguna Beach, Riverside, and Point Loma reflected the same conservatism, with few exceptions. The Theosophical community at Point Loma attracted English and central European artists who produced symbolistic and complex allegorical paintings, but they were not among the "acceptable" painters of San Diego.[88]

Landscape painting dominated the art world of San Diego, with the artists

Maurice Braun and Charles Arthur Fries serving as the major contributors. The San Diego Art Association, founded in 1904, encouraged the landscapists and their employment of Impressionism. In 1915 the Panama-California Exposition offered an opportunity to introduce modernism, but Alice Klauber, who formed the art gallery for the fair, broke little new ground. A landscape painter from a prominent San Diego family, Klauber had studied with William Merritt Chase and Robert Henri. She asked the latter to help her organize the art gallery, which he did. Henri obtained paintings from his students and fellow members of the "Ash Can School," and the galley walls were graced by the works of John Sloan, William Glackens, Ernest Lawson, and George Luks. Paintings by Childe Hassam and Guy Péne du Bois substantiated the urban-realist aesthetic, but nothing appeared from the post-Impressionists or those in the modernist current. Klauber and Henri stayed with the safe and acceptable.[89] Determined to create an art life in San Diego, Klauber chose not to risk local support for her goal of an art museum by antagonizing a public unprepared for a *Nude Descending a Staircase*. Klauber's goal of an art museum for San Diego would be achieved in the mid-1920s.

In her efforts to create an art museum, Klauber mirrored women in the East and Midwest. Yet even though women led the fight to establish art museums in New York, New England, and Chicago, they often found themselves marginalized as men later took over as trustees and members of the museum boards. Women were willing to take greater risks than men in their endeavors, but even those with wealth and power could not maintain great influence.[90] The experiences of women in the Southwest proved far different. In Houston, San Antonio, and Dallas, women created art museums and played major roles in their development and management.

In Houston, Mrs. Robert S. Lovett, spouse of a prominent citizen, held a meeting in her home in 1900 to organize an art league. Forty-seven women joined together to promote art in the public schools. By 1909 their ranks had grown to over six hundred, and four years later they became the Houston Art League, with the goal of establishing a permanent art collection and a museum. After a site was donated in 1916, they began to raise funds for the building, which would ultimately open in 1924. The Houston Art League officers were largely women, and the board of directors in 1913 consisted of three men and sixteen women. Four years later, seven men served with nineteen women. Male business leaders in Houston recognized the importance of the Houston Art League's goals, even if they failed to appreciate the art the building would house.[91] Of the museum, the community leader F. M. Law declared, "Representing the businessmen of Houston, I can say that this is . . . distinctly and definitely of material and commercial value."[92] An art museum was good for business; it symbolized a well-rounded, progressive city.

Meanwhile, the art life of San Antonio was dominated by the painter Eleanor Onderdonk. With her creative talent, organizational skills, and strong personality, Onderdonk labored—through the San Antonio Museum Association, the San Antonio Art League, and other groups—to acquire an art collection and a building to house it. In 1922 Onderdonk and her friend and colleague Ellen Quillin acquired a largely scientific collection, which they displayed in empty schoolrooms. A bequest from Alfred G. Witte, plus funds raised by Quillin and Onderdonk and the San Antonio Art League, led to the Witte Memorial Museum. Onderdonk served as art curator from 1927 to 1958, and Quillen served as director from 1926 to 1960. Onderdonk built a collection of nineteenth-century regional art, and Quillen acquired the concrete for the building. Together with the women of San Antonio, they created a museum for the city.[93]

The art world of Dallas gained some institutional structure in 1893 with the help of Eleanor's father. Robert Onderdonk formed the Dallas Art Students League and organized art exhibitions at the Texas State Fair. Fellow painter-teacher Frank Reaugh helped to create the Dallas Art Association in 1903. The impetus and financial support for an art museum came not from the art community, however, but from prominent women in the city. After the new Carnegie Library opened in Dallas in 1900, Mrs. Henry Exall urged that a permanent art organization should be created to place paintings in a room set aside for an art gallery. Reaugh made the original suggestion for an art display, but Mrs. Exall proceeded to act. The Dallas Art Association purchased paintings, held lectures, and sponsored touring exhibitions. A board of twenty-one included nearly every leading family in the city. Mrs. A. H. Bello, the first major benefactor, donated funds to purchase a painting by Childe Hassam, initiating the permanent collection. By 1909, the association had acquired the Fine Arts Building at the Texas State Fair Grounds, a large fireproof structure designed in a Beaux Arts style. From 1909 until 1926, Mrs. George K. Meyer served as acting director and president of the Dallas Art Association. She raised funds, organized exhibitions, and chaired meetings; she was the dominant force of the organization. Mrs. Meyer assembled exhibits of paintings from New York galleries for possible purchase by Dallas citizens; the works would eventually come to the museum, she hoped. After Mrs. S. I. Munger donated $50,000 in 1925, funds for acquisitions grew, as did the permanent collection. These women brought to Dallas a museum that made the city the foremost art center in the region.[94]

In Los Angeles, "art was the monopoly of the Women," wrote one observer, but unlike their contemporaries in Dallas and Houston, the women in Los

Angeles met with limited success.[95] The construction of the Science and Art Museum in Exposition Park in 1910 provided space for exhibitions organized by the Fine Arts League. Mrs. Harvey Housh led the league, which sought financial support and donations of art. There were few contributors, and some paintings donated were of questionable authenticity. Although Mrs. Housh succeeded in obtaining space from the county supervisors, she received little support from the community. When William P. Harrison moved from Chicago to Los Angeles, he donated contemporary art that formed the basis for a collection, but the struggle for institutional art in the city languished, with one major exception: the private gallery established by Henry E. Huntington.[96]

The nephew of the fabled railroad magnate Collis P. Huntington, Henry left his uncle's railroad empire to embark on a career in southern California, where he built an electric traction system that eventually extended throughout Los Angeles County and opened the way for suburban development. Huntington owned vast tracts of land, which he converted from orange groves into miles of streets and homes. Although he had not gone beyond public high school in terms of a formal education, Huntington appreciated fine objects and began to acquire a substantial collection of books and manuscripts, particularly from Elizabethan England. Huntington spent over $1 million in 1911 alone. He commissioned the premier architects of Los Angeles, Myron Hunt and Elmer Grey, to design an English manor house in San Marino for him and his growing collection. Hunt and Grey produced a huge home comparable to Kenwood House in London. Using highly skilled craftsmen, the architects modeled the interior after eighteenth-century English and French rooms. Constructed in 1910–11, the house gained a new mistress two years later when Huntington married Arabella Huntington, the widow of his uncle Collis. Two vast fortunes were consolidated, and Arabella, then sixty years old, brought with her a large collection of Renaissance paintings. Guided by the London art dealer Sir Joseph Duveen, Arabella purchased paintings by Rembrandt, Hals, Velasquez, and Bellini. Henry Huntington added works by the English artists Romney, Reynolds, Turner, and Constable and a large group of paintings by Thomas Gainsborough. Henry purchased Gainsborough's famous *Blue Boy* in 1922. The couple filled the house with European art of high quality and acquired an enormous collection of books and manuscripts. On the vast estate, a botanical garden surrounded the house and the library that Huntington built to hold his purchases. After Arabella's death in 1924, he added a memorial wing to the library for her art collection. On his death in 1927, Huntington left $8 million to endow the library, gallery, and gardens. Thus southern California acquired one of the great research libraries of the world and an exceptional art collection. Visitors could view Thomas Lawrence's

FIGURE 19

FIGURE 19
The legacy of Henry E. Huntington lives on in his art collection, library, and gardens and the architecture of Myron Hunt and Elmer Grey. Author's collection.

Pinkie, stroll through five acres of camellias, or view folios of Shakespeare and Chaucer.[97] The Huntington Library, Art Collections, and Botanical Gardens was the first of many great "vanity museums" in the Southwest, and for decades it served southern California in the absence of any other major art collection.

Meanwhile, the average American viewed the Southwest not through art collections but largely through the pages of novels and short stories. The popularity of narratives about cowboys, desperados, cattle drives, bank robberies, and prostitutes with hearts of gold continued unabated. Indeed, it seemed that Westerns translated into silent films enhanced the market for such novels and short fiction. Readers turned away from the cheap "dime novels" in pursuit of better-written stories with more plausible plots. They demanded that the stories be realistic but that the language and the descriptions of the land be romantic and nostalgic. Owen Wister's highly successful novel *The Virginian* established a new genre of serious western fiction, stimulated by the popularity of the writings of Charles Lummis and George Wharton James.

In 1903, a New York dentist, Zane Grey, published his first Western and subsequently became a leading novelist of the Southwest for three decades. A conservationist who visited Arizona frequently, Grey based his novels on the residents of that state. He rode and camped with ranchers; he visited the Hopi and Navajo country; and he studied the physical setting. *Riders of the Purple Sage* (1912), *The Light of Western Stars* (1914), and *Man of the Forest* (1920) emphasized the traits Grey thought of as "western": endurance, manliness, loyalty, and courage. Grey emphasized the physical beauty of the land, which he visited before writing each novel. His nonfictional publications, essays about hunting trips, also emphasized the land and its people. Over 130 million of Grey's books were sold, and more than one hundred films were produced based on his writings. A Social Darwinist, Grey viewed southwesterners as struggling for survival in a land that shaped their lives and personalities. The region served as a repository for the national values of individualism and optimism. Grey's fiction focused on the natural beauty of the Sonoran desert, the forests of the Mogollon Rim, and the chasms of the Grand Canyon. The people living in those settings possessed simplicity, believed in individualism, and accepted hard work. Their American values had deep roots in the Arizona soil. Grey's heroic language, lengthy and detailed descriptions of the land, and emphasis on morality established an image of the region for millions of Americans.[98]

Many of these same characteristics appeared in the stories and novels written by Eugene Manlove Rhodes, who published his first book in 1910. The Rhodes family had moved from Nebraska to the Tularosa Basin of New Mexico in 1881, when "Gene" was thirteen years old. He became a cowboy and almost an outlaw while homesteading in the San Andreas Mountains. The young rancher loved to play poker, frequenting saloons to find a game, though not liquor. The pugnacious Rhodes also often found himself in brawls.

He began to write after two years at the College of the Pacific. He found both an outlet in *Land of Sunshine* and a friend in the magazine's editor, Charles Lummis. Lummis encouraged Rhodes and became his mentor for a decade. Rhode's true success came when the *Saturday Evening Post* accepted his short stories about the southwestern corner of New Mexico. From his ranch in the mountains he submitted stories to the *Post* and other magazines, but because of warrants issued for his arrest, Rhodes eventually fled to New York. (The extent of his "immoral conduct" is not clear.) Yet even though he left, his love for New Mexico and its people remained.[99]

Like Grey, Rhodes emphasized the settings of his stories, especially the mountains that stood in sharp contrast to the nearby deserts. His characters spoke in authentic dialects as his plots gradually unfolded. The stories often had reversed values as a theme—his cowboys were often Robin Hood in chaps. *Pasó por Aquí* (1926), a short novel considered by many to be his best book, tells the story of Ross McEwen, a cowboy fleeing from Sheriff Pat Garrett. McEwen stops to save a diptheria-stricken Hispanic family, even though he knows that offering succor means capture. The story is as gritty as the alkali desert in which it is set. Rhodes wrote a Western in which there were neither fights nor killings. He employed western virtues of courage, good humor, self-reliance, independence, and eternal optimism. In this and other stories, Rhodes described in detail the White Sands, Sierra Blanca, and the cottonwoods along the creeks. Where a tenderfoot saw snakes, scorpions, dust, glare, and loneliness, Rhodes found beauty.[100] An avid reader of literary classics, Rhodes abhorred the works of Ernest Hemingway, D. H. Lawrence, and Sherwood Anderson. He brought to his New Mexico stories the values he found in Theodore Dreiser, G. K. Chesterton, and Hilaire Belloc.[101] Some critics suggested that geography and a sense of place limited writers such as Rhodes, who created heroes to match the immense space. But Rhodes did not see the land as threatening; rather it provided the opportunity to awaken the human spirit.

Another Lummis protegée, Mary Austin, brought to the desert country of southern California a similar appreciation of the land. Austin had left her Illinois home in 1888 when she was only twenty years old. For more than a decade she lived in the Owens Valley, and her early books and essays centered on this valley and on the Mojave Desert country below the southern Sierra Nevada. A failing marriage led her to Los Angeles, where she published short pieces in *Land of Sunshine,* and ultimately to Carmel, New York, Europe, and in the 1920s, Santa Fe.

From an early age, Austin communed with nature; she drew strength from "the spirit in the fields." In *The Land of Little Rain* (1903), Austin produced tales, sketches, and nature studies of the desert country. With the precision of the geologist, she observed the mesas and canyons, alpine lakes, and mountain ranges. With the eye of the botanist, she wrote of the plant life and the natural adaptation of desert plants and pine forests. Hawks, coyotes, deer, mice, and reptiles populated her pages. Austin wanted to discover things for the sake of knowing, but more important, she felt that these observations helped her and her readers to see the place of human society in the physical environment. To understand oneself and humankind, one needs to know the land and the procession of life each year.[102] The key to her early writings was adaptation, the way in which the human spirit engaged the land and the sky: "Out West, the west of the mesas and the unpatented hills, there is more sky than any place in the world. It does not sit flatly on the rim of earth, but begins somewhere out in the space in which the earth is poised, hollows more, and is full of clean winey winds."[103]

The desert country became Austin's laboratory for literature, and she brought to her pages a sensitivity for the land, the flora and fauna, that captivated readers.

From 1903 until 1917, she published novels about the struggles of farmers in this arid land and the fight over water rights in the Owens Valley. She wrote of a lost heiress disguised as a shepherd boy at the Carmel Mission in old California, of desperate women who mistook chivalry for love, and of the impact of speculation in oil leases. Austin's writings always drew from the land: "I may not know how to write, nor how to delineate character, nor even how to tell a story. The one thing I am sure about myself is that I know the relation of letters and landscape, of life and environment."[104]

In an essay titled "Art Influence in the West," Austin used language and imagery that, consciously or unconsciously, reflected her conception of writing about the Southwest. She described what motivated her work:

> The total effect of bright sun, rich-toned landscapes, and a life spent largely in the open air.
>
> A lurking preference of the land for color. . . .
>
> Extraordinary definition of form in the landscape.
>
> Everything seemed more dramatic in the Southwest—light, shadows, storms, and sun. The topography consisted of bold outlines and sharp edges.
>
> These two, then, must be thought of as affecting the final form of Western art—color and high simplicity of form combined with great intricacy of detail.[105]

For Austin, people had to come into harmony with the land, with nature. The California writings developed her sense of the landscape as a major element in human affairs, and without resorting to literary devices, she developed a sharply honed narrative skill. When Austin moved to New York, she found critical acceptance and joined Mabel Dodge's salon, but happiness and contentment eluded her, and true satisfaction came only when she returned to the Southwest and established residence in Santa Fe. Her creative spirit revived in New Mexico, where she believed a new regional culture would arise. There, she argued, the land made such a dramatic and almost immeasurable impact on the people that a new civilization would emerge.

Others shared her view of the importance of the southwestern landscape. One of these was Willa Cather, who grew up in the farm country of south-central Nebraska just as Austin came of age in Illinois. Cather too interacted with the land and nature. Her first trip to the Southwest, in 1912, shaped her writing even as she became one of the nation's finest novelists. By that year Cather had given up her job as an editor at *McClure's* to devote herself full-time to producing fiction. She published poetry and short stories, and while she was

CULTURE *in the* AMERICAN SOUTHWEST

FIGURE 20
*Willa Cather's visit to Mesa Verde
in 1915 inspired three novels about
the Southwest. Photograph
furnished by Evelyn Funda.
Published courtesy Helen Cather
Southwick.*

visiting her brother Douglass, who worked for the Santa Fe Railway in Winslow, Arizona, Cather's first novel appeared. She toured the Grand Canyon during her stay and ventured into the Hopi and Navajo country. Fascinated by the region, Cather returned to Arizona in 1914 and during the next two years visited New Mexico and Mesa Verde in Colorado. Even before seeing the Southwest, she had used a regional legend in her short story "The Enchanted Bluff." Now she saw the Southwest in an intensely personal way. She talked with residents, listened to stories, read books about the region, and traveled by train, car, wagon, and horseback across the deserts and mountains. Cather visited Frijoles Canyon and the Española Valley in New Mexico, but Walnut Canyon near Winslow appeared first in her fiction.[106]

Douglass Cather had roamed the Southwest and spoke tolerable Spanish, and he and a fellow railroad worker, a man named Tooker, helped Cather explore both the physical landscape and the landscape of the mind. Walnut Canyon, with its cliff dwellings, stirred memories of Willa's childhood speculations and her thoughts about the Anasazi peoples. Douglass introduced her to Hispanics in Winslow, including a handsome young man named Julio, who escorted her to dances and sang songs and played the guitar for her. The local Catholic priest took Cather on long drives across his parish and told her Hispanic and Indian legends. At this point Cather had not planned a novel about the Southwest, but Tooker, Julio, and Walnut Canyon formed ideas for her.[107]

Initially the Southwest may have overwhelmed Cather. She wrote to her friend Elizabeth Shepley Sergeant that she feared the bigness of the West. The landscape of the West was "big, bright, and consuming."[108] Nevertheless, Cather returned to Winslow in 1914, and the following year she visited Mesa Verde. Riding the narrow-gauge train over La Veta Pass to Durango and then to Mancos, Cather sat on the rear platform of her coach, absorbing the scenery. She hired a team to reach Mesa Verde, where she spent a week hiking through the ruins of the cliff dwellings. On an excursion to the Tower House, Cather and her companions became lost, but before they were rescued she watched the moon rise over the canyon and the moonlight play across the ruins. All the while she collected memories and information, and she listened to patterns of speech. Cather did the same in Taos, her next stop, where she spent a month riding over the plateau, going to the pueblo, and visiting the small Hispanic settlements nearby. Although Cather had been to Santa Fe and Lamy on her trips to Arizona, this was her first experience in northern New Mexico. She would return to Taos the following year, for Cather "was intensely alive to the country," observed her companion Edith Lewis. "She loved the Southwest for its own sake." Initially her visits were not to collect material, but indeed she did.[109]

Cather loved music, and one of her favorite singers, Olive Fremstad, became "Thea Kronberg" in Cather's book *The Song of the Lark* (1915). Thea grew up in Moonstone, Colorado, fascinated by the Hispanic community at the edge of town. She found life and vitality there, especially with "Spanish Johnny," a young man who sang and played the guitar for her. Embarking on a musical career, Thea moved to Chicago, where she met a wealthy businessman, Fred Ottenburg. Should she marry and give up her career? How was she to know? Ottenburg took Thea to his ranch in Arizona near Panther Canyon. At the ranch, Thea found herself in a world of aspens and piñon pines, a world of bright earth colors and vast sky. When Thea ventured out to the canyon, her life was transformed. She reflected on the ancients, the cliff dwellers and their society. The symbolic landscape, a soaring eagle, and a mystic sunrise unleashed her artistic vitality and imbued her with a sense of freedom and independence. "The Cliff-Dwellers had lengthened her past. She had older and higher obligations."[110] The ancients taught her the hardness of human life and gave her back her sources of gladness. Invigorated by her sojourn in Panther Canyon, Thea determined to go to Germany to study opera. Thea wanted a career. Arizona and Moonstone provided the intangibles of her life: the light on the desert, the smell of sage-brush after a rain, and "a new song in that blue air which had never been sung in the world before."[111] Cather would return to the Southwest in the 1920s to write two of her major novels, but *The Song of the Lark* made clear the force the region and its peoples had on her. As she wrote to her friend Annie Adams Fields: "I long to tell you about Wonderful Arizona. I really learned there what Balzac meant when he said, 'In that desert there is everything and nothing — God without mankind.'"[112] Cather combined her love of music and her sensitivity for the Southwest to create in Thea a personality strengthened by the land and by the myths of its ancient inhabitants.

Cather's passion for music had been developed in Red Cloud, Nebraska, and like many residents of the small towns and cities in the Southwest, she constantly sought to hear the classics. After 1900, a few southwestern communities gained the financial strength to develop their own orchestras and opera companies, but most still depended on touring musical groups. Dallas (1900), Houston (1913), and Los Angeles (1919) obtained symphony orchestras, and throughout the region, women's organizations and federations of music clubs labored tirelessly to promote orchestras and operas. In many instances their efforts received a boost when musicians from other parts of the nation, or from Europe, came to the Southwest as performers and teachers. By 1920, it was possible to hear classical music played by trained professionals in much of the region.

In Dallas, Mrs. W. H. Abrams organized the Dallas Symphony Club in 1900 and arranged for Hans Kreissig to conduct twenty-one violinists for the first concert. Stranded in Houston when his touring orchestra failed, in 1887 the German-born Kreissig went to Dallas, where he taught music and led the Dallas Philharmonic Society, a group of amateur players. Kreissig and Mrs. Abrams kept their symphony alive for only two years, but there was both a need and a desire for an orchestra in Dallas. The Beethoven Symphony Orchestra formed in 1907, and four years later, under the baton of Carl Venth, it became the Dallas Symphony Orchestra. The founder of the Brooklyn Symphony, Venth led the Dallas Symphony from 1911 until 1914, when it collapsed financially. Revived in 1918, the orchestra played under Walter Fried until 1924. Like most other cities that tried to build symphonies, Dallas discovered that the costs often exceeded the community's initial fund-raising abilities. But by the mid-1920s, the city was able to create a permanent professional organization. In the meantime, audiences listened to Nellie Melba and Ignacy Paderewski or attended Wagner's *Parsifal* performed by the Metropolitan Opera or heard the Chicago Opera Company with Luisa Tetrazzini in *Lucia di Lammermoor* or with Mary Garden in *Thais*. The audience for the latter filled the 4,500 seats at the coliseum.[113]

The thirst for classical music brought touring performers and orchestras to communities as small as Austin, Texas. Paderewski played before a capacity audience in 1900 and would return again and again to perform Liszt, Chopin, Schumann, and Beethoven. The Lambardi Italian Opera Company offered selections from *Rigoletto* and *Cavaleria Rusticana*. Mrs. Robert G. Crosby led the Austin Music Festival Association, which brought the Chicago Symphony, the St. Louis Symphony, and the Russian Ballet with Anna Pavlova to the state capital. Ernestine Schumann-Heink performed seven times between 1903 and 1931. Efforts to create an Austin Symphony failed, but large audiences heard the St. Louis Symphony perform Franck, Haydn, Sibelius, and Wagner. Austinites possessed musical tastes sophisticated enough that conductors could play both Bach and contemporary composers to receptive listeners.[114]

The indefatigable Mrs. Eli Hertzberg organized the San Antonio Symphony Orchestra in 1904 and obtained the services of Carl Hahn as conductor for the next decade. Mrs. Hertzberg formed a committee of San Antonio women to support the orchestra, and they imported brass players to augment the strings and woodwinds. Guest artists included the composer and pianist Percy Grainger. The orchestra was dissolved in 1909 but was revived under the baton of Julian Blitz from 1916 until 1922. Like Dallas and Austin, San Antonio depended on touring performers and symphonies to fill voids in the city's musical life.[115]

After Mrs. Nell Johnson came to El Paso from St. Louis, she sought to make the community a regional music center. Aided by Dorrance Roderick, the publisher of the *El Paso Times,* she organized musical events and promoted an annual Mexican Concert season. Mrs. Johnson found El Paso audiences sophisticated and knowledgeable. In 1907, when a touring opera company substituted for the advertised tenor in *The Barber of Seville* and omitted one scene in Act I and several scenes in Act II, the audience rioted. The manager of the company insisted that the performance was exactly the same as presented in other cities. The audience was not appeased even when soprano Alice Nelson sang "Swanee River," "Coming through the Rye," and "Annie Laurie." Hisses and howls followed, and the refunds demanded were received only after the police arrived.[116]

The Hispanic population of El Paso also demanded quality performances and brought companies from Mexico City and Spain. A middle-class audience developed for opera, and when the Colón Theater opened in 1919, it offered *Rigoletto* as the first program. The Mercedes Navarro Company also performed plays written by Europeans. The Mexican Revolution of 1910 brought large numbers of exiles to El Paso, many of whom were well educated. A "high culture" developed quickly as the population of the city swelled to 80,000, half of whom were Hispanics.[117]

But not all members of southwestern audiences possessed the sophistication necessary to appreciate contemporary music. Walter Damrosch brought the New York Symphony Orchestra and soloists to Oklahoma City in 1904. He presented excerpts from Wagner's *Parsifal,* which had been presented only recently at Bayreuth and in New York City. As the orchestra concluded the prelude, the theater manager rushed onstage to announce: "Ladies and gentlemen: I am proud to see so many of you here to-night and to take this opportunity of announcing to you that I have already made arrangements for next season for a course which will be in every respect better than the one I am giving you this year! I would also like to announce that Stewart's Oyster Saloon will be open after the concert."[118] Damrosch then proceeded with *Parsifal.* Many in the audience greeted the presentation with "enthusiastic approval," although one young man commented, "This show ain't worth thirty cents."

Other citizens of Oklahoma Territory did appreciate the fine arts, and a classical music program emerged at the territory's college for African Americans at Langston. The Colored Agricultural and Normal University was created in 1897, and Dr. Inman E. Page served as president. His daughter, Zelia N. Page Breaux, taught music at the college, where she emphasized the classics. Breaux formed an orchestra in 1902 and offered music by Bach, Mozart, and Chopin. She presented few non-European selections, and later, as the supervisor of music in the segregated Oklahoma City schools, she urged her students to avoid jazz. Breaux owned the only African American theater in Oklahoma City, where she brought musicians, theatrical groups such as the Lafayette Players, and eventually, jazz and the blues. The writer Ralph Ellison, one of her students, said that Breaux created a "cultural nexus" for the African American community. The interaction of art forms helped the community deal with racism and a changing culture.[119]

At the same time Tulsa, a town of only 3,500 in 1904, acquired a musical culture when Jane Heard Clinton and nine other women formed the Hyechka Club, named after a Creek word for music. Clinton served as president of the club for seventeen years, bringing to Tulsa Madam Schumann-Heink, the New York Symphony Orchestra, and the Minneapolis Symphony Orchestra, among others. The club created a Spring Music Festival, sponsored talented young people, and eventually brought the Chicago Civic Opera to Tulsa each year. In 1924 Tulsans heard Mary Garden sing Massenet's *Cleopatre,* for example. The Grand Opera House served as the hub of Tulsa's cultural life.[120]

Farther west, the rapidly growing city of Los Angeles also benefited from touring opera companies and symphony orchestras, but the Los Angeles Symphony Society emerged slowly as a local professional organization. Beginning in 1897, the violinist Harley Hamilton pulled together a group of players from theater orchestras and the Seventh Regiment Band and presented concerts. Mrs. John C. Mossin, later called "the mother of the Los Angeles Symphony," sponsored his efforts, and when the orchestra had serious financial problems in 1900, Mrs. Emily Earl pledged $3,000 yearly to keep it alive. By 1900, the orchestra had doubled in size and could offer Tchaikovsky's *Pathétique*. The repertoire included Brahms, Dvořák, and Haydn, but Hamilton also presented music by local composers and other Americans. In 1913, Adolph Tandler, a Viennese musician, became the conductor, and he substantially expanded the repertoire. He conducted Beethoven's Ninth Symphony for the first time in Los Angeles and introduced Berlioz's *Harold in Italy*. Like Hamilton, he also offered works by contemporary American composers.[121]

As successful as Tandler had been, the quality of the orchestra did not please a new resident of southern California, William Andrews Clark. The *Los Angeles Evening Express* announced on June 11, 1919, that W. Andrews Clark proposed to establish a new, salaried professional orchestra. The impressario L. E. Behymer spoke for Clark and declared that the city, growing at the rate of 100,000 people yearly, deserved a quality orchestra. Clark's Los Angeles Philharmonic Orchestra would be equal to the major symphonies in the country, those with annual budgets in excess of $250,000. Only forty-two years old, the shy and reserved Clark had inherited over $100 million from his father, the Montana copper king Senator W. A. Clark. An amateur musician and art patron, the younger Clark had moved to Montecito near Los Angeles and continued his study of the violin. Clark's commitment to the Philharmonic included an initial $1 million, and by 1934 he had contributed another $2 million. Each year the Philharmonic's deficits, often as much as $200,000, were guaranteed by Clark. He sought to hire Sergei Rachmaninoff as the conductor, but when the composer declined, he employed Walter Henry Rothwell. The best musicians from the Los Angeles Symphony Orchestra joined the Philharmonic, which moved into Philharmonic Auditorium in 1920.[122] Clark gave the city a highly talented and successful symphony orchestra.

The desire for quality musical performances reflected the craving for classical drama and comedies on the stages of southwestern theaters. Touring companies found packed houses in the larger cities and even in the smaller towns. Minnie Maddern Fiske appeared in Arizona Territory in 1907 and 1908, with performances in Phoenix, Tucson, Bisbee, and Globe. Her audiences cheered all the productions, except one. When she presented Ibsen's *Rosmersholm* in Phoenix, a sparse house made it clear that the community was not ready for heavy Scandinavian drama.[123] Houston audiences lauded Otis Skinner in *Kismet* and the Dolly sisters in *The Merry Countess*. Performers in Houston included Ethel Barrymore,

Sarah Bernhardt, Eva Tanguay, and Gaby Deslys. Broadway hits came to the Southwest almost immediately after opening in New York.[124] Anita Loos recalled that the stock company her father organized in San Diego pirated plays by placing stenographers in Broadway houses, where they took the dialogue in shorthand, then typed the scripts and mailed them to California. Miss Loos appeared in *East Lynne* and *Little Lord Fauntleroy* with the company before becoming a screenwriter.[125] The stage of Henry Overholser's Opera House in Oklahoma City saw Julia Marlow, E. H. Sothern, Thomas Keene, and other notables in *Hamlet, Richard III,* and *The Comedy of Errors.* Overholser formed a theatrical circuit that booked George M. Cohan, Joseph Jefferson in *The Rivals,* and a grand-scale production of *Ben Hur.*[126] Even the remote town of Santa Fe, New Mexico, hosted Ethel Barrymore and Tom Terriss, and when the touring companies failed to appear frequently enough for theatergoers, they organized the Santa Fe Community Theater in 1919 to present their own productions.[127]

Anglo American theatrical longings differed little from those within the Hispanic community. In the border cities of El Paso and Tucson, Hispanic theater continued to generate substantial audiences, and it was particularly vibrant in San Antonio. Theaters in San Antonio drew from both the Spanish and the Mexican traditions, with touring companies from Mexico presenting dramas, comedies, and musicals from Mexico and Iberia. A performance often included a serious drama and then an afterpiece of a short comic relief or a zarzuela. The latter incorporated dialogue, music, and dancing, usually with a comic theme. Companies produced plays in Mexico City and then toured larger cities in Mexico before coming to San Antonio. Often the plays were productions of avant-garde Spanish dramas by José Echegaray, who wrote in an Ibsen-like vein. There were melodramas and comedies but also plays dealing with family relations, the role of the Roman Catholic Church, and political themes. These contemporary Spanish or Mexican plays reinforced a pride in language and culture and spoke to Hispanic values and aspirations.[128]

Hispanics in San Antonio organized their own companies and produced plays that toured other Texas cities. Compañia Juan B. Padilla leased the Teatro Zaragoza, where it performed plays by Luis Iza of Mexico City and mounted a production of *The Barber of Seville.* All eight hundred seats were filled for *Othello* performed in Spanish. Francisco Solórzan formed a resident company, purchased a theater, and offered dramas, musicals, and comedies. Compañia Villalongín benefited greatly when actors fleeing the Mexican Revolution joined the troupe. The company mounted high-quality productions, with the famous actress Concepcíon Hernandez (Concha) taking major roles. Teatro Nacional brought films, vaudeville, and dramas to San Antonio after 1917, providing a large house for touring companies such as that of Virginia Fábregas, a very popular Mexican actress. Theatro Nacional also sponsored local productions, becoming a significant aspect of Hispanic culture in Texas.[129]

In 1915, the Tucson entrepreneur Carmen Soto Vásquez built a fourteen-hundred-seat theater, the largest and most elegant in the community. Teatro Carmen provided a venue for touring companies from Mexico and Los Angeles. Dramas, comedies, and zarzuelas brought an elegantly dressed audience to the theater. Famous Mexican performers such as Virginia Fábregas played the house. Teatro Carmen symbolized culture for the upper- and upper-middle-class Hispanics in Tucson. Performances of classical Iberian plays in Spanish affirmed their cultural heritage.[130]

Southwesterners did more than simply import theater. The impresarios Oliver Morosco and L. E. Behymer also originated productions in Los Angeles, took the plays and operas on tour, and sent a few directly to Broadway. Oliver Morosco arrived in Los Angeles in 1899 and proceeded to create a theatrical empire. Theater flourished in Los Angeles in the 1890s, and Morosco moved quickly to establish a stock company of talented performers. He initially leased theaters, but in 1909 he purchased the five-year-old Belasco Theater as a venue for his company. With the actor Lewis Stone as his leading man and a series of talented actresses, Morosco produced *When Knighthood Was in Flower, The Admirable Crichton, Candida,* and *Undertow.* He sent the last production to New York, where it became a hit. New plays such as *The Half Breed* and *The Judge and the Jury* received tryouts in Los Angeles before opening on Broadway. Morosco produced *The Bird of Paradise* in 1911, and this smash toured the United States and Canada. Laurette Taylor's *Peg of My Heart* moved from Los Angeles to New York, giving Morosco one of his greatest hits. West Coast business leaders financed the plays, since Morosco proved to be a talented producer.[131]

The tireless and ambitious Lynden Ellsworth Behymer served as the leading impresario of Los Angeles for over forty years. "The Bee," as he was known, brought Bernhardt, Eleonora Duse, Edwin Booth, and others to Los Angeles, as well as Isadora Duncan and the Metropolitan Opera. When Behymer imported "The Met" to Los Angeles in 1900, Walter Damrosch conducted a cast of 253 that included Nellie Melba and Lillian Nordia. The overwhelming response led Behymer to emphasize opera rather than theater, and in 1915 he formed the Los Angeles Grand Opera Company. He brought conductors and principals to California, organized the productions, and then sent them on tours across the West and the South. His company performed in Denver, Houston, Dallas, Fort Worth, and San Antonio.[132] The successes of Behymr and Morosco symbolized a shift of significant magnitude: the Southwest could export culture; it could originate high-quality theatrical and operatic productions that generated the respect of audiences and critics alike.

Between 1900 and 1920, the trends that had developed in the previous two decades accelerated. The Southwest became more urbanized and even more ethnically diverse. Cultural institutions appeared in the major cities while artists and writers discovered the riches of the deserts and the mountains and their inhabitants as subject matter. A substantial influx of people from the Midwest and Northeast brought demands for the cultural trappings of western European society. Business leaders recognized that symphonies, museums, operas, and theater contributed to the economic well-being of the cities. The convergence of many factors fueled the rise of a culture that began to move toward a higher level, toward creation rather than emulation. Families in the East and Midwest—living in "California bungalows," sitting in Mission Revival furniture, reading a story by Eugene Rhodes or listening to a recording of the Los Angeles Grand Opera Company, with a reproduction of a painting by William R. Leigh on the wall—unconsciously embraced the culture of the Southwest.

CHAPTER 4

A Regional Culture
Is Formulated

1920–1940

During the Roaring Twenties, the nonagricultural economy of the Southwest boomed as petroleum, real estate and construction, diversified small-scale manufacturing, the aviation industry, and tourism fueled rampant growth. Like their contemporaries across the nation, southwesterners followed the bull market on the New York Stock Exchange, listened to "hot music" on the radio, and purchased small electrical appliances on credit from chain stores. They acquired automobiles to drive to church and to the bootlegger, as well as to the new suburban shopping areas. Some joined the Ku Klux Klan and supported the National Origins Act, which slammed closed "the Golden Door" to immigrants. But most residents of the region concentrated on financial gain, and that meant moving to the cities, which held both economic opportunities and cultural institutions. The urban Southwest formed the basis for the creation of a regional culture.

The rapid growth of Los Angeles continued, and the rates of expansion in Houston, Dallas, Oklahoma City, Fort Worth, and Tulsa soon were among the highest in the nation. At the same time, the culture maven Mable Dodge settled in Taos, arguing for a new American culture based on the simplicity of life among the New Mexico Pueblos. Others in the region sought out the architect Frank Lloyd Wright to design organic homes with Meso-American themes. Modernism in art flourished in Los Angeles and New Mexico while young Kiowas in Oklahoma created a new Native American art motif. Strong cultural crosscurrents and tensions continued unabated in the 1920s.

The institutional cultural dynamism of the 1920s shattered with the coming of the Great Depression. Although the worst ravages of the economic collapse came late to the urban Southwest, the depression smashed many of the cultural institutions created during the previous, heady decade. The New Deal for the arts employed artists, writers, actors, and musicians in the region, but the small programs were generally lost opportunities. Conservative legislators and governors, provincial community norms, and the absence of resources meant limited achievements in maintaining and creating viable cultural institutions.

Nevertheless, southwesterners took advantage of New Deal programs to form symphony orchestras, community theaters, and incipient art museums. Writers and playwrights, such as Lynn Riggs, seized on the economic travails of the region as themes. Artists, touched by the plight of farmers and the dispossessed, combined social realism with a sense of place and produced art reflecting a region in despair. New Deal programs provided Native American artists with opportunities to gain critical recognition for their paintings and pottery. The New Deal encouraged Hispanic theater, which flourished in Los Angeles, in San Antonio, and in the valley of the Rio Grande. Before the outbreak of World War II the Southwest longed to emulate the national culture, but financial restraints and essentially conservative communities limited those aspirations.

The dichotomy between those who sought a dynamic, growing Southwest and those who wished to preserve the alleged serenity and simplicity of an earlier society continued in the two decades before World War II. Intellectuals came to New Mexico and southern California seeking solitude, inspiration, and after 1933, a refuge from fascism. Others came to participate in the economic expansion. These divergent goals were all based on the land and its people. The "dean of Texas letters" J. Frank Dobie declared: "If people are to enjoy their own lives, they must be aware of the significance of their own environment. The mesquite is, objectively, as good and as beautiful as the Grecian acanthus. . . . We in the Southwest shall be civilized when the roadrunner as well as the nightingale has connotations."[1] The English dramatist and literary critic J. B. Priestley stayed at a ranch near Wickenburg, Arizona, and wrote in a small shack. The distant horizon and the vast space impressed him, but he noted, "Arizona is something more than a collection of natural marvels and multi-coloured landscapes." The people made Arizona appealing, wrote Priestley. "They were our sort of folk."[2] The native son of Texas and the English intellectual defined the basic elements of southwestern society and culture, both of which were increasingly urban.

After 1920, rapid population growth occurred almost exclusively in southwestern cities, especially the smaller metropolitan centers. Between the end of World War I and the outbreak of war in Europe in 1939, Dallas grew from 159,000 people to 294,000 while its rival, Fort Worth, expanded from 106,000 to 177,000. Houston mushroomed from 138,000 to 384,000, and San Antonio grew from 161,000 to 253,000. The petroleum boom caused Oklahoma City and

Tulsa to double in size, the former increasing from 91,000 to 204,000, and the latter from 72,000 to 142,000. A modest-sized town in 1920 with 29,000 people, Phoenix reached 65,000; meanwhile Tucson increased to 35,000 from 20,192. Albuquerque grew in population from 15,157 in 1920 to 35,000 in 1940.[3] These substantial population increases stimulated construction and real estate markets and demands for paved roads, sewer and water systems, and a larger commercial infrastructure.[4]

Opportunities to create a regional architecture thus abounded, and designers responded by taking international motifs and giving them a southwestern flavor. In the 1920s, European architectural currents came to the United States in the forms of Art Deco and Art Moderne, motifs embraced by southwestern designers. Architects using Art Deco took their cues from the Exposition des Arts Décoratifs in Paris in 1926 or from German expressionists. Setback buildings, reflecting New York City zoning requirements, received facades that were hard-edged and geometrical, with low-relief ornamentation around doors and windows and along roof edges. Architects emphasized vertical lines using metals such as copper as well as glazed bricks, mosaic tiles, and zigzag banding. Ornamentation was often constructed in the same material as the building itself. Stylized figure sculptures, sunrise patterns, chevrons, and floral images decorated walls and openings. By the 1930s, Art Moderne offered softer, rounded corners, smooth wall finishes, and a streamlined effect, usually with strong horizontal lines. Aluminum and stainless-steel trims appeared around doors and windows, but in nondecorative forms.[5] Southwestern architects found clients clamoring for the newest concepts in designs as the cities entered major construction booms. As a consequence, Los Angeles, Tulsa, Phoenix, Oklahoma City, Fort Worth, and other cities acquired skyscrapers, hotels, theaters, department stores, and residences in both the Art Deco and the Art Moderne styles.

The skyscraper symbolized the economic success of a city and of the corporations located there. Land values in southwestern cities generally did not justify structures twenty or thirty stories in height, but the desire for such buildings was not based on economics. Banks, petroleum companies, and investors wanted the tallest buildings in the most advanced styles for symbolic reasons. In 1924 in Phoenix, Henry C. Trost designed a ten-story structure, the Luhrs Building, a Sullivanesque conception with strong vertical lines. But five years later, when the Luhrs Tower appeared, Trost provided a stepped-back design complete with Art Deco chevrons and floral patterns in cast-stone details. A near twin, the Bassett Tower in El Paso (1930) also featured setbacks, strong vertical lines, and spare ornamentation on its fifteen-story facade. Though finished on all four sides, the Bassett Tower's decorations were even more spartan in detail, with a

FIGURE 21

*A busy street in downtown Phoenix shows the evolution of the skyscraper
in the region: from Chicago "commercial" in the early 1900s to Art Deco
in the 1920s to the International Style of the 1960s. Author's collection.*

zigzag motif.[6] In Oklahoma City two Art Deco buildings rose across the street
from each other in 1928, using totally different exterior materials. The thirty-
three-story First National Bank's Bedford limestone veneer rose to a sloping
aluminum roof. Weary and Alford, Chicago architects, used aluminum decorations at the main entrance, which led to an elaborate Art Deco lobby. The oilman
W. R. Ramsey's tower of the same height employed strong vertical lines and a
brick facade not unlike that of the future Rockefeller Center in New York.[7] The
Phillips brothers of Tulsa built the Philtower and the Philcade Building to house
their petroleum offices and those of other oil companies. Stepped towers with
magnificent Art Deco public spaces, these office buildings were but two examples
of Art Deco in "The Oil Capitol."[8] The Richfield Building in Los Angeles

sported black terra-cotta walls with gold stripes, representing the "black gold" in that city. The Sinclair Building brought the zigzag Art Moderne motif to Fort Worth, with cubist eagles in panels on the upper floors and Mayan-inspired decorations at the entrance.[9] Spanish-derived Art Deco ornamentation graced the exteriors of the Casino Club and the Smith-Young Tower in San Antonio.[10]

These "cathedrals of commerce" soon had new neighbors. Tourism generated demands for hotels in southwestern cities large and small. The Wooten Hotel in Abilene (1930) and the Settlers Hotel in Big Spring (1930) dominated the skylines of those Texas towns as Art Deco towers of fifteen and seventeen stories rose above the prairie.[11] Oklahoma City's Hotel Black (1928) received a profusion of Art Deco ornamentation based on Native American designs. New Mexico's only Art Deco skyscraper, the ten-story Hotel Clovis, was a monument to the aspirations of the town of Clovis. Built in 1931, the facade of the hotel incorporated stone heads of Plains Indians in its facade. It was "a place nice folks went."[12]

"Nice folks" also attended films and plays at Albuquerque's KiMo Theater, purchased clothes at Bullock's on the Miracle Mile in Los Angeles, bought train tickets at Art Deco railway stations in Tulsa, Fort Worth, and Oklahoma City, and checked out books from the Los Angeles Public Library, all testaments to the range of Art Deco. The architect Carl Boller of Los Angeles created rich Art Deco decorations using Native American symbols on the KiMo Theater (1927). Bold colors and patterns in stucco and terra-cotta produced a splendidly gaudy form of "Pueblo Deco," a concept that soon could be found across the Southwest.[13] The Texas & Pacific Railroad's passenger terminal in Fort Worth (1931) had Art Deco and Moderne elements drawn from both Native Americans and the Egyptians, while the Santa Fe Railway station in Oklahoma City had much plainer elements in decorative metals. Bullock's Department Store also eschewed the excesses of Art Moderne for a streamlined effect, but the Los Angeles Public Library, designed by Bertram Goodhue, featured a pyramid-shaped central tower covered in brilliant Spanish tile with various exotic motifs.[14] Homes, airport terminals, service stations, and courthouses appeared in Art Deco and streamlined Moderne forms for those southwesterners who demanded the avant-garde in architecture.

Achieving the avant-garde often included commissioning Frank Lloyd Wright, *the* American architect of the era, to produce a building. The petroleum heiress Aline Barnsdall met Frank Lloyd Wright in Chicago, where she codirected a theater company. She produced plays in Los Angeles in 1916 and 1917, and on the death of her father, she received a huge inheritance. Barnsdall purchased thirty-six acres of land north of downtown Los Angeles and in 1919 hired Wright

FIGURE 22

The Lawyers Title Building, Albuquerque, combined Spanish Colonial Revival motifs with Moorish influences to create an ahistorical style. Author's collection.

to design her home and eventually more than forty buildings at Olive Hill and elsewhere. Always avant-garde, Barnsdall produced plays using sets designed by the modernist Norman Bel Geddes, and she wanted to create at Olive Hill an artistic colony to further her interests. Wright laid out a cultural center with her home, Hollyhock House, at its heart. Hollyhocks were Barnsdall's favorite flower, and Wright incorporated the flower into a concrete-block system that served as the basic structural material for her home. He placed the house at the crown of Olive Hill surrounding an exterior garden court. Wright moved beyond his Prairie house concept as he worked with masses of concrete blocks with flat, unadorned surfaces.[15] The Los Angeles landscape shaped Wright's organic design, but he rejected the prevalent styles in the area, declaring: "All was flatulent or fraudulent with a cheap opulence. Tawdry Spanish Medievalism was now rampant."[16] Hollyhock House had pre-Columbian roots: Wright sought a natural, organic appearance using cast-concrete details. Mayan influences appeared even as Barnsdall and Wright fought over his blueprints. Despite their artistic differences, Hollyhock House and the related buildings were a triumph and won Wright additional commissions in Los Angeles.

Although Wright had gained an international reputation as a consequence of his Imperial Hotel in Tokyo, clients were few in the United States because of his nontraditional designs. But Alice Millard of Chicago, like Barnsdall, hired Wright *because* of his concepts. An avid art collector, Millard wanted a fireproof house in Pasadena for her collection. Wright responded with another concrete-block house that would be warm in the winter, cool in the summer, and protective of the art collection. In a jungle-like ravine, Wright placed La Miniatura, an inexpensive, durable, and strong house. Over the next several years Wright found more clients in Los Angeles for his concrete-block houses. The Storer House (1923–24) employed square blocks and steel reinforcing rods in a two-story design. The Freeman House (1923) of concrete blocks had two-story, mitered-glass, corner windows that offered spectacular views of the city, and the Ennis House (1924) looked like a vast Mayan temple or fortress, with elegant geometric patterns in the blocks. Wright called the latter "the little palace." His houses grew out of the sand and the gravel of their sites as he literally mixed those soils into the concrete for color and texture.[17] Wright found a region where he could experiment, along with clients who were willing to take risks.

Wright went to Tulsa in 1929 to design a home for his cousin, the publisher Richard Lloyd Jones. The house, Westhope, rose from the red Oklahoma soil in the form of large concrete pillars and blocks cast at the site. Mayan-influenced patterns in the blocks and vertically stacked windows repeated elements of his Los Angeles houses. Large open interior spaces, a flat roof, and a modular construction technique represented the beginning of what Wright called "Usonian architecture." He dramatically balanced glazed and masonry surfaces in abstract forms.[18]

Two years before he built Westhope, Wright had visited Arizona for the first time. It changed his life. A former student, Albert Chase McArthur, brought Wright to Phoenix to help design the Arizona Biltmore Hotel in Scottsdale. McArthur sought Wright's advice in using molded-concrete blocks for the hotel. Palm leaves and Aztec and Mayan patterns on the gray blocks created dramatic spaces, but Wright and McArthur argued about cost overruns and design differences. The lushly landscaped hotel nevertheless opened in 1929 to critical acclaim.[19]

With continuing personal problems and professional disappointments, Wright returned to Phoenix in 1937. He sought to establish a winter design school replicating the work done at his studio in Wisconsin. After a year of searching, he found a site northeast of Phoenix. "On up to a great mesa in the mountains, on the mesa just below McDowell Peak, we stopped, turned, and looked around. The top of the world from Maricopa Hill. . . . Well, that was to be our place on the mesa." Wright and his students constructed Taliesen West of orange, ocher, and flint-gray rocks set in concrete. Roofs, doorways, and windows of redwood

FIGURE 23
The desert inspired and provided materials for Frank Lloyd Wright's
Taliesin West in Arizona. Author's collection.

sustained the natural colors of the walls. Translucent light, first through canvas
and then through plastic panels, flooded the studios. "Taliesen West had to be
absolutely according to the desert," Wright declared. The buildings were simple
and noble, sculptured like the land. Wright's complex emerged from the eight
hundred acres he had purchased, and he reveled in driving his Cherokee Red
Lincoln Zephyr across the land. The Southwest had a profound impact on
Wright and his students.[20]

Wright's influence in the region extended beyond his own work, as architects
adopted his philosophy of organic architecture. One such young designer, Bruce
Goff of Tulsa, fell in love with Wright's architecture. Goff first entered an architect's office in 1915 as a part-time draftsman, when he was eleven years old. Graduating from high school seven years later, he began to design simple, rectangular

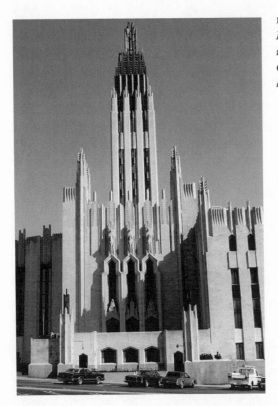

FIGURE 24
*Boston Avenue Methodist Church
in Tulsa made architect Bruce
Goff's reputation as an innovative
designer. Author's collection.*

buildings with abstract geometrical details. He helped produce the Tulsa Club (1927) with Art Deco ornamentation, but Goff's Riverside Music Studio (1928) broke cleanly from traditional architecture. The geometric lines in white stucco and the brown steel casement windows suggested the impact of Wright as well as German and French architecture of the 1920s. Goff's masterpiece, the Boston Avenue Methodist Church, established his reputation. Bedford limestone ashlor blocks, buff-colored terra-cotta spandrels, and a 255-foot tower topped with copper and glass created a dramatic structure. Goff used native Oklahoma flowers in the interior decorations, another reflection of Wright's influence. With an exterior that hinted of the Art Deco and even the Gothic, the church broke with tradition in a city that had rarely taken risks in architecture. Modernism had arrived in the region, and southwestern architects sought to combine it with traditional forms and motifs.[21]

John Gaw Meem seemed an unlikely defender of both traditional regional designs *and* modernism, but for three decades he practiced imaginative architecture, fought to preserve the Pueblo missions of New Mexico, and spoke for utilizing native materials and building techniques. "Some old forms are so honest, so completely logical and native to the environment that one finds — to his delight and surprise — that modern problems can be solved and are best solved by the use of forms based on tradition."[22] Born in Brazil and educated at Virginia Military Institute, Meem was a veteran of World War I. He originally came to New Mexico because of tuberculosis. In Santa Fe, the artist Carlos Vierra interested him in local architecture, and after he mended, Meem went to Denver to study with the firm of Fisher and Fisher. Meem admired Irving Gill's cubist forms and blended blocks and masses with few openings, and he combined these concepts with elements drawn from the pueblos. Buildings should be logical and clean, he wrote, and should be constructed of native materials.

The commission that Meem received from Alice Bemis Taylor in 1932 allowed him the freedom to turn these ideas into a brilliantly successful design. Taylor collected Native American and Hispanic arts, and she wanted to build a museum in Colorado Springs to house them. Known as "Lady Bountiful," Taylor donated $400,000 to initiate the project. She contacted the Broadmoor Academy of Art about a site for the museum, and with Mrs. Meridith Hare, chairperson of the academy's building committee, she proposed a structure to incorporate both the museum and the school. The Colorado Springs Fine Arts Center emerged, with Meem as its architect.[23] On a particularly difficult site, Meem placed a building designed to carry out many functions. "I am thrilled at the opportunity of designing a building strictly in keeping with modern times, something I have not yet undertaken," he declared.[24] Meem created an exterior of setback blocks that evoked the pueblos, but in an asymmetrical grouping. He used concrete, colored with Cripple Creek rhyolite, poured into wooden forms. When the concrete dried, it retained the imprint of the wood grain and the striped effect of the forms. Abstract Pueblo motifs decorated the exterior. Doors, windows, and balcony railings were made of unadorned aluminum. Classical proportions, terraces, geometric shapes, and earthen colors won praise from the *Architectural Forum*. The building was not a "fake Pueblo" but was "modern, monumental, and unlabored."[25] The artist Andrew Dasberg told Meem that he had "designed one of the purist buildings in America."[26]

Taylor's largess and Meem's talents produced a building that blended traditional southwestern architecture and the International Style. The latter, a concept that would dominate architecture in the 1930s, had come to the United States from Germany, France, and Scandinavia after World War I. Architects and designers created a new form wholly devoid of ornamentation. They employed flat roofs, smooth walls, large expanses of glass, and projecting or cantilevered balconies and upper floors. Metal casement windows set flush in white walls, roofs without eaves, and exposed structural members created dramatic buildings. In the 1920s, Rudolph Schindler, Richard Neutra, and Kem Weber brought the International Style to southern California, and it soon spread across the Southwest.

Los Angeles in the 1920s became "a paradise for realtors and a refuge for the rheumatic," but it was also a place where architects found clients willing to experiment with the newest concepts. Rudolph Schindler, a Viennese designer, arrived in Los Angeles in 1920 to supervise the construction of Hollyhock House for Wright and Barnsdall. Educated at the Vienna Academy of Fine Arts and the Imperial Institute of Engineering, Schindler had first come to the United States in 1914, bringing the influence of Otto Wagner and Adolf Loos and their non-decorative architecture. A train trip to New Mexico, Arizona, and California in 1915 gave Schindler a strong appreciation for Pueblo architecture. Moving to California in 1922, he built a tilt-slab concrete home in Hollywood and began to produce houses in the International and Moderne styles. In 1925–26, he designed a beach house for the health fanatic Dr. Phillip Lovell at Newport Beach. The house consisted of a concrete frame and great expanses of glass looking out toward the ocean. With its unadorned facade, the house looked like plastic volumes and forms rising above the sand.[27]

That same year, Schindler's fellow Austrian Richard Neutra joined him as a partner, sharing his practice. Neutra had graduated from a technical school in Vienna, served in the military during World War I, and after a brief period of study, came to the United States to work with Wright. The Schindlers took the Neutras on tours of southern California, where, Neutra wrote to a friend, a person could find "ocean, forest, desert, snow, palm trees, South Sea fishes all in 2–3 hours driving time."[28] The land affected him deeply, as did the people. He said: "[In] Southern California, I found what I had hoped for, a people who were more 'mentally footloose' than those elsewhere, who did not mind deviating opinions . . . where one can do most anything that comes to mind and it is in good fun. All this seemed to me a good climate for trying something independent of hidebound beatification."[29]

Neutra's clients included the same Dr. Lovell and his wife, Leah. Because of their views on health, they asked for a house open to the sun, with balconies and terraces. The Lovell house of 1928–29 floated above a canyon, with a steel frame supporting three floors of strong horizontal lines. Cantilevered above the canyon, the house featured large areas of glass and an open, informal interior. The Lovell house won praise from critics and brought more clients to Nuetra, who had by now broken away from Schindler to establish his own practice. For the next four decades he expanded on the concepts of the Lovell house.[30] Neutra contended that humankind "loves to immigrate to the South, or conquer it."

He added, "Like all Nordic barbarians, we want to go to sunny Helas, or to the land where the lemon blooms and no icy storms trouble us."[31] He created an architecture for the "Nordic barbarians" of southern California.

Another major contributor to design in southern California was Karl Emmanuel Martin ("Kem") Weber. Born in Germany, Weber studied at the Academy of Applied Arts in Berlin, honing his skills as a designer. He came to the United States in 1914 to work on the German exhibit at the Pan-Pacific Exposition in San Francisco. When war broke out, he stayed in California. He joined the design studio of Barker Brothers in Los Angeles, where he produced interiors and furniture in the streamlined Moderne style. His interiors paralleled motion picture sets in the 1930s, with their use of polished metals and stone, rare woods, and colored glass in highly stylized representations of flora and geometric designs. He created tubular furniture and experimented with recessed fluorescent lights. Weber did not push his designs beyond the curve of public acceptance, but his work as a teacher and as a set designer at Paramount Studios allowed him an opportunity to mold public taste.[32] Furthermore, Weber's furniture and interiors harmonized with the houses designed by his friends Neutra and Schindler. Weber, Neutra, Schindler, and Harwell Harris thus created a "Los Angeles School" of architecture in the 1930s. They blended indoor and outdoor living, using large areas of glass, sliding glass doors, and balconies and terraces.

Like modernism in architecture, modernism in art came to the Southwest after 1920. The impact of post-Impressionism and the rise of modernism first entered the region through northern New Mexico in the years following the New York Armory Show of 1913. Robert Henri arrived in 1916 to paint portraits of the Native Americans whom he had seen at the San Diego exposition two years before. Enchanted with New Mexico, Henri urged his New York students and colleagues to join him, and they did. George Bellows and Leon Kroll came in 1917, and John Sloan arrived two years later after hearing of the glories of the area from Marsden Hartley, who had visited and painted there in 1918. Andrew Dasburg, John Marin, Edward Hopper, Stuart Davis, and Georgia O'Keeffe came in the 1920s, and all but Davis and Hopper returned.[33] A few became permanent residents. To varying degrees, the New Mexico experience altered their styles even as the area provided landscapes and people as subjects of their work. The land exerted an abstract power while the character of the Native American and Hispanic peoples offered entirely different personalities to explore on canvas.

"It was a great day for John Sloan when he discovered New Mexico," wrote Sloan's fellow artist Walter Pach. "But it was also a great day for New Mexico."[34] For almost thirty years Sloan came to the state to paint and reflect. Sloan had studied at the Pennsylvania Academy of Fine Arts in the 1890s and later with Henri in New York City. He exhibited with "The Eight," urban artists who had rejected Impressionism, and helped to mount the Armory Show. Until he came to New Mexico, his primary subject was urban life, expressed with a dark palette. After he bought a house in Santa Fe, worked with the city's Fiesta Committee on the elaborate floats used in the annual celebration and parade, visited the pueblos, and toured the land, his subject matter was transformed, as were the colors on his palette. Of the pueblo at Tesuque he wrote: "Within nine miles of a Europeanized city for three hundred years the little Pueblo of Tesuque has made a noble fight against combined poverty and civilization [sic]. The population is small and on the day we saw the ceremony [Eagle Dance] a mere handful appeared as spectators."[35]

The land inspired him as well. "I like the colors out there." He noted: "The ground is not covered with green mold as it is elsewhere. . . . Because the air is so clear you feel the reality of things in the distance."[36] Sloan explained: "The desert landscape with its ancient geometrical formations was of profound inspiration to me in a new chapter of work. I was carrying on ideas assimilated from study of the post-impressionists, in the New Mexico landscape."[37] He commented on one of his works, *Chama Running Red,* painted in 1925: "The river is running like pink tomato soup to the Rio Grande and the Gulf of Mexico, carrying off the good red earth."[38] The years in New Mexico shaped Sloan's art and his life.

Marsden Hartley knew even before going to New Mexico that he "wanted to be an Indian, . . . go to the west, and face the sun forever."[39] This was a strange sentiment for a young man from Cleveland, Ohio, who had studied with William Merritt Chase and at the National Academy of Design. The gallery owner Alfred Stieglitz had sponsored Hartley's visit to Germany, where Hartley saw the work of avant-garde painters such as Wassily Kadinsky. Even in Berlin, Hartley tried painting an Indian scene, using artifacts.[40] The American West beckoned, and returning to the United States, he visited New Mexico in 1918 and 1919. He discovered that it was not "a country of light on things, but a country of things in light."[41] Invited to the Taos home of Mabel Dodge Sterne (better known by her later name, Mabel Dodge Luhan), he was overcome by the beauty of the area. Hartley wrote to Stieglitz: "The country outside of Taos is simply too beautiful. I have never seen anything so lovely in my life. It is not the kind of thing I thought I would see, . . . these long chains of blue grey mountains, and the miles of sage-brush plains in front of them, and here and there rising out of the sage in the distance, clear blue hills standing alone, mesas they call them in this land, . . . and over all this acres of blue sky; well, I give you my word, I have never seen anything lovelier."[42]

The art critic Leo Stein, the brother of Gertrude Stein and also a guest of Mabel Dodge Sterne's, urged Hartley to settle in Taos. Hartley found the realist painters of Taos to be "cheap artists" who applied academic styles to the Native Americans and the landscape. He sought a totally different approach: "I am an American discovering America. I like the position and I like the results."[43] He was inspired by the land, all stark and grandiose. He used pastels to capture the vivid colors and added regional design elements to his compositions. When he returned to Germany in 1921–22, Hartley continued to paint scenes of New Mexico, naturalistic representations of the land. For Hartley, the Southwest was a sculptural country where the land and the architecture merged. When he visited southern California briefly, the effect was not the same: "No landscape to speak of. Mostly scenery. It has the look of a stage set."[44] New Mexico provoked his creativity and made his painting more abstract and vivid.

Similarly, two other artists — George Bellows and John Marin — found subjects for their canvases and new ways to express their ideas in New Mexico, even though they painted almost a decade apart. Bellows's wife, Emma, hated the Southwest and disliked both the Native American and the Hispanic peoples. Yet the land inspired Bellows. He brought to New Mexico a modernism that used nondescriptive colors. A critic in Santa Fe denigrated "Bellows's Green Cow," but his style and his presence demonstrated the vitality of American art.[45] Mabel Dodge Luhan brought John Marin to Taos in 1929, and he returned the following summer. A painter of New York City streets, the coast of Maine, and the White Mountains of New England in abstract forms, Marin was not prepared for New Mexico. "If you think you know what light is, then go to New Mexico and you'll find light many times more intense."[46] He wrote to Stieglitz in 1929: "The *One* who made this country, this big level seeming desert table land cut out slices. They are the canyons, then here and there he put mountains atop. Astanding here you can see six of seven thunderstorms going on at the same time."[47]

Again writing to Stieglitz, Marin declared: "Big Sun heat. Big Storm. Big Everything. — A leaving out of that thing called *Man*."[48] The next summer he wrote that he had painted a dance of the San Domingo Indians: "Certain passages in the dance itself are so beautiful that to produce a something having seen it — becomes well nigh worthless — it's like grafting on to perfection — it's like rewriting *Bach*."[49] Marin did not paint abstract landscapes; his paintings reflected how he saw the land. He found a place he liked, then he painted "a kind of frame around it."[50] Working in watercolors, he brightened his palette and pursued strong expressionist elements — that is, the paintings were more geometric and formal.

Not all artists found in the Southwest new subjects and techniques. The abstract painter Stuart Davis proclaimed: "It's a place for an ethnologist, not an artist. Not sufficient intellectual stimulus. Forms made to order, to imitate. Colors — but I never went there again."[51] Overwhelmed by the scale of the land and all its "great dead population," Davis rejected heroic landscapes and romantic narratives. Edward Hopper, the realist painter of melancholy urban life, visited New Mexico and painted little except a watercolor: *Locomotive, D&RG.* The subjects that inspired Hopper apparently did not exist in New Mexico.[52] It is a pity he did not go further west, to Los Angeles, seeking urban subjects.

Perhaps Hopper and Davis simply did not find the stimulus that moved Georgia O'Keeffe to return to New Mexico and make it her home. At the age of forty-one, at the height of her creative powers, O'Keeffe returned to the Land of Enchantment. By the summer of 1929, she had become one of America's foremost artists. From the time Stieglitz exhibited her watercolors at his gallery, 291, she had gained popular and critical acclaim. Bored and feeling confined in New York, she accepted Mabel Dodge Luhan's invitation to visit Taos. Subsequently she would spend part of each year in New Mexico until 1946, when she moved permanently to her home at Ghost Ranch. Her second summer in New Mexico found O'Keeffe painting landscapes near Espanola, Taos, and Abiquiu. Traveling by car over rutted dirt roads, she found the desert and canyon country irresistible.[53] She wrote to the critic Henry McBride: "You know I never feel at home in the East like I do out here — and finally feeling in the right place again — I feel like myself — and I like it."[54] Mabel Dodge Luhan brought many artists and writers to Taos, but few responded as dramatically as O'Keeffe. "Well! Well! Well!" she exclaimed. "This is wonderful. No one told me it was like *this.*" As they drove across the tableland near Taos, she murmured over and over, "Well! Well! Well!"[55]

The Taos desert thrilled her, but the eroded canyons and bluffs of Ghost Ranch became the heartland, "Her country." She wrote: "A red hill doesn't touch everyone's heart as it touches mine and I suppose there is no reason why it should. The red hill is a piece of the bad lands where even the grass is gone. Bad lands roll away outside my door — hill after hill — red hills of apparently the same sort of earth that you mix with oil to make paint. All of the earth colors of the painter's palette are out here in the many miles of bad lands."[56] The space, wind, and land of New Mexico transformed O'Keeffe's art as she found the hottest sun, the brightest moonlight, and the biggest sky.

The roadside crosses of the Hispanic peoples, the rough-textured doors, the rounded adobe of the church at Ranchos de Taos, the giant tree at D. H. Lawrence's ranch, the bleached bones of animals, and the Taos Pueblo all appeared in vivid abstractions on her canvases. She commented, "Anyone who doesn't feel crosses doesn't get the country."[57] Describing an early-morning setting, she wrote: "I wish you could see what I see outside my window. The earth pink and yellow cliffs to the north—the full pale moon about to go down in an early morning lavender sky behind a very long beautiful tree covered mesa to the west—pink and purple hills in front and the scrubby fine dull green cedars—and a feeling of space."[58] In one of her letters, she noted: "At five I walked—I climbed way up on a pale green hill where I could look all around at the red, yellow, purple formations—miles all around—the color all intensified by the pale grey green I was standing on. It was wonderful."[59] She wrote to her friend Dorothy Brett: "I think of your house up on the side of the mountain—of Frieda's [Lawrence] house at the ranch—the walk along the ditch—and wish I could be walking along the ditch without any clothes on—or sitting up among the trees in a sunny spot—alone with just me and the wind and the trees and the pine needles on the ground."[60]

For nearly six decades O'Keeffe painted the land and the sky of New Mexico. "God told me," she said, "that if I painted that mountain [Pedernal Peak] enough, I could have it."[61] What O'Keeffe called "The Faraway County" became hers and the focus of her art. "I'm lucky to have found my time—not everybody does," she said. She also found her place, New Mexico: "It was a new world, and I thought this was my world."[62]

While O'Keeffe, Sloan, and other modernists found their world, the Taos painters continued to produce realistic landscapes and portraits of Native Americans and Hispanics. Although a few additional painters joined the original Taos Society of Artists, their styles remained representational and, in some cases, formulaic. The vibrancy of Taos passed to Santa Fe in the 1920s as five young men—Jozef Bakos, Fremont Ellis, Walter Mruk, Willard Nash, and Will Schuster—formed Los Cincos Pintores. They built studios and houses along Camino del Monte Sol, where they shared an enthusiasm for modernism. They drew inspiration for their landscapes and figure studies from the work of post-Impressionists such as Paul Cézanne. These artists, plus Randall Davey, Sheldon Parsons, and others, formed the heart of the Santa Fe colony. They established the community's reputation as an art center and as a place where modernism in art flourished.[63]

By contrast, Impressionism continued to dominate the art world in southern California well into the 1940s. The lag in style was due in part to the lack of

FIGURE 25
With Canon Synchromy
(Orange) *and similar works,*
Stanton Macdonald-Wright
brought modernism to Los
Angeles. Collection Frederick R.
Weisman Art Museum at the
University of Minnesota,
Minneapolis. Gift of Ione and
Hudson Walker.

support for art generally, for as collector William Preston Harrison noted in 1921, "The city's women's clubs are virtually the only outside encouragement to art development here."[64] Captivated by the geography and the climate, artists in the area failed to move forward. There were a few exceptions. Stanton Macdonald-Wright helped to organize the Group of Independents, which embraced modernism. He grew up in Santa Monica, studied at the Los Angeles Art Students League, and left for Paris in 1907. Between 1911 and 1913 he created Synchronism, in which Cubist geometric forms were reinterpreted as swirling fragments of color. Macdonald-Wright returned to California in 1919 and, as director of the Art Students League in Los Angeles, introduced his brand of modernism to students. By the 1930s, several Los Angeles artists had created a post-Surrealism that drew from literary and theatrical sources, and Millard Sheets offered urban subjects in a style suggestive of Edward Hopper.[65] Discouraged by the failure of the Los Angeles Museum of History, Science, and Art to develop a strong program, the Los Angeles Art Association sponsored fresh and exciting exhibitions, especially the 1937 Loan Exhibition of International Art, a huge success.[66] Nevertheless, the art world of southern California lacked vibrancy and vitality before World War II.

In Oklahoma, art life blossomed in the 1920s and 1930s because of the emergence of Native American artists who created entirely new forms and styles. The Kiowa Nation had roamed the southwestern plains before the second conquest, but late in the nineteenth century the federal government had placed them on a reservation in Oklahoma Territory. At the Anadarko Indian Agency a field matron, Susan Ryan Peters, saw the wide range of Kiowa arts, which included col-

FIGURE 26
Professor Oscar B. Jacobson and five of his Kiowa artists posed in 1929, at the time that their new approach to Native American painting was gaining international notice. Western History Collection, University of Oklahoma Libraries.

orful and elaborate images. Trained as an artist, Peters recognized that several young people in the tribe possessed considerable talent. Indeed, some were already selling crayon drawings to dealers. She arranged for an art teacher to work with the youngsters, and in 1923 she initiated an effort to have them admitted to the University of Oklahoma's School of Art. Finally, in 1928, aided by Professor Oscar B. Jacobson, she obtained permission for five of them to work in the university's art studios, with funds provided by the oilman Lew Wentz. Monroe Tsa Toke, Stephen Mopope, Spencer Asah, Jack Hokeah, and Louise Bou-Ge-Tah Smokey, the only woman, studied with Jacobson and Edith Mahier, both of whom encouraged their aspirations.[67]

The Kiowa painters used vivid colors and substantial detail in a highly stylized format. Figure studies often emphasized ceremonials, dances, and Native American arts and crafts. James Auchiah replaced Smokey in the group, which rejected the conservative landscape style practiced by Jacobson. There was humor and lyricism in their paintings, which soon drew critical notice. The Kiowas exhibited first in Oklahoma, then in Czechoslovakia, where European critics lauded their bold, colorful paintings. When a publisher in France printed a folio of their work the following year, the artists generated further attention.

The "Kiowa School" and its success brought other Native American art students and painters to the University of Oklahoma, where Jacobson urged them not to emulate western European art but to build on their own traditions. Acee Blue Eagle, Woodrow Crumbo, Dick West, and others joined the Kiowa painters in seeking to create a new Native American artistic expression. Trained at the Chilocco Indian School, Acee Blue Eagle used watercolors to create brilliant designs of strong colors in paintings that depicted his Creek-Pawnee heritage. He later chaired the art department at Bacone College near Muskogee, Oklahoma, where he promoted Native American painting and dance. "Woodie" Crumbo, a Potawatomie, studied with Jacobson before teaching at Bacone College. Using a "flat" style with a two-dimensional simplicity, Crumbo painted murals that spoke to the history of his people. Dick West, a Southern Cheyenne, studied with Blue Eagle at Bacone and then with Jacobson. His work, like that of other Native American artists in Oklahoma, was illustrative, anecdotal, and nostalgic. Cheyenne tribal lore and activities gave his paintings a Brueghel-like quality. West also taught at Bacone College, and the art department there produced many young painters trained in the new mode.[68]

The work of the Oklahoma artists soon came to resemble "The Studio" style developed by Native American artists at Santa Fe. Edgar L. Hewett, both at the School of American Research and at the Museum of New Mexico in Santa Fe, encouraged Native American artists before the 1920s. He commissioned Crescencio Martínez to paint dances at San Ildefonso, and that successful effort led him to hire two Hopi painters, Fred Kabotie and Otis Polelonema, and a Zia painter, Velino Herrera. They joined Awa Tsireh, of San Ildefonso, to create a historical record of their peoples. The paintings drew the attention of the artist John Sloan, the writer Mary Austin, and the poet Alice Corbin Henderson, who began to promote Native American arts.[69]

Although rituals and ceremonies initially served as the subject matter for the paintings, after Dorothy Dunn created the art program at the Santa Fe Indian School, the range of subjects expanded substantially. Dunn sought not only to foster traditional art but also to create new motifs, styles, and techniques. Because of tribal criticism generated by some of Hewett's painters, Dunn encouraged her students to maintain both tribal and individual distinctions. They were taught that their native art was *art,* not something that was simply part of everyday life. Dunn's "studio" influenced not only the young artists who studied there but also the older, self-trained painters such as Awa Tsireh. Cross-fertilization arrived in the form of the Kiowa artist Jack Hokeah, who came to Santa Fe to work with the students. A "true art" emerged as Native American painters moved away from the traditional idea that everyone was an "artist." Nevertheless, their work remained highly personal. As Sloan wrote: "When Awa Tsireh sits down to paint a leaping deer he remembers not only the way a deer looks leaping over a log but feels himself leaping in the dance with antlers swaying on his forehead and two sticks braced in hands for forelegs."[70] Sloan organized the Exposition of Indian Tribal Arts in New York in 1931, which produced not only an outpouring of interest in Native American painting but also the support Dunn needed to formally establish the art program at the Indian School.

The students at the Indian School came from the Pueblos as well as from the Hopi, Navajo, and Apache tribes. They observed the animal and stylized figure studies produced in vivid colors by Awa Tsireh. Velino Herrera's portraits with their rich colors interested them, as did his genre and hunting scenes. But the students moved beyond the self-trained generation. For example, Tonita Peña, a member of the traditionalists, told the students they could paint ceremonial figures that were people, not spirits. Her paintings were of lusty, fat figures, dancing and playing drums without symbolism or mysticism. The Navajo paint-ers at the school, such as Harrison Begay and Gerald Nailor, established their own concepts. Begay painted landscapes of northern Arizona — the cliffs and the red rocks — and scenes of tribal life. Nailor experimented with bright colors, then shifted to a palette of brown tones for depictions of traditional Navajo life inspired by sand painting. Allan Houser, an Apache and grandson of Geronimo, painted dramatic two-dimensional scenes filled with color. The Pueblo, Hopi, Navajo, and Apache painters emphasized tribal life, bringing together the people and the land in a new artistic form that preserved their traditional view of the world. They became the "caretakers of the earth."[71]

In the Native Americans' view of the earth and their relationship to it, Mabel Ganson Evans Dodge Sterne found the peace that had escaped her for three decades. Two failed marriages, years in Florence, Italy, and the creation of a famous salon in New York never fulfilled her psychologically. In 1918 she arrived in New Mexico, planning to visit for two weeks; she stayed for forty-four years. With her third husband, the painter Maurice Sterne, and her son John Evans, she went to Santa Fe and immediately responded to the town and its artistic community. Never one to share the limelight, however, Mabel Dodge Sterne decided to venture the seventy miles over primitive roads to Taos in a rented Model T. The land and the sky overwhelmed her. "'Holy! Holy! Holy!' I ex-claimed to myself. 'Lord God Almighty!' I felt a sudden recognition of the reality of natural life that was so strong and so unfamiliar that it made me feel unreal. I caught a fleeting glimpse of my own spoiled and distorted nature, seen against the purity and freshness of the undomesticated surroundings."[72]

For the first time in her life, Mabel Dodge Sterne recalled, she heard the voice

FIGURE 27
*Mabel Dodge Luhan listens as Tony Luhan plays the drum, Taos, New Mexico, 1924. This
item is reproduced by permission of the Huntington Library, San Marino, California.*

of "the One coming from the Many." She determined to create in Taos a center
of culture based on the human response to the land and the Native American
view of society, as she understood it. For Mabel Dodge Sterne, the mountain
behind Taos "was alive, awake, and breathing." The mountain told her, "I am
what I am — nothing can add to me or take away from me my own being."[73]

Mabel Dodge Sterne decided to be her own being. She began to construct
the first of several houses, to which she invited writers, musicians, artists, poets,
dancers, composers, photographers, and philosophers. She met a leader of the
Taos Pueblo — the tall, handsome Tony Luhan — and the two began a love affair
that led them to divorce their respective spouses so that they could marry. Mabel
Dodge Luhan and her husband created a salon of international renown in Taos.
The first years in New Mexico saw Mabel Luhan supervising construction of a
house, becoming the center of the town's artistic community, and mailing many
letters of invitation to potential guests. To Mary Austin, she wrote: "I am deter-

mined to get back to my original idea of having this place a creative centre—not just a place for people to retreat into—or to go to sleep in—or to barge in for just a good time. I want people to use it freely, but for creative purposes."[74] She added: "I feel strongly something wonderful will come out of the Taos Valley yet. There is a great and powerful enchantment here."[75]

She brought a wide range of guests to Taos, she or Tony drove them around the countryside, and she urged them to write, compose, and paint—under her guidance, of course. Strong-willed, bright, verbal, and domineering, Mabel Luhan filled the Taos Valley with the talented. John Sloan, John Marin, and Georgia O'Keeffe came to paint; Mary Austin and Willa Cather wrote, or tried whenever Mable left them alone; the poet Robinson Jeffers arrived from Carmel; and the psychologist Carl Jung came to study the Native Americans. But Mabel Luhan's prize was the English writer D. H. Lawrence, who came to Taos in 1922 at her urging. Unfortunately for her hope to monopolize Lawrence, he brought along his wife, Frieda, and shortly a friend, the painter Lady Dorothy Brett arrived. There would be no peace in paradise as the three women each sought his attention and affection.[76]

Novelist, poet, essayist, romantic figure, and world traveler, D. H. Lawrence came because Mable Luhan feared that Taos would become spoiled and exploited. She wanted him to write, to certify her view of Taos as a creative center, as a place to launch a new civilization. Lawrence eventually responded that he would join her. The impact of New Mexico on the English writer was all that Luhan could have wanted: "I think New Mexico was the greatest experience from the outside world that I have ever had. It certainly changed me for ever. Curious as it may sound, it was New Mexico that liberated me from the present era of civilization, the great era of material and mechanical development. The moment I saw the brilliant, proud morning shine high up over the deserts of Santa Fe, something stood still in my soul, and I started to attend."[77] New Mexico liberated Lawrence geographically and sensually: "Very nice, the great Southwest, put on a sombrero and knot a red kerchief round your neck to go out in the great free spaces."[78]

Mabel Luhan, Frieda Lawrence, and Dorothy Brett gave Lawrence little freedom and peace of mind with their constant bickering and jealousy, but he nevertheless wrote, visited the pueblos, and eventually acquired Kiowa Ranch north of Taos. There he found "a sense of space" and an escape from "the petty-fogging narrowness of England."[79] With Tony Luhan he visited the Jicarilla Apache reservation, where he was enthralled by a festival. His three muses—Mabel, Frieda, and Dorothy—kept his life in turmoil, but Lawrence produced short stories and novellas portraying the primitive world of the Sangre de Cristo Mountains. He

FIGURE 28

*D. H. Lawrence (right), Frieda Lawrence, and the poet Witter Bynner enjoy
a good story on a New Mexico rooftop in the 1920s. Literary Files, Harry
Ransom Humanities Research Center, the University of Texas at Austin.*

returned to New Mexico in 1924 and 1925, gathering material, writing drafts,
and editing the results. Lawrence wanted to establish a utopian society in New
Mexico — which he called Rananim — where writers and artists would live a monastic life. The contrast with his own hedonistic wanderings was palpable.

Frieda Lawrence shared her husband's enthusiasm for New Mexico, if not
for their demanding hostess. She too was overwhelmed by the land when they
arrived: "The next morning we drove up through the vast wonderful desert
country with its clear pure air, driving through the Rio Grande canyon deep
down by the river and then coming up on the Taos plateau. Coming out of the
canyon to the mesa is a wonderful experience, with all the deep mountains sitting mysteriously around in a ring, and so much sky."[80]

And so much Mabel. Frieda made her husband give up a novel about their
hostess, who subsequently appeared in several short stories. But it was the Native Americans and the land that inspired Lawrence, not his bickering muses.
"The Indian Pueblo is still, earth-brown, and in a soft, sun-soaked way aborigi-
nal. I like it."[81] Lawrence believed that a simple society would triumph over the
skyscraper: "Oh, yes, in New Mexico the heart is sacrificed to the sun, and the
human being is left stark, heartless, but undoubtedly religious."[82] His *padrona*
lamented her inability to redirect Lawrence's life, but he longed to return shortly
after each visit. It was like falling onto the moon, but a moon complicated by
the presence of Mabel, Frieda, and Lady Brett, the trio now referred to as the
"Three Dis-Graces." After 1925, Lawrence never returned to New Mexico, but

until his death five years later, his writing reflected the "primitive" world of bright light he had found in Taos.[83]

Mabel Luhan's ever-expanding adobe houses filled with other guests, creating what cynics later called "Chaos in Taos." Only a few of these guests established permanent residence in the town. Lady Dorothy Brett, who had arrived with the Lawrences on their second visit, stayed, becoming an American citizen in 1938. Brett, the daughter of Viscount Esher, was a friend of the English writers Katherine Mansfield, Virginia Woolf, Bertrand Russell, and Robert Graves. Trained as an art student, she found the Pueblo Indians totally fascinating. She recalled, "Much of our lives were bound up with the Indian life."[84] She had decided to visit New Mexico after she met Willa Cather in New York with the Lawrences in 1924 and heard of the writer's delight in the Southwest. Brett began to paint shortly after her arrival. She developed an empathy with the people of the pueblos, and she painted their ceremonies in an abstract but formal manner. Brett visualized the ceremonies but did not fully experience their sounds because of her hearing loss. Nevertheless she sensed the rhythm and cadence of the dancers, and aided by her ear trumpet, "Toby," she felt the drums and bells. Painting intuitively and with great feeling, Brett captured the ceremonies and dances in universal terms that appealed to viewers in this country and in Europe.[85] Brett attributed her ability to understand the Native Americans to her commitment to Jungian psychology, probably a consequence of Carl Jung's presence in Mable Luhan's Taos salon.

Jung came to New Mexico, interviewed Pueblo people, and was intrigued by their view of the world and their relationship to the environment. The Pueblo chief Ochwiay Biano explained to Jung that his people did not think with their heads, as whites did, but with their hearts. Startled, Jung carefully considered this revelation and concluded that the Taosan offered great insights. The linkage of the Pueblos to the earth, the sacred mountains and lakes, the Pueblo reverence for animals, and their vision of plant life struck Jung as a new way to view the human existence. "For the first time in my life," Jung wrote, "so it seemed to me, someone had drawn for me a picture of the real white man."[86] Jung's experience was not unique among those who enjoyed Mabel Luhan's hospitality. Others saw the Native American society as more humane, a society absent of rapaciousness and a people concerned with external values. This romantic idealism enthused Mabel Luhan, who implored her guests to write about this model for the world.

The growing body of writers and poets in Taos and Santa Fe in the 1920s established a literature that drew on the native peoples and the land. The playwright Maxwell Anderson's *Night over Taos* depicted the tragedy of the Pueblo

FIGURE 29
*Alice Corbin Henderson and
William Penhallow Henderson
helped create the intellectual society
of Santa Fe. Photograph by Will
Connell, Courtesy Museum of
New Mexico, Santa Fe, Negative
59757.*

revolt. This poetic drama of the clash of two civilizations was presented by the
Group Theater in New York and soon became a staple of community theaters
and university playhouses.[87] The poet Alice Corbin Henderson drew to Santa
Fe a group that included Witter Bynner, Haniel Long, Lynn Riggs, and Willard
"Spud" Johnson. In addition to the resident writers, poets such as Carl Sandburg
and novelists came for shorter stays, which led to significant works. Henderson,
cofounder with Harriett Monroe of *Poetry,* came to New Mexico because of ill
health. With her husband, the artist William Penhallow Henderson, she encouraged her coterie to interpret the Native American and Hispanic cultures. She
wrote two books of poetry about the societies of New Mexico and edited a
third, *The Turquoise Trail,* that included poems by writers lured to New Mexico:
Bynner, Long, Riggs, Lawrence, and Paul Horgan. Her collection *Red Earth*
included poems about Native Americans, Hispanics, and her response to New
Mexico. For Henderson, there was an organic relationship between the land and
the people, but the desert was a female image that could never be mastered.[88]
The wealthy, Harvard-educated poet Bynner wrote not only of the land but also
its peoples. He produced *Cake,* a bitter satire about Mabel Luhan. His lover,
"Spud" Johnson, edited *Laughing Horse,* an irregular journal that included con-

tributions by Santa Fe and Taos writers with two basic themes: the power and beauty of the western landscape and the uniqueness of the native peoples.[89] Riggs contributed "The Arid Land," which celebrated the dry wasteland, "under its iron band of sky," a place that "we yet may love."[90] A publication devoid of racism or sexism, *Laughing Horse* symbolized the openness of the artistic and literary communities in Taos and Santa Fe. The unbridled, high-spirited literary magazine published Lawrence's letters, poems, and essays, and its artwork included drawings by Brett, Andrew Dasburg, and Miguel Covarrubias, among others. The Santa Fe writers recognized that their surroundings stirred their creative juices, for as Long wrote, "Call the Southwest a spiritual experience or not, it has forced people to face the realities of existence."[91] His friend Oliver LaFarge sought to penetrate that reality with his novel *Laughing Boy,* which dealt with the cultural tensions between the Native Americans and the occupants of their lands. Although highly romanticized and nostalgic, LaFarge's novel won the Pulitzer Prize in 1930 and brought even greater attention to the literary world of the Southwest.[92]

This creative ferment in the late 1920s pleased Mabel Luhan, who earlier in the decade had despaired of the efforts of the Santa Fe writers. She had implored Austin: "Please get busy and write — write — write. *No one* but Alice Corbin & [Witter] Bynner is writing in Santa Fe. All the other work there is secretarial."[93] Luhan encouraged Frank Waters to write of the Native Americans as they saw themselves — not as LaFarge did, through a "white psyche."[94] She lobbied editors to publish stories, essays, and poetry about the Southwest, and she continued her efforts to bring established writers to the region.[95] Two of her greatest recruiting successes were Willa Cather and Mary Austin.

Cather returned to New Mexico in 1925, a response to a long-felt desire stimulated by her meeting with the Lawrences in New York. Arriving in the summer, Cather had no book in mind, but while she was in Santa Fe the outline of *Death Comes for the Archbishop* emerged as she read of Archbishop John Baptist Lamy and visited the cathedral he had built. She responded to Mabel Luhan's persistent urges and went to Taos, occupying "The Pink House," where the Lawrences had stayed. She spent a week at a ranch in the Espanola Valley reading proofs for *The Professor's House* before reaching Taos. Perhaps the section of that novel entitled "Tom Outland's Story," about the ruins at Mesa Verde, had stimulated her desire to return to the Southwest. Tony Luhan drove Cather and her companion Edith Lewis into the mountains to visit small Hispanic communities, and Cather came to admire the tall, handsome Luhan, who became the character "Eusabio" in *Death Comes for the Archbishop.* For two weeks Cather enjoyed Mabel Luhan's hospitality, and after she was finally left alone to think and write, she determined to return the following summer. From her room at La Fonda Hotel, Cather could see the statue of Archbishop Lamy near the cathedral, and she began to formulate the novel in which he would be the central figure.[96]

Cather returned to spend the summer of 1926 in New Mexico. She visited Acoma and Mesa Encantada, spent a week at Laguna Pueblo when a cloudburst blocked the clay road leading back to Santa Fe, and after a period at La Fonda, moved into Mary Austin's house, La Casa Querida, where she wrote much of *Death Comes for the Archbishop*. In the restful quiet of Austin's library, Cather brought together the Catholic priests, Native Americans, and her love of the land. Vivid word pictures of Acoma, the Sangre de Cristo Mountains, and the desert lands at Laguna emerged. The land and the heavens were principal elements in the narrative,[97] and her characters spoke of a sky in motion: "There was so much sky, more than at sea, more than anywhere else in the world"; "Brilliant blue of stinging air"; "Elsewhere the sky is the roof of the world; but here the earth was the floor of the sky."[98] Whereas Native Americans removed all signs of their passage across the land, Europeans determined to conquer the landscape, to leave a mark of their sojourn. Indians vanished into the landscape; whites stood in relief against it. The Native Americans drew from the land their inspirations for decoration and design, but they placed no mark on the land. They lived with nature, and they had no desire to master it. *Death Comes for the Archbishop* proved to be a critical and popular success because of the strength found not only in Cather's characters but also in the rapt descriptions of the land itself. Landforms and colors, storms, heat, tamarisk in bloom, piñons and aspens, and streams of clear water provided the setting and the mood of the novel. Stories told to her by Tony Luhan, conversations with the people of Laguna, a visit to Canyon de Chelly, and the small Hispanic communities in the mountains established Cather's views of New Mexico and the parameters of her story. Geography and human history merged in her story of the archbishop and his "Midi Romanesque" cathedral, so incongruous in the flat-roofed adobe town. Old-world architecture and new-world native stone brought together cultural traditions and the landscape.[99]

"Tom Outland's Story" in *The Professor's House* drew from Cather's earlier visit to Mesa Verde and her desire to tell a contemporary story that included the ancients of "Cliff City." Tom Outland's discovery of the cliff dwellings came from the story of the Wetherill family, who had found the ruins at Mesa Verde, and about their efforts to obtain help from the government to preserve the dwellings and their antiquities. Tom Outland represented the strong, masculine, quiet, reserved southwestern man that Cather identified with her brothers; the Native

Americans of her narrative displayed the dignity and respect for the land she so admired. Cather contrasted Outland and his passion for the esthetic with Professor Godfrey St. Peter, who had lost that verve forever.[100] Criticizing the crass materialism of the 1920s and lauding the simplicity of the world of the ancients, Cather depended on place to establish for her readers the vast differences in the two civilizations. "And the air, my God, what air! — Soft, tingling, gold, hot with an edge of chill on it," she wrote, "full of the smell of piñons — it was like breathing the sun, breathing the colour of the sky."[101] For many easterners and midwesterners, the Southwest came alive on the pages of Cather's novels. She recognized that the region inspired her best work. In a letter to the writer Zoë Akins a few years before her death, Cather declared: "I was working in New York, but the most real and interesting part of my life through all those years, I spent in the West with my brother."[102] The child of Nebraska transferred her sense of place to the Southwest, and her novels helped generate a national awareness of the region and its culture.

Mary Austin, who saw herself as the center of Santa Fe's literary world, criticized Cather's interpretation of Archbishop Lamy and his cathedral, displaying a jealousy that neither diminished Cather's achievement nor enhanced Austin's own. In *Land of Journey's Ending* (1924), Austin compared contemporary life in the United States with the Pueblo culture and found the former wanting. Arguing in *The American Rhythm* (1931) and *Starry Adventure* (1931) that literature had to spring from the environment, Austin emphasized the Pueblo and Hispanic cultures and their interaction with the land. Place was important to Austin in both the geographical and the environmental senses.[103] She wrote to Daniel T. MacDougal, a botanist with the Carnegie Institution, of her relationship to the region:

> Now I see what you mean by your insistence that I should come to the Southwest until the same transaction takes place between my spirit and the spirit of the land. . . .
>
> And I know that I shall die unsatisfied if that does not happen. I have seen enough of the Southwest to understand that what would come to me there would be immensely more radiant and splendid than what came in California. I long for it with all my soul, as if it were something I was dedicated to before I was born, and can not fulfill myself without having.[104]

Illness had brought Austin to New Mexico in 1919, and she had recuperated at Mabel Luhan's home in Taos. There she determined to live in New Mexico, finally settling in Santa Fe. *The Land of Journey's End* stood as a monument to her delight in the Southwest. Austin's trips to Tucson, Phoenix, Zuni, and El Morro introduced her to a terrain unlike that of the Owens River valley of her earlier books. The wind, earth, sky, and water represented unspoiled beauty where she could celebrate life.[105] The pueblos filled Austin with a sense of peace and a sense of place: "There is another sort of beauty playing always about the Pueblo country, beauty of cloud and rain and split sunshine. . . . Everywhere peace, impenetrable timelessness of peace, as though the pueblo and all it contains were shut in glassy fourth dimension, near at the same time inaccessibly remote."[106]

For Austin, the southwestern landscape housed three cultures that had the potential to reproduce the glory of ancient Greece. The cultures existed "in a land whose beauty takes the breath like pain." The land was mysterious and naked; the atmosphere was stimulating; the society represented the integrated experiences of many peoples.[107] Regionalism offered a response to the vastness of America, and the Southwest provided an opportunity to reinvigorate the national culture. Austin saw the impact of the region on individuals as diverse as Jung and the dancer Agnes DeMille, and she believed that the Native American sense of "folk" could enrich the larger society with a new awareness of the land. Regional culture became a way of living and thinking.[108] "Art is naturally the product of a *way of life*," she said, and Austin spent her last years trying to establish a regional culture in the Southwest.[109] Austin believed, "A regional culture is the sum, expressed in ways of living and thinking, of the mutual adaptations of a land and a *people*. In the long run the land wins."[110] Austin also encouraged younger authors to explore the region for universal themes, and between the world wars, a southwestern literature began to emerge.[111]

The writers of the Southwest were consumed by the land and its peoples, the sense of place. Oliver LaFarge's only significant literary success, *Laughing Boy,* drew from his knowledge of the Navajo people, their culture, and the land they inhabited. A Harvard-trained anthropologist, LaFarge worked at digs in the Four Corners area during his college summers, and after graduation he took long horseback trips through the Navajo country. His poignant story emphasized the role of the family, the clan, and the interrelationship between the young Navajo man Laughing Boy and the ancient beliefs of his people.[112] Like LaFarge, Haniel Long came to New Mexico from the East after a Harvard education, and the land and its people inspired his introspective and romantic poetry. Long found the Pueblos unpretentious, simply of the earth, and the piñon forests refreshed his soul. His lyrical verses were filled with references to the Native Americans, the environment, and their interactions. Long joined with LaFarge, Austin, Bynner, and others to fight for the rights of Native Americans, to promote Hispanic folk arts, to preserve the mission churches, and to tightly restrict construction in Santa Fe, to maintain its "style."[113]

Elsewhere in the state and the region other writers pursued similar goals. One of the strongest statements about the Southwest came from the pen of Ross Calvin, a Harvard doctoral graduate in English and an Episcopal priest. When his health faltered, Calvin moved to New Mexico, where he lived for forty-three years in Silver City, Clovis, and Albuquerque. In 1934 he published *Sky Determines*, in which Calvin argued that the climate of the region determined its history and culture. Walking the desert, he sought to understand the responses of plants and animals to heavy rains or to drought. Clouds, hail, and storms established the rhythm of his life. In the desert he found the conflicts between humankind and the earth, and he discovered beauty in winter rainbows in the mountains and a hawk sweeping out of the sky to snatch a field mouse. Navajo sings and Pueblo dances confirmed for Calvin his observations. The Native Americans understood the relationship of the earth to the people, and "the sky" determined life in the region.[114]

Adaptation to the often harsh and cruel land also permeated the writings of Ross Santee. Born in Iowa and educated at the Art Institute of Chicago, Santee did not see the Southwest until he was twenty-five years old. But when he came to the Gila country of southwestern Arizona, he found a land and a people for his pen and his paintbrushes. Santee wrote of his reaction to the Southwest: "The country itself dwarfed everything. The little ranch house in the distance could hardly be defined against the great expanse of country and the great dome of the sky. . . . It was the spring of 1915, and it was my first trip west."[115] Santee watched a cowboy and his horse from a train window west of El Paso, and that fascination became the theme of Santee's life. He found work as a wrangler on a ranch and began to sketch and write about the cowboys and their occupation. In simple language, but with humanity and compassion, Santee described, for both adult and juvenile readers, the making of the cowboy. His stories were filled with dust, grime, and loneliness, but there was also pride in accomplishments, friendships, and the glory of the land. The cowboys adapted to the earth and the sky of the Gila country.

Writers in Oklahoma in the period between the world wars also drew from the land for their stories and poetry. The vast space was primitive, it challenged the human spirit, and it offered opportunity for the demonstration of individualism as well as responsibility to the community. The raw nature of the state presented a clean slate for those who would write of this land. The historian E. E. Dale noted the opportunities that existed in the 1920s: "Physically speaking, materially considered, frontier conditions in Oklahoma have gone forever. But culturally we are yet pioneers living upon our intellectual frontier. The material wilderness has been conquered, it yet remains to complete the conquest of the cultural and intellectual wilderness."[116]

Novels and short stories about pioneer life and the settlement of Oklahoma emphasized individualism, independence, opportunity, and freedom. An open society offered hope for a new life. A prevailing theme was the attachment to the land. In Nola Henderson's *This Much Is Mine* (1934) and Cecil Brown Williams's *Paradise Prairie* (1935), farmers struggled to succeed, with the economy and the Dust Bowl working against them. The endurance of a people bound to the earth, sustained by a strong system of values, permeated the literature of the era.[117]

Whereas Oklahoma fiction generally dealt with white farmers and ranchers, a mixed-blood Osage, John Joseph Mathews, wrote two major novels about his people and the intersection of the two cultures. Born on a ranch in Osage County, Mathews attended the University of Oklahoma, served as an officer of the Flying Service during World War I, and studied at Oxford University for three years. He attended the University of Geneva and traveled throughout Europe and Africa before returning to a ranch in the Osage country in 1929. Although Mathews served on the Osage Tribal Council, he was considered re-clusive, and he visited the nearby town of Pawhuska infrequently. At his ranch, Mathews wrote *Wah' Kon-Tah: The Osage and the White Man's Road* (1932) and *Sundown* (1934), novels about his people and their reactions to the culture of whites. His first book revealed the feelings of a young Osage man forbidden by his family to marry an Arapaho girl. In simple and elegant language, Mathews revealed the strong emotions hidden behind a mask of stoicism. The novel, praised by Mary Austin and critics, became a Book-of-the-Month Club selection and provided many readers their first experience with Native American litera-ture. Published two years later, *Sundown* told of a young Osage who left the reservation for a university education and a life in the business world. Again, the Native American responds with disbelief at the machinations of the white soci-ety. The Osage people on the pages of Mathews's books cannot fathom the deg-radation of the land by the whites and the whites' cynical attitudes toward each other. Mathews produced what some consider the best novel written about Oklahoma in *Wah' Kon-Tah*, and he found both critical and popular success.[118]

The literary ferment in the Sooner State ranged from the founding of journals to the recognition of an "Oklahoma Manner" among its poets by H. L. Mencken. *Books Abroad*, established in 1927, reviewed books not published in English, and it achieved international fame for its critiques. B. A. Botkin, best known as a folklorist, founded *Folk-Say*, a regional literary journal. Mencken published Oklahoma poets in *The American Mercury* in 1926, and the sixteen poems by Botkin, Lynn Riggs, Stanley Vestal, and others ranged in subject matter from nature to ancestors and academics. The poems won Mencken's praise, a rare commodity.[119]

A member of the English department at the University of Oklahoma, Walter S. Campbell, who used the pen name Stanley Vestal, wrote studies of Native Americans. Campbell believed that the society of the Native Americans could not be understood without seeing their relationship to nature, to the land. Oklahoma's first Rhodes Scholar, Campbell based his novels, biographies, and historical works on sound factual research. Thus his review of Edna Ferber's *Cimarron* (1929) denounced the novel as fantasy. Although a popular success, the novel reflected a two-week visit by Ferber to Oklahoma and was based largely on talks with Elva Shartel Ferguson, the wife of a former territorial governor. Campbell noted Ferber's lack of understanding of the mores of the Sooners, and he noted that although she told a good story, she was not a Willa Cather, who captured the spirit of the Southwest.[120]

Far closer to Campbell's ideal was *The Wind,* by the Texan Dorothy Scarborough. Published in 1925, *The Wind* established Scarborough's reputation as an important regional novelist. In *The Wind,* she captured young Letty Mason's struggle to create a farm on the plains near Sweetwater, Texas. No soft, helpless southern belle, Mason stood up against the wind and the sand and the blizzards, and when she was attacked by a jealous man, she shot him and buried the body. The first sentence of the novel established the theme: "The Wind was the cause of it all."[121] This primal force shaped Mason's destiny. "In the old days, the winds were the enemies of women. Did they hate them because they saw in them the symbols of that civilization which might gradually lessen their own power?"[122] Men improved the land, but women created civilization, Mason believed. At the end of a hard day's labor, she waited for the pageant of color at sundown, "a wild richness of sky."[123] Denounced by many West Texans when it was published, *The Wind* became a classic southwestern book. Although Scarborough, the holder of a Columbia University doctorate, wrote other novels about the cotton farms of the Brazos River valley, this was her only book strongly rooted in the geographical Southwest that she knew from her childhood in Sweetwater. Her view of life on the plains contrasted sharply with the themes of Eugene Manlove Rhodes and even Willa Cather. Letty Mason exhibited courage, perseverance, faith, and hope, but she could not conquer the wind. Once more the land won.

In the 1920s and 1930s, Texas authors struggled to create a "regional literature" and to decide if they were of the South or of the West. George Sessions Perry felt that a regional literature had to come from "trouble, anguish and dismay."[124] His novel *Hold Autumn in Your Hand* owed much more to William Faulkner's South than to the Southwest. Its plot and characters are sharply etched, but they speak of cotton, farm tenancy, and crop liens, a way of life transported from the South and one dying in Texas even as Perry wrote. Similarly, Katherine Anne Porter, who came to maturity in rural Texas near San Marcos, adamantly maintained that she was a southerner. Disregarding her obvious West Texas upbringing, she declared: "It is quite all right to regard me as a southern, specifically a Texas writer. I know that Texas is south*west*, but my origins were really southern. I do not think my family have been in Texas more than seventy-odd years. . . . I have lived out of the south since I was nineteen . . . , but southerner just the same, and will be."[125]

Even as Perry and Porter struggled to keep their intellectual and creative roots in the South, a flagship literary journal, the *Southwest Review,* called for a regional distinctiveness while reaching for the national cultural mainstream. Eschewing its earlier provincial title, the *Texas Review,* the journal took the new name in 1924 to reflect its commitment to a "new regionalism."[126] The *Southwest Review* published regional authors, organized symposiums to define "culture" and the "Southwest," and sought out young, unpublished writers. One of the contributors to the *Southwest Review,* J. Frank Dobie, championed regionalism and used his talents to take its folktales and stories to a national audience. Dobie contended, "The Southwest has inherited a turn of idiom, a history, a tradition of character, a flavor of the soil that are highly individual."[127] *Coronado's Children* made him famous as he spun yarns of buried treasures and lost mines. Neither a historian nor a folklorist, Dobie conceived of a southwestern literature that drew from the people and the earth. His description of cowboys evoked the passion of his prose: "Their eyes are used to looking through heat devils shimmering over drought-browned mesas and at mountains a look and a half away. Without knowing it, something of the tonic of sagebrush aroma has passed into the very corpuscles of their blood and something of the assurance belonging to the quietness of sky and earth has entered their mental attitudes."[128] Dobie romanticized the Southwest and its peoples, and he aided young authors, encouraging them to write with his intensity about the region.

While Dobie and others tried to formulate a southwestern literature that drew its strength from individual farmers and ranchers, others sought to institutionalize a musical culture within the region's cities. Urban growth, cultural aspirations, and economic vitality in the Southwest produced renewed efforts to establish viable symphony orchestras and to bring opera to the region. Southwesterners sought to end a legacy of musical colonialism, but the coming of the Great Depression thwarted those ambitions. Texas offers a clear example of the

CULTURE *in the* AMERICAN SOUTHWEST

tastes for classical music, opera, and dance and of the range of opportunities for audiences in the 1920s. Small towns provided venues for Madame Ernestine Schumann-Heink and the Great Lakes Quartet, while cities such as Fort Worth hosted Enrico Caruso. Houston audiences heard the San Carlo and Chicago Grand Opera Companies, and Dallas welcomed Mary Garden, Fritz Kreisler, the New York Philharmonic Orchestra, and Isadora Duncan's dance company.[129] Business leaders such as Jesse H. Jones and Ross S. Sterling joined bankers and retailers to bring the German Grand Opera to Houston in 1930. A company of 150 presented Wagner's *Der Ring Des Nibelunger* in four evening performances. The Houston Committee for the German Grand Opera Company, made up entirely of women, reported a profit of $129 on the venture. Throughout the decade following the end of World War I, Houston provided large audiences for operas, Anna Pavlova and the Ballet Russe, and Jascha Heifetz.[130]

Creating a symphony orchestra in Houston proved far more difficult. Ima Jane Hogg, the daughter of Governor James S. Hogg, led the effort to form a major orchestra. A trained pianist and music teacher, Ima Jane Hogg sought to revitalize the Houston orchestra that had collapsed during World War I. Throughout the 1920s, she and other prominent women in the city sponsored concerts for visiting orchestras and raised funds to support musical activities. Finally, in 1931 the Houston Symphony Association announced the formation of an orchestra led by the Italian conductor Uriel Nespoli. He sought to build an audience by offering dramatic programming, but he tried too hard, presenting major works by Wagner, Saint-Saëns, Schumann, and Beethoven played by a largely amateur orchestra. The association fired him after two years, but thanks to the efforts of "Miss Ima Jane," the Houston Symphony Orchestra was launched.[131]

At the other end of the Lone Star State, El Paso struggled to establish a viable symphony orchestra. Concerts in the 1890s and early 1900s indicated that an audience existed for classical music, but efforts to create a permanent organization failed. Between 1917 and 1925, eighteen concerts led by three different conductors kept the idea alive. Local talent increased as musicians came to the city for reasons of health. In 1930, Hine Arthur Brown, a violin teacher from the Julliard School, joined the faculty at New Mexico College of Agriculture and Mechanical Arts in Las Cruces and agreed to conduct an orchestra in nearby El Paso. With significant community support, sixty musicians were recruited. The next year Brown conducted works by Sibelius, Vivaldi, and Beethoven in the first performance. Brown arranged to broadcast the concerts to broaden the audience base, and he brought in guest artists to generate attendance. Isaac Stern, Helen Traubel, Lauritz Melchior, Yehudi Menuhin, and Artur Rubinstein came to the Pass of the North during the years Brown conducted the El Paso Symphony Orchestra. The Julliard Foundation initially subsidized Brown's salary as the conductor, but when that support ended in 1937, the city raised funds to continue the orchestra. El Paso, still a small city, wanted classical music.[132]

Support for the musical arts and dance in Texas ranged from appearances of the dancers Ted Shawn and Martha Graham in Austin in 1921 to presentations by the Metropolitan Opera in Dallas in 1939. Austin welcomed Shawn and Graham, selling out the Hancock Opera House, where ticket prices ranged from $.75 to $2.50 for box seats. But the composer David Guion lamented throughout the 1920s that Dallas was failing to support the arts, particularly music. He believed that famous performers drew audiences to mediocre programs but that talented local artists were ignored. His observation held true for several decades as the Dallas Symphony struggled to stay alive. The desire for the highest of "high culture" led the department store executive Arthur L. Kramer to lobby the Metropolitan Opera to visit Dallas on its annual tour. From 1930 to 1939, Kramer cajoled and pleaded until at last the Met told him it would come in 1939 if he guaranteed $65,000 for four performances. Kramer led a fund-raising effort that generated $136,000, and Dallasites heard Grace Moore sing *Manon* and *La Bohéme,* as well as productions of Wagner's *Tannhäuser* and Verdi's *Otello.* The Met returned to Dallas nearly ever year until 1984, bringing grand opera to the Southwest.[133]

The region also produced musicians of the quality necessary to perform with organizations like the Metropolitan Opera. The seventeen-year-old Oklahoma farmboy Joseph Benton left his hometown of Sayre to enter the University of Oklahoma, and after receiving degrees in the arts and music, he went to France to study and to sing. "Giuseppe Bentonelli" performed in Paris and Florence, becoming one of the first American singers to gain a reputation in Europe. A leading tenor with opera companies on the continent, Benton returned to the United States in 1934 to sing with the Chicago Opera, and two years later he debuted at the Met. Benton paved the way for other musicians, and after returning to the University of Oklahoma as a professor of music, he trained young singers and sustained a program in opera with his fellow teacher Dame Eva Turner. The maturation of quality musical performance in the region moved forward, if at a glacial pace.[134]

Fledgling communities such as Phoenix, Tucson, and Albuquerque recognized the need to create musical organizations and to sponsor concerts. Business leaders realized the value of cultural activities in the promotion of their communities. Located on major transcontinental railroad lines and graced with warm winter climates, the cities highlighted their locations to obtain professional musicians traveling to or from California. Orchestras, opera companies, and musical performers played during stopovers. Mrs. Archer E. Linde brought Marian Anderson, Eleanor Steber, and Risë Stevens to Phoenix, as well as the San Francisco Ballet and the Ballet de Monte Carlo; other promoters developed similar programs. The Phoenix Music Club sponsored the Phoenix Civic Orchestra in its first performance in 1930, but a major orchestra was decades away.[135]

In Tucson, the Women's Club led a drive to create the Temple of Music and Art, a facility to house art exhibits and provide a venue for musical performances. They constructed the temple in 1927 and organized the Tucson Symphony Orchestra the next year, with Madeline Heineman leading the drive for both. Drawing on talent from the University of Arizona and the community, the Belgian musician Camil Van Hulse conducted the first concert. Heineman led Tucson's efforts to develop a program of classical music for more than three decades. She raised funds, sponsored concerts, and presided over the temple. The community recognized her work and that of the other women who labored with her.[136] As one observer noted: "The Temple of Music and Art is the work of women. . . . It is built on a foundation of caliche, true, but its firmer foundation rests on [women's] ideals and the need of something to lift us to better and higher things of life."[137] The slender, handsome young pianist and composer Camil Van Hulse raised his baton before an audience of nearly 1,000 on January 13, 1929, bringing classical music to the Sonoran desert community.

Like Van Hulse, Grace Thompson Edminister came to the Southwest because of poor health. In 1925 she settled in Albuquerque as head of the School of Music of the University of New Mexico and soon founded an orchestra. Filled with energy and enterprise, trained at the American Conservatory and at Julliard, she brought enthusiasm and talent to the community. The Albuquerque Civic Symphony performed under her direction for almost a decade and then again for two years during World War II. Although the orchestra had only 435 season-ticket holders in 1935, it survived the Great Depression and World War II, touring the state and presenting concerts from Raton to Silver City.[138]

San Diego did not have the musical leadership displayed in other cities. Although its art museum and art life flourished in the 1920s, efforts to create an orchestra lagged. A city of almost 150,000 people, San Diego possessed geographical attributes that seemed to auger well for civic and cultural growth. One observer commented hopefully: "Certainly San Diego seems the most logical spot on the coast for the development of a regional culture. It may not be too much to hope that within a few years it will begin to flower there."[139] The Amphion Club continued to bring performers such as Lawrence Tibbett and Lily Pons to San Diego, and the city hosted major opera companies. The Columbia Grand Opera Company presented *Carmen, Il Trovatore, Rigoletto, Lucia di Lam-*

mermoor, I Pagliacci, Cavalleria Rusticana, and *La Traviata* in one week to large and enthusiastic audiences.[140] An amateur production of choruses from three operas in 1925 led the *San Diego Union* to cry, "Press forward for culture."[141] European immigrants infused the musical life of San Diego between the wars and revived the idea of an orchestra. The Italian-born Nino Marcelli formed the San Diego Symphony in 1927. Under his leadership, the musicians became the San Diego Symphony Orchestra five years later. They presented a formal season and played in Balboa Park during the summer. Over 11,000 people heard their concert with Ernestine Schumann-Heink in 1928, and the summer series attracted thousands to each performance. Concertmaster Enzo Pascorella, a graduate of the Royal Conservatory of Music in Naples, prepared the players for guest conductors such as Arnold Schoenberg, Pierre Monteaux, and Otto Klemperer. The Ford Motor Company constructed the Ford Bowl in Balboa Park and gave it to the orchestra in 1935, and annual attendance at the outdoor concerts soon exceeded 76,000. Yet the demands of World War II halted the progress of the orchestra, the U.S. Navy took over the park, and financial problems loomed large. The orchestra and its summer program would not be revived until after 1945.[142]

To the north, in Los Angeles, the world of music expanded. Emigré musicians came to the City of Angels to work in the motion-picture industry, especially when "talkies" made music an integral part of films. Lynden Ellsworth Behymer, "the Bee," kept opera alive in Los Angeles in the 1920s even as he served as the business agent for the Philharmonic. The Los Angeles Grand Opera Association organized performances after 1924 and mounted a successful production of *Andrea Chenier.* A "Women's Committee" sold 35,000 tickets for the company. Gaetano Merola, a leader in the association, had created the San Francisco Grand Opera Association, but opera lovers in Los Angeles wanted their own, independent organization. They did not want to simply bring the San Francisco company to Los Angeles with a different name. They severed ties with Merola, who then formed the California Opera Company. The city suddenly had two rival operas mounting major performances. The clash of civic pride, artistic personalities, and urban rivalries ultimately cooled, and the companies began to cooperate, sharing costs and staffs. Los Angeles did not lack for opera in the 1920s, but the depression decade that followed saw suspended seasons and major deficits.[143]

The Los Angeles Philharmonic Orchestra thrived in the 1920s with William Andrews Clark as financial backer and with Walter H. Rothwell as musical director. By 1926, some concerts were selling out during the twenty-eight-week season. Ensembles and chamber music groups formed, based on talented players from the Philharmonic. After Rothwell stepped down as director in 1927, the orchestra had two unsuccessful leaders. Clark then recruited Otto Klemperer in 1933 after he fled from Germany. Under his stern hand, the Philharmonic began to flourish musically, but Clark despaired at the lack of community support and withdrew his subsidy. When Clark died in 1934, he left no bequest for the orchestra. The Community Development Association then assumed responsibility for the orchestra. Klemperer hired eighty-five musicians, and over 42,000 people attended the 1934–35 season. The city and county governments provided financial support for the "Keystone in the cultural arch of the West." Clark's legacy continued as Klemperer brought major soloists to play with the Philharmonic and introduced modern music to the repertoire. Los Angeles audiences heard Hindemith, Stravinsky, Shostakovitch, and Mahler regularly, when their compositions were played only rarely by other major orchestras. Under Rothwell and then under Klemperer, the Philharmonic Orchestra kept ticket prices low and played many free concerts. In an effort to reach an even larger audience, the orchestra began to appear at the Hollywood Bowl.[144]

The site of the Hollywood Bowl had been in use since before World War I, when a sheltered valley in the Hollywood Hills was discovered that formed a natural amphitheater with excellent acoustics. In May, 1916, a charity production of *Julius Caesar* drew a huge throng to Beachwood Canyon to see Douglas Fairbanks, Mae Murray, and other motion-picture stars. Other productions followed, and in 1918 the Theater Alliance was formed, guided by Behymer, to create an outdoor venue for music and drama. Artie Mason Carter led the effort, aided by productions organized by Christine Wetherill Stevenson. These women, supported by D. W. Griffith, Ted Shawn, and Mira Hershey, began to negotiate for the property. Hershey owned the site, which she sold to the Alliance after Marie Rankin Clarke and Stevenson each extended loans. Carter organized programs, and the Alliance converted itself into the Community Park and Art Association. Volunteers solicited funds to build the Hollywood Bowl, and Behymer arranged for the Philharmonic to play there for two months each summer. The leaders agreed that the Bowl was not to be a film industry entity and that it would be a place for classical music. Carter led the Hollywood Bowl Association, and with the financial support of Mrs. Leiland Atherton Irish and others, the association reconstructed the facility. The architect Lloyd Wright designed a temporary shell, built in 1927, and then erected a permanent, concrete shell in 1929. Tickets for the 20,000 seats at the Bowl sold for as little as twenty-five cents. Tens of thousands of people came to the Bowl for the symphony, ballet, and internationally known soloists. The Bowl made money even in the depression years; for example, in 1936 over 29,000 heard Lily Pons. The Hollywood

Bowl proved to be a popular success, generating support for the Philharmonic Orchestra and for classical music. The shell hosted many musicians who fled from Europe after 1933, often after they established residence in southern California. Once again a dedicated band of women created an organization and a site for the promotion of musical life in the Southwest.[145] When the writer Thomas Mann came to Los Angeles in the summer of 1940, he lauded the violin sonata by Handel that he heard one evening, as well as the Bach *partia* and a quartet led by a Hungarian composer. A dinner companion, the actor Charles Laughton, recited from *The Tempest*. "Neither Paris nor Munich of 1900 could have provided an evening so rich in intimate artistic spirit, verve and merriment," Mann declared.[146]

By the end of the 1930s, the Southwest had developed a cultural life that supported not only opera companies and symphony orchestras but also theatrical groups. Throughout the United States, the Little Theater movement flourished between 1918 and the early 1930s. Resident stock companies fell victim to films and the radio, and local theaters became parts of national chains that booked only their own productions. Touring companies declined in number, and only a few stars could generate the packed houses of previous decades. The continuing desire for live performances led to the flowering of the Little Theater movement as actors, actresses, producers, and directors formed local theatrical groups. Although the casts were usually amateurs, some Little Theaters brought in professionals to play leads or to direct a production. The Little Theaters offered classical plays, recent Broadway hits, and occasionally, original productions. The movement came to the Southwest early in the 1920s and flourished for a decade. Some of the Little Theaters, such as those in Dallas and Albuquerque, became nationally famous for their offerings.[147]

The Dallas Little Theater, founded in 1921, gained recognition under the direction of Oliver Hinsdale. Subscribers built a theater seating over 200 people in 1924, the year the Dallas Little Theater won the Belasco Cup of the National Little Theater League in New York for its production of *Judge Lynch* by John William Rogers. The Dallas performers also won the cup in 1925 and 1926. Audiences grew quickly, and a new theater, seating 650, was opened in 1928. That year it played before 3,000 people monthly and raised pledges of over $100,000 for its new facility. The Dallas Little Theater offered George Bernard Shaw and Eugene O'Neill, as well as contemporary playwrights such as Paul Green. Civic leaders provided financial support despite the presentation of plays often considered controversial. The Dallas Little Theater's professionalism destroyed the last stock company in the city; it simply could not compete with the quality of the amateur performances. The depression ended the success of the Dallas Little

Theater, however; it lost its building in 1937, reorganized and regained its facility, but closed in 1942. The war and a loss of artistic vigor led to its final demise.[148]

The Albuquerque Little Theater did not appear until after the Great Depression began, but in the midst of economic misfortunes it succeeded. The talented Broadway actress Kathryn Kennedy came to New Mexico because of health problems, and there she met and married the Irishman James O'Connor, another health-seeker, who had acted in England and Ireland. Determined to bring quality theater to Albuquerque, Kathryn O'Connor joined with a local journalist, Irene Fisher, to establish the Albuquerque Little Theater in 1930. They offered their first play, a comedy with the young actress Vivian Vance in the cast, at the KiMo Theater. Using her Broadway connections, O'Connor brought recent hits directly to the Southwest. In 1933, for example, she received permission to produce the smash *Of Thee I Sing*. The civic leader and future U.S. Senator Clinton Anderson served as president of the theater's board of directors, and he obtained Works Progress Administration (WPA) funds to build a theater. His successor, the newspaper heiress Ruth Hanna McCormick, secured the gift of a site, and the architect John Gaw Meem designed the building. Donated materials, WPA labor, and O'Connor's tenacity created a facility. WPA Director Harry Hopkins came from Washington, D.C., in 1936 for the first performance, Lynn Riggs's play *Russet Mantle*. The Albuquerque Little Theater paid its debts, attracted military personnel from nearby bases during World War II, and began to bring celebrities to the city as leads. Leo G. Carroll, Edward Everett Horton, Zasu Pitts, Linda Darnell, Jane Darwell, and Hugh Marlow joined local performers in a wide-ranging repertoire.[149] O'Connor had only one regret: "One of the disappointments of my life was that I was never able to find a play about the Southwest that would picture New Mexico with the bright clarity and strength of a Peter Hurd or Kenneth Adams painting, or a play that would mirror any of the fine gallant features of our Spanish inhabitants."[150] For forty years O'Connor led the Albuquerque Little Theater, which by the 1970s had more than 10,000 season subscribers. Other southwestern cities also formed Little Theaters, but few found such continuing success.

Women also led the way in the creation of Little Theaters elsewhere in the region. In San Antonio the actress Sarah Barton Luke Bindley taught drama after coming to the city in 1910. She organized a club that became a Little Theater workshop. She produced plays throughout the 1920s, creating a Little Theater in 1926.[151] Three women formed the Lubbock Little Theater in 1925, producing plays for four years. Their initial effort foundered during the depression, but in 1948 another group of women re-created the Little Theater and by

1953 acquired a playhouse.[152] Mary Waldo persuaded fifty people in Houston to donate $25 each to launch the Green Mask Players. Drawing on Little Theater advisers from across the nation, Waldo mounted productions of Shaw, John Galsworthy, Anton Chekhov, and Anatole France, using Rice Institute faculty and students in her casts.[153] In Arizona, Maie Heard, Katherine McClusky, and Harry Belin organized the Phoenix Players in 1921, using the Heard family's carriage house as a theater. They reorganized as the Phoenix Little Theater in 1924 and offered Shaw's *Arms and the Man,* Noel Coward's *Hay Fever,* and Maxwell Anderson's *Night over Taos,* as well as Ibsen and Shakespeare. Surviving the depression, the theater had a budget of over $2,000 in 1937. The Phoenix Little Theater moved to a new playhouse in 1951, serving as a venue for live drama in Phoenix for four decades.[154] Oklahoma City, Tucson, and Tulsa acquired Little Theaters in the 1920s, meeting the needs of their communities for live drama.

The two major theatrical successes of the era were in California: the Old Globe Theater in San Diego and the Pasadena Playhouse. San Diego community leaders planned a major exposition for 1935, hoping that it would stimulate the local economy as the fair of 1915–16 had done. They used Balboa Park as the venue, centering the exhibits around the Spanish Colonial buildings remaining from the fair. A successful venture at Chicago's Century of Progress of 1933 had been a replica of Shakespeare's Old Globe Theater in London, where the Bard's plays had been performed. San Diego brought the director of the Chicago production, Thomas Wood Stevens, to California to replicate the concept. A prototype Elizabethan theater emerged in Balboa Park, and Stevens employed some of his Chicago troupe in the cast. When the California Pacific International Exposition opened in 1935, the Old Globe Theater proved to be a hit. Presenting shortened versions of Shakespeare's plays, the actors performed six times each day. Its success led some residents of San Diego to urge that the Old Globe be made a permanent part of Balboa Park and the basis for a resident theater. Swift action saved the facility from destruction, and a local group, the San Diego Community Theater, was formed to perform in the park. WPA labor rebuilt the theater for permanent use, and "The Globe" opened in 1937. The repertoire included the classics and modern plays while melodramas brought in profits to sustain the playhouse. Concerts added to revenues, as did guest film actors. The U.S. Navy occupied the park during World War II, but when the war ended, "The Globe" shifted from the Little Theater concept to a community theater, which was no longer a club for local actors. During the late 1940s the productions ranged from the classics to avant-garde plays performed in the Tavern Building. By the 1950s, "The Globe" had become famous for its summer Shakespeare Festival and for the quality of its performances.[155]

CULTURE *in the* AMERICAN SOUTHWEST

In Los Angeles, a theatrical boom swept the city in the 1920s as a consequence of rapid growth and the rise of the film industry. Community leaders encouraged the construction of new theaters, and Los Angeles investors financed new productions. A large box office developed when stage and screen performers starred in local productions. Ambitious producers and directors developed new plays and brought playwrights to California to create vehicles. The producer Thomas Wilkes tried out plays in Los Angeles and then took the survivors to New York. Sophisticated productions of cutting-edge dramas were mounted and then exported to Broadway. The rise of local productions led to the opening of six new theaters in 1926–27 alone. A former movie house, the Lincoln Theater, was converted to stage productions in 1928 for the Lafayette Players, an all African American troupe of professional actors. Their productions soon traveled widely across the country. The Los Angeles Repertory Theater presented six plays each year and brought Theater Guild productions from New York. During the 1920s, theater in Los Angeles existed independently of the motion picture industry, not as a sideshow; indeed, film industry executives complained about the competition.[156]

One of the brightest lights in this renaissance was the Pasadena Playhouse. Its founder, Gilmor Brown, came to Pasadena in 1916 after traveling all across the country in his career as an actor. He admired the climate of Pasadena and the largely midwestern people of the community. Brown founded the Community Players of Pasadena, at first in league with the Savoy Stock Company, but he soon abandoned the concept of stock players. When the Savoy Stock Company failed, the residents of Pasadena asked him to start again. A supportive, sophisticated audience developed, and Brown — as actor, director, and producer — created a quality theater for them. Originally playing in an old burlesque theater, in 1925 the Pasadena Playhouse moved into its own facility, a $380,000 venue designed by Elmer Grey in the Spanish Colonial Revival style. Early supporters included Aline Barnsdall and Eleanor Bissell, with the latter providing substantial financial support. For his productions, Brown recruited local actors and directors. He also organized dramas for public schools and reached out to the community in a variety of ways. He brought dance as well as drama to the Playhouse and featured Martha Graham and Agnes DeMille. There were lectures by theatrical luminaries such as Thornton Wilder and John Masefield. Although the Playhouse was entirely amateur, Brown produced Ibsen, O'Neill, and Galsworthy and eventually the complete Shakespeare canon of thirty-seven plays. The contents of a few of the dramas offended some of the conservative residents of Pasadena, but when it came time to raise money for the new theater, contributions both large and small arrived at the Playhouse. The quality of Brown's productions led to an invitation to join the New York Drama League, and New York critics declared the Playhouse one of the nation's strongest Little Theaters. Brown premiered plays such as O'Neill's *Lazarus Laughed,* and he "found" talented performers like Victor Jory and Lurine Tuttle, who went on to the stage and screen. New York producers tried out productions at the Playhouse, and touring companies played the venue. The Pasadena Playhouse created a School of the Theater to train actors, and it formed an Experimental Workshop to perform new works and to use a stage-in-the-round. Over the next thirty-five years, the Playhouse produced more than 3,000 plays, 135 of which were world premieres, including Franz Kafka's *The Trial.* The Playhouse functioned as a democracy, with all members allowed to vote on major decisions. The spark plug was Brown, for as one critic wrote, "His life *is* the theatre."[157] The Pasadena Playhouse added to the prestige of the theater in the Southwest.

Hispanic theater in the region was equally vibrant, especially in San Antonio, Tucson, and Los Angeles. *La Prensa* of San Antonio urged its readers to attend the opera, especially the Civic Opera of Chicago when it came on tour, but the paper also asked that they listen to classical music on the radio, "Música Simfónica." To create a cohesive Hispanic community, *La Prensa* told its readers to attend Mexican films, lectures by Mexican and Spanish intellectuals, and the theater. Some Hispanics, especially the "rico" immigrants from Mexico, desired to retain their national roots, Lo Mexicano, whereas many middle-class, Spanish-speaking San Antonio residents preferred to create their own cultural traditions. The upper class founded Club Mexicano de Bellos Artes to further the goals of Lo Mexicano while middle-class Hispanics attended plays about life in the United States. With nearly 100,000 Spanish-speaking people, San Antonio supported an active Spanish-language theater.[158]

Tucson's Hispanic community also attended musical and theatrical performances in large numbers. Teatro Carmen offered plays and musical events. Julia Rebeil, trained as a pianist in Chicago, New York, and Europe, joined the University of Arizona faculty in 1920 to teach piano. A member of one of Tucson's elite families, Rebeil brought classical music to the Spanish-speaking community, as did Manuel Monijo, Jr., a violinist with the Tucson Symphony. They and other members of the Spanish community attended performances of touring companies from Mexico, as well as locally produced plays.[159]

Particularly popular in communities such as Tucson were zarzuelas, Spanish operettas from the seventeenth to the nineteenth centuries. Emigrés from Mexico brought zarzuela manuscripts, and productions were mounted in the Southwest. The zarzuelas featured speaking and singing parts, music and dancing.

Traveling zarzuela companies visited Tucson, El Paso, Laredo, San Antonio, and Los Angeles.

The *colonias* of Los Angeles supported zarzuelas as well as live drama.[160] Directors, actors, and actresses arrived in substantial numbers after the revolution in Mexico in 1910, organizing stock companies, writing plays, and by the 1930s operating five theaters. The plays focused on contemporary events, social and political criticism, and humor. The *revistas* plays dealt with the cultural shocks of the immigrants. Esteban Elías Gonzales and Gabriel Navarro wrote or directed plays for the growing Hispanic community in Los Angeles.[161] After 1932 the Mexican Players at the Padua Hills Theater near Claremont offered musical and theatrical performances, largely based on folk stories and designed to preserve the culture of early Hispanic California. The Hispanic community of southern California could see both contemporary and historical plays in this vibrant atmosphere.[162]

The Great Depression did not harm the Mexican Players, but economic collapse resulted in unemployed architects, artists, actors, and musicians in the Southwest. Cultural institutions succumbed as the wave of economic disaster spread across the nation. Franklin Roosevelt's New Deal contained some programs for the arts, however. After March, 1933, federal funds provided support for artists, theaters, musicians, and writers, but the money was always limited, and state and community responses were not always enthusiastic. Governments in the region reacted conservatively to the New Deal arts programs, and the "liberalism" or "radicalism" of some of the participants led to protests. Local leadership in the arts often made the difference between the success or failure of these New Deal programs.

As part of the federal government's economic-stimulus efforts, vast construction projects employed thousands of workers who built federal office buildings, post offices, courthouses, airport terminals, university facilities, and public schools. Early in the New Deal, artists were employed to paint murals or to provide paintings for these structures. After 1935, the WPA continued this program and also hired artists to teach classes in painting and sculpture. Competitions within the region provided artists with opportunities to paint, and most of those awarded contracts resided in the Southwest. The federal, state, and local governments, as well as the public, wanted positive, traditional subjects and executions that were realistic. The American Scene style of Thomas Hart Benton, Grant Wood, and John Steuart Curry proved very popular. In New Mexico and Oklahoma, Native American themes were often requested, whereas residents of Texas and California preferred preindustrial paintings with a historical content.

WPA art emphasized a pastoral regional history, not violence, turmoil, or social realism. Community involvement was encouraged in the choice of subject matter and even in the selection of artists. The WPA also financially supported the creation of art centers in cities to display and teach art in programs that were either of low cost or free to participants. These activities kept art life alive in the Southwest.[163]

In Arizona, the Public Works of Art Project of the Treasury Department and the WPA Federal Art Project employed about fifty artists. Gunnar Widforss provided watercolors of the Grand Canyon and the Salt River valley for federal buildings, and Lon Megargee painted murals for facilities of the University of Arizona. Megargee supervised the WPA Federal Art Project in the state but was able to find relatively few commissions for individual artists. Far more significant was the creation of the Phoenix Federal Art Center, which offered classes for adults and children and sponsored art exhibits. A city of over 60,000, Phoenix had little art life and no art museum. When the Federal Art Center opened in 1937, response was so enthusiastic that the project became the basis for the Phoenix Art Museum. Although some patrons reacted negatively to the presence of poor, dirty children in the studios, the staff welcomed everyone. Local amateur painters found trained artists as teachers, and a few publicly owned paintings brought to the center formed the nucleus of a collection. The Phoenix Federal Art Center made a valuable contribution.[164]

Oscar Jacobson directed the Public Works of Art Project in Oklahoma, and Nan Sheets supervised the Oklahoma WPA Federal Art Project. These vigorous leaders made the Sooner State a flagship in the programs. Jacobson found commissions for Native American artists he had trained. Acee Blue Eagle, Stephen Mopope, James Auchiah, Spencer Asah, and others provided murals and paintings with Native Americans as subjects. Viewers sought representational art with historical themes that did not include the degradations of the conquests. Jacobson and Sheets made sure that women artists received work, and one-third of the commissions went to female painters. Their themes included pioneer farmers, ranchers, and settlers on the plains. Small-town post offices received murals by Oklahoma and New Mexico artists portraying the Run of 1889, the coming of the railroad, and in the eastern part of the state, the Trail of Tears. The last depicted the heroic survivors among the Cherokees forced to march from Georgia to Indian Territory in 1839, not the thousands who died. The New Deal art in Oklahoma reflected a search for "American values," not a portrayal of social and economic crisis.[165]

Sheets had come to Oklahoma City in 1915, and she soon became the community's advocate for art. Not only a trained artist but also a skilled leader, she organized art exhibits, promoted artists in the state, and reviewed art for the city's leading newspaper. When asked to supervise the Oklahoma WPA Federal Art Project and create an art center in Oklahoma City, she thought it was a joke. She later noted, "It was too good an opportunity to miss."[166] A gallery located in a space donated by the chamber of commerce drew 40,000 visitors in 1936. She raised funds, moved into larger quarters, presented lectures, and taught classes. Sheets obtained loans of art owned by residents of the city and presented an exhibition that included paintings by El Greco, Jean Corot, Thomas Sully, John Sloan, George Inness, and Edward Potthast, among others. Oklahomans discovered painting at the art center, which eventually evolved into a permanent museum.[167]

The federal arts programs in New Mexico focused on Hispanics and Native Americans, with considerable success. Nina Otero Warren, a suffragist, politician, educator, and entrepreneur, worked with Mary Austin, John Gaw Meem, and others to revive Spanish Colonial arts in northern New Mexico. They sought commissions for wood-carvers, potters, weavers, and metalworkers. Programs were devised that employed artisans who produced furniture, metal decorations, and hangings for federal and state facilities. The artists found second incomes beyond farming and raising sheep. Twenty-four communities established craft schools, where instruction was provided. The Anglo teachers and supervisors determined what was "authentic," and they "improved" the designs by limiting subject matter and colors. Nevertheless, the projects created income and revived colonial arts in remote villages.[168]

John Collier, the commissioner of Indian affairs during the New Deal, persuaded Congress to create the Indian Arts and Crafts Board in 1935 to stimulate Native American culture. The program's financial and preservation goals quietly ended the suppression of Indian cultural life. The Arts and Crafts Board held exhibitions, promoted sales, and established artistic standards for blankets, jewelry making, and other crafts. A major exhibition at the Golden Gate International Exposition in San Francisco in 1939 featured the work of New Mexico and Arizona Native Americans. Pueblo, Zuni, Hopi, and Navajo artists received commissions for paintings that decorated federal buildings in the region and in Washington, D.C. These federal programs enhanced art education and training for Native Americans.[169]

Artists in Taos and Santa Fe, faced with a substantial loss of patronage in the 1930s, eagerly sought commissions from the WPA and other federal relief agencies. They painted murals in communities across the Southwest and sold paintings for new governmental buildings. Traditionalists such as Oscar Berninghaus, Theodore Van Soelen, and Victor Higgins had no problem providing realistic

FIGURE 30
*Unlike other members of the Taos
Society of Artists, Victor Higgins
embraced elements of modernism
in his work. Courtesy Museum of
New Mexico, Santa Fe, Negative
40394.*

paintings of historical events. Some of the modernists, such as Randall Davey
and Raymond Jonson, had to avoid social themes that might upset the public.
Western exploration, ranching, pioneer life, and the coming of industry were
acceptable themes that the agencies sought for conservative communities. Although Emil Bisttram painted *Transgression,* an allegorical scene of death and
punishment, for the Taos County Courthouse, and Bert Phillips depicted a hand-
cuffed prisoner with a weeping wife in *The Shadow of Crime,* these were rare
examples of social realism in New Deal art in the region.[170]

The art projects in southern California provided employment for painters
and sculptors, but the programs displayed little vigor. Stanton Macdonald-
Wright led the WPA Federal Art Project in Los Angeles, and he found some
work for artists in post offices in Venice and Beverly Hills. Here too, the American Scene style and historical themes prevailed. The influence of Mexican muralists such as Diego Rivera appeared in some of the large paintings but only in
technique, not subject matter. The projects in southern California included more
sculptures than elsewhere, with historical themes. Controversy reigned here as
elsewhere. Critics found Donal Hord's statue of a pioneer woman in San Diego

to be "too Mexican," and the sculptor had to produce his Anglo model in response. Community conventions limited the impact of these programs.[171]

The success of New Deal art projects varied enormously from state to state. In Texas, for example, there were few opportunities for artists. Although some commissions became available, there was no WPA Federal Arts Project in the Lone Star State. The WPA director for Texas, Harry P. Drought, did not want an art project, he said, because there were only twenty-three artists in the entire state, according to his count![172] Ironically, Texas was witnessing an artistic renaissance in Dallas even as Drought declared his opposition to the program.

The fate of the art programs often paralleled that of the music projects. The WPA Federal Music Project employed only 4,000 musicians in the entire American West and made minimal contributions in the Southwest, with a few significant exceptions. The Federal Music Project did leave major legacies in Oklahoma, where it created a symphony orchestra, in San Diego, where it revived a moribund orchestra and created an opera, and in Los Angeles, where it brought classical music to large audiences. Oklahoma City had been without an orchestra since 1929, when an amateur group led by Dean Frederick Holmberg of the University of Oklahoma had folded. The Federal Music Project in the community received $50,000 in WPA funds in 1937, and the next year the Oklahoma City Symphony Orchestra, led by Ralph Rose, presented its first concert. Trained at the Curtis Institute in Philadelphia, Rose determined to provide a quality program of Tchaikovsky and Listz. The following year, twenty-two-year-old Victor Allesandro became the conductor of the sixty-five-member orchestra. A graduate of the Eastman School of Music and a winner of awards at Salzburg and of a Prix de Rome fellowship, Allesandro raised the quality of his orchestra and took it on statewide tours. A skilled conductor and astute manager, Allesandro played children's concerts and Starlight performances, reaching 55,000 people in his premier season. With ticket prices ranging from twenty-five to fifty-five cents, Allesandro generated widespread community support for the symphony. By the time the Federal Music Project ended in 1942, the Oklahoma Symphony Society had 3,000 members and the orchestra was firmly launched. The WPA had turned "hellish want into heavenly harmony."[173]

The California State Emergency Relief Administration created music programs before the WPA entered the scene, and in San Diego it organized an orchestra, a chorus, and a dance band. The WPA Federal Music Project took over the program in 1935, inheriting 350 musicians who were rehearsing two operas. The Federal Music Project did not encourage operas because of the cost, but San Diego managed. The WPA Sewing Project produced costumes, and a crew constructed inexpensive sets. The lead singer of the Royal Opera Company of Mexico, Jose de Arrotia, came to take a major role. The project scheduled two performances of *Cavalleria Rusticana* and was overwhelmed by the response. In a city of about 150,000, the run had to be extended for five more appearances as 15,000 people attended the opera. San Diego Federal Music Project Director William Dean then prepared William S. Gilbert and Sir Arthur Sullivan's *Gondoliers* and took it on a bus tour. *The Mikado* sold out in 1936, and by 1940, the season included five operas. When the Federal Music Project in Washington, D.C., banned all operas, San Diego protested and was allowed to continue. The project offered the music of Johann Strauss, Gioacchino Rossini, and Franz Lehar to enthusiastic audiences in southern California. Understanding the need to build support by singing in English and offering familiar operas, Dean thus generated community enthusiasm for music, including the San Diego Symphony. Many of the players in the opera orchestra were also part of the symphony. Veterans of the Federal Music Project in San Diego also formed the core of the Starlight Theater, which continued operatic performances in San Diego after 1945.[174]

The omnipresent L. E. Beymer served on the Los Angeles County Federal Music Project Advisory Board, and through his efforts a major program reached out to the community. He recruited singers and musicians from among the European immigrants who came to Los Angeles in the 1930s, many of whom had extraordinary credentials. Although some were too proud to go on relief, the project needed them, and Behymer persuaded the musicians to apply to the WPA. In 1936, the Los Angeles Federal Music Project Symphony offered concerts that included music by Bach, Schumann, and Beethoven, as well as Ernst Bacon's Pulitzer Prize–winning symphony conducted by Bacon himself. The project soon had 1,600 musicians enrolled, and they presented over five hundred performances, many of which were free. The project organized a Hispanic "Tipica Orchestra" and an African American Chorus, which Behymer declared to be the best he had ever heard. Indeed, he argued that the quality of the music in the project was higher and more professional than that which the city had experienced before the depression. The programs generated intensely enthusiastic audiences for music ranging from works by Stephen Collins Foster to Verdi's *La Traviata*.[175] The Federal Music Project in Los Angeles achieved the exact goal of the WPA: it took quality music to the masses. Unfortunately, there were few other such examples in the Southwest.

The history of the WPA Federal Theater Project in the region is also a story of missed opportunities and conservative reactions to dramas of social criticism. In the West some 13,000 people participated in the Federal Theater Projects, but at least one-third were in Los Angeles. Problems in the project limited its effectiveness throughout the region. Because Oklahoma had few professional actors, Director John Dunn created units for Little Theater, marionettes, and research. The last unit collected regional dramatic materials. When Dunn tried to produce the antifascist *It Can't Happen Here,* local criticism blocked his plan. Nevertheless, his touring players covered the state, driving cars confiscated from bootleggers.[176] With low levels of funding, the four theatrical units in Texas— Dallas, Fort Worth, Houston, and San Antonio—lasted only one year. Texas WPA Director Harry Drought opposed the concept, and there was little public support.[177] In Los Angeles, however, the Federal Theater Project blossomed under the direction of Gilmor Brown of the Pasadena Playhouse. He leased theaters, organized companies, hired directors, and produced plays in English, Yiddish, and French. An African American unit offered *Black Empire, Noah,* and *John Henry.* The Hearst newspapers attacked the project because of the "leftist" plays offered in some theaters. The director of the state WPA demanded the right to review all scripts because of complaints of "communism" and "immorality" in the plays, and Brown was dismissed. Nevertheless, the Los Angeles Federal Theater Project continued until 1939, developing scripts for "Los Pastores," producing an all-black cast for *Macbeth,* and offering Shaw, Shakespeare, and O'Neill at very low ticket prices.[178] When the Federal Theater Project decided to cancel the "mediocre" unit in San Diego, local business and religious leaders demanded its continuation. Twenty thousand citizens sent letters and petitions to Washington in protest, and the decision was reversed. It was a "political choice," however, and not a vote for theatrical excellence.[179]

The New Deal programs for the arts employed thousands and created some lasting cultural institutions. The success or failure of the projects rested on the desire of communities for the arts as well as on strong local leadership. As the depression decade came to an end, two indigenous achievements set the tone for the future of art and the theater in the region: the emergence of the Dallas Nine painters and of the southwestern voice in plays by Lynn Riggs.

In 1936, Dallas presented a pageant, "The Cavalcade of Texas," which celebrated the century since Texas had declared its independence from Mexico. The *Dallas Morning News* said, "The work must not be judged by the standard of Salzburg, Chicago or Baltimore spectacles, but as a sumptuous achievement of our young but ambitious theatre."[180] The newspaper reporter verbalized the pride that Texas felt for what had been achieved culturally, but also the fear of being criticized by external standards. Nine artists in Dallas rejected that point of view and asked to be judged as artists in a global sense. From New York critics to the artist Thomas Hart Benton, the evaluations proved positive, almost lyrical. In 1932, these nine struggling artists, all under the age of thirty, sustained each other even as the coming of the depression made their goals harder to achieve. Members of the Dallas Artists League, they were modernists whose work paralleled the "New Regionalism" spawned by Thomas Hart Benton, John Steuart Curry, and Grant Wood. The Dallas Nine used the environment and people of the Southwest to express eternal truths and values. Although they felt Benton, Curry, and Wood to be insular and superficial, they drew themes and sometimes composition from the American Scene paintings. The Dallas Nine worked largely in oil on Masonite, depicting social and rural scenes and often employing distorted objects or perspective in a surrealistic mood. Their paintings contained dreamy and mysterious objects mixed with spirit-filled characters. Richly detailed, their pictures often had a sharp edginess in the depiction of industrialization, soil erosion, poverty, the rape of the land, the greed for oil, and the Dust Bowl. An exhibition of part of the S. H. Kress Collection of early Italian Renaissance paintings in Dallas in the 1930s also influenced their choices of subject matter and composition. The Dallas Nine sought to reach out to larger audiences, and they made lithographs of their paintings that could be sold at low prices.[181] Most of all, they painted the world around them, the people and the land. As one of their leaders, Jerry Bywaters, wrote in response to Benton's plea for regional art: "We were already regionalists. That was the natural thing to do. We were just doing what we were destined to do — what we'd been responding to all our lives."[182]

The Dallas Public Art Gallery's exhibition of paintings by the Dallas Nine in 1932 demonstrated the vitality of their work. Bywaters, John Douglass, Otis Dozier, Lloyd Goff, William Lester, Perry Nichols, Everett Spruce, Alexandre Hogue, and Thomas Still were joined by other area painters who sought to depict the harsh realities of life in the Southwest in the midst of economic travail. A strong camaraderie developed among the members of the Dallas Artists League as they formulated a regional style of painting. Simultaneously they tried to rid themselves of the influence of the Impressionist "Blue Bonnet School" and of outside forces such as the "Social Realists" of the East. Suitable subjects abounded: the cracked earth, abandoned farms, dead livestock, sharecroppers, the unemployed in the cities, oil-field prostitutes, and the poverty of Hispanics in the barrios and of blacks in rural Texas. The roots of "Lone Star Regionalism" were rural, but the painters labored to reproduce the realities of urban life as well. When they exhibited collectively, a stunning panorama of the contemporary Southwest emerged.[183]

Bywaters and Hogue led the group with their obvious artistic talents and their drive to produce quality regional art with eternal themes. Born in Paris, Texas, in 1906, Bywaters had studied art in Dallas and at the Art Students League in New York with John Sloan. He learned technique but wanted to create his own style. A visit with the muralist Diego Rivera in Mexico led Bywaters to conclude, "I know now that art, to be significant, must be a reflection of life; that it must be understandable to the layman; and that it must be part of a people's thought."[184]

For sixty years Bywaters promoted this view of art. He led the Dallas Museum of Fine Arts for two decades, actively encouraging artists in the region. His own work suffered because of his commitment to developing art in the Southwest, but from 1933 to 1943 a burst of creativity produced remarkable paintings. Clean, bright, unsentimental images of dusty main streets, small-town life, and sweating sharecroppers filled his canvases. *Oil Field Girls* of 1940 depicted two hitchhiking prostitutes against a background of billboards and oil derricks. The subject matter was not atypical of Bywaters and the Dallas Nine.[185]

Undoubtedly the strongest talent in the group belonged to Hogue. Born in Missouri but brought to Texas at the age of six weeks, Hogue grew up in Denton. He studied art in Minneapolis after graduating from high school but returned to Dallas to train as an illustrator. While living in New York in the 1920s, he studied in the galleries and museums, but by 1926 Hogue was painting during the summer at Taos or in Texas. Returning to Dallas, he joined with Bywaters and the regionalists to create a new style. He soon gained national recognition: Hogue's paintings of the Dust Bowl were featured in *Life* magazine in 1937, and *Fortune* commissioned him to produce a series of paintings of the oil industry. The Jeu de Poume Museum in Paris purchased one of his paintings, and critics praised his graphic scenes of the Southwest. Painting in the Texas Panhandle or on the prairies northwest of Dallas, Hogue created works depicting the destruction of the land by humankind. He painted not only the beauty of the land but also the human exploitation of the earth.[186]

Hogue's paintings *Mother Earth Laid Bare, The Crucified Land,* and *Drouth Survivors* brought the effects of the Dust Bowl and soil erosion to millions. Humankind had abused the land and now was paying the consequence. The agents who had brought life to the land had actually destroyed it. *Mother Earth Laid Bare* showed a gigantic female figure revealed in the curvaceous landscape of an abandoned farm, with a plow serving as a phallic symbol of the rape of the land. *Drouth Survivors,* with its graphic view of the effect of the drought on the cattle industry, so outraged West Texas ranchers that they tried to purchase it so that the painting could be burned. Hogue vehemently denied that he was a social realist: "I did the Dust Bowl because I was there and could see the sinister beauty of it with my own eyes."[187]

Hogue's inspirations came from his respect for the land. His mother's garden

FIGURE 31

Alexandre Hogue's Erosion No. 2: Mother Earth Laid Bare, *1936,*
depicted the rape of the land made evident in drought-stricken Texas.
Courtesy the Philbrook Museum of Art, Tulsa, Oklahoma.

and her feeling for nature influenced his work. He noted that she had tried to
instill in him "a respect for the soil, and no doubt she succeeded." He added, "I
began to imagine a great female form lying there under the ground."[188] Summers spent on a ranch in the Texas Panhandle as a teenager left an impression of
"the most luscious grassland on earth," but "sad to relate, the grassland is gone
forever."[189] When his Dallas teacher Frank Reaugh took Hogue to the Big Bend
country, his view of the landscape solidified: "In that crisp atmosphere nothing
is ambiguous—I was called a hard edge painter. Atmosphere elsewhere in the
country becomes fuzzy in the distance, yet in the Big Bend forms at great distance are as clear as nearby. You have to see it to believe it. Distance is achieved
by greater color contrast in nearby forms. The forms are hard edge *mass*."[190] The
colors of the earth intrigued Hogue, whether in northern New Mexico, Palo
Duro Canyon, the prairies of northern Texas, or the Big Bend: the vermilion,
yellow, ocher, and greens on canyon walls or against strong red-clay soils, the
blues of trees at a distance, and the colors of the skies, ranging from dark blue
to bright red, orange, and purple. Hogue's friendship with Frank Dobie and his

respect for Dobie's writings caused his "roots [to] sink still deeper into the soil of the Southwest."[191]

It was not enough for Hogue to paint the region. He also used his pen to write forceful articles advocating regional art, architecture, and literature. In contributions to Dallas newspapers, the *Southwest Review,* and *El Palacio,* he pleaded for art that honestly represented the region. He wrote about Victor Higgins, "And so the American artist in general will come of age only when he has the stamina to blaze his own trails thru the part of the country where he lives."[192] For Hogue, the rolling plains of Texas compared favorably to the turbulence of great mountains: "Like still waters they run deep. But under the surface are extraordinary possibilities for the artist who masters interpretation of them."[193] Hogue's art depended on his interrelationship with the earth and the sky. "Every existing thing / Even the sky / Has a voice for me / If I but listen."[194]

Hogue and the Lone Star Regionalists won praise and awards at exhibitions in San Francisco, New York, Paris, and elsewhere. Donald Bear, director of the Denver Art Museum, wrote: "These Texas artists . . . have not only caught the breadth of the country which they paint, but have conveyed in terms of true social meaning something of the character of the people and their relation to the land. . . . They have created Texas art."[195] *Art Digest* devoted its entire June, 1936, issue to art in Dallas and lauded the creators of the paintings that conveyed the "startling effects of light and air—the subtle tones of the desert, the turquoise sky, the sense of freedom that goes with wide, unfenced spaces."[196] The Dallas Nine and their colleagues brought national attention to the quality of their art and to the vitality of creativity in the region.

The views of the Dallas Nine echoed the words of those actors and actresses who, on stages across the nation, were performing in the plays of Lynn Riggs. Raleigh Lynn Riggs, son of a rancher father and a one-eighth-Cherokee mother, was born three miles southwest of Claremore, Indian Territory, in 1899. The family moved to town when Riggs was six, and he attended a small preparatory school, from which he graduated in 1917. Riggs hopped a cattle train to Chicago after working as a cowboy but returned to Tulsa and a job at the *Oil and Gas Journal.* He left to live in New York briefly, before enrolling at the University of Oklahoma. Small-boned, frail, meticulously dressed, and gentle of manners, Riggs blossomed at the university.[197] Faculty in the strong English department encouraged him to write for campus literary magazines. A brilliant talker as well as writer, he wrote a farce, *Cuckoo*—presented by the University Playhouse in 1921—which incorporated music, mainly pioneer ballads.[198] He discovered poetry, publishing in *Smart Set* and *Poetry* in 1922 while teaching English classes.

FIGURE 32

During his sojourn in New Mexico, the playwright Lynn Riggs went "native" while drafting dramas about the people of the region. Photograph by Carl Van Vechten, reproduced by permission of the Van Vechten Trust. Print from Literary Files, Harry Ransom Humanities Research Center, the University of Texas at Austin.

Riggs met Witter Bynner when the poet visited the university, and after Riggs developed tuberculosis, he moved to Santa Fe and lived with Bynner. He fell under the spell of New Mexico and the artists and writers of the community, but not of Mabel Dodge Luhan, who he felt "played" with people: "She's a meddler. She thinks she is God."[199] Riggs wrote a one-act play, *Knives from Syria,* which was performed by the Santa Fe Players and was published by Samuel French in New York. Encouraged, Riggs returned to New York City, where the American Laboratory performed his *Big Lake* in 1927. This was the first of eighteen plays based on the people of Oklahoma and New Mexico.

A Guggenheim Fellowship the next year found Riggs first in Paris, where he began to write *Green Grow the Lilacs* at a bar, and then in the south of France, where he finished the play. But he longed for the Southwest. He wrote Alice

Corbin Henderson in Santa Fe, "Now I'm so homesick for your bright hills, even Paris cannot compensate."[200] Yet he did not have to be in Oklahoma to write about it. When asked if the farmhouse in *Green Grow the Lilacs* was authentic, he responded, "It ought to be because it was where I was born."[201] His plays appeared in New York in rapid succession: *Roadside, Green Grow the Lilacs, The Domino Parlor, Cherokee Nights,* and *Russet Mantle.* The last, a comedy about Santa Fe sophisticates, showed a gift for humor, but the other plays about Oklahoma carried "a slight-edge beyond realism."[202] New York audiences were stunned by his use of violence, fury, incest, and murder in plays that also often contained folk music and ballads. He subordinated plot to "mood and feeling," but his use of dialect, geography, and nostalgia set his work apart.[203] When the Theater Guild produced *Green Grow the Lilacs* in 1931, Riggs had his first hit. A mixed cast of Lee Strasberg, Franchot Tone, and Tex Ritter brought to life the people of Indian Territory at the turn of the century. Interludes of "Git Along, Little Dogies," "Home on the Range," and "The Chisholm Trail" heightened the contrast between the love story and the violence represented by Jud Fry.[204] Love and hunger for the land created a nostalgic glow, "but in dramatic dialogue more than song." Riggs wrote, "The great range of mood . . . characterized the old folk songs and ballads I used to hear in Oklahoma in my childhood."[205] Riggs found "quaintness, sadness, robustness, simplicity, heart and bawdy humor" in the speech of southwesterners.[206] But the land too became part of his plays. To the dramatist Paul Green he wrote: "Like you, I carry my own state with me. . . . Some day I am going to write a play called *More Sky,* after I've found a little more of myself. . . . There's some pretty wide air out there, and more sky than is allotted to most sections of the country. You'll gather that I'm beginning to find out where I live."[207]

Riggs visited Europe, bought a house in Santa Fe, and briefly wrote film scripts in Hollywood, but his best work, which ended by 1940, centered on the people of Oklahoma. "The range of life there is not to be indicated, much less its meaning laid bare, by a few people in a few plays. Some day, perhaps, all the plays I have written, taken together, may constitute a *study* from which certain things may emerge and be formulated into a *kind of truth* about people who happen to be living in Oklahoma."[208] Although Riggs delighted in the poetic speech and melodious flow of words, his characters also represented values he admired. "Curly" in *Green Grow the Lilacs* is not an educated young man, but he is honest, hardworking, devoted, and loyal. Riggs celebrated the raw edge of life, but the folk wisdom of "Aunt Ellie" contained the virtues and morality of his family and neighbors in Claremore. The characters in his dramas were people he knew; his friend Betty Kirk appeared as "Betty" in *Big Lake*.[209] They were boisterous but lonely, loving but capable of jealousy. A gifted playwright with a vivid memory, Riggs wrote of the people and their land.

Only a few thousand theatergoers in New York saw the plays of Riggs, but millions came to know "Curly," "Laurie," "Jud Fry," "Aunt Ellie," and "Adoo Annie" through Riggs's collaboration with Richard Rodgers and Oscar Hammerstein II in *Oklahoma!* Rodgers and Hammerstein retained the language and flavor of *Green Grow the Lilacs* in a production that integrated dialogue, music, and dance for the first time. The nation had been at war for two years when *Oklahoma!* opened on Broadway, and the American people thirsted for a story and music that reinforced the values of democracy and the common people. *Oklahoma!* won a Pulitzer Prize, ran for 2,212 performances, and made Riggs a wealthy man. His characters and dialogue brought the people and the land of the Southwest to the world.[210] Few knew that his play had been written in Europe at the outset of the depression; only a handful knew that the tensions and drama were heightened by Riggs's confrontation with his homosexuality.[211] Produced by repertory theaters, high schools, university playhouses, and off-off-Broadway companies, Riggs's plays helped establish the legitimacy of the Southwest as a contributor to the national culture.

The Santa Fe writer Kyle Crichton observed, "Culture is not a thing which may be manufactured synthetically; it grows out of a rich background and from a sound philosophy."[212] At the end of the Great Depression, the people of the Southwest had formulated the basis for a regional culture. Economic expansion during the next two decades would allow for the growth of cultural institutions and would provide a place where architects, artists, musicians, theatrical producers, and writers could thrive. As Rodgers and Hammerstein understood, southwesterners had established a relationship with the soil: "We know we belong to the land, / And the land we belong to is grand."

CHAPTER 5

Nationalization of a Regional Culture

1940–1960

World War II transformed the Southwest. Federal spending created wealth and an industrial infrastructure. Migration patterns accelerated the process of urban growth as cities came to dominate the regional economy. Defense plants spawned other industries, which in turn led to larger banks, insurance companies, food processors, and manufacturers of clothing, furniture, and appliances. When the war ended, most defense-related factories shifted to domestic commercial products, but the coming of the cold war led to even larger federal expenditures in the region. Petroleum and petroleum-based firms burgeoned, as did the transportation system that moved their products to national and international markets. As a consequence, smaller cities such as Albuquerque and Tucson became major urban centers. The largest cities in the region soon dominated the lists of the nation's ten largest metropolitan areas. Urban growth and civic pride, based on the vibrant regional economy, vastly expanded cultural resources that not only reflected national trends but also began to shape those currents.

In the two decades between 1940 and 1960, the culture of the Southwest altered markedly due to the economic expansion and urban growth. A rural-based literature became more urban oriented as writers focused on the city rather than the farm or the ranch. Urban growth produced an architecture drawn largely from the International Style as major firms sought signature buildings for their corporate headquarters. Rising incomes meant discretionary spending could be directed to art museums, symphony orchestras, opera productions, and exciting new theatrical companies. Wealth, urban expansion, and the desire of elites to emulate the social and cultural leadership in cities outside the Southwest led to the nationalization of the regional culture. Success in creating orchestras, theaters, and museums of quality produced demands for the even higher levels of achievement that the rampant economic growth would fund from the 1960s through the 1980s. As the *Dallas Morning News* critic John Rosenfield noted, "The arts were nothing more than spiritual and recreational comfort until the post–World War II period."[1]

As noted, regional demographic patterns shifted massively after 1940. During the Great Depression the rural Southwest lost hundreds of thousands of farmers, ranchers, sharecroppers, and tenant farmers who were blown off the land by the Dust Bowl or tractored off in land consolidations. They migrated to southwestern cities and to California, a trend that continued after World War II broke out, as defense plants sought workers to meet production goals. The region witnessed increased migration from the East and Midwest as well as a large influx of Europeans, especially to California. Many of these recent arrivals were highly educated and deeply involved in the arts. They sought to enrich the cultural institutions of the Southwest, and they introduced a new vitality. Not content with simply emulating museums, symphonies, and theaters elsewhere, they sought to be creative, not derivative. The war simply postponed their yearnings. Innovation and experimentation awaited the coming of peace.

Migration patterns also altered the racial composition of southwestern cities. Native Americans in Oklahoma, New Mexico, and Arizona moved to urban areas, particularly Los Angeles and Phoenix, as their total number rose from about 340,000 in 1950 to more than 520,000 in 1960. Hispanics abandoned farms and ranches to move to San Antonio, El Paso, Tucson, Phoenix, and urban areas in southern California. Hispanics represented almost 15 percent of California's population by 1960. Federal programs brought Mexican nationals to work in the Southwest during the war, and many stayed, swelling the population of the barrios. World War II sharply accelerated the movement of African Americans into the Southwest: some 600,000 blacks left the South and headed west, largely to Texas and California. Job opportunities in a more fluid society offered hope for economic advancement for blacks as well as for middle-class whites.

The southwestern economy boomed after 1940, and highly educated technical workers added to an evolving labor force. Job-training programs transformed farmers into skilled industrial employees building airplanes, producing sophisticated communications gear, and creating new petrochemicals. The aviation industry built huge facilities in Oklahoma City, Fort Worth, Tulsa, Phoenix, and southern California. States largely devoid of heavy industry suddenly had thousands of blue-collar workers. By 1950 Los Angeles trailed only New York City and Chicago as a manufacturing center.

Raw numbers barely hint at the revolutionary changes that took place from 1940 to 1960. Phoenix grew from a small city of 65,000 to a large metropolitan center of 440,000. Although the entire state of Oklahoma lost population in the 1930s and 1940s, its cities swelled between 1940 and 1960: Oklahoma City grew from 204,000 to 324,000 and Tulsa from 142,000 to 261,000. The towns of Tucson and Albuquerque leaped from about 35,000 people to 212,000 and 201,000 respectively. In Texas, El Paso's defense facilities helped create a major city of 276,000 from a community of only 96,000 two decades earlier. Houston's petroleum, shipping, and agricultural-processing facilities attracted immigrants, who pushed the city's population from 384,000 in 1940 to 938,000 in 1960. Dallas swelled from 294,000 to 680,000 while rival Fort Worth grew from 177,000 to 356,000. San Antonio surged from 253,000 to 587,000. Suburbs, shopping centers, freeways, congestion, and urban sprawl became common experiences of all southwestern cities. Air conditioning, widespread ownership of automobiles, vast tracts of affordable housing, and numerous employment opportunities made the urban Southwest a magnet for millions.[2]

The war and postwar expansion linked the region economically, solidifying a southwestern identification. Aircraft industries located in southern California established major plants in Oklahoma and Texas, with frequent exchanges of personnel and technology. Texas petroleum companies established oil-production facilities in the rest of the Southwest, sending executives and technicians to Oklahoma, California, and New Mexico. Southwestern retail chains appeared in regional shopping centers; buyers in Los Angeles had to know what would sell in El Paso or Amarillo. As per capita incomes rose to the national average and then beyond, banks acquired capital to extend more and larger loans. Insurance companies in Dallas, Houston, and Los Angeles loaned money to ship-builders in Corpus Christi, clothing manufacturers in El Paso, and food processors in Albuquerque and Oklahoma City. As the percentage of the population that was urban reached more than half of the regional total, industrial output, retail sales, bank deposits, manufacturing output, and personal income soared. The internal regional identification solidified with the movement of Texans and Oklahomans to California, New Mexico, and Arizona.

After the war ended, tourism again became a major growth industry. Many visitors came for brief visits and stayed, or returned in retirement. One writer noted in the 1930s that Tucson, a county-seat town with a state university, was "the only city of comparable size in the world without visible means of support."[3] With nearly a quarter of a million people in 1960, Tucson boasted a huge air force facility, tourism, large-scale trade with Mexico, and many small manufacturing and commercial firms. It served as a microcosm for the region.[4]

The 1940s and the 1950s transformed the Southwest far more than had the Great Depression. The regional sense of optimism, the willingness to innovate and to take risks, the strong entrepreneurial spirit, and the desire to compete carried over into the realm of cultural life. The incipient cultural institutions of the prewar era received greater attention, larger budgets, and an influx of eager supporters. The culture of the Southwest blossomed after 1945, providing architects, artists, musicians, thespians, dancers, and writers with opportunities that had never existed before. Ironically, even as these opportunities appeared, the regional distinctiveness waned as the Southwest became more fully integrated into the national culture.[5] Preservation of a regional identity was threatened by cultural successes.

Architecture provided a highly visible illustration of the region's cultural vitality after 1945 as rising office towers transformed the urban landscape. The enormous growth of Tucson and Phoenix, for example, led to urban sprawl and signature buildings at their centers. Local architects such as Lewis Place of Place and Place designed new buildings for banks, utilities, and savings and loan companies. The University of Arizona developed a professional course in architecture in 1958, producing locally trained designers. The Arizona Land Title Building in Tucson opened that year, an office tower with balconies and an open promenade at the street level. Both communities developed leaders who solicited external investment, particularly from Texas and Los Angeles, even though some residents of Phoenix decried the city's "Californication."[6]

In Tulsa, Oklahoma City, Austin, and Albuquerque, skyscrapers built in the International Style announced the economic successes of the postwar decade. The twenty-story First National Bank of Tulsa, built in 1950, soon had neighbors housing Skelly Oil Company and the Fourth National Bank. Those structures and the Liberty Towers were all in a modified International Style, devoid of decoration. In Oklahoma City, Tom and Lee Sorey and Alfred Hill designed many buildings for the heart of the downtown. The firm engaged in "pragmatic styling": the International Style with strong vertical lines.[7] When the internationally recognized architect Edward Durrell Stone designed the Westgate in Austin in 1965, he shattered the city's low horizon with an International Style building not unlike the CBS office tower in New York.[8] A similar transformation occurred in Albuquerque, which had been largely a one-, two-, or three-story town. Even in "the busiest districts, as in all the Southwest, the sky predominates," Erna Fergusson wrote in 1947.[9] New architects arrived in Albuquerque, bringing the International Style with them. The Albuquerque National Bank, the Simms Building of twelve stories, and the Federal Building changed the skyline as towers of glass-and-metal panels pierced the sky. Sterile, boxlike structures dominated the void between the West Mesa and the mountains to the east.[10]

The British author J. B. Priestly recognized the urban boom in the Southwest when he toured Texas in 1955: "But why Texas? Because there, . . . may be found the latest men, living in what are for their size the richest and most rapidly expanding cities in our Western world. If our newest urban civilization cannot be found here, then where can it be found? . . . Dallas and Houston represent the newest, the most prosperous, the most 'progressive' America, just as American life itself represents a pattern of society to which all our urban Western Civilization is beginning to conform."[11]

Priestly stood in awe of the new Dallas skyline — the Republic Bank Building of forty stories; the twenty-nine-story Adolphus Tower; the Southland Building at forty-seven stories — all built between 1954 and 1959. They were the vanguard of thirty major office buildings constructed between 1945 and 1980. The glass-clad Southland Center, the tallest building west of Chicago in 1958, included a separate hotel building and retail shops. The "skin" of the Republic National Bank — aluminum panels — reflected the Texas sun by day and looked like a giant metal sculpture at night. None of these buildings moved beyond critically acceptable concepts, but their mere presence symbolized the massive economic changes in the postwar Southwest.[12]

Another symbol, suburban sprawl, meant tens of thousands of pseudo–ranch style houses, mock stucco casas, and ersatz English castles. The ever cynical novelist Nathaniel West denounced Los Angeles as a city of "Mexican ranch houses, Samoan huts, Mediterranean villas, Egyptian and Japanese temples, Swiss Chalets [and] Tudor cottages."[13] Despite the jerry-built appearance of Los Angeles and other southwestern cities, some fine architecture could be found in the postwar boom. A lack of imagination in urban housing dominated, but several thoughtful architects brought quality materials and creativity to their designs. In Houston, John Staub produced dozens of homes for the nouveau riche in River Oaks and other subdivisions. Staub used historical models from England, France, and Italy for traditional homes constructed of fine materials. Rich, ornate, and decorative, his homes reflected his clients' desire for instant lineage.[14]

The African American architect Paul R. Williams designed similar homes in Los Angeles, gracing Palos Verdes with houses in the Williamsburg style. His clients in the motion-picture industry wanted traditional homes or houses in the Art Deco or streamlined Art Moderne modes. Trained as a traditionalist at the Beaux Arts Institute of Design, Williams broke from that heritage, producing houses that reflected the International Style. Unlike Staub, Williams also designed homes for the middle class and public housing. He collaborated on the Pueblo del Rio project, which incorporated horizontal bands of windows to bring indoors the garden plots and fruit trees surrounding the two-story units. A major contributor to the growth of Los Angeles, Williams had $20 million in projects under way in 1948 alone.[15]

Similarly, O'Neil Ford brought to Texas architecture a commitment to quality materials and a desire to build upon the historical designs of the state and region. Apprenticed as an architect in Dallas during the Great Depression, Ford struggled to survive, but clients soon came when they saw his employment of limestone and cedar for both the landscape and the building materials in his designs. Ford moved to San Antonio, where his tours of rural areas made him want to utilize in his concepts the ideas of the early settlers. After service in the U.S. Air Corps during World War II, Ford used his flying skills to criss-cross Texas, meeting prospective clients. He experimented with lift-slab technology in concrete but retained his passion for natural materials that were integrated into the site.[16] The impact of individuals such as Staub, Williams, and Ford could be seen across the region.

In New Mexico and Colorado the influence of John Gaw Meem continued to shape the desires of clients and to inspire young architects. While Meem labored to save the mission churches and embraced the use of adobe in buildings, he also accepted Eliel Saarinen's call for fundamental forms as a composite of culture; traditional forms could be molded to fit contemporary building requirements. Tradition and modernism were not antipodal. While other architects in the region rejected the approach used by Meem and totally embraced the International Style, some, such as Antoine Predock, turned away from absolute functionalism and, by the early 1960s, had begun to adapt buildings to the environment and to employ natural materials.[17] A small but eloquent Los Angeles structure designed by Lloyd Wright, the son of Frank Lloyd Wright, showed how the simple could be made extraordinary. His Wayfarers' Chapel in Palos Verdes incorporated large sheets of glass, laminated redwood framing, and local stone for the base, creating a religious greenhouse. Using his training as a landscape architect, Wright placed trees and plants and a small waterfall in and around the chapel. Wright believed that there was a spiritual basis in nature, and his chapel reflected that view.[18]

The Wrights, father and son, deeply influenced southwestern architecture in the postwar era. At Taliesen West, Frank Lloyd Wright's students heard his insightful and acerbic comments about regional architecture. "A doctor can bury his mistakes," Wright declared, "but an architect can only advise his client to plant vines."[19] When asked why design should be studied, he answered: "Great architecture is great civilization. Always. Without it? No civilization. Art alone gives vitality and true appreciation of life to human desire. With Art and Architecture a civilization is alive — 'quick.' Without Art and Architecture, a civilization has no soul: dies like an animal."[20] But even as Wright influenced young architects, the Southwest shaped his organic concepts. "I, too, have discovered this America that is Arizona," he said. "It is the grandeur of this great desert-garden that is Arizona's chief asset. . . . The Arizona desert is no place for the hard box-walls of the houses of the Middle West and East."[21] Wright added: "Living in the desert is the spiritual cathartic a great many people need. I am one of them."[22]

The desert, the sky, and the southwestern trees and plants shaped Wright's designs in the 1950s as he produced homes in Arizona, Texas, and California, as well as the spectacular Price Tower in Oklahoma. For his son David he designed a round, cantilevered "citrus orchard" house. For Harold Price, he created a sprawling home in Camelback, Arizona, using desert colors, extended porches, and deep overhangs. Concern for color, texture, and geometry marked his southwestern houses; the Lykes house, for example, seemed to grow out of a mountainside.[23] For the proposed Burlingham home near El Paso, he used adobe in a rounded design of curves and arches, resulting in what Wright called "the pottery house." The house was eventually built near Santa Fe by another client.[24] In Amarillo, Dallas, and Houston, Wright employed red bricks, limestone, or concrete blocks with large expanses of glass, copper roofs that weathered jade green, and terrazzo floors. He told his client Dorothy Ann Kinney, "The only thing an architect can do is not offend nature anymore than is absolutely necessary."[25] Regional architects and their clients found inspiration in his works and philosophy.

Among the last of Wright's major commissions, only the Guggenheim Museum received as much attention as the Price Tower in Bartlesville, Oklahoma. Harold C. Price developed a technique to use arc welding in petroleum pipeline construction, and from a small welding shop he built an international firm. Risk-takers, Price and his son Joe also loved beautiful objects. Harold Price's experience with Wright as the architect on his Arizona home led him to commission an office building for his firm. Wright returned to a project he had proposed in New York in 1929 and created a design for a sixteen-story building based on four concrete fins from which the floors were cantilevered. The non-load-bearing walls of tan masonry, gold glass, and copper plates and screens rested on the floors. Interior modules as parallelograms suggested open spaces on the office floors and the eight apartments at the top of the tower. The interior colors were those of nature; when asked what color he desired for the floor coverings, Wright bent over, gathered a handful of red Oklahoma soil, and handed it to the contractor.[26] Wright totally rejected the International Style and proclaimed,

"Now the skyscraper comes into its own on the rolling plains of Oklahoma."[27] Visible from sixteen miles away, the tower added dramatically to the vast horizon, especially at night, when it looked like a lighted sculpture.

Wright understood that the opportunity to produce this new form of construction came only because of Price's vision and his willingness to take risks. Wright told a reporter, "That's the job for you fellows, to find the Prices of this world, if we ever have a culture of our own."[28] Clients with verve and nerve were required: "Lieber Meister (the late Louis H. Sullivan) used to say to me, 'Wright, why are the American people so G— — D— — credulous?' So they are. But they are not dead yet, witness this release of the skyscraper from slavery (commercial bondage) to a humane freedom by Hal Price."[29] The new skyscrapers rising in southwestern cities failed to impress Wright, who declared, "Downtown Dallas buildings have about as much life as a rubber doormat."[30]

Ever the egoist, Wright castigated the work of most other designers, but he encouraged the pioneering of admirers such as Bruce Goff. The ubiquitous postwar ranch-style house received an imaginative challenge from Goff, who continued to break with convention. He combined natural colors and native materials with unusual shapes. As a professor at the University of Oklahoma School of Architecture from 1947 to 1955, Goff designed houses that stunned the locals. The Ledbetter-Taylor House had a circular floating roof, structural suspension cables, freestanding elements, masonry walls that seemed to rise out of the red clay soil, and disks suspended over the carport and patio. An "open house" of this structure in 1948 attracted 14,500 people, at a time when the town had a population of 22,000. Goff used native Oklahoma stone, cedar, dark wood trim, and serpentine walls in a utilitarian and functional home. The Bavinger House of 1950 incorporated a continuous curving limestone wall, ninety-six feet long, which formed a spiral around a steel pole that supported a suspended roof. The Bavingers were willing to risk the wrath of neighbors living in traditional houses.[31]

After Goff left the university, his students, especially Herb Greene, continued to design stunning houses that defied convention. Greene produced the "Buffalo House" and the "Prairie House" near Norman in 1962 and 1965. The latter served as a metaphor for beasts and caves. His organic approach used rhythms in shingles and boards. Greene explained, "In designing the Prairie House, I made a serious attempt to evoke a sense of time by including in the image a range of references that span the ages from the primordial past to an intimated future."[32] The houses also became tourist attractions, though not by the architect's intent.

Wright and Goff's organic architecture was echoed in Los Angeles and southern California by the Case Study Houses. Initiated by the editor of *Arts and Architecture* magazine, John Entenza, this project led to the creation of thirty-six experimental houses between 1945 and 1966. Most of the designs were built to serve as models for the vast expansion of home construction in the area. Some leading architects participated in the program, with designs furnished by Charles Eames, Pierre Koenig, and Craig Ellwood, among others. The Case Study Houses often had steel frames and large expanses of glass. Single-family homes, they incorporated advance designs in layouts, appliances, heating and cooling systems, and building materials. The concepts sprang from the prewar contributions of Richard Neutra and Rudolph Schindler. The houses seemed like "machines in the garden" with their technical marvels set in lush vegetation or perched on the side of a hill. The Case Study Houses proved that affordable housing did not have to be ugly or constructed with cheap materials. The project served to raise the aesthetic aspirations of home builders and venturesome architects as they abandoned historical sources and hard-and-fast rules.[33]

Unlike the innovative southwestern architects, regional authors in the postwar era, with a few notable exceptions, failed to equal in quality of output the work produced during the two previous decades. Initially, writers continued to focus on the rural nature of the region even as the rate of urbanization accelerated. Moreover, novels, short stories, and plays dwelled on the past, particularly the nineteenth century. Conrad Richter, Paul Horgan, Frank Waters, and others produced critically acclaimed books that often sold well, but younger authors such as Richard Bradford and Larry McMurtry called for a focus on the contemporary Southwest. Too, some promising authors — such as Don Blanding, Marquis James, and Paul Wellman — left the region to find different subject matter or a different muse. But as the settler "Big Jim" Murphy along Horse Creek in central Oklahoma argued: "Iv'rthing that iver happened anywhere has happened at Mar-rshall Oklahoma."[34]

Perhaps the initial problem was a lack of readership. Maybe Aunt Eller in *Green Grow the Lilacs* was right about her neighbors: "They had rather have a smokehouse full of meat than a book full of writing."[35] In *Sky Determines,* Ross Calvin discerned that the Southwest was not merely a place to live but also a manner of life.[36] That manner, that life, had to be discovered by writers within the region.

One of the most productive and profound of regional authors, Frank Waters, found his muse in northern New Mexico. Born in Colorado Springs in 1903 to an Anglo mother and a part-Cheyenne father, Waters knew the Southwest intimately. Before his father's death in 1914, Waters went to the Navajo Reservation with him for a summer. Waters labored in the family coal mine, as a telephone lineman in California's Imperial Valley, and as a writer for the U.S. Army during World War II. He started a novel in 1927 and published three autobiographical works of fiction between 1935 and 1940. Waters sought to reconcile the differences between the cultures of the Anglo-Europeans and that of the Native Americans. Aided by Tony Luhan, he studied Indian lore, writing several novels that contrasted Native American and white societies. *Masked Gods* (1950) challenged the European concept of progress and argued for an Anglo–Native American unity based on Eastern metaphysics. The book provided an in-depth account of Pueblo and Navajo religion. *The Woman at Otowi Crossing,* his novel about Edith Warner, who operated a tearoom near the Los Alamos Laboratory, related her transcendence and his belief that individual enlightenment and the harmony of diverse cultures were one and the same. His novels about the Pueblo Indians established his reputation, and over fifty years later, many of these works remain in print.[37]

Two of Waters's novels, *The Man Who Killed The Deer* (1942) and *People of the Valley* (1941), explored the conflict between the Anglo and Native American societies in terms of values. To Waters, European cultures appeared to be rationalistic, masculine, and aggressive. The Native American cultures seemed non-rational, feminine, and passive. *The Man Who Killed The Deer* portrayed the monastic Indian culture using italicized passages. These sections were the inner voice of the tribe. Dedicated to "Mabel and Tony," the novel concerned Martiniano, a young Indian arrested by Anglo officials for killing a deer. Martiniano had been to federal Indian schools, but he refused to abandon his beliefs. His life centered on Mother Earth, Father Sun, Brother Deer, and the Sacred Lake. He studied the mysteries of the seasons and determined to create a farm in the piñon forest. When the deer ate his corn, he freed himself from his fear of the deer by killing the animal. The trader Rodolfo Byers aided Martiniano because the Anglo merchant hated the sickly sentimentality of the female tourists, the greed of museum collectors, the mock gravity of the anthropologists, and the false idealism of the intellectual escapists. *People of the Valley* focused on Hispanic villagers threatened by a dam that would harness their river. Waters emphasized the land, the beauty of the valley, and the mingling of the three cultures destroyed by progress. The displaced people survived when they exercised faith and commitment and entered yet another valley, to begin again.[38]

Although these two works and Waters's twenty other books did not immediately receive critical acclaim, his reputation for dealing with basic values through cultural integration led to translations in many languages. Land served as the basic unifying force in his work. In *Below Grass Roots* (1937), Waters described the chief character: "He eats, sleeps and rides still further into the land that is a vast emptiness without a frame, a monotone that is never monotonous. And thus without perspective he remembers only the old jutting fragments as of a dream of time."[39] By the end of the 1980s, Waters took solace in the writings of southwesterners who sought universality of thought and a belief in this transcendent unity. He saw a new objectivity and a depth of wisdom that he had helped to launch.[40]

Conrad Richter shared Waters's enthusiasm and concern for universality and a search for values, although he did not approach his fiction metaphysically. Born in Pennsylvania in 1890, Richter had, by 1914, published short stories notable for their graceful style, strong sense of detail, and authenticity. His wife became ill, and he moved to Albuquerque in 1928. Five years later he began to write again. Ultimately winning the Pulitzer Prize (1951) and the National Book Award (1961), Richter lived and wrote in Albuquerque for twenty-two years.[41] After returning to the East in 1950, Richter declaimed: "I've often asked myself, why do we feel about our Southwestern country as we do? On first being exiled here we may fiercely dislike it. Let us stay a while, and we can scarcely bear to leave it. Away from it, we seldom fail to remember it without longing."[42]

The history and geography of the region and the land — "one is always aware of the land" — dominated Richter's *The Sea of Grass* (1937) and *The Lady* (1957), his principal novels of the Southwest. Though written twenty years apart, their themes are similar. Vibrant female characters draw strength from the land, the mountains, the bosques, the grasslands, the sky — horizon, colors, clouds — and the cycles of life. The land determined life for Anglo ranchers and their Hispanic colleagues and workers. The narrator of *The Sea of Grass* comments, "The free wild life we lived on that shaggy prairie was to me the life of gods."[43] Lutie Cameron Brewton in that novel and Doña Ellen Johnson y Campo Sessions in *The Lady* possess strong wills and intelligence and bring culture to the land through books and music. When Doña Ellen mounts her horse and rides across the prairie, the narrator describes the scene: "Riding out, we were prisoners suddenly escaped to the unfettered world of land and sky. . . . We breathed air never before tasted by a human being."[44]

Richter avoided melodrama in novels that told of the end of the great cattle ranches. Strong themes and mastery of language carried his narratives. But the inspiration came from the land, the sky, and the people. He stated, "In my own case, the most helpful thing I found in writing of the Southwest was the Southwest itself, its brilliant light, wide spaces, mountains and deserts, particularly its great sky and finer air which lift a man into a more rarefied and stimulating world of life and thought inhabited by certain lessor gods called Southwesterners."[45]

Paul Horgan, another immigrant from the East, was born in New York in 1903, came to Albuquerque as a young boy, and lived in New Mexico off and on for fifty years. He shared Waters's desire for a universality in fiction and Richter's passion for the region and its people. His history of the Rio Grande won the Pulitzer and Bancroft Prizes in 1954, establishing his critical reputation and answering the question of whether southwesterners could write excellent books about their own region. Horgan described the boosterism of Albuquerque in *The Common Heart,* deploring the changing city's abandonment of "real virtues." But Horgan also wrote about clashes between Anglos and Native Americans in novels such as *The Enemy Gods*(1937). From *No Quarter Given* (1935) to *Lamy of Santa Fe* (1975), he explored, through the people of the Southwest, inner and personal conflict as well as conflict between cultures. Author, artist, actor, and musician, Horgan served as the librarian at New Mexico Military Institute at Roswell from 1926 to 1942, where he not only came to know students and their families from across the region but also reestablished his friendship with the artists Peter Hurd and Henriette Wyeth Hurd, who lived nearby. Horgan's experiences and contacts led to the formation of his "Heroic Triad," a regional

FIGURE 34

The writer Paul Horgan interpreted the cultures of the Southwest in fiction, historical works, and essays for three decades. Photograph by Carl Van Vechten, reproduced by permission of the Van Vechten Trust. Print from the Harry Ransom Humanities Research Center, the University of Texas at Austin.

interpretation based on images of the mission/hacienda Hispanics, the Native Americans, and the cowboys/ranchers. These cultural icons shaped popular views of the Southwest, though they were often factually in error.[46]

From the time his family moved to Albuquerque, Horgan sensed the importance of place and people:

> After a year or so getting used to the swift and amazing change in the condition of my childhood environment, the values I began to absorb had to do with the vast land and its great river nearby, the mountains off there, and the golden sunlight that seemed to hold the past as well as the present in its power of revelation. Because the land was so vacant, and its form so huge and abiding, it seemed that what men and women had enacted there long ago could still be seen if you looked hard enough with eyes closed, as it were. And if history did not tell enough about what people did in that land, then what they did must be invented.[47]

Like Richter, Horgan made women some of his major characters, such as Vicky Cochran in *Whitewater* (1970), who brought culture to small West Texas or New Mexico towns. Cochran invited the brightest high school students into her home, exposed them to literature, art, and music, and provided scholarships for those who wanted to go to college. When she drove through the hazy dust of the countryside with a student, she remarked: "I thought we would drift through the country together and see the plains. I never get tired of them." Young Phil Durham, his eyes opened emotionally and intellectually, responds, "No, nor do I, though I didn't know it until now!"[48] For Horgan, the great constancy in his work was the land and what the human spirit felt there. The grandeur and power of the earth shaped the people and the characters in his novels. The land nourished his imagination.[49]

Between 1940 and the mid-1960s, regional authors pursued themes, largely historical, that failed to convey the extraordinary demographic and economic changes of the era. Benjamin F. Capps produced a series of novels, masterfully written, that dealt with the frontier Southwest. *Hanging at Comanche Wells* (1962), *The Trail to Ogallah* (1964), and others focused on the Plains Indians and the Anglo conquest. His portraits of Native Americans treated them as equals; there was no condescension in his work. Capps wrote about the time and place where his roots lay. He saw in the conflicts of the plains a microcosm of the human predicament, but he did not write about the cities, where many of his readers lived.[50] The only major novel about urban life in the Southwest in the 1950s, Madison Cooper's *Sironia, Texas,* won the Houghton-Mifflin Literary Award and, when published at 1,730 pages, was one of the longest works of fiction in modern times. Working for eleven years in the third-floor turret of his home, the author drafted a narrative about life in Waco ("Sironia") between 1900 and 1920. The Texas equivalent of Sinclair Lewis's *Main Street,* Cooper's novel *Sironia, Texas* sold 25,000 copies in a few months and then disappeared.[51] Although Cooper maintained that Sironia was a southern—not western—city, and indeed the social satire in the novel ridicules the snobbishness and pomposity of families who identified with the Old South, not the Southwest, longtime residents of Waco could identify many people, places, and events found in the novel.[52]

The absence of novels about industrialization, urbanization, and politics—an absence lamented by Texas critics—was felt across the region. One of the greatest changes in the Southwest was the oil boom from Texas to California, and it found no voice. Instead, the rest of the nation saw Texas on the pages of Edna Ferber's *Giant*. Allegedly Ferber, on a flight from New York to Los Angeles, sent a message to the pilot as they passed over the Lone Star State:

CULTURE *in the* AMERICAN SOUTHWEST

"Please fly a little lower; I want to write a book about Texas."[53] Critics and Texans saw her popular novel as misguided and misinformed.

The enormous ferment in the region simply escaped literary notice for decades. Short-story writers later spoke of the young people who abandoned the farms and ranches and fled to the cities seeking fulfillment, culture, and the opportunity to move beyond Herefords and wheat fields. In the funny and perceptive story "My Brother Is a Cowboy," Carolyn Osborn's heroine, Gay Lane, escapes the family ranch to go to San Antonio, where she joins the opera chorus and meets her husband at a rehearsal of *La Traviata*.[54] John Graves captured the end of the range-cattle industry in "The Last Running" when the aged rancher Tom Bird exclaims to his great-nephew: "Damn you, boy. . . . Damn you for not ever getting to know anything worth knowing. Damn me, too. We had a world once."[55] But there were constants. The poet William Goyen celebrated the coming of spring and the land in a prose poem written at Spud Johnson's house at Placita, New Mexico: "In the morning the little river was clear and sprightly and glisting in the sunlight like a polished silver collar round the neck of our little village."[56]

The land remained overwhelming, especially to easterners such as Joseph Wood Krutch. Drama editor for *The Nation,* Columbia University professor, naturalist, and ecologist, Krutch came to the Sonoran desert each summer for many years before constructing a home in Tucson in 1952. He "felt the lifting of the heart" in the desert, and his books *The Desert Year* and *The Voice of the Desert* graphically portrayed its flora and fauna. For Krutch, "a new, undreamed of world was revealed" in the Southwest.[57] But the very qualities that he found appealing were under siege by urban sprawl and the exploitation of the desert peoples. His constants were sun, aridity, and the land: "Life is everywhere precarious, man everywhere small."[58]

The philosophical truths that Krutch discovered in the desert differed marginally from those discovered by the only significant urban writers of the period: James M. Cain and Raymond Chandler. From the mid-1930s to the late 1940s, Cain and Chandler chronicled the life of Los Angeles in hard-hitting novels that displayed a strong sense of cynicism about life in general and urban society in particular. They saw Los Angeles as a city based on the automobile, a city filled with restless people constantly on the move. It was a "department store city" in a department store West. "The most of everything, the best of nothing," wrote Chandler.[59] Cain's *Double Indemnity, The Postman Always Rings Twice,* and *Mildred Pierce* revealed a Los Angeles of seedy, mean streets." Staccato dialogue, strong language, and stories of adultery and questionable business ethics filled Chandler's pages, as did tainted money and violence. Chandler's *Farewell My*

Lovely contended that these traits spilled over into small-town California. The novels by both authors contained detailed descriptions of Los Angeles—its architecture, home designs, fashions, businesses, parks, and the transit system. The books were anchored in time and place with "the open road," a metaphor for freedom. Cain and Chandler saw a Los Angeles in love with speeding cars, joy rides, and escapism by automobile. Scene after scene took place on the Pacific Coast Highway. Landscape set the mood for these novels, a mood that would continue in the works of Joan Didion and others. The character Mildred Pierce gains control of her life by racing down the highway and watching the speedometer needle rise even as Chandler's Philip Marlow ruminates in his car about crime, criminals, and the city. The fluidity of the society, the movement across the land, and Los Angeles as the shattered "Golden West" dream provided themes for both Cain and Chandler. Their novels about the urban Southwest stood alone for almost twenty years. They pioneered the genre and showed the importance of the city in the region.[60] Yet even with the urban decadence, Chandler wrote: "I'll take the big, sordid, dirty city."[61]

That "dirty city" also served as the home for a rising artistic movement in the Southwest: abstract expressionism. The abstract expressionists emphasized color, design, rhythm, and application, without concern for specific or recognizable objects. The concept came from Europe to the United States in the 1930s as some of its leading practitioners fled fascism. Those painters who lived in the Southwest and adopted abstract expressionism as a style rarely revealed a true sense of place. Even the painters who turned to a world of things—a style known as "assemblage"—failed to identify their found objects with the region. An assemblage accumulated and rearranged reality, but that reality did not have a geographical base. Los Angeles art galleries frequently offered art not unlike that found in New York, an art without a sense of belonging.[62]

Max Ernst and Adolph Gottlieb stand as major exceptions to this trend. Ernst reached the United States in 1941, a refugee from Germany. Having read of the American West as a child, he wanted to see the Southwest, which he visited for the first time in 1943. An abstract expressionist with an eye for form and spatial relationships, Ernst was unprepared for the vastness of the region and for the impact of Native American art. At a ranch near Sedona, Arizona, he saw the "exuberance of the colours," the Ponderosa pines, and the very shape of the rocks as images for his work. The Hopi people fascinated him, as did their concepts of art. In 1946 he returned to Sedona, built a cabin, and began to paint the land. "There I found once again the landscape which had always been in my mind and which is to be found time and time again in my early pictures."[63] *Phases of the Night,* painted that first year, contained landscape elements, masks, and personal

CULTURE *in the* AMERICAN SOUTHWEST

mystical pieces. Over the next fifteen years Ernst's geological fantasies mixed the rugged terrain of central Arizona with a mysterious spiritual view of nature.[64]

Gottlieb, a native New Yorker, came to Arizona only briefly, but that short visit altered his abstract concepts. A winter and spring spent in Tucson in 1938 found him initially unable to paint. For Gottlieb, being out in the desert was like being at sea. He gave up trying to paint landscapes and turned to still life, using desert plants as inspirations. He juxtaposed a cactus with a watermelon to symbolize the aridity of the desert, for example. Slowly he began to paint the desert itself. "I think I've got the hang of landscape at last," he wrote.[65] As a consequence of his Arizona experience, Gottlieb shifted dramatically from subjects of social realism to questions about nature, and his work became even more abstract. When his New York colleagues commented on the change in his art, Gottlieb responded, "I simply felt that the themes I found in the Southwest required a different approach from what I had used before."[66]

The land and its people shaped the art of both those who came *from* the Southwest and those who came *to* the region. The abstract painter Beatrice Mandelman and her husband, Louis Ribak, moved to Taos from New York in 1944. A social realist who switched to abstraction after seeing Russian constructivism, Mandelman came from the intellectual world of German and Austrian Jewish leftists. But even with such a background, her art reflected the impact of the Southwest. "I've always been a nature lover. I've always been interested in prehistory, Chaco Canyon, Canyon de Chelly, Mesa Verde, the mystery of the land and sky, and the light of Taos . . . that's what it's all about. How does one relate to this vast, vast emptiness of the landscape?"[67]

Four Texas abstract expressionists of the 1950s shared some of Mandelman's concerns even as they gained critical acclaim in New York. Exhibited in leading galleries along with Jackson Pollock, Mark Rothko, and Robert Motherwell, three of these Texans — Forrest Bess, Joseph Glasco, and Ben L. Culwell — were vanguard artists in the 1940s and 1950s who incorporated regional motifs into their paintings.[68] The fourth Texas artist, Coreen Mary Spellman, brought elements of precisionism to her abstractions, which had sharply focused detail. "I feel that my best work is that concerning my own environment. I am definitely of Texas and the Southwest of which I am a part."[69]

While abstract expressionism and assemblages entered the art life of the region in a modest way, the average southwesterner tended to label such works a "hunk of junk." The city of Dallas built a new public library in 1955, and the architect George Dahl commissioned Harry Bertoia to design a huge mural in the form of a metallic sculpture of gilded steel. When it was installed, Mayor Robert L. Thornton denounced the work of the famous sculptor: "It looks to me like a bunch of junk painted up." Under siege by the Dallas City Council, the mural was taken down. The *New York Times* and art journals derided the city. When an Abilene banker offered to purchase the mural, an embarrassed Thornton agreed to its reinstallation if private funds paid for the mural. Bertoia's work became a symbol of the rejection of abstract art. Similarly, the Dallas Museum of Fine Arts came under significant pressure from reactionaries to remove paintings by Pablo Picasso, Diego Rivera, and other contemporary artists who were seen as leftists or communists. These paintings came down, but later the museum board quietly put them back up on the gallery walls.[70]

Texans and other southwesterners generally preferred traditional, representational art such as that produced by Peter Hurd, Henriette Wyeth Hurd, and Tom Lea. Born on the plains of New Mexico in 1904, Peter Hurd grew up singing *vaquero* songs. He attended New Mexico Military Institute and then West Point. After failing mathematics, he transferred to Haverford College. Hurd studied painting with Nathaniel C. Wyeth and at the Pennsylvania Academy of Fine Arts. As a student of Wyeth's, he met the artist's daughter, Henriette, whom he married. After seven years in the East, Hurd returned to the Hondo Valley of southeastern New Mexico, where he painted the land and its people. A realist who chose the common people for portraits, Hurd also painted the environment around his ranch at San Patricio. He gave his neighbors dignity, and he found beauty in their lives.[71] Hurd explained: "It is the huge accident of weather, light, the shapes of the land and the happenstance of what people look like, that makes the beauties which we see in nature."[72]

Deeply influenced by his surroundings, Hurd discovered an array of subjects. He noted, "Here everything is drama. . . . If the effects of light and vapor and water seem infinite in their variety of mood, so does the terrain."[73] His portraits and landscapes in egg tempera received widespread praise not only for their delicacy of technique but also for their depth of feeling. When painting, Hurd drove out on the plains and read books of history about the region. The magnificence of the sky and thunderstorms sweeping across the plains reminded him of "avenging angels in a renaissance painting."[74]

Hurd had some doubts about bringing Henriette, a sensitive eastern painter, to New Mexico, but she too found inspiration. "I loved this valley immediately. The Southwest gave me a whole new language — new vistas to paint."[75] She wrote to her parents: "This place is excitingly and brilliantly beautiful, the air so curiously clear and sterescopic [*sic*]. White very *Wyeth* clouds float over the hills in a pulsating blue, and you feel you can touch them, pull them down. . . . I want to paint it — I am surprised at myself for having this urge, which grows stronger each hour."[76] On the 2,500 acres of Sentinel Ranch she found a land that reminded her of southern Spain. Despite deep roots in New England, the Southwest of "Petey" Hurd became her land too. For Henriette, art was like a religious quest, for the studio was her church. "You must become part of what you are doing," she said. Her portraits and landscapes reflected her life in the Hondo Valley.[77] The National Academy of Art recognized her work, her style, and the universality of her subject matter.[78]

Like the Hurds, Tom Lea used a traditional, representational style to paint the region he knew so well. Recognized as much for his books as for his art, Lea accomplished significant achievements in both fields. *The Brave Bulls* (1949), *The Wonderful Country* (1952), and *The Hands of Cantu* (1964) won him honors as a writer. He illustrated many books with drawings that emphasized the vast scale of the land and a sense of history and place. As a teenager, Lea had studied art in Chicago and Paris, and he later painted in Santa Fe and in his hometown of El Paso. There he found his place: "It has always seemed to me that I was fortunate in being born on the border in a town where two nations and two peoples meet, where more than one mode of life and one mode of thought are in constant confrontation to test and to broaden and to deepen one's view of the world."[79] But why paint the Southwest? "First I say I was born in it, then I say, furthermore I love it for the intensity of its sunlight, the clarity of its sky, hugeness of its space, its revealed structure of naked earth's primal form, without adornment."[80] Lea brought a sensitivity for the land and its history to his representational art.

Interestingly, even as the traditionalists of the Southwest found buyers and acclaim for their paintings, the landscapes of the region's cities were being altered with the creation of major art museums filled with paintings often far removed from the styles of the Hurds and Tom Lea. The artist, writer, and critic Walter Pach's state-by-state guide to art museums in 1948 made it clear how far the Southwest lagged at the outset of the postwar era. Arizona and Oklahoma were not even listed; New Mexico had a one-sentence entry for museums in Santa Fe; California and Texas had several brief statements about museums in Los Angeles, San Diego, Dallas, Fort Worth, Houston, and San Antonio. Detroit, Toledo, Boston, and other cities in the East and Midwest received extended treatments.[81] If a similar survey had been published twenty years later, readers would have discovered that a virtual boom in art museums in the Southwest had occurred, part of a national trend that saw more than 320 museums constructed between 1941 and 1969. As early as the mid-1950s, when the French writer André Malraux toured the United States, he was asked if he agreed with the British author Rebecca West's statement that America's cathedrals were its railway stations. "No," he responded quickly, "her cathedrals are her museums."[82] The construction of "art palaces" for the masses after 1945 saw more museums built in California than in all of western Europe.[83] In the Southwest, new art monuments rose at a breathtaking pace. The confluence of economic expansion and urban growth and, more important, a determination to demonstrate cultural maturation led to the employment of the art museum as a civic artifact, a symbol of regional development.

Civic leaders directed efforts to build art museums designed by internationally acclaimed architects in order to demonstrate that the region was not a cultural backwater. As Earl Powell, the director of the Los Angeles County Museum of Art, noted: "Here it has to do with the growth of the city. Cultural development follows economic development."[84] Southwesterners became convinced that civilization indeed was the art of living in cities. No longer should the leadership of a southwestern city be forced to apologize for its community while visiting New York or entertaining potential investors from abroad. If a southwestern city had a new, expansive, and expensive art museum designed by a prestigious international architect and filled with recently acquired major pieces paid for at extraordinary prices, it would be the equal of any metropolis. The cities of the region labored to create symbols of cultural adornment, with the hope of being accepted into the realm of mature urban centers.[85]

Art museum architecture influenced the appearance of entire communities as it came to represent a concrete example of urban cultural aspirations. The landscape altered dramatically as museum trustees found glamour in commissioning architects of world prominence to design buildings underscoring the community's economic success and cultural attainments. As one cynic noted, "A provincial city anxious to attract tourists will not go wrong by commissioning a leading architect to design an art museum."[86] Leaders of southwestern cities built upon museums established before World War II for these new examples of the "edifice complex," but these cultural jewels dwarfed their antecedents in size and quality. The scale of construction and the boldness of design reflected both the affluence and the naiveté of the region's cultural benefactors.[87]

Before World War II, the major art repositories in the Southwest ranged from Henry Huntington's treasure trove in San Marino to budding museums in Dallas and Houston. The San Diego Fine Arts Gallery, the Philbrook Art Center in Tulsa, and the McNay Art Museum in San Antonio represented core facilities around which significant collections could be built. Again, women played major roles in formulating art museums, as they had in other cultural endeavors — Alice Bemis Taylor in Colorado Springs, Millicent Rogers in Taos, and the Putnam sisters in San Diego. In city after city throughout the Southwest, individual benefactors left a personal stamp on collections and entire museums. The region

CULTURE *in the* AMERICAN SOUTHWEST

would ultimately have a number of "vanity museums" as a consequence of a combination of generosity and ego. But the region also was home to major institutions produced by groups with members from across the community.

One of these major institutions was begun in 1900 when five women in Houston began to collect reproductions of famous paintings to be circulated in the public schools. By 1913, the social leader Corinne Abercrombie Waldo had persuaded the developer George Hermann to donate the site for a museum, and a fund-raising drive began for a building. The women in the Houston Art League collected money and pledges for the museum even as they solicited donations of original works of art. The architect William Ward Watkins, who had come to Houston to supervise the building of Rice Institute for its Bostonian architect Ralph Adams Cram, won the commission to design the Houston Museum of Fine Arts. He selected a Beaux Arts Revival style not unlike that of museums recently built in Detroit and Toledo. Watkins produced drawings for a small structure with eight Ionic columns and a narrow loggia across the facade. The symmetrical design called for two splayed wings extending on either side. Construction of the central portion was completed in 1924, and Will C. Hogg, brother of "Miss Ima Jane," raised the money for the wings, which were added two years later. Thus Houston had a small traditional art museum that acquired an eclectic collection of paintings and sculpture. But by the 1950s, civic pride and cultural aspirations demanded much more.[88]

Houston, wanting to be on the cutting edge, chose as its design model the Museum of Modern Art in New York City, with its International Style facade. In 1954, the Houston museum hired Ludwig Mies van der Rohe to expand its facility. The most famous architect in the world after Frank Lloyd Wright, Mies sought to find a place to employ his concepts of an art museum. As early as 1942 he had advocated that the structure should have glass walls and a vast open space to provide maximum flexibility. Curators should shape the interior volume, he said. Mies proposed to fill the area between the Houston museum's wings with one vast space: a pie-shaped addition with a curving glass wall thirty-three feet high. A successful fund-raising drive by the city's leaders and foundations funded Cullinan Hall, the first stage of Mies's plan. The curving gray-glass wall dominated an enormous room that dwarfed the art it contained. The old Grecian portico of 1924 became the museum's back door as visitors instead entered the new addition.[89] Critics condemned the overpowering vastness of Cullinan Hall, and when the Brown Pavilion opened in 1974 the negative chorus sang even louder. The Pavilion, designed to hold the European art collection, enveloped Cullinan Hall with a new curving glass wall three hundred feet long.

Mies's rigorous rationalism and concept of universal space proved controver-

sial, but the architect was not concerned: "It is such a huge hall that of course it means great difficulties for the exhibiting of art. I am fully aware of that. But it has such potential that I simply cannot take those difficulties into account."[90] Though shocked by the critical assaults on their new cultural jewel, Houston boosters and art patrons marched forward to fill the city with buildings in the International Style. Miesian-influenced office towers, apartment buildings, and even churches quickly spread across the city.

While Houston constructed its first art museum in the 1920s, a building of totally different architectural style rose in San Diego and soon housed a marvelous collection of European art, thanks to the Putnam sisters. In the 1920s, the growing city of San Diego wanted to create in Balboa Park an art museum that would harmonize architecturally with the buildings designed by Bertram Goodhue for the 1915 Panama-California Exposition. The local architects William Templeton Johnson and Robert W. Snyder designed the San Diego Fine Arts Gallery in the Spanish Colonial style, with a two-story stone-and-stucco facade and a balanced entrance rotunda. Neo-Plateresque details around the entrance were both ornate and delicate.

The museum emerged as one of the region's finest buildings, and it soon displayed a marvelous collection. The Putnam family had arrived in San Diego in 1913 and soon prospered in real estate, hardware, and banking. The sisters Anne, Irene, and Amy Putnam grew up in a reclusive environment of private education in the classics. After the sisters inherited the family's holdings, the San Diego Museum of Art (the facility's new name) began to receive anonymous gifts of European Old Master paintings. Throughout the 1930s, the museum director Reginald Poland hung outstanding works by Goya, El Greco, Titian, Vandyke, Reubens, and Rembrandt on the walls of the museum. He knew the identity of the benefactors, of course, and arranged for them to visit the galleries at night to see "their" paintings. Taking advantage of the horrific conditions in Europe in the 1930s and 1940s, the Putnam sisters sent a virtual flood of Spanish Baroque, Italian Renaissance, and Dutch Old Master paintings to Poland, but when the director retired in 1950, the flood receded. The sisters continued to purchase art but loaned it to the Metropolitan Museum of Art, the National Gallery of Art, and other museums. Fearful that the collection would be lost, the San Diego Museum built a new, jewel-box-like building to house only the Putnams' paintings. The Timkin Gallery became a monument to the sisters, who gave San Diego an international reputation with one of the nation's finest collections of European art.[91]

The Dallas Museum of Fine Arts did not gain a collection comparable to that in San Diego, but it did acquire a new museum as part of the Texas Centennial of 1936. The fledgling art museum at Fair Park had garnered a solid collection of art in the 1920s and 1930s, but its location and limited facilities inhibited growth and patronage. By the late 1920s, the museum's board of directors included representatives of the city's leading families. They hired a new director, brought in touring exhibitions, and when the city decided to build new buildings for the centennial, they made sure the plan included a new art museum. Bonds in the amount of $500,000 were sold, and an association of architects, with Paul Cret of Philadelphia as consultant, produced a simple Art Deco building of straight lines and smooth walls. A rectangle of Cordova cream stone, the museum faced a small lake. The architects fulfilled their charge to create a functional building that allowed the works of art to be seen without architectural interference. A blockbuster show of over six hundred works of art filled the air-conditioned museum when it opened. Over the next two decades the museum hosted exhibitions of art from Latin America and Europe even as it acquired a larger and more distinguished collection of its own. Acquisition fund drives and donations of art created a holding that ranged from American Impressionism to modernists such as Jackson Pollock and Alexander Calder. By the time Mrs. Eugene McDermott became president of the museum in 1961, the rate of acquisi-

FIGURE 36
*In addition to collecting exquisite
examples of Native American arts
and crafts, Millicent Rogers also
dyed her own velvet. Courtesy
Millicent Rogers Museum
Archives.*

tions had accelerated to the point that the facility, even with a new wing, was no longer adequate. Agitation began for a new building, preferably in the heart of the city—a goal that would be achieved in the next decade.[92]

Like the art museums in San Diego, Colorado Springs, and Houston, the Millicent Rogers Museum in Taos owes much to a woman and her sense of beauty. The museum celebrates the connoisseurship of Millicent Rogers, granddaughter of the Standard Oil partner Henry H. Rogers. Tall, elegant, and sophisticated, Rogers was a high-society debutante in the Jazz Age. Married and divorced three times, she moved to California to escape New York. A friend, the actress Janet Gaynor, asked Rogers to join her on a journey to New Mexico, and Rogers fell in love with the region. She moved to Taos and began to purchase Native American jewelry, pottery, blankets, and baskets. Long known for her excellent taste, Rogers bought only the highest-quality items and soon possessed an outstanding collection. She filled her adobe home with the very best arts of the Southwest. After her death in 1953, the Rogers family formed the museum, whose holdings reflected Rogers's keen mind and intellectual bent. The collec-

CULTURE *in the* AMERICAN SOUTHWEST

tion showed the aesthetic emergence of a multicultural society, the goal Millicent Rogers had set.[93]

Not surprisingly, a woman was also the founder of an art museum in Phoenix. In 1895, Dwight B. Heard and Maie Bartlett Heard had arrived in Phoenix; he came from Boston, she from a prominent Chicago family, and together they raised the cultural level of the city and Arizona. She soon operated a "bookmobile," distributing books to ranching families from her buggy. She helped organize the Little Theater and encouraged local artists. An inveterate world traveler, Maie Heard collected crafts from many countries. After Dwight Heard's death in 1929, she moved to establish a museum for Phoenix. She had the firm of Green and Hall design a Spanish Colonial building for the museum, and for the next two decades she filled it with Native American arts and crafts, some 75,000 objects. After her death in 1951, the Heard Museum continued to expand, adding the Barry Goldwater collection of Hopi Kachinas and the Fred Harvey Fine Arts Collection. By the 1980s, some 300,000 visitors were coming each year to see one of the largest holdings of Native American arts and crafts in the country. Maie Heard left her adopted city and state a major legacy that could not be duplicated.[94]

Marion Koogler McNay shared the enthusiasm of Maie Heard and Millicent Rogers for Native American and Spanish Colonial arts and crafts, but she moved far beyond the Southwest in her quest to acquire the beautiful in painting and sculpture. The daughter of a Kansas physician, she studied painting in Chicago and was captivated by the exhibit of the Armory Show at the Art Institute in 1913. Subsequently she married a Texas doughboy ten years her junior and moved to San Antonio, where she remained after her husband's death during World War I. The discovery of oil on her father's lands in Kansas gave her the resources to collect art for thirty years. She studied art in Taos and was briefly married to a New Mexico painter, but McNay expanded her holdings beyond the region. She commissioned Atlee B. Ayres and Robert M. Ayres to design a Spanish Revival home for her in San Antonio. Built to showcase her collection, gallery-like rooms surrounded an enclosed patio and pool. One of the leading architectural firms in the region, Ayres and Ayres created a delightful home that McNay transformed into an enchanting museum. A discriminating collector, McNay filled her home with outstanding examples of French Impressionist and post-Impressionist paintings. Her virile tastes were revealed in the house, its arrangement, and its art treasures. After her death in 1950, the collection formed the heart of a museum boasting works by Renoir, Cézanne, Gauguin, and Picasso, as well as American watercolors, prints, and drawings. McNay left the

FIGURE 37
In Taos, New Mexico, Marion Koogler McNay painted, studied, and collected art for her home and future museum. Courtesy the McNay Art Museum Library and Archives, San Antonio, Texas.

home, the collection, and an endowment to acquire more paintings to the city of San Antonio. Subsequent additions to the museum and gifts from San Antonio collectors formed a diverse collection of high quality. The museum and surrounding gardens stand as a monument to McNay and her generosity.[95]

Other twentieth-century Medicis in the Southwest included the Oklahoma oilmen Waite Phillips and Thomas Gilcrease, who created entirely different, but complementary, museums in Tulsa. Southwestern entrepreneurs collected art the same way they acquired business enterprises—that is, with determination and zeal for gaining a prize—and they often had resources to purchase art at times when others could not. Their wealth allowed them a means of self-expression and later provided the basis for gifts that guaranteed a kind of immortality. Some, like Phillips, donated their homes for a museum. Private egos and federal tax laws favored the creation of these "art palaces." As one critic wrote, "People who live in palace-museums don't need them. People who don't, do."[96]

The conversion of Phillips's mansion into the Philbrook Art Center in Tulsa created a museum with a diverse holding of European and American art. The cofounder of Phillips Petroleum Company, Phillips hired the Kansas City architect Edward B. Delk to design an Italian Renaissance villa on twenty-three acres of land in southern Tulsa. Trained in the academic style, Delk produced a man-

FIGURE 38

*Marion Koogler McNay's Spanish Colonial Revival home in San Antonio became
a treasury of European and southwestern art and sculpture. Author's collection.*

sion of brilliant-white stucco with limestone trim. Oversized Italian tiles on the
roof, loggias, and terraces established the tone. Phillips lived in the house for a
decade, filling it with art until he donated it as a museum in 1938. The Philbrook
Art Center received additional bequests, leading to subsequent expansions of
the facility, but its regal European character remained unblemished. The architecture of Philbrook had a significant impact on housing designs in Tulsa, but
more important, Phillips's generosity gave the city a major art museum.[97]

Thomas Gilcrease also lavished affection and great wealth on art and manuscripts, but for a very different purpose. His vast collection of American art,
manuscripts, books, and Native American artifacts did not laud the Anglo conquest of the frontier but celebrated the cultures of both societies. The quiet and
unassuming Gilcrease, born in Louisiana in 1890, later moved with his parents
to Indian Territory. One-eighth Creek Indian, Gilcrease obtained an allotment
of tribal lands that was located in the heart of the Glen Pool oil field, near Tulsa.
By 1917 more than thirty wells on his farm formed the basis for a major fortune.
He used his wealth to purchase petroleum production and exploration firms,
banks, and real estate. By the mid-1920s he had established an office in Europe
and made extensive tours of the continent. While in Paris, he decided to create a
collection of materials to record the history of the American Indian. He acquired

Nationalization of a Regional Culture

FIGURE 39
*The Italian Renaissance–style Philbrook Art Center looms over
the formal gardens behind the museum. Author's collection.*

manuscripts, books, and artifacts in the United States and Europe and soon owned an outstanding collection. He also began to purchase western American art, then available at very low prices in a market that denigrated its importance.[98]

Living briefly in San Antonio, Gilcrease exhibited his paintings but found little interest there. Discouraged, he returned to Tulsa and established the Thomas Gilcrease Institute of American History and Art in 1949. Gilcrease constructed a small, U-shaped building with quonset-hut beams forming a vault to span the space between the wings. The design suggested an Indian long-house. Employing Native American labor and using local sandstone, Gilcrease completed the museum and opened it to the public. He continued his program of acquisitions until he faced bankruptcy in 1953. With Gilcrease nearing financial collapse, the city of Tulsa moved to prevent the loss of his collection. It acquired Gilcrease's holdings and assumed responsibility for the museum. Later additions to the museum also used natural materials, and the ocher-sandstone exterior and the long-room vault of a 1987 expansion repeated the motif of the first structure, now absorbed into the core. The architecture did not overwhelm the art.[99] Although dealers thought Gilcrease eccentric, his good friend Frank Dobie called him "one of the islands of humanity." The art critic Thomas Hoving described the collection of 70,000 books, 300,000 artifacts, and thousands of paintings as "the most outstanding collection of American painting and Indian art in the country."[100] The repository Gilcrease created reflected his heritage and personality. The Southwest gained a significant museum because of his connoisseurship.

Similar private collections were housed in southern California, but the city of Los Angeles failed to appreciate them and for decades let major holdings disappear at auctions or watched as benefactors donated art to museums elsewhere. The stream of German and Austrian exiles and British expatriots to Los Angeles in the 1930s and 1940s created a substantial international colony. The composers Arnold Schoenberg and Igor Stravinsky, the conductors Bruno Walter and Otto Klemperer, the playwright Berthold Brecht, the writer Christopher Isherwood, the novelists Aldous Huxley and Erich Maria Remarque, the film director Josef von Sternberg, and others brought with them paintings of enormous cultural worth. Remarque owned works by Cézanne, Delacroix, Degas, and Utrillo, to name a few. Sternberg came with a collection of German expressionist art.[101] Leading actors and actresses began to emulate the Europeans, and the actor Vincent Price soon opened an art gallery to stimulate this taste for "modern" art. In one day, visitors to his gallery included Huxley, the novelist Thomas Mann, and the composer/conductor/pianist Sergei Rachmaninoff.[102] Soon bankers, producers, developers, oilmen, and other community leaders made acquisitions as art galleries in New York and Los Angeles sold them American paintings, Barbizon School landscapes, European Old Masters, and post-Impressionist works. But the city lacked an art museum that could bring together such holdings. Efforts to create a separate art museum failed in 1938, and the public art collection remained in the vast polyglot holdings of the Los Angeles County Museum of History, Art, and Science. The result was a tragedy. After Aline Barnsdall died, her heirs sold and dispersed her collection of modern French art. Sternberg's holdings were sold at an auction in New York. The wealthy collectors Walter and Louise Arensberg offered their massive holding of modern art, mainly Cubism, to the county museum, but it was rejected as too avant-garde. The collection went to the Philadelphia Museum of Art. A nasty divorce prompted the actor Edward G. Robinson to place his collection of French Impressionist paintings on the market. When neither the museum nor local buyers showed interest, it was auctioned in New York. Paintings owned by the directors Hal Wallis and Billy Wilder were also lost.[103]

This roll call of disaster continued until the 1940s when William R. Valentiner, a new codirector for the art collection, arrived at the county museum. A German immigrant with a Teutonic personality, Valentiner had been with the Metropolitan Museum in New York, where he worked with J. P. Morgan, and at the Detroit Institute of the Arts, where he served as director from 1924 to 1945. Arriving in Los Angeles in 1946, he quickly established a relationship with William Randolph Hearst, boding well for the museum. Preston Harrison had been the art museum's main benefactor until his death in 1940, giving the collection a number of pieces of American art.[104] Now Hearst became the major source of support. Through the Hearst Foundation, the Hearst Corporation, and the publisher himself, the museum acquired classical sculptures, paintings by Rembrandt, Vandyke, Reubens, Veronese, Fragonard, and others, and an acquisitions fund established by Hearst. The Hearst Fund filled gaps as the museum built a comprehensive collection. Paintings from the Italian and Spanish Baroque joined the Hearst decorative arts holdings. After retiring from the museum, Valentiner continued as a consultant, obtaining gifts from J. Paul Getty and other Los Angeles collectors.[105]

Not until 1961 was the goal of a separate art museum realized in Los Angeles. But now that the directors of the museum faced the prospect of a new building, they began public bickering when each of the three major donors for the facility demanded that the new building be named for them. In a compromise, the architect William L. Pereira and his associates were directed to design three buildings on county-owned land near the La Brea tarpits. The absence of bedrock forced Pereira to use floating foundations, with gardens and pools between the buildings. The museum occupied the three pavilions in 1965, but the largest museum west of the Mississippi River proved inhospitable. The pools leaked oil from the tarpits and had to be filled in, and the building exteriors, said to be based on "commodity, firmness, and delight," were harshly criticized as "Hollywood Wedding Cakes." The screens of nonstructural columns created uncomfortably narrow porches that one critic called the "worst mistake of the 1960s." The new museum buildings failed in their chief purpose: they were not hailed by eastern critics as great architecture; indeed they were vilified. Local art patrons divided their loyalties and contributions, and the continued fighting led two major art collectors to create their own vanity museums.[106]

Thankfully, the Los Angeles Philharmonic did not suffer the same fate as the city's art museum. It and other orchestras in the region reached higher levels of maturity after World War II. The musical foundations laid during the Great Depression provided a basis for expanding the size of these professional orchestras and elevating the quality of musicianship. Civic pride, prosperity, and a desire for cultural recognition combined as orchestra associations sought leading conductors, recruited players, and planned elaborate new symphony halls. Snaring a well-known European conductor, importing internationally recognized soloists, and taking the orchestra on tour became major goals. Recording contracts

CULTURE *in the* AMERICAN SOUTHWEST

and opera productions enhanced the reputations of the orchestras and their communities. The cities of the Southwest determined to move their symphonies into the front rank.

No city made greater advances than Houston. From an ensemble of 35 musicians and a budget of $1,500 in 1913, the Houston Symphony Orchestra became a professional organization of 97 players with a budget of $7.5 million by the 1980s. In its early years, the symphony society served largely as the host for visiting orchestras, but between 1918 and 1931 substantial strides were made in improving the quality and in lengthening the season. Under the baton of Ernst Hoffmann from 1935 until 1947, the orchestra achieved full professional status. These gains were not made without crisis, however. Although concerts often attracted audiences of 2,000 or more, financial problems grew. The Houston Symphony Orchestra Association, aided by newspaper boosterism, tried to recruit 3,000 new members in the 1930s, with some degree of success. Oveta Culp Hobby, whose family owned a major newspaper, served as an officer of the association, as did the oilman H. R. Cullen; the president of Humble Oil Company held a vice presidency in the association. But even with such supporters, a crisis in 1940 almost took the orchestra under.[107] The orchestra needed $35,000, and the editor of the *Houston Post* took the city to task: "In matters artistic, Houston suffers from a blighting inferiority complex. It appears to have started when we had a self-conscious and overgrown town. . . . It is time to drop the bush league attitude. If the Houston Symphony Orchestra can free us from one of a lingering hick town character, it is worth ten times what it costs."[108] The community rallied to save the symphony, and within two years the annual budget reached $52,000.

During World War II the orchestra toured military bases and gave free concerts for civilians. H. R. Cullen led the effort to raise funds each year, and in 1944–45 he personally underwrote the $125,000 budget. His commitment reflected the influence of his spouse, Lillie Cullen, a longtime symphony supporter. But when H. R. had to write a personal check for $45,000 to cover a deficit, he resigned, and another crisis loomed. Ima Jane Hogg came to the rescue, as she had in the 1920s, and served as president of the society for a decade. She presided, negotiated, mediated, and donated. She worked with the business elite, society matrons, and conductors. When the Hungarian conductor Ferenc Fricsay quit in midseason, she obtained the services of Sir Thomas Beecham to finish the concerts. Then, in a stroke of genius and audacity, she recruited the legendary Leopold Stokowski as the conductor.[109]

Stokowski made the orchestra a first-rate symphony between 1955 and 1961. He broadened the repertoire, added outstanding musicians, and charmed the community. During his six-year tenure, Stokowski was determined to carry out a goal: "I see in Houston the possibility of building one of the great orchestras of the world."[110] He premiered new works, obtained a recording contract, and had the old Music Hall rebuilt while a new auditorium, Jones Hall, was under construction. But in 1960, when he wanted to use the all African American choir from Texas Southern University for Arnold Schoenberg's *Gurrelieder*, the symphony board said no, and he left. Racism precluded efforts to build the world-class orchestra Stokowski had envisioned. Nevertheless, the leaders of the symphony continued his quest by hiring Sir John Barbirolli as his replacement. Sir John built on the work of his predecessor, took the orchestra on tour, and persuaded the symphony society to increase the budget.[111] By the end of the 1960s, Houston had one of the nation's leading orchestras.

Elsewhere in Texas, the San Antonio Symphony owed its birth to a European émigré and its maturation to a young, native-born Texan. Dr. Max Reiter, an Austrian refugee, arrived in New York in 1938, learned English, and with money borrowed from the Jewish Relief Fund bought a bus ticket to Texas. Hearing that there was a need for trained musicians in the Southwest, he sought a job first in Waco and then in San Antonio. Armed with a suitcase filled with newspaper clippings, he met Pauline Washer Goldsmith, San Antonio's musical leader. Charmed by the thirty-three-year-old Reiter, she guaranteed a concert, and he organized a program played at the Sunken Garden Theater. He recruited musicians from across the region, and the concert received a great response. Goldsmith arranged for funds to guarantee a full season, and the San Antonio Symphony was launched. Reiter built the orchestra using European refugees as guests; he recruited professional musicians from Dallas, Houston, and Waco; and he offered traditional programming. He used his prewar contacts to bring musicians such as Jascha Heifetz to San Antonio. During the second year some 3,600 season tickets were sold, and by 1943 Reiter had moved to create a full, professional symphony. Adroit at booking guests who generated audiences, he brought Grace Moore and Jeanette McDonald to the city to sold-out concerts. For eight years Reiter and the symphony were one. He gained national recognition with stories in *Time* and *Newsweek* and praise from Arturo Toscanini. Reiter organized the San Antonio Opera Festival in 1945, presenting Grace Moore in *La Bohéme*. The festival also offered *Cavalleria Rusticana* and *Pagliacci*. Intense civic pride emerged, and Reiter responded with Risë Stevens and other leading singers in productions of *Aïda, Carmen,* and *La Traviata.*[112]

When Reiter died in 1950, San Antonio music lovers feared the worst, but the Symphony Society recruited the young Victor Alessandro, conductor of the Oklahoma City Symphony, to replace their beloved maestro. Alessandro's great

CULTURE *in the* AMERICAN SOUTHWEST

success in Oklahoma had brought him to the attention of the San Antonio Symphony. From 1951 until 1976, he moved beyond the repertoire developed by Reiter and gained even greater recognition for the orchestra. He continued to use major names in the operas and also experimented, premiering Verdi's *Nabucco* a year before a Metropolitan Opera production. The Symphony Society generated one of the largest budgets in the region, reaching $530,000 in 1963–64. Special fund-raising efforts covered the small annual deficits. As early as 1950, the guest conductor Dimitri Mitropoulos said, "This orchestra can compete with any orchestra in this country or Europe." Sir Thomas Beecham also praised Reiter's efforts to build a major symphony.[113] Under Alessandro, the orchestra offered diverse programming that appealed to the city's multicultural community. He presented programs that included German composers as well as music from Mexico and South America. During his twenty-five-year career in the city, the orchestra became the central cultural asset of San Antonio.

Meanwhile the Dallas Symphony Orchestra — a victim of deficits, lost personnel, and little community support — suspended operations after 1942. The Dallas banker D. Gordon Rupe, Jr., decided to relaunch the orchestra, and in 1945 he sold 150 founder memberships at $1,000 each and 1,000 regular memberships at $100 each. With these funds, he hired Antal Dorati as conductor, and three months later eighty-three musicians presented the first concert. Dorati opened the season with Beethoven's *Eroica,* and soon the personable, energetic conductor had a recording contract with RCA Victor. He created a broad repertoire that often included contemporary music; a performance of Stravinsky's *Le Sacre du Printemps,* a modernist composition, created a controversy that took months to calm. For seven seasons Dorati raised the quality of the orchestra and the musical tastes of symphony supporters. The budget rose to $200,000, then climbed again. The music critic John Rosenfield of the *Dallas Morning News* praised the conductor and his programming in this audience-building effort.[114] When a financial crisis loomed in 1951, two years after Dorati left to become the conductor of the Minneapolis Symphony Orchestra, the banker R. L. Thornton led a successful effort to save the symphony. But Dallas still had a long way to travel. As Thornton himself commented: "I think a symphony is a good thing for the town, and I am for it. I'll do anything for it but go to hear it."[115] The symphony survived the crisis. Though one writer suggested that Dallas had "undertaken to become the Athens of the alfalfa fields, the cultural capital of the Southwest," the city did desire quality music.[116] A series of short-lived contracts with conductors produced a revolving door over the next decade until the arrival of Eduardo Mata in 1977 returned stability and brought aspirations for greatness.

Smaller cities in the region also saw their orchestras take major strides immediately after the war ended. The Oklahoma City Symphony Orchestra had hired Victor Alessandro as its conductor in 1938, and for thirteen years he built the organization. Warm and charming, Alessandro took a mixed group of professionals and amateurs and created an orchestra that played on programs for the National Broadcasting System and the Voice of America. When he resigned to go to San Antonio, the symphony hired Guy Fraser Harrison of the Rochester Civic Orchestra. Born in England and a graduate of the Royal Academy of Music, Harrison used a standard repertoire and guest artists to build an audience. For twenty-one years he conducted a symphony that toured the state and presented national radio broadcasts. Harrison and the orchestra also recorded prize-winning original compositions that gained critical praise.[117]

Although not organized until 1947, the Phoenix Symphony Orchestra became a significant factor in the cultural life of that city. Originally formed simply to provide a source of classical music, as Phoenix grew so did its ambitions for the orchestra. From a program of three concerts and 1,682 season tickets in a city of 87,000, the orchestra expanded to eight sold-out concerts each year and a budget in excess of $500,000, which funded musicians' contracts for twenty-six weeks. John Barnett led the orchestra initially, but the orchestra blossomed under Leslie Hodge (1952–59) and Eduardo Mata (1971–77). A Ford Foundation grant of $850,000, to be matched with $500,000 raised locally, established a firmer financial base. Internal controversies between the symphony's board and the conductors created administrative chaos, however, even though the symphony income rose to $420,000 by 1970–71 and to $1 million in 1976. Obviously, the principal fund-raising arm of the symphony, the Women's Guild, was successful in its primary responsibility. Not yet a major orchestra, largely because of internal problems, the symphony nevertheless improved in quality. In 1964 when the orchestra moved into Grady Gammage Auditorium, designed by Frank Lloyd Wright, attendance rose. But as some observers noted, retirees and "snowbirds" living in Phoenix often gave more money to orchestras in their former hometowns of Chicago, Cleveland, and Detroit than they did to the Phoenix Symphony.[118]

The Southwest witnessed an effort by smaller cities to form symphony orchestras that, though not made up entirely of professional musicians, brought quality classical music to their communities. From Lubbock, Texas, to La Jolla, California, orchestras appeared after 1945. The year after World War II ended, Lubbock created a "Little Symphony," soon dropping the "Little." The first concert brought 1,500 people to hear Grieg and Beethoven.[119] Corpus Christi acquired an orchestra in 1955, the same year that the East Texas Regional Symphony began to perform in Tyler, Longview, and Marshall.[120] The Bulgarian conductor Peter Nicoloff came to La Jolla in 1954 and formed a group that became the La Jolla Civic Orchestra. The season grew from one concert per year to four. After the University of California at San Diego added a music department in 1967, the number of professional musicians increased, and the orchestra began to offer programs of experimental music.[121] Indeed, throughout southern California, communities formed orchestras, often providing university faculty and students with opportunities to perform. Symphonies appeared in Claremont, Compton, Long Beach, Pasadena, Redlands, Riverside, Wittier, and the San Fernando Valley. They were often multiclass and multicultural in structure, offering an alternative to the Los Angeles Philharmonic. Conductors and players brought to these orchestras rich backgrounds in music from across the United States and Europe. Patrons who could not afford to attend the Philharmonic or who refused to drive into the city found quality music in their own communities.[122]

The Los Angeles Philharmonic Orchestra thrived under Otto Klemperer in the 1930s as émigré musicians augmented its ranks. The influx of immigrants to Los Angeles meant that young musicians could play with George Piatigorsky, Artur Rubinstein, Heifetz, and Stravinsky. After Klemperer's departure from the orchestra following the 1939–40 season, guest conductors such as Bruno Walter, Sir Thomas Beecham, Sir John Barbirolli, and Leopold Stokowski led the symphony. Alfred Wallenstein became the permanent conductor in 1943, and over the next thirteen years he produced a major symphony orchestra. Born in Chicago but raised in Los Angeles, Wallenstein transformed the organization, which offered an extensive repertoire in ninety concerts each season. He presented huge choral performances in association with the director Roger Wagner. At the same time, Wallenstein built an audience. When the Los Angeles Philharmonic played Beethoven's Ninth Symphony in Shrine Auditorium in 1958, 6,600 listeners filled the hall. Because of ill health, Wallenstein retired in 1959, and three years later Zubin Mehta moved the orchestra into the top ranks as a firm financial base and promises of a new concert hall brought even finer players to the symphony. Mehta's musicianship attracted international notice for himself and the Los Angeles Philharmonic, but ironically recognition came slowly in Los Angeles and California. After 1957–58, Californians led New Yorkers in financial support of the radio broadcasts of the New York Philharmonic.[123] The regional inferiority complex remained.

Los Angeles supported other music ventures, however. In 1939 Peter Yates and his spouse, the pianist Frances Mullen, founded "Monday Evening Concerts," a distinguished music series. Known as "Evenings on the Roof" after 1954, the series premiered many new compositions, and extraordinary musicians performed. Evenings were often devoted to one composer such as Béla Bartók, Charles Ives, Arnold Schoenberg, or Roy Harris. The Los Angeles County Museum of Art sponsored the concerts, which focused on modern music and celebrity artists. John Cage, Aaron Copland, Henry Cowell, and Paul Wittgenstein, the one-armed Viennese pianist, appeared in the series. Audiences grew from 100 seated on the second floor of the Yates home in 1939, to theaters, and then to an auditorium at the University of Southern California. The musicians included many of the principals from the Philharmonic, and the audience included literary figures, theatrical and film industry personalities, and a growing segment of the general public. The concerts attracted national notice by the 1950s.[124]

Also in the 1950s, John O'hea Crosby created the Santa Fe Opera, which brought additional international attention to the Southwest. Rudolph Bing, director of the Metropolitan Opera, dismissed Crosby's achievement with the snide question "Where is Santa Fe?" and with his own response: "There is no opera in America worth seeing outside of New York City." But he was wrong.[125] As a child, John Crosby had vacationed with his family in New Mexico. Because of ill health, he went to preparatory school in Los Alamos before going to Yale University and then Columbia University, where he studied conducting. The family-owned ranch brought him back to New Mexico after service in World War II; Crosby said New Mexico gave him a "sense of place."[126] Thirty years old, ambitious, and eager to produce opera, he created the Santa Fe Opera in 1956. In a natural amphitheater north of the community, with the audience seated on benches, he brought grand opera to a town of 30,000 people. Along with *Madam Butterfly* were operas by Richard Strauss and Stravinsky. With a budget of $100,000, Crosby built an audience. Half the funds came from the box office, the other half from local contributions. By 1967 the budget reached $400,000. When a fire swept through the opera site, a new facility arose within a year, and the opera reopened in 1968. *Time* magazine commented, "Santa Fe has shelled out for opera as though it were investing in big-league baseball."[127]

In this dramatic site, with the Jemez Mountains as a backdrop, the opera played before capacity houses to rave reviews. A bold repertoire became even more daring during the twenty-six years Crosby served as conductor. He introduced young singers, premiered operas written by composers from around the globe, and launched numerous careers in the process. In a theater of radical and innovative design, Crosby proved Rudolph Bing to be a poor geographer and an even poorer critic. By 1961 Santa Fe Opera productions were touring Europe, and the Berlin press hailed this "vital opera." Audiences came from across the United States and abroad to hear music in a venue with spectacular acoustics at 7,000 feet elevation.[128]

The nationalization of the culture of the Southwest included not only the development of major symphonies and the Santa Fe Opera but also the creation of music by one of the nation's leading composers, Roy Harris. Born in a log cabin on Lincoln's birthday in 1896, Harris grew up with the sounds of American music. From the farm his family homesteaded near Chandler in Oklahoma Territory, the Harrises moved to California. The family played and sang the songs of the frontier, music that became part of Harris's life. He played the clarinet and the piano, farmed in the San Gabriel Valley, served in World War I, and composed music at night. Harris entered the University of California as a special student and then in 1926 went to Paris to study composition aided by a Guggenheim Fellowship.

In 1929 Harris returned to the United States, where he became a major composer. Before he died in 1979, Harris had written sixteen symphonies and over two hundred other compositions. Though modern in concept, his music was effused with the songs of the Southwest.[129] *Johnny Comes Marching Home, Farewell to Pioneers, American Creed, Cimarron,* and *Symphony, 1933* were filled with "a mood of adventure and physical exuberance," he said.[130] The critic Paul Rosenfeld referred to him as an "awkward, serious young plainsman."[131] His *Symphony, 1933* and *Second Symphony* were well received, and his music was widely played in Europe. A Chicago critic noted that there was still "something of the crudeness and strength of pioneer America" in his compositions, which were "as completely outside European experience as the prairie morning itself."[132] Harris wrote, conducted, taught, and filled concert halls with music derived from the southwestern frontier. Like the composer Charles Ives, he heard the sound of his music as part of the American experience. Harris employed popular melodies, folk tunes, and jazz rhythms in an individualistic style. "A prophet from the Southwest," as one musicologist called him, the tall, lanky, rawboned Harris spoke in a "drawling Southwestern" idiom.[133] The *Folk Song Symphony* and others drew from the tunes his father had whistled in the fields on their farm. One of the most important figures in the establishment of American symphonic music, Harris understood his roots and their impact: "Our people are more than pleasure-loving. We also have qualities of heroic strength — determination — will to struggle — faith in our destiny. We are possessed of a fierce driving power — optimistic, young, rough and ready."[134] Harris brought the music of the region to the world in symphonic form. Sometimes difficult to listen to and often dissonant, his music compelled attention. In the 1940s and 1950s it made millions aware of the sounds of the American Southwest.

One of the most important regional contributions to the national culture after 1945 was the southwestern theater. Two women — Margo Jones and Nina

Vance—made Theater '47 and its successors in Dallas and the Alley Theater in Houston showcases for modern drama. They encouraged the early efforts of the playwrights Tennessee Williams, William Inge, Preston Jones, and Beth Henley. Creating and then employing the concept of the theater-in-the-round, or arena theater, they influenced not only the Mummers Theater in Oklahoma City but also the Arena Stage in Washington, D.C., and The Circle in the Square in New York City. Indeed, their concepts came to dominate theatrical companies in Louisville, Milwaukee, and other American cities. Starting with a handful of volunteers and a vision, these two women revolutionized theater in this country.

Born in Livingston, Texas, in 1911, Margo Jones decided at the age of eleven that she wanted to direct theater. Enrolling at Texas State Women's College four years later, she studied drama and psychology and frequently went to Dallas and Fort Worth to see plays. After graduation, she directed the Ojai Community Players and worked at the Pasadena Playhouse in southern California. Returning to Texas after a trip around the world, she became assistant director of the Federal Theater in Houston. Jones organized the Houston Community Theater in 1936. An innovator from the beginning, she produced Elmer Rice's *Judgement Day* in a courtroom. She offered plays by Ibsen, Shakespeare, Maxwell Anderson, and Chekhov and also produced plays by local authors such as the future Hollywood scriptwriter Cy Howard. Jones discovered talented local actors, such as Ray Walston, many of whom moved on to the professional theater or films. Before the theater ended its run in 1942, she had produced sixty plays. After briefly instructing in drama at the University of Texas, Jones moved to Dallas and organized a repertory theater in 1945. That same year she codirected her first major Broadway success, Tennessee Williams's *The Glass Menagerie*. Later she would produce *Summer and Smoke* in Dallas before Williams took the play to New York.[135]

This "Texas Tornado," a bundle of ambition and talent, had a messianic zeal. She explained: "Theatre in Texas is my job and I must do something about it. What I am doing here is not enough. I must see what I can do about pulling the curtain up on the next era."[136] Jones did precisely that when she opened Theater '47, and then Theater '48, and so on. At this theater—the first nonprofit, professional, residential theater in the country—she produced plays for the theater-in-the-round concept. Since it was a nonprofit company, she could raise money beyond the box office. And since it was a professional theater, she could employ talented, trained thespians. With a proscenium-less theater she could put her audience next to the stage and experiment with unique production techniques. She refused to create a repertory of light Broadway comedies and in the

CULTURE *in the* AMERICAN SOUTHWEST

first year produced an early version of William Inge's *Dark at the Top of the Stairs*. As both the artistic director and the managing director, Jones selected the plays and designed the productions, and in so doing, she made a major contribution to American theater. Directors, producers, playwrights, community playhouse leaders, and actors and actresses came to Dallas to see the revolution. For as Jones stated, "Everything in life is theatre."[137]

Jones constantly encouraged William Inge and Tennessee Williams and solicited their plays for Dallas productions; several of their works were among the eighty-six plays she premiered.[138] Armed with a Rockefeller Foundation grant and supported by the Dallas community, Jones launched her arena concept. Why Dallas? She noted: "All roads pointed to Dallas. . . . It is in a new, fresh, rich, pioneering part of the nation; it is a city already rich in theatre tradition; it had always been a good road town; . . . it was my home territory."[139] When, in January, 1955, a group of theater supporters proposed to create the Dallas Theater Center to incorporate her theater-in-the-round, Jones simply shouted: "Glory be to Betsy! I second the motion. Let's get started."[140] Tragically, Jones died in an accident that year. Her company staggered on until 1959, but the vitality was gone.

Yet Bea Handel refused to let the idea of the Dallas Theater Center die. Before moving to Dallas, Handel had spent ten years working at the Cleveland Playhouse; theater was part of her life. Aided by the *Dallas Morning News* columnist and critic John Rosenfield, she pushed Jones's concepts. Eventually Robert Stecker, a department store executive, resigned his position to head the Dallas Theater Center, and Paul Baker at Baylor University agreed to serve as the managing director. A native Texan with excellent credentials, Baker had built at Baylor a theatrical program that developed a national reputation, and he, like Jones, believed in integrating all art forms into the theatrical experience. Handel hosted meetings, raised funds, and developed plans for a permanent home. She obtained a donated site on Turtle Creek and, with considerable audacity, contacted Frank Lloyd Wright and asked him to design the theater.[141] The architect resisted at first, then agreed. Wright told her: "I wanted to be an actor when I was young, and I became busy with other things. I do not have a theater in the world which I have designed. Yes, indeed, I will be there. . . . If you people have the money, you can rest assured that I'll build it."[142]

Handel raised the money. Mrs. R. W. Humphreys gave $100,000 to honor her late daughter Kalita, who had studied with Baker. Eventually Handel acquired over $750,000 to build Wright's experimental structure. When the Kalita Humphreys Theater opened in 1959 with *Of Time and the River,* the play and the

FIGURE 40
*Nina Vance, the founder of the
Alley Theater in Houston,
brought both contemporary drama
and the classics to the Bayou City.
Courtesy the Alley Theater.*

facility received rave reviews. The boldly sculptured building on a sloping site featured an interplay of curves, sharp angles, and broad overhangs. The interior had some poor sightlines and the lighting had to be altered, but Wright provided Baker and his company with a place to experiment.[143] Wright had declared, "I will build a building that Paul Baker can work in and grow in, and that those who follow him can work and grow in."[144] Until he retired in 1981, Baker used the Dallas Theater Center to continue the goals of Margo Jones, with such success that the theater attracted international attention.[145]

In Houston, Nina Vance developed the Alley Theater even as Margo Jones created Theater '47. Vance had worked in Jones's Houston Community Theater, admired her mentor, and became a disciple. Born in Yoakum, Texas, in 1914 and educated at Texas Christian University, the University of Southern California, and the American Academy of Dramatic Arts in New York, Vance determined to fill the theatrical void in Houston after Jones left. In 1947 she mailed 214 penny postcards asking for contributions to create a professional theater in a ballet studio. Why 214? Because that was all the coins she had in her purse.[146] "If I am going to have a theater that's really professional I am going to have it here," she later declared.[147] Thirty-seven donors sent $20 each, and Vance was under way. Her first meeting brought one hundred volunteers, who helped re-model the facility where she opened the first production six weeks later. For the next eight years Vance produced and directed plays that grew increasingly more professional in quality. The company moved to an old fan factory in 1948, retaining the arena concept. Vance offered Broadway "flops" in new productions as well as successes by Clifford Odets, Lillian Hellman, and Arthur Miller.

In 1954, Vance tore the company apart by insisting on professional actors. Many of the volunteers left in a fury, but through a contract with the Actors' Equity Association, Vance created a purely professional company in 1961–62. By 1958, Alley Theater had drawn national attention, and a Ford Foundation grant the next year helped pay the salaries of the new company. Three years later the Ford Foundation offered a $2.1 million challenge grant for a new theater, and local contributors added $1 million more. In 1968 the Alley Theater moved into a new venue; designed by Ulrich Franzen, it won several architectural awards. A postmodern design in rich-colored brick and stone, the theater drew even greater attention to Vance and her company.[148] She said, "I'm just a country woman from a little Texas town. . . . Almost every character in a play, every action, has its Yoakum counterpart."[149] Asked to move the Alley to New York, Vance adamantly refused: "I like the environment where I can see the sky meet the earth. When that is present, the human being stands taller in my mind, and I can see and remember him better in order to put him on stage."[150]

By the time of Vance's death in 1981, the Alley Theater had a yearly budget of nearly $4 million, with 30,000 subscribers. The Alley's new director, Patricia Ann Brown, also a native Texan, took the company into bolder, new productions, much like the Alley of the 1970s. Vance had realized that there were those who questioned women as directors and producers, but she had a response: "Femininity [is a resource] too valuable to dissipate by apeing [sic] masculine techniques. . . . The gentleness of womanhood can be a powerful weapon. Granted this gentleness must be accompanied by steel, but when there is such a combination, the highest artistry is possible."[151] Vance also rejected the concept of "regional theater." She declared: "We are not regional (I think the term is second-class sounding). . . . Until we aim our own thinking toward a conviction that we have some international importance — whether we do or don't — we are downgrading our goals."[152] The Ford Foundation agreed and directed numerous grants to strengthen theater outside of New York.

Whereas the Ford Foundation succeeded in Houston, its efforts couldn't save the Mummers Theater in Oklahoma City. When Mack Scism, the founder of the Mummers Theater, and some friends erected a tent in 1948 and produced the melodrama "The Drunkard," the Oklahoma City Police charged them with being a public nuisance. They moved their production to a small space in the Municipal Auditorium, and for the next four years Scism directed plays performed by an amateur company. They moved to a warehouse and, with advice from Margo Jones, created a theater-in-the-round.[153] A sparkplug of the company, Mayde Mack Jones said of their first offering, "Oklahoma City is built on oil and beef, so let's give them some corn to feed on."[154] But Scism and the company desired to replicate the Cleveland Playhouse—with solid drama, the classics, and contemporary theater. They played melodramas in the summer to raise funds but moved to serious drama in the regular season. After Mayde Mack Jones died, they took the name Mayde Mack Mummers and then simply the Mummers Theater.

Scism became the full-time director in 1952, and the company grew in size and quality. By the end of the decade, Scism made clear his goal to develop a full professional company, leading to a split in the organization. He pursued that goal aided by a Ford Foundation grant of $1,250,000, to be matched locally with $750,000. This was a huge sum for a regional theater, but the money was raised. The Ford Foundation provided $240,000 more to support a professional season of seven plays. A paid staff of sixteen began to plan a new theater complex.[155] On land cleared by urban renewal, a striking theater, designed by John M. Johansen of New York, opened in 1970. Although the building won a national design award, it proved controversial at the outset with nearly all the mechanical elements painted in bright colors outside the Bauhaus brutalist walls. Scism defended Johansen's building: "His designs are not environmentally inspired, but functional sculptures."[156] The building, huge operating costs, large Equity salaries, the avant-garde productions, and the loss of community players soon doomed the Ford Foundation's pet project, and the Mummers folded in 1971. The theater had offered 150 plays in over twenty years to generally enthusiastic audiences, but the rapid growth led to its demise. The $3 million theatrical complex sat idle. When the theater first opened, Scism had declared: "Thousands of people who have never attended a play before will come here to see our home. Our task is to be good enough that they'll want to come back for more."[157] Yet the Mummers failed to achieve Scism's goal. The Oklahoma Theater Center, formed after the Mummers Theater closed, took over the complex, but the facility never met the aspirations that Scism and the Ford Foundation had sought.[158] The Mummers was too much of a good thing brought from the outside, not a theater built from within the community.

Other playhouses and community theaters in the region fared better in the postwar decade, but few were of a quality to rival the enormous successes in

Dallas and Houston. The Phoenix Little Theater survived the Great Depression and World War II and by 1957–59 was operating in the black. When the opportunity came to be part of a cultural complex that included a new public library and an art museum, the Little Theater built a facility that generated larger revenues and audiences.[159] The Tucson Little Theater became the Tucson Community Theater in 1957 and, nine years later, the Arizona Civic Theater. A resident professional company in Tucson, the group traveled statewide and by 1980 had an audience of 70,000.[160] The Tulsa Little Theater entered the 1950s with 5,000 members, its own theater, and virtually no debt. An elaborate committee system created a broad range of support across the community.[161]

One of the great success stories of the postwar period was San Diego, where the Old Globe Theater thrived. Respected members of the community served on the board, giving stability and prestige to the theater. Establishing a broader base through an expanded repertoire, the Old Globe Theater gained season-ticket holders and a stronger financial base. The artistic director Craig Noel came aboard in 1945 and stayed for three decades, providing strong and continuous leadership. In the winter season the Old Globe drew its cast from the community; in the summer it was a professional house. The summer Shakespeare Festival drew large audiences, as did popular plays. In 1953, a production of *Mr. Roberts* generated 27,000 ticket sales in twelve weeks. By 1958 the Old Globe was a full-time, professional, Equity company that soon drew national attention for its quality. A city of 260,000 when the Old Globe had opened in 1937, San Diego counted 1.6 million people in 1975, enough to support a vastly expanded theater.[162]

The accolades for the theater in the Southwest were not unlike those received by five Oklahoma ballerinas who took the world of dance by storm. In the 1940s and 1950s, these five ballet dancers startled audiences in New York and Paris with their skill and poise. All of the ballerinas were Native Americans, and critics contended that the dancers' heritage could be seen in their dignity, control, love of beauty, and sense of freedom. They had begun to dance as children and had trained with leading ballet instructors. Their parents took them to California, New York, and Europe to work with the best coaches and choreographers. Rosella Hightower, a Choctaw, studied in Kansas City, and after a performance of the Ballet Russe de Monte Carlo there, an audition was arranged. Invited to join the company, she returned with them to Europe, where she emerged as a prima ballerina. After retirement as a dancer, she became the artistic director of the Paris Opera Ballet and then opened her own school in Cannes. Moscelyne Larkin, a Shawnee-Peoria Indian, studied in New York and at age fifteen joined the original Ballet Russe. She felt that the experience with the Ballet Russe inspired each of the "Indian Ballerinas." Larkin later became the coordinator of the Tulsa Civic Ballet. Of Cherokee heritage, Yvonne Chouteau joined the Ballet Russe when she was only fourteen years old, the youngest American to participate in the company. She married her fellow dancer Miguel Terekhov, and after retirement they became artists-in-residence at the University of Oklahoma. Maria and Marjorie Tallchief, granddaughters of an Osage chief, were taken as young girls to California to study with Madame Nijinska. Maria became a prima ballerina with the Ballet Russe, met and married the choreographer George Balanchine, and joined his New York City Ballet. Marjorie Tallchief danced with the Ballet Russe and the Harkness Ballet and became the first American prima ballerina with the Paris Opera Ballet.[163] In 1967, four of the ballerinas performed in a commissioned ballet by the Oklahoma-born, Native American composer Louis Ballard: *The Four Moons*. Chouteau said, "You could see so clearly the Indian heritage." It was, she thought, uncanny. "Only an Indian could touch like that."[164]

Chouteau's observation was similar to comments made over two decades about the five ballerinas. Acclaimed as "the finest American-born classical ballerina the twentieth century has produced," Maria Tallchief referred to her Native American roots when asked about her feeling for dance.[165] Ballanchine created *Firebird* for her, and rave reviews spoke of "the beautiful dancing Osage." Even though Maria and her sister Marjorie had attended Osage dances, part of the tribal tradition, their parents had emphasized European music and ballet. Hence they shared two cultures. On stage the Indian ballerinas — with their tall, slender, strong bodies, olive skin, dark eyes, high cheekbones, and clouds of dark hair — drew gasps even before they took a step. When they danced in *The Four Moons*, the ballet critic Walter Terry spoke of a "savage aristocracy" about their performance.[166] The ballerinas discussed among themselves how they had reached such achievements, and simultaneously they concluded that their Native American heritage and their southwestern roots were factors. Chouteau said: "I've talked to each of the girls about it, and we all feel very strongly that there was an influence from our Indian Heritage. There must be something there."[167]

In dance, as in other areas, the culture of the region entered the mainstream of American life after World War II. And yet, an inferiority complex not unlike that described by the *Houston Post* in 1940 continued to permeate the region. There remained a reluctance to make the kind of financial commitment necessary to sustain large cultural institutions. Writers, artists, theatrical producers, and conductors recognized the conservative limits of the cultural tastes in the Southwest. After spending several months in the region in 1955, the English author J. B. Priestly concluded about one major city, Dallas: "Culture is not neglected; there is a gallant symphony orchestra, a tiny theatre-in-the-round, some museums. . . . But rather too much is claimed for Dallas as a cultural centre; the oil tycoons do not seem to throw their millions in that dubious direction."[168]

But in the 1970s and 1980s, the Dallas "oil tycoons" and their counterparts across the region did "throw their millions" at culture. The Dallas and the Southwest of 1955 were far different from what they would become three decades later. Perhaps the Southwest changed because, as one writer claimed, cultural organizations goaded "the Western conscience, trying to grasp Aaron Copland and Tennessee Williams without losing Johnny Ringo and Wyatt Earp."[169]

CHAPTER 6

Institutional Culture/ Creating Icons

1960–1980

The 1960s and 1970s witnessed sweeping changes as southwestern cities became some of the largest in the nation. Economic growth brought millions of immigrants from Mexico, Central America, and Asia, as well as migrants from the Midwest and Northeast. Factories, distribution centers, corporate headquarters, and research facilities spread across the region, bringing surging incomes, a massive construction boom, and increasing financial independence. Cityscapes altered dramatically as a spate of International Style towers punctured skylines. Indeed, these skyscrapers became symbols of the regional prosperity. New cultural icons represented financial success and a continuing search for critical acceptance. Art museums, especially "vanity museums," attracted international acclaim, as did new concert halls and theaters. National tours by southwestern symphony orchestras and opera and ballet companies played to packed houses in New York City and Washington, D.C., and to generally positive critical reception. Novels by "regional" authors found places on best-seller lists even as plays by and about southwesterners found homes on Broadway and in the nation's capital. At long last, those who had tried to establish institutional cultural artifacts, as well as writers, artists, dancers, and musicians, gained notice and reputation. These distinct voices came from within the Anglo, Hispanic, and Native American communities, but they shared such common features as an emphasis on the land, traditions, and sense of place. Cultural growth and economic expansion moved in tandem for two decades, creating vibrant institutional cultural icons.

The pastoral image of the region waned as its cities became national or even international leaders in both size and cultural attributes.[1] Growth alone spoke to this transformation by the time of the 1980 census. Standard metropolitan statistical areas in the Southwest mushroomed as Los Angeles claimed over

7 million people, Houston and Dallas–Fort Worth almost 3 million each, and Phoenix 1.5 million. San Diego soared to nearly 2 million people while Oklahoma City had over 800,000 and Albuquerque more than 450,000. San Antonio drew both Hispanics from below the Rio Grande and midwesterners as it sprawled to more than 1 million people.[2] Huge metropolitan centers physically and psychologically diminished the conceptions of a Southwest of farms, ranches, and deserts.

Economic expansion accelerated with the growth of the aviation and aerospace industries, federal government establishments, energy-based corporations, financial institutions tied to urban promotion, consumer-goods manufacturers, agribusinesses and food processors, and companies linked to trade with Mexico. Newly arrived scientists, engineers, corporate executives, and bankers added to the demand for cultural amenities. The Sandia Laboratory in Albuquerque and the Johnson Space Center in Houston symbolized the new research facilities and their highly trained staffs. Numerous corporate headquarters shifted to the Southwest, with Dallas acquiring American Airlines, Diamond Shamrock, National Gypsum, and J. C. Penney. Executives from outside the region arrived with spouses who were experienced leaders in cultural institutions and who expected quality orchestras, theaters, museums, and operas. The impact of these changes could be seen across the region, but Houston serves as a clear example. In 1970 the Bayou City ranked seventy-sixth among all U.S. cities in per capita income; in 1980 it ranked sixteenth![3] Similar economic growth elsewhere fueled the drive for the expansion of cultural institutions.

A small regional community with a fledgling state university, Tucson had 35,000 people when World War II broke out. In 1980, some 330,000 Tucson residents could attend theatrical performances, the ballet, and symphony concerts and could visit an emerging art center. The vast growth of the University of Arizona, the presence of a major military installation, and expanding financial institutions spawned a substantial boom, as did the arrival of tens of thousands of retirees. The University of Arizona helped to supply a rich program in the arts for the new arrivals. Dependence on copper, cattle, and cotton ended in Tucson as well as in Phoenix. Over 70 percent of Arizona's population lived in these two cities by 1980.[4] The so-called Sunbelt Revolution transformed Arizona and the region.

Corporate elites arriving in the Southwest found a lower cost of living and lower taxes, but often they also found an entrenched urban leadership that was initially reluctant to accept "outsiders." Shell Oil Company executives who transferred to the new corporate tower in Houston found Rice University to be an excellent school for their children and discovered fine shopping at the Galleria, but they did not gain immediate places on symphony and museum boards.[5] The resistance soon ended, however, as old elites withdrew or were pushed aside by the new corporate leadership. In Phoenix, the boomers and promoters of the prewar community gave way to newspaper editors, company presidents, and industrial executives. When new corporate headquarters arrived in Phoenix in the decades after 1960, an infusion of talent led to the expansion of city services, skyscrapers, vast suburbs, and unrelieved urban sprawl.[6] But cultural institutions changed too, and when English Professor Rita Dove at Arizona State University won the Pulitzer Prize in poetry, the school's president could safely declare the event "as exciting as the Rose Bowl, and it's more significant."[7] Some alumni winced, but the quip contained a message about the importance of culture to the institution and to the future growth of metropolitan Phoenix.

Some residents of the Southwest refused to laud the sweeping changes and longed for the quiet, genteel aspects of the urban society before its transformation. The writers Harvey Fergusson and his sister Erna, as well as the reporter Ernie Pyle, waxed eloquent about Albuquerque before the boom. It had been a city that worshiped its past, a place where rabbit families inhabited lawns, a city small enough that you could greet acquaintances downtown.[8] But their city grew from just over 200,000 in 1960 to more than 320,000 two decades later. A vast immigration from rural areas and from out of the state created a major city on the banks of the Rio Grande, a city with substantial populations of Hispanics and Native Americans.[9] The Albuquerque of the Fergussons and Pyle joined a regional network of cities that heightened identification with place.

At several levels, between 1960 and 1980 the urban centers of the Southwest formed links that drew residents of the region closer. As early as 1974, university students in Texas saw the Lone Star State and the Golden State joined through economic and cultural ties. "The region of which they were the center consisted of themselves and California."[10] Cultural ties developed between southern California and the artist colonies in Santa Fe and Taos, and writers such as Larry McMurtry bridged the various areas of the region with novels and screenplays that ranged geographically from the Pacific Coast to the "third coast" of Texas.

The demographic changes wrought in these two decades served to emphasize the cultural pluralism of the Southwest as the African American and East Asian populations also grew rapidly. Without efforts to assimilate or to force cultural conformity, these new ingredients added zest to the mixture. Having begun in the 1940s, the historic migration of blacks to southern California accelerated in the 1960s, but African Americans also arrived in large numbers in Dallas, Phoenix, and other regional cities. Simultaneously, the Hispanic population in the

CULTURE *in the* AMERICAN SOUTHWEST

Southwest reached almost 4 million, with the largest concentrations in California and Texas. The migration of Native Americans paralleled that of African Americans as Los Angeles, Tulsa, Oklahoma City, Albuquerque, and Phoenix acquired the largest concentrations of Indians in the country. Although many Navajo, Hopi, Zuni, and Pueblo peoples remained on reservations or on tribal lands, the young began to seek college degrees and an urban environment. There they found Filipinos, Chinese, Japanese, Koreans, and Vietnamese as students, professionals, and business owners who added to the cultural diversity of southwestern cities.[11]

Demographic changes, economic growth, urbanization, and industrialization revolutionized the region. Yet a feeling of inferiority continued to fuel the drive to make manifest the region's maturity, and how better to achieve that goal than with glass-clad towers — designed by internationally recognized architects — rising above the vast reaches of southwestern cities? Houston epitomized the commitment to the skyscraper as a symbol of economic success and cultural achievement. Between 1960 and 1970, six new high-rise buildings housing banks, energy companies, and petroleum corporations rose above the Bayou City. One Shell Plaza reached fifty-one stories in 1971, the tallest structure west of the Mississippi River. After designing the Teneco Building in 1962–63, a thirty-three-story tower with subtly screened facades, Skidmore, Owings, and Merrill of New York and San Francisco won the commission for One Shell Plaza when that corporation moved to Houston.[12] Not to be outdone in the prestige of architectural firm or in the pathbreaking design of its headquarters, Pennzoil hired Philip Johnson and John Burgee to create twin towers in the form of trapezoids with their opposing ends angled at forty-five degrees. The wedged-shaped towers established an exquisite tension above the expansive Pennzoil Plaza. Board Chairman J. Hugh Liedtke wanted the structure "to soar, to reach and a flat-top doesn't reach."[13] He wanted "no cigar box or wedding cake."[14] The Houston builder-developer Gerald D. Hines responded with dramatic structures separated by only a ten-foot-wide slot. Pennzoil Plaza served as a harbinger of a new concept, the skyscraper as sculpture, a concept that would be emulated in Los Angeles, Dallas, and Phoenix and then across the country. Johnson and Burgee, along with Hines, collaborated on other projects equally as dramatic, and equally as profitable. They effectively married art and business.[15]

In the next decade Hines and other developers in Houston continued to commission nationally and internationally known architects — Johnson and Burgee; I. M. Pei; Skidmore, Owings, and Merrill; and Cesar Pelli — for even taller, more dramatic towers. A five-sided, pale-gray, granite Texas Commerce Plaza by Pei rose seventy stories, while Skidmore, Owings, and Merrill produced the Allied Bank Building, a semicircular, blue-green tube sliced lengthwise and standing 970 feet above the street. With the spread of the city and rising land values, developers moved to the west of downtown, creating not just one structure but clusters of towers.[16] Echoing the Allen Center in the heart of the city, new "downtowns" arose along major boulevards and expressways. Designed by Hellmuth, Obata, and Kassabaum, the Galleria — a massive, climate-controlled shopping area with an ice-skating rink at its center — became a magnet for office towers, hotels, and other retail stores. Hines used Milan's Galleria Vittorio Emmanuele as the model, but some of the nearby buildings, such as the Neiman-Marcus Department Store, turned to Le Corbusier's brutalism for inspiration.[17] Intense competition between business executives, developers, and retail chains transformed Houston and influenced the rest of the Southwest. The *New York Times* architectural critic Ada Louise Huxtable called Houston "the American city of the second half of the twentieth century."[18]

The writer Max Apple, a newcomer to the city, satirized the compulsion of Houstonians to acquire land and build upon it. In the short story "My Real Estate," the principal character, Jack Spenser, wants a house. "I told her the simple truth. 'I want a house because my people have owned land and houses in Texas for four generations. We have lived here with the Mexicans and the Indians. I'm the first Spenser who hasn't owned a tiny piece of Texas.'" But when poor Jack ultimately finds a place to live, it's inside the Astrodome, on land once owned by his father. His domicile is the world's first fully enclosed, air-conditioned stadium, a symbol of Houston's obsession with size and unique architectural expression.[19]

If Houston led the way, other cities in Texas and the region soon followed, each attempting to use architecture as a symbol of its economic and artistic prowess. When San Antonio hosted the 1968 HemisFair to celebrate its 250th anniversary, the architect O'Neil Ford urged that the existing structures on the ninety-two-acre site be retained to preserve "the old San Antonio." Civic leaders and HemisFair organizers rejected that idea and leveled the old neighborhood to erect a convention center, the Institute of Texan Cultures, and the Tower of the Americas. The last soared above the exposition grounds, the Riverwalk, and La Villita, the oldest quarter of the city. Any sensitivity toward preservation was swept away to create an urban monument.[20]

In Dallas, Fort Worth, and El Paso, enthusiasm for giantism in architecture produced variations on the Houston themes. Hines constructed Dallas buildings emulating his triumphs in the Bayou City while the local developer Trammel Crow moved to build even more daring structures. In nearby Fort Worth, the "edifice complex" contributed to Skidmore, Owings, and Merrill's First National Bank tower of 1960, with a green granite sculpture by Isamu Noguchi on its plaza. Rival Continental Bank had thrown up a thirty-one-story tower four years earlier. Both were soon shaded by the Atlanta architect John Portman's Fort Worth National Bank, a thirty-seven-story, glass-sheathed tower with a pyramidal base. "Eagle," a forty-foot-tall, red-orange steel stabile by Alexander Calder, guarded the entrance. Even the city government joined the parade, with a new city hall designed by the international stylist Edward Durrell Stone. El Paso gained banks and a hotel as phallic symbols rising above the Rio Grande. In cities with relatively low-cost land at their cores, structures were erected largely without regard for financial considerations.[21] Business and community leaders wanted "signature" architecture.

Sharing in the population explosion and fiscal boom of the period, Phoenix lost its essentially low-scale center to a massive reconstruction effort. Three bank-owned skyscrapers, including the forty-story Valley National Bank, led the way. Each sentinel stood literally and figuratively as a reflection of the International Style: glass, metal, and concrete rectangles rising above parking garages. The Phoenix Civic Plaza project of the 1970s included a Hyatt Regency Hotel, a convention center, a symphony hall, and underground parking, all abutting a skid-row area. Again emulating Houston, a "new" downtown — the Rosensweig Center — emerged north of the old. Four large, bland towers housed the Greyhound, Armour, and Del Webb corporate facilities and a hotel. A new shopping center, La Borgata, which opened in the far northeastern quadrant of the metropolitan area in 1981, was a copy of the Tuscan village of San Gimignano; the architectural firm of Jones and Mah brought a little drop of Italy to Phoenix. Whereas the Arizona Biltmore and the Luhrs Tower had foreshadowed architectural trends in the 1920s and 1930s, buildings in Phoenix now followed the accepted modes in the 1960s and 1970s. Only Heritage Square, a collection of preserved structures, gave the city a sense of architectural history.[22] Yet one needed to look only a few miles to the east, toward Tempe, to see imaginative design. There Michael and Kemper Goodwin created a municipal building in 1971 in the form of an inverted pyramid. Set in a plaza at a forty-five-degree angle from true north, the inverted dark-glass walls — also at a forty-five-degree angle — rose above promenade decks and bridges. The award-winning design created "a cone of insulation."[23]

Unfortunately, Tucson shared the architectural traits and tastes of Phoenix rather than those of Tempe. The blue-glazed-brick, International-style Home Federal Savings and Loan building of 1966 was joined a decade later by the city's tallest tower, the Arizona Bank Plaza. Using features from the Citicorp Building in New York, the architects Friedman and Jobusch set the white-ribbed prism

FIGURE 41

*The City Hall at Tempe, Arizona, an inverted pyramid, contrasts sharply
with the stale designs in nearby Phoenix. Author's collection.*

at an angle to the street. Forty exterior columns framed silver reflective glass.
There was no pioneering in conception or execution, but Tucson could proclaim
that it too had arrived.[24]

The impact of the International Style reached the prairies of Oklahoma as
the state's two largest urban areas shared in the region's prosperity and in its
love affair with skyscrapers. Local architects created the Cities Service Building
(1969–71), and One Williams Center (1978) in Tulsa. These were sterile boxes,
but with a difference. Both towers rose above gardens, pools, and fountains that
formed "people places." Similarly, Frankfort-Short-Emery-McKinley, architects
in Oklahoma City, designed the McGee Tower (1973) with an adjacent park
containing an amphitheater. Set back from the street with a garden entry, the
thirty-story slab featured ever-larger patterns of windows reaching to its height.
The variegated facade and the green space at street level offered a different approach to the International Style that so dominated the Southwest in the period.[25]

Other regional voices in architecture—such as James H. Garrott in Los
Angeles and George Clayton Pearl and Antoine Predock of Albuquerque—
eschewed these trends. Garrott apprenticed in architectural offices before being
licensed in 1928. Until obtaining his degree from the University of Southern
California in 1945, he generally designed homes in Westwood Hills and Hollywood in the Spanish Colonial Revival and Art Deco styles. But Garrott soon
joined a community of architects practicing the International Style, which he

FIGURE 42

A gold-toned geodesic dome and a gold-finned office tower made Citizens National Bank of Oklahoma City a prominent landmark. Photo by John Powell. Courtesy the Pledger Collection.

adopted. An African American who was well acquainted with the need for imaginative public housing, he created designs that incorporated parks, playgrounds, and extensive "people places." His clients were no longer the wealthy and famous but were those who occupied housing projects or used public buildings. Emphasizing the concepts of the International Style, but incorporating the landscape, Garrott created livable spaces and places.[26]

In Albuquerque, George Clayton Pearl designed university buildings, schools, hospitals, office buildings, and libraries while experimenting with new construction techniques and materials. He also accepted commissions to preserve older buildings, such as the Albuquerque Main Library of 1925. Pearl incorporated landforms in his designs, but his primary concerns were the client and the site: "I think architecture is seldom a proper medium for self-expression. Most architects should write verse or paint pictures or whatever they need to do to express themselves. The client's needs and the physical and cultural context of the site are the proper subject matter of architecture, not the architect's current preferences."[27] Trained at the University of Texas, Pearl spent summers in Arizona and practiced in New Mexico. His feelings for the land and its people led to a design for the Ácoma-Laguna-Cañoncito Hospital at Ácoma Pueblo. The hospital included an "Earth, Fire, and Sky Ritual Room" for curing ceremonies for the two pueblos and for the Navajo patients. The contemporary exterior incorporated pottery designs as well as solar energy panels.

Pearl's determination to link architecture to the landscape received an enthusiastic response from the young Antoine Predock, whose La Luz housing project drew national attention. His philosophy echoed that of Pearl: "The concept of La Luz involves a basic attitude toward the land: An urban environment and large natural open areas should exist together, especially in New Mexico. Existing natural patterns should be recognized and reinforced rather than eliminated. The delicate balance of plant and wild life need not be destroyed by development."[28] Similar views were being voiced by other designers by the end of the 1980s. While the race to build ever upward continued, a sensitivity to the needs of site and client emerged as well.

In Los Angeles, the repeal in 1957 of the city ordinance restricting the height of buildings led to a frenzied competition to construct skyscrapers not only in the downtown district but also along Wilshire Boulevard and in areas north and west of the city's core. Civic leaders of Los Angeles applauded the new skyline, but only a few recognized that the city still lacked a true cultural center. The Los Angeles Philharmonic played in an antiquated facility, and there were limited venues for theatrical productions. The absence of a modern physical facility for cultural activities grated, and yet the community remained deeply divided over the site, the sources of funding, and the occupants of such a center. Efforts to create an opera house and an auditorium failed when voters refused to approve bond issues.[29]

Yet Dorothy Buffum Chandler would not accept defeat, and she organized a campaign to give Los Angeles a first-class cultural center. The spouse of Norman Chandler, publisher of the *Los Angeles Times,* "Buff" Chandler had led the fight to save the Hollywood Bowl in 1951, raising $100,000 in twelve days to keep the summer season alive. Now she organized the community to make a music center a reality. Los Angeles County created a committee to spearhead this effort and agreed to provide a site on Bunker Hill. An urban-renewal project would remove slum housing from Bunker Hill, over one hundred acres located northwest of the central business district. The space would become twenty-five "super-blocks" for government offices, commercial towers, and a music and theatrical center. Chandler went to work. In one evening she obtained pledges of $400,000, and by 1959 she had commitments in excess of $4 million. A broadly based citizens group led the drive, and Chandler made sure that "newcomers" to Los Angeles were included. In addition to the "old money" in the city, she went after executives and business leaders who had come to Los Angeles during the postwar economic boom. Lacking financial support from the federal and state governments, she sought funds from the private sector. Women's organizations played a major role in the campaign, in which Chandler ultimately raised $18.5 million. The composer John Green called her "the greatest fund raiser since Al Capone."[30] Some donations were very large, such as those from two businessmen, Mark Taper and Howard Ahmanson, who initially pledged $1 million each, but Chandler sought to include virtually all of southern California in this remarkable effort.

As president of the Southern California Symphony Association, Chandler wanted not only the cultural center but also a permanent conductor for the orchestra, an individual with an international reputation who would bring audiences to a state-of-the-art concert hall. She got both. The architect Welton Becket of Los Angeles proposed three buildings for the Bunker Hill site: the Dorothy Chandler Pavilion for the Philharmonic; the Ahmanson Theater for dramatic productions; and the Mark Taper Forum for experimental theatrical works. The Dorothy Chandler Pavilion, with black-granite walls behind soaring white columns, opened in 1964. The Philharmonic moved into its new home under the baton of the young Zubin Mehta, whose father conducted the Bombay Symphony Orchestra. Chandler had her venue and her international star. She had maneuvered gracefully to appease the savings-and-loan rivals Mark Taper and Howard Ahmanson, who were both determined to have their names on separate theaters. The result was a complex of halls housing organizations ranging from the Hollywood Bowl to the "light opera." When the Ahmanson Theater was dedicated in 1967, the actor Gregory Peck declared: "Since we didn't inherit great cultural monuments, we had to create our own."[31]

Dorothy Chandler found more than 3,000 donors for the Music Center, which ultimately cost over $24 million, but more important, she put Los Angeles on the nation's cultural map. No longer would Los Angeles be seen as simply the place where films were made. The Center aided the rise of the Los Angeles Philharmonic Orchestra as one of the nation's leading symphonies, and the Ahmanson Theater's stage served as a venue for new productions and revivals that moved to New York and toured the country. For example, José Quintero directed a production of Eugene O'Neill's *More Stately Mansions* starring Ingrid Bergman and Colleen Dewhurst. The Mark Taper Forum became a venue for experimental theater and a place for aspiring playwrights, directors, and actors to gain exposure. John Houseman's Theater Group from the University of California at Los Angeles formed the nucleus of the company, which premiered works by John Whiting, Heiner Kipphardt, and Conor Cruise O'Brien. The

New Theater for Now workshop productions included plays by John Guare, Lanford Wilson, and Adrienne Kennedy. The theaters made Los Angeles a serious rival of Broadway both in drama and in musical comedy.[32]

Time Magazine in 1964 described Chandler's role in creating the Music Center as "the most impressive display of virtuoso money-raising and civic citizenship in the history of U.S. womanhood." When Zubin Mehta greeted her from the stage at the opening of the Pavilion, he declared, "Unlike the princes of Florence and the Pharaohs of Egypt, she is a dignified, simple lady."[33] The audience responded with a four-minute ovation. By 1989, the Music Center Foundation had an endowment of $50 million to carry on her work. Although some architectural critics called the hall elitist and sterile, it drew capacity crowds to hear music created by Mehta and the Philharmonic.

The Los Angeles Philharmonic Orchestra in the 1960s represented a trend found across the region. Many cities built new concert halls, hired well-known conductors, recruited musicians from home and abroad, and attracted sizable audiences and subscribers. In addition, some of these orchestras ran substantial risks in their efforts to build reputations. Again, the Los Angeles Philharmonic was a trend-setter. The Philharmonic had contracted with the legendary George Solti to conduct thirteen weeks each year. But in 1961, the twenty-four-year-old Zubin Mehta electrified the musicians when he conducted without a score while substituting for Fritz Reiner. At Chandler's urging, the Philharmonic board hired him as assistant to Solti. In Europe, Solti was outraged that Mehta had been hired without his approval: the young man had to go or Solti would resign. The board accepted his resignation. Mehta developed the Philharmonic into an internationally acclaimed symphony.[34]

Few regional orchestras could claim equal successes, but the 1960s and 1970s saw a vast expansion of symphonic music in the Southwest, as well as a meteoric rise in the quality of the orchestras. Civic leaders, urban boosters, and symphony supporters in Phoenix did not aim as high as Los Angeles but did endure financial and organizational problems in the 1960s and 1970s. The Phoenix Symphony Orchestra hired Guy Taylor in 1959 to build a professional orchestra. The former conductor of the Nashville Symphony Orchestra, Taylor proved to be an excellent musician who was well received by the community.[35] The first year was a sellout, with people turned away. Season-ticket sales almost tripled by 1964, when the orchestra moved into Grady Gammage Auditorium on the Arizona State University campus. George Szell, conductor of the Cleveland Symphony Orchestra, declared that Gammage was "probably the greatest hall of the twentieth century."[36] Supported by several leading citizens of Phoenix, Taylor created a major orchestra with a budget in excess of $500,000. But a player crisis devel-

FIGURE 43

*Frank Lloyd Wright's Grady Gammage Auditorium at Arizona State University,
Tempe, mixed earth tones with magical shapes. Author's collection.*

oped in 1964, and several principals departed. A Ford Foundation grant in 1966
for some $850,000, including $600,000 to be matched locally, provided an infusion of funds that allowed Taylor to continue his plan. The symphony board
wanted more rapid growth, however, and a "name" conductor. It fired Taylor in
1968, creating a furor in Phoenix.[37]

After two years of guest conductors, the board hired Eduardo Mata in 1971.
The symphony's leaders raised the matching funds for the Ford grant and obtained a young and talented conductor. Only twenty-nine years old, Mata had
served as conductor of the National University of Mexico orchestra for five
years. He arrived in Phoenix, fired twenty-two players, and with great confi-
dence began to form his symphony. Members included professionals as well as
community players, which posed problems for Mata's goal of a major national
symphony. He introduced Latin American composers to Phoenix and American
audiences and broadened the repertoire, especially after the orchestra moved
to its own Symphony Hall in 1972.[38] The Phoenix Symphony Association also
sponsored an opera series, which Mata did not conduct, and the money-losing
operas undermined the association's financial well-being. Season-ticket sales grew
and income exceeded $1 million, but the strain of the losses generated by the
operas created another crisis.[39]

In 1978 Mata resigned to become the conductor and musical director of the
Dallas Symphony, and the Phoenix Symphony found itself in dire straits. Mata

had not been able to move beyond a semiprofessional orchestra, and many members of the audiences did not agree with the always favorable symphony reviews written by the critic Anson B. Cotts of the *Arizona Republic*.[40] By the early 1980s the orchestra was in serious trouble, with no infusion of "old money" and with meager local government support. In 1983–84, recognizing the crisis, the city of Phoenix provided a grant of $650,000 to keep the symphony alive. Although there were constant references to the orchestra as the "jewel in the Valley," Symphony Association President David R. Johns admitted in 1986 that problems remained: "The symphony is one of the key cultural indicators in the city and the state. It is also a way of promoting our community and making people aware that there is more to Phoenix than just cactus."[41] The ambitions of Mata and of some community leaders could not be realized without a larger, stronger fiscal commitment.

In the 1960s, the Women's Committee of the San Diego Symphony Association seized the initiative to enhance the quality of that city's orchestra. From the end of World War II to 1959, the musicianship of the symphony had not changed greatly, and it certainly had not kept pace with the vast growth of San Diego. A major transformation began with the hiring of Earl Bernard Murray as conductor and music director. Murray, challenged to create a "new" orchestra, was aided by the Women's Committee, which sold tickets and raised funds for the next six years. The 1,600 members held Viennese Balls and other events, and their efforts were recognized in 1966 when the American Symphony Orchestra League honored their successful campaign. The former associate conductor of the San Francisco Symphony, Murray recruited musicians and gave San Diego an orchestra of talent. When the symphony moved into a rehabilitated Civic Theater in 1965, the singer Dorothy Kirsten joined the orchestra for opening night.[42] The momentum of the 1960s began to falter, however, and the next decade saw events not unlike those in Phoenix.

The San Diego Symphony board in 1959–60 had included only eight leaders of the community, with few from major firms. A decade later, a huge board of eighty-three contained more influential citizens but proved unwieldy. San Diego, the ninth-largest city in the United States, stood thirty-second in support of its orchestra.[43] A population swollen by retirees, by military personnel often in residence only briefly, and by recent immigrants from Mexico did not present a strong base upon which to build the symphony. Clearly the entire community needed to be marshaled. The 1970s saw struggles over programs, the replacement of Murray, and a strike by the musicians. A line of credit from local banks kept the symphony alive as its annual budget rose to nearly $1 million. The cultural aspirations of San Diego exceeded the efforts of the Combined Arts and

Educational Council, a fund-raising umbrella for arts organizations as well as for the symphony.[44] "Pops" concerts in the summer with popular vocalists and conductors generated additional revenues, but San Diego, like Phoenix, could not support a major orchestra. The pool of musicians lacked depth, and hiring a "name" conductor did not instantly create an orchestra of national repute. Ambitions simply outran resources.

There were regional triumphs in these years, however, with the notable example of Sir John Barbirolli and the Houston Symphony Orchestra. Houston lavished funds and praise on the English conductor, who built a strong organization. In the mid-1960s the orchestra moved into Jesse H. Jones Hall for the Performing Arts, a venue described by *Architectural Record* as "the most sophisticated building of its kind anywhere in the world." The local architects Caudill, Rowlett, Scott wrapped Italian travertine behind the hall's peristyle of thin piers and created a finely tuned auditorium.[45] The year before, Barbirolli had taken the orchestra to New York's Philharmonic Hall, where an audience of 2,500 demanded four curtain calls at intermission and six at the conclusion. Many concert-goers stood on their seats, and others gathered at the stage to hail the orchestra. Alan Rich, critic at the *New York Herald Tribune* wrote: "Clearly the state of Texas, and specifically the city of Houston, deserves inclusion among the [cultural] centers."[46] Such praise and audience responses were precisely what the region's cultural mavens and business leaders wanted so desperately.

In El Paso, Tucson, and Albuquerque the models adopted were less those of the Houston Symphony Orchestra and the Los Angeles Philharmonic and more along the lines of the Phoenix and San Diego symphonies, but without over-wrought ambitions. For twenty years the Italian conductor Orlando Barera led the El Paso Symphony, but in 1975 the symphony hired Abraham Chavez as conductor and music director. A native of El Paso, Chavez had played in the orchestra at age fourteen. He left to study at the Los Angeles Conservatory of Music and then became a faculty member at the University of Colorado. The symphony and the University of Texas at El Paso provided Chavez with dual appointments, and he gave El Paso a well-received orchestra. He won the community's support as ticket sales rose, and he introduced a much broader reper-toire with selections by modernists such as Béla Bartók, Darius Milhaud, and Igor Stravinsky. By 1981 the orchestra could present a highly creditable perfor-mance of Dimitry Shostakovich's difficult Tenth Symphony. The orchestra's suc-cess reflected the talents of Chavez and his personal role in the musical life of the community.[47]

Tucson's experience, nearly the reverse of El Paso's, was one of conflict and struggle. The Symphony Orchestra hired Gregory Millar in 1966 to raise its quality. Formerly the conductor of the Kalamazoo and Grand Rapids orchestras, Millar proved energetic but also, in the eyes of some, undisciplined. Two years of controversy in 1974–76 led to his departure in a frenzy of bad publicity. The orchestra then recruited George Trautwein from the Savannah Symphony. Traut-wein set out to raise professional standards and musicianship, and soon subscrip-tions reached nearly 3,000 as the budget rose to $500,000. As part of an urban-renewal project, a downtown barrio had been demolished and a new music hall opened in 1971. The site included a theater, a sports arena, and an exhibition hall. The venue helped generate larger audiences, but it was the improved or-chestra that produced community support. The quality continued to rise when William McGlaughlin became the conductor in 1982, but the players remained underpaid, part-time musicians,[48] a problem that plagued other regional sym-phonies as well.

The Albuquerque Civic Symphony Orchestra became the Albuquerque Sym-phony Orchestra and then, in 1976, the New Mexico Symphony Orchestra as it sought to become a professional organization. A brief flirtation with a "name" conductor, the pianist José Iturbi, proved unsuccessful, but from 1970 to 1984, under Yoshimi Takeda, the symphony gradually became fully professional. He led a youthful group of more than eighty players who performed throughout the state and Mexico.⁴⁹ The name change and the concerts outside of Albuquerque generated a broader base of support for the orchestra.

Simultaneously with the region's efforts to build symphonies arose a campaign for chamber music. The internationally acclaimed Santa Fe Chamber Music Festival led the way beginning in 1973, with similar summer festivals appearing later in Taos and Angèl Fire, New Mexico. Smaller communities found that a chamber orchestra demanded less financial support than a full symphony. Midland-Odessa, Texas, established the Touvenel String Quartet, and an endowment by Sybil Harrington of $1.6 million supported the Harrington String Quartet at West Texas State University in Canyon. String ensembles in Houston, Austin, and Dallas also won widespread acclaim. The Houston String Quartet played in the Kennedy Center in Washington, D.C., and toured Asia. The African American Scott Joplin Chamber Orchestra, organized by Anne Lundy in 1983, played not only music by Joplin but a wide-ranging repertoire. Maturing musical audiences supported the Voices of Change, a Dallas–Fort Worth ensemble that played modernists such as Bartok and Arnold Schoenberg. The composers John Cage and Toru Takemitsu attended concerts when their music was performed. It was possible to find audiences for the music of the Baroque, of Joplin, and of Cage in a region with cultural aspirations that often outran the resources to support them.⁵⁰

A slightly different pattern emerged with the formation of opera companies in the Southwest as strong fiscal support allowed for the development of major organizations in Houston, Dallas, and San Diego. Indeed, the Houston Grand Opera mounted productions that moved on to Washington, D.C., and New York City. Founded in 1955 by Elva Lobit, the Houston Grand Opera Association hired Walter Herbert from the New Orleans Opera and raised $40,000 to offer three operas each season. Lobit and her supporters knew that the Houston Music Hall was a poor venue, but they struggled through the 1950s and 1960s, offering solid productions of well-known operas. A woman of means and sound judgment, Lobit encouraged Herbert to bring new, young performers to Houston. Audiences heard future stars such as Beverly Sills, Placido Domingo, and Sherrill Milnes in highly professional productions. Nevertheless the opera seasons generated deficits, and audience support frequently lagged. The Houston Grand Opera leaders sought even higher quality. The new Jones Hall provided excellent facilities, with its huge movable ceiling and vast array of theatrical equipment. To take advantage of the hall and to mount stellar productions, the association brought twenty-nine-year-old David Gockley to Houston.⁵¹

Gockley gave the association all it asked for and more. He told Houstonians, "We want to combat the image of opera as a medium for only the wealthy and elite." He reached out to the community with operas designed to broaden the base of support. Sills returned for *Daughter of the Regiment* as Gockley increased the season to six productions. A lavish *Porgy and Bess* went to New York, where it won a Tony Award. In 1975 a production of Scott Joplin's *Treemonisha* toured the country before going to New York. Critics acclaimed a new production of *Der Rosenkavalier,* and audiences grew larger with operas featuring internationally recognized performers. Gockley's enthusiasm for opera broadly defined meant that his repertoire included Lehár, Verdi, and Wagner as well as *Showboat.* By 1976, Gockley had a production of *Rigoletto* in Houston, *Porgy and Bess* in New York, and *El Capitan* on tour. Talented and insightful, Gockley had apprenticed at the Santa Fe Opera, had been a fund-raiser at Lincoln Center in New York, and was also a trained musician. His broad range of experiences proved valuable as he created an opera company with an international reputation. With a budget in excess of $7 million annually, he began to offer either a world premiere each season or a contemporary masterpiece. Houston audiences heard Berg's *Lulu* and *Wozzeck* and Britten's *Peter Grimes* and premieres of *Willie Stark* and the *Seagull.*[52] By the early 1980s the Houston Grand Opera could be considered a grand success, a triumph for Elva Lobit and the women who had joined her campaign over two decades earlier.

Not to be outdone by Houston, opera lovers in Dallas took advantage of a split at Chicago's Lyric Theater to lure Lawrence Kelly as general manager and Nicola Rescigno as music director to the Dallas Civic Opera in 1957. The twenty-nine-year-old Kelly raised $25,000 for a deficit fund and produced a brilliant *L'Italiana in Algeri* by Rossini with sets by Franco Zeffirelli and lighting by Jean Rosenthal, both outstanding designers. As a precursor to the opening, Maria Callas sang in concert with the Dallas Symphony Orchestra, enthralling the audience. A reviewer for *Newsweek* enthused, "For a couple of nights running . . . Dallas, Texas, was the operatic capital of the United States."[53] Callas returned the next year to sing *La Traviata* (with Zeffirelli sets) and followed with *Media* by Cherubini. Alexis Minotis from the Greek National Theater served as stage director for the latter production, which moved on to London and great acclaim. Callas returned yearly, provoking snide comments about the "Callas Civic Opera" or "Callas in Dallas," but she was not the only diva to sing in the huge State Fair Park Music Hall. For example, La Fenice in Venice loaned a production of Handel's *Alcina* for Joan Sutherland in 1960. Referring to Mozart's *Don Giovanni,* also part of the 1960 season, the irrepressible social gadfly Elsa Maxwell remarked: "It's really incredible—incredible—the greatest opera in the world in a little town like Dallas."[54] Her comment about Dallas won no praise from opera supporters or civic leaders. They believed the city "must have the performing arts to be the model of a modern, major metropolis."[55]

Although far from being a major metropolis in 1950, San Diego gained a new cultural organization that year when Mrs. Edgar A. Luce, the spouse of a local judge, used her talents to form the San Diego Opera Guild. The Guild brought the San Francisco Opera Company to the city from 1952 to 1965 as its original 30 members grew to over 1,300. By 1965 it was possible to mount a local, professional production of *La Boheme* directed by Walter Herbert of Houston. The ambitious company produced the American premiere of Henze's *Der Junge Lord* in 1967 in a season that included *Aïda, Tosca,* and *La Traviata.*[56] In 1975 Tito Capobianco became the opera's director, and he offered Beverly Sills in the world premiere of Menotti's *La loca.* Other stars followed in fifty productions by twenty-five composers. Capobianco established a Verdi Festival in 1987, and the Guild commissioned Leonardo Balada to write an opera based on the life of the Mexican patriot Emiliano Zapata.

While the repertoire expanded and the quality of the San Diego Opera soared, its financial situation worsened. The Combined Arts and Educational Council had provided half of the opera's funds, but by 1980 only 13 percent of the budget came from that source. When banks refused to loan money to the opera in 1970, Margaret Ridout, a leading supporter of the company, rallied the troops. Seven women went quietly around the city and raised $65,000 to produce *La Traviata.* The season was cut from four productions to two, but the company survived. Grants from the Ford Foundation and the National Endowment for the Arts enhanced local fund drives.[57] By 1977, all of the performances sold out: the city at last saw the opera as a major cultural institution.

The success of the San Diego Opera came in the midst of a larger drive in the city to expand support for the arts. The Old Globe Theater sold over 200,000 tickets and won a Tony Award for Excellence. The Repertory Theater generated a budget of nearly $2 million by 1976. The Museum of Art saw its membership grow from 4,000 to 10,000 and its budget increase by 400 percent between 1976 and 1986. Although the San Diego Ballet closed in 1980, the La Jolla Playhouse ceased operation, and the San Diego Symphony faced runaway deficits, arts budgets climbed from $7,750,000 in 1976 to $40 million a decade later.[58] Cultural icons cost huge sums, and even the most generous of communities found that excellence could not be achieved in all areas of the arts. Opera companies, theaters, symphony orchestras, ballets, and museums competed for funds that even a booming city such as San Diego could not provide. Perhaps it was true that even if arts organizations had unlimited budgets, there would never be enough money.

Musical organizations emerged across the region between 1960 and 1980 as symphony orchestras and opera companies appeared in major cities and smaller communities. Tucson and Fort Worth developed well-received opera companies even as nonprofessional orchestras could be heard in Waco, Bryan–College Station, and Wichita Falls, Texas. High schools boasted of "orchestra kids," and string teachers trained young musicians to enter local symphonies. Civic pride and boosterism credited these organizations with qualities they often did not possess. When the renowned cellist Yo-Yo Ma came to Wichita Falls to play with its orchestra, a native son entered the musician's dressing room to reassure him: "I know you're probably nervous playing with the symphony, you want a beer or something?"[59]

Provincialism, however, did not preclude the quest for cultural attainment in the region. In its march toward a cultural renaissance, the Southwest continued to erect great "art palaces" in the 1960s and the 1970s. Some national observers believed that soaring prices for paintings and sculptures and the escalation of construction costs for new museum buildings meant that the era of national expansion had ended. The critic Paul Goldberger proclaimed: "That the great era of museum building is over is, clearly, beyond argument. The boom period that permitted the art rush of the 1960s is not likely to return for some time."[60] The cultural writer Brian O'Doherty echoed that sentiment: "The museum age, which reached its Augustan apogee with the post-World War II boom in art education, in special exhibitions, in collecting, in museum-building, is finally over."[61]

But the prognosticators were wrong. The boom continued, with new wings at the Metropolitan Museum of Art and the National Gallery of Art, a new building for the High Museum in Atlanta, and the creation of the Terra Museum of American Art in Chicago. Yet even these facilities paled in comparison with the rampant growth of museums in the Southwest. In the states of Texas, Oklahoma, Colorado, New Mexico, and Arizona and in southern California, new art monuments arose at an astonishing rate. Thirty new buildings were constructed in Texas alone. The confluence of economic expansion, urban growth, and more important, a determination to demonstrate cultural maturation led to the use of the art museum as a civic artifact and as a symbol of regional development.

The great architectural success of the Museum of Modern Art in New York set the initial tone for art museums in the Southwest in these years, as seen in Mies van der Rohe's additions to the Houston Museum of Fine Arts: Cullinan Hall and the Brown Pavilion. The architects Philip Goodwin and Edward Durrell Stone had designed a new building for the Museum of Modern Art based on the International Style. The building emphasized volume, regularity, and fine proportions in elegant materials and technical perfection. Its facade was a plain, non-load-bearing skin.[62] While the practitioners of the International Style did not solve all of the problems created for museums by Beaux Arts buildings, their innovative concepts signaled a new approach to museum design, as seen in the Timkin Gallery at the San Diego Museum of Art, a rectangular glass box.

Distinguished museum directors such as William Valentiner of the Detroit Institute of Arts became convinced that since "museums are the most peaceful and enduring institutions on earth," the classical style was inappropriate. "The museum should be built in the modern style," Valentiner declared.[63] Southwesterners embraced architectural experimentation in their public and commercial buildings and in their homes as they sought cultural acceptance from those advocating the avant-garde in critical circles. They enthusiastically adopted the International Style for the art museums that proliferated after World War II. Indeed, the development of art museum architecture in the Southwest closely followed national trends until the 1960s, when the region moved to the cutting edge of art museum design.

Coinciding with a thirst for art museum buildings of architectural distinction was the creation of "vanity museums" across the region. A major factor in the emergence of the art museum as a cultural artifact in the Southwest has been the individual patron or family who either creates a vanity museum or shapes a public museum's collection through sheer weight of generosity. Many of these twentieth-century Medicis were not natives of the region but came to the Southwest to establish fortunes in petroleum, real estate, banking, newspaper publishing, or agribusiness. Their largess became the basis upon which art collections were formed and buildings were erected, creating institutions of national and international reputation. Indeed, several of the art museums of the Southwest owed their prominence to their personalized nature. The region exhibited a strong dependence on the patronage of individuals rather than art associations or government appropriations. The use of dedicated trusts to establish a museum and to endow its operations and collection development is an American phenomenon that reached its apogee in the Southwest. As Lewis Mumford wrote, the museum became "a manifestation of our curiosity, our acquisitiveness, our essentially predatory culture."[64]

Cities in the region, struggling for recognition, eagerly accepted these gifts in a quest to create an instant culture. As a leading scholar of museum history has written, somewhat cynically, "The magnificent flowering of museums in the United States in less than half a century is the spontaneous creation of the American public whose richest citizens have thus acquitted their debt to the less fortunate."[65] Yet critics asked, what was the quality of these artistic repositories? Was it possible in this century to acquire works of art that would establish a collection worthy of comparison to the older museums in Europe or even to the museums in the eastern United States?

In his syndicated newspaper column, Edward J. Sozanski spoke to these questions: "A private art collection is a private indulgence, and, as such, it does not have to satisfy any public obligations or expectations. Nor need its owners rationalize its form or apologize for any of its perceived excesses or deficiencies. But, when such a collection enters the public domain, particularly as a self-contained museum, it invites closer scrutiny. The vanity museum is the highest form of ego gratification to which an aesthete can aspire."[66] To provide justification for its existence, the personal museum needed to demonstrate distinction through exceptional concentration in a specific type or period of art, an exemplary model of connoisseurship, or a refined or contemplative ambience. The Southwest provided numerous museums to which these criteria could and would be applied.

One such example was the Amon Carter Museum of Art in Fort Worth. Working within the boundaries of the new formalism, the architect Philip Johnson produced a distinguished structure for the museum. Situated high on a bluff, with a vista east to downtown Fort Worth, the museum facade reflected its founder's personality. Amon Carter had come to Fort Worth in 1905 and four years later established the *Fort Worth Star-Telegram*. The paper prospered and so did Carter. He began to collect western American art, and by 1945, when he established the Amon G. Carter Foundation, he had acquired a major holding. At his death, Carter's will instructed his children to create an art museum for the city, in what Carter called an "artistic enterprise." Using the Foundation as the financial vehicle, the Carter children hired Johnson to design the museum building while they developed a retrospective collection of some 6,000 works of high-quality American art.

A leading figure in formulating the International style in homes, commercial buildings, and museums, Johnson abandoned the stark steel-and-glass boxes of his earlier designs. A porch across the museum's facade supported by five segmental arches on tapered columns formed a modern stoa or loggia behind which a glass wall separated the art from the city. Using Texas honey-colored shell stone with bronze and teak details, Johnson projected a sense of peace and order within and outside the museum. Opened in 1961, the building won praise from critics and made Johnson the architect of choice for developers and builders in Texas.[67] Johnson and his partner, John Burgee, began to design the skyscrapers

CULTURE *in the* AMERICAN SOUTHWEST

FIGURE 45

The Amon Carter Museum of Art by Philip Johnson overlooks Fort Worth. Author's collection.

that brought architectural critics from around the world to see the wonders of the Southwest.

Amon Carter's initial collection reflected his love of the West — its geography, its heritage, and its values. Carter and other collectors sought art that portrayed what William Goetzmann has called "the West of the imagination."[68] They purchased sculpture and paintings that depicted the courage and tenacity of the settlers and their triumphs over the weather, wild animals, and the native population. Carter and others formed major collections of western and frontier art and presented their holdings to the public in an effort to preserve the concept of a heroic past and to maintain the virtues seemingly represented by the frontier experience.

Another such collector, the Fort Worth millionaire Sid Richardson, eschewed the opportunity to move beyond the world of Frederic Remington and Charles Russell and built a collection almost exclusively of their works. Born in Athens, Texas, in 1891, Richardson entered the oil business at age twenty-two and within two decades acquired a fortune based on petroleum, land, and cattle. He bought his first Russell painting in 1942 and told Bertram M. Newhouse of the Newhouse Gallery in New York City to form a collection. During the next five years, Newhouse built the Richardson holdings to more than eighty paintings, which

were transferred to the Sid Richardson Foundation. Although it had access to enormous assets, the Foundation did not acquire additional artworks after the death of its founder but did create a small, handsome gallery in downtown Fort Worth to display the Richardson Collection. This would have pleased its developer, who "didn't like western landscape artists — he wanted cowboys, Indians and horses in his paintings." In Russell and Remington, Richardson found the vitality and motion that he associated with the West.[69]

Whereas some regional vanity museums remained as repositories of art seeking to reflect the Southwest and the West, Fort Worth acquired the Kimbell Art Museum, which in its architecture and its collection became an internationally recognized institution. As director of the Los Angeles County Museum of Art, Richard Fargo Brown had observed the disastrous consequences of its new home near the La Brea tarpits and decided that if he ever had the opportunity to create a new museum building again, it would be with the total support of the museum board, with a careful and detailed plan of needs, and with a sensitive architect committed to a structure of absolute excellence. He got the chance in 1964 when the trustees of the Kimbell Art Foundation asked him to come to Fort Worth as the first director of the Kimbell Art Museum. Brown assumed the leadership of what was then the wealthiest museum in the nation. Founded

FIGURE 47

Velma Kimbell (left) and Mr. and Mrs. Louis I. Kahn presided over the opening of
the Kimbell Art Museum in 1972. Courtesy Kimbell Art Museum, Fort Worth, Texas.
Photographer Robert Wharton.

by the shy, modest Fort Worth entrepreneur Kay Kimbell, the foundation received Kimbell's estate at his death, and his wife, Velma Fuller Kimbell, donated
her share of their community property to form an endowment of $100 million
for a museum of the "first class." Brown turned to the controversial architect
Louis I. Kahn of Philadelphia to design a building, but not until a clear and
cogent prearchitectural plan had been drafted.[70] Brown took a perilous course,
for even though Kahn had designed other art museums, his structures were often brutal concrete monoliths lacking warmth or charm.

With a yearly acquisitions budget of nearly $7 million, Brown assembled a monumental art collection and simultaneously sought from Kahn a building that would match the prizes it was to house. The architect did not fail at the task. He responded with a design of six cycloid semibarrel concrete vaults more than three hundred feet long. Abandoning the brutalism long associated with his work, Kahn decided to bring into the galleries natural light at once diffused and silver in quality. "We are born of light," he declared, "to me, natural light is the only light because it has mood."[71] From plexiglass skylights in the top of the lead-covered vaults, light poured down upon polished-aluminum reflectors that projected the brightness against the curves of the interior ceiling. Magic sunlight, satin travertine, honey-colored oak, and blue stainless steel gave the interior a majestic warmth. The "liquid stone" concrete exterior defied easy classification, though the long porches hinted at classical roots. Kahn declared: "You know what's so wonderful about those porches? They're so unnecessary."[72] The architect had not created a "Greek Garage" but rather a "flawless success."[73] Arata Isozaki, the leading architect of Japan, called the Kimbell Art Museum simply "the best building in the United States."[74] At last the goals of the boosters and art patrons were being realized. The Kimbell Art Museum was lauded by critics, by museum directors, and by patrons. Architectural magazines, eastern newspapers, and cultural journals featured this remarkable building and its outstanding collection.

Perhaps the region had arrived because of Kay Kimbell's enthusiasm for art. In 1935 his wife, Velma, had persuaded Kay to accompany her to a Fort Worth Art Association exhibit. There the quiet entrepreneur found an eighteenth-century English hunting painting that so appealed to him that he knew he had to have it. Bertram Newhouse sold Kimbell the first of many paintings, and over the next two decades Newhouse and his sons guided the Kimbells on a quest for the best in Renaissance, British, and nineteenth-century French painting. Born in rural Texas in 1886, the hardworking Kimbell had mastered the marketplace in flour and grain and built a business empire. By the 1960s, from his headquarters in Fort Worth, Kimbell led some seventy corporations in food manufacturing and distribution, petroleum, real estate, and insurance. From the time he acquired his first painting, Kimbell became an inveterate museum-goer. On every business trip he visited museums, and he and his wife continued to purchase paintings that soon overwhelmed their home. Loans to colleges, universities, and libraries did not achieve Kimbell's desire to "share what he had with others."[75]

The Kimbells created the Kimbell Art Foundation in the 1930s to own the art. Realizing that his good friend Amon Carter was forming a major collection of western American art and that the Fort Worth Museum of Art desired to build a modern art collection, Kimbell decided to fill the void with European paintings and sculpture. The directors of the Kimbell Foundation built on the core collection of two hundred pieces, using the Foundation's resources to buy paintings from the Renaissance and scrolls from the Orient as well as pre-Columbian art. The collection was broadened after 1981 with the acquisition of works by Velásquez, Chardin, Watteau, and Picasso, many of them masterworks in prime condition. As early as 1982, the cultural critic Thomas Hoving called the Kimbell "America's best small museum." Thus the modest Kimbell and his wife provided Fort Worth with a museum that carried out his plan, a serene place of silver light to house the best and the most beautiful, an art museum truly of the first rank.[76]

Urban boosters in the region continued to seek large-scale architectural statements. As a consequence, throughout the 1960s and into the 1980s, internationally known architects produced dozens of art museums in the Southwest, though none reached the greatness of Kahn's Kimbell. Alden Dow at Phoenix, Philip Johnson at Corpus Christi, Gunnar Birkerts at Houston, and Edward Larrabee Barnes at Dallas produced buildings reflecting the struggles between the proponents of the International Style, who followed the model of Mies van der Rohe, and the postmodernists, who wanted to reintroduce classical elements into American architecture. With each building, they also struggled to attain the wishes of the community for a statement, a symbol, a concrete notice that the city was a center of both commerce and culture.

One of the best examples of the explosion of the sunbelt was Phoenix, a community that grew from a town of 60,000 people with virtually no art life in the 1930s into the nation's ninth-largest city by the mid-1980s. As Phoenix matured, its community leaders desired to create an art museum as part of a civic center complex. Frank Lloyd Wright had made a major impact on the city with the creation of Taliesin West, so it was not surprising that the directors of the Phoenix Art Museum turned to a Wright disciple to design their new museum. Alden B. Dow of Michigan had studied with Wright in the 1930s and gained an appreciation for the decorative effects of natural materials. With attention to careful detailing and integrity with the site, Dow produced a "Wrightian" design with a prevailing horizontality. Only three windows broke the facade of the building, which had large, open gallery spaces. Civic boosters offered the new museum as proof that Phoenix was indeed a city with culture.[77] Although the Phoenix Art Museum gained no single, major benefactor and although its permanent collection was neither broad nor deep, the city continued its inexorable growth, and by the end of the 1980s, civic leaders pressed forward with a major expansion of both the museum and its holdings.

Corpus Christi obtained a museum resembling a brilliant-white Greek island block when the Art Museum of South Texas commissioned Philip Johnson and John Burgee to produce a relatively small building, but one with a dramatic presence. Located on the shore of the bay, the reinforced concrete structure was an abstract object. The exterior seemed sliced out of concrete like an eroded square while the three-level interior had broad expanses of pure white with huge windows overlooking the seascape.[78] Of the bronze-trimmed monolith, Johnson said, "I tried to design a space that in itself without any pictures, without any reason for being, would be exciting."[79] The architects succeeded at their task. The building was exciting, and the museum had virtually no significant paintings in its permanent collection. The Corpus Christi experience demonstrated another hazard of the art museum building boom: major resources were directed to concrete and glass with unsuccessful efforts to raise nonvisible endowments. The community also had few art collectors and even fewer major donors. Thus the museum depended on traveling exhibitions for its gloriously light-filled galleries.

If Corpus Christi acquired a brilliant, small solitaire by the sea, Dallas wanted a new art museum that would serve as the dazzling, multijeweled crown of a monumental arts district. The art museum at Fair Park could no longer exhibit its growing holdings; that area of the city suffered from urban blight, and Dallas needed to make a cultural statement that would mitigate nearly two decades of negative publicity. By 1977, museum trustees had the noted architect Edward Larrabee Barnes at work on a design for a huge edifice to be built on the near-north side of the business district. Barnes had produced other art museums, but this was an opportunity to make an eloquent postmodernist statement. The directors organized a massive fund-raising effort for the new building in a city then in the midst of economic expansion. A bond issue provided $25 million, and the fund drive raised $20 million in cash and in gifts of paintings, sculpture, and decorative arts. This was culture with a vengeance. Against the dramatic backdrop of downtown Dallas, Barnes produced a low-keyed building of limestone blocks containing flowing galleries and courtyards separated by a series of steps. A long barrel vault paid homage to Kahn's Kimbell Museum. But even as Barnes brought the project to closure, Director Harry Parker and his board members obtained the Wendy and Emery Reves Collection, appraised at nearly $30 million, doubling the value of the museum's holdings. They then directed

Barnes to add a $5 million decorative arts wing on the second floor for the Reves Collection.[80]

The Reves Collection reflected the connoisseurship of Wendy Reves—New York model, international socialite, and art collector—and of her late husband. Born Wyn-Nelle Russell in Marshall in rural eastern Texas, Wendy Reves became a John Robert Powers model in New York and joined the international set in the years before World War II. In 1949 she began a life with Emery Reves, although they were not married until fifteen years later. Emery Reves (originally Revexz), a Hungarian Jew, formed an antifascist news syndicate in the 1930s and became a confidant of Winston Churchill and other allied leaders. He wrote extensively and prospered as a publisher and editor. Emery and Wendy Reves purchased Coco Chanel's home in the south of France and filled it with art and distinguished guests. The Reveses acquired paintings by Cézanne, Monet, Gauguin, Renoir, Van Gogh, and Degas, as well as Chinese porcelains, ironwork from the Middle Ages, Spanish and Middle Eastern carpets, rare books, and decorative arts. They also held a large body of Winston Churchill memorabilia.[81]

After the death of Emery Reves in 1981, it became known that the collection might be available to a museum. The aggressive trustees of the Dallas Museum of Art acted quickly. Civic leaders and the museum's young director, Harry Parker, courted Wendy Reves assiduously and won a commitment.[82] The museum agreed to her terms in order to obtain what it did not have—a major collection of seventy Impressionist and post-Impressionist paintings. Dallas had no Renoirs; Reves was offering eight! But the price was steep. She demanded that the museum re-create six of the principal rooms of her home, Villa La Pausa, with the furniture, paintings, tapestries, and other furnishings just as she had them arranged. Furthermore, the collection would include the ironworks, Churchill memorabilia, and decorative arts, to be displayed as a unit. The Reves gift significantly increased the value of the museum's permanent collection, but at some sacrifice: the Reves Collection was a strange combination of extraordinary paintings, decorative pieces, tapestries, and memorabilia. Still, the museum's acquisition was an obvious accomplishment. As one New York art authority noted: "Texas museums are perceived as being on the make. They're energetic and extremely well heeled."[83]

Texas was one example of the rise of the Southwest as a force in the international art world as powerful, wealthy collectors came to dominate the marketplace. But perhaps nowhere was this as obvious as in Los Angeles with the opening of the Norton Simon and J. Paul Getty museums and their insatiable donors who purchased art at a phenomenal rate. Southern California benefited from the creation of two of the finest vanity museums in the world. Simon, Getty, and their foundations not only formed museums of extraordinary range and quality but also continued to acquire works of art at an astonishing pace and at astonishing prices. The result was the creation of an entirely new art atmosphere in southern California.

Although not a native of the region, Norton Simon made his home in southern California after becoming a highly successful entrepreneur. Born in Portland, Oregon, in 1907, Simon moved to San Francisco as a young man. There he developed a food-processing firm and in 1943 formed Hunt Foods, turning it into a $1 billion conglomerate during the next three decades. In 1954 Simon bought his first paintings for a new home—a Gauguin, a Bonnard, and a Picasso. "I was hooked," he recalled.[84] Simon read art books voraciously, visited museums, and met with gallery owners. By the mid-1960s he prepared to enter the international art market with a vengeance. He purchased the entire Duveen Brothers art gallery and the building in which it was housed for $15 million and then bought, at record-setting prices, works by Rembrandt, Raphael, Monet, Degas, and other masters. Soon Simon had spent over $100 million on art. Angered by the policies of the Los Angeles County Museum of Art and the feuding among his fellow directors, Simon resigned from the board and in 1974 prepared to create his own museum.

Fortunately for Simon, the Pasadena Museum of Modern Art had grossly overextended itself in constructing a large building without an endowment to maintain the facility. Its desperate directors asked him for aid. Simon agreed to pay their debts, to repair and remodel the building, and to continue to display their small but impressive collection of modern art. But they had to accept his terms: changing the name to the Norton Simon Museum of Art and giving him total control of the policies of the museum. They agreed, and when the museum reopened in 1975 it housed the Norton Simon holdings, and Simon's wife, the former actress Jennifer Jones Simon, chaired a handpicked board of directors. Simon thus seized the opportunity to "pick up" a museum in the same way that he had acquired food processors for the conglomerate. He told reporters that he wanted "to clarify unmistakably" that the museum was "to become an institution of the type of the Frick Collection in New York."[85]

With assets in excess of $100 million, the Norton Simon Foundation acquired outstanding Dutch and Flemish works, then added some seventeenth-and eighteenth-century paintings of major importance. The collection was broadened to include Matisse, Utrillo, and Modigliani and was strengthened in French Impressionism. Degas bronzes, Barbizon landscapes, and Picasso's

CULTURE *in the* AMERICAN SOUTHWEST

Woman with Book helped form an impeccable and increasingly comprehensive holding. Simon proved not to be an adventurous collector, but he was consumed with a restless energy to locate and acquire the very best works and he demonstrated a passion for purchasing blockbuster masterpieces. By 1987, the Simon holdings had an estimated value of $750 million and the museum had become one of the most remarkable art collections in the world.[86]

The furor over soaring prices for art increased dramatically with the rising fiscal strength of the J. Paul Getty Trust and its voracious appetite. Born in Minneapolis in 1892, J. Paul Getty moved with his family in 1903 to Oklahoma Territory, where his father entered the petroleum business. Educated at the University of Southern California, the University of California at Berkeley, and Oxford University, Getty toured the National Gallery in London and the Louvre in Paris as a young man, beginning a lifelong interest in art. He worked on his father's oil properties in Oklahoma during the summers and developed his own petroleum holdings. A millionaire by age twenty-three, Getty divided his time between his homes in Los Angeles and Europe. After the outbreak of the Great Depression, he began to purchase works of art then available at very low prices. After buying his first painting in 1931, Getty fell in love with English and French furniture and by the late 1930s was collecting in earnest. Getty read widely in art books and journals and made a decision to collect Greek and Roman antiquities, Renaissance paintings, eighteenth-century French furniture, and classical carpets. The growing Getty fortune allowed him to increase his rate of acquisition, particularly after he moved permanently to England in 1957. Vast profits from Middle Eastern oil investments encouraged Getty to furnish several homes with his growing treasury.[87]

In 1953 he created a trust to build a museum in southern California, and plans were developed to construct the facility on his Malibu ranch. There Getty desired to display part of his holdings in what he referred to as "my Taj Mahal." A $17 million museum would house a collection worth $200 million. Having developed his collection largely in a depressed market and in several areas not favored by contemporary tastes, and taking advantage of American and British tax laws, Getty ordered that a reproduction of a Roman villa be erected on a hill overlooking the Pacific Ocean. He did not want some "tinted glass and stainless-steel monstrosity" for his collection. Opened in 1974 to less-than-positive notices, the Getty Museum was criticized for both its architecture and the unevenness of its collection. Getty never saw the museum before his death in 1976, but he undoubtedly felt the slings and arrows of its detractors, who noted that he had refused to enter competition for the finest Old Master paintings and that

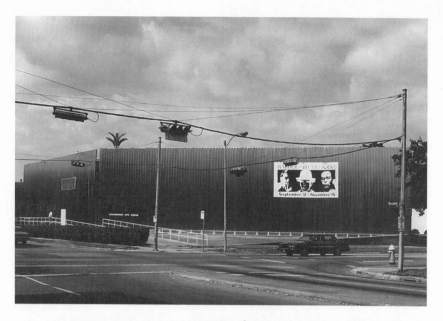

FIGURE 48

*The architect Gunnar Birkerts provided Houston's Contemporary Arts Museum with a
corrugated metal skin denounced by one critic as a "metal shack." Author's collection.*

the collection did not compare in quality to the collections of Kimbell or Simon. Getty defended the building: "What could be more logical than to display [classical art] in a classical building?"[88]

The museum staff and trustees of the foundation assumed that they would benefit from a Getty endowment, but they were unprepared for the largess provided in his will. Getty gave the museum his private art collection and his entire fortune, worth $700 million. That sum soared to $1.25 billion when Getty Oil Company was sold. Federal law required that the trust spend almost $100 million per year on its activities, and consequently the trustees engaged in a policy of major purchases and initiated the construction of a huge new museum complex in Brentwood. They also developed programs in the areas of art education, art history, and preservation.[89] Nevertheless, the richest museum in the world remained under assault for the quality of its holdings and for the "modest" nature of its acquisitions. Regardless of the criticism, few museums in the country so closely reflected the personality of their benefactors as the Getty. Its Roman villa stood in sharp contrast to the trends in museum architecture in the region.

Two strong currents in American architecture could be seen across the Southwest, as nationally and internationally recognized designers produced buildings in both the modernist and the postmodernist styles. For example, the Contem-

CULTURE *in the* AMERICAN SOUTHWEST

porary Arts Museum of Houston turned to the Latvian immigrant architect Gunnar Birkerts to design a new building. Birkerts had worked in the office of Eero Saarinen as a young architect and was deeply influenced by Saarinen and the International Style. In 1970, he initiated work on the Houston commission, and the result was a large parallelogram with an unbroken stainless-steel skin. The site contributed to the decision regarding the building's shape, but critics attacked the design as a "corrugated metal shack." Interestingly, Birkerts's building stood directly across the street from the Houston Museum of Fine Arts and the curved Miesian wall of the Brown Pavilion. Although the contents of the museums were distinctly different, the intellectual and aesthetic sources of their architecture were not.[90] Perhaps of greater importance, Houston could now claim a place in the world of contemporary art. The Museum of Fine Arts housed a growing collection of traditional paintings and sculpture, whereas the Contemporary Arts Museum exhibited avant-garde works from New York, Los Angeles, and Europe, as well as from Houston's own art community. The city was not just a warehouse for the arts of the past but was a creator of the art of the present.

Economic growth, expanding urban places, and unrelieved ambitions came together in the Southwest from the 1960s to the early 1980s. New cultural institutions emerged and older organizations expanded as high-quality art museums and symphony orchestras, as well as striking architecture, shaped the institutional culture. Urban spaces acquired icons of glass and marble to demonstrate their maturity. Simultaneously, regional artists, writers, musicians, thespians, and dancers gained additional critical reknown for the Southwest.

CHAPTER 7

A Renaissance with
Many Voices

1960–1980

Even as southwesterners created new or expanded institutional cultural icons, a number of individual artists, writers, dancers, and thespians were producing an astonishing array of paintings, sculptures, novels, plays, short stories, and ballets. Works by Native Americans and Chicanos enriched the culture of the region as a growing sense of ethnic pride emphasized the role of the arts in their societies. Critics in the United States and Europe noted this outpouring, both its quality and its quantity. A new awareness of the region emerged by the 1980s, much of this consciousness resulting from the rich sounds of the many voices echoing across the Southwest.

Artists produced paintings and sculpture that encompassed trends international in scope but also reflective of the geography and the peoples of the region. The most significant changes included the abandonment of provinciality in styles and a growing acceptance by collectors as well as gallery visitors. As early as 1963, an observer of the art scene in southern California declared: "Provincialism, the curse of so many gifted American artists, has died on the vine in Los Angeles."[1]

The City of Angels became "America's Second Art City." Sculpture in southern California achieved new creative heights in the 1970s as rampant eclecticism swept the region. Art forms based on ingenuity and the application of creative energy emerged from highly individualistic studios. California sculpture reflected East Asian influences, but assemblages using a vast array of materials and methods reflected regional themes. Artists in southern California stood in the mainstream of American art and often directed its currents. They launched savage attacks on racism, conventional sexual mores, police violence, and the war in Southeast Asia. Galleries along La Cienega in Los Angeles hosted experimental artists among the avant-garde. Pop art, often bizarre, mocked societal values using epoxy resins or plastics, symbols of an age of materialism.[2]

Postmodernists in Texas also eschewed traditional landscapes, still lifes, and portraiture as they embraced an artistic freedom that a newly educated audience could accept. John Alexander, David Bates, Melissa Miller, and James Surls, among others, led the wave. Houston in particular became a place to which artists migrated to participate in the revolution. The Contemporary Arts Museum (CAM) came to the fore as a venue for the "new" Texas art. The exhibition "Fire!" organized by Surls at the CAM in 1979 drew one hundred Texas artists. The show won critical and public acclaim. Validation of the quality of the work being produced came in 1984 with the landmark exhibit "Fresh Paint: The Houston School" at the Museum of Fine Arts. The movement of paintings and sculptures across the street from the CAM to the Fine Arts Museum represented a giant leap for contemporary Texas artists.[3]

The Kimbell Art Museum held a retrospective for Melissa Miller, displaying her work along with selections from the museum's holdings. Her folk-tale subjects painted in a Japanese brush-and-ink manner produced mythical figures in a misty golden light. One critic described her work as "Hieronymous Bosch meets West Texas animal life." Miller returned to the Indian dancers she had seen in New Mexico as a child for the world of dreams she created. Her paintings, and those of her contemporaries, served to demonstrate how far removed art in the Southwest was from the Taos School of the 1920s.[4] Another Texas artist, the Port Arthur–born Robert Rauschenberg, fled to New York to avoid "terminal neglect," yet his paintings, drawings, and minimalist constructions found places in southwestern museums, galleries, and homes.[5] Experimentation in the use of materials and styles marked the cultural renaissance occurring simultaneously among Anglo, Native American, Hispanic, and African American artists.

After 1945, Native American painters and sculptors had abandoned the iconographic orthodoxy of their training in Santa Fe, the University of Oklahoma, and Bacone College. A dramatic shift occurred as they moved away from traditional watercolor paintings to mainstream easel art. Tonita Peña and her son Joe Herrera of Cochiti Pueblo combined elements of the old and the new styles, but other artists adopted a nonderivative modernism that employed traditional symbols while totally reorganizing them on canvas. There was a collective rejection of the "Bambi art" of the 1930s.[6]

The Hopi people had a strong tradition of painting, as seen in the works of Fred Kabotie and Otis Polelonema, pioneer tribal artists three decades earlier, but by the 1970s young Hopi painters had developed a synthesis of the conventional symbols and postmodernist styles. Ancient Hopi legends and representations emerged in abstract expressions or in cubist forms. Some experimented with pop art, particularly to satirize aspects of Hopi life and the Anglo world. The Hopi artists lived and worked in the villages, participated in the ceremonies and rituals, and related their people and their land to their work. They put tribal symbolism in new forms that celebrated the Hopi "Way and Spirit." The young artists abandoned the clichéd style found in shops and galleries catering to tourists. They explored their heritage in forms fresh and exciting.[7]

No other Native American artist had as much impact in the 1960s and 1970s as Fritz Scholder.[8] Although one-quarter California Mission Indian (Luiseño), Scholder rejected the term "Native American artist." He declared, "I do not call myself an Indian artist . . . everyone else does."[9] Yet the subject matter of his brilliantly ironic canvases was American Indians. His father, an employee of the Bureau of Indian Affairs, moved the family to South Dakota, where as a high school student Fritz studied with the Sioux painter Oscar Howe. When the family moved to California, young Scholder attended Sacramento City College and the state college. One of his teachers, Wayne Thibaud, exposed him to the English painter Francis Bacon's work, which had a major impact on his emerging style. After receiving a master's degree from the University of Arizona, Scholder taught from 1964 to 1969 at the Institute of American Indian Arts in Santa Fe. There he revolutionized the form and content of the curriculum.

Both gifted and technically proficient, Scholder placed works in galleries where his ethnicity became irrelevant. His "discovery" of the Southwest while a graduate student in Tucson shaped his art, which Scholder saw as "autobiographical." He wrote: "I do not feel the pull of the dichotomy of two cultures. However, I am aware of the incongruous nature of the two cultures." His art referred to Native Americans engulfed by a European culture.[10] His subjects destroyed traditional, historical masks to reveal the contemporary Indian. Scholder's use of humor and poignancy produced highly critical responses by some Native Americans, who saw the paintings as grotesque and insulting. That, of course, was not the artist's intent. Scholder combined a form of Bacon's expressionism with pop art in order to state his personal and political attitudes about Native Americans. Huge canvases in vibrant colors depicted "regalia-clad warriors wearing sunglasses or drinking a can of beer. Other paintings seem filled with alienation and rage; they were even hostile and menacing. Many young Indian artists, both conscious and unconscious protégés, followed his example to create a contemporary Indian art."[11]

T. C. Cannon, a Caddo-Kiowa from Oklahoma, adopted Scholder's approach. Cannon saw a new form to express ancient traditions: "I dream of a great breadth of Indian art to develop that ranges through the whole region of our past, present and future, something that doesn't lack the ultimate power we possess. . . . From the poisons and passions of technology arises a great force with which we must deal as present-day painters."[12] Cannon built on Scholder's aesthetic, blending abstract expressionism and pop art to expose the plight of his people stranded between two cultures. His paintings moved from radical political statements to satire as a vehicle to challenge the mythology forced on Native Americans by an Anglo society.

If Scholder led the way in painting, Allan Houser (in Apache, "Ha-o-zous") became the patriarch of Native American sculptors. A Chiricahua Apache from Oklahoma, Houser learned the traditions of his tribe from a family of storytellers and singers. Only nineteen years old when he began to study at the Indian School in Santa Fe, Houser sculpted first in wood and then turned to bronze and stone. After studying with Dorothy Dunn, Houser worked in construction, painted murals, and illustrated children's books. He returned to the Indian School as a teacher in 1962 and began a series of sculptures that won international recognition. His fully contoured, representational portrayals of women and children emphasized beauty and dignity. "It all comes back to Mother Earth," he said.[13] "I could never turn away from my history. That's the part of me that made me what I am now. The strength that I have is my pride in who I am. My heritage."[14] Houser saw sculpture in the rocks of Canyon de Chelly, Monument Valley, and the cliff dwellings at Puyé. The earth and his people provided Houser with materials, subject matter, and inspiration. "That's why I stay in New Mexico. The weather is good. The sagebrush and cedars are typical of Apache country. What more could anyone ask for?"[15] Houser shaped Native American sculpture as effectively as Scholder gave life to contemporary Indian painting.

Neither Houser nor Scholder received the popularity of R. C. Gorman, however. A bumper sticker in the Southwest in the 1970s asked, "Who is R. C. Gorman?" Rudolph Carl Gorman's work seemed ubiquitous. Prints, notecards, posters, stationary, and paintings with his work appeared everywhere. Gorman, a Navajo, produced traditional figurative subjects in monochromatic colors on delicate backgrounds. Borrowing from the Mexican painter José Clemente Orozco, he combined academic elegance with subjects that reflected his heritage and the region. Financial success made Gorman an Indian jet-setter; he appeared on television talk shows wearing a blazer from Brooks Brothers and an Indian headband. As his lithographs and prints sold in larger numbers at ever-higher prices, Gorman carefully cultivated an image enhanced by an exuberant life-style in

Taos.[16] A dedicated modernist, Gorman found his muse in the earth. "Real Indian art is not made on easels, its on rocks, as in Canyon de Chelly. . . . The forms of the earth rubbed off on me. . . . The canyon was filled with images. The impressions never left me."[17] Gorman's success as an artist depended on his employment of figures and the landscape in works that seemed both timeless and traditional, without the anger or anxiousness of Scholder.

Even as Native American artists created new voices in the 1960s and 1970s, many Mexican Americans, Hispanics, Mexicanos, and Latinos found an awareness of kinship that led to the Chicano movement, an ethnic and political identity often expressed in art and literature. In cultural centers, studios, and galleries in San Diego, Los Angeles, San Antonio, and El Paso, the Chicano art movement emerged in the 1960s. Artists of Mexican ancestry achieved a self-awareness as members of a distinct group whose ethnicity strongly influenced their work. They sought to establish an identity and a relevance as painters. Strongly influenced by artistic trends from Mexico, young Chicano painters found models in the works of Mexican muralists and modernists. They filled physical space with symbols and myths resurrected from the south. In Tucson, for example, Antonio Pazos led a group that placed murals in the old Presidio as well as in the barrio. Some Chicano painters expressed passionate support for itinerant farmworkers and the downtrodden and called for political activism, but others focused on portrayals of the Hispanic people and their place in the Southwest. Paintings of "zootsuiters," collections of folk art, and assemblages of ordinary household items helped define "El Movimiento." Huge, painterly, bright, abstract expressionist works contrasted sharply with traditional santos. By the 1970s, Chicano art had attained critical acclaim for its inventiveness and strong statements on a broad range of issues.[18]

The sculptor Luis Jimenez epitomized the emergence of Chicano art with his large, garishly colored statues in fiberglass and epoxy. Born in El Paso in 1940, Jimenez worked in his father's sign business from the age of six, learning how to mold concrete, weld steel, blow glass, spray paint, work tin, and form neon lights. An architecture student, first at El Paso and then at the University of Texas at Austin, Jimenez shifted his major to art. A three-month visit to Mexico shaped his style and his career. "I guess what really impressed me about Mexican art was somehow it seemed relevant. I thought I had to be relevant to the society," he said.[19] Following five largely unsuccessful years in New York, Jimenez returned to the Southwest, where the oilman, painter, and art patron Donald Anderson provided him with work space, living quarters, and financial assistance in Roswell, New Mexico. For the next six years Jimenez created the *Progress*

FIGURE 49
Vaquero, *by Luis Jimenez, stands
in Moody Park near one of
Houston's barrios. Author's
collection.*

sculptures — large, complex southwestern images. The fiberglass figurative sculptures, soon to be his signature, dealt with racism, the Hispanic female form, and
the Mexican American subculture fixation on "Low Riders." Jimenez produced
a stylized *Vaquero* for a Houston barrio and *Howl,* a coyote, for Wichita State
University, but he also produced *Old Woman with Cat,* which affectionately captured the image of the Hispanic *madre.* By the early 1980s Jimenez had presented
one-man shows at prestigious galleries across the country and had received several awards and fellowships, including a stint at the American Academy in Rome.
Returning to Roswell after several years in El Paso, he established a studio in
nearby Hondo, where he continued to use his sculptures as statements about
contemporary society. Art as polemic became his theme, whether he depicted
cowboys or Aztecs. The neon lights that he added to the brightly colored fiberglass produced even more graphic statements about the age of machines and

FIGURE 50
Southwest Pieta, *by Luis Jimenez, dominates Martineztown Park
in Albuquerque. Author's collection.*

technology, its force and power. Motorcycles and television sets became part of his pieces.[20] The Metropolitan Museum of Art and the Chicago Art Institute added his works to their permanent collections.

Melesio Casas's paintings shared characteristics with the sculptures by Jimenez. With a pop art sensibility, he created "humanscape" paintings that used a movie-theater format to project images of advertisements and to suggest the absence of reality in their content. Born in El Paso in 1929 and educated at Texas Western College and the University of the Americas in Mexico City, Casas taught in El Paso before moving to San Antonio. By 1970, he began to paint specifically Chicano themes, often as visual puns.[21] A painting of Indians, Chicanos, and chocolate cakes became *Brownies of the Southwest*. The director of Houston's Contemporary Arts Museum, James Harithas, said: "Using *pachuco* logic, *barrio* humor, and a piercing intellectual approach to integrate the message content, Casas establishes a sophisticated didactic painting."[22] Casas saw Mexican American artists as outsiders, neither Mexican nor Anglo, a position that he thought fortunate, for it defined their art. He explained, "I can combine English and Spanish to give a more colorful expression than I would if I said it all in English or all in Spanish."[23] Contemporary television commercials mixed with

Aztec legends in paintings satirical and humorous gave Casas a voice that won recognition among Chicanos and Anglos.

The early work of Chicano artists generated critical acclaim, but Chicana painters found acceptance harder to obtain. Ysela Provenicio O'Malley of El Paso, Anita Rodríguez of Taos, and Carmen Rodríguez of Austin explored themes of the land interacting with the people. They drew from folk traditions and gender roles to produce distinct cultural forms. The deep spirituality in their paintings and drawings came from landforms and the desert. Anita Rodríguez declared, "Mud is the flesh of the earth, and stones are the bones." But not until the 1980s did Chicana artists find the acceptance that had come to Chicano painters and sculptors a decade earlier.[24]

The African American art community also became a vibrant part of the regional culture by the 1960s. John Biggers painted life in Houston's Third Ward, where deep poverty moved him to record its history on canvas. The urban black experience formed the core of his work, which as early as 1950 won a prestigious competition at the Museum of Fine Arts. The twenty-six-year-old artist could not attend the reception to honor him, however, since the museum was segregated. Two years later he won the Dallas Museum of Art's Neiman-Marcus Purchase Prize, but when he went to collect his check, it was presented to him at the door: he could not enter the museum. Biggers became both a spokesman for and a historian of the African American society in Houston. He borrowed from Thomas Hart Benton and Diego Rivera as he painted large murals and small, quiet, elegant pieces. Biggers drew on a sense of place and an ethnicity that emphasized family, religion, traditions, ceremonies, and work. A teacher at Texas Southern University for many years, Biggers influenced young artists who came to study with him. African themes, human values, and a work ethic permeated his art and that of his protégés. As important, Biggers became the nucleus of a group of Houston-based African American artists who garnered critical praise while depicting the history of the black community. In 1995, the Museum of Fine Arts presented a retrospective of the work of Biggers in its main gallery.[25]

The crosscurrents in the region's architecture and art mirrored a literary renaissance that swept the Southwest in the 1960s and 1970s. Regional writers maintained a national consciousness in works that used southwestern locales, peoples, and cultures. While part of a larger literary framework, the regionalists found in specific times and places a means to enhance American themes.[26] Although the period began with Larry McMurtry wearing a T-shirt emblazoned with the words "Minor Regional Novelist," by the early 1980s, he and other southwestern writers had won international recognition for a body of extraordinary work. Eastern critics had refused to acknowledge the quality of regional literature, other than that produced in the American South, in reviews and essays. In turn, southwesterners lamented the provincialism of the cultural literati who believed civilization ended on the east bank of the Hudson River. Eastern seaboard intellectuals drew this line in critiques published in *New Yorkers Review Each Other's Books,* as outlanders referred to the *New York Review of Books.* Initially, southwestern writers produced traditionally oriented novels and short stories with a focus on the land, ranches, and farm life. Paul Horgan and Elmer Kelton wrote historical fiction that, though it was often harsh and realistic, embraced geographical symbolism and incorporated Hispanics and Native Americans. McMurtry, Joan Didion, and others turned to the urban Southwest to describe the emerging boomtowns of Houston and Los Angeles. Native American and Hispanic voices emerged to critical acclaim for a fiction of peoples long only shadows in Anglo literature. By the end of the 1980s, sophisticated bookstores on Madison Avenue in New York City not only stocked southwestern novels on their walnut or cherry shelves but also had Willie Nelson singing "Stardust" on the sound system above their espresso bars.

Perhaps the most startling shift in southwestern literature came from the typewriters of Edward Abbey, William Eastlake, and John Nichols, who used the power of words to decry ecological disasters in the region. Strongly influenced by a literary tradition extending from Henry David Thoreau to Wallace Stegner, the trio used anger, violence, and moral outrage to express their dismay at the "rape of the land." While some of their plots often employed stereotypes and showed political naivete, their voices stirred a regional sense of environmental loss. Passion sometimes merged with slapstick comedy, and characters often lacked credibility, but Abbey, Eastlake, and Nichols won readers, if not always converts.[27]

Edward Abbey's ouvre included the novels *Fire on the Mountain* and *The Monkey Wrench Gang,* as well as *Desert Solitare,* a study of environmental change. But whether in fiction or in essays, he revealed the impact of the region on his career. "I would have been a writer wherever I lived, but the deserts, mountains, rivers and canyons of the American Southwest have been my home and spiritual center since I first saw them in 1944. In that sense, the landscape has been a part of my writing, as of my life, for more than forty years."[28] Born in Pennsylvania in 1927, educated at the University of New Mexico and the University of Edinburgh, Scotland, Abbey became a U.S. Park Service ranger after military duty. Subsequently he joined the U.S. Forest Service as a fire lookout. Beginning with *The Brave Cowboy* (1957), he published novels, essays, and social criticism that reflected a distinct perspective on the world in which he lived: "I am an enemy of the modern military-industrial state; all of my books, fiction and non-fiction, are written in defense of human liberty and for the greater glory of the natural world."[29]

Abbey's "natural world" included *The Monkey Wrench Gang,* a group of comical ecological saboteurs. These merry marauders threw monkey wrenches into machines and blasted dams in an effort to save the environment. More satisfying as a work of literature is *Fire on the Mountain,* in which John Vogelin, the owner of a small ranch near White Sands, New Mexico, fights the federal government, which sought his land for a missile range. With his grandson Billy Vogelin Starr and friend Lee Mackie, John Vogelin represents determinism, independence, and pride in the land. Abbey develops the narrative against a landscape filled with heat, bright light, and animals, both domestic and wild. Vogelin, like Charlie Flagg in Elmer Kelton's *The Time It Never Rained* or the Texas panhandle ranchers in Larry McMurtry's *Horseman, Pass By,* loves the land and the freedom it brings. The enemies are the federal government and the large corporations that threaten the survival of a way of life, a mode of thinking.[30] Life in Abbey's "natural world" could be humble and serene or it could become arrogant and predatory as he confronted contemporary problems in a vision both brilliant and bleak.[31] Verbally blasting the Glen Canyon Dam on the Colorado River, Abbey declared: "Civilization is the wild river. Culture, 592,000 tons of cement."[32]

Where Abbey used comedy and pathos, William Eastlake turned to satire that echoed Thomas Pynchon, Kurt Vonnegut, and Joseph Heller. In novels such as *Go in Beauty, The Bronc People, Portrait of an Artist with Twenty-six Horses,* and *Dancers in the Scalp House,* Eastlake employed bitter humor and nihilism to depict life in his adopted Southwest. Using both satire and whimsy, Eastlake populated his novels with Indians and cowboys, rich tourists and rodeo stars, all caught up in a search for American values in a world in which words such as *honor* and *justice* are all but undefinable.[33] Born in Brooklyn in 1917 and raised in New Jersey, Eastlake graduated from high school during the Great Depression. Hoboing across the country, he found work in Stanley Rose's Book Shop in Los Angeles, where he met Theodore Dreiser, Nathaniel West, and William Saroyan. Rose and these literary luminaries influenced Eastlake to write, and for two decades he struggled. After service in France during World War II, he visited his brother-in-law, a paleontologist living in the Jemez Mountains of New Mexico.[34] Thus began a love affair, revealed in the opening of *Go in Beauty:* "Once upon a time there was time. The land here in the Southwest had evolved slowly and there was time and there were great spaces. Now a man on horseback from atop a bold mesa looked out over the violent spectrum of the Indian Country— into a gaudy infinity where all the colors of the world exploded, soundlessly. 'There's not much time,' he said."[35]

Eastlake settled on a ranch near Cuba, New Mexico, and began a series of novels about that land and its peoples. With a fresh perspective and vigorous writing, he captured the essence of "Indian Country." He sought to expose the excesses of American society in episodic novels and short stories that gained acclaim among eastern critics. Members of the Bowman family, the protagonists of his first three New Mexico novels, illustrate themes of life in the Southwest. Through them, Eastlake lauded the simplicity of Native American culture and deprecated the excesses of contemporary civilization. When a group of Navajos unite to fight a dam project in *Dancers in the Scalp House*, Eastlake used satire, irony, and even fantasy to depict a struggle against "progress."[36]

Another expatriate, John Nichols, also adopted the Southwest, where he, like Abbey and Eastlake, used the land and its native peoples to explore the travails of a nation torn by a war in Southeast Asia, racism, and rapacious capitalism. Born in New York in 1940, Nichols grew up in New York, Connecticut, and Virginia, first coming to New Mexico as a sixteen-year-old prep-school student. A stalled writing career and disillusionment with the war in Vietnam later brought him back to the Southwest. After publishing the widely acclaimed *The Sterile Cuckoo* (1965), Nichols seemed to lose his vision until moving to Taos in 1969. There he produced lyrical prose poems about fly fishing, nature, and the changing environment, as well as polemical tracts. Living in a ramshackle house without indoor plumbing, Nichols roved the Rio Grande valley, which he chronicled in *If Mountains Die* and *On the Mesa*. The latter included his photographs of the landscape and natural wonders.

Readers of these quiet, environmentally sensitive essays were often stunned when they bought copies of Nichols's novels that savagely attacked developers and the federal government. Beginning with *The Milagro Beanfield War* (1974) and *The Magic Journey* (1978), Nichols produced a three-volume New Mexico trilogy about the people and their quality of life in the Taos area. The former depicted the efforts of one man to preserve the rural way of life in a fight with a conglomerate backed by Santa Fe politicians. Nichols cast his novel with people from Costilla and Taos in a struggle between good and evil that included strange plot twists and mystical occurrences. He sought to defend the poor and the downtrodden, conceiving the area as little more than a Third World country: "Taos is sort of like a little outpost in the Amazon."[37] Both novels move at a frenetic pace as Hispanic villagers fight to preserve their traditions and save their land. The third volume in the trilogy, *The Nirvana Blues* (1981), continued the saga of the political and social development of northern New Mexico, with Nichols calling for "balance" in what he characterized as "a life and death struggle."[38] Never one to use serene terms if bombast would do, Nichols's position was clear: "I view the world from a Marxist perspective . . . our economic system is responsible for cultural genocide."[39]

Idealist, activist, and a colorful character, Nichols sustained himself by selling film options on his novels to major Hollywood studios. These payments allowed him to write lyrical essays about the Rio Grande valley and polemical novels defending the small villages situated at the vortex of Anglo and Hispanic clashes. The country that gave him, as a teenager, "the most fabulous summer" he had "ever had" also provided a locale for eminently readable novels that offered scathing views of contemporary America.[40] Yet in each of his novels, Nichols could not escape from the land that had so enthralled him as a wealthy prep-school boy: "The Córdova sons and daughters had scattered, as the saying goes, to the four winds. Or actually, only to the three winds, eastward being anathema to the children of Milagro whose Mississippi was the Midnight Mountains, that chain running north and south bare a mile or two from all their backyards."[41]

Native American novelists and short story writers also sought to expose Anglo readers to their culture and the traditions of their peoples. To do so, they turned to the legends, myths, and folklore of their tribes to develop a sense of place and to evoke their spiritual roots. Native American writers probed the experiences of their people, particularly the young Indians torn between two cultures, the Native and Anglo worlds. Novels, short stories, and poetry revealed an intimate relationship to the region's landscape as the physical forms of the earth served as more than a backdrop — the land and the people were one.

The first Native American author to win a Pulitzer Prize, N. Scott Momaday presented, in *House Made of Dawn* (1968), a series of Kiowa tales that incorporated the earth, sky, moon, sun, and seasons as part of the narrative. Born in Lawton, Oklahoma, in 1934, of a Kiowa father and a Cherokee mother, Momaday grew up in New Mexico and Arizona before his parents moved to the Jémez Pueblo as schoolteachers. He received a bachelor's degree from the University of New Mexico and a doctorate from Stanford University, subsequently teaching at the University of California at Santa Barbara, Berkeley, and Stanford before joining the faculty at the University of Arizona.[42] After publishing *House Made of Dawn,* he authored *The Way to Rainy Mountain, The Names,* and *The Ancient Child.* In these books he combined Native American mythology with autobiographical elements. The oral traditions of the Kiowa provided sources and ideas for his fiction and his art. Yet Momaday denied that he was an "Indian writer." As a novelist, poet, and artist, Momaday did not reject his "Indianness," but he refused to defend the Pueblo villages he saw as "anachronistic clusters," and he did not chart a career to preserve "the old ways" and reservation life.[43] His parents had provided a strong sense of his ancestry in their art, and his extended family shared the stories, tales, and myths of the Kiowas. Momaday brought this heritage to Jémez, where he realized the significance of the interaction of the Native Americans and the landscape. "I came to know the land by going out upon it in all seasons, getting into it until it became the very element in which I lived my daily life."[44]

The works that followed used nature and the landscape to give meaning to the narrative. "Having grown up in the Indian world," Momaday said, "I came to understand that there is a great deal of experience, an accumulation of knowledge and an exercise of the imagination that is indigenous to North America." The writer "is the intelligence of his soil."[45] Momaday's Kiowa name, Tsoatalie, meaning "Rock-Tree Boy," was given to him by the Kiowa storyteller Old Wolf and further linked him to the land and his heritage.[46] Momaday wrote of his time and place, and his investment in that time and place, and although he was intrigued during his travels by the foothills of central Asia and by northwestern Greenland, he made a conscious decision as to where to live and where to compose: "But the Southwest, the Southwest is mine."[47]

Like Momaday, Leslie Marmon Silko, Simon Ortiz, Joy Harjo, Luci Tapahonso, and Linda Hogan found inspiration for their novels, short stories, and poetry in the region and their Native American heritage. In the 1960s and 1970s they also found receptive audiences among Native Americans and among some Anglos whose consciousness and interest had been piqued by Dee Brown's *Bury My Heart at Wounded Knee* and by the activities of the American Indian Movement. Publishers discovered a market for Native American literature, and young Indian writers in the Southwest produced works of reality often edged with anger and sorrow.

Leslie Marmon Silko found in the Laguna Pueblo inspiration, experience, and a source for her stories and novels. Born in Albuquerque in 1948 of mixed Laguna, Hispanic, and Anglo ancestry, Silko attended private schools in Albuquerque before moving to Laguna. A graduate of the University of New Mexico, she briefly studied law before settling in the pueblo as a writer. Strongly influenced by grandparents who had attended the Carlisle Indian school, she combined a traditional education with learning to breed cattle and hunt deer.[48] A mixed-blood at the edges of three cultures, Silko made clear her sense of place: "I am of mixed-breed ancestry, but what I know is Laguna. This place I am from is everything I am as a writer and human being."[49] Silko's *Ceremony* (1978), a novel about a mentally exhausted war veteran at Laguna, was typical of her spare, controlled narratives. She dramatized the conflicts between Pueblo religious views and Christianity as her mixed-blood protagonist, Tayo, seeks personal peace in the high mesa country. A Navajo medicine man saves Tayo, in a tale that draws from the "grail romance" style.[50] But for Silko, the novel is simply the narrative of a good storyteller: "Implicit in that is the whole idea that all of my heritage, my background, was gathered, is a part of being a storyteller."[51]

Women are powerful figures in the Laguna clans, and Silko's female characters, such as Tayo's grandmother, exert influence both temporal and spiritual.[52] Silko's females draw strength from the landscape, as does she: "So long as the human consciousness remains *within* the hills, canyons, cliffs and the plants, clouds and the sky, the term *landscape,* as it has entered the English language is misleading." For Silko, the dictionary definition of *landscape* as what a human being can comprehend in a single view was inadequate. "This assumes the viewer is somehow *outside* or *separated from* the territory he or she surveys. Viewers are as much a part of the landscape as the boulders they stand on."[53]

Other writers of the Native American experience echoed her views. Simon Ortiz, dean of American Indian poets, lived in California, Colorado, Arizona, and elsewhere, but Ácoma Pueblo, where he was born and raised, remained his inspiration. "Ácoma is my home in the deepest sense. It is my identity, my cultural heritage, my community; in other words, Ácoma is who I am. I see through the perspective of being a native of this land, culture, and community. Without that, my work would not have the distinct identity it does."[54] Teacher, storyteller, and activist, Ortiz published poetry and short stories filled with references to the oral traditions and myths of his land and people. He used "Indian humor," which often escaped Anglo readers, in stories that expressed cynicism about white culture. His poetry was of wind, rain, and light, employing powerful language to describe the darkness of contemporary society. Yet an optimism remained; the masses will reaffirm their humanity. For Ortiz, everything is story, the epic of life. Images of desert landscape, dry plains, and vast expanses of porcelain-blue sky fill his works. Oral traditions of Ácoma blend with the reality of the modern Southwest, illuminating Ortiz's world of the "Sky City" as well as literary workshops in faraway cities.[55]

Another Native American writer, Joy Harjo, a member of the Creek Nation, was born in Tulsa. Harjo found her voice while a student at the University of New Mexico. A teacher in Arizona and Colorado, she wrote of heritage but also of place. "The compelling spirit, or at least a powerful and recognizable force behind what I write is certainly the Southwestern landscape."[56] Poems from *She Had Some Horses* and other collections appeared frequently in anthologies, where readers found selections shaped by her interest in the Navajo language and the land. "Wherever I write, I stand in this beautiful and bittersweet country, the land that triggered the curious and terrifying place within me that forces me to write."[57] For Harjo, the landscape formed the mind and voice that was Native American, female, and southwestern.

Luci Tapahonso and Linda Hogan carried these visions into the 1980s with poetry that sprang from Navajo and Chickasaw roots. Born at Shiprock on the Navajo Reservation, Tapahonso received bachelor's and master's degrees from the University of New Mexico, where she also taught. In three volumes of poems, some in English and others in Navajo, she paid homage to her people. She wrote of "Tse bi tah, old birdshaped rock . . . our Mother who brought the people here on her back," drawing from the mythology of the Navajos.[58] Small of body and soft of voice, Tapahonso often sang her poems, which spoke of bread-baking, dances, feast days, mesas, horses, and the sunrise. "The place where we're from is really who we are," she declared.[59] "The land is an integral part of my history, my life and even my name. . . . The landscape plays an important role in my writing because it is part of the Navajo consciousness and lifestyle."[60]

Linda Hogan shared that vision. "People always think of Oklahoma as the dust bowl, but it's really a very rich land. It's very beautiful, and in comparison to the other places I've lived, a strange and almost surrealistic landscape. The colors are intense. . . . Why, when the sun sets, the light's so red for so long and the way it lays across the land."[61] Hogan's poems, and her novel *Mean Spirit,* incorporated the landscape of her native Oklahoma and the tales of the Chickashaw, Osage, and other tribes. She wrote of urban-rural conflicts, collisions of cultures, and stress between generations. The beautiful and the tragic are interwoven in works that speak of animal spirits, bat medicine, and the impact of technology on ancient peoples. Born in Denver in 1947 and educated in Colorado and Oklahoma, Hogan straddled two worlds in a military family constantly moving. But she developed "a genetic memory" of Oklahoma, which became what she called "my *heart* home."[62] She explained, "[Oklahoma] was where magic lived for me, and still does, in the fireflies, and in the breezy motion of trees, and the stillness."[63] The land and the voices of the Chickashaws inspired and enriched *Seeing through the Sun* (1985) and other collections.

Even as Hogan, Silko, Momaday, and other Native Americans found muses in the myths of their people and the land they occupied, Chicano and Chicana writers discovered a rich literary heritage and a broader audience. Chicano literature of the 1960s sprang from both Iberian and Mexican roots. The native population of Mexico had developed a body of oral literature that incorporated myths, the landscape, and folklore. The Spanish conquerors imposed a culture and language then at its creative height. The conquistadores brought Cervantes

CULTURE *in the* AMERICAN SOUTHWEST

and Lope de Vega to the "new world," and educated officers performed classical plays at remote outposts in New Spain. The *corrido,* a fast-paced narrative ballad, laid the basis for much of Chicano literature. *Corridos* spoke of historical events, family loyalty, and the love of the land, concepts that filled the short stories of Mexican American writers into the twentieth century. By the time of World War I, mainstream journals such as *The Century* and *American Magazine* were publishing sketches and stories by María Cristina Mena and others. But because many Hispanic writers published only in Spanish, their talents went largely unnoticed by Anglo readers and critics. Anglos sought romantic, charming Mexicans as an antidote to the "greasers" portrayed by Bret Harte, Helen Hunt Jackson, and Gertrude Atherton. Thus by the 1930s a Mexican American literature had emerged that spoke of an imaginary past, of lives filled exclusively with dignity and civility.[64]

The practice of writing solely for Anglo tastes ended after World War II, in the midst of a vast migration of Mexicans to the United States and of Mexican Americans to the cities of the Southwest. Hispanics who had served in the military during the war often returned with strong beliefs in democracy and equality and with an invigorated ethnic pride. They wanted to enter the mainstream of American life and, simultaneously, to establish and maintain a separate cultural identity. Mario Suárez of Tucson began to publish short stories about the barrio, about the people of El Hoyo ("The Hole"). The barrio, with its unique culture, teemed with life, sights, and sounds far removed from the Anglo world. Suárez filled his stories with people who spoke of the need to maintain fundamental "Mexicanness." The first truly Chicano writer, Suárez was joined by those who shared his vision and generated enough interest to justify the creation of Quinto Sol Publishers in Berkeley as an outlet for their writings.[65]

Authors published by Quinto Sol rejected Anglo modes, turning to Borges and García Márquez. Their cultural ties were to Mexico and Latin America and to the concept of Aztlán, a land inhabited by the true ancestors of the Aztecs. They reproduced the speech patterns of the borderlands in vigorously written sketches, short stories, and novels. They captured the vitality of a resilient people in realistic narratives almost void of romanticism. The critic Tomás Rivera called it a "fiesta of the living."[66] A leading student of this work offered a clear definition: "Chicano literature is that body of work produced by US citizens and residents of Mexican descent for whom a sense of ethnicity is a critical part of their literary sensibility and for whom the portrayal of their ethnic experience is a major concern of their art."[67]

Chicano literature embraced the social and political activism of the 1960s as the concept of La Raza, a Mexican American race, emerged. A self-identity that emphasized "Spanishness" and "Indianness" generated plays, novels, and poetry calling for social action to liberate the people economically, politically, and culturally. But those who embraced La Raza as an idea fragmented on basic issues. Some writers emphasized diversity within La Raza. Others argued that their work was an art form, not a political expression. While some sought liberation from the authority of Roman Catholicism, others saw the church as part of the culture's core.[68] Yet even with these basic divisions, there was a commitment to the concept of the Southwest as the lost homeland. Aztlán represented a home and a culture that predated even the Aztecs. Carlos Vélêz-Ibáñez, a scholar of Mexican culture in the Southwest, saw this as a quest for "enduring space and place." The common thread that united Hispanic writers was "the basic existential search for place, space, and connections, and just as important cultural creation and invention." Chicano activists and more conservative authors agreed that literature could create ethnic pride for a long-oppressed people.[69]

Chicano writers, especially the more polemic, initially focused on the plight of migrant workers and rural families, but slowly a shift in emphasis took place. Increasingly the Chicano population lived mostly in urban areas, in sprawling cities that threatened the good earth and the rivers of life. Chicanos refused to be prisoners of the city and poverty, however, and many of them conceived of the barrio not as a ghetto but as the center of life. The barrio replaced the traditional village. Chicano families needed to resist Anglo middle-class values or they would disintegrate, wrote José Antonio Villareal in *Pocho*. But in *Chicano*, Richard Vasquez found no redeeming values in the city for Hispanic families. Urban life proved a trap for the Sandoval family in his anti-urban novel. But even as some Chicano authors attacked urban life and its effect on the people, the barrio sustained admirable traits.[70] The barrio provided warmth, sharing, comradeship, and pleasure. The message was clear: the Chicano was alienated not from self but from urban life. The rituals of the barrio would cause the people to "feel like shouting, *Yo Soy Mexicano,* in the middle of a crowded street."[71]

Ironically, the Hispanic writer who achieved the greatest commercial success in the 1970s, Rudolfo A. Anaya, brought together rural and urban themes in a varied voice far less strident and angry. Born in Pastura, New Mexico, a small village on the Llano Estacado in 1937, Anaya grew up in the town of Santa Rosa. After receiving two degrees from the University of New Mexico, he taught English in Albuquerque public schools before joining the faculty of the university in 1974. His first novel, *Bless Me, Ultima* (1971), won the Premio Quinto Sol Award and became a classic in Hispanic literature. *Heart of Aztlán* and *Tortuga* followed, creating a trilogy about Hispanic life in modern New Mexico. Edited volumes, short story collections, screenplays, and dramas led to additional awards and national recognition.[72]

A child of the Llano, an academic in Albuquerque, and a writer of the Hispanic experience, Anaya voiced the sounds of the village and the barrio. "I was born in Pastura, New Mexico, a small village on the llano. . . . It is a harsh environment. I remember most the sense of landscape which is bleak, empty, desolate, across which the wind blows and makes its music. My work is full of references to the land and the landscape; it can't help but be."[73] Like the Spanish classicists of the sixteenth century, Anaya found his muse in the traditions of his people and their interaction with the land. "And always there is the interplay of people on the stage of life with the elements of nature. . . . I can't think of very many things I have written that do not have a reference to those natural forces and that earth and people which nurtured me."[74] There was the overwhelming presence of the landscape in his life and in his writing. "Here I can look around and have a feeling that these hills, these mountains, this river, this earth, this sky is mine."[75]

A progression occurred in Anaya's fiction—the movement from the Llano, to the village, and on to the barrio. Essentially this was the story of a large percentage of New Mexico's Chicano people. Through this progression, he stressed respect for the elderly, the old ones, and for their wisdom. In *Bless Me, Ultima,* young Antonio Marez respects his parents and Ultima, the *curandera* ("healer"). With their care and strength he comes to grips with the stresses in his family during World War II. The novel, filled with dreams and superstitions, also reveals the turmoil in Latin American theology. When Antonio's brothers return from the war, they move to Santa Fe, rejecting the Llano of their father and the village of their mother. But Antonio learns to honor his heritage without being destroyed by it. His cultural identity helps develop his individual spirit. Throughout the story, the small boy interacts with his family and the land; Anaya uses the words *la tierra* because they convey a deeper relationship with place.[76]

In a more recent novel, *Alburquerque* (1992), Anaya explores the barrio of the city named for a Spanish nobleman. In urban places, Anglos see the land as lots for homes and buildings, but the Chicanos and the Pueblo Indians retain their view of the land as the spirit and the soul of the people. When Abrán González, a "Barrio Boy," visits a northern New Mexico village to meet his girlfriend's family, he finds his roots. "He [Abrán] paused and they realized what they took for granted, generations of living in the same villages of the Sangre de Cristo and roots that went deep into the soil and the spirit of the people, he did not have."[77] Ben Chávez, a writer and Abrán's unrecognized father, moves among

Albuquerque's wealthy Anglos and realizes the barriers of urban life. "Wealthy Anglos . . . were great supporters of the City Symphony. . . . They had all of the amenities of Southwest living without ever having to meet the natives. Class lines, ethnic lines, Ben thought. Borders in our own backyard."[78] When developers threaten to turn the center of Albuquerque into a Disney-like theme park, Ben, Abrán, and the Chicanos of the barrio prevent the destruction of the urban core and the planned diversion of the Rio Grande. In the novel's end, those who respect the land and preserve the integrity of the family triumph over materialism run rampant.[79]

Like Anaya, Rolando Hinojosa eschewed polemic in favor of dialogue, irony, and cultural interaction. In a Faulknerian mode, Hinojosa created Klail City, Belken County, Texas, in the Rio Grande valley. Based on the area around his birthplace in Mercedes, the novels of the Klail City Death Trip Series feature wry, pragmatic Hispanics living among paternalistic and racist Anglos. Hinojosa saw both cultures at home — from his father, a refugee from the Mexican Revolution, and his mother, an Anglo — as well as in the community. He graduated from the University of Texas, served in the army in Korea, and taught at Brownsville High School. After receiving a master's degree from New Mexico Highlands University, he earned a doctorate at the University of Illinois. An academic career took him to Trinity University in San Antonio, Texas A&I University in Kingsville, and the University of Minnesota before he was offered a chair in creative writing at his alma mater. Regardless of his location, Hinojosa produced novels and stories in the 1970s and 1980s set in the Rio Grande valley. Writing in Spanish, he won recognition and awards for *Estampas del Valle y Otras Obras* (1973) and *Claros Varones de Belken* (1986). With *Rites and Witnesses* (1973), he began to publish in English. All of his novels and short stories focused on the lives of his characters, their cultural values and traditions, and their prescribed roles in closely knit families. Using unhurried rhythms and elliptical narratives, often without a narrator, Hinojosa re-created the racial and class tensions of his homeland. Soft Spanish and slang and Hispanicized English words conveyed his messages in a fictionalized South Texas.[80] Witty, precise, and eloquent, Hinojosa produced a mythological county not unlike that populated by William Faulkner's Snopse family in Mississippi. And, as in Faulkner's stories, humor and irony often appear to be the monopoly of the ethnic minority. The Southwest figures prominently, almost exclusively, in all of his work: "The place and people are not only important, they are essential to me and to my writing."[81]

Chicana writers embraced their people and their land also, but from a feminist perspective that added yet another dimension to the search for ethnic identity. An early Chicana novelist, Fabiola Cabeza de Baca, published *We Fed Them*

Cactus in 1954. She described the Llano Estacado at a time when Hispanic families were moving from the plains but were also leaving behind a legacy of language and place-names. The families suffered a sense of loss, yes, but also found a determination to survive in a harsh and angry land. "It is a lonely land because of its intensity, but it lacks nothing for those who enjoy Nature in her full grandeur. The colors of the skies, of the hills, the rocks, the birds and the flowers are soothing to the most troubled heart. It is loneliness without despair."[82] The people drew from the land courage and contentment.

The playwright and novelist Denise Chávez found her muse in the land as well, but also from *los pastores* and *las posadas,* the traditional Christmas plays. Born in Las Cruces, New Mexico, in 1948, Chávez grew up in the borderland desert. "My internal landscape is the desert," she said. "I know it very well, I know the heat, I know the lack of rain, and the joy that one experiences when you do have rain."[83] She studied drama with the playwright Mark Medoff at New Mexico State University and then received an M.F.A. from Trinity University in San Antonio. Educated, energetic, and articulate, Chávez wrote with inspiration from oral history, folk dramas, and the tales of the storytellers. But she also developed a strong sense of place. "I feel as if I am New Mexico, as well as Texas, my mother's homeplace. . . . To understand me is to know this land I love."[84] Her one-character play *El Santero de Cordova* demonstrated her ability to blend Spanish and English, the poetic and the feminist, while employing the riches of the southwestern culture.

Other Chicana authors shared her vision of the Southwest. Jovita González, from Rio Grande City, Texas, based her narratives on Hispanic folklore, while Fermina Guerra, from Laredo, wrote of ranch life along the Rio Grande and her people's feelings about that land.[85] The poetess and short story writer Bernice Zamora found in her birthplace, a village in Aguilar County, Colorado, the oral traditions that infused her work. Written in strong street language, her carefully crafted poems ranged from narratives about the Spanish Peaks of southern Colorado to the lives of urban Hispanics.[86] In 1971, Estela Trambley Portillo published her play *Day of the Swallows,* for which she received the Quinto Sol Award in literature. Born in El Paso in 1936, she taught English in high school before turning to a writing career. She edited an issue of *El Grito* in 1973, containing the first collection of literature by Mexican American women. Portillo sought to use her pen to advocate the complete liberation and full equality of women. Her characters are rebels against ritualized behavior, but all too often they fail; thus Portillo creates a Hispanic tragedy. In her work, passionate Chicanas, repressed by males, both Hispanic and Anglo, seek outlets for their talents. More recently Sandra Cisneros used similar themes in *Woman Hollering Creek* (1991), set in metropolitan San Antonio. The MacArthur Foundation awarded Cisneros a major prize for her treatment of the lives of Hispanic women. Translated into a dozen languages, collections of her work received widespread critical praise. *The House on Mango Street,* forty-four sketches and vignettes, sold over 500,000 copies. Chicana authors constantly used family and *la tierra* as basepoints and frequently saw the earth in a female form. As Chicana Lucinda Oso says in *Alburquerque,* "The landscape reminds me of a Georgia O'Keeffe painting. . . . The earth becomes the woman's body."[87]

Just as Hispanic literature arose from a sense of place, space, and folk, so too did the novels and short stories produced by Anglo writers in the Southwest in the 1960s and 1970s. The range of subject matter expanded as authors found in the cities and larger towns themes and characters that could be used to express universalities. Richard Bradford, a southerner transplanted to Santa Fe, produced *Red Sky at Morning,* which explored a white adolescent's coming of age. Young Joshua Arnold discovered the Hispanic and Indian cultures as well as the artistic colony in Santa Fe even as he found his sense of identity. The novel took place where "the thick-walled house seemed to grow naturally from the brown earth."[88] Bill Brammer, Senator Lyndon B. Johnson's press aide, found in Austin and Texas politics a place and a subject that explored the region's modern character. Governor Arthur Fenstermaker, the central character in *The Gay Place* (1961), had many of the personality traits of Senator Johnson, but moving beyond a story about the profane and rambunctious politician, Brammer captured the essence of a state and region in transition, a predominantly urban society.[89] Thomas Thompson, a journalist and native Texan, explored both Fort Worth and Los Angeles in *Celebrity.* The novel tracked three young men as they followed their careers as a writer, as a football hero and movie star, and as a religious cult leader. Adolescence in "Cowtown" shaped their lives.[90] In a series of novels about young people in Tulsa, Susan Eloise Hinton explored the violent nature of urban life in the Southwest. Only seventeen years old when *The Outsiders* was published in 1967, Hinton wrote from the perspective of teenagers living through an era of significant and rapid change in the society in which they lived.[91]

Whereas younger authors found sustenance in the cities, established writers remarked on the decline of the farms and small towns, and the developing urban focus of southwestern literature did not go unchallenged by those who lamented the passing of a rural way of life. With grace and eloquence, John Graves spoke of the ambiance of the Brazos River and the impact of urbanization. *Goodbye to a River* (1960), *The Last Running* (1974), and *Hard Scrabble* (1974) romanticized a rural Texas that was rapidly disappearing. *Goodbye to a River,* according to

Graves, was "a bit of nostalgic provincial non-fiction," but it spoke to his dismay about urbanization.[92] People in Los Angeles were, Graves felt, "hellbent on present and future."[93] Benjamin Capps, Al Dewlin, and Max Evans shared Graves's desire to recapture rural southwesterners' feelings for the earth and the virtues that allowed them to settle and survive in a hostile and unforgiving land. Capps explored the lives of pioneers and cattlemen as well as Native Americans. *The Trail to Ogallala* (1964) established his credentials as an author of insight, one who understood the two competing and clashing cultures.[94] The Texas Panhandle provided Al Dewlin with eccentric characters for *The Bone Pickers* (1958) and with a lurid murder trial for *Twilight of Honor* (1961). While these novels, and others, were more contemporaneous, they borrowed heavily from the past. For *Twilight of Honor,* Dewlin studied not only the legal aspects of the judicial system but also the speech patterns and expressions of the lawyers, judges, and jurors in courtrooms. There could be no doubt that the setting was the Texas panhandle.[95] Another Texan, the painter, miner, cowboy, rancher, and writer Max Evans, sought to "put down the humor, tragedy, loneliness, and adventure" as he had "lived and loved it" during his lifetime.[96] The cowboy protagonists in *The Rounders* (1965) are losers, funny but doomed. With rib-cracking humor, Evans makes it clear that Dusty Rhodes and Wrangler Lewis are trapped in their environment and can never escape. Evans did not view his characters with contempt but simply described how they dealt with the danger, pain, and violence of the New Mexico cow country. The country was, he argued, a metaphor for the world.

The growing regional literary dichotomy could be seen in the universes created by Joan Didion in Los Angeles and by Elmer Kelton in West Texas. Born in Sacramento in 1934, Didion moved to New York after graduating from the University of California. Following her marriage to the writer John Gregory Dunne, she returned to California in 1964 and became an accomplished essayist, short story writer, screenwriter, and novelist. In novels reminiscent of Nathaniel West, Didion wrote of a Los Angeles of crowded freeways, earthquakes, and Santa Ana winds. In her novels, even the weather in Los Angeles is apocalyptic.[97] In *Play It As It Lays* (1970), Maria Wyeth drives the freeways in a compulsive rage, but she ultimately surrenders to this omnipresent facet of urban life. She becomes a total participant in the highway culture. Maria's personality disintegrates, a symbol of the social disintegration in the City of Angels. Her abortion and sterility parallel the author's view of Los Angeles. Neurotic women populate Didion's novels, such as *Run River* (1963) — women harried by complex social relationships and urban chaos. The experiences of her heroines are those of a region of rapid growth without a concomitant maturation. Only when Maria successfully maneuvers through a freeway interchange and crosses four lanes of traffic at a diagonal without braking or missing a beat on the radio can she find exhilaration: "That night [she] slept dreamlessly."[98]

The urban world seemingly without urbanity would also resonate in the Houston of Larry McMurtry's novels, but both worlds lay far away from Elmer Kelton's West Texas. The son of a foreman, Kelton grew up on a ranch near Crane, Texas. Born in 1926, he served in World War II and then studied journalism at the University of Texas, graduating in 1948. For the next two decades Kelton lived in San Angelo, writing about agriculture and ranching for the local newspaper, then working as an editor of ranching journals. In his spare moments he wrote formulaic western stories for pulp magazines and novels for paperback publishers. After the publication of *The Day the Cowboys Quit* (1980), Kelton devoted himself exclusively to serious fiction.[99] In *The Time It Never Rained* (1973), Kelton captured the world of Charlie Flagg, a rancher whose pride will not allow him to take federal aid in the midst of a terrible drought in the 1950s. Charlie, a man of integrity and stubbornness, takes a paternalistic view of his Mexican American workers, but he respects them as well as the traditions of Native Americans. What brings Flagg to this position? All three cultures love this arid, desolate land.[100] Kelton's historical novel *The Wolf and the Buffalo* created two characters of depth and feeling: Gray Horse Running, a Comanche warrior, and Gideon Ledbetter, an African American "buffalo soldier." The warrior finds solace in the spirit of the land even as his people are forced to leave. The wolf and the buffalo are his spiritual advisers. But Gray Horse Running, like Didion's urban heroines, is doomed by a changing world over which he has no control. Gideon comes to respect his adversary, whose dreams of the Comanches returning to the plains are doomed. Kelton understood the nuances of the thoughts and language of his characters.[101] "I can't write about heroes seven feet tall and invincible," he said. "I write about people five foot eight and nervous."[102] The heroes of Kelton's novels are indeed nervous, but they share a sense of place, a focus on values, and a respect for the earth.

In his early novels, Larry McMurtry's protagonists, like those of Kelton, battled the elements and raged against governmental interference, but they continued to struggle on the windswept plains of northwestern Texas. Later novels, set largely in Houston, found young graduate students and older matrons coping with the vagaries of urban life, but often with the same reserve and resilience. Two characteristics found in McMurtry's novels were a strong sense of place and powerfully drawn portraits of women.[103] The latter became even clearer in the film versions of *Horseman, Pass By* and *Terms of Endearment*. McMurtry's shift in locales from ranches and small towns to the Bayou City mirrored the rapid

urbanization of the region as well as his enthusiasm for the urban Southwest and its people.

Born in Wichita Falls in 1936, McMurtry came of age in Archer City, a small town a few miles to the south. After receiving an undergraduate degree at North Texas State University and a graduate degree at Rice, he studied writing at Stanford University. He taught English, operated a book business, married, had a child, divorced, and wrote. *Horseman, Pass By* (1961), his first novel, painted a stark portrait of the pathos of life on a small Texas ranch. Five years later, *The Last Picture Show* described the grim reality of life in a dying Texas town. The novel created an uproar in Archer City. McMurtry created a literary firestorm with a highly critical collection of essays, *In a Narrow Grave* (1968), wherein he described Texans as not only simply vulgar but also boring. Later he denounced the provinciality of regional literature, having the temerity to bash Texas icons such as Walter Prescott Webb, J. Frank Dobie, and Roy Bedichek. Perhaps some of this bluster came as a consequence of publishing six successful novels in fourteen years, receiving a Guggenheim Fellowship, and finding material success as well as fame in Hollywood.

Ironically, McMurtry repeatedly admitted that his novels drew directly from a childhood on the family ranch, an adolescence in Archer City, and graduate student years in Houston. "My writing comes as much out of the place as it does out of anything else. It's a particular place that I'm trying to describe and render. . . . You reach what is common in human experience through attention to what is local."[104] In an address to the Texas Institute of Letters only a year after *Horseman, Pass By* was published, McMurtry sought to explain the problems of being a Texas writer or a writer in Texas: "I believe that one of the strongest assets a fiction writer can have is a sense of place and of the uniqueness of place. As writers, our place is always to some extent both then and now, both this Texas we daily encounter and that Texas we daily put behind us to fuel our nostalgia. I have felt sometimes — in spite of all the talk about our exaggerated home pride — that the Texas writer is a bit too apt to be embarrassed and apologetic about his regionalism; that at times he is almost scared to be as regional as he needs to be."[105] Yet he also warned of the narrowness that precluded the writing of great literature.

McMurtry's ambivalence had seemed to end with his return to his ranch after a stint in California in 1961. "Well am back on my native acres, and the country boy in me is rising to the top like cream. Doubt I'll ever leave agin [*sic*] for longer than a month at a time."[106] Yet six novels later, he left Texas to open a bookstore in Georgetown because of the loss of a sense of place. He was "sucking air."[107] The District of Columbia, Las Vegas, even New York City gave McMurtry new "places," but critical reaction to these novels never approached his earlier acclaim. Whereas McMurtry had previously denounced "Creeping California" and the impact of Los Angeles on Tucson and Houston, he declared now that he liked "bigger and better cities."[108] He said, "I like nature, but I still feel as if I am part of it, that I have never really separated from it, even in the city." But it was not until he returned to the Southwest, literally and fictionally, that he regained a strong voice and won a Pulitzer Prize.[109] McMurtry returned to Archer City when his famous cross-country driving sprees were no longer necessary to find his muse. He found his place and new voices, ranging from "Billy the Kid" to "Pretty Boy Floyd" to the trail riders of *Lonesome Dove*. He found his roots again.

Working in an entirely different genre, Tony Hillerman produced award-winning and best-selling mysteries that mixed a thorough knowledge of the Navajo people with graphic landscape portraits of the Four Corners area of New Mexico and Arizona. Many readers became convinced that Hillerman is a Native American because of the depth of his understanding of the Navajos. His principal characters, the Navajo policemen Joe Leaphorn and Jim Chee, solved cases using the philosophy and logic of the Dineh, their knowledge of land, and their training as anthropologists. But Hillerman is "a redneck from a small cotton gin town in Oklahoma," who found "good old boys" like himself among the Navajos. Because of his success in writing authentically about the Navajos, the tribe made him a "Special Friend of the Dineh."[110]

Their special friend grew up in rural Oklahoma, won a Silver Star in World War II, graduated from the University of Oklahoma, and became a journalist. As a reporter, Hillerman worked in Oklahoma, Texas, and New Mexico until 1962 when, at age thirty-seven, he entered graduate school. After receiving a master's degree from the University of New Mexico in 1965, Hillerman joined the faculty, where he taught until 1986. His novel *The Blessing Way* (1970) launched a series that beguiled mystery enthusiasts as well as readers interested primarily in the analysis of Navajo culture and descriptions of the Navajo homeland. Although a *belogana* ("white guy"), Hillerman developed a sensitivity to Native Americans, transcending ethnic boundaries.[111] "I really think there is something about the Southwestern landscape and Southwestern culture and society that fosters creativity in a lot of people. There are some who feel oppressed by the vast distances, the space. But others, and I am one of them, are stimulated by this. It's simply — you look out at a countryside that doesn't seem as it if were designed for human occupation, yet here we are. The view alone puts things in a different perspective."[112] The land had a mystique for Hillerman, whether it was the rushing water in San Juan River Canyon, the White Sands at night, Toltec Gorge after a summer rain with the smell of ozone in the air, or the dry emptiness of Chaco Mesa. He noted of the earth, the sky, the people: "All of them have made a mark on my memory." The environment gave him perspective: "a very small human in a very large landscape."[113]

Writers of fiction in the Southwest in the 1960s and the 1970s had an even greater range of subject matter than authors of earlier eras. The booming cities and economic growth created stresses and tensions that cried out for interpretation. Max Apple — essayest, short story writer, and author of screenplays — came to Houston to teach at Rice University and discovered a rich lode of material. The great cities of the Southwest seemed to be accidental diversions from the seductive emptiness surrounding them. "While the writers of more settled areas explore the nuances of manners," he wrote, "in the Southwest it sometimes seems that geography is destiny."[114] Apple found unity in the diverse geography and peoples: "There are no boundaries to regionalism; when you see the Southwest you are seeing everything. The local language and customs, the small matters that separate us, these things, properly noticed, become the bond that unites us."[115]

Southwestern playwrights, meanwhile, seized on language and customs to present dramas and comedies that explored the whole range of human behavior. In so doing, they sent plays to New York and London and then across the nation. Their works conveyed, through regional images, the universalities sought by southwestern novelists. Their range extended from D. L. Coburn's Pulitzer Prize–winning *The Gin Game* to Larry King and Peter Masterson's *The Best Little Whorehouse in Texas* and to Jack Hefner's *Vanities*. Dallasite Coburn's play about the unsentimental life of the elderly in a nursing home could have been set anywhere, but it resonated with regional rhythms. With Carol Hall's music, *The Best Little Whorehouse in Texas* contrasted the southwestern demand for individual expression with the constraints of public morality and "decency." Extended runs in New York, Washington, and London led to national tours. In *Vanities,* Jack Hefner focused on three young women from Texas at various stages of their lives. It too was well received by critics and audiences.[116]

New York critics did not appreciate Preston Jones's *A Texas Trilogy,* however, with its "quaint" characters in heavily accented dialogue, but the three plays succeeded elsewhere. Jones created "Bradleyville, Texas — population 6,000 — a small dead West Texas town in the middle of a big dead West Texas prairie between Abilene and San Angelo. The new highway has bypassed it and now the world is trying to."[117] At age forty, Jones began to write plays after years of work with Paul Baker's Dallas Theater Center. Born and raised in New Mexico, Jones studied with Baker at Baylor University and, encouraged by his mentor, began to write. *The Oldest Living Graduate* premiered in 1974 and was followed by *The Last Meeting of the Knights of the White Magnolia* and *Lu Ann Hampton Laverty Oberlander.* With their roots in nonurbanized Texas, the plays rested on speech common to the region to express the decline of rural and small-town life in an age of rapid technological change. In 1976 the plays broke box office records at the Kennedy Center in Washington, D.C., and Jones won numerous awards.[118] The comedy, sympathy, and irony in his work left his audience laughing and crying. Tragically, Jones died in 1979, only forty-three years old. In his plays he confronted racism, economic change, and the plight of a young woman whose dreams turn to total boredom. Jones referred to *The Texas Trilogy* as "A Long Day's Journey into West Texas" and found great advantages in being a southwesterner. "Since I live in Texas that's where I set my plays. I do that because I know the country and the people."[119] But audiences found themselves in the characters Jones created.

Plays by Jones, Hefner, Coburn, and other southwesterners found venues across the nation but especially in the Southwest itself, where a theatrical renaissance occurred in the 1960s and 1970s. In Los Angeles, for example, the Ahmanson Theater and the Mark Taper Forum developed productions that often moved

CULTURE *in the* AMERICAN SOUTHWEST

to New York or began national tours. The Los Angeles Theater Center opened in a former bank building on Spring Street and by 1985 had 26,000 subscribers. The revived La Jolla Playhouse groomed *Big River* for Broadway, while the Performing Arts Society of Los Angeles premiered African American dramas for a decade.[120] Over two dozen theaters in greater Los Angeles offered productions that often included motion-picture performers working at minimum salaries. Writers, directors, actors, stage designers, and other talents joined forces to make theater in southern California second only to theater in New York.

A major exception to this continuing success story was the famed Pasadena Playhouse, which fell on hard times. In the 1930s and 1940s the Playhouse had developed huge deficits that threatened to end the company. Mrs. Fannie E. Morrison stepped in many times to retire the debt, ultimately providing nearly $500,000.[121] After the death of the theater's founder, Gilmor Brown, the Playhouse entered a long period of decline financially — but not theatrically, at least not for a while. In 1966 the Internal Revenue Service closed the theater, which then raised funds to continue the season. Well-known actors played the stage at scale, but audiences stayed away. The Pasadena Playhouse declared bankruptcy in 1969. Costumes were auctioned, and vandals set the boarded-up theater afire. When the mortgage holder threatened to raze the facility, the city of Pasadena purchased the theater. Restored and reopened, the Pasadena Playhouse began to flourish in the 1980s with revivals and premieres; the theater was now not unlike Gilmor Brown's vision six decades earlier.[122]

California's oldest professional theater, the Old Globe of San Diego, survived a disastrous fire in 1978 to become a venue not only for Shakespeare but also for premieres and revivals of the classics. Retirees, professionals, military personnel, and technocrats buoyed audiences who came to see *Richard III* directed by John Houseman and similar productions. When an arsonist destroyed the original complex, over $500,000 in contributions arrived in a month, and within twenty months the Globe raised $6.5 million. The city, county, and state governments contributed, as did foundations, but the fund swelled through individual contributions. Helen Edison, the spouse of Simon Edison, a wealthy retailer, made a major contribution, and the complex received his name. The new theater opened in 1982 with *As You Like It,* and two years later the "new" Old Globe had over 40,000 season-ticket holders.[123]

Another regional jewel shone brightly in the period as Paul Baker and his colleagues left Baylor University in 1962, moving to Trinity University in San Antonio. While at Baylor, Baker had obtained Carlotta O'Neill's permission to stage the first university production of her husband's play *Long Day's Journey into Night,* but she refused Baker's request to cut the profanity. Baylor's president closed the production, and Baker and thirteen faculty members walked. The fourteen faculty had built an internationally recognized theater program, but the Southern Baptist school demanded censorship. *Time* magazine had called the Baylor program "one of the most fertile experimental theaters in the U.S.," but now Trinity's program won those accolades.[124] Baker had also served as director of the Dallas Theater Center and with some of his former colleagues and their students proceeded to create an extraordinary ensemble there. Playgoers could see work by local playwrights such as Preston Jones or Dylan Thomas's *Under Milk Wood* directed by the actor Burgess Meredith. Nearly four hundred professional actors in the Dallas area found work at the Theater Center and at six other year-round theaters in the metropolis.

In Houston, Nina Vance and her Alley Theater moved into a new, turreted complex in 1968. The main stage, without a proscenium, carried forward the idea of theater-in-the-round. Strongly ideological plays, experiments in costuming and productions, and plays without stars — characteristics that doomed other regional theaters across the country — did not deter Houston theatergoers. The Alley had over 11,000 subscribers by the 1980s, making the theater one of the largest in the country. Not even the death of Vance in 1980 slowed the development of the Alley Theater into a national showcase for playwrights and actors.[125]

Nonprofessional theater also flourished in the Southwest as strong companies emerged, often linked to drama programs at nearby colleges and universities. The Zachary Scott Theater of the University of Texas launched a dramatic renaissance in Austin, while companies in Tucson and Phoenix employed students and faculty from the University of Arizona and Arizona State University respectively. Other successes resulted from the efforts of one person to bring theater to their communities. Marjorie Morris led a one-woman crusade to construct a reproduction of London's Globe Theater in Odessa, Texas, and succeeded in 1966. Paul Baker's Dallas Theater Center opened the "Globe of the Southwest" with *Julius Caesar.* Audiences from Odessa, Midland, and other West Texas communities came to hear and see Shakespeare in an authentic setting.[126] Few of the citizens of Preston Jones's "Bradleyville" were in attendance.

Paralleling the resurgence in Chicano literature, Hispanic theater emerged in the region in the 1960s and 1970s. Venues included labor union halls, the streets, and community theaters in the barrios. Teatro Campesino, founded by Luis Valdez, formed part of César Chávez's labor movement. Teatro Chicano took to the streets with student actors while Teatro Urbano drew its casts from the community. Demands for social and economic justice resonated in these productions, which contained powerful political messages and also a sense of pride in Iberian and Hispanic culture. José Rodríguez, a professional actor from Puerto

Rico, formed La Compañía de Teatro de Alburquerque in 1979. Employing casts ranging in age from five to eighty, Rodríguez demanded professional quality. He produced the classics by Lorca in Spanish and plays by New Mexico playwrights. The contemporary dramas often drew from traditional folk plays. The company performed in Spanish and then in English, and some productions were bilingual. The first Hispanic graduate of the Royal Academy of Dramatic Arts, Rodríguez made clear his determination that the company would be of the highest quality. "We're doing real theater," he declared, "not quaint, folklorish, picturesque garbage."[127] The comment symbolized the regional desire for recognition and achievement in the theater, a quest that seemed within reach by the 1980s.

Similar advances in the formation of regional ballet companies and their professionalization occurred in the 1970s. Although founded in 1955, the Houston Ballet did not become a professional resident company until 1969. But three years later it made a significant national tour and by 1980 had an annual budget of $3.5 million. Ben Stevenson assumed the position of artistic director in 1976 and created a company of almost fifty dancers. The repertory included the classics and original works by permanent choreographers.[128] The Houston Ballet became internationally recognized by the 1980s.

Southwesterners embraced ballet with more enthusiasm than grand opera, perhaps because ballet productions proved less costly. Audiences grew across the region as ballet companies were established in El Paso, Oklahoma City, Tucson, Fort Worth, and Dallas. When the civic leaders of El Paso established a set of community goals, they included a ballet company, since it was the most popular performing art in the city. A foundation was established to support Ballet El Paso. Performances began in 1957, and by 1977 a varied repertory drew guest artists and choreographers. Ballet El Paso toured Mexico four times, with a wide range of productions.[129] Yvonne Chouteau and Miguel Terekhov directed the Oklahoma City Ballet in the 1960s, and in 1972 the company left the umbrella of the symphony orchestra as an independent agency. The next year Conrad Ludlow and Joy Feldman came from the New York Ballet, with the former serving as artistic director, and soon the company was giving eleven performances per season.[130] Tucson hired Richard Holden of the Metropolitan Opera Ballet Company to direct its dancers, who formed the Arizona Dance Theater. Ballet enthusiasts discovered that bringing well-known directors and guest performers would result in fund-raising dollars that far exceeded earlier efforts.[131]

The Fort Worth Ballet found a "financial angel" in Anne Bass, the spouse of Sid Richardson Bass. A Vassar graduate, Bass became "the Empress of Fort Worth" as she led fund-raising efforts for the symphony and the art museum. A devotee of the ballet, she served on the board of the School of American Ballet of the New York City Ballet. Close to George Balanchine, Mikhail Baryshnikov, and Peter Martens, she publicly fought with Lincoln Kirstein, who succeeded Balanchine on the latter's death. Despite the turbulence in New York, Bass determined to create her own company and chose to revitalize the Fort Worth Ballet. She became a member of the ballet's board, selected the artistic directors, and brought the company nearly $300,000 in grants from the Sid Richardson Foundation. A resident company was created, and by the 1980s Fort Worth had a quality ballet.[132]

Dallas lacked a "Medici de ballet." But the famed director George Skibine came to Dallas from New York in 1968 to stage *Firebird,* and impressed with the local talent, he stayed. He formed the Dallas Civic Ballet and led it as the Dallas Ballet until his death in 1981. Without its artistic soul the company languished, folding in 1988. Its successor, the Ballet Dallas, led by Skibine's associate Thom Clower, brought dance back to the city in 1989.[133]

The Southwest experienced enormous cultural growth and maturation for two decades. Rapid urbanization and seemingly unending economic expansion spawned major new institutions and the revitalization of older museums, symphonies, and theaters. Individual artists, writers, and architects produced a cornucopia of works that spoke about and to the region. Southwesterners took great pride in what they had achieved, but their elation came before a serious economic fall, which would temporarily set back efforts to develop a mature regional culture.

CHAPTER 8

The Exportation of a Regional Culture

1980–1995

In the mid-1980s, the Southwest experienced a financial collapse that continued into the first years of the next decade. It was particularly severe in southern California. By the mid-1990s, however, economic revival in Texas, Oklahoma, New Mexico, and Arizona allowed for a renewal of the drive for cultural recognition and critical acclaim. There had been casualties, of course, with the demise of symphonies in San Diego and Oklahoma City and of theatrical and ballet companies elsewhere. But once more the major cities led the way with the renewed expansion of real estate markets, banking, technology firms, and petroleum companies. The receptive business climate and the presence of cultural resources enticed more corporations to abandon the Northeast and Midwest and move their headquarters to the Southwest. The influx of professionals and corporate executives, and their spouses, fueled the drive for greater achievements in institutional culture. New opera houses in Houston and Dallas, bold new art museums across the region, and rising ballet companies symbolized the rejuvenation of the cultural renaissance. In architecture, literature, and theater, southwesterners won prestigious awards and critical recognition. The culture became universal in goals and international in modes and themes, but its roots remained southwestern. The region became a national pacesetter as it sent novels, orchestras, operas, and plays into the mainstream, and its architecture became the subject of international acclaim for its vivacity and daring.

The architectural critic Ada Louise Huxtable recognized early the importance of architecture as the symbol of urbanization: "A city, in its most real sense, is its buildings. Whatever the life, spirit, activity, or achievements of the city may be, they are expressed in the mass of asphalt, bricks, stone, marble, steel and glass that has been accumulated during the city's existence."[1] Likewise promoters,

FIGURE 52

International Style skyscrapers surrounded and obscured the Art Deco buildings of Tulsa by the 1980s. Photograph by Don Sibley, Tulsa Chamber of Commerce.

developers, entrepreneurs, political leaders, and increasingly the general public understood that the physical city symbolized progress, growth, and economic viability. The skyscraper remained the most visible sign of capitalism, but by the early 1980s, a simple glass-sheathed box would not do. The commercial temple had to be produced by a major architectural firm in a postmodern form that dramatically punctured the skyline. A distinct relationship developed between the physical corporate headquarters and the business activity of the firm. "Only the skyscraper offers business the wide-open spaces of a man-made Wild West, a frontier in the sky," wrote one critic.[2] In Houston, Dallas, and Los Angeles, towers in many forms rose to greater heights, but so did buildings in smaller metropolises such as Austin.

The negative reaction to the sterile International Style glass boxes emerged in the early 1980s. Philip Johnson's AT&T Building in New York, completed in 1979 with its "Chinese Chippendale" cornice, and Michael Graves's structures, with their irregular lines and bright colors, ushered in the "postmodern era." Robert Venturi, Kevin Roche, and Helmut John reached back to Palladio and

CULTURE *in the* AMERICAN SOUTHWEST

classical architecture for designs incorporating arches, columns, and cornices. Round windows, colorful tiles, irregular shapes, and even Romanesque detailing produced buildings of character and distinction. Always desiring to be on the cusp of change, southwesterners embraced postmodernism with the same zeal they had greeted the International Style three decades earlier.

In the 1980s, the poet Lorenzo Thomas noted that Houston residents were so passionate about their new skyscrapers that it was "a town where high school children on the bus discourse on architecture."[3] Philip Johnson and John Burgee led the way in creating a new Houston that even teenagers could recognize. Although Johnson had named the "International Style" and had practiced that mode for three decades, in the 1980s he and Burgee teamed to create postmodern designs for Houston and other cities. Sophisticated and outgoing, Burgee organized and managed the firm and also contributed some of the duo's most controversial designs, such as the broken pediment of the AT&T Building. Beginning with the "seashell" art museum in Corpus Christi in 1969, Johnson and Burgee brought their daring concepts to the Southwest. Allied with the developer Gerald Hines, they produced Pennzoil Place (1976), the Transco Tower (1985), and the Republic Bank Center (1984) in Houston, among others. The Crescent in Dallas (1985) and the Garden Grove Community Church in southern California (1980) carried their signatures across the region.[4] As they added new shapes and colors to Houston's skyline, Johnson described the city as "a world's fair of skyscrapers."[5] A stunning piece of commercial architecture, Pennzoil Place changed American concepts of the skyscraper. Far more dramatic than a single seventy-story tower would have been, the thirty-five-story twin towers broke American architecture "out of the box."

A few steps away, Johnson and Burgee designed the Republic Bank Center, a Flemish Gothic, granite-clad skyscraper. The architects and Hines sought to re-create a post-Reformation banking house in the twelve-story financial hall with its ribbed and gabled roof and finials. Grand Romanesque arches greeted customers passing down an awesome concourse leading to the fifty-six-story attached tower. Red Vermont granite, cut in Italy and shipped to Houston, created the thin skin of the tower. The steeply stepped roof lines of the skyscraper diminished its neighbors, including Pennzoil Place. Not even the seventy-one-story Allied Bank Plaza by Skidmore, Owings, and Merrill, with its two quarter-circles slipped off center, rivaled the Republic Bank. Allied Bank Plaza, with its green reflective glass in great curves, still echoed the International Style, as did the silver glass of the fifty-story Four Allen Center of 1983.[6]

The crown jewel of Houston's economic boom in the 1980s—the Transco Tower (1983), by Johnson and Burgee with Morris Aubrey Architects—stood like a campanile above the coastal plain. Rising 900 feet over the Galleria area, the tower reminded viewers of the great Art Deco buildings of New York of the 1920s and 1930s, but its gray-tinted panels seemed to float in the bright light of the Texas sun. Seen from all sides, the symmetrical structure featured projection-like bay windows rising above its huge arched doorway of pink granite. A beacon on top pierced the night skies, reminding residents twenty miles away of this symbol of economic expansion and corporate success.[7]

Determined to project corporate images equal to or more extravagant than those of its rival to the south, Dallas financial institutions created glossy geometrical sentinels that rose like giant sculptures above the prairie. The glass-sheathed Allied Bank Tower at Fountain Plaza extended sixty stories above a four-acre water garden (1985). The upper floors formed a triangle while a giant diagonal slash across the facade formed an offset. Henry Cobb of I. M. Pei & Partners based the design on a double square, subtracted sections, and produced "what's left after carving into a square prism." The vitality of the enormous green-glass wedge led to a commission for the new symphony hall.[8]

Richard Keating of Skidmore, Owings, and Merrill designed the Texas Commerce Tower of fifty-five stories with a "window" — twenty-seven feet wide and seventy-four feet high — separating the upper six floors (1987). Offsets, curved walls, and a notched arch at the top created a dramatic signature structure. The "hole at the top" lessened wind resistance and thus reduced the size and cost of the structural system. Investors maximized leasable space while architects engaged in theatrical image-making for the bank.[9] The sheer audacity of the concept drew architects, engineers, and entrepreneurs from around the world, and soon similar structures appeared in Europe and East Asia.

Johnson and Burgee gave Dallas a postmodern building that hinted of France during the Second Empire. Drawing from historical sources, Johnson and Burgee produced three related structures of eighteen and nineteen stories in a broad arc. The Crescent dominated the north side of downtown Dallas with its mansard roof and ornamental grillwork (1986). Offices, shops, and a hotel rose around a courtyard of heroic scale. Limestone walls, a slate-colored roof, black dormers, and wrought iron suggested Paris in the 1880s.[10] From the Crescent, office workers, shoppers, and hotel guests could see the 564-foot Reunion Tower on the west side of downtown and its geodesic dome covered with hundreds of exterior lights. Even nearer, the LTV Center extended fifty stories above a $3 million collection of bronze sculptures by Auguste Rodin, Antoine Bourdelle, and Aristide Maillol.[11] It was no longer sufficient to hire world-famous designers for a structure; it became necessary to surround the base with works of art that simply shouted "culture" and "wealth."

Southern California joined Texas cities in the race to create spectacular and innovative architecture in the last two decades of the twentieth century. Those who designed buildings in the southern third of the Golden State went there "attracted by opportunity and some images. The images included some physical qualities such as the sky, the light, and the landscape . . . but most of all we were attracted by the great promise to make a new city."[12] So wrote Cesar Pelli, dean of the School of Architecture at Yale University and a former resident of Santa Monica. Pelli believed that he and others designed for a pristine blue sky, for a bright light that cast deep shadows, and for a flat land punctuated by palm trees. A "City of Tomorrow" could be produced, a metropolis of the future, for the real Los Angeles existed only in the future.

Angeleños sought to give the city of sprawl a core, and the old downtown became a glass-and-concrete forest of postmodernist structures. Soon, the City of Angels had buildings that looked "like refugees from Houston."[13] Indeed, the Bayou City appeared to be the model. Beginning in the 1970s, one tower after another announced the presence of major petroleum firms and banks. The twin ARCO Tower and the Bank of America (1972), each fifty-one stories, rose above a large plaza. The Union Bank (1966) hid its parking garage behind a screen while other skyscrapers placed their automobile decks below ground. Trying to create "green space" in the city of the automobile, the fifty-five-story, granite-faced Security Pacific Bank (1974) overlooked a large park. For pure kitsch, John Portman's Bonaventure Hotel (1975–77) could not be topped. Five glass cylinders, the tallest reaching thirty-five floors, contained Portman's signature concepts of vast volumes of open space, pools and flowing water, and a collection of shops and restaurants.[14] The Bonaventure established an atmosphere leading to a spate of tall, irregularly shaped, and strongly hued commercial buildings in the postmodernist mode.

Churches and public buildings also appeared in forms that both shocked and delighted the senses. Johnson and Burgee provided the evangelist Robert H. Schuller with his Crystal Cathedral in Garden Grove (1977–80). The mirrored, truncated, crystalline form of 10,000 panes of glass housed 3,000 worshipers seated below 11,000 crystal stars. The presence of the latter dismayed the architects but pleased their client. Silver-coated glass-and-steel trusses painted white created an atmosphere that brought the sky, the light, and the landscape inside.[15]

A few miles away Michael Graves produced the San Juan Capistrano Public Library as a postmodern delight with Egyptian and Moorish influences (1983). Filled with dramatic interior spaces, the building included fountains to reduce the street noise. A fairy-tale castle of vivid colors, turrets, and pergolas, the structure created illusions of different times and places. When Graves designed the

Hyatt Regency Hotel in La Jolla (1990), he used red Indian sandstone and maize-and-tan stucco. A slab crowned by a low arc, the hotel adjoined an office building and other facilities with rich colors and strong geometric forms. The hotel complex was but one of several striking facilities in the area, others being the Orange County Performing Arts Center in Costa Mesa and the Newport Center with its dramatic office buildings designed by several leading architects. Southern California gained numerous examples of cutting-edge architecture.[16]

Unfortunately, home designs in Los Angeles, Houston, and the rest of the region generally failed to demonstrate the same degree of imagination and verve. In her novel *The Nowhere City,* Allison Lurie spoke of the sky, the light, and the landscape, but also of the sterility of the homes in Los Angeles: "He described the wonderful climate, the dry light, the white-walled houses with their orange and lemon trees, the Santa Monica mountains rising smoky green and brown against the north edge of the sky." But, the character added: "All the houses on the street were made of stucco in ice cream colours: vanilla, lemon, raspberry, and orange sherbet. Moulded in a variety of shapes and set down next to the other along the block, behind plots of flowers much larger and brighter than life, they looked like a stage set for some lavish comic opera."[17] A few architects, such as Hugh Jefferson Randolph of Austin, continued to subscribe to the ideas of O'Neil Ford, emphasizing natural materials, flowing open spaces, and concern for placing houses in a site with sensitivity to the environment. Most residents of the urban Southwest in the 1980s and 1990s concerned themselves less about housing designs, however, than the need to have architectural masterpieces on their major thoroughfares.

Nowhere in the region was the rage for postmodernist towers more apparent than in Austin in the 1980s. In an age of heroic developers and playful architects, banks and investment groups fought over prime real estate on which to erect monuments. Congress Avenue, extending south from the state capitol to Town Lake, lost its low-scale, pedestrian-oriented facades to the $80 million, thirty-story One Congress Plaza and to 100 Congress Avenue at $60 million and twenty-two levels. Granite and bronze-tinted glass competed with sunset-red native Texas granite and rose-colored windows. The latter matched the shade of the developer's spectacles. These two towers joined four other buildings in excess of twenty floors located within two blocks of each other. Echoing Houston and Dallas signature pieces, the Austin buildings stood as nonrectangular slabs with set-back corners and stepped roofs. Pedestrians entered the towers through arcades with arches or overwhelming plazas at the street level. The Austin Center and the San Jacinto Center incorporated hotels within the office complexes, erected in a frenzy of overbuilding. A "genteel" cityscape gave way to glass-barrel

FIGURE 53

Postmodern office towers in Austin overshadowed the Texas
State Capitol by the mid-1980s. Author's collection.

vaults and atria hung with massive Art Deco lamps. The various elements created a "kaleidoscopic survey of historical architecture."[18] Within a brief period, ownership of these postmodernist confections passed into the hands of federal agencies, rival hotel chains, and out-of-state banks.

The cities of the Southwest lost much of their core architectural heritages in the 1980s as megablock developments overshadowed or destroyed the business and shopping districts of older downtown areas. Fort Worth's historic Sundance Square, with its modestly scaled masonry buildings, looked like a set of toys against the nearby glass boxes. The Americana Hotel and the City Center's towers with cutouts and massive facades overwhelmed the historic structures.[19] Similarly, the $85 million NBC Bank Plaza in San Antonio rose above the Riverwalk like a 1940s jukebox. With three offsets on each side, a recessed area at the twenty-fifth and twenty-sixth floors, and a bar across the top at the thirty-first level, the building suggested a "mighty Wurlitzer."[20]

Yet there were examples of dramatic postmodernist designs that in conception and scale established high marks for regional architects. Ricardo Legorreta, the leading architect of Mexico, gave San Antonio a remarkable new central library. A bold, bright "Enchilada Red" structure, the library's broken walls — with irregular openings and windows, "stairs" in the walls, cylinders, pyramids,

FIGURE 54

The postmodern San Antonio Library, with its many shapes and bright colors, stunned the public and some critics. Author's collection.

and cubes—played with shape and color. Splashes of deep blue and bright yellow enlivened an exterior that reached back to the city's Hispanic past.[21] Similarly, the Lucille Halsell Observatory by Emilio Ambasz gave the Alamo city an extraordinary set of clear-glass pyramids, cones, and conic sections nestled in a green hill. The clear globes held rare trees and flowers in an environment controlled and protected from the bright light and cloudless skies.[22]

"Houstonitis" spread across the region, seeming to transform commercial architecture. Phoenix, Tucson, Oklahoma City, San Diego, and Tulsa joined the Bayou City as centers of postmodernism. The Denver architect Curtis Fentress produced the United Bank Tower in Tucson with historical references. The twenty-three-story octagonal structure used setbacks borrowed from nearby St. Augustine Cathedral and a pink color taken from the peeling paint of El Adobe Mexican restaurant. Fentress obtained pink granite from Finland and pink glass from Belgium and added "Tucson Blue" window frames based on a color used in the adobes of the presidio.[23] Few designers emulated this effort to tie the new to the old.

Yet Bart Prince, a fourth-generation New Mexican, turned to the organic architecture of Native Americans, Frank Lloyd Wright, and his mentor Bruce Goff to create a unique style that had a global impact. Born in Albuquerque and

CULTURE *in the* AMERICAN SOUTHWEST

FIGURE 55
The United Bank Tower in Tucson wedded pink granite and pink glass to the regional blue of the window frames. Author's collection.

educated at Arizona State University, Prince met Goff at Tempe when the latter came as a guest lecturer. Goff admired Prince's designs and invited him to join "the American school" in his office. The young architect collaborated with Goff and absorbed his sculptural concepts. Prince produced houses with organic shapes constructed of space-age materials.[24] Individuality became Prince's hallmark: "True architecture comes as a result of a creative response to the needs of the client" and originates in "an *idea* which depends on the creative use of space and materials."[25] His houses acquired names that reflected their shapes or materials. The Hanna House became "Escargo," while the Worley residence became "The Hen." His own house and studio in Albuquerque looked like a spaceship, a three-story oblong aloft on four cylinders. Dramatic and provocative forms and shapes created pools of space. Yet he did not reject the region—"I knew I wanted to live in the Southwest"—or its architectural heritage.[26] "I've always loved Taos and San Ildefonso pueblos. A lot of people think I'm reacting against them with my architecture, but I think it's because I like them so much that I don't want to see all those fake quotations of them. We ought to be doing some-

FIGURE 56
In an Albuquerque neighborhood of one-story stucco houses, Bart Prince's
postmodern studio and home provided a cultural shock. Author's collection.

thing as great as those buildings were and still are."[27] When Goff died, it was
Prince who completed the Shin' enKan Pavilion of Japanese Art for the Price
Collection in Los Angeles. A circle had been closed—the Oklahoma pipeline
company executive Joe Price's collection of Japanese screens found a home at
the Los Angeles County Museum of Art in a structure designed by Oklahoman
Bruce Goff and completed by Bart Prince of New Mexico.

The international architectural giants Walter Gropius, Paul Rudolph, and
Eero Saarinen influenced Judith Chafee of Tucson, whose "least architecture"
brought numerous awards. A native of Tucson with degrees from Bennington
College and Yale University, Chafee created houses for the desert. Both intellectual and combative, Chafee resisted modern architectural clichés. She incorporated historical treatments from older Tucson homes and placed the structures in
the desert. Rejecting revivalism, her houses became "ramadas with glass walls."
Sensitive to the land and the sky, Chafee declared: "Well, I still have a sense of
frontier about this part of the world. . . . Our climate's so brutal that structure
is more important than in temperate climates. They're kind of refuges." Bold
and confident masses, her houses were not fragile. Chafee said, "We like to say
they have balls."[28]

That comment about architecture, and the forceful personality it reflected,

FIGURE 57
*Simple lines, ferro concrete "leaves," and cypress siding gave the Menil Collection
in Houston dignity and classical proportions. Author's collection.*

also conveyed some of the drive, talent, and experimentation that characterized
the ongoing proliferation of the new "art palaces" in the region. Although the
economy of the Southwest suffered greatly by the late 1980s, the construction
of vanity museums continued unabated. Though only a few of the public art
treasuries could expand in this period, privately funded museums kept an international spotlight on the Southwest.

The arrival of John and Dominique de Menil in Houston in the 1930s would
later revolutionize that city's art world. The opening of the Menil Collection in
1987 culminated their efforts to focus attention on European art of the twentieth
century. They had come to the Bayou City as "Pioneer cultural wildcatters" and
became the "Medicis of Modern Art."[29] Although wooed by New York and
Paris, the Menils decided early to locate their treasury in their adopted city. "I
wanted Houston. I had always wanted Houston," Dominique declared. "It is
my city."[30]

Although final judgment on the Menil Collection is years away, John and
Dominique de Menil strongly influenced art in the Southwest. Long before
their museum opened in Houston, John de Menil was an adviser to the Kimbell
Art Museum. Dominique served on the board of directors of the Museum of
Contemporary Art in Los Angeles and was also chairman of the Centre Georges

Pompidou in Paris. Their connoisseurship underlay the Menil Collection, and its disparate holdings, a $150 million art treasure that now resides in a building designed by the Genoese architect Renzo Piano, who also produced the Pompidou Center. The collection ranges from paleolithic times to the twentieth century, with an emphasis on expressionist and post-expressionist art. The 10,000 objects reflect the Menils' interests in Greek and Roman antiquities, African art, and the Cubists and Surrealists. When asked what characterized the collection, Dominique de Menil responded, "Maybe a passionate curiosity for the past and also a vulnerability to poetry — the poetry of a Cubist collage that sings a miraculous song, poetry of images revealing the beauty and mystery of the world, whether the image is a small and tender Vuillard or a stunning Magritte."[31]

Born in Paris in 1908, the daughter of a physicist, Conrad Schlumberger, Dominique de Menil inherited a substantial fortune in the oil-servicing company Schlumberger Limited. She married the Parisian banker Jean (changed to John in 1962) de Menil, and in the late 1930s they began to purchase art. When John paid $2,000 for a Cézanne watercolor, Dominique was shocked, and her mother soon feared their acquisitions would lead them to poverty. But their discovery of Max Ernst (from whom they bought one hundred works), Joan Miro, and Georges Braque simply whetted their appetite. "We became totally unreasonable," Dominique recalled. "It was folly. We borrowed money to buy art."[32] Forced to flee to the United States when the German Army occupied Paris, the Menils moved to Houston, became U.S. citizens, and continued to add to their art collection. They became a force in the Houston Museum of Fine Arts and created art history centers at the College of St. Thomas and Rice University. These "modern Medicis" demanded control over the programs they supported, and if they did not receive it, they moved on to other projects.

Using the Menil Foundation as a vehicle, they spent thirty years acquiring their impeccable pieces. Known to Houston civic leaders and to art dealers as the "steeled butterfly," Dominique de Menil decided, after her husband's death in 1973, to use their fortune, estimated at $200 million, and the assistance of several local foundations to create a museum in Houston to house their collection. The architecture of the $25 million building reflected the collaboration of Dominique de Menil and Renzo Piano. She had spoken with other architects, such as Philip Johnson, who had designed her home, but she turned first to Louis Kahn because of his success with the Kimbell Art Museum. Following Kahn's death, she negotiated with Piano. His concept for the building mirrored her wishes: no monumental structure, the use of natural light in the galleries, and large storage areas. She demanded a treasure house that was small outside and big inside and that would "keep the light alive."[33] Piano and his Houston collaborator, Richard Fitzgerald, responded with a museum of monastic simplicity and geometric rigor.

The structure featured a facade of white steel girders and gray-stained cypress, roofed by unique ferro-concrete leaves. The leaves functioned as roof trusses, gallery ceilings, and giant louvres allowing sunlight to filter into the sleek white galleries. Glass-walled tropical gardens interspersed throughout the building contrasted with the African and oceanic sculpture, antiquities, and expressionist art.[34] When the collection was placed within the museum, even Dominique was shocked. "My, my goodness, we did buy a lot of things," she declared.[35] One of the last great private collections in the United States, the Menil Collection brought critics from around the world to visit the quiet, dignified building and its noncomprehensive holdings. Serenity, light, spaciousness, and elegance characterized the structure, and it won immediate critical acclaim. "The architecture here is not secondary to the art; it is in splendid balance with it," said the *New York Times*. The *Wall Street Journal* called it "intimate, low-key, flooded with light and intelligence."[36] The Menil Collection brought to Houston, and Texas, the realization that architecture need not be flamboyant to be arresting, that size and beauty were not synonymous, and that classical elements and natural materials surpassed the sleek and sterile when handled deftly.

Taking an entirely different direction was the new J. Paul Getty Museum in Los Angeles, on an enormous site in Brentwood. Pavilions of travertine, glass, and soft-beige metal panels were "silhouetted against the brilliant California sky."[37] While its architect, Richard Meier, paid homage to the natural light of the area, the structures were monumental in scale. One critic called the new museum "an oasis of civility," but others found the massive complex overwhelming. Constructed at a cost of $1 billion, the Getty incorporated not only museum spaces but also facilities for conservation, art education, and administration. Reaching for the ambiance of an Italian hill village, Meier incorporated bridges, courtyards, balconies, terraces, gardens, and a circular pool. The creamy white walls could appear "chilly," but "the golden light washes over this space and casts deep shadows upon . . . pristine walls." Meier developed a strong sense of place; as he put it, "The golden light of California is intoxicating." His postmodern "secular monastery" provided an enormous boost to the quest by Los Angeles for cultural recognition.[38]

Meanwhile the Los Angeles County Museum of Art remained under siege, not only because of the competition created by the new Getty but also because of its loss of major collections and the continued fighting among its board members. When the ninety-one-year-old industrialist Armand Hammer announced in 1989 that he would not give his extensive collection to the museum, the mu-

seum trustees removed him from the board, on which he had served for twenty-one years. When the board had refused to construct a new building for the Hammer Collection, he built his own museum on Wilshire Boulevard next to the headquarters of his Occidental Petroleum Company. In a building designed by Edward Larrabee Barnes, Hammer placed his trove of art, largely purchased in the former Soviet Union in the 1930s. Old Master works and nineteenth-century paintings valued at $250 million graced the walls of yet another vanity museum.[39]

Across town, when the trustees of the Virginia Steele Scott Foundation decided to donate its collection of American art, the recipient was the Huntington Library, not the Los Angeles County Museum of Art. Scott had developed a premier holding of American art from the colonial period to the modernists of the 1920s. Paintings by Mary Cassatt, John Singleton Copley, Edward Hopper, John Sloan, and others were placed in a double-winged neoclassical pavilion. Set in a coppice — the Shakespeare Garden — the Scott Gallery added to the extraordinary range of the Huntington's holdings.[40]

The art museum boom continued in Los Angeles even as the California economy entered a deep recession. Creating a new, permanent home, the Los Angeles Museum of Contemporary Art embraced the postmodernism of Japan's foremost architect, Arata Isozaki. In 1979, strongly influenced by several wealthy and prominent collectors of contemporary art, Mayor Tom Bradley initiated a scheme to build a museum as part of the $2 billion California Plaza redevelopment project on Bunker Hill in downtown Los Angeles. In a unique arrangement, the promoters of California Plaza had to provide 1 percent of the project cost, some $20 million, and the museum and the museum board raised $14.5 million for an endowment. Located in the midst of office buildings, commercial spaces, residential buildings, and a hotel, the museum needed to blend into the site and yet relate to the entire plaza. Because of intense bickering by museum board members, Isozaki threatened to quit before winning approval for a series of geometrical volumes with pure lines.[41] His plans involved pyramids, a cylinder, and cubic forms covered in red sandstone from India and green-metal panels. Long considered to be Japan's "guerrilla architect," Isozaki created balance and mass that was both serene and witty, and occasionally irreverent.[42] The exterior formed a small village with unpolished natural surfaces. Most critics praised the commodious galleries, but one saw the exterior as "Egypto–Romanesque–Hot Rod" in style.[43] The architectural critic Paul Goldberger called the museum "a powerful formal composition" exquisitely crafted.[44] Indeed, the response to what Isozaki called a "signature" building was overwhelmingly positive; words used to describe it included "complex," "intimate," "intellectual," and "highly approachable."[45] This new exhilarating design clearly demonstrated the importance of the West Coast in contemporary American art; New York, and its museums and galleries, could not ignore the growing prominence of artists and collectors in southern California.

If Isozaki scored a home run in downtown Los Angeles, there was simultaneously a strikeout on Wilshire Boulevard at the Los Angeles County Museum of Art. Trying desperately to overcome the loss of Norton Simon's collection and other potential donations, the leaders of the museum proved successful in filling the gallery spaces in the original complex. A seed grant of $3 million from Atlantic Richfield Company initiated a drive to raise more than $50 million for an expansion program. The board hired Hardy Holzman Pfeiffer Associates of New York to design a building along Wilshire Boulevard to give the complex a new entrance and to house contemporary art. The structure, designated the Robert O. Anderson Building, masked the three original pavilions and gave the museum an entirely new appearance. The architects produced a monolithic, stepped facade with a monumental arch five stories high that served as a ceremonial entrance portal. Designed to provide an aesthetic unity to the whole, the building offered a "new front door" of stone, terra-cotta tile, and glass brick.[46] While the design hinted at the strong Art Deco presence along Wilshire, one critic dismissed the style as "Deco-Babylonian."[47] Another called it a rare slip by distinguished architects, noting that the building "looks like something out of a

FIGURE 59

The "Deco-Babylonian" entrance to the Los Angeles County Museum of Art
failed to win the praises its leaders sought. Author's collection.

musical comedy borrowed from bad old Hollywood."[48] Yet another critic said
simply, "New Babylon meets Wilshire Boulevard," commenting that the portal
could have been cribbed from Cecil B. DeMille.[49] In the style of its structure,
and in the quality of its collections, the county museum could not compete with
the local vanity museums.

The advancement of the art world of Los Angeles continued to suffer as the
trustees of the Los Angeles County Museum of Art publicly feuded. They lost
their director, Earl A. "Rusty" Powell, the collection of the producer David
Geffen, and the opportunity to exhibit the Barnes Collection from Philadelphia.
Powell went to the National Gallery of Art, Geffen resigned from the board and
donated his paintings to the Museum of Modern Art in New York, and Joe
Price removed part of his Japanese holdings to create his own research center
because the board refused to form a research facility as Price felt he had been
promised. The museum faced a series of crises in the mid-1990s, creating an
artistic leadership vacuum that other regional cities leaped to fill.[50]

San Antonio moved to create a new art museum, but unlike other southwestern cities, it did not hire an internationally known architect to produce a blockbuster structure. Rather, the San Antonio Museum of Art decided to recycle an
older industrial building of historical value. The museum might be the only

FIGURE 60
From brewery to "cultural palace,"
the San Antonio Museum of Art is
a unique example of adaptive use
in the region. Author's collection.

regional example of such a project, but it was a substantial success. There had been an art presence in San Antonio since the founding of the Witte Memorial Museum in the 1920s, but that institution became a hodgepodge of paintings, decorative arts, natural science, and regional history. The San Antonio Museum Association decided to move its fine arts collection to a new location. Simultaneously, the city government of San Antonio sought to expand tourism by extending the Riverwalk beyond the central city. One of the sites for redevelopment included a complex of facilities built by the Anheuser-Busch interests beginning in 1883. The Lone Star Brewing Company (no connection to the present firm of that name) had occupied the buildings until the Prohibition era. By the 1970s, some of the structures were in disrepair and others were the home of small businesses.

The San Antonio Museum Association conceived the idea of turning the large open spaces of the brewery into galleries. The plan left the yellow-brick Romanesque Revival details of the facade intact but substantially altered the interior. The facade combined the Romanesque with Italianate and even Gothic elements, and the addition of colorful awnings and glazed-blue windows highlighted the eclecticism. The museum board hired Cambridge Seven Associates of Boston to redesign the facility, and the result was a national-award-winning museum. The "creative yet respectful transformation" was acclaimed by *Time* as one of the five best architectural designs in 1981, echoing an award presented by *Progressive Architecture* two years earlier.[51] The success of the museum sparked an effort in the city to end the demolition of historic structures in the downtown area and to recycle the buildings into hotels, condominiums, and commercial spaces.

Success eluded neighboring Austin for more than a decade as a grand scheme for an art museum in the downtown area outstripped resources. The small Laguna Gloria Art Museum, located in the 1916 home of Clara Driscoll Sevier and H. H. Sevier, could no longer represent a city of more than 500,000 people. The museum hired the distinguished firm of Venturi, Rauch and Scott Brown in 1986, and announced that the facility would open in 1989. On a major site near Congress Avenue, the architects proposed a large four-story structure using native Austin limestone and red and blue tiles. Even as Robert Venturi and Scott Brown worked on the Austin project, they were designing the new Seattle Art Museum and the Sainsbury Wing of London's National Gallery of Art. Leading the revolt against the International Style, Venturi declared, "Less-is-not-more!" Alas, the collapse of leading Austin financial institutions, the local real estate market, and some technology firms ended work on the museum. Finally, in 1994 the city of Austin purchased a site, and a referendum by voters provided $11 million for the project. The Austin Museum of Art would occupy a new facility, but with new architects and a different concept.[52]

The economic revival of the mid-1990s fueled a new wave of museum growth and expansion. The Museum of Fine Arts in Houston began construction of a new facility designed by Rafael Moneo of Spain at a cost of $115 million. Following major gifts of modern art by James and Mari Michener, the University of Texas announced the construction of the Jack S. Blanton Museum of Art, a $42 million project. The Micheners provided over $40 million in paintings and cash for the museum. The city of San Antonio, several foundations, and the Rockefeller family developed the Nelson A. Rockefeller Center for Latin American Art at the San Antonio Museum of Art. The El Paso Museum of Art had a new $14 million building under way, and aided by the Bass family, the Modern Art Museum of Fort Worth was expanded with a $60 million addition.[53] But when the trustees of the Kimbell Art Museum in Fort Worth proposed to vastly expand Louis Kahn's masterpiece, critics, architects, and an outraged citizenry terminated the scheme. Meanwhile the Dallas Museum of Art opened the Nancy and Jake Hamon Gallery for the Art of the Americas.[54] Across the street, the collector

Raymond D. Nasher created a sculpture garden and filled it with works by Calder, Miró, Moore, Rodin, and others. He declined requests for the collection by the Smithsonian, the Guggenheim, and the Tate Gallery in London. Twenty to thirty pieces would be exhibited as the collection rotated through the two-acre site. Nasher spent $32 million of his own funds to create the garden.[55]

The expansion of museums throughout the Southwest spoke not only to a revitalized economy but also to a regional enthusiasm for new or larger art palaces. Edward Mazria and Associates created the Museum of Indian Arts and Culture in Santa Fe, a passive solar structure, to display part of the 50,000-piece collection of the Laboratory of Anthropology. The Philbrook Museum of Art in Tulsa added a new wing, as did the Thomas Gilcrease Institute. The University of Oklahoma built the Fred Jones Museum of Art and subsequently acquired the Richard and Adeline Fleischaker Collection of twentieth-century art for the facility. The Fort Worth art maven Anne W. Marion, the daughter of Anne Burnett Tandy, used the Burnett Foundation as a vehicle to form the Georgia O'Keeffe museum in Santa Fe.[56] The long lines of gallery-goers across the Southwest on Sunday afternoons testified to the positive public response to these cultural monuments.

Regional economic leaders saw the art museums as good business. Often desperately seeking outside capital to respark the growth of their cities, the business elite needed visible cultural symbols to motivate New York, Philadelphia, and Boston investors not only to build new plants and facilities in their communities but also to move there. They had to have a symphony, a ballet, an opera company, and elegant art museums. The buildings to house these cultural palaces represented newly acquired wealth and a veneer of sophistication but, more important, often gave new life to downtown districts suffering from losses of department stores, shops, restaurants, theaters, and hotels. The art museums brought commuters back to the heart of the city on weekends and created a sense of urban vibrancy. The bold architectural thrust of the museums also encouraged business and urban leaders to abandon traditional architectural forms for skyscrapers, shopping centers, apartments, hotels, and civic buildings, resulting both in creating striking skylines and accelerating urban sprawl.[57] Cultural needs, aspirations for economic growth, and the desire to escape an aura of provinciality motivated southwesterners to erect cultural edifices of monumental cost at an astonishing rate.

The great expansion and diversity of museum buildings after 1970 demonstrated the pluralism of contemporary architecture and the longings of southwestern cities. Each institution sought a unique identity in its building, and the structures served as catalysts for bold and provocative designs. The Japanese architect Arata Isozaki declared: "In the past, religious buildings had a strong role in society. Now art is coming to take over the position where the gods are no more. . . . Even the activity of raising funds and collecting art for the museum is like the religious activity of the past."[58] Art museums became a major architectural presence in southwestern cities, and as the architect Philip Johnson said: "Once you could tell a lot about a community by its church. It was the place the city took pride in. Now it is the cultural center, the museum as monument."[59]

The strategy for the enhancement of symphonic music paralleled that of the art museum promoters. Although faced with adverse economic conditions, Houston, Dallas, Fort Worth, and Los Angeles built enormously expensive symphony halls and hired new conductors in a quest for national and international recognition. The successful orchestras found individuals or foundations who gave huge sums for buildings, salaries, and endowments. The results were triumphant orchestral halls and symphonies of great quality.

Christoph Eschenbach, a forty-nine-year-old German-born conductor, took the helm of the Houston Symphony Orchestra in 1987 and led it to greater heights. He played a very public role in the city as part of an effort to regain the momentum of the 1970s. The Houston Grand Opera and the Houston Ballet were moving into the $70 million Wortham Theater Center, and in response, the symphony trustees fought to continue to make the orchestra the city's cultural flagship. Trained by the famed George Szell in Cleveland, Eschenbach sought to produce an orchestra that would win not only the support of Houstonians but also international acclaim. A shy, short man, the conductor soon became a common figure in Bayou City social circles. A $6 million challenge grant from the Cullen Foundation initiated a drive to build a $30 million endowment.[60] Referring to himself as "head of an assembly of artists," Eschenbach recruited new players even as he lengthened the season.[61] He took the symphony on national and international tours, to positive critical notice. Left as the sole occupant of Jones Hall, an aging facility, the symphony began an effort to construct a new venue. As the quality of the orchestra rose, and as attendance grew, the drive for a new symphonic hall took form with substantial grants from the Hobby family and the Houston Endowment. The supporters of the Houston Symphony covered their bet on Eschenbach by giving the orchestra a new home.[62]

The Dallas Symphony Orchestra moved into the Meyerson Symphony Center in the fall of 1989, and its conductor, Eduardo Mata, made the most of the $200 million hall. The architect I. M. Pei's stunningly elegant building housed the Eugene McDermott Concert Hall, which the symphony filled with warm, crisp tones. With its glass-and-limestone skin, the structure added one more signature building to the Dallas Arts District.[63] With onyx-panel trim, cherry-wood walls, brass accents, and a sky-blue ceiling, McDermott Hall was praised for its beauty and acoustics by musicians, critics, and engineers. The residents of northern Texas responded to the hall and the orchestra with six consecutive sold-out seasons, both the classical and the "pop" series. Over 90 percent of subscribers renewed each season, some 28,700 orders. After Andrew Litton took over as conductor in 1995, the orchestra's repertoire was expanded, and a new, fuller sound emerged.[64] The Dallas Symphony had arrived.

While Dallas celebrated its newest cultural jewel, Fort Worth voters turned down a $20 million bond issue to convert the aging Will Rogers Auditorium into a modern, multipurpose hall. The Bass brothers — Sid, Edward, Robert, and Lee — and others had pledged $30 million for the proposal, but preservationists and angry taxpayers said "no!" Undaunted, Ed Bass chaired a fundraising effort to build a new $60 million hall in the downtown district. With the solid support of the Bass family's Sid Richardson Foundation, the Nancy Lee and Perry R. Bass Performance Hall soon rose ten stories above Commerce Street. Designed by the architect David Schwarz and three other firms, the more than 180,000-square-foot building, constructed of green granite and tan Texas limestone, would house the Fort Worth Symphony Orchestra, the Van Cliburn International Piano Competition, the Fort Worth Ballet, and the Fort Worth Opera. A horseshoe-shaped hall seating over 2,000 occupied the center of the huge structure. The north exterior wall was graced by two trumpet-blowing angels made of Texas limestone, symbolizing the triumph of inherited wealth over vox populi.[65]

Ignoring the recession in California, fund-raisers labored for a decade to generate $220 million to build Walt Disney Concert Hall as part of the Los Angeles Music Center. The architect Frank Gehry conceived a sensuous exterior of curving stone forms, producing a billowing shape. The Los Angeles Philharmonic, led by its baby-faced director Esa-Pekka Salonen, prepared to occupy the hall. Hired in 1992 and only thirty-three years old, Salonen immediately put his stamp on the orchestra. An early concert showed the demands of the Finnish conductor, who brought the Philharmonic closer to the audience with a bigger, brighter, and better-blended sound.[66] Like Houston and Dallas, Los Angeles bet on a new hall and a new conductor to enhance its symphony.

Symphonic music all but disappeared, however, in San Antonio, San Diego, and Oklahoma City in the late 1980s. In the city of the Alamo, old, wealthy families had long dominated the San Antonio Symphony Board. Gradually they were replaced by business leaders with little interest in or knowledge of music. The concerns of these leaders were the ongoing deficits and dwindling audiences. From 1984 to 1987 the orchestra had no music director, managing director, or development officer. Early in 1987 the board canceled the next season. Musicians took severe wage cuts, but the debt continued to grow. Despite these problems, the quality of the orchestra remained high. Mayor Henry Cisneros pleaded with the board to appeal to the city's large Hispanic population with programs of Iberian and Latin American classical music, but to no avail. The symphony lurched from one crisis to another. Christopher Wilkins became the music director, providing some stability at the podium. In 1994, the symphony used its endowment to repay a bank loan of $5 million, leaving only about $1 million in the fund. The music director took another salary cut as the board reduced the budget. A city of over one million people had a symphony with a budget of only $6.2 million.[67] The orchestra's board simply refused to accept the demographic realities of San Antonio, and the fiscal crisis worsened.

The San Diego experience echoed that of San Antonio. An ambitious drive to create a superior symphony began in the mid-1970s. By 1980 the American Symphony Orchestra League named the San Diego Symphony a "major" orchestra as the budget reached $2 million. But a financial crisis the following year led to an emergency fund drive, a situation that would be repeated several times. When the symphony moved into the rehabilitated Fox Theater, the restoration effort fell $2 million short. Yearly deficits and a labor conflict led to the cancellation of the 1986–87 season; refunds could not be made to subscribers, since the money had been spent. Marketing strategies failed, endowment funds were tapped to pay operating costs, and musicians, already poorly paid, refused to accept salary cuts. Concerts resumed in 1987, but with a shortened season. In an effort to reduce the orchestra's debts, the board used an anonymous gift of $2.5 million to settle with banks holding loans in excess of $6.8 million. Not even a series of summer concerts could generate additional funding, and in 1996, the orchestra board moved to declare bankruptcy.[68] The San Diego Symphony Orchestra could not find an audience among its huge metropolitan population.

Other southwestern cities suffered similarly as their symphonies struggled in the 1980s. The Oklahoma City Symphony Orchestra floundered with heavy debts that not even a Ford Foundation grant could erase. Yearly deficits led to efforts to reduce salaries, and a bitter labor dispute forced the orchestra to disband in 1988. In Arizona, a supporter of the Phoenix Symphony complained, "We still have people who will give money to the Cleveland Symphony but who don't give any to the Phoenix Symphony." The Tucson Symphony survived a series of crises, including large deficits, leading its conductor, Robert Bernhardt, to reduce the size of the orchestra rather than cut salaries. In October, 1994, the New Mexico Symphony Orchestra could not cover its payroll, and the board of trustees sought funds from the legislature to pay for statewide concerts.[69]

Clearly, some southwestern cities simply established unattainable goals as they sought cultural acclaim.

Houston, however, was not one of these cities. On May 10, 1987, more than 2,300 of Houston's social and economic elite celebrated the completion of the Gus S. Wortham Center, the first major opera house opened since the Kennedy Center in Washington, D.C. Built at a cost in excess of $70 million, paid for entirely with private-sector funds, the hall vindicated the hopes of a city coming back from near economic collapse. Opera stars, pop singers, a ballet, and a production of *Aïda* provided music for every taste. In the Brown Theater, those individuals who had contributed $240,000 or more and held season tickets occupied one tier of boxes. The boxes above were for corporate donors. Over seven difficult years, more than $66 million had been raised for the huge opera house made of dark-red brick and rose-colored granite. The vaguely Romanesque building sat on two blocks of prime downtown real estate; the roof was the size of three football fields — a point the press made for nonopera buffs. The Alice and George Brown Theater, with 2,200 seats, hosted the Houston Grand Opera, while the Houston Ballet occupied the 1,100-seat Cullen Theater.[70] The awesome size of the Wortham Center led one observer to declare that it had the "monumentality of some great old European train station."[71] The architects Pete Ed Garrett and Reginald L. Mach of Morris Architects created an exterior design harmonious with Philip Johnson's First Republic Bank across the street. The theaters were equipped with large prosceniums, deep stages, and elaborate mechanical features. Opening with *Aïda* proved apt.

The Houston Grand Opera thrived under David Gockley, and now it had a worthy home. Patrons entered Wortham Center under an eighty-eight-foot Romanesque arch, which symbolized the success of the opera and of Houston's ability to raise funds in the midst of economic reversal. Italian-silk wall hangings, bronze doors, and the chandelier from the Helen Hayes Theater in New York conveyed visual messages to operagoers and critics. Although the city of Houston donated the site, valued at $35 million, the quest for the opera house was achieved through contributions from local foundations, corporations, and individuals. As the *Christian Science Monitor* noted: "The Wortham Center will be a red-brick monument to the self-help style that has made Houston the sprawling, up-from-the-bootstraps giant it is."[72] That was precisely the effect Houston's civic leaders had sought.

The Houston Grand Opera rose to the challenge of the new hall with productions of "old warhorses" such as *Aïda* and *Tannhäuser,* but Gockley also offered *Nixon in China* by the modernist John Adams. By the mid-1990s, the season would include *La Bohéme* and *Norma* as well as *Four Saints in Three Acts.* The

Opera Studio experimented with Ricky Ian Gordon's *The Tibetan Book of the Dead*. The Houston audiences offered mixed responses to some of the productions, but civic pride overcame dissonant chords. Wealth and determination, plus an imaginative general director, made the Houston Grand Opera a rival to companies in New York and Europe.[73]

Even though Houston had few operatic competitors in the Southwest, or in the nation, regional companies continued to offer quality productions. The Santa Fe Opera expanded its repertoire and presented premieres as well as works infrequently heard. Contemporary operas included the Finnish composer Aulis Sallinen's *The King Goes Forth to France,* a grim allegory whose score drew from musical history ranging from Verdi to Weill. The Arizona Opera Company, based in Tucson, collaborated with thirteen other companies in OPERA America to hold down production costs. Director Glynn Ross paid off the Arizona Opera Company's debt, balanced the budget, and presented sold-out productions of *La Bohéme* and *The Barber of Seville*.[74] Southwestern audiences wanted to hear and see quality opera in the 1990s as ardently as they had in the 1890s. Now, however, the performances were first-rate, were heard in lavish halls, and were offered by their own companies. Too, the productions often toured across the nation, to Europe, and to Asia.

By the outset of the 1990s, theatrical companies in the region had begun to recover from the doldrums of the economic slump. The long-dormant former home of the Mummers Theater in Oklahoma City became the Oklahoma Theater Center operated by the city's Arts Council. Benefactor John Kilpatrick paid the mortgage, and the facility reopened. Oklahomans also supported the Jewel Box Theater, which celebrated thirty seasons of community theater, while the Carpenter Square Theater offered risky, avant-garde plays. The Arizona Theater Company provided Tucson and Phoenix with performances in a professional, nonprofit format. More than 100,000 people attended six plays each season, with offerings ranging from Shakespeare to David Mamet. Phoenix provided a new venue in the $12 million Herberger Theater Center. To encourage regional drama, television, and film in New Mexico, the actress Greer Garson donated $3 million to the College of Santa Fe to construct a communication arts facility with theater and film production studios.[75]

Texas and California remained the dominate theatrical centers. The Alley Theater in Houston and the Dallas Theater Center each had budgets in excess of $4 million by the early 1990s and about 10,000 season subscribers. The Alley offered the Texas premiere of Corpus Christi native Terrence McNally's *Love! Valour! Compassion!,* the 1995 Tony Award winner. It produced Waco-born Steve Martin's *Picasso at the Lapin Agile* for Houston audiences.[76] After bringing Lynn

Redgrave for a one-woman show in 1994, the Alley's next season offered Vanessa Redgrave as the director and star of *Anthony and Cleopatra,* and Corin Redgrave directed and starred in *Julius Caesar.* These joint productions with the Redgraves' Moving Theater initiated an ongoing collaboration. "We in England know how unique this [the Alley Theater] is," professed Vanessa Redgrave.[77]

Dallas patrons also appreciated the uniqueness of their theater, the Dallas Theater Center, but the subject matter of some contemporary plays drove audiences away. Classics by Shakespeare and Eugene O'Neill generated subscribers, but *Fool for Love,* a play about incest, led to massive cancellations. The center's director, Adrian Hall, a native Texan, tried to rebuild the subscription list, but by the early 1990s, the company was in serious trouble. The center's board brought Richard Hamburger to Dallas as artistic director with the specific purpose of recreating an audience. A trained actor and director, Hamburger offered conventional plays in solid productions. He demanded excellence from the casts, who praised him as a director. Local actors resented the presence of out-of-town cast members, but the Dallas Theater Center moved out of the doldrums under his management.[78]

Theatrical producers in Dallas and Houston recognized that they had to reach out to all segments of their cities. Successful drama did not mean all-white casts playing before all-white audiences. Pressured by outside forces, Dallas Theater Center commissioned the African American playwrights Vinnette Carroll and Micki Grant to write an original musical. The two had previously written *Don't Bother Me, I Can't Cope* and *Your Arm's Too Short to Box With God,* and their new work, *Ups and Downs* was well received.[79] Based on a Jamaican folktale, the new musical had an all-minority cast. The African American playwright Celeste Colson-Walker, a native of Houston, produced and starred in several plays, including *Sister Sister.* Esther Rolle played the lead in its Los Angeles production. Colson-Walker's *Camp Logan,* about African American soldiers in World War I, and *Reunion at Batersville* won many awards. She exhibited a strong sense of place in her plays, which featured sudden plot turns, tight dialogue, and acute social observations. Colson-Walker's dramas became part of the repertoire of playhouses across the country.[80]

Theater in southern California survived and even prospered in the late 1980s and early 1990s. The Pasadena Playhouse, now the State Theater of California, premiered plays such as Rupert Holmes's *Solitary Confinement* and Mark St. Germain's *Camping with Henry and Tom.* Holmes, who had also written *The Mystery of Edwin Drood,* and St. Germain turned to the Playhouse and its excellent productions to polish their work. The Old Globe Theater won a special Tony Award in 1985 and that year sold $1 million in subscriptions. Its production of *The Skin of Our Teeth* was the first Public Broadcasting System satellite telecast of a live drama. The Edison Center in Balboa Park hosted the Globe, the Cassius Carter Center Stage with its theater-in-the-round, and the open-air Lowell Davis Festival Theater. All three venues offered significant productions by a distinguished resident acting company that drew large crowds to the park.[81]

The Mark Taper Forum's artistic director, Gordon Davidson, spoke about theater in Los Angeles in 1991: "As the city has grown, more cultural entities have taken root. One feels a sense of expansion and, to a lesser extent, a deepening. . . . Twenty years ago, mine was the only theater. It's not the only theater today. Twenty years ago, Los Angeles was still a two-week turn for road shows. You can't send tired road show companies here any longer. Los Angeles is either a beginning place or an ending place."[82] After Davidson first opened the Mark Taper in 1970, he took risks with untried plays and playwrights, but backed by Dorothy Buffum Chandler, he succeeded. The Taper generated additional venues for live drama in Los Angeles and southern California. His productions, and those of other theaters, often moved directly to New York stages.

Recognition of regional drama produced by southwestern theatrical companies included Hispanic organizations as well. In 1984, Joseph Papp's Public Theater invited La Compañía de Teatro de Alburquerque to present Denise Chávez's play *Plaza* in New York. La Compañía continued its tour for a one-week run at the International Theater Festival in Edinburgh, Scotland.[83]

The exportation of culture included not only entire companies but also the plays of writers such as Mark Medoff. When Medoff joined the faculty of New Mexico State University in 1966, he had severe doubts about his decision. He was "truly unable to imagine [that] a Jewish kid from Miami Beach by way of Stanford was going to find happiness in an ag school in southern New Mexico." Twenty years later, having received Tony, Drama Desk, Obie, and Best Play of the London Season Awards, Medoff admitted, "Here I am, and of course now they'd have to dynamite me out."[84] The New Mexico landscape and the mythology of the Southwest provided both a physical and a psychological home for the prolific playwright. His early works — *Doing a Good One for the Red Man: A Red Farce* and *When You Comin' Back, Red Ryder?* — explored western themes. "I try to start all my work here," Medoff declared. "Both figuratively and literally, I've written a lot about New Mexico."[85]

Born in Illinois in 1940, and educated at the University of Miami and Stanford University, Medoff seemed an unlikely author of dramas about the Southwest. Yet the region supplied inspiration, colleagues, audiences, and theatrical facilities. Produced first in San Antonio by the Dallas Theater Center, his initial play later moved to off-off Broadway. When his greatest success, *Children of a*

FIGURE 61

*The playwright Mark Medoff and the actress Phyllis Frelich, the inspiration for
the Tony Award-winning* Children of a Lesser God, *rehearse a play in 1984.
Courtesy of New Mexico State University, Las Cruces.*

Lesser God, premiered in 1979, it opened at the Mark Taper Forum in Los Angeles
before a lengthy run in New York. Like most of his other plays, this drama
focused on the difficulty of human communication.[86]

As head of the Theater Arts Department at New Mexico State University,
Medoff not only wrote award-winning plays but also formed the semiprofessional American Southwest Theater Company. The company drew audiences
from El Paso as well as Las Cruces and premiered some of the playwright's work,
such as *The Heart Outright.* The company attracted talented students who found
a teacher enamored with a southwestern aesthetic. What he admired "was the
combination of liberalism and provincialism in the best sense." He noted, "I
found a kind of vestigial old pioneer civility that still existed here, and I also
liked the three cultures."[87] The land also contributed: "The seeming simplicity
of it. . . . It's not barren; it's wonderfully, interestingly populated in terms of
plant and animal life."[88] Even as he moved to a successful career as a screenwriter, Medoff conveyed his sensibilities about the Southwest to his audiences.
"Anybody's notion that New Mexico is some sort of backwoods area is incor-
rect. I just love living here. I wasn't born in New Mexico, but I am a New Mexican."[89] The region became a trusted friend or parent, embracing him and his
plays.

Eastern audiences reacted warmly to plays by Medoff and Sam Shepard, another adopted southwesterner, and they also applauded regional ballet companies, especially the Houston Ballet. From the time Ben Stevenson assumed leadership of this company in 1976, the Houston community responded with patronage and financial support. The budget exceeded $9.5 million by the end of the 1980s, when the endowment stood in excess of $18 million, the highest in the country. The new venue in the Wortham Center hosted the fifth-largest ballet company in the United States.[90] Critics commented not only on the dancers' American exuberance and energy but also on their "English" deportment. A former dancer with the Royal Ballet, Stevenson brought English choreographers to the staff, giving the company an unusual style. Their *Sleeping Beauty* made a triumphal national tour, and beginning in 1986, the Houston Ballet made regular appearances across the country. It toured Europe, the United Kingdom, and Canada and, in 1995, became the first American ballet invited to perform in the People's Republic of China.[91]

The ballet companies in Dallas and Arizona could not achieve the renown of the Houston Ballet, but their success demonstrated the region's commitment to dance. The Dallas Ballet overcame a large debt in the late 1980s with a major fund-raising effort and moved toward a forty-week season.[92] The merger of three young companies in 1986 produced Ballet Arizona, which performed in Tucson and Phoenix. A company of twenty-four dancers, recruited by Director Jean-Paul Comelin, came from Europe, Asia, and Latin America, as well as the United States.[93] The regional enthusiasm for ballet produced semiprofessional companies in many cities and generated large audiences. Although these organizations did not tour extensively, they often won critical notice for their quality.

The urban Southwest not only cultivated the theater and the ballet but also nurtured a literary life that drew even greater attention to the region and its writers. Interestingly, with the obvious exception of Larry McMurtry, female novelists received the greatest critical recognition and generated the most substantial readership among mainstream authors. Shelby Hearon, Beverly Lowry, Laura Furman, and Sarah Bird in Texas and Joan Didion in southern California wrote of the contemporary Southwest from a feminist perspective and with a strong sense of the impact of urbanization on women and their families. Often weathering the vagaries of marriage, divorce, financial stress, child rearing, and constantly threatened career goals, these writers and their subjects revealed the internal turmoil of a region in the midst of monumental change.

Shelby Hearon, born in Kentucky, had moved to Texas as an adolescent. After graduating from the University of Texas, she married, had children, and divorced. A single parent living in Austin, she began to write novels with a strong sense of place and character. The most intellectual among her contemporaries, Hearon's subject matter and style ranged widely. Whereas some of her autobiographical novels dealt deftly and humorously with careers beset by teenagers and former spouses, she could also employ black comedy, as in *Hannah's House*. By the early 1990s she had published twelve novels, won numerous awards, and moved first to New York and then to Vermont.[94] But her fiction never lost its Texas and southwestern compass. With a wicked wit and tart tongue, Hearon barbed Texas pretentiousness. At a cocktail party in *Owning Jolene* (1990), guests discuss and debunk efforts to form cultural icons:

> Houston spent $1,000,000 to bring in 250 pictures of "Wyeth's girl friend."
> Fort Worth invested $1,000,000 to turn its Stockyards into "The Williamsburg of the West."
> San Antonio invested $6,000,000 in a "Fern Barn" [The Botanical Garden].
> Reflecting the economic downturn, one guest complained, "The only thing in this state that's making money is cul-chure."[95]

Hearon's style and verve took her to creative writing programs at the University of Houston, Bennington College, and the University of California at Irvine. Her short stories won the NEA/PEN Short Story Prize five times. With a near-perfect ear for regional speech, Hearon constructed witty exchanges at a variety of levels. Even when her heroines leave Texas, as she did, they do not escape the Southwest. Lutie Sayre, the protagonist in *Group Therapy*, moves to New York City, but when she cooks, Lutie bakes buttermilk pies and fries chicken. Her grandmother's house on the Guadalupe River remains the center of her life.[96] This novel, like others from Hearon's pen, used Texas women and generational conflict to explore the human condition. From *Armadillo in the Grass* in 1968 to her novels of the 1990s, Hearon's identification with her gender and her adopted home shaped and molded a significant body of work.

While Hearon employed Austin, San Antonio, and the Texas hill country as her geographical base, Beverly Lowry found Houstonians as fascinating and complex as Tolstoy's Muskovites. Novelist, short story writer, and actress, Lowry left her native Memphis, moving first to Houston and then to the Texas hill country. She taught at the University of Houston and there perfected her skills as a novelist of contemporary Texas. In her fictional town of Eunola, she found the voices of the rural community residents whom she graphically portrayed in *Daddys Girl*.[97] That novel won awards and critical notice, but Lowry portrayed the restless female urbanite with an even clearer voice in *The Perfect Sonya*. The heroine, Pauline, a sensual and intelligent actress, comes to terms with herself as she moves from coastal Texas to Houston, Austin, and New York. From her

FIGURE 62
*Beverly Lowry produced
southwestern novels that were both
urbane and urban. Photo by Bill
Wittliff. Southwestern Writers
Collection/Southwest Texas State
University.*

uncle, Will Hand, a teacher and writer in San Marcos, Pauline gains a deeper understanding of the land and accepts her feelings of love and passion. Like the role she plays in Chekhov's "Uncle Vanya" — portraying what a critic described as "the perfect Sonya" — Pauline examines her life and copes with painful memories and buried secrets.[98] Lowry argued that Houstonians saw themselves as Texans but that residents of the Bayou City were no longer southwesterners, since cosmopolitanism had replaced regionalism. Yet Pauline and Lowry's other characters *are* truly Texans.[99]

Lowry's view of Houston as simply another large metropolitan center was echoed by Laura Furman in *The Shadow Line*. Although that novel was of and about Houston, almost a roman-à-clef, Liz Gold, the heroine, is a Jewish writer from New York. The story belongs to Gold, not Houston, but Furman filled the novel with details about the city. Furman's life in Texas included stints as a teacher at the University of Houston, Southern Methodist University, and the University of Texas. During that period she won numerous awards and a Guggenheim Fellowship. Although the highly acclaimed *Tuxedo Park* returned Furman to her native New York, her novels and short stories continued to reflect her sojourn in the Southwest. Like Hearon and Lowry, Furman created characters and stories based in the region, but with a universality that transcended geography.[100]

Just as Larry McMurtry gave up wearing the T-shirt with its slogan mocking his "regional writer" status, other writers of the Southwest shook off their sense of provincialism to explore the universal. But they did so in voices aware of the land, its peoples, and its history. Sarah Bird, in a style filled with wry humor, mocked the pretentions of Austinites. Yet her characters were clearly part of the multidimensional culture emerging in the Southwest in the 1980s. Whereas McMurtry returned to the nineteenth and early twentieth centuries for his fiction in the late 1980s, other writers used the contemporary Southwest to sustain their exploration of the human condition. Novelists, playwrights, and short story writers took the region to a national — indeed, an international — audience.

Demographic changes of enormous significance could be seen not only in the response of Anglos to vast urban growth but also in the growing impact of the Hispanic community. The presence of Mexican- and Spanish-born peoples had given shape to the regional culture for four centuries. The arrival of millions of immigrants from Mexico, the Caribbean, and Central America after the 1970s simply enhanced their contributions to the Southwest. As noted by José David Saldívar and Carlos Vélêz-Ibáñez, scholars of the Mexican American society, there has never been a cultural border or frontier between Mexico and the United States. Mexican American and Hispanic American cultures came from the south and constantly moved northward. These peoples and their societies did not see a political border; their families may have lived in the Mexican state of Sonora, in the area of the Gadsden Purchase, or in Arizona, but there was always an ongoing cross-fertilization of cultures.[101]

In the years after 1980, Anglos and others discovered the vitality of the Hispanic culture, particularly its art. The Houston Museum of Fine Arts originated the exhibition "Hispanic Art in the United States," and the 180 works toured the country as well as Mexico City. The paintings and sculptures destroyed the idea of a monolithic Hispanic culture but revealed the strong differences between Hispanic art and Anglo art. Hispanic artists and sculptors found their roots in family and communal values, the Roman Catholic Church, and pre-Columbian myths. Passionate art, religious forms, unconventional details and humor, deliberately abused color harmonies, and distortions of space marked a vibrant exhibit. Residents of Los Angeles, Laredo, El Paso, Tucson, and other cities near the border were neither shocked nor surprised by this artistic display, since they had already observed the effects of "barrioization" in areas of their cities. Cultural segregation produced a vitality that found outlets in murals, sculptures, and other art forms. Museum visitors in Washington, D.C., and New York City flocked to see yet another example of the exportation of southwestern culture.[102]

From the arrival of the earliest occupants of the Southwest to the end of the twentieth century, the regional culture has been shaped by the natural environment. Since the 1880s, the built environment has also contributed to the conception of a region set apart from the rest of the nation.[103] The idea of a "Southwest" drew from an understanding of the process of settlement by Anglos moving from the eastern seaboard to the Pacific Ocean. But even though the term had a geographic connotation initially, it came to mean much more. For some Anglo residents and visitors to the region it meant a "desert aesthetic," a changing middle-class response to a land both alien and enchanting.[104] Such a concept had no meaning to a Hopi, a Navajo, or a resident of Ácoma Pueblo, however. For them, the people and the land were one, they were of the earth. Even with such diverse conceptions of their relationship to the land, Native Americans, Hispanic Americans, and Anglo Americans formed a bond with the Southwest. Their affection for place, their consciousness of the land and the sky, created their "topophilia."[105] They were westerners, but there were "many Wests," and the Southwest stood apart.[106] Simultaneously, they belonged to a society and a place, and that awareness produced a self-identity.[107] From that self-identity as southwesterners, they have produced architecture, art, literature, music, and dance directly related to the land and to their societies. Just as salsa has challenged ketchup as the nation's leading condiment, the peoples of the Southwest have created a culture that has altered and shaped the national American culture. Southwesterners know they belong to the land with its vast sky; the dramatic presence of that land shapes their lives and their cultures.

NOTES

INTRODUCTION

1. Paul Shepard, *Man in the Landscape* (New York: Alfred A. Knopf, 1967), pp. 29, 39–40. See also Yi-Fu Tuan, *Topophilia: A Study of Environmental Perceptions, Attitudes, and Values.*
2. Yi-Fu Tuan, *Space and Place: The Perspective of Experience,* pp. 3, 6, 7, 54.
3. Artist Alan Gussow quoted in the introduction to Wayne Franklin and Michael Steiner, eds., *Mapping American Culture* (Iowa City: University of Iowa Press, 1992), 4; Carl O. Sauer, "The Morphology of Landscape," no. 2 of *University of California Publications in Geography* (Berkeley: University of California Press, 1925), p. 53: D. W. Meinig, *Southwest: Three Peoples in Geographical Change,* p. 3. For a recent effort to define western American regionalism, see David M. Wrobel and Michael C. Steiner, eds., *Many Wests: Place, Culture, and Regional Identity.*
4. William Balassi, John F. Crawford, and Annie O. Eysturoy, eds., *This Is about Vision: Interviews with Southwestern Writers,* p. 1.
5. Robin W. Winks, "Regionalism in Comparative Perspective," in William G. Robbins, Robert J. Frank, and Richard E. Ross, eds., *Regionalism and the Pacific Northwest* (Corvallis: Oregon State University Press, 1983), pp. 26–27. See also Michael L. Johnson, *New Westers: The West in Contemporary American Culture,* for an interpretation of the creation of a "West" in popular culture.
6. Georgia O'Keeffe quoted in Elizabeth Cunningham, "Visions of a Big Sky," *Natural History* 94 (Nov., 1985): 65.
7. Robin W. Doughty, *At Home in Texas: Early Views of the Land,* pp. 6–8, 135–39. See also Leonard Lutwack, *The Role of Place in Literature* (Syracuse, N.Y.: Syracuse University Press, 1984), 142–81.
8. Witter Bynner, "Desert Harvest," *Southwest Review* 14 (summer, 1929): 493–94; Harriet Monroe, "In Texas and New Mexico," *Poetry* 16 (Sept., 1920): 328.
9. Stuart B. James, "Western American Space and the Human Imagination," *Western Humanities Review* 24 (spring, 1970), 147–55; Lawrence Clark Powell, *Southwest Classics: The Creative Literature of the Arid Lands,* pp. 3–4: Michael James Riley, "Picturing the Southwest Reframed: An American Cultural Landscape and the Social Negotiation of Art, Ethnicity, and Place" (Ph.D. diss., University of Texas, 1993).
10. Cultural anthropologist Clark Wissler quoted in Walter S. Campbell [Stanley Vestal], *The Book Lover's Southwest: A Guide to Good Reading* (Norman: University of Oklahoma Press, 1955), 16.
11. Ross Calvin, *Sky Determines: Interpretation of the Southwest,* pp. xi–xvi, 1–2, 28, 63, 284–314.

12. Larry McMurtry, *All My Friends Are Going to Be Strangers* (New York: Simon and Schuster, 1972), p. 176.

13. Richard West Sellars, "The Interrelationship of Literature, History, and Geography in Western Writing," *Western Historical Quarterly* 4 (Apr., 1973): 185.

14. For an extended discussion of "where" the Southwest is located, see James W. Byrkit, "Land, Sky, and People: The Southwest Defined," *Journal of the Southwest* 34 (autumn, 1992): 365–66, 377, 380, 382.

15. Lawrence R. Clayton, "The Southwest and Its Culture," *Journal of American Culture* 14 (summer, 1991): 7–8.

16. Bruce Bigelow, "Roots and Regions: A Summary Definition of the Cultural Geography of America," *Journal of Geography* 79 (Nov., 1980): 218–29: Powell, *Southwest Classics,* pp. 5–6.

17. Howard W. Odum and Harry Estill Moore, *American Regionalism* (New York: Henry Holt and Company, 1938), pp. 594–617.

18. Meinig, *Southwest,* pp. 3, 55–56, 61.

19. Erna Fergusson, *Our Southwest* (New York: Alfred A. Knopf, 1940), p. 18.

20. Michael J. Riley, "Constituting the Southwest, Contesting the Southwest, Reinventing the Southwest," *Journal of the Southwest* 36 (autumn, 1994), pp. 222–23.

21. John Chávez, *The Lost Land: The Chicano Image of the Southwest,* pp. 1–5.

22. J. Frank Dobie, *Guide to Life and Literature of the Southwest* (Dallas: Southern Methodist University Press, 1952), p. 37.

23. D. H. Meinig, "The Continuous Shaping of America: A Perspective for Geographers and Historians," *American Historical Review* 83 (Dec., 1978): 1205: John Crowe Ransome, "The Aesthetic of Regionalism," *American Review* 2 (Jan., 1934): 293–94.

24. David Potter, *The South and the Sectional Conflict* (Baton Rouge: Louisiana State University Press, 1968), p. 4: Kirkpatrick Sale, *Power Shift: The Rise of the Southern Rim and Its Challenge to the Eastern Establishment* (New York: Random House, 1980); John W. Caughey, "The Spanish Southwest," in Merrill Jensen, ed., *Regionalism in America* (Madison: University of Wisconsin Press, 1951), pp. 175–76.

25. Clyde A. Milner II, "The View from Wisdom: Four Layers of History and Regional Identity," in William Cronon, George Miles, and Jay Gitlin, eds., *Under an Open Sky: Rethinking America's Western Past,* p. 204. Chris Wilson has shown how one southwestern community formed an ahistorical past; see *The Myth of Santa Fe: Creating a Modern Regional Tradition.*

26. Lon Tinkle, "Texas Theatre from the Imported to the Indigenous," in Leonard E. B. Andrews, ed., *Dallas Theater Center* (Dallas: Dallas Theater Center, 1963), n.p.

27. Robert V. Hine, *Community on the American Frontier: Separate but Not Alone* (Norman: University of Oklahoma Press, 1980); Louis B. Wright, *Culture on the Moving Frontier* (Bloomington: Indiana University Press, 1955): Richard C. Wade, "Urban Life in Western America, 1790–1830," *American Historical Review* 64 (Oct., 1958): 14–30.

28. Lawrence W. Levine, *Highbrow/Lowbrow: The Emergence of Cultural Hierarchy in America,* pp. 230–31; D. H. Meinig, "American Wests: Preface to a Geographical Introduction," *Annals of the Association of American Geographers* 62 (June, 1972): 159–84. See also James Clifford, *The Predicament of Culture: Twentieth-Century Ethnography, Literature, and Art* (Cambridge: Harvard University Press, 1988), p. 235.

29. Neil Harris, *Four Stages of Cultural Growth: The American City* (Indianapolis: Indiana Historical Society, 1972), pp. 26–27; Robert F. Berkhofer, Jr., "Space, Time, Culture, and the New Frontier," *Agricultural History* 38 (Jan., 1964): 25, 30.

30. Gerald D. Nash, *The American West in the Twentieth Century: A Short History of an Urban Oasis,* pp. 2–3; Johnson, *New Westers,* p. 129.

31. Levine, *Highbrow/Lowbrow,* pp. 223–33, 244, 255.

32. Ronald L. Davis, "Culture on the Frontier," *Southwest Review* 53 (autumn, 1968): 383–403.

33. James Bryce, *The American Commonwealth,* vol. 2 (London: Macmillan, 1889), p. 681.

34. Quoted in Donald William Looser, "Significant Factors in the Musical Development of the Cultural Life in Houston, Texas, 1930–1971" (Ph.D. diss., Florida State University, 1972), p. 367.

35. Quoted in Eloise Spaeth, *American Art Museums and Galleries: An Introduction to Looking* (New York: Harper and Brothers, 1960), 169.

CHAPTER 1. CULTURES AND CONQUESTS

1. Peter Nabokov and Robert Easton, *Native American Architecture,* pp. 352–53.

2. Frederick J. Dockstadter, *Indian Art in America: The Arts and Crafts of the North American Indian,* pp. 34–35.

3. "Casa Grande" (Washington, D.C., National Park Service, 1985).

4. Joseph Franklin Sexton, "New Mexico: Intellectual and Cultural Developments, 1885–1925, Conflict among Ideas and Institutions" (Ph.D. diss., University of Oklahoma, 1982), pp. 15–18.

5. Nabokov and Easton, *Native American Architecture,* pp. 325–26.

6. Ibid., pp. 322, 324.

7. Thomas J. Noel, "Colorado's Architecture: The Design of a State," *Colorado Heritage,* summer, 1992, pp. 20–21; Nabokov and Easton, *Native American Architecture,* pp. 356–57.

8. Nabokov and Easton, *Native American Architecture,* p. 150.

9. Ibid., pp. 348, 350–51; Dockstadter, *Indian Art in America,* p. 17.

10. Thomas J. Lyon, ed., *A Literary History of the American West* (Fort Worth: Texas Christian University Press, 1987), p. 11; Frank G. Applegate, *Indian Stories from the Pueblos* (Philadelphia: J. B. Lippincott, 1929).

11. Lawrence Clark Powell, *Southwestern Book Trails* (Albuquerque: Horn and Wallace Publishers, 1963), p. 55; J. J. Brody, *Anasazi and Pueblo Painting;* J. J. Brody, *Indian Painters and White Patrons,* pp. 14–15, 30–32, 37–38; Lance Chilton et al., *New Mexico: A New Guide to a Colorful State* (Albuquerque: University of New Mexico Press, 1984), p. 139; Andrew Hunter Whiteford et al., *I Am Here: Two Thousand Years of Southwest Indian Arts and Culture* (Santa Fe: Museum of New Mexico Press, 1989).

12. Brody, *Indian Painters and White Patrons,* pp. 14–15.

13. Dockstadter, *Indian Art in America,* pp. 43–44.

14. Chilton et al., *New Mexico,* pp. 142–43; Margery Bedinger, *Indian Silver: Navajo and Pueblo Jewelers,* p. vii; Arthur Woodward, *Navajo Silver: A Brief History of Navajo Silversmithing* (Flagstaff: Northland Press, 1971); Whiteford et al., *I Am Here.*

15. Fred G. Sturm, "Aesthetics of the Southwest," in Nicholas C. Markovich, Wolfgang F. E. Preiser, and Fred G. Sturm, eds., *Pueblo Style and Regional Architecture* (New York: Van Nostrand Reinhold, 1990), p. 14; Nabokov and Easton, *Native American Architecture,* p. 351.

16. Ray B. West, Jr., ed., *Rocky Mountain Cities* (New York: W. W. Norton and Company, 1949), p. 24; George C. Kubler, "Two Modes of Franciscan Architecture: New Mexico and California," *Gazette des Beaux Arts* 23 (Jan., 1943): 39–48.

17. Kubler, "Two Modes of Franciscan Architecture," pp. 39–42.

18. "Salinas" (Washington, D.C., National Park Service, 1989).

19. Lawrence W. Cheek, "Arizona's Architecture," *Arizona Highways* 60 (May, 1984): 7–8; Stryker McGuire, "Arizona's Sistine Chapel," *Newsweek,* Nov. 27, 1995, p. 88A; Prent Duell, *Mission Architecture As Examplified in San Xavier del Bac* (Tucson: Arizona Archaeological and Historical Society, 1919).

20. G. E. Kidder Smith, *The Architecture of the United States,* vol. 3, *The Plains States and the Far West* (Garden City: Anchor Press/Doubleday, 1981), pp. 50–51; Louis R. Caywood, "Tumacacori," *Arizona Highways,* Feb., 1943, pp. 20–27.

21. Ralph E. Parachek, *Desert Architecture* (Phoenix: Parr of Arizona, 1967); Hunter D. Scott, "Pueblo-Mission Architecture: A Distinctive Product of the Southwest," *Masterkey* 2 (July-Aug., 1928): 15–24; Calvin, *Sky Determines,* pp. 142–99.

22. Calvin, *Sky Determines,* pp. 200–24.

23. Doughty, *At Home in Texas,* pp. 100–102.

24. Noel, "Colorado's Architecture," pp. 21–22; Robert Adams, *The Architecture and Art of Early Hispanic Colorado* (Denver: Colorado Associated University Press, 1974).

25. Dockstadter, *Indian Art in America,* pp. 43–44.

26. Chilton et al., *New Mexico,* pp. 142–43; Bedinger, *Indian Silver.*

27. Chilton et al., *New Mexico,* pp. 139–41; Alice Marriott, *María: The Potter of San Ildefonso;* Larry Frank, *Indian Silver Jewelry of the Southwest* (Boston: New York Graphic Society, 1978).

28. Kate Peck Kent, *Navajo Weaving: Three Centuries of Change* (Santa Fe: School of American Research, 1985); Charles Avery Amsden, *Navaho Weaving: Its Technic and History* (Chicago: Rio Grande Press, 1964).

29. Anthony Berlant and Mary Hunt Kahlenberg, *Walk in Beauty: The Navajo and Their Blankets,* pp. 3–6; Kent, *Navajo Weaving;* Chilton et al., *New Mexico,* pp. 136–37.

30. Jacob Jerome Brody, "Indian Painters and White Patrons" (Ph.D. diss., University of New Mexico, 1970).

31. Chilton et al., *New Mexico,* pp. 137–38.

32. Lane Coulter and Maurice Dixon, Jr., *New Mexican Tinwork, 1840–1940.*

33. *Flow of the River/Corre el Rio* (Albuquerque: Hispanic Culture Foundation, 1992), p. 23; Charles L. Briggs, *The Wood Carvers of Cordova, New Mexico: Social Dimensions of an Artistic "Revival."*

34. José Griego y Maestas, comp., *Cuentos: Tales from the Hispanic Southwest* (Santa Fe: Museum of New Mexico, 1980); Howard Swan, *Music in the Southwest, 1825–1950* (San Marino, Calif.: Huntington Library, 1952), pp. 86–107; Mabel Major, T. M. Pearce, and Rebecca Smith, *Southwestern Heritage: A Literary History and Bibliography* (Albuquerque: University of New Mexico Press, 1972), pp. 150–51.

35. Lota M. Spell, *Music in Texas: A Survey of One Aspect of Cultural Progress* (Austin: n. p., 1936), pp. 3–22; Theodore H. Hittlell, *History of California* (San Francisco: Pacific Press Publishing House, 1885), vol. 2, pp. 499–512.

36. Ibid.

37. David J. Weber, "The Spanish Legacy in North America and the Historical Imagination," *Western Historical Quarterly* 23 (Feb., 1992): 6–8, 17–19.

CHAPTER 2. THE IMPORTATION OF ANGLO CULTURE, 1850–1900

1. Rodman W. Paul, *The Far West and the Great Plains in Transition, 1859–1900,* p. 16.

2. Frances Brown Moore, "A History of Cultural Development in San Antonio, Texas" (master's thesis, Colorado State College, 1938), p. 8.

3. Howard N. Rabinowitz, "Continuity and Change: Southern Urban Development, 1860–1900," in Blaine A. Brownell and David R. Goldfield, eds., *The City in Southern History: The Growth of Urban Civilization in the South* (Port Washington: Kennikat, 1977), pp. 92–93; Kenneth W. Wheeler, *To Wear a City's Crown: The Beginnings of Urban Growth in Texas, 1836–1865,* pp. 165–66.

4. Gerald D. Nash, "Stages in California's Economic Growth, 1870–1970: An Interpretation," *California Historical Society Quarterly* 51 (winter, 1972): 315–30; Paul, *Far West and the Great Plains,* p. 15; Franklin D. Walker, *A Literary History of Southern California* (Berkeley: University of California Press, 1950), pp. 72–73.

5. Bradford Luckingham, "The Southwestern Urban Frontier, 1880–1930," *Journal of the West* 18 (July, 1979): 40; Lawrence H. Larsen, *The Urban West at the End of the Frontier,* p. 8.

6. Clarence Alan McGrew, *City of San Diego and San Diego County* (Chicago: American Historical Society, 1922), vol. 1, pp. 117–41, 206–15, 290–94; *San Diego: A California City* (San Diego: San Diego Historical Society, 1937), p. 49.

7. Bradford Luckingham, "The Urban Dimension of Western History," in Michael P. Malone, ed., *Historians and the American West* (Lincoln: University of Nebraska Press, 1983), pp. 327–28; Paul, *Far West and the Great Plains,* pp. 121–23; D. W. Meinig, *Imperial Texas: An Interpretive Essay in Cultural Geography,* pp. 64–65, 56–57; Meinig, *Southwest,* pp. 27–37.

8. Paul, *Far West and the Great Plains,* pp. 3–4, xiii–xiv; Meinig, *Imperial Texas,* pp. 7–8.

9. Paul, *Far West and the Great Plains,* pp. 20–21, 23, 153–57; Bradford Luckingham, "Urban Development in Arizona: The Rise of Phoenix," *Journal of Arizona History* 22 (summer, 1981): 197–234; Mening, *Southwest,* pp. 48–52.

10. Wheeler, *To Wear a City's Crown.*

11. *Tombstone Epitaph,* Mar. 29, 1882.

12. Richard W. Etulain, "Western Art and Architecture," *Montana: Magazine of the West* 40 (autumn, 1990): 3.

13. Josiah Gregg, *Commerce of the Prairies: A Selection,* ed. David Freeman Hawke (New York: Bobbs-Merrill Company, 1970), p. 64.

14. Charles H. Shinn, "Current Comment," *Overland Monthly* 2 (Dec., 1883): 657, 658.

15. Bryce, *The American Commonwealth,* vol. 2, p. 372.

16. Ibid., p. 681.

17. Josiah Strong, *Our Country* (1885; reprint, Cambridge: Harvard University Press, 1963), p. 182.

18. David J. Weber, "The Spanish Legacy in North America and the Historical Imagination," *Western Historical Quarterly* 23 (Feb., 1992): 12–13; E. Boyd, "Domestic Architecture in New Mexico," *El Palacio* 79 (Dec., 1973): 12–15; Bainbridge Bunting and John P. Conron, "The Architecture of Northern New Mexico," *New Mexico Architecture* 8 (Sept.–Oct., 1966): 14–31, 33–35, 39–49; Dora P. Crouch, Daniel J. Garr, and Axel L. Mundigo, *Spanish City Planning In North America* (Cambridge: MIT Press, 1982).

19. Bruce Ellis, *Bishop Lamy's Santa Fe Cathedral* (Albuquerque: University of New Mexico Press, 1985), p. 6.

20. Bunting and Conron, "The Architecture of Northern New Mexico"; Adams, *The Architecture and Art of Early Hispanic Colorado*.

21. Byron A. Johnson, *Old Town, Albuquerque, New Mexico: A Guide to Its History and Architecture* (Albuquerque: Albuquerque Museum), pp. 1–51; Susan Dewitt, *Historic Albuquerque Today: An Overview of Historic Buildings and Districts* (Albuquerque: Historic Landmarks Survey of Albuquerque, 1978).

22. Boyd C. Pratt, "Homesteading the High Plains of New Mexico: An Architectural Perspective," *Panhandle-Plains Historical Review* 63 (1990): 1–33.

23. Glenn Chesney Quiett, *They Built the West: An Epic of Rails and Cities* (New York: Appleton-Century, 1934), pp. 256–57; John W. Reps, *Cities on Stone: Nineteenth Century Lithograph Images of the Urban West* (Fort Worth: Amon Carter Museum, 1976), plate 12; Charles L. Brace, *The New West; or, California in 1867–1868* (New York: G. P. Putnam and Son, 1869), p. 278; Oscar Osburn Winther, "The Rise of Metropolitan Los Angeles," *Huntington Library Quarterly* 10 (Aug., 1947): 391.

24. *Portals at the Pass: El Paso Area Architecture to 1930* (El Paso: El Paso Chapter, A.I.A., 1984), pp. 15–17; *South El Paso Street/Historic American Buildings Survey* (Washington, D.C.: National Park Service, n.d.).

25. Wheeler, *To Wear a City's Crown*, pp. 126–28; Moore, "A History of Cultural Development in San Antonio, Texas," pp. i–x; Gary Cartwright, "The Snootiest Neighborhood in Texas," *Texas Monthly*, June, 1986, pp. 110–16, 164–74.

26. Willard B. Robinson, *Texas Public Buildings of the Nineteenth Century* (Austin: University of Texas Press, 1974), pp. 56–62.

27. Letterbook, Nicholas J. Clayton Papers, University of Texas Center for American History, Austin; Stephen Fox, "The Master Builder," *Texas Monthly*, Jan., 1986, p. 151.

28. Kenneth Hafertepe, *Abner Cook: Master Builder on the Texas Frontier* (Austin: Texas State Historical Association, 1992); Drury Blakeley Alexander, *Texas Homes of the Nineteenth Century* (Austin: University of Texas Press, 1966), p. 263.

29. Robinson, *Texas Public Buildings*, pp. 62–65, 107–50.

30. Smith, *Architecture of the United States*, 3:676–77.

31. William L. McDonald, *Dallas Rediscovered: A Photographic Chronicle of Urban Expansion, 1870–1925*, pp. 7–52.

32. Leonard Sanders, *How Fort Worth Became the Texasmost City* (Fort Worth: Amon Carter Museum of Western Art, 1973), pp. 26, 51, 110.

33. Adams quoted in Sandra L. Myres, "Fort Worth, 1870–1900," *Southwestern Historical Quarterly* 72 (Oct., 1968): 206.

34. Jay C. Henry, *Architecture in Texas: 1895–1945*, pp. 13–27.

35. Elizabeth Skidmore Sasser, *Dugout to Deco: Building in West Texas, 1880–1930* (Lubbock: Texas Tech University Press, 1993).

36. Willard B. Robinson, *Gone From Texas: Our Lost Architectural Heritage*, pp. 187–242; Sasser, *Dugout to Deco*, pp. 58–74; Dorothy Knox Howe Houghton et al., *Houston's Forgotten Heritage: Landscape, Houses, Interiors, 1824–1914* (Houston: Rice University Press, 1991).

37. Larry Booth and Jane Booth, "A Glimpse at Nineteenth Century San Diego," *American West* 16 (Sept./Oct., 1979): 20–21; Larry Booth, Roger Olmsted, and Richard F. Pourade, "Portrait of a Boom Town: San Diego in the 1880s," *California Historical Quarterly* 50 (Dec., 1971): 363–94.

38. Karen Johl, *Timeless Treasures: San Diego's Victorian Heritage* (San Diego: Rand Editions, 1982), pp. 24–29; Harold P. Simonson, "The Villa Montezuma: Jesse Shepard's Lasting Contributions to the Arts and Architecture," *Journal of San Diego History* 19 (spring, 1973): 39–42; Georgia Heine and William M. Thomas, "A Survey of Victorian Residential Architecture within the City of San Diego" (manuscript, San Diego Historical Society, San Diego, California, 1981).

39. Johnson, *Old Town, Albuquerque;* Harriett Hall, comp., *Albuquerque Historic Homes and Districts: A Handbook of Resources* (Albuquerque: New Mexico Arts Commission, 1977).

40. "Mr. W. R. Norton," *Southwest Illustrated Magazine* 1 (June, 1895): 113; Geoffrey P. Mawn, "Phoenix, Arizona: Central City of the Southwest, 1870–1920" (Ph.D. diss., Arizona State University, 1979), pp. 173–74.

41. *Arizona Daily Star* (Tucson), July 25, 1976; *New York Tribune,* Nov. 22, 1896; *Buildings of Architectural Significance in Tucson: A Guide to Old and New Buildings* (Tucson: A.I.A., Southern Arizona Chapter, 1960).

42. Louise Harris Ivers, "The Montezuma Hotel at Las Vegas Hot Springs, New Mexico," *Journal of the Society of Architectural Historians* 33 (Oct., 1974): 206–13.

43. *Denver Post,* May 24, 1987.

44. Patricia Carr Bowie, "The Cultural History of Los Angeles, 1850–1967: From Rural Backwash to World Center" (Ph.D. diss. University of Southern California, 1980), pp. 35–58; John W. Reps, *Cities of the American West: A History of Frontier Urban Planning* (Princeton: Princeton University Press, 1979), p. 283; Robert M. Fogelson, *Fragmented Metropolis: Los Angeles, 1850–1930* (Cambridge: Harvard University Press, 1967), p. 139.

45. Sam Hall Kaplan, *LA Lost and Found: An Architectural History of Los Angeles,* pp. 50–51.

46. Smith, *Architecture of the United States,* 3:102–103; Kevin Starr, *Material Dreams: Southern California through the 1920s,* pp. 181–83.

47. Quotations from Joanne West Dodds, *Pueblo: A Pictorial History* (Norfolk: Donning Company, 1982), p. 86; Robert Twombly, *Louis Sullivan: His Life and Work* (Chicago: University of Chicago Press, 1987), p. 244; Robert Twombly, "Beyond Chicago: Louis Sullivan in the American West," *Pacific Historical Review* 54 (Nov., 1985): 414–17.

48. Alex Traube, *Las Vegas, New Mexico: A Portrait* (Albuquerque: University of New Mexico Press, 1984); Chris Wilson, "Preserving Architectural Riches in Las Vegas," *El Palacio* 91 (winter/spring, 1986): 4–7; Elmo Baca, "Stone Masons Leave Their Mark on Las Vegas," *New Mexico Magazine*, Feb., 1988, pp. 47–51.

49. Arn Henderson, "Low-Style/High Style: Oklahoma Architectural Origins and Image Distortion," in Howard F. Stein and Robert F. Hill, eds., *The Culture of Oklahoma* (Norman: University of Oklahoma Press, 1993), pp. 160, 162, 173–76; Arn Henderson and Deborah M. Rosenthal, *Guthrie: A Plan for Historic Preservation* (Norman: School of Architecture, University of Oklahoma, 1978).

50. Helen F. Holmes, *Homes of Historic Guthrie* (Guthrie: Docents of the State Capital Publishing Museum and the Logan County Historical Society, 1987); Arn Henderson, "Joseph Foucart, Territorial Architect," in Howard L. Meredith and Mary Ellen Meredith, eds., *Of The Earth: Oklahoma Architectural History* (Oklahoma City: Oklahoma Historical Society, 1980), pp. 72–85.

51. Archibald Edwards, "Recollections of Oklahoma Venacular Architecture," in Meredith and Meredith, eds., *Of The Earth*, pp. 45–46, 47–49; Arn Henderson, Frank Parman, and Dorthea Henderson, *Architecture in Oklahoma: Landmark and Vernacular* (Norman: Point Riders Press, 1978); Bob Blackburn, Arn Henderson, and Melvena Thurman, *The Physical Legacy: Buildings of Oklahoma County, 1889 to 1931* (Oklahoma City: Southwest Heritage Press, 1980).

52. H. Wiley Hitchcock, *Music in the United States: A Historical Introduction* (Englewood Cliffs, N.J.: Prentice-Hall, 1969), p. 45.

53. Ronald L. Davis, "Sopranos and Six-Guns: The Frontier Opera House as a Cultural Symbol," *American West* 7 (Nov., 1970): 10–11, 15–16.

54. Henry W. Splitter, "Music in Los Angeles," *Historical Society of Southern California Quarterly* 38 (Dec., 1956): 308, 310–12; Swan, *Music in the Southwest, 1825–1950,* pp. 110–46; Bowie, "The Cultural History of Los Angeles," pp. 2–29.

55. Paul, *Far West and the Great Plains,* p. 141; Heather S. Hatch, "Music in Arizona Territory," *Journal of Arizona History* 12, no. 4 (1971): 263–80.

56. Spell, *Music in Texas,* pp. 23–33, 36–42, 72–76; Terry Jordan, "The German Settlement of Texas after 1865," *Southwestern Historical Quarterly* 73 (Oct., 1969): 193–212; Theodore Albrecht, "More Than Polkas and Prosit!," *Texas Humanist* 7 (July-Aug., 1985): 26–27, 41.

57. Donald Wagner Pugh, "Music in Frontier Houston, 1836–1876" (Ph.D. diss., University of Texas, 1970), pp. 91–95, 1–9.

58. Gladys Williams, "Orchestras and Bands: El Paso Music, 1880–1960" (master's thesis, University of Texas at El Paso, 1960).

59. Davis, "Sopranos and Six-Guns," p. 63.

60. Swan, *Music in the Southwest,* pp. 151–69, 187–89; Neil Erman Wilson, "A History of Opera and Associated Educational Activities in Los Angeles" (Ph.D. diss., Indiana University, 1968), p. 24; Splitter, "Music in Los Angeles," pp. 324–26; Levine, *Highbrow/Lowbrow,* pp. 85–87.

61. Lynn Moody Hoffman, "Starlit Trails" (manuscript, Lynden Ellsworth Behymer Papers, Huntington Library, San Marino, California); Splitter, "Music in Los Angeles," pp. 340–43.

62. William J. Perlman, "From the Pueblos to the Movies," in Richard Saunders, ed., *Music and Dance in California and the West* (Hollywood: Bureau of Musical Research, 1948), pp. 24–25; Splitter, "Music in Los Angeles," pp. 321–22, 334.

63. "Music," Vertical File; Waldo F. Chase, "Memoirs of Waldo F. Chase," typescript; Mrs. W. H. Porterfield, "I Remember When," typescript; and Loleta L. Rowan Scrapbook; all in San Diego Historical Society. Gertrude Gilbert, "Music in San Diego," *San Diego Magazine*, Sept., 1927, pp. 24–25, 29; *San Diego Union*, Dec. 3, 1939.

64. Moore, "A History of Cultural Development in San Antonio, Texas," pp. 183–85; Adel Speiser, "The Story of the Theater in San Antonio" (master's thesis, St. Mary's University, 1948), pp. 39, 62–85; Barbara Rabke, "Theatre in San Antonio, 1886–1891" (master's thesis, Trinity University, 1964), pp. 37–39.

65. Spell, *Music in Texas*, pp. 78–79, 101–106; Joe Edgar Manry, *Curtain Call: The History of the Theatre in Austin, Texas: 1839 to 1905* (Austin: Waterloo Press of the Austin History Center, 1985), pp. 3–5; Box 1, Ephemera Collection, University of Texas Center for American History, Austin.

66. Quoted in John Dizikes, *Opera in America: A Cultural History* (New Haven: Yale University Press, 1994), p. 225.

67. Box 1, Ephemera Collection, University of Texas Center for American History.

68. Angelo C. Scott, *The Story of Oklahoma City* (Oklahoma City: Times-Journal Publishing Company, 1939), p. 103.

69. Levine, *Highbrow/Lowbrow*, p. 37; Richard A. Van Orman, "The Bard in the West," *Western Historical Quarterly* 5 (Jan., 1974): 29–38.

70. Michael John Barnes, "Trends in Texas Theatre History," (Ph.D. diss., University of Texas, 1993), pp. 11–60; Joseph S. Gallegly, *Footlights on the Border: The Galveston and Houston Stage before 1900;* Waldo F. McNeir, "The Reception of Shakespeare in Houston, 1839–1980," in Philip C. Kolin, ed., *Shakespeare in the South: Essays on Performance* (Jackson: University Press of Mississippi, 1983), pp. 175–83.

71. Manry, *Curtain Call*, pp. 1–3, 6–19, 43–52.

72. Donald Vincent Brady, *The Theatre in Early El Paso, 1881–1905* (El Paso: Texas Western College, 1966); Harriett Howze Jones, ed., *El Paso: A Centennial Portrait* (El Paso: Superior Printing Company, 1972), pp. 239–43.

73. Speiser, "The Story of the Theater in San Antonio," pp. 3–12, 19–43; Christa Luise Carvajal, "German Theaters in Central Texas, 1850–1915" (Ph.D. diss., University of Texas, 1977); Moore, "A History of Cultural Development in San Antonio, Texas," p. 236; Charles Bennett Myler, "A History of English-Speaking Theatre in San Antonio before 1900" (Ph.D. diss., University of Texas, 1968); Rabke, "Theatre in San Antonio," pp. 60–119.

74. Clair Eugene Willson, "Mines and Miners: A Historical Study of the Theater in Tombstone," *University of Arizona Bulletin* 6, no. 7 (1935); Pat M. Ryan, *Tombstone Theatre Tonight: A Chronicle of Entertainment on the Southwestern Mining Frontier* (Tucson: University of Arizona Press, 1966).

75. *Arizona Daily Star* (Tucson), July 21, 1985.

76. Edwina Romero, "Footlights in the Foothills: The Drama of Las Vegas, New Mexico," *El Palacio* 95 (spring/summer, 1990): 56–63.

77. *Los Angeles: A Guide to the City and Its Environs* (New York: Hastings House, 1951), pp.

132–33; Alan Lambert Woods, "The Interaction of Los Angeles Theatre and Society between 1895 and 1906: A Case Study" (Ph.D. diss., University of Southern California, 1972).

78. Ralph Freud, "Frank A. Miller: Theatre Manager," *Historical Society of Southern California Quarterly* 41 (Mar., 1959): 5–10; "Theater," Vertical File, San Diego Historical Society; Rebecca Elizabeth Lytle, "People and Places: Images of Nineteenth Century San Diego in Lithographs and Paintings" (master's thesis, San Diego State University, 1978), p. 21.

79. Nicolás Kanellos, ed., *Mexican American Theatre: Then and Now*, p. 19; Nicolás Kanellos, ed., *Hispanic Theatre in the United States* (Houston: Arte Publico Press, 1984), pp. 8, 179–80; Nicolás Kanellos, *A History of Hispanic Theatre in the United States: Origins to 1940*, pp. 6–7; Elizabeth C. Ramiréz, *Footlights across the Border: A History of Spanish Language Professional Theatre on the Texas Stage, 1875–1935*, pp. 7–29.

80. Henry Winifred Splitter, "Literature in Los Angeles before 1900," *Journal of the West* 5 (Jan., 1966): 91–104; Arnold L. Rodríguez, "New Mexico in Transition: Cultural Development," *New Mexico Historical Review* 24 (Oct., 1949): 267–84; McGrew, *City of San Diego*, pp. 290–93.

81. William C. Bartlett, "Literature and Art in California: A Quarter-Centennial Review," *Overland Monthly* 15 (Dec., 1875): 533.

82. Ibid., pp. 544–45.

83. Trueman O'Quinn, "O. Henry in Austin," *Southwestern Historical Quarterly* 43 (Oct., 1939): 143–57.

84. Edgar Carlisle McMechen, "Literature and the Arts," in James H. Baker and Leroy R. Hafen, eds., *History of Colorado*, vol. 3 (Denver: Linderman Company, 1927), pp. 1231–86.

85. Edwin R. Bingham, *Charles F. Lummis, Editor of the Southwest* (San Marino, Calif.: Huntington Library, 1955); Powell, *Southwest Classics*, pp. 43–54; Turbesé Lummis Fiske and Keith Lummis, *Charles F. Lummis: The Man and His West* (Norman: University of Oklahoma Press, 1975).

86. Charles F. Lummis, *The Land of Poco Tiempo;* Charles F. Lummis, *Mesa, Cañon, and Pueblo;* Charles Fletcher Lummis, *A New Mexico David and Other Stories and Sketches of the Southwest* (New York: Charles Scribner's Sons, 1891).

87. Quoted in Weber, "The Spanish Legacy," p. 14.

88. Dudley Gordon, *Charles F. Lummis: Crusader in Corduroy* (Los Angeles: Cultural Assets Press, 1972), pp. 175–88; "Autobiographical Fragment," Box 2, Charles Fletcher Lummis Papers, Special Collections, University of Arizona Library, Tucson.

89. Powell, *Southwest Classics*, pp. 315–27.

90. Charles F. Lummis, "The Artists' Paradise," *Out West* 28 (June, 1908): 451.

91. Gerald Nash and Richard W. Etulain, eds., *The Twentieth Century West: Historical Interpretations*, pp. 384–85.

92. Keith L. Bryant, Jr., "The Atchison, Topeka, and Santa Fe Railway and the Development of the Taos and Santa Fe Art Colonies," *Western Historical Quarterly* 9 (Oct., 1978): 436–53.

93. Doris Ruddell DuBose, "Art and Artists in Arizona, 1847–1912" (master's thesis, Ari-

zona State University, 1974); Katherin L. Chase, "Brushstrokes on the Plateau: An Overview of Anglo Art on the Colorado Plateau," *Plateau* 56, no. 1 (1984): 2–33.

94. Quoted in Patricia Trenton and Peter H. Hassrick, *The Rocky Mountains* (Norman: University of Oklahoma Press, 1983), pp. 245–46, 263–64. The letter from Whittredge is found on pp. 215, 219.

95. Henry Winifred Splitter, "Art in Los Angeles before 1900," *Historical Society of Southern California Quarterly* 41 (Mar., 1959): 44–45, and "Art in Los Angeles before 1900," *Historical Society of Southern California Quarterly* 41 (June, 1959): 121–22.

96. *Overland Monthly*, 2d series, 2 (Dec., 1883): 658.

97. William H. Gerdts, *Art across America: Two Centuries of Regional Painting*, 3:298–300; Patricia Trenton, "'Islands on the Land': Women Traditionalists of Southern California," in Patricia Trenton, ed., *Independent Spirits: Women Painters of the American West*, pp. 42–50.

98. Gerdts, *Art across America*, 3:293.

99. Splitter, "Art in Los Angeles," 41 (June, 1959): 136, 137.

100. Ibid. 41 (Sept., 1959): 247–50.

101. Kevin Starr, *Inventing the Dream: California through the Progressive Era*, pp. 120–21.

102. Gerdts, *Art across America*, 3:325.

103. Lytle, "People and Places"; Bruce Kamerling, *100 Years of Art in San Diego* (San Diego: San Diego Historical Society, 1991); Martin E. Petersen, "Maurice Braun: Master Painter of the California Landscape," *Journal of San Diego History* 23 (summer, 1977): 20–40.

104. Gerdts, *Art across America*, 2:113–17.

105. Cecilia Steinfeldt, *Art for History's Sake: The Texas Collection of the Witte Museum* (Austin: Texas State Historical Association, 1993), pp. 80–81.

106. Gerdts, *Art across America*, 2:116–20; Cecilia Steinfeldt, *The Onderdonks: A Family of Texas Painters* (San Antonio: Trinity University Press, 1976).

107. Gerdts, *Art across America*, 3:123–27.

CHAPTER 3. CITIES AND CULTURE, 1900–1920

1. Meinig, *Imperial Texas*, pp. 79–82.

2. Nash, *The American West in the Twentieth Century*, pp. 11–12, 16–18, 65–66, 77–82.

3. Nash and Etulain, eds., *The Twentieth Century West*, p. 46; U.S., Department of Commerce, Bureau of the Census, *Statistical Abstract of the United States, 1946* (Washington, D.C.: Printing Office, 1946).

4. Nicholas Vachel Lindsay, *The Art of the Moving Picture* (1915; reprint, New York: Liveright, 1970), pp. 247–48.

5. Robert W. Rydell, "Architectural Frontiers: An Introduction," *Pacific Historical Review* 54 (Nov., 1985): 397.

6. Constance M. Greiff, ed., *Lost America: From the Mississippi to the Pacific*, pp. 146–47; Howard L. Meredith and George H. Shirk, "Oklahoma City: Growth and Reconstruction," *Chronicles of Oklahoma* 55 (fall, 1977): 293–308; Blackburn, Henderson,

and Thurman, *The Physical Legacy,* pp. 24–26; Mary Jo Nelson, "Solomon Layton: Architect," in Meredith and Meredith, eds., *Of the Earth,* pp. 87–104.

7. Marianne Weber, *Max Weber: A Biography* (New York: John Wiley and Sons, 1975), pp. 291–92.

8. William Butler, *Tulsa 75: A History of Tulsa, Oklahoma* (Tulsa: Metropolitan Tulsa Chamber of Commerce, 1974); Glen Roberson and Courtney Ann Vaughn-Roberson, *City in the Osage Hills: A History of Tulsa, Oklahoma* (Boulder: Pruett Publishing Company, 1984), p. 120.

9. McDonald, *Dallas Rediscovered,* pp. 63–101; *The Prairie's Yield,* pp. 22–23, 26–27; Patricia Evridge Hill, "Origins of Modern Dallas" (Ph.D. diss., University of Texas, 1990), p. 30.

10. Theo B. Billings, "The Museum of Fine Arts, Houston: A Social History" (Ph.D. diss., University of Houston, 1994), p. 108.

11. Ruby Schmidt, ed., *Fort Worth and Tarrant County: A Historical Guide* (Fort Worth: Texas Christian University Press, 1984), pp. 12–13; Sanders, *How Fort Worth Became the Texasmost City,* p. 153; Alar R. Sumner, ed., *Dallasights: An Anthology of Architecture and Open Spaces* (Dallas: Dallas Chapter of the American Institute of Architects, 1978), pp. 180–81.

12. Henry, *Architecture in Texas,* p. 133: Jamie Louise Lofgren, "Early Texas Skyscrapers: A History of Skyscraper Style" (master's thesis, University of Texas, 1987), pp. 6–25.

13. Henry, *Architecture in Texas,* pp. 74–101.

14. Larry Booth and Jane Booth, "A Glimpse at Nineteenth Century San Diego," *American West* 16 (Sept./Oct., 1979): 28–29; *San Diego, A California City* (San Diego: San Diego Historical Society, 1937), pp. 20, 22.

15. John C. Orneby Austin, comp., *Architecture in Southern California* (Los Angeles: H. T. Grace, 1905); Patricia Carr Bowie, "The Cultural History of Los Angeles, 1850–1967: From Rural Backwash to World Center" (Ph.D. diss., University of Southern California, 1980), pp. 35–58, 79–109.

16. Lawrence W. Cheek, "Arizona's Architecture," *Arizona Highways* 60 (May, 1984): 2–9, 12–15, 18–22; Gary David Matthews, *Holmes and Holmes, Architects, Tucson, Arizona, 1905–1912* (Tucson: College of Architecture, University of Arizona, 1969); Mary P. Davis and Michael J. Rock, *Huning Highland Neighborhood Walking Tour and Arm Chair Guide* (Albuquerque: Albuquerque Historic Landmarks Survey, n.d.).

17. Carl Abbott, *The Metropolitan Frontier: Cities in the Modern American West,* pp. 131–32.

18. Clay Lancaster, *American Bungalow, 1880–1930* (New York: Abbeville Press, 1985), p. 151.

19. William Jordy, *American Buildings and Their Architects: Progressive and Academic Ideals at the Turn of the Twentieth Century,* pp. 220–45; Karen Current, *Greene & Greene: Architects in the Residential Style* (Fort Worth: Amon Carter Museum of Western Art, 1974).

20. "The Gamble House" (Friends of the Gamble House, Pasedena, n.d.).

21. Walton Bean, *California: An Interpretive History* (New York: McGraw-Hill, 1973), p. 459.

22. Henry, *Architecture in Texas,* pp. 248–53; Sasser, *Dugout to Deco;* Sandra Dallas, *Colorado Homes* (Norman: University of Oklahoma Press, 1986), p. 197.

23. George Devereaux, "In the Land of the Bungalow," quoted in Kaplan, *LA Lost and Found,* p. 45.

24. Quoted in Randell Makinson, *Greene & Greene: Architecture as a Fine Art* (Salt Lake City: Peregrin Smith, 1977), p. 34.

25. David Gebhard, "The Myth and Power of Place: Hispanic Revivalism in the American Southwest," in Markovich, Preiser, and Sturm, eds., *Pueblo Style and Regional Architecture*, pp. 143, 148, 156–57.

26. Benton quoted in ibid., p. 143.

27. David Gebhard, "Architectural Imagery, The Mission, and California," *Harvard Architectural Review* 1 (1980): 137–39, 140–41; Karen J. Weitze, *California's Mission Revival* (Los Angeles: Hennessey and Ingalls, 1984).

28. Sara Holmes Boutelle, *Julia Morgan: Architect;* Lucinda Liggett Eddy, "Lilian Jeannette Rice: The Lady Architect" (master's thesis, University of San Diego, 1984); Harriet Rocklin, "Among the First and the Finest: California Architects: Julia, Hazel, Lilian, Lutah, Edla" (research paper, n.d.), San Diego Historical Society; Sally Bullard Thornton, *Daring to Dream: The Life of Hazel Wood Waterman* (San Diego: San Diego Historical Society, 1987); *Directory of San Diego Architects* (San Diego: University of San Diego, 1984), 130–31.

29. George Wharton James, *Arizona, The Wonderland* (Boston: Page Company, 1917), pp. 442–48; Bradford Luckingham, *Phoenix: The History of a Southwestern Metropolis,* pp. 132–34; *A Guide to the Architecture of Metro Phoenix* (Phoenix: Central Arizona Chapter of the American Institute of Architecture, 1983), p. 177.

30. Sylvanus Griswold Morley, "Development of the Santa Fe Style of Architecture," *Old Santa Fe* 2 (Jan., 1915): 281; Lloyd C. Engelbrecht and June Marie Engelbrecht, *Henry C. Trost; Architect of the Southwest* (El Paso: El Paso Library Association, 1981), p. 94; Jocelyn Lieu, "The Casteñada," *New Mexico Magazine* 69 (Feb., 1981): 70–73; ibid., "Architecture and the Fred Harvey Houses," *New Mexico Architect* 4 (July-Aug., 1962): 11–13, 15–17; David Gebhard, "Architecture and the Fred Harvey Houses: The Alvarado and La Fonda," *New Mexico Architect* 6 (Jan.-Feb., 1964): 18–25.

31. Wister quoted in Virginia L. Grattan, *Mary Coulter: Builder upon the Red Earth;* William K. Bare, "Mary E. J. Coulter: Architect and Designer," *Arizona Highways* 60 (May, 1984): 16–17.

32. "A Bostonian Finds a New Home," *Out West Magazine* (Jan., 1906).

33. Doughty, *At Home in Texas,* p. 89.

34. Gregory Montes, "Balboa Park, 1909–1911: The Rise and Fall of the Olmsted Plan" *Journal of San Diego History* 28 (winter, 1982): 46–67; Richrd W. Amero, "The Making of the Panama-California Expositon, 1909–1915," *Journal of San Diego History* 36 (winter, 1990): 1–47; Carleton Monroe Winslow, Jr., "The Architecture of the Panama-California Exposition, 1909–1915" (master's thesis, University of San Diego, 1976); G. Aubrey Davidson, "History of the Panama-California Exposition of 1915 and the Panama-California International Exposition of 1916," in Carl D. Heilborn, ed., *History of San Diego County* (San Diego: San Diego Press Club, 1936), pp. 401–406.

35. Richard Oliver, *Bertram Grosvenor Goodhue* (New York: Architectural History Foundation and M.I.T. Press, 1983).

36. Quoted in Robert W. Rydell, *All the World's a Fair: Visions of Empire at American International Expositions, 1876–1916* (Chicago: University of Chicago Press, 1984), p. 209.

37. Eugen Neuhaus, *The San Diego Garden Fair* (San Francisco: Paul Elder and Company, 1916), p. 76.

38. Christopher Wilson, "The Spanish Colonial Revival Defined, 1904–1921," *New Mexico Studies in the Fine Arts* 7 (1982): 24–30.

39. J. K. Shishkin, *An Early History of the Museum of New Mexico Fine Arts Bulding* (Santa Fe: Museum of New Mexico Press, 1968); Carl D. Sheppard, *Creator of the Santa Fe Style: Isaac Hamilton Rapp, Architect* (Albuquerque: University of New Mexcio Press. 1988).

40. Ibid.; Lummis, *Mesa, Cañon, and Pueblo,* pp. 423–24.

41. Quoted in "The New Museum Is a Wonder . . . Museum of Fine Arts to Reopen," press release, 1981, Museum of Fine Arts Library, Santa Fe, New Mexico.

42. Edgar Lee Hewett quoted in "50th Anniversary Exhibition, November 12, 1967– February 18, 1968," catalogue, Museum of New Mexico, Santa Fe, New Mexico. See also Beatrice Chauvenet, "A New Era Begins," *El Palacio* 88 (summer, 1982): 29–30.

43. Irving Gill quoted in Harold Kirker, "California Architecture and Its Relation to Contemporary Trends in Europe and America," *California Historical Quarterly* 51 (winter, 1972): 302.

44. Quoted in Esther McCoy, *Five California Architects* (New York: Reinhold Publishing, 1960), p. 61.

45. Ibid.

46. Quoted in Bruce Kamerling, *Irving Gill: The Artist as Architect* (San Diego: San Diego Historical Society, 1979), p. 2.

47. Ibid.; Helen McElfresh Ferris, "Irving John Gill; San Diego Architect: The Formation of an American Style of Architecture," *Journal of San Diego History* 17 (fall, 1971): 1–19.

48. Engelbrecht and Englelbrecht, *Henry C. Trost.*

49. Henry C. Trost, "Architecture," in *Trost & Trost, Architects* (El Paso: Trost & Trost, 1907), pp. 2–3.

50. Henry, *Architecture in Texas,* pp. 44–48; Henry C. Trost, Gustavus Adolphus Trost, and George E. Trost, "Folios of Drawings," Harry Ransom Research Center for the Humanities, University of Texas, Austin.

51. Lloyd C. Engelbrecht and June-Marie Engelbrecht, "The Trost Touch: Henry Trost and the Bhutanese Architecture," *Texas Civil Engineer* 55 (May, 1985): 20–22; "Bhutanese Style Architecture," Box 33, Archives, University of Texas at El Paso.

52. Engelbrecht and Engelbrecht, *Henry C. Trost,* p. 102.

53. George H. Edgell, *The American Architecture of To-Day* (New York: Charles Scribner's Sons, 1928), pp. 340–41.

54. Anne Farrar Hyde, *An American Vision: Far Western Landscape and National Culture, 1820–1920* (New York: New York University Press, 1990), p. 304.

55. Everett Carroll Maxwell, "The 'Great Southwest' as the Painters of That Region See It," *Craftsman* 20 (June, 1911): 270.

56. Albert A. Boydon, Jan. 13, 1905, Fernand Lungren Papers, Huntington Library, San Marino, California.

57. Wister to Lungren, Sept. 21, 1910, ibid.

58. Michael Ennis, "Longhorn Leonardo," *Texas Monthly,* Jan., 1986, p. 157.

59. Steinfeldt, *Art for History's Sake,* pp. 200–201.

60. Emily Fourmy Cutrer, *The Art of the Woman: The Life and Work of Elisabet Ney* (Lincoln: University of Nebraska Press, 1988); Henry B. Dielmann, "Elisabeth Ney, Sculptor," *Southwest Historical Quarterly* 45 (Oct., 1961): 157–83.

61. William R. Leigh, "My Life," manuscript autobiography, n.d., William R. Leigh Collection, Thomas Gilcrease Institute of American History and Art, Tulsa, Oklahoma.

62. Dixon quoted in Katherine Plake Hough and Michael Zakian, *Transforming the Western Image in 20th Century American Art* (Palm Springs: Palm Springs Desert Museum, 1992), p. 19; see also Wesley Burnside, *Maynard Dixon: Artist of the West* (Provo: Brigham Young University Press, 1974); Wilbur Hall, "The Art of Maynard Dixon," *Sunset Magazine*, Jan., 1921, pp. 44–45.

63. Quoted in Sarah J. Moore, "No Woman's Land: Arizona Adventurers," in Trenton, ed., *Independent Spirits*, p. 133.

64. Ibid., p. 134.

65. Kay Aiken Reeve, "The Making of an American Place: The Development of Santa Fe (Ph.D. diss., Texas A&M University, 1977); Arrell M. Gibson, *The Santa Fe and Taos Colonies: Age of the Muses, 1900–1942*.

66. Ernest L. Blumenschein, "Origin of the Taos Art Colony," *El Palacio* 20 (May, 1926): 191.

67. Quoted in Dorothy Skousen Black, "A Study of Taos as an Art Colony and of Representative Taos Painters" (master's thesis, University of New Mexico, 1949), p. 8.

68. W. Herbert Dunton, "The Painters of Taos," *American Magazine of Art* 13 (Aug., 1922): 247.

69. A. N. Jensen, "The Academie Julian and the Academic Tradition in Taos," *El Palacio* 79 (Dec., 1973): 37–42.

70. Keith L. Bryant, Jr., "The Atchison, Topeka, and Santa Fe Railway and the Development of the Taos and Santa Fe Art Colonies," *Western Historical Quarterly* 9 (Oct., 1978): 436–53.

71. Ernest L. Blumenschein and Bert B. Phillips, "Appreciation of Indian Art," *El Palacio* 6 (May, 1919): 178–79; Frank Waters, "Indian Influence on Taos Art," *New Mexico Quarterly* 21 (summer, 1951): 173–80.

72. Quoted in Mary Witter Booth, "The Taos Art Colony," *El Palacio* 53 (Nov., 1946): 322.

73. W. Herbert Dunton, "The Painters of Taos," *El Palacio* 13 (Aug., 1922): 46.

74. David L. Witt, "Art Pioneers," *New Mexico Magazine* 65 (May, 1987): 21–24; Gerdts, *Art across America*, 3:161–64.

75. Birger Sandzen, "The Southwest as a Sketching Ground," *Fine Arts Journal* 33 (Aug., 1915): 335–52; Patricia Janis Broder, *The American West: The Modern Vision*, pp. 29–42.

76. Quoted in Anita Pollitzer, *A Woman on Paper: The Letters and Memoir of a Legendary Friendship*, p. 146.

77. Lloyd Goodrich and Doris Bry, *Georgia O'Keeffe* (New York: Praeger, 1970), p. 9.

78. John F. Matthews, "The Influence of the Texas Panhandle on Georgia O'Keeffe," *Panhandle-Plains Historical Review* 56 (1984): 114.

79. Georgia O'Keeffe to Anita Pollitzer, Sept. 11, 1916, in Pollitzer, *A Woman on Paper*, p. 145.

80. Quoted in Clive Giboire, ed., *Lovingly, Georgia: The Complete Correspondence of Georgia O'Keeffe and Anita Pollitzer* (New York: A Touchstone Book, 1990), p. 183.

81. Quoted in Dan Flores, *Caprock Canyonlands: Journeys into the Heart of the Southern Plains* (Austin: University of Texas Press, 1990), pp. 128–29.

82. Quoted in Jeffrey Hogrefe, *O'Keeffe: The Life of an American Legend,* p. 48.

83. Quoted in Pollitzer, *A Woman on Paper,* p. 158.

84. Ibid., p. 159.

85. *Masterworks of California Impressionism: The FFCA, Morton Fleischer Collection* (Tulsa: Thomas Gilcrease Institute of American History and Art, 1988).

86. Ernest A. Batchelder, quoted in Robert Judson Clark and Thomas S. Hines, *Los Angeles Transfer: Architecture in Southern California, 1880–1980* (Los Angeles: William Andrews Clark Memorial Library, 1983), p. 4.

87. Mabel Urmy Seares, "The Spirit of California Art," *Sunset Magazine* 23 (Sept., 1909): 266.

88. Gerdts, *Art across America,* 3:296–98.

89. Bruce Kammerling, "Painting Ladies: Some Early San Diego Women Artists," *Journal of San Diego History* 32 (summer, 1986): 147–91; Bruce Kammerling, "Alice Ellen Klauber: San Diego Artist," *Western States Jewish History Journal* 20 (Apr., 1988): 247–49; Bruce Kammerling, "The Start of Professionalism: Three Early San Diego Artists," *Journal of San Diego History* 30 (fall, 1984): 241–51.

90. Kathleen D. McCarthy, *Women's Culture: American Philanthrophy and Art, 1830–1930* (Chicago: University of Chicago Press, 1991), pp. 115, 244.

91. Stella Hope Shurtleff, *A Brief Review of Art Progress in Houston as Part of the Art Development of America, 1900–1925* (Houston: N. p. 1926); Billings, "The Museum of Fine Arts, Houston," p. 170.

92. Quoted in ibid., p. 169.

93. Steinfeldt, *Art for History's Sake,* p. ix; Nathaniel Burt, *Palaces for the People: A Social History of the American Art Museum* (Boston: Little, Brown, and Company, 1977), pp. 378–79.

94. Jerry Bywaters, *Seventy-Five Years of Art in Dallas.*

95. Winifred Haines Higgins, "Art Collecting in the Los Angeles Area, 1910–1960" (Ph.D. diss., University of California, Los Angeles, 1963), p. 7.

96. Benjamin Chambers Brown, "The Beginnings of Art in Los Angeles," *California Southland* 6 (Jan., 1924): 7–8; Nancy Dustin Wall Moure, *Dictionary of Art and Artists in Southern California before 1930* (Los Angeles: Privately printed, 1975).

97. "The Huntington Art Gallery" (1984), Huntington Library, Art Collection, and Botanical Gardens, San Marino, California; J. M. Fenster, "The Huntington's Triple Treasures," *New York Times,* Nov. 25, 1990; Spaeth, *American Art Museums and Galleries,* pp. 207–10; Burt, *Palaces for the People,* pp. 398–99.

98. Candice C. Kant, *Zane Grey's Arizona* (Flagstaff: Northland Press, 1984).

99. W. H. Hutchinson, *A Bar Cross Man: The Life and Personal Writings of Eugene Manlove Rhodes;* May Davison Rhodes, *The Hired Man on Horseback: My Story of Eugene Manlove Rhodes* (Boston: Houghton Mifflin Company, 1938); Powell, *Southwest Classics,* pp. 161–73.

100. Eugene Manlove Rhodes, *Pasó Por Aquí* (Norman: University of Oklahoma Press, 1973).

101. Rhodes to Betty Luther, [?] 14, 1930, and Dec. 11, 1930, Eugene Manlove Rhodes Papers, Zimmerman Library, University of New Mexico, Albuquerque.

102. Esther Lanigan Stineman, *Mary Austin: Song of a Maverick* (New Haven: Yale University Press, 1989); Augusta Fink, *I-Mary: A Biography of Mary Austin.*

103. Mary Austin, *The Land of Little Rain* (Albuquerque: University of New Mexico Press, 1974), p. 100.

104. Austin to Carey McWilliams, Apr. 29, 1932, Mary Austin Papers, Zimmerman Library, University of New Mexico, Albuquerque.

105. Mary Austin, "Art Influence in the West," *Century Magazine* 89 (Apr., 1915): 829–30.

106. Edward A. Bloom and Lillian D. Bloom, "The Genesis of *Death Comes for the Archbishop,*" *American Literature* 26 (Jan., 1955): 479–506; E. K. Brown, *Willa Cather: A Critical Biography.*

107. Edith Lewis, *Willa Cather Living: A Personal Record* (New York: Alfred A. Knopf, 1953), pp. 80–83.

108. Cather to Elsie Sergeant [Elizabeth Shepley Sergeant], Apr. 20 and May 21, 1912, Willia Cather Collection, Pierpont Morgan Library, New York City.

109. Lewis, *Willa Cather Living,* pp. 93–96, 99–102.

110. Willa Cather, *The Song of the Lark* (Boston: Houghton Mifflin Company, 1937), p. 383.

111. Ibid., p. 277.

112. Cather to Annie Adams Fields, June 27, 1912, Annie Adams Field Papers, Huntington Library, San Marino, California.

113. John William Rogers, *The Lusty Texans of Dallas* (New York: E. P. Dutton, 1960), p. 233; Spell, *Music in Texas,* pp. 109–10; Ronald L. Davis, *A History of Opera in the American West,* pp. 114–17.

114. Mint O. James-Reed, *Music in Austin, 1900–1956* (Austin: Von Boeckmann-Jones Company, 1957), pp. 1–2, 8–11, 35–37, 104–109; Playbills, Ephemera Collection, University of Texas Center for American History, Austin.

115. Spell, *Music in Texas,* pp. 107–12; Sharrard H. Douglas, "A History of the San Antonio Symphony Orchestra" (master's thesis, Incarnate Word College, 1971), pp. 15–16.

116. Duncan Aikman, "El Paso: Big Mountain Town," in West, Jr., ed., *Rocky Mountain Cities,* p. 101; Levine, *Highbrow/Lowbrow,* pp. 180–81.

117. Mario T. García, *Desert Immigrants: The Mexicans of El Paso, 1880–1920,* pp. 197–220, 235–36.

118. Walter Johannes Damrosch, *My Musical Life* (New York: Charles Scribner's Sons, 1924), pp. 192–93.

119. Linda Williams Reese, "Race, Class, and Culture: Oklahoma Women, 1890–1920" (Ph.D. diss., University of Oklahoma, 1991), p. 130; Ralph Ellison, *Going to the Territory* (New York: Random House, 1986), pp. 134–37.

120. "Hyechka Club," Vertical File, Oklahoma Historical Society, Oklahoma City; Glen Romaine Roberson, "City on the Plains: The History of Tulsa, Oklahoma" (Ph.D. diss., Oklahoma State University, 1977), pp. 39–40, 85–86; Butler, *Tulsa 75.*

121. John H. Mueller, *The American Symphony Orchestra: A Social History of Musical Taste* (Bloomington: Indiana University Press, 1951); Caroline Estes Smith, *The Philhar-*

monic *Orchestra of Los Angeles: The First Decade, 1919–1929* (Los Angeles: United Printing Company, 1930), pp. 27–38.

122. John Orlando Northcutt, *Symphony: The Story of the Los Angeles Philharmonic Orchestra.*

123. Rosemary Gipson, "Mrs. Fiske Tours Arizona," *Journal of Arizona History* 22 (autumn, 1981): 277–94.

124. Hubert Roussel, *The Houston Symphony Orchestra, 1913–1971*, p. 17.

125. Anita Loos, "Those Were the Days," *Saturday Review of Literature*, May 13, 1961, p. 44.

126. K. Kay Brandes, "Theatrical Activities in Oklahoma City from 1889 to 1964" (master's thesis, University of Oklahoma, 1964).

127. *Santa Fe New Mexican*, Jan. 19, 1915; Mary Austin, "Santa Fe's Community Theatre," *El Palacio* 6 (1919): 26–27.

128. Ramírez, *Footlights across the Border*, pp. 38–60.

129. Weldon B. Durham, ed., *American Theatre Companies, 1888–1930* (Westport, Conn.: Greenwood Press, 1987), pp. 353–58, 413–16, 449–53: Michael John Barnes, "A Survey of Historic Theatre Structures in Texas" (master's thesis, University of Texas, 1987), p. 169.

130. Thomas E. Sheridan, *Los Tucsonenses: The Mexican Community in Tucson, 1854–1941*, pp. 200–202.

131. Helen M. Morosco and Leonard Paul Dugger, *The Oracle of Broadway: The Life of Oliver Morosco* (Caldwell, Idaho: Caxton Printers, 1944).

132. Typescript, Lynden Ellsworth Behymer Papers, Huntington Library, San Marino, California; Swan, *Music in the Southwest, 1825–1950*, p. 202; Neil Erman Wilson, "A History of Opera and Associated Educational Activities in Los Angeles" (Ph.D. diss., Indiana University, 1968), pp. 36, 96–98.

CHAPTER 4. A REGIONAL CULTURE IS FORMULATED, 1920–1940

1. Quoted in Bryan Woolley, "Voice of a Mythical Land," *Texas Monthly* (Jan., 1986), p. 176.

2. J. B. Priestley, "Remembering Arizona," *Arizona Highways* 25 (Dec., 1949): 5–7.

3. U.S. Department of Commerce, Bureau of the Census, *Statistical Abstract of the United States* (Washington, D.C.: U.S. Government Printing Office, 1946).

4. Angie Debo, *Tulsa: From Creek Town to Oil Capitol* (Norman: University of Oklahoma Press, 1943), p. 105.

5. Carol Willis, "Zoning and Zeitgeist: The Skyscraper City in the 1920s," *Journal of the Society of Architectural Historians* 45 (Mar., 1986): 47–59; Wayne Andrews, *Architecture, Ambition, and Americans: A Social History of American Architecture* (New York: Free Press, 1978), p. 221.

6. *A Guide to the Architecture of Metro Phoenix* (Phoenix: Central Arizona Chapter of the American Institute of Architects, 1983); Marcus Whiffen and Carla Breeze, *Pueblo Deco: The Art Deco Architecture of the Southwest* (Albuquerque: University of New Mexico Press, 1984), pp. 35, 37, 61; Lloyd C. Engelbrecht, "Henry Trost: The Prairie School in the Southwest" *Prairie School Review* 4 (1969): 28.

7. Blackburn, Henderson, and Thurman, *The Physical Legacy*, pp. 45–78.

8. Glen Romaine Roberson, "City on the Plains: The History of Tulsa, Oklahoma" (Ph.D. diss., Oklahoma State University, 1977), pp. 158–59.

9. Patricia Carr Bowie, "The Cultural History of Los Angeles, 1850–1967: From Rural Backwash to World Center" (Ph.D. diss., University of Southern California, 1980), pp. 132–65; Henry, *Architecture in Texas*, pp. 218–28; Judith Singer Cohen, *Cowtown Moderne: Art Deco Architecture of Fort Worth, Texas*, p. 10.

10. Ibid.

11. Henry, *Architecture in Texas*, pp. 218–28.

12. Sandra D. Lynn, "Architect's Design Solutions Help Shape the State," *New Mexico Magazine*, Apr., 1992, pp. 76–80, 82, 84–85.

13. Dewitt, *Historic Albuquerque Today*, pp. 78–79; Ellen Threinen, *Historic Architecture of Albuquerque's Central Corridor* (Albuquerque: Task Force of Albuquerque Center, 1977), pp. 47–109.

14. Kaplan, *LA Lost and Found*, p. 89.

15. Moure, *Dictionary of Art and Artists in Southern California before 1930*, p. xvii; Kathryn Smith, "Frank Lloyd Wright, Hollyhock House, and Olive Hill, 1914–1924," *Journal of the Society of Architectural Historians* 38 (Mar., 1979): 15–33; David S. Gebhard, *Romanza: The California Architecture of Frank Lloyd Wright* (San Francisco: Chronicle Books, 1988).

16. Susan Vaughn, "Taking a Spin around the Concrete Block," *Los Angeles Times*, May 12, 1991.

17. Gebhard, *Romanza*.

18. *Tulsa Art Deco: An Architectural Era*, pp. 91–95; David B. Brownlee and David G. DeLong, *Louis I. Kahn: In the Realm of Architecture* (New York: Rizzoli International Publications, 1991), p. 94; Charles R. Goins and John W. Morris, *Oklahoma Homes: Past and Present* (Norman: University of Oklahoma Press, 1980), p. 131.

19. Marilyn Kluger, "Taliesen West — Frank Lloyd Wright's Arizona Retreat," *Gourmet*, Mar., 1991, pp. 86–89, 136, 138, 140–41; *A Guide to the Architecture of Metro Phoenix*.

20. Quotations from Kluger, "Taliesen West," pp. 88, 136. See also Smith, "Frank Lloyd Wright, Hollyhock House, and Olive Hill," 35, 37–38.

21. Bill E. Peavler, "Bruce Goff's Riverside Music Studio," in Meredith and Meredith, eds., *Of the Earth*, pp. 105–14; *Tulsa Art Deco*, pp. 68–91; Smith, *Architecture of the United States*, 3:574–75.

22. Bainbridge Bunting, *John Gaw Meem: Southwestern Architect* (Albuquerque: University of New Mexico Press, 1983), p. 24. See also Meem to George P. Day, Mar. 13, 1929, in Mary Austin Papers, Huntington Library, San Marino, California.

23. Arthur L. DeVolder, "John Gaw Meem, F.A.I.A.: An Appreciation," *New Mexico Historical Review* 54 (July, 1979): 209–25.

24. Quoted in Chris Wilson, "In the Modern Spirit: John Gaw Meem's Design for the Colorado Springs Fine Arts Center," *New Mexico Architecture* 27 (Mar./Apr., 1986): 18.

25. Quoted in Stanley L. Cuba and Elizabeth Cunningham, *Pike's Peak Vision: The Broodmoor Art Academy, 1919–1945* (Colorado Springs: Colorado Springs Fine Arts Center, 1989), p. 63.

26. Quoted in Wilson, "In the Modern Spirit," 18.

27. David Gebhard, *Schindler* (New York: Viking Press, 1972).

28. Thomas S. Hines, "Los Angeles Transfer: Rationalism and Reintegration, 1920–1980," in Clark and Hines, eds., *Los Angeles Transfer,* p. 79.

29. Ibid., p. 78.

30. Kaplan, *LA Lost and Found,* p. 108.

31. Quoted in Esther McCoy, *Richard Neutra* (New York: George Braziller, 1960), pp. 7–8.

32. David Gebhard and Harriette von Breton, *Los Angeles in the Thirties, 1931–1941* (Salt Lake City: Peregrine Smith, 1975); David Gebhard, "Kem Weber: Moderne Designs in California, 1920–1940," *Journal of Decorative and Propaganda Arts* 2 (summer/fall, 1986): 20–31.

33. Van Deren Coke, "Why Artists Came to New Mexico," *Artnews* 73 (Jan., 1974): 22–24.

34. Walter Pach, "John Sloan," *New Mexico Artists, Series 3* (Albuquerque: University of New Mexico Press, 1952), p. 3.

35. John Sloan, *Gist of Art* (New York: American Artists Group, 1939).

36. Ibid., p. 147.

37. Quoted in James Kraft and Helen Farr Sloan, *John Sloan in Santa Fe* (Washington, D.C.: Smithsonian Institution, 1981), foreword.

38. David Scott, *John Sloan, 1871–1951* (Boston: Boston Book and Art Publishers, 1972), p. 172.

39. Brian W. Dippie, "The Visual West," in Clyde A. Milner II, Carol A. O'Connor, and Martha A. Sandweiss, eds., *Oxford History of the American West,* pp. 695–96.

40. Charles Eldredge, Julie Schimmel, and William H. Truettner, *Art in New Mexico: Pathways to Taos and Santa Fe, 1900–1945,* p. 197.

41. Sheldon Reich, "John Marin and the Piercing Light of Taos," *Artnews* 73 (Jan., 1974): 16.

42. Jeanne Hokin, *Pinnacles and Pyramids: The Art of Marsden Hartley* (Albuquerque: University of New Mexico Press, 1993), p. 39.

43. Broder, *The American West,* p. 138.

44. Hokin, *Pinnacles and Pyramids,* p. 42.

45. Broder, *The American West,* p. 73.

46. Reich, "John Marin and the Piercing Light of Taos," 16.

47. Ibid., p. 16.

48. Ibid.

49. Marin to Stieglitz, Aug. 4, 10, and 14, 1930, John Marin Papers, Zimmerman Library, University of New Mexico, Albuquerque.

50. Sheldon Reich, *John Marin: A Stylistic Analysis and Catalogue Raisonné,* vol. 1 (Tucson: University of Arizona Press, 1970), pp. 183–84.

51. Broder, *The American West,* p. 118.

52. Coke, "Why Artists Came to New Mexico," 22–24.

53. Doris Bry, "O'Keeffe Country," in Doris Bry and Nicholas Calloway, *Georgia O'Keeffe: In the West* (New York: Alfred A. Knopf, 1989), pp. 99–105.

54. Quoted in *Georgia O'Keeffe, 1887–1986* (New York: Metropolitan Museum of Art, 1988), n.p.

55. Mabel Dodge Luhan, "Georgia O'Keeffe in Taos," *Creative Art* 9 (June, 1931): 407.

56. Georgia O'Keeffe, *About Myself* (New York: An American Place, 1939).

57. Hogrefe, *O'Keeffe,* p. 153.

58. Ibid., p. 167.

59. Pollitzer, *A Woman on Paper,* pp. 224–25.

60. O'Keeffe to Brett, n.d., Dorothy Brett Papers, University of Texas Harry Ransom Humanities Research Center, Austin.

61. Bry and Calloway, *Georgia O'Keeffe.*

62. "O'Keeffe: Her Time, Her Place," *New Mexico Magazine,* May, 1986, p. 52.

63. Gerdts, *Art across America,* 3:166–67.

64. Winifred Haines Higgins, "Art Collecting in the Los Angeles Area, 1910–1960" (Ph.D. diss., University of California, Los Angeles 1963), p. 25.

65. Gerdts, *Art across America,* 3:319–22, 322–25.

66. Nancy Dustin Wall Moure, *Painting and Sculpture in Los Angeles, 1900–1945* (Los Angeles: Los Angeles County Museum of Art, 1980), pp. 28–34; Paul J. Karlstrom, "Los Angeles in the 1940s: Post-Modernism and the Visual Arts" *Southern California Quarterly* 69 (winter, 1987): 301–28.

67. Arthur Silberman, *100 Years of Native American Painting* (Oklahoma City: Oklahoma Museum of Art, 1978), pp. 15–17; Dorothy Dunn, *American Indian Painting of the Southwest,* pp. 218–19; O. R. Landelius, "Oscar B. Jacobson, pedagog och konstnär," *Utlandssvenskarna* 17 (Nov. 11, 1955): 14–16; A. M. Gibson, "The Oscar Jacobson Legacy: A Preservation Imperative," *Chronicles of Oklahoma* 70 (spring, 1992): 84–89.

68. Bess England, "Artists in Oklahoma: A Handbook" (master's thesis, University of Oklahoma, 1964); Green Peyton, *America's Heartland: The Southwest* (Norman: University of Oklahoma Press, 1948), pp. 257–58; Willie Jordan Misner, "An Evaluation of Art Activity in Oklahoma during Its First Thirty Years of Statehood" (master's thesis, University of Oklahoma, 1940), p. 42; Howard L. Meredith, "The Bacone School of Art," *Chronicles of Oklahoma* 58 (spring, 1980), 92–98.

69. Brody, *Indian Painters and White Patrons,* pp. 85–87, 101–102, 128–29; Silberman, *100 Years of Native American Painting,* pp. 19–20; Dunn, *American Indian Painting,* pp. 29–30.

70. Rennard Strickland, "Where Have All The Blue Deer Gone? Depth and Diversity in Post-War Indian Painting," *American Indian Art Magazine* 10 (spring, 1985): 43.

71. Dunn, *American Indian Painting,* p. 235; John Anson Warner, "The Individual in Native American Art: A Sociological View," in Edwin L. Wade, ed., *The Arts of the North American Indian* (New York: Hudson Hills Press, 1986), pp. 190–96; Jamake Highwater, *Song from the Earth: American Indian Painting,* pp. 46, 48, 52, 85, 89; Eldredge, Schimmel, and Truettner, *Art in New Mexico,* pp. 191, 200, 201; Ina Sizer Cassidy, "Art and Artists of New Mexico: Indian Artists," *New Mexico Magazine,* Nov., 1938, pp. 22, 32–33.

72. Mabel Dodge Luhan, *Edge of the Taos Desert: An Escape to Reality,* pp. 32–33.

73. Ibid., pp. 71–72.

74. Luhan to Austin, n.d., Austin Papers, Huntington Library.

75. Ibid., [1921?].

76. Emily Hahn, *Mabel: A Biography of Mabel Dodge Luhan;* Lois Palken Rudnick, *Mabel Dodge Luhan: New Woman, New Worlds.*

77. D. H. Lawrence, "New Mexico," *Survey Graphic* 66 (May 1, 1931): 153.

78. Ibid.

79. Lawrence to S. S. Koteliansky, Sept. 18, 1922, quoted in Harry T. Moore, ed., *Collected Letters of D. H. Lawrence,* vol 2 (New York: Viking Press, 1962), p. 715.

80. Frieda Lawrence, *"Not I, but the Wind . . ."* (New York: Viking Press, 1934), p. 135.

81. Lawrence to E. H. Brewster, Sept. 22, 1922, quoted in Moore, *Collected Letters,* 2:717.

82. Lawrence, "New Mexico," p. 154.

83. Luhan to Austin, Nov. 28, [1922], Austin Papers, Huntington Library; D. H. Lawrence, "Indians and an Englishman," *The Dial,* Feb., 1923, pp. 144–52; Luhan to Dorothy Hoskins, Mar. 31, 1932, Brett Papers, University of Texas Harry Ransom Humanities Research Center.

84. Dorothy E. Brett, "Autobiography: My Long and Beautiful Journey," *South Dakota Review* 5 (summer, 1967): 60.

85. Broder, *The American West,* p. 210; Frank Waters, *Masked Gods: Navajo and Pueblo Ceremonialism* (Chicago: Swallow Press, 1950), p. 275; Folder 1, Box 4, Dorothy Eugenie Brett Papers, Zimmerman Library, University of New Mexico, Albuquerque.

86. C. G. Jung, "The Pueblo Indians," in Aniela Jaffe, ed., *Memories, Dreams, Reflections* (New York: Random House, 1963), as reprinted in Tony Hillerman, ed., *The Spell of New Mexico* (Albuquerque: University of New Mexico Press, 1976), p. 39.

87. Major, Pearce, and Smith, *Southwestern Heritage,* p. 153.

88. Correspondence with William H. Simpson, Alice Corbin Henderson Papers, University of Texas Harry Ransom Humanities Research Center, Austin; Witter Bynner and Oliver LaFarge, "Alice Corbin: An Appreciation," *New Mexico Quarterly Review* 19 (spring, 1949): 34–79; Shelley Armitage, "New Mexico's Literary Heritage," *El Palacio* 90, no. 2 (1984): 20–29; Elizabeth S. Sergeant, "The Santa Fe Group," *Saturday Review of Literature,* Dec. 8, 1934, pp. 352–54; Lois Rudnick, "Re-Naming the Land: Anglo-Expatriate Women in the Southwest," in Vera Norwood and Janice Monk, eds., *The Desert Is No Lady: Southwestern Landscape in Women's Writings and Art* (New Haven: Yale University Press, 1987), pp. 12–15.

89. Donald A. Barclay, "The Laughing Horse: A Literary Magazine of the American West," *Western American Literature* 27 (spring, 1992): 47–55; Hogrefe, *O'Keeffe,* p. 160; Ron Kampfe, "Laughing Horse Man," *New Mexico Magazine,* May, 1986, pp. 43–45.

90. Barclay, "The Laughing Horse," 50.

91. Haniel Long, *Piñon Country* (New York: Duell, Sloan, and Pierce, 1941), p. 30.

92. Nash, *The American West in the Twentieth Century,* p. 126.

93. Luhan to Austin [1922?], Austin Papers, Huntington Library.

94. Luhan to Waters, n.d., Frank Waters Papers, Zimmerman Library, University of New Mexico, Albuquerque.

95. Mabel Dodge Luhan to Forbes-Watson, Editor of *The Arts,* n.d., Mabel Dodge Luhan Papers, Zimmerman Library, University of New Mexico, Albuquerque.

96. Lewis, *Willa Cather Living,* pp. 138–42; Brown, *Willa Cather,* pp. 251–52.

97. Lewis, *Willa Cather Living,* pp. 144–46; Cather to Austin, June 26, 1926, Austin Papers, Huntington Library.

98. Willa Cather, *Death Comes for the Archbishop* (New York: Vintage Books, 1971), p. 232.

99. Ibid.; John Charles Scott, "Between Fiction and History: An Exploration into Willa Cather's *Death Comes for the Archbishop*" (Ph.D. diss., University of New Mexico, 1980); Mabel Dodge Luhan, "Paso por Aqui!," *New Mexico Quarterly* 21 (summer,

1951): 139; Richard West Sellars, "The Interrelationship of Literature, History, and Geography in Western Writing," *Western Historical Quarterly* 4 (Apr., 1973): 184–85.

100. Willa Cather, *The Professor's House* (New York: Alfred A. Knopf, 1925).

101. Ibid., p. 240.

102. Cather to Akins, Jan. 3, 1946, Zoë Akins Papers, Huntington Library, San Marino, California.

103. Fink, *I-Mary*.

104. Quoted in Fink, *I-Mary*, pp. 195–96.

105. Mary Austin, *The Land of Journey's End* (New York: Century, 1924).

106. Mary Austin, *Taos Pueblo* (San Francisco: Grabhorn Press, 1930), p. 6.

107. Mary Austin, "Why I Live in Santa Fe," *Golden Book Magazine* 16 (Oct., 1932): 306, 307.

108. Mary Austin, "Regionalism in American Fiction," *English Journal* 21 (Feb., 1932): 97–107; Mary Austin, "Indian Detour," *Bookman* 68 (Feb., 1929): 653–58; Austin to Carey McWilliams, Sept. 1, 1931, Mary Austin Papers, Zimmerman Library, University of New Mexico, Albuquerque.

109. Mary Austin, "Democracy and Criticism," [1934], typescript, Austin Papers, Huntington Library.

110. Mary Austin, "Regional Culture in the Southwest," *Southwest Review* 14 (summer, 1929): 474.

111. Mary Austin, *Earth Horizon* (Boston: Houghton Mifflin Company, 1932), p. 359.

112. Oliver LaFarge, *Laughing Boy* (Boston: Houghton-Mifflin, 1929); John Gaw Meem, "untitled tribute" to Oliver LaFarge, Mar. 23, 1965, typescript, Oliver LaFarge Papers, University of Texas Harry Ransom Humanities Research Center, Austin; "New Mexico: The Pool of Time," notes and outline by Oliver LaFarge, LaFarge Papers.

113. Powell, *Southwest Classics*, pp. 109–18.

114. Ross Calvin Diaries, May 23, 1933, and Mar. 5 and 6, 1936, and "Moods of Earth and Sky," manuscript, Ross Calvin Papers, Zimmerman Library, University of New Mexico, Albuquerque.

115. Powell, *Southwest Classics*, p. 177.

116. Edward Everett Dale, "The Spirit of Soonerland," *Chronicles of Oklahoma* 1 (June, 1923): 177.

117. Anne Hodges Morgan, "Oklahoma in Literature," in Anne Hodges Morgan and H. Wayne Morgan, eds., *Oklahoma: New Views of the Forty-Sixth State* (Norman: University of Oklahoma Press, 1982), pp. 184–85.

118. Ibid., pp. 181–82; Mary Hays Marable and Elaine Boylan, *A Handbook of Oklahoma Authors* (Norman: University of Oklahoma Press, 1939), 20.

119. "Oklahoma Poets," *American Mercury*, May, 1926, pp. 14–17.

120. Marable and Boylan, *A Handbook of Oklahoma Authors*, pp. 35–37; Stanley Vestal, "Miss Ferber's Myth," *Saturday Review of Literature*, Mar. 22, 1930, p. 841.

121. Dorothy Scarborough, *The Wind* (New York: Harper and Brothers, 1925), p. 1. For a recent study of Scarborough, see Sylvia Ann Grider, "Dorothy Scarborough," in Sylvia Ann Grider and Lou Halsell Rodenberger, eds., *Texas Women Writers: A Tradition of Their Own*, pp. 134–40.

122. Scarborough, *The Wind*, p. 3.

123. Ibid., pp. 258–59.

124. "Will Texas Develop a Real Regional Literature?" manuscript, George Sessions Perry Papers, University of Texas Harry Ransom Humanities Research Center, Austin.

125. Porter to Perry, Feb. 5, 1943, Perry Papers.

126. Jay B. Hubbell, "The New Southwest," *Southwest Review* 10 (Oct., 1924): 91–99.

127. J. Frank Dobie, "True Culture Is Eclectic, but Provincial," *Southwest Review* 14 (summer, 1929): 482.

128. J. Frank Dobie, *Prefaces* (Austin: University of Texas Press, 1982), p. 51.

129. Spell, *Music in Texas,* pp. 144–46; Playbills, Ephemera Collection, University of Texas Center for American History, Austin.

130. Donald William Looser, "Significant Factors in the Musical Development of the Cultural Life in Houston, Texas, 1930–1971" (Ph.D. diss., Florida State University, 1972), pp. 17–18; Playbills, Ephemera Collection, University of Texas Center for American History.

131. Roussel, *The Houston Symphony Orchestra,* pp. 8–29, 38–55.

132. Gladys Williams, "Orchestras and Bands: El Paso Music, 1880–1960" (master's thesis, University of Texas, El Paso, 1960); Neal M. Weaver, *Abraham Chavez: El Paso's Maestro* (El Paso: Musical Friends of the Maestro, 1992), pp. 14–20.

133. David W. Guion, "Is the Southwest Musical?," *Southwest Review* 14 (Apr., 1928): 344–50; Rogers, *The Lusty Texans of Dallas,* pp. 239–43; Davis, *A History of Opera in the American West,* pp. 117–18; "The Met Does Dallas," *Texas Monthly,* Jan., 1986, p. 153.

134. Joseph Benton, *Oklahoma Tenor: Musical Memories of Giuseppe Bentonelli* (Norman: University of Oklahoma Press, 1973).

135. Michael John Kotlanger, "Phoenix, Arizona, 1920–1940" (Ph.D. diss., Arizona State University, 1983), pp. 270–72; Programs, Grace Alexander Papers, Arizona State University Library, Tempe.

136. *Arizona Daily Star* (Tucson), Sept. 28, 1980; Joseph Lemos Cordeiro, "A Century of Musical Development in Tucson, Arizona, 1867–1967" (D. of M. A. diss., University of Arizona, 1968); Jack L. Cross, Elizabeth H. Shaw, and Kathleen Scheifele, eds., *Arizona: Its People and Resources* (Tucson: University of Arizona Press, 1960), p. 315; C. L. Sonnichsen, *Tucson: The Life and Times of an American City* (Norman: University of Oklahoma Press, 1982), pp. 174–77.

137. Sarah J. Moore, "No Woman's Land: Arizona Adventurers," in Trenton, ed., *Independent Spirits,* pp. 144, 146.

138. Albuquerque Civic Symphony Orchestra Papers, Fine Arts Library, University of New Mexico, Albuquerque; Marc Simmons, *Albuquerque: A Narrative History* (Albuquerque: University of New Mexico Press, 1982), p. 361; Phillip Hart, *Orpheus in the New World: The Symphony Orchestra as an American Cultural Institution* (New York: W. W. Norton and Company, 1973), pp. 246–47.

139. Aubrey Burns, "Regional Culture in California," *Southwest Review* 17 (July, 1932): 373–94.

140. *San Diego Union,* Nov. 1, 1940; Music, Opera, Vertical File, San Diego Historical Society.

141. Quoted in *San Diego Union,* Mar. 18, 1973.

142. Mildred Lyman Tracy, "The Development of the San Diego Symphony Orchestra"

(master's thesis, San Diego State College, 1962); Music, Opera, Vertical File, San Diego Historical Society; Alice Barnett Stevenson Scrapbooks, San Diego Historical Society; *San Diego Jewish Press,* Nov. 4, 1977.

143. John Sanders, "Los Angeles Grand Opera Association: The Formative Years, 1924–1926," *Southern California Quarterly* 55 (1973): 261–302; Bowie, "The Cultural History of Los Angeles," pp. 206–11, 258–61; Receipts Report, California Grand Opera, 1925, Lynden Ellsworth Behymer Papers, Huntington Library, San Marino, California.

144. John Orlando Northcutt, *Magic Valley: The Story of the Hollywood Bowl* (Los Angeles: Osherenko, 1967); "Los Angeles Philharmonic Orchestra," speech manuscript, Behymer Papers, Huntington Library; Mueller, *The American Symphony Orchestra,* pp. 165–69.

145. Northcutt, *Magic Valley;* Isabel Morse Jones, *Hollywood Bowl* (New York: G. Schimer, 1936), pp. 1–60; "Hollywood Bowl," manuscript, Theodore Gerson Papers, Huntington Library, San Marino, California. (Gerson served as director of the Hollywood Bowl Association.)

146. Quoted in Tom Dardis, *Some Time in the Sun: The Hollywood Years of Fitzgerald, Faulkner, Nathaniel West, Aldous Huxley, and James Agee* (New York: Charles Scribner's Sons, 1976), p. 14.

147. Major, Pearce, and Smith, *Southwestern Heritage,* p. 152.

148. Henry Nash Smith, "Culture," *Southwest Review* 13 (Jan., 1928): 249–55; Rogers, *Lusty Texans of Dallas,* pp. 211–15; Davis, *A History of Opera in the American West.*

149. Kathryn Kennedy O'Connor, *Theatre in the Cow Country* (South Bend: Creative Service for Publishers for the Albuquerque Little Theater, 1966); David Richard Jones, ed., *New Mexico Plays,* pp. 10–12; Robert Turner Wood, "The Transformation of Albuquerque, 1945–1972" (Ph.D. diss., University of New Mexico, 1980); Ray Terry, "The Albuquerque Little Theatre: Its 30 years," *New Mexico Quarterly* 30 (spring, 1960): 11–25.

150. Quoted in Jones, ed., *New Mexico Plays,* p. 11.

151. Felix Diáz Almaráz, Jr., *Standing Room Only: A History of the San Antonio Little Theatre, 1912–1962* (Waco: Texian Press, 1964).

152. Lawrence L. Graves, ed., *A History of Lubbock* (Lubbock: West Texas Museum Association, 1962), pp. 573–74.

153. Vaughn S. Albertson, "The Green Mask Players," *Southwest Review* 16 (winter, 1931): 164–77.

154. Kotlanger, "Phoenix, Arizona," pp. 276–77; Grace Alexander Papers, Arizona State University Library.

155. John Eugene Donnelly, "The Old Globe Theater at San Diego, California: An Historical Survey of Its Origin and Development" (master's thesis, University of California, Los Angeles, 1957).

156. Camille N. R. Bokar, "An Historical Study of the Legitimate Theatre in Los Angeles, 1920–1929, and Its Relation to the National Theatrical Scene" (Ph.D. diss., University of Southern California, 1973).

157. Gail Leo Shoup, Jr., "The Pasadena Community Playhouse: Its Origins and History from 1917 to 1942" (Ph.D. diss. University of California, Los Angeles, 1968); Zoë Akins, "Playwright's Paradise," *Theatre Arts* 36 (Aug., 1952): 36–37, 91; Harriet L.

Green, ed., *Book of the Pasadena Community Playhouse* (Pasadena: Pasadena Playhouse Press, 1934).

158. Richard Amado Garcia, *Rise of the Mexican-American Middle Class: The Making of the Mexican-American Mind, San Antonio, Texas, 1929–1941* (College Station: Texas A&M University Press), pp. 94–107, 233–37.

159. Sheridan, *Los Tucsonenses,* pp. 99, 197–99.

160. Mary Montaño Army, "*Zarzuelas:* Spanish Operetta in the New World," *El Palacio* 91 (fall, 1985): 18–25.

161. Kanellos, ed., *Mexican American Theatre,* pp. 27–33.

162. Pauline B. Deuel, *Mexican Serenade: The Story of the Mexican Players and the Padua Hills Theatre* (Claremont: Padua Institute, 1961).

163. Sally B. Soelle, "New Deal Art: The Section of Fine Arts Program in the Great Plains States" (Ph.D. diss., University of Oklahoma, 1993); Marlene Park and Gerald E. Markowitz, *Democratic Vistas: Post Offices and Public Art in the New Deal* (Philadelphia: Temple University Press, 1985).

164. Daniel A. Hall, "A WPA Art Center in Phoenix, 1937–1940," in John Franklin White, ed., *Art in Action: American Art Centers and the New Deal* (Metuchen, N.J.: Scarecrow Press, 1987), pp. 114–30; Philip C. Curtis, "The Phoenix Art Center," in Francis V. O'Connor, ed., *The New Deal Art Projects: An Anthology of Memoirs* (Washington, D.C.: Smithsonian Institution Press, 1972), pp. 221–23; Peter Bermingham, *The New Deal in the Southwest: Arizona and New Mexico* (Tucson: University of Arizona Museum of Art, 1980).

165. Oliver Gough Meeks, "The Federal Art Program in Oklahoma (1934–1940)" (master's thesis, University of Oklahoma, 1941); Nicholas A. Calcagno, *New Deal Murals in Oklahoma* (Miami, Okla.: Pioneer Printing, 1976); Sally B. Soelle, "New Deal Art Projects in Oklahoma, 1933–1943" (master's thesis, University of Oklahoma, 1984).

166. Quoted in Kathleen Grisham Rogers, "Incidence of New Deal Art in Oklahoma: An Historical Survey" (master's thesis, University of Oklahoma, 1974), p. 40.

167. Ibid.; Leonard Good, "Oklahoma's Art in the 1930s: A Remembrance," *Chronicles of Oklahoma* 70 (summer, 1992): 194–209; Nicholas A. Calcagno and Barbara K. Scott, "The Federal Art Gallery System in Oklahoma: A Successful Experiment," in White, *Art in Action,* pp. 37–78; England, "Artists in Oklahoma."

168. Charlotte Whaley, *Nina Otero-Warren of Santa Fe* (Albuquerque: University of New Mexico Press, 1994); Suzanne Forrest, *The Preservation of the Village: New Mexico's Hispanics and the New Deal* (Albuquerque: University of New Mexico Press, 1989), pp. 105–25; Sarah Deutsch, *No Separate Refuge: Culture, Class, and Gender on an Anglo-Hispanic Frontier in the American Southwest, 1880–1940,* pp. 188–96.

169. Robert Fay Schroder, *The Indian Arts and Crafts Board: An Aspect of New Deal Indian Policy* (Albuquerque: University of New Mexico Press, 1983).

170. Bermingham, *The New Deal in the Southwest;* D'Lyn Ford, "Depression Era Art Still Lifts Spirits," *New Mexico Magazine,* Nov., 1990, pp. 38–47.

171. Moure, *Painting and Sculpture in Los Angeles,* pp. 42–54; *Southern California Creates* (Los Angeles: Federal Art Project of Southern California, [1939]); Steven M. Gelber, "Working to Prosperity: California's New Deal Murals," *California History* 58 (summer, 1979): 103.

172. Kenneth E. Hendrickson, Jr., "The WPA Arts Projects in Texas," *East Texas Historical Journal* 26, no. (1988): 3–13.

173. Carol Wilmoth, "Heavenly Harmony: The WPA Symphony Orchestra," *Chronicles of Oklahoma* 64 (summer, 1986): 35–51; Suzanne H. Schrems, "New Deal Culture in Oklahoma: The Federal Theatre and Music Projects," *Heritage of the Great Plains* 19 (winter, 1986): 1–13; Kenneth E. Hendrickson, Jr., "Politics of Culture: The Federal Music Project in Oklahoma," *Chronicles of Oklahoma* 63 (winter, 1985–86): 361–75.

174. Peter Mehren, "San Diego's Opera Unit of the WPA Federal Music Project," *Journal of San Diego History* 18 (summer, 1972): 12–21; *San Diego Union,* Nov. 5, 1972; *San Diego Sun,* July 19, 1939.

175. Behymer to Nikolai Sokoloff, Jan. 2, and Feb. 28, 1936; letters from musicians to Behymer, 1936–1938; concert programs, 1936; all in Behymer Papers, Huntington Library.

176. Schrems, "New Deal Culture in Oklahoma"; K. Kay Brandes, "Theatrical Activities in Oklahoma City from 1889 to 1964" (master's thesis, University of Oklahoma, 1964).

177. Hendrickson, "The WPA Arts Projects in Texas."

178. Jane DeHart Mathews, *The Federal Theatre, 1935–1939: Plays, Relief, and Politics* (Princeton: Princeton University Press, 1967), pp. 245, 163–64; Robert Holcomb, "The Federal Theatre in Los Angeles," *California Historical Society Quarterly* 41 (summer, 1962): 134–47.

179. Mathews, *The Federal Theatre,* p. 247.

180. Quoted in Paul Burka, "Between the Lines," *Texas Monthly,* Jan., 1986, p. 8.

181. *Houston Post,* Sept. 7, 1986; Susie Kalil, *The Texas Landscape: 1900–1986* (Austin: University of Texas Press, 1986); Rick Stewart, *Lone Star Regionalism: The Dallas Nine and Their Circle,* p. 20; Michael B. Ennis, "Deep in the Art of Texas," *Houston Post Family Weekly,* May 26, 1985, pp. 11–13; Lea Rosson DeLong, *Nature's Forms/Nature's Forces: The Art of Alexandre Hogue;* Francine Carraro, *Jerry Bywaters: A Life in Art* (Austin: University of Texas Press, 1984).

182. Quoted in Kalil, *The Texas Landscape,* p. 35.

183. Anne Dingus, "Brush with Fame," *Texas Monthly,* Jan., 1995, pp. 128–31; Alexandre Hogue, "All Texans Do Not Paint 'Wild Flowers,'" *Art Digest* 2 (mid-Apr., 1928): 3.

184. Quoted in Stewart, *Lone Star Regionalism,* p. 21.

185. Carraro, *Jerry Bywaters.*

186. Alexandre Hogue, "The Making of an Artist: Autobiography of Alexandre Hogue," Alexandre Hogue Papers, University of Tulsa McFarland Library, Tulsa, Oklahoma.

187. Quoted in DeLong, *Nature's Forms/Nature's Forces,* p. 3.

188. Hogue, "Making of an Artist," p. 18.

189. Hogue to Matthew Baigell, June 14, 1967, quoted in Sandra Lea Rosson, "The Career of Alexandre Hogue" (Ph.D. diss., University of Kansas, 1983), p. 9.

190. Handwritten comment by Hogue on a copy of Sandra Lea Rosson's "Career of Alexandre Hogue," Hogue Papers, University of Tulsa McFarland Library.

191. Hogue, "Making of an Artist," p. 22.

192. Alexandre Hogue, "Victor Higgins: Some Opinions of an Opothegmatic Artist," *Southwest Review* 14 (winter, 1929): 259.

193. Alexandre Hogue, "A Texas View," *Art Digest,* Jan. 1, 1933, p. 26.

194. Alexandre Hogue, "Cathedral Voices," quoted in *Art and Auction,* Oct., 1994, p. 88.

195. *Dallas Journal,* June 9, 1936.

196. *Art Digest,* June 1, 1936, p. 14.

197. Charles Edward Aughtry, "Lynn Riggs, Dramatist: A Critical Biography" (Ph.D. diss., Brown University, 1959); *New York World-Telegram,* Feb. 27, 1931.

198. Joseph Benton, "Some Personal Remembrances about Lynn Riggs," *Chronicles of Oklahoma* 34 (autumn, 1956): 296–301.

199. Riggs to Betty Kirk, July 24, 1924, Raleigh Lynn Riggs Papers, University of Oklahoma Western History Collection, Norman.

200. Riggs to Henderson, Sept. 17, 1928, Henderson Papers, University of Texas Harry Ransom Humanities Research Center.

201. Quoted in Aughtry, "Lynn Riggs, Dramatist," p. 31.

202. Felix Sper, *From Native Roots: A Panorama of Our Regional Drama* (Caldwell, Idaho: Caxton Printers, 1948), 218.

203. Anne Andrews Hindman, "The Myth of the Western Frontier in American Dance and Drama: 1930–1943" (Ph.D. diss., University of Georgia, 1972), p. 105.

204. Phyllis Cole Braunlich, *Haunted by Home: The Life and Letters of Lynn Riggs* (Norman: University of Oklahoma, 1988).

205. *New York World-Telegram,* Feb. 27, 1931.

206. Ibid.

207. Quoted in Braunlich, *Haunted by Home,* p. 87.

208. Ibid., p. 390.

209. Riggs to Kirk, July [15], 1926, Riggs Collection.

210. Thomas A. Erhard, *Lynn Riggs: Southwest Playwright* (Austin: Steck-Vaughn, 1970).

211. Riggs to Kirk, June 23, 1944, and note attached written by Kirk, Riggs Collection.

212. Kyle Crichton, "Cease Not Living," *New Mexico Quarterly* 5 (May, 1935): 71.

CHAPTER 5. NATIONALIZATION OF A REGIONAL CULTURE, 1940–1960

1. Nash and Etulain, eds., *The Twentieth Century West;* Nash, *The American West in the Twentieth Century,* pp. 218–25, 256–57; Carol A. O'Connor "A Region of Cities," in Milner, O'Connor, and Sandweiss, eds., *The Oxford History of the American West,* pp. 553–56; John Rosenfield quoted in Grider and Rodenberger, eds., *Texas Women Writers,* p. 325.

2. Michael P. Malone and Richard W. Etulain, *The American West: A Twentieth Century History,* pp. 120–26.

3. Sherman R. Miller, *Tropic of Tucson* (Tucson: Rutz Press, 1964), p. 8.

4. June Caldwell, "Tucson: The Folk Industry," in West, Jr., ed., *Rocky Mountain Cities,* pp. 208–10.

5. Nash, *The American West in the Twentieth Century,* p. 268.

6. *A Guide to the Architecture of Metro Phoenix* (Phoenix: Central Arizona Chapter of the American Institute of Architects, 1983); *Arizona: Its People and Resources* (Tucson:

University of Arizona Press. 1972), pp. 307–309; *Buildings of Architectural Significance in Tucson.*

7. Butler, *Tulsa 75;* Tom Sorey, Jr., "Sorey Hill and Sorey: Architects with a Civic Conscience," *Chronicles of Oklahoma* 71 (winter, 1993–94): 356–75.

8. Hank Todd Smith ed., *Austin: Its Architects and Architecture 1836–1986* (Austin: Austin Chapter, American Institute of Architects, 1986), pp. 14–27.

9. Erna Fergusson, *Albuquerque* (Albuquerque: Merle Armitage Editions, 1947), pp. 2–3.

10. Edna Hetherington Bergman, "The Fate of Architectural Theory in Albuquerque: Buildings of Four Decades, 1920–1960" (master's thesis, University of New Mexico, 1978), pp. 217–411.

11. J. B. Priestly and Jacquetta Hawkes, *Journey down a Rainbow* (New York: Harper and Brothers, 1955), p. xii.

12. *The Prairie's Yield,* pp. 44–46; David Dillon and Doug Tomlinson, *Dallas Architecture, 1936–1986,* pp. 35–36.

13. Nathaniel West, *Miss Lonely Hearts* and *The Day of the Locust* (New York: New Directions, 1962), p. 61.

14. Howard Barnstone with Stephen Fox, Jerome Iowa, and David Courtwright, *The Architecture of John Staub: Houston and the South* (Austin: University of Texas Press, 1979).

15. Wesley Howard Henderson, "Two Case Studies of African-American Architects' Careers in Los Angeles, 1890–1945: Paul R. Williams, FAIA, and James H. Garrott, AIA" (Ph.D. diss., University of California, Los Angeles, 1992); David Gebhard and Robert Winter, *A Guide to Architecture in Los Angeles and Southern California,* pp. 71, 125, 243.

16. Mary Carolyn Hollers George, *O'Neil Ford, Architect;* John Pastier, "Texas Architecture: Mythmakers and Realists," *Texas Journal* 8 (fall/winter, 1985–86): 12–13.

17. Christopher Wilson, "Regionalism Redefined: The Impact of Modernism in New Mexico," *Mass,* spring, 1983, pp. 16–21.

18. Smith, *Architecture of the United States,* 3:134–36.

19. Quoted in *Arizona Highways* 60 (May, 1984): 1.

20. Frank Lloyd Wright, "Architecture: Organic Expression of the Nature of Architecture," *Arizona Highways* 32 (Feb., 1956): 16.

21. Frank Lloyd Wright, "To Arizona," *Arizona Highways* 16 (May, 1940): 8, 10.

22. Frank Lloyd Wright, "Living in the Desert," *Arizona Highways* 25 (Oct., 1949): 12.

23. Wright, "Architecture," pp. 23–24.

24. Keith Raether, "Shaping the Pottery House," *New Mexico Magazine,* Apr., 1986, pp. 34–41.

25. Lisa Germany, "Texas Meets Mr. Wright," *Domain,* winter, 1987, pp. 56–57.

26. *Bartlesville Advertiser,* Feb. 9, 1956; Smith, *Architecture of the United States,* 3:559–61; press kit issued at the opening of the Price Tower, Feb. 10, 1956 (author's collection).

27. Frank Lloyd Wright, *The Story of the Tower: The Tree That Escaped the Crowded Forest* (New York: Horizon Press, 1956), n.p.

28. Quoted in Roy P. Stewart, "Famous Architect Is Worth Hearing," *Daily Oklahoman* (Oklahoma City), newspaper clipping, author's possession.

29. Quoted in press kit, Feb. 10, 1956.

30. Quoted in Dillon and Tomlinson, *Dallas Architecture*, p. 32.

31. David Gibson De Long, *The Architecture of Bruce Goff: Buildings and Projects, 1916–1974;* Jeffrey Cook, *The Architecture of Bruce Goff* (New York: Harper and Row, 1978), pp. 30–35; Goins and Morris, *Oklahoma Homes,* 1980.

32. Herb Greene, *Mind and Image: An Essay on Art and Architecture* (Lexington: University Press of Kentucky, 1976), p. 46.

33. Elizabeth A. T. Smith, ed., *Blueprints for Modern Living: History and Legacy of the Case Study Houses;* Paul Robinson Hunter and Walter L. Reichardt, *Residential Architecture in Southern California* (Los Angeles: Southern California Chapter, A.I.A., 1939).

34. Angie Debo, *Prairie City: The Story of an American Community* (New York: Alfred A. Knopf, 1944), p. vii.

35. Quoted in Anne Hodges Morgan, "Oklahoma in Literature," in Morgan and Morgan, eds., *Oklahoma,* p. 203.

36. Calvin, *Sky Determines,* pp. 315–17.

37. Balassi, Crawford, and Eysturoy, eds., *This Is about Vision,* p. 15; Fred Erisman and Richard W. Etulain, eds., *Fifty Western Writers: A Bio-Bibliographical Sourcebook* (Westport: Greenwood Press, 1982), pp. 509–13; John R. Milton, "The American West: A Challenge to the Literary Imagination," *Western American Literature* 1 (1967): 278–79.

38. Frank Waters, *The Man Who Killed the Deer* (New York: Farrar and Rinehart, 1942); Frank Waters, *People of the Valley* (New York: Farrar and Rinehart, 1941).

39. Quoted in John R. Milton, "The Land as Form in Frank Waters and William Eastlake," *Kansas Quarterly* 2 (spring, 1970): 104–109.

40. Frank Waters, "The Southwest: Vision and Revisions," *Book Talk* 16 (Apr., 1987): 5.

41. Robert J. Barnes, *Conrad Richter* (Austin: Steck-Vaughn, 1968); Carolyn V. Platt, "Conrad Richter and the Big Trees," *Timeline* 12 (Oct., 1995): 2–15.

42. Quoted in John T. Flanagan, "Conrad Richter: Romancer of the Southwest," *Southwest Review* 43 (summer, 1958): 190.

43. Ibid.; Conrad Richter, *The Sea of Grass* (New York: Alfred A. Knopf, 1949), p. 5.

44. Conrad Richter, *The Lady* (New York: Alfred A. Knopf, 1957), p. 91.

45. Quoted in Campbell [Stanley Vestal], *The Book Lover's Southwest,* p. 19.

46. James Kraft, "No Quarter Given: An Essay on Paul Horgan," *Southwestern Historical Quarterly* 80 (July, 1976): 1–32; Charles D. Biebel, "Paul Horgan's Early Albuquerque: Notes on a Southwestern City in Transition," *New Mexico Humanities Review* 3 (summer, 1980): 35–45; Peyton, *America's Heartland,* pp. 227–28; David Farmer, *The Collector's Eye: Selections from the Sally Zaiser Collection of Paul Horgan* (Dallas: DeGolyer Library, Southern Methodist University, 1991).

47. Paul Horgan, *Mountain Standard Time* (New York: Farrar, Straus, and Cudahy, 1962), p. 594.

48. Paul Horgan, *Whitewater* (New York: Farrar, Straus, and Giroux, 1970), p. 251.

49. Paul Horgan, *Figures in a Landscape* (New York: Harper and Brothers, 1940), pp. 2–3.

50. James Vinson, ed., *Twentieth-Century Western Writers* (Detroit: Gale Research Company, 1982), pp. 142–43.

51. Madison Cooper, *Sironia, Texas* (Boston: Hougton Mifflin, 1952).

52. "A Boom in Books about Texas and by Texas Authors," *Publishers Weekly* 162 (Dec. 20, 1952): 2368–69.

53. Frank H. Wardlaw, "Texas Is Bursting with Creativity," *House and Garden,* Jan., 1958, p. 15.

54. Carolyn Osborn, "My Brother Is a Cowboy," in Max Apple, ed., *Southwest Fiction* (New York: Bantam Books, 1981), p. 247.

55. John Graves, "The Last Running," in ibid., p. 131.

56. "April in Taos," typed manuscript dated 1947, William Goyen Papers, University of Texas Harry Ransom Humanities Research Center, Austin.

57. Joseph Wood Krutch, *The Desert Year* (New York: William Sloan Associates), 1952, p. 5.

58. Ibid., p. 270.

59. Raymond Chandler, *The Little Sister* (New York: Ballantine Books, 1971), p. 88.

60. Linda Venis, "L.A. Novels and the Hollywood Dream Factory: Popular Art's Impact on Los Angeles Literature in the 1940s," *Southern California Quarterly* 69 (winter, 1987): 349–69; Tom S. Reck, "J. M. Cain's Los Angeles Novels," *Colorado Quarterly* 22 (winter, 1974): 375–87; David M. Fine, "James M. Cain and the Los Angeles Novel," *American Studies* 20 (spring, 1979): 25–34; David Fine, "Running Out of Space: Vanishing Landscapes in California Novels," *Western American Literature* 26 (fall, 1991): 209–18; Raymond Chandler, "Writers in Hollywood," *Atlantic Monthly,* Nov., 1945, pp. 50–54.

61. Quoted in Edward Thorpe, *Chandlertown: The Los Angeles of Philip Marlowe* (New York: St. Martin's Press, 1983), p. 83.

62. Anne Bartlett Ayers, "Los Angeles Modernism and the Assemblage Tradition, 1948–1962" (Ph.D. diss., University of Southern California, 1983).

63. Quoted in Broder, *The American West,* pp. 280–81.

64. Jon Manchip White, *A World Elsewhere: One Man's Fascination with the American Southwest* (New York: Thomas Y. Crowell, 1975), pp. 16–17.

65. Quoted in Hough and Zakian, *Transforming the Western Image in 20th Century American Art,* p. 47.

66. Ibid.

67. Robert Hobbs, *Beatrice Mandelman: Taos Modernist* (Albuquerque: University of New Mexico Press, 1995), p. 2.

68. Susan Chadwick, "Art," *Houston Post,* July 12, 1987.

69. Coreen Mary Spellman to Nan Sheets, 1953, quoted in Susan Landuer with Becky Duval Reese, "Lone Star Spirits," in Trenton, ed., *Independent Spirits,* p. 199.

70. A. C. Greene, "A Bunch of Junk," *Texas Monthly,* Jan., 1986, pp. 124, 126, 128.

71. Peyton, *America's Heartland,* pp. 244–46.

72. Quoted in Paul Horgan, "Peter Hurd," *New Mexico Magazine,* Jan., 1961, p. 8.

73. Peter Hurd, "New Mexico," *New Mexico Magazine,* Jan., 1961, pp. 12, 34, 36, 38.

74. Peter Hurd to Henriette Wyeth Hurd, July 21, 1935, quoted in Robert Metzger, ed., *My Land Is the Southwest: Peter Hurd Letters and Journals* (College Station: Texas A&M University Press, 1983), pp. 142–43.

75. Quoted in Sandra D'Emilio and Sharyn Udall, "Inner Voices, Outward Forms: Women Painters in New Mexico," in Trenton, *Independent Spirits,* p. 155.

76. Wyeth to Mr. and Mrs. N. C. Wyeth, Sept. 22, 1937, quoted in Metzger, *My Land Is the Southwest,* p. 187.

77. Quoted in Nena Singleton, "Henriette Wyeth: Grand Dame of Art's First Family," *New Mexico Magazine,* May, 1988, p. 68.

78. Henriette Wyeth Hurd to Theodore Van Soelen, May 15, [1954?], in the Theodore Van Soelen Papers, Huntington Library, San Marino, California.

79. Quoted in Lou Rodenberger, "Tom Lea, Artist and Novelist: Interpreter of Southwestern Border Life," *Southwest Heritage,* summer, 1980, p. 5.

80. Tom Lea, *The Southwest: It's Where I Live* (Dallas: DeGolyer Library, Southern Methodist University, 1993), n.p.

81. Walter Pach, *The Art Museum in America* (New York: Pantheon Books, 1948), pp. 270–88.

82. Karl E. Meyer, *The Art Museum: Power, Money, Ethics* (New York: William Morrow and Company, 1979), pp. 127–28.

83. Max Kozloff, "The Contemporary Museum: Under the Corporate Wing," in Brian O'Doherty, *Museums in Crisis* (New York: George Braziller, 1972), p. 159.

84. *Los Angeles Times,* May 23, 1986.

85. Keith L. Bryant, Jr., "The Art Museum as Personal Statement," *Great Plains Quarterly* 9 (spring, 1989): 100–17.

86. Meyer, *The Art Museum,* p. 128.

87. Keith L. Bryant, Jr., "Roman Temples, Glass Boxes, and Babylonian Deco: Art Museum Architecture and the Cultural Maturation of the Southwest," *Western Historical Quarterly* 22 (Feb., 1991): 45–71.

88. Lorimer Rich, "Planning Art Museums," *Architectural Forum,* 47 (Dec., 1927): 553–78; William C. Agee, *The Museum of Fine Arts, Houston* (Houston: Museum of Fine Arts, 1981).

89. Franz Schulze, *Mies Van Der Rohe: A Critical Biography* (Chicago: University of Chicago Press, 1985), pp. 230–31; Peter C. Papademetriou, "Varied Reflections in Houston," *Progressive Architecture* 56 (Mar., 1975): 52–57.

90. Schulze, *Mies Van Der Rohe,* p. 309.

91. "San Diego Museum of Art," *Apollo* 115 (June, 1982): 7–65; Spaeth, *American Art Museums and Galleries,* pp. 196–98; *San Diego Museum of Art* (San Diego: San Diego Museum of Art, 1985).

92. Bywaters, *Seventy-Five Years of Art in Dallas;* Kenneth B. Ragsdale, *The Year America Discovered Texas: Centennial '36,* pp. 176–207.

93. "Description of Resources: Physical Facilities," files of the Membership and Development Department, Millicent Rogers Museum, Taos, New Mexico; Jim Sagel, "A Cultural Gathering: Millicent Rogers Museum," *New Mexico Magazine,* May, 1986, pp. 36–41; Tricia Hurst, "Millicent Rogers," *Interview,* Jan., 1987, pp. 54–56.

94. Kathryn Coe, "The Heard Museum," *Journal of the West,* 19 (Apr., 1980): 86–90; Luckingham, *Phoenix,* pp. 90–92; Paul Coze, "The Heard Museum," *Arizona Highways* 13 (Feb., 1965): 6–15.

95. Les Krantz, "Marion Koogler McNay Art Institute," *Texas Art Review* (Houston: Gulf Publishing Company, 1982), pp. 18–19; Burt, *Palaces for the People,* p. 379; Spaeth, *American Art Museums and Galleries,* pp. 186–87.

96. Burt, *Palaces for the People,* p. 14.

97. Carol Haralson and Raakel Vesanen, *Villa Philbrook* (Tulsa: Philbrook Art Center, 1976); "History of Philbrook Art Center," 13, 13A-13L, TS, Philbrook Art Center Library, Tulsa, Oklahoma.

98. David Randolph Milsten, *Thomas Gilcrease* (San Antonio: Naylor Company, 1969), pp. 313–17; Aline B. Saarinen, *The Proud Possessors* (New York: Random House, 1958), pp. 107–325; Fred A. Myers, *Thomas Gilcrease and His National Treasure* (Tulsa: Gilcrease Museum, 1987).

99. Martin Wenger, "Thomas Gilcrease," *Chronicles of Oklahoma* 40 (summer, 1962): 94–98; "Thomas Gilcrease," typescript, Gilcrease Institute Library, Tulsa, Oklahoma; Francine Du Plessix and Cleve Gray, "Thomas Gilcrease and Tulsa," *Art in America* 52, no. 3 (1964): 64–73.

100. Dobie quoted in Plessix and Gray, "Thomas Gilcrease and Tulsa," p. 71; Hoving quoted in "Gilcrease Museum," brochure, Gilcrease Museum Library, Tulsa, Oklahoma.

101. Patricia Carr Bowe, "The Cultural History of Los Angeles, 1850–1967: From Rural Backwash to World Center," (Ph.D diss., University of Southern California, 1980), pp. 178–83, 281–90, 263–66; Nash, *The American West in the Twentieth Century,* pp. 192–93; Barbara Isenberg, "The Art of Hollywood's Other Deals," *Los Angeles Times,* May 21, 1991.

102. Nash, *The American West in the Twentieth Century,* pp. 192–93.

103. Winifred Haines Higgins, "Art Collecting in the Los Angeles Area, 1910–1960" (Ph.D. diss., University of California, Los Angeles, 1963).

104. Ilene Susan Fort, "American Painting and Its Development," *Apollo* 124 (Nov., 1986): 42–47.

105. "Los Angeles County Museum of Art," *Apollo* 124 (Nov., 1986): 7–10; Spaeth, *American Art Museums and Galleries,* pp. 190–94.

106. Bryant, "Roman Temples, Glass Boxes, and Babylonian Deco," pp. 59–60; "William L. Pereira & Associates, Architects," *Arts and Architecture* 82 (May, 1965): 16–17; Katharine Kuh, "Los Angeles: Salute to a New Museum," *Saturday Review,* Apr. 3, 1965, pp. 29–30, 35.

107. Leopold L. Meyer Papers, Houston Metropolitan Research Center, Houston, Texas: Financial Records of the Houston Symphony Society; "Houston Symphony Society," typed manuscript dated 1943; and George A. Butler to L. L. Meyer, May 22, 1945.

108. *Houston Post,* clipping, 1940, in ibid.

109. Roussel, *The Houston Symphony Orchestra.*

110. Quoted in Francis Loewenheim, "False Crescendo," *Texas Monthly,* Jan., 1986, p. 168.

111. Ford Hubbard, Jr., to Leopold L. Meyer, Mar. 21, 1969, Meyer Papers, Houston Metropolitan Research Center.

112. Sharrard H. Douglas, "A History of the San Antonio Symphony Orchestra" (master's thesis, Incarnate Word College, 1971), pp. 21–34; "Success in Texas," *Time,* July 14, 1947, p. 68; Sam Woolford, ed., "History of the San Antonio Symphony Orchestra," *San Antonio: A History for Tomorrow* (San Antonio: Naylor Company, 1963), pp. 72–75; Davis, *A History of Opera in The American West,* p. 148.

113. *San Antonio Express,* Mar. 6, 1950; Marcia Pelton Holliman, "The Development of the San Antonio Symphony Orchestra, 1939–1966" (master's thesis, Trinity University, 1966), pp. 68–69.

114. Ronald L. Davis, *A History of Music in American Life,* vol. 3, *The Modern Era, 1920–Present* (Melbourne, Fla.: Krieger Publishing Company, 1981), pp. 25–26; George Sessions Perry, *Cities of America* (New York: McGraw-Hill, 1947), pp. 60–61; Peyton, *America's Heartland,* 199.

115. Davis, *A History of Music in American Life,* 3:24–25.

116. Perry, *Cities of America,* p. 59.

117. Holliman, "The Development of the San Antonio Symphony Orchestra," pp. 174–76; "Guy Fraser Harrison," Vertical File, Oklahoma Historical Society, Oklahoma City; Gaston Litton, *History of Oklahoma,* vol. 2 (New York: Lewis Historical Publishing Company, 1957), pp. 218–19.

118. Bryan Carrol Stoneburner, "The Phoenix Symphony Orchestra, 1947–1978: Leadership, Criticism, and Selective Commentary" (master's thesis, Arizona State University, 1981); Programs and Ephemera, Grace Alexander Papers, Arizona State University Library, Tempe.

119. Graves, ed., *A History of Lubbock,* pp. 571–72.

120. Frank Goodwyn, *Lone-Star Land: Twentiety-Century Texas in Perspective* (New York: Alfred A. Knopf, 1955), pp. 42–43, 166–67.

121. Clifford L. Graves, "The First Twenty Years: A History of the La Jolla Civic-University Orchestra and Chorus Association," unpublished paper, San Diego Historical Society.

122. Edward Clinton Tritt, "The Community Symphony Orchestra: A Study of the Historical Development, Present Activities, Personnel, and Inner Organization of Eight Community Orchestras in Southern California" (Ph.D. diss., Indiana University, 1961).

123. Patricia Carr Bowie, "The Cultural History of Los Angeles, 1850–1967: From Rural Backwash to World Center" (Ph.D. diss., University of Southern California, 1980), pp. 313–14; Neil Morgan, *Westward Tilt: The American West Today* (New York: Random House, 1961).

124. Dorothy Lamb Crawford, *Evenings on and off the Roof: Pioneering Concerts in Los Angeles, 1939–1971* (Berkeley: University of California Press, 1995).

125. Hugo Hamilton, "The Santa Fe Opera: A Brief History," *Journal of the West* 22 (July, 1983): 78.

126. Dizikes, *Opera in America,* p. 510.

127. Quoted in Dizikes, *Opera in America,* p. 511.

128. Davis, *A History of Opera in the American West,* pp. 142–47.

129. Jeanette Hayden Hollman, "Oklahoma Composers" (master's thesis, University of Oklahoma, 1941), pp. 32–35.

130. Quoted in John Tasker Howard, *Our American Music* (New York: Thomas Y. Crowell, 1965), p. 436.

131. Ibid., p. 435.

132. Angie Debo, *Oklahoma: Foot Loose and Fancy Free* (Norman: University of Oklahoma Press, 1949), p. 213.

133. John Tasker Howard, *Our Contemporary Composers: American Music in the Twentieth Century* (New York: Thomas Y. Crowell, 1941), pp. 133, 137.

134. Quoted in Davis, *A History of Music in American Life*, 3:172.

135. *Houston Post*, May 9, 1988; Margo Jones, *Theatre-in-the Round* (New York: Holt, Rinehart and Winston, 1951), pp. 40–63.

136. Margo Jones to David Stevens, May 20, 1944, quoted in June Bennet Larsen, "Margo Jones: A Life in the Theatre" (Ph.D. diss., City University of New York, 1982), p. 262.

137. Gerald M. Berkowitz, *New Broadways: Theatre across America, 1950–1980* (Totowa, N.J.: Rowman and Littlefield, 1982), pp. 57–59; James Leslie This, "The Old Globe Theatre and Carter Centre Stage, San Diego: An Analytical and Historical Study" (Ph.D. diss., University of Southern California, 1978), pp. 31–35 (quotation is from p. 35).

138. Correspondence with William Inge and Tennessee Williams in 1945 and 1946, Margo Jones Papers, University of Texas Harry Ransom Humanities Research Center, Austin.

139. Quoted in Goodwyn, *Lone-Star Land*, p. 224.

140. Andrews, ed., *Dallas Theater Center*, n.p.

141. Joyce Burke Cory, *The Dallas Theater Center: An Idea That Was Too Big to Die* (Dallas: Dallas Theater Center, 1980), p. 11.

142. Quoted in ibid.

143. Dillon and Tomlinson, *Dallas Architecture*, p. 35.

144. Quoted in Andrews, *Dallas Theater Center*, n.p.

145. Carl John Marder III, "A History of the Development and Growth of the Dallas Theater Center" (Ph.D. diss., University of Kansas, 1972), pp. 263–67; Cory, *The Dallas Theater Center*, p. 4.

146. Nina Jane Stanley, "Nina Vance: Founder and Artistic Director of Houston's Alley Theatre, 1947–1980" (Ph.D. diss., Indiana University, 1990).

147. Quoted in Clifford Pugh, "The Alley Theater Goes to New York," *Texas Journal* 8 (fall/winter, 1985–86): 44.

148. Stanley, "Nina Vance"; Nina Vance, "The Alley Theater — Houston, Texas," *Theatre Arts*, Dec., 1950, pp. 54–55.

149. Quoted in Stanley, "Nina Vance," pp. 1, 2.

150. Ibid., pp. 147–48.

151. Ibid., pp. 149–50.

152. Quoted in Joseph Wesley Zeigler, *Regional Theatre: The Revolutionary Stage* (Minneapolis: University of Minnesota Press, 1973), p. 199.

153. K. Kay Brandes, "Theatrical Activities in Oklahoma City from 1889 to 1964" (master's thesis, University of Oklahoma, 1964); "Oklahoma Theater Center, History, 1972–1982," Mummers Theater Collection, Oklahoma Historical Society, Oklahoma City.

154. Brandes, "Theatrical Activities in Oklahoma City," p. 80.

155. "Oklahoma Acquires a Theatre," *New York Times*, Dec. 4, 1970; "Order of the Day," pamphlet, Mummers Theater Collection, Oklahoma Historical Society; This, "Old Globe Theatre," pp. 81–83.

156. "Oklahoma Theater Center, History, 1972–1982," Mummers Theater Collection, Oklahoma Historical Society.

157. Quoted in "Oklahoma Acquires a Theatre."

158. Lyle Dye, Jr., "Oklahoma Theatre Center," *Players Magazine,* fall/winter, 1974, pp. 6–11, 44–45.

159. Michael Konig, "Phoenix in the 1950s: Urban Growth in the 'Sunbelt,'" *Arizona and the West* 24 (spring, 1982): 25; Moyca Manoil, "The Phoenix Little Theatre," *Arizona Highways,* Jan., 1960, pp. 22–23, 32–35.

160. *Arizona: Its People and Resources* (Tucson: University of Arizona Press, 1972), 321; Sonnichsen, *Tucson,* p. 307.

161. Lucy M. Smith, "The Tulsa Little Theatre," *Wisconsin Idea Theatre Quarterly* 4 (spring, 1950): 8–11.

162. This, "Old Globe Theatre."

163. *Daily Oklahoman* (Oklahoma City), Nov. 15, 1987; Elizabeth P. Myers, *Maria Tallchief: America's Prima Ballerina* (New York: Grossett and Dunlap, 1966); "Talented Tallchief: We Find Our Own Ballerina," *Newsweek,* Oct. 11, 1954, p. 102; Tobi Tobias, *Maria Tallchief* (New York: Thomas Y. Crowell, 1970); Anne Doyle, "Maria and Marjorie Tallchief," manuscript, vertical files, Oklahoma Historical Society, Oklahoma City.

164. *Daily Oklahoman* (Oklahoma City), Nov. 15, 1987.

165. "Talented Tallchief," 102.

166. Walter Terry, "Four Moons: Oklahoma Indian Ballerina Festival," *Saturday Review of Literature,* Nov. 18, 1967, p.61.

167. *Oklahoma Gazette* (Oklahoma City), Mar. 15, 1989.

168. Priestly and Hawkes, *Journey down a Rainbow,* p. 42.

169. Konig, "Phoenix in the 1950s," p. 25.

CHAPTER 6. INSTITUTIONAL CULTURE/CREATING ICONS, 1960–1980

1. Abbott, *The Metropolitan Frontier,* p. xii.

2. Richard M. Bernard and Bradley R. Rice, *Sunbelt Cities: Politics and Growth since World War II,* pp. 8–9.

3. Ibid., p. 201.

4. Malone and Etulain, *The American West,* pp. 254–55.

5. Carol A. O'Connor, "A Region of Cities," in Milner, O'Connor, and Sandweiss, eds., *The Oxford History of the American West,* pp. 556–58.

6. G. Wesley Johnson, "Generations of Elites and Social Change in Phoenix," in Jessie L. Embry and Howard A. Christy, eds., *Community Development in the American West* (Provo, Utah: Charles Redd Center for Western Studies, 1985), pp. 79–110.

7. Richard Etulain, "Contours of Culture in Arizona and the Modern West," in Beth Luey and Noel J. Stone, eds., *Arizona at Seventy-five: The Next Twenty-five Years* (Tucson: Arizona State University Public History Program and the Arizona Historical Society, 1987), p. 42.

8. Harvey Fergusson, "Old Town and New," pp. 84–87, and Ernie Pyle, "Why Albuquerque?," pp. 80–81, both in Hillerman, ed., *The Spell of New Mexico.*

9. Bradford Luckingham, *The Urban Southwest,* p. 108; Warren A. Beck, *New Mexico: A History of Four Centuries* (Norman: University of Oklahoma Press, 1962), pp. 283–84.

10. Winks, "Regionalism in Comparative Perspective," in Robbins, Frank, and Ross, *Regionalism and the Pacific Northwest,* p. 21.

11. Nash, *The American West in the Twentieth Century,* p. 297; Nancie L. González, *The Spanish-Americans of New Mexico,* p. ix; Rennard Strickland, *The Indians in Oklahoma,* p. 6; and Malone and Etulain, *The American West,* pp. 66–67.

12. Quoted in Smith, *Architecture of the United States,* 3:677–79, 693–95.

13. Ibid., p. 694.

14. Lawrence W. Speck, *Landmarks of Texas Architecture,* p. 110.

15. Stephen Fox, *Houston: Architectural Guide,* pp. 26, 40, 231–32.

16. David G. McComb, *Houston: A History* (Austin: University of Texas Press, 1981), pp. 133–35.

17. Fox, *Houston,* p. 235.

18. Quoted in John Pastier, "Texas Architecture: Mythmakers and Realists," *Texas Journal* 8 (fall/winter, 1985–86): 15.

19. Max Apple, "My Real Estate," in Max Apple, ed., *Southwest Fiction* (New York: Bantam Books, 1981), pp. 21–33.

20. Lisa Germany, "Fair or Foul?," *Texas Monthly,* Jan., 1986, p. 254.

21. Pastier, "Texas Architecture," pp. 15–16; Oliver Knight, *Fort Worth: Outpost on the Trinity* (Fort Worth: Texas Christian University Press, 1990), pp. 250–52; Sumner, ed., *Dallasights,* p. 174; W. H. Timmons, ed., *Four Centuries at the Pass* (El Paso: City of El Paso, 1981), p. 112.

22. Bradford Luckingham, "Urban Development in Arizona: The Rise of Phoenix," *Journal of Arizona History* 22 (summer, 1981): 198; "Phoenix Civic Plaza," *Arizona Architect* 15 (July-Aug., 1972): 13–17; Carol Osman Brown, "Phoenix 1975: A City of Builders," *Arizona Highways,* May, 1975, pp. 4–7, 10–13; *A Guide to The Architecture of Metro Phoenix* (Phoenix: Central Arizona Chapter of the American Institute of Architects, 1983), p. 127; *Arizona Republic* (Phoenix), Feb. 27, 1983.

23. "Tempe Municipal Building," *Arizona Architect* 14 (Sept.-Oct., 1971): 14–15.

24. "Super Structure for Tucson," *Builder Architect Contractor Engineer* 38 (Jan., 1976): 24–25; "Super Structure," *Tucson,* Jan., 1977, pp. 59–62; John Bret Harte, *Tucson: The Story of a Desert Pueblo* (Woodland Hills, Calif.: Windsor Publications, 1980), p. 161.

25. Smith, *Architecture of the United States,* 3:575–76, 570–71; Henderson, Parman, and Henderson, *Architecture in Oklahoma,* p. 170.

26. Wesley Howard Henderson, "Two Case Studies of African-American Architects' Careers in Los Angeles, 1890–1945: Paul R. Williams, FAIA, and James H. Garrott, AIA" (Ph.D. diss., University of California, Los Angeles, 1992).

27. Sandra D. Lynn, "Architect's Design Solutions Help Shape the State," *New Mexico Magazine,* Apr., 1992, p. 76.

28. *Albuquerque Journal,* Mar. 10, 1968.

29. Patricia Carr Bowie, "The Cultural History of Los Angeles, 1850–1967: From Rural Backwash to World Center" (Ph.D. diss., University of Southern California, 1980), pp. 349–53, 398–412; Tamara Constance Asseyer, "The Development of the Los Angeles Music Center Project" (master's thesis, University of California, Los Angeles, 1968); Northcutt, *Symphony.*

30. *Los Angeles Times Magazine,* Sept. 10, 1989, p. 10.

31. Quoted in Bowie, "The Cultural History of Los Angeles," p. 438.

32. Berkowitz, *New Broadways,* pp. 66–69.

33. *Los Angeles Times Magazine,* Sept. 10, 1989, p. 10.

34. Bowie, "The Cultural History of Los Angeles," pp. 412–16; Northcutt, *Symphony.*

35. Bryan Carrol Stoneburner, "The Phoenix Symphony Orchestra, 1947–1978: Leadership, Criticism, and Selective Commentary" (master's thesis, Arizona State University, 1981), pp. 33–56.

36. Ibid., p. 41.

37. Ginger Arlington Hutton, "The Phoenix Symphony: At the Crossroads," *Phoenix,* Aug., 1968, pp. 12, 14, 40–41.

38. "Phoenix Symphony's Young Maestro," *Phoenix,* Oct., 1973, pp. 41–43, 78.

39. Stoneburner, "The Phoenix Symphony Orchestra," pp. 61–72.

40. The Anson B. Cotts Papers, Arizona State University Library, Tempe, contain copies of the always-favorable reviews written by Cotts.

41. Luckingham, *Phoenix,* p. 251.

42. *San Diego Sun,* Oct. 25, 1960; *San Diego Union,* June 20, 1966; Records of the Women's Committee, Box 4, San Diego Symphony Orchestra Association Papers, San Diego State University Library; *San Diego Evening Tribune,* Jan. 9, 1965.

43. David Estes and Robert Stock, *The San Diego Symphony: Problems of Institutional Building* (San Diego: School of Public Administration and Urban Studies, San Diego State University, 1978).

44. Minutes of the Board of Directors, Boxes 8 and 10, 1962–1980, San Diego Symphony Orchestra Association Papers; "History of the Old Globe Theatre," manuscript, Old Globe Theater Papers; both in San Diego State University Library.

45. Quoted in Smith, *Architecture of the United States,* 3:679–80.

46. Quoted in McComb, *Houston,* p. 183.

47. Weaver, *Abraham Chavez.*

48. *Tucson Citizen,* Nov. 18, 1978; Sonnichsen, *Tucson,* p. 288; "Tucson Community Center," *Arizona Architect* 15 (Nov.-Dec., 1971): 14–16; Marjorie Sherrill, "William McGlaughlin Plots an Eclectic Season," *Tucson,* Apr., 1982, pp. 22–26.

49. Hart, *Orpheus in the New World,* pp. 239–63; H. Wiley Hitchcock and Stanley Sadie, *The New Grove Dictionary of American Music,* vol. 1 (New York: Macmillan, 1986), p. 26.

50. Chester Rosson and W. L. Taitte, "Fine Tuning," *Texas Monthly,* Dec., 1990, pp. 135–37, 152, 154.

51. Robert I. Giesberg, *Houston Grand Opera: A History; Houston Post,* Sept. 28, 1986; Dizikes, *Opera in America,* pp. 513–14; Sue Dauphin, *Houston by Stages: A History of Theatre in Houston* (Burnet, Tex.: Eakin Press, 1981), p. 281.

52. Roussel, *The Houston Symphony Orchestra,* pp. 160–61.

53. Quoted in Davis, *A History of Opera in the American West,* p. 122.

54. Ibid., p. 131.

55. Dizikes, *Opera in America,* p. 513.

56. Programs and manuscripts, Musical Merit Foundation Scrapbooks, San Diego Historical Society; *San Diego Union,* July 21, 1968; *San Diego Tribune,* Feb. 4, 1967; William Sullivan, "Bravo San Diego Opera," *San Diego Magazine,* May, 1980, p. 186.

57. *San Diego Union,* Oct. 18, 1971.

58. Hilliard Harper, "Arts Grow Despite Some Setbacks," *Los Angeles Times,* newspaper clipping, n.d., San Diego Opera Collection, Box 1, San Diego Historical Society.

59. Skip Hollandsworth, "Music to My Ears," *Texas Monthly,* July, 1985, p. 175.

60. Paul Goldberger, "What Should a Museum Building Be?," *Art News* 74 (Oct., 1975): 37.

61. Brian O'Doherty, "Introduction," *Museums in Crisis,* p. 2.

62. Helen Searing, "International Style: The Crimson Connection" *Progressive Architecture* 63 (Feb., 1982): 88–91.

63. William Valentiner, "The Museum of Tomorrow," in Paul Zucker, ed., *New Architecture and City Planning* (New York: Philosophical Library, 1944), p. 656. For an extended discussion of the value of the new approach by one of its practioners, see Philip C. Johnson, "American Museum Architecture," *Indian Architect* 5 (June, 1963): 32–34, 37–38.

64. Herbert Katz and Marjorie Katz, *Museums, U.S.A.: A History and Guide* (Garden City: Doubleday and Company, 1965); Roberto Aloi, *Musei: Architettura-Tecnica* (Milano: Ulrico Hoepli, 1962), pp. 167–69; Saarinen, *The Proud Possessors;* Daniel M. Fox, *Engines of Culture: Philanthropy and Art Museums* (Madison: State Historical Society of Wisconsin, 1963), pp. 1–2, 5, 27; Eugene Smolensky, "Municipal Financing of U.S. Fine Arts Museums: A Historical Rationale," *Journal of Economic History* 46 (Sept., 1986): 757–68; Lewis Mumford, *Sticks and Stones* (New York: Dover Publications, 1955), p. 150.

65. Germain Bazin, *The Museum Age* (New York: Universe Books, 1967), p. 261.

66. Edward J. Sozanski, "The Menil Collection," *Bryan–College Station (Texas) Eagle,* Oct. 16, 1987.

67. News release, June 30, 1986, Amon Carter Museum, Fort Worth, Texas; Linda Ayres et al., *American Paintings: Selections from The Amon Carter Museum* (Birmingham: Oxmoor House, 1986), pp. vi–vii; John M. Jacobus, Jr., *Philip Johnson* (New York: George Braziller, 1982), pp. 39–40; Charles Noble, *Philip Johnson* (New York: Simon and Schuster, 1972); and Aloi, *Musei,* pp. 492–96. See also Jerry Flemmons, *Amon: The Life of Amon Carter, Sr., of Texas* (Austin: Jenkins Publishing Company, 1978).

68. William H. Goetzmann and William N. Goetzmann, *The West of the Imagination.*

69. *Annual Report,* Sid Richardson Foundation, Fort Worth, Texas, 1985; Jan Brenneman, director of the Richardson Collection, quoted in typescript, "Sid Richardson Collection of Western Art," brochure, Richardson Collection, Fort Worth.

70. "Kay Kimbell," personal data sheet, n.d., library, Kimbell Art Museum, Fort Worth, Texas; *Kimbell Art Museum: Handbook of the Collection* (Fort Worth: Kimbell Art Foundation, 1981), pp. viii–ix; Thomas Hoving, "Money and Masterpieces: Rating the Acquisitions of the Two Richest Museums," *Connoisseur* 216 (Dec., 1986): 92–99; Heinz Ronner et al., *Louis I. Kahn: Complete Works, 1935–1974* (Boulder, Colo.: Westview Press, 1977), pp. 343–51; Lawrence W. Speck, "Evaluation: The Kimbell Museum," *AIA Journal* 71 (Aug., 1982): 36–43; Catherine Chadwick, "The Museum," *Texas Monthly,* Jan., 1986, p. 242. See also *In Pursuit of Quality: The Kimbell Art Museum — An Illustrated History of the Art and Architecture* (Fort Worth: Kimbell Art Foundation, 1987).

71. Quoted in Ronner et al., *Louis I. Kahn,* p. 345.

72. Quoted in Nell E. Johnson, comp., *Light Is the Theme: Louis I. Kahn and the Kimbell Art Museum* (Fort Worth: Kimbell Art Foundation, 1975), p. 28.

73. Thomas Hoving, "A Gem of a Museum," *Connoisseur* 210 (May, 1982): 90.

74. Quoted in Phil Patton, "Japan's Best Architect Gives Los Angeles a Great Museum," *Connoisseur* 216 (Nov., 1986): 125.

75. "Kay Kimbell," personal data sheet; *Kimbell Art Museum Catalogue* (Fort Worth: Kimbell Art Museum, 1972), pp. iii–iv; Chadwick, "The Museum," p. 242.

76. Hoving, "A Gem of a Museum," 88; Edmund Pillsbury, "Recent Painting Acquisitions: The Kimbell Art Museum," *Burlington Magazine* 124 (Jan., 1982): i–vii; Emily J. Sano, "Recent Asian Acquisitions: The Kimbell Museum," *Burlington Magazine* 126 (Jan., 1984): i–viii; Meyer, *The Art Museum*, pp. 159–60.

77. Philip C. Curtis, "The Phoenix Art Center," in Francis V. O'Connor, ed., *Art For the Millions* (Greenwich, Conn.: Graphic Society, 1973), pp. 221–23; "Historical Overview of the Phoenix Art Museum," and James K. Ballinger, "Phoenix Art Museum," manuscripts in the files of the Phoenix Art Museum Library, Phoenix, Arizona; Marcus Whiffen, *American Architecture since 1780: A Guide to the Styles* (Cambridge: MIT Press, 1969), pp. 263–68; *Arizona Republic* (Phoenix), Nov. 15, 1959.

78. Carleton Knight III, *Philip Johnson/John Burgee: Architecture, 1979–1985* (New York: Rizzoli, 1985), pp. 168–69.

79. Quoted in Paula Eyrich Tyler and Ron Tyler, *Texas Museums: A Guidebook* (Austin: University of Texas Press, 1983), p. 49.

80. Robert V. Rozelle, Steven A. Nash, and David T. Owsley, *The Wendy and Emery Reves Collection* (Dallas: Dallas Museum of Fine Arts, 1985); *Houston Post*, Dec. 7, 1985.

81. Rozelle, Nash, and Owsley, *The Wendy and Emery Reves Collection;* Helen Dudar, "An Art-Filled Villa Finds a Special Setting in Texas," *Smithsonian*, Jan., 1987, pp. 50–59; *The Wendy and Emery Reves Collection at the Dallas Museum of Art* (Dallas: Dallas Museum of Art, 1986); Clifford Pugh, "Wendy Reves," *Houston Post*, Dec. 29, 1985.

82. Bywaters, *Seventy-Five Years of Art in Dallas;* Anne R. Bromberg, *Dallas Museum of Fine Arts: Selected Works* (Dallas: Dallas Museum of Fine Arts, 1983); Helen Searing, *New American Art Museums* (New York: Whitney Museum of American Art, 1982), pp. 89–91.

83. Quoted in Julie Vorman, "Texas Aims to Strike It Rich Culturally with Museums," *Houston Post*, Dec. 7, 1985.

84. Meyer, *The Art Museum*, p. 154.

85. Ibid., p. 158.

86. "The Norton Simon Museum of Art at Pasadena," *Connoisseur* 193 (Nov., 1976): 161–240; "Norton Simon Museum of Art," brochure, and "Historical Sketch" in "Dedication of the Pasadena Museum, November 24, 1969," Norton Simon Museum of Art files, Pasadena, California.

87. J. Paul Getty, *How to Be Rich* (New York: Playboy Press, 1965); J. Paul Getty, *As I See It: The Autobiography of J. Paul Getty* (Englewood Cliffs, N.J.: Prentice-Hall, 1976); *Handbook of the Collections of the J. Paul Getty Museum* (Malibu: J. Paul Getty Museum, 1986), pp. 1–10; Robert Lenzner, *The Great Getty: The Life and Loves of J. Paul Getty, Richest Man in the World* (New York: Crown Publishers, 1986), pp. 178–96.

88. Getty quoted in David Gebhard and Robert Winter, *Architecture in Los Angeles: A Complete Guide* (Salt Lake City: Peregrine Smith Books, 1985), p. 38.

89. *Handbook of the Collections of the J. Paul Getty Museum*, pp. vii–ix; "Building for the

Future," *J. Paul Getty Trust Bulletin* 1 (fall, 1986); Helen Dudar, "Onward, Upward, and Westward with the Fine Arts," *Smithsonian,* June, 1986, pp. 96–97. For critical comments, see Lenzner, *The Great Getty,* pp. 178–96; David Shaw, "J. Paul Getty's Dream Museum: Critics Pan It, Public Loves It," *Smithsonian,* May, 1974, pp. 28–35.

90. Cheryl A. Brutvan et al., *In Our Time: Houston's Contemporary Arts Museum, 1948–1982;* Meyer, *The Art Museum,* p. 131; Peter C. Papademetriou, "Varied Reflections in Houston," *Progressive Architecture* 56 (Mar., 1975): 52–57.

CHAPTER 7. A RENAISSANCE WITH MANY VOICES, 1960–80

1. Jules Langsner, "America's Second Art City," *Art in America* 51 (Mar.–Apr., 1963): 128.

2. Richard Armstrong, *Sculpture in California, 1975–1980* (San Diego: San Diego Museum of Art, 1980); Richard Cándida Smith, *Utopia and Dissent: Art, Poetry, and Politics in California.*

3. Michael Ennis, "Local Color," *Texas Monthly,* Feb., 1993, pp. 212–15.

4. Michael Ennis, "Double Visions," *Texas Monthly,* Nov., 1991, pp. 76, 78, 80, 82, 84.

5. Michael Ennis, "Rauschenberg Relics," *Texas Monthly,* Feb., 1986, pp. 126, 128–29.

6. Rennard Strickland, "Where Have All The Blue Deer Gone? Depth and Diversity in Post-War Indian Painting," *American Indian Art Magazine* 10 (spring, 1985): 36–45; Brody, *Indian Painters and White Patrons,* p. 160.

7. Patricia Janis Broder, *Hopi Painting: The World of the Hopi.*

8. Joshua Charles Taylor et al., *Fritz Scholder* (New York: Rizzoli International Publications, 1982), p. 277; Brody, *Indian Painters and White Patrons,* pp. 203–204.

9. Quoted in Highwater, *Song from the Earth,* p. 96.

10. Quoted in Taylor et al., *Fritz Scholder,* p. 350.

11. Jamake Highwater, "Controversy in Native American Art," in Wade, ed., *The Arts of the North American Indian,* pp. 238–41.

12. Quoted in Highwater, *Song from the Earth,* p. 119. See also *Two American Indian Painters: Fritz Scholder and T. C. Cannon* (Washington: Smithsonian Press, 1972).

13. Quoted in Barbara H. Perlman, *Allan Houser (Ha-o-zous),* p. 12.

14. Ibid., p. 52.

15. Ibid., p. 46. See also Willie Jordan Misner, "An Evaluation of Art Activity in Oklahoma during Its First Twenty Years of Statehood" (master's thesis, University of Oklahoma, 1940), p. 67.

16. Stephen Parks, *R. C. Gorman: A Portrait* (Boston: New York Graphic Society, 1983), pp. 33, 38.

17. Quoted in ibid.

18. Jacinto Quirarte, "Mexicans and Mexican American Artists in the United States, 1920–1970," in Luis R. Cancel, ed., *The Latin American Spirit: Arts and Artists in the United States, 1920–1970,* p. 64; Michael Ennis, "Moving Pictures," *Texas Monthly,* July, 1993, pp. 52, 54–57; Mary Montaño Army, "El Arte," *New Mexico Magazine,* July, 1988, pp. 37–42; Carlos Vélêz-Ibáñez, *Border Visions: Mexican Cultures of the Southwest United States,* p. 244.

19. Quoted in Jacinto Quirarte, *Mexican American Artists,* p. 117.

20. John Beardsley, Jane Livingston, and Octavio Paz, *Hispanic Art in the United States* (New York: Abbeville Press, 1987), pp. 190, 193; Camille Flores-Turney, "Roswell Museum Embraces Cutting-Edge Artists," *New Mexico Magazine*, May, 1997, pp. 44–49; Eva Cockcroft, "The United States and Socially Concerned Latin American Art," in Cancel, ed., *The Latin American Spirit*, p. 220; Michael James Riley, "Picturing the Southwest Reframed: An American Cultural Landscape and the Social Negotiation of Art, Ethnicity, and Place" (Ph.D. diss., University of Texas, 1993), pp. 154–64; Gregory Curtis, "Art," *Texas Monthly*, May, 1997, p. 46.

21. Cockcroft, "The United States and Socially Concerned Latin American Art," p. 220; Quirarte, *Mexican American Artists*, pp. 80–85.

22. Quoted in Cockcroft, "The United States and Socially Concerned Latin American Art," p. 220.

23. Quoted in Quirarte, *Mexican American Artists*, p. 85.

24. Quoted in Marianne L. Stoller, "Peregrinas with Many Visions: Hispanic Women Artists of New Mexico, Southern Colorado, and Texas," in Norwood and Monk, eds., *The Desert Is No Lady*, pp. 125–45.

25. *Austin American-Statesman*, May 25, 1995.

26. Nash and Etulain, eds., *The Twentieth Century West*, pp. 361–63.

27. James W. Byrkit, "Land, Sky, and People: The Southwest Defined," *Journal of the Southwest* 34 (autumn, 1992): 270–72.

28. Edward Abbey, quoted in Cynthia Farah, *Literature and Landscape: Writers of the Southwest* (El Paso: Texas Western Press, 1988), p. 2.

29. Quoted in William T. Pilkington, "Edward Abbey," in Vinson, ed., *Twentieth-Century Western Writers*, p. 8.

30. Edward Abbey, *Fire on the Mountain* (New York: Avon Books, 1982).

31. Ann Ronald, "Edward Abbey," in Erisman and Etulain, eds., *Fifty Western Writers*, pp. 3–4, 8.

32. Edward Abbey, *Desert Solitare: A Season in the Wilderness* (New York: McGraw-Hill, 1968), p. 277.

33. George Walsh, "William Eastlake," in Vinson, ed., *Twentieth-Century Western Writers*, pp. 257–59.

34. Gerald Haslam, "William Eastlake," in Erisman and Etulain, eds., *Fifty Western Writers*, pp. 89–90.

35. William Eastlake, *Go in Beauty* (New York: Harper, 1956), p. 1.

36. William Eastlake, *Dancers in the Scalp House* (New York: Viking Press, 1975).

37. Jon Bowman, "John Nichols: Taos Author Savors Life on the Edge," *New Mexico Magazine*, Jan., 1988, p. 41.

38. Balassi, Crawford, and Eysturoy, eds., *This Is about Vision*, p. 119.

39. Deborah Aydt, "An Interview with John Nichols," *El Palacio* 90 (1984): 58.

40. David King Dunaway and Sara L. Spurgeon, *Writing the Southwest* (New York: Plume/Penguin Books USA, 1995), p. 125.

41. John Nichols, *The Milagro Beanfield War*, excerpted in Max Apple, ed., *Southwest Fiction* (New York: Bantam Books, 1981), p. 222.

42. John Nizalowski, "N. Scott Momaday," *New Mexico Magazine*, Aug., 1990, pp. 21–25;

Balassi, Crawford, and Eysturoy, *This Is about Vision,* pp. 59, 66; Erisman and Etulain, eds., *Fifty Western Writers,* pp. 313–15.

43. Matthias Schubnell, *N. Scott Momaday: The Cultural and Literary Background* (Norman: University of Oklahoma Press, 1985), p. 9.

44. Quoted in ibid., p. 18.

45. Quoted in Richard Mahler, "Momaday Emerging as a True Renaissance Artist," *New Mexico Magazine,* Oct., 1992, p. 19.

46. N. Scott Momaday, "American Indian Literature," in Charlotte Heth and Michael Swarm, eds., *Sharing a Heritage: American Indian Arts* (Los Angeles: American Indian Studies Center, University of California, 1984), p. 177.

47. Quoted in Farah, *Literature and Landscape,* p. 56.

48. Per Seyersted, *Leslie Marmon Silko,* Western Writers Series no. 45 (Boise: Boise State University, 1980).

49. Quoted in ibid., p. 15.

50. Alan R. Velie, *Four American Indian Literary Masters,* pp. 106–107.

51. Quoted in Seyersted, *Leslie Marmon Silko,* p. 39.

52. Vera L. Norwood, "Thank You for My Bones: Connections between Contemporary Women Artists and the Traditional Arts of Their Foremothers," in Joan M. Jensen and Darlis A. Miller, eds., *New Mexico Women: Intercultural Perspectives* (Albuquerque: University of New Mexico Press, 1986).

53. Leslie Marmon Silko, "Landscape, History, and the Pueblo Imagination," *Anateus* 57 (autumn, 1986): 84.

54. Jo Ann Baldinger, "The Write Stuff: Place Continues to Shape the Written Word," *New Mexico Magazine,* Mar., 1994, p. 23.

55. Dunaway and Spurgeon, *Writing the Southwest,* pp. 142–43, 150–51.

56. Quoted in Farah, *Literature and Landscape,* p. 32.

57. Ibid. See also Baldinger, "The Write Stuff," p. 20, and Balassi, Crawford, and Eysturoy, *This Is about Vision,* p. 171.

58. Jo Ann Baldinger, "Navajo Poet: Tapahonso Holds Home in Her Heart," *New Mexico Magazine,* Aug., 1992, p. 31.

59. Ibid., p. 32.

60. Quoted in Farah, *Literature and Landscape,* p. 86. See also Balassi, Crawford, and Eysturoy, *This Is about Vision,* pp. 195, 197.

61. Quoted in Dunaway and Spurgeon, *Writing the Southwest,* p. 86.

62. Quoted in Balassi, Crawford, and Eysturoy, *This Is about Vision,* p. 144.

63. Ibid., p. 145. See also Dunaway and Spurgeon, *Writing the Southwest,* pp. 78–79, 86–87.

64. Raymund A. Paredes, "The Evolution of Chicano Literature," *Melus* 5 (summer, 1978): 71–110.

65. Ibid., pp. 89–93.

66. Tomás Rivera, "Chicano Literature: Festival of the Living," *Books Abroad* 49 (1975): 439–52.

67. Paredes, "The Evolution of Chicano Literature," p. 104.

68. Cecil Robinson, *Mexico and the Hispanic Southwest in American Literature* (Tucson: University of Arizona Press, 1977), pp. 308–31; Vélêz-Ibâñez, *Border Visions,* pp. 213–14.

69. Chávez, *The Lost Land*.

70. Vernon E. Lattin, "The City in Contemporary Chicano Fiction," *Studies in American Fiction* 6 (spring, 1978): 93–100.

71. Amado Muro, "Maria Tepache," in Ludwig Santibanez and James Santibanez, eds., *The Chicanos* (Baltimore: Penguin Books, 1971), p. 130.

72. Matt S. Meier and Feliciano Rivera, *The Chicanos: A History of Mexican Americans* (New York: Hill and Wang, 1972), pp. 8–9.

73. Quoted in Juan D. Bruce-Novoa, *Chicano Authors: Inquiry by Interview* (Austin: University of Texas Press, 1980), p. 184.

74. Ibid., p. 185.

75. Ibid., p. 186.

76. Rudolfo Anaya, *Bless Me, Ultima* (Berkeley: TQS Publications, 1972).

77. Rudolfo Anaya, *Alburquerque* (New York: Warner Books, 1994), p. 171.

78. Ibid., p. 67.

79. Paredes, "The Evolution of Chicano Literature," pp. 101–102.

80. James Ward Lee, *Classics of Texas Fiction* (Dallas: E-Heart Press, 1987), p. 67; Carlota Cárdenas de Dwyer, "Cultural Regionalism and Chicano Literature," *Western American Literature* 15 (fall, 1980): 187–94; Bruce-Novoa, *Chicano Authors,* pp. 49–65.

81. Quoted in Farah, *Literature and Landscape,* p. 36. For a recent interpretation, see Joyce Glover Lee, *Rolando Hinojosa and the American Dream*.

82. Fabiola Cabeza de Baca, *We Fed Them Cactus* (Albuquerque: University of New Mexico, 1979), pp. 1–3.

83. Quoted in Dunaway and Spurgeon, *Writing the Southwest,* p. 32.

84. Quoted in Farah, *Literature and Landscape,* p. 18. See also William B. Martin, "Emerging from the Wings: Texas Women Dramatists," in Grider and Rodenberger, eds., *Texas Women Writers,* pp. 336–37.

85. Américo Paredes and Raymund Paredes, *Mexican-American Authors* (Boston: Houghton-Mifflin, 1972), pp. 8, 17.

86. Bruce-Novoa, *Chicano Authors,* pp. 203–18; Olivia Castellano, "Of Charity and the Moon: A Study of Two Women in Rebellion," *De Colores* 3 (1977): 25–29.

87. Anaya, *Alburquerque,* p. 154.

88. Richard Bradford, *Red Sky at Morning* (Philadelphia: J. G. Lippincott, 1968), p. 22. See also Scotty King, "Richard Bradford: Gray Sky at Morning," *New Mexico Magazine,* Feb., 1980, pp. 48–49.

89. Bill Brammer, *The Gay Place* (Boston: Houghton-Mifflin, 1961).

90. Thomas Thompson, *Celebrity* (New York: Doubleday and Company, 1982).

91. S. E. Hinton, *The Outsiders* (New York: Viking Press, 1967); S. E. Hinton, *Rumble Fish* (New York: Delacorte Press, 1975); S. E. Hinton, *That Was Then, This Is Now* (New York: Viking Press, 1971).

92. John Graves to Gordon Lish, Apr. 23, 1966, John Graves Papers, University of Texas Harry Ransom Humanities Research Center, Austin.

93. Graves to Lish, Jan. 25, 1964, ibid.

94. James W. Lee, "Benjamin Capps," in Erisman and Etulain, eds., *Fifty Western Writers,* pp. 42–43.

95. Lee, *Classics of Texas Fiction,* pp. 31–33; manuscripts and research notes for *Twilight of*

Honor, Al Dewlin Papers, University of Oklahoma Western History Collection, Norman.

96. Quoted in Vinson, ed., *Twentieth-Century Western Writers,* p. 279.

97. Mark Royden Winchell, *Joan Didion* (Boston: Twayne Publishers, 1989).

98. Joan Didion, *Play It As It Lays* (New York: Bantam Books, 1971), p. 14.

99. Dorys C. Grover, "Elmer Kelton," in Erisman and Etulain, eds., *Fifty Western Writers,* pp. 237–39.

100. Elmer Kelton, *The Time It Never Rained* (Garden City: Doubleday, 1973).

101. Elmer Kelton, *The Wolf and the Buffalo* (Garden City: Doubleday, 1980).

102. Quoted in Anne Dingus, "The Good Old Boy," *Texas Monthly,* Dec., 1995, p. 88.

103. Kerry Ahearn, "Larry McMurtry," in Erisman and Etulain, eds., *Fifty Western Writers,* pp. 280–83.

104. Larry McMurtry, "A Novelist of Characters and Place," *Humanities Interview* 7 (summer, 1989): 2.

105. "Dallas, 1962," mimeograph copy, Larry McMurtry Papers, University of Texas Harry Ransom Humanities Research Center, Austin.

106. McMurtry to David Meltzer, June 11, 1961, Larry McMurtry Papers, University of Texas Center for American History, Austin.

107. Larry McMurtry, "The Texas Moon and Elsewhere," *Atlantic Monthly,* Mar., 1975, pp. 29–36.

108. McMurtry to Dorthea Oppenheimer, Nov. 20, 1964, McMurtry Papers, University of Texas Harry Ransom Humanities Research Center; *Houston Post,* Oct. 30, 1966.

109. *Houston Post,* Oct. 30, 1966.

110. Patricia O'Connor, "Chief of Detectives: Unraveling the Mystery of Tony Hillerman," *Spirit,* May, 1992, pp. 31–33, 44, 46–67.

111. "Vita," Tony Hillerman Papers, Zimmerman Library, University of New Mexico, Albuquerque.

112. "Conversation with Tony Hillerman," ibid.

113. Tony Hillerman, "Mystique of the Land," *New Mexico Magazine,* Jan., 1987, p. 39.

114. Apple, *Southwest Fiction,* p. ix.

115. Ibid., p. xix.

116. *A Literary History of the American West* (Fort Worth: Western Literature Association, 1987), p. 1239.

117. Preston Jones, *A Texas Trilogy* (New York: Hill and Wang, 1976), n.p.

118. Program Notes, "The Oldest Living Graduate," Kennedy Center, Washington, D.C., 1976.

119. Quoted in Mark Busby, *Preston Jones,* Western Writers Series (Boise: Boise State University, 1983), pp. 14, 15.

120. Margaret B. Wilkerson, "The Black Theatre Experience: PASLA," in Dunbar H. Ogden, Douglas McDermott, and Robert K. Sarlós, eds., *Theatre West: Image and Impact* (Amsterdam: Rodopi, 1990), pp. 69–83; Patterson Greene, "Theatre US: Los Angeles," *Theatre Arts* 45 (June, 1961): 66–71.

121. Gail Leo Shoup, Jr., "The Pasadena Community Playhouse: Its Origins and History from 1917 to 1942" (Ph. D. diss., University of California, Los Angeles, 1968).

122. Diane Alexander, *Playhouse* (Los Angeles: Dorleac-MacLeish, 1984), pp. 151–68.

123. "History of the Old Globe Theatre," typescript, n.d.; press release, June 11, 1979; "Ten Year Plan, 1978"; file on reconstruction, Box 7; all in Old Globe Theater Papers, San Diego State University Library.

124. Alice Gordon, "Eugene O'Neill," *Texas Monthly*, Jan., 1986, p. 153; Henry Hewes, "Broadway Postscript: 'Father Courage,'" *Saturday Review of Literature*, June 4, 1960, p. 30; Jerome Weeks, "Alley Theatre Dominates in Houston While Others Struggle to Survive," *Dallas Morning News*, Aug. 18, 1991.

125. Smith, *Architecture of the United States*, 3:681–82; Weeks, "Alley Theatre Dominates in Houston."

126. Earl L. Dachslager, "Shakespeare at the Globe of the Southwest," in Kolin, ed., *Shakespeare in the South*, pp. 264–77.

127. Quoted in Jones, ed., *New Mexico Plays*, p. 15. See also Jorge A. Huerta, "Labor Theatre, Street Theatre, and Community Theatre in the Barrios, 1965–1983," in Kanellos, ed., *Hispanic Theatre in the United States*, pp. 62–70.

128. "Brief History of the Houston Ballet," files, Houston Ballet, Houston, Texas.

129. "Goals for El Paso: A Position Paper," manuscript, Southwest Collection, El Paso Public Library, El Paso, Texas; "History of Ballet El Paso," files, Ballet El Paso, El Paso, Texas.

130. Allied Arts Council Files, Mummers Theater Collection, Oklahoma Historical Society, Oklahoma City; K. Kay Brandes, "Theatrical Activities in Oklahoma City from 1889 to 1964" (master's thesis, University of Oklahoma, 1964).

131. *Tucson Star*, Feb. 22, 1986; *Arizona Daily Star* (Tucson), Mar. 7, 1992.

132. John Davidson, "The Empress of Fort Worth," *Texas Monthly*, Feb., 1987, pp. 80–85, 130–33.

133. "Ballet Dallas Organizational History," manuscript, Ballet Dallas files, Dallas, Texas.

CHAPTER 8. THE EXPORTATION OF A REGIONAL CULTURE, 1980–1995

1. Ada Louise Huxtable, quoted in *Tulsa Art Deco: An Architectural Era*, n.p.

2. Rem Koolhaas, *Delirious New York* (New York: Oxford University Press, 1984), p. 72.

3. Lorenzo Thomas, quoted in Gerald Asher, "Houston," *Gourmet* Oct., 1987, pp. 70,72.

4. Quoted in Knight, *Philip Johnson/John Burgee*, pp. 166–87.

5. Ibid., p. 7.

6. Joel Warren Barna, *The See-Through Years: Creation and Destruction in Texas Architecture and Real Estate, 1981–1991*, pp. 9–14; Fox, *Houston*, pp. 30–31.

7. Fox, *Houston*, pp. 235–36; Knight, *Philip Johnson/John Burgee*, 74; Steve Brady, *Presence: The Transco Tower*.

8. Barna, *The See-Through Years*, pp. 3, 4, 14–15.

9. Ibid., pp. 162–67.

10. Thomas Hine, "Philip Johnson in Texas," *Bryan Eagle*, July 19, 1986; Gregory Curtis, "Behind the Lines," *Texas Monthly*, Nov., 1985, pp. 5–6; Knight, *Philip Johnson/John Burgee*, p. 132.

11. Smith, *Architecture of the United States*, 3:655–56.

12. Quoted in Esther McCoy, *The Second Generation*, pp. xi–xiii.

13. Paul Goldberger, *On The Rise: Architecture and Design in a Post-Modern Age* (New York: New York Times Book Company, 1983), p. 89.

14. Smith, *Architecture of the United States,* 3:119–20.

15. Knight, *Philip Johnson/John Burgee,* pp. 7–8, 16; Paul Goldberger, "Raising the Architectural Ante in California," *New York Times,* Oct. 14, 1990.

16. *Houston Post,* Jan. 24, 1987.

17. Allison Lurie, *The Nowhere City* (New York: Coward-McCann, 1965), pp. 14, 3–4.

18. Michael Ennis, "Post-Modern Times: Shoot-out at First and Congress," *Texas Monthly,* Sept., 1986, pp. 14, 16; "Austin," *Texas Monthly,* Dec., 1986, pp. 207–23; Douglas Davis, "Raiders of the Lost Arch," *Newsweek,* Jan. 20, 1986, pp. 66–68; Barna, *The See-Through Years,* pp. 140–46.

19. David Dillon, "Darth Vader at the O. K. Corral," *Architecture* 72 (Nov., 1983): 66–67.

20. *Houston Post,* July 8, 1987.

21. "Around the State," *Texas Monthly,* June, 1995, p. 16; "You Say Tomato, I Say I Hate It," *Newsweek,* Feb. 27, 1995, p. 7; Jan Russell, "Seeing Red," *Texas Monthly,* Nov., 1995, p. 16.

22. Douglas Davis, *The Museum Transformed* (New York: Abbeville Press, 1990), p. 209.

23. *Tucson Star,* July 23, 1986.

24. V. B. Price, *A City at the End of the World* (Albuquerque: University of New Mexico Press, 1992), p. 37.

25. Quoted in Christopher Mead, *Houses by Bart Prince: An American Architecture for the Continuous Present,* p. 4.

26. Ibid., p. 16.

27. Ibid., p. 11.

28. *Tucson Citizen,* Oct. 8, 1985.

29. Grace Glueck, "The de Menil Family: The Medici of Modern Art," *New York Times,* May 18, 1986.

30. Quoted in Jacqueline M. Pontello, "Graffiti," *Southwestern Art* 17 (June, 1987): 12.

31. Dominique de Menil quoted in "Comments on the Menil Collection and Museum," typescript, the Menil Collection, Houston, Texas.

32. Quoted in Clifford Pugh, "The Magnificent Obsession," *Houston Post,* May 31, 1987.

33. E. M. Farrelly, "Piano Practice: Picking up the Pieces (and Running with Them)," *Architectural Review* 181 (Mar., 1987): 34.

34. Bertrand Davezac, "The Museum of the Menil Collection," manuscript; "Renzo Piano," manuscript; and "The Menil Collection: The Museum," manuscript; all in Menil Collection; *Houston Post,* Nov. 23, 1986.

35. Dominique de Menil quoted in Susan Chadwick, "Sneak Peek," *Houston Post,* June 4, 1987. See also Michael Ennis, "Art: New Kid on the Block," *Texas Monthly,* June, 1987, pp. 142–45; Cathleen McGuigan, "A Private Passion for Art," *Newsweek,* June 15, 1987, pp. 68–69; "Houston Comes to Paris," *Newsweek,* Apr. 23, 1984, pp. 60–62; and Ann Holmes, "Dominique de Menil: From Jeune Fille to 'Renaissance Woman,'" *Art News* (Jan., 1983), pp. 80–85.

36. *New York Times,* June 14, 1987; *Wall Street Journal,* June 16, 1987.

37. Cathleen McGuigan, "A Place in the Sun," *Newsweek,* Oct. 13, 1997, p. 73.

38. Cathleen McGuigan, "A Lavish Place in the Sun," *Newsweek,* Oct. 21, 1991, p. 64.

39. *Cleveland Plain Dealer,* June 12, 1989; *Houston Post,* Jan. 22, 1988.

40. William R. Wilson, *The Los Angeles Times Book of California Museums* (New York: Harry N. Abrams, 1984), p. 210; "An Introduction to the Virginia Steele Scott Gallery of American Art," files of the Huntington Library, Art Collection, and Botanical Gardens, San Marino, California.

41. "Biography: Arata Isozaki," "Interview of Arata Isozaki, April 30, 1986," "A History of the Museum, September 29, 1986," "The MOCA Building," and Sherri Geldin, "One Very Lucky Museum," all in the files of the Museum of Contemporary Art, Los Angeles, California.

42. Geldin, "One Very Lucky Museum."

43. *Los Angeles Times,* May 23, 1986.

44. *New York Times,* Oct. 26, 1986.

45. As examples, see the following: Cathleen McGuigan and Janet Huck, "Picasso in Lala Land," *Newsweek,* Nov. 24, 1986, pp. 86–88; Joseph Giovannini, "Arata Isozaki: From Japan a New Wave of International Architects," *New York Times Magazine,* Aug. 12, 1986, pp. 27–31, 53, 62, 65; and Helen Duda, "Onward, Upward, and Westward with the Fine Arts," *Smithsonian,* June, 1986, pp. 91–92.

46. Wilson, *Los Angeles Times Book of California Museums,* pp. 17, 137–38; Earl A. Powell III, "A Master Plan for a New Museum," *Apollo,* Nov., 1986, pp. 12–13; "Robert O. Anderson Building," brochure, Los Angeles County Museum of Art, Los Angeles.

47. *Los Angeles Times,* May 23, 1986.

48. Douglas Davis, "Winging It: Does Adding On Add Up," *Newsweek,* Feb. 23, 1987, p. 71; Davis, "Raiders of the Lost Arch," pp. 66–68.

49. *Los Angeles Times,* Nov. 15, 1987.

50. William Boot, "LACMA Loses Its Way," *Buzz,* Dec./Jan., 1995, pp. 70–75, 125.

51. "Museum of Art," manuscript, library, San Antonio Museum of Art, San Antonio, Texas; Richard L. Tuve, "The San Antonio Museum of Art: The Adaptive Re-use of the Old Lone Star Brewery," *Technology and Conservation* 5 (winter, 1980): 31; "San Antonio Museum of Art," *Interior Design,* July, 1981, pp. 194–203; Arbon Jack Lowe, "The San Antonio Museum of Art," *Americas* 35 (May/June, 1983): 42–45.

52. "Austin," *Texas Monthly,* Dec., 1986, pp. 207–23; *Houston Post,* Jan. 9, 1988; *Austin American,* May 25, 1994.

53. Rebecca S. Cohen, "Art Beat," *Texas Monthly,* May, 1997, p. 26.

54. *Texas Journal* 14 (fall/winter, 1991): 37.

55. Kathryn Jones, "Raymond Nasher," *Texas Monthly,* Dec., 1997, p. 105.

56. "Philbrook Museum of Art," Philbrook Museum of Art, Tulsa, Oklahoma; Ree Sheck, "New Museum Opens Doors to Indian Culture," *New Mexico Magazine,* July, 1987, pp. 54–58; George Lang, "A Lasting Legacy," *Oklahoma Gazette,* Nov. 14, 1996.

57. One study shows the relationship of urban design to the evolutionary process of architectural change. See Wayne Attoe and Donn Logan, *American Urban Architecture: Catalysts in the Design of Cities* (Berkeley: University of California Press, 1989).

58. Quoted in *Los Angeles Times,* May 23, 1986.

59. Quoted in Paul Goldberger, "What Should a Museum Building Be?," *Art News* 74 (Oct., 1975): 37.

60. *Cleveland Plain Dealer,* May 25, 1989.

61. *Houston Post,* Mar. 4, 1988.

62. Chester Rosson, "Sound Investments," *Texas Monthly,* Nov., 1989, pp. 140, 142, 144.

63. Ibid.; Barna, *The See-Through Years,* pp. 199–207; Cathleen McGuigan, "The Perfectionist," *Newsweek,* Sept. 25, 1989, pp. 60–64.

64. John Ardoin, "Litton Puts His Imprint on Orchestra," *Dallas Morning News,* May 21, 1995.

65. *Dallas Morning News,* May 29, 1994; *Fort Worth Star-Telegram,* Sept. 28, 1996.

66. *Los Angeles Times,* Feb. 8, 1992.

67. *San Antonio Express-News,* June 1, 1994; Lawrence Wright, "Culture Club," *Texas Monthly,* June, 1987, pp. 118–19, 161–67.

68. Manuscript, n.d., Box 1, File 1, San Diego Opera Collection, San Diego Historical Society; Mark Lusvardi, "A Marketing Study of the San Diego Symphony Orchestra" (master's thesis, San Diego State University, 1983); John Willett, "The Symphony's Foxy Move," *San Diego Magazine,* Apr., 1984, pp. 125–27, 291; *San Diego Union,* Dec. 3, 1985, and Feb. 10, 1991; *New York Times,* June 3, 1987.

69. *Daily Oklahoman* (Oklahoma City), Mar. 19, 1989; *Arizona Republic* (Phoenix), June 1, 1986; *Tucson Citizen,* Apr. 30, 1981; *Arizona Daily Star* (Tucson), Sept. 20, 1987, Dec. 3, 1988; *Albuquerque Journal,* Oct. 21, 1994.

70. "Rite of Passage," *Texas Monthly,* July, 1987, pp. 86–87; Paul Cunningham, "The Worth of the Wortham," *Houston Post,* May 10, 1987.

71. Paul Cunningham, "Curtain Up at Wortham," *Houston Post,* May 3, 1987.

72. *Houston Post,* May 10, 1987.

73. Dizikes, *Opera in America,* pp. 533–34.

74. "Making Music on the Mesa," *Newsweek,* Aug. 11, 1986; San Diego Opera Collection, San Diego Historical Society; "Tucson," *Horizon,* May, 1987, p. 48.

75. *Daily Oklahoman* (Oklahoma City), May 18, 1992; "Tucson," *Horizon,* May, 1987, p. 44; Jon Bowman, "Greer Garson: Actress Takes Leading Role in State's Communication Arts," *New Mexico Magazine,* Nov., 1990, pp. 22–29.

76. *Dallas Morning News,* Aug. 18, 1991; Renee Boensch, "Theatre," *Texas Monthly,* May, 1997, p. 50; *Houston Post,* May 3, 1987.

77. Quoted in Jack Kroll, "Deep in the Heart of Texas," *Newsweek,* Feb. 12, 1996, p. 82.

78. *Dallas Morning News,* Oct. 17, 1993.

79. W. L. Taitte, "Desire and Memory," *Texas Monthly,* Dec., 1985, pp. 200, 202, 203.

80. Patricia R. Williams, "Literary Tradition in Works by African-American Playwrights," in Grider and Rodenberger, eds., *Texas Women Writers,* pp. 253–54.

81. Programs, Pasadena Playhouse, 1990–1991 season; Beth Mohr, "The Old Globe Theatre: Highlights from Fifty Years," *Journal of San Diego History* 31 (spring, 1985): 87–120; *Denver Post,* May 24, 1987.

82. Quoted in Leonard Gross, "L.A.: Let's Take It Seriously," *Condé Nast Traveller,* Sept., 1991, pp. 195–96.

83. Jones, ed., *New Mexico Plays,* pp. 16–17, 82–83.

84. Quoted in Sharon Niederman, "Mark Medoff," *New Mexico Magazine,* Nov., 1988, p. 75.

85. Ibid., p. 77.

86. Balassi, Carpenter, and Eysturoy, eds., *This Is about Vision,* pp. 109, 111.

87. Quoted in Niederman, "Mark Medoff," p. 77.

88. Ibid.

89. Ibid., p. 81.

90. "Brief History of Houston Ballet," files of the Houston Ballet, Houston, Texas.

91. *Houston Post,* Oct., 1985; *Dallas Morning News,* May 21, 1995.

92. *Houston Post,* Sept. 14, 1986.

93. "Ballet Arizona: Company History," files, Ballet Arizona, Phoenix, Arizona.

94. Patrick Bennett, "Laura Furman, Beverly Lowry, and Shelby Hearon," in Grider and Rodenberger, eds., *Texas Women Writers,* pp. 151–54.

95. Shelby Hearon, *Owning Jolene* (New York: Warner Books, 1990), pp. 87–88.

96. Shelby Hearon, *Group Therapy* (New York: Warner Books, 1990).

97. Bennett, "Laura Furman," pp. 151–54.

98. Beverly Lowry, *The Perfect Sonya* (New York: Penguin Books, 1988).

99. Beverly Lowry, "Us," in Rita Saylors, ed., *Liquid City* (San Antonio: Corona Publishing Company, 1987), p. 43.

100. Laura Furman, *The Shadow Line* (New York: Viking Press, 1982); *Houston Post,* Sept. 28, 1986.

101. José David Saldívar, *Border Matters: Remapping American Cultural Studies* (Berkeley: University of California Press, 1997); Vélêz-Ibáñez, *Border Visions.*

102. Mark Stevens, "Devotees of the Fantastic," *Newsweek,* Sept. 7, 1987, pp. 66–68; Michael Ennis, "We Are the World," *Texas Monthly,* Dec., 1995, p. 58; Bradford Luckingham, *Minorities in Phoenix: A Profile of Mexican American, Chinese American, and African American Communities, 1860–1992,* p. 193.

103. John M. Findlay, "Far Western Cityscapes and American Culture since 1940," *Western Historical Quarterly* 22 (Feb., 1991): 40–43.

104. David W. Teague, *The Southwest in American Literature and Art: The Rise of a Desert Aesthetic.*

105. Yi-Fu Tuan, *Topophilia.*

106. For a recent effort to define the West, see Wrobel and Steiner, eds., *Many Wests.*

107. William Viteck and Wes Jackson, eds., *Rooted in the Land: Essays on Community and Place* (New Haven: Yale University Press, 1996), p. 132.

SELECTED BIBLIOGRAPHY

In the course of nearly two decades of research, I examined almost 7,000 manuscript collections, newspaper and vertical files, books, articles, essays, dissertations, and theses. A traditional bibliography would tax not only the patience of the reader but also the resources of the publisher, without suggesting the importance of individual entries. In an effort to provide guidance for those wanting to pursue topics included in the book, I have prepared a bibliography of the most significant manuscript collections and those secondary sources that helped shape the basic themes and interpretations. In the footnotes, scholars will find references to more specific and often fugitive sources.

MANUSCRIPT COLLECTIONS

Arizona State University Library, Tempe
    Grace Alexander Papers
    Anson B. Cotts Papers
El Paso Public Library, El Paso, Texas
    Southwest Collection
Houston Metropolitan Research Center, Houston, Texas
    Leopold L. Meyer Papers
    Houston Symphony Orchestra Scrapbooks
Huntington Library, San Marino, California
    Zoë Akins Papers
    Mary Austin Papers
    Lynden Ellsworth Behymer Papers
    Annie Adams Field Papers
    Theodore Gerson Papers
    Charles Lummis Papers
    Fernand Lungren Papers
    Pasadena Playhouse Papers
    Theodore Van Soelen Papers
Oklahoma Historical Society, Oklahoma City
    Mummers Theater Collection
San Diego Historical Society, San Diego, California
    Musical Merit Foundation Scrapbooks
    Loleta L. Rowan Scrapbook
    San Diego Opera Collection
    Alice Barnett Stevenson Scrapbooks

San Diego State University Library, San Diego, California
  Old Globe Theater Papers
  San Diego Symphony Orchestra Association Papers
Thomas Gilcrease Institute of American History and Art, Tulsa, Oklahoma
  William R. Leigh Collection
Tucson Public Library, Tucson, Arizona
  Tucson and Arizona Cultural Files
University of Arizona Library, Tucson
  Charles Fletcher Lummis Papers.
  Francis Douglas Papers
University of New Mexico, Albuquerque
  Fine Arts Library
    Albuquerque Civic Symphony Orchestra Papers
  Zimmerman Library
    Mary Hunter Austin Papers
    Dorothy Eugenie Brett Papers
    Ross Calvin Papers
    Tony Hillerman Papers
    Mabel Dodge Luhan Papers
    John Marin Papers
    John Gaw Meem Papers
    Eugene Manlove Rhodes Papers
    Frank Waters Papers
University of Oklahoma Western History Collection, Norman
  Al Dewlin Papers
  Oscar B. Jacobson Papers
  Raleigh Lynn Riggs Papers
University of Texas Center for American History, Austin
  Nicholas J. Clayton Papers
  Ephemera Collection
  Larry McMurtry Papers
University of Texas Harry Ransom Humanities Research Center, Austin
  Dorothy Brett Papers
  Witter Bynner Papers
  William Goyen Papers
  John Graves Papers
  Alice Corbin Henderson Papers
  Spud Johnson Papers
  Margo Jones Papers
  Oliver LaFarge Papers
  Larry McMurtry Papers
  George Sessions Perry Papers
  Henry C. Trost Papers
University of Tulsa McFarland Library, Tulsa, Oklahoma
  Alexandre Hogue Papers

Calvin, Ross. *Sky Determines: Interpretation of the Southwest.* New York: Macmillan, 1934.

Cronon, William, George Miles, and Jay Gitlin, eds. *Under an Open Sky: Rethinking America's Western Past.* New York: W. W. Norton, 1992.

Davis, Ronald L. *A History of Opera in the American West.* Englewood Cliffs, N.J.: Prentice-Hall, 1965.

Deutsch, Sarah. *No Separate Refuge: Culture, Class, and Gender on an Anglo-Hispanic Frontier in the American Southwest, 1880–1940.* New York: Oxford University Press, 1987.

Doughty, Robin W. *At Home in Texas: Early Views of the Land.* College Station: Texas A&M University Press, 1987.

Etulain, Richard W. *Re-Imagining the Modern American West: A Century of Fiction, History, and Art.* Tucson: University of Arizona Press, 1996.

Johnson, Michael L. *New Westers: The West in Contemporary American Culture.* Lawrence: University Press of Kansas, 1996.

Levine, Lawrence W. *Highbrow/Lowbrow: The Emergence of Cultural Hierarchy in America.* Cambridge: Harvard University Press, 1988.

Limerick, Patricia. *The Legacy of Conquest: The Unbroken Past of the American West.* New York: W. W. Norton and Company, 1987.

Meinig, D. W. *Southwest: Three Peoples in Geographical Change.* New York: Oxford University Press, 1971.

Milner, Clyde A., II., Carol A. O'Connor, and Martha A. Sandweiss, eds. *The Oxford History of the American West.* New York: Oxford University Press, 1994.

Paul, Rodman W. *The Far West and the Great Plains in Transition, 1859–1900.* New York: Harper and Row, 1988.

Powell, Lawrence Clark. *Southwest Classics: The Creative Literature of the Arid Lands.* Los Angeles: Ward Ritchie Press, 1974.

Teague, David W. *The Southwest in American Literature and Art: The Rise of a Desert Aesthetic.* Tucson: University of Arizona Press, 1997.

Tuan, Yi-Fu. *Topophilia: A Study of Environmental Perception, Attitudes, and Values,* Englewood Cliffs, N.J.: Prentice-Hall, 1976.

———. *Space and Place: The Perspective of Experience.* Minneapolis: University of Minnesota Press, 1977.

White, Richard. *"It's Your Misfortune and None of My Own": A New History of the American West.* Norman: University of Oklahoma Press, 1991.

Wrobel, David M., and Michael Steiner, eds. *Many Wests: Place, Culture, and Regional Identity.* Lawrence: University Press of Kansas, 1997.

CHAPTER 1. CULTURES AND CONQUESTS

Bedinger, Margery. *Indian Silver: Navajo and Pueblo Jewelers.* Albuquerque: University of New Mexico Press, 1973.

Berlant, Anthony, and Mary Hunt Kahlenberg. *Walk in Beauty: The Navajo and Their Blankets.* Boston: New York Graphic Society, 1977.

Briggs, Charles L. *The Wood Carvers of Cordova, New Mexico: Social Dimensions of an Artistic "Revival."* Knoxville: University of Tennessee Press, 1980.

Brody, J. J. *Indian Painters and White Patrons.* Albuquerque: University of New Mexico Press, 1971.

———. *Anasazi and Pueblo Painting.* Albuquerque: University of New Mexico Press, 1991.

Coulter, Lane, and Maurice Dixon, Jr. *New Mexican Tinwork, 1840–1940.* Albuquerque: University of New Mexico Press, 1990.

Dockstadter, Frederick J. *Indian Art in America: The Arts and Crafts of the North American Indian.* Greenwich: New York Graphic Society, 1961.

Goetzmann, William H., and William N. Goetzmann. *The West of the Imagination.* New York: W. W. Norton and Company, 1986.

Marriott, Alice. *María: The Potter of San Ildefonso.* Norman: University of Oklahoma Press, 1948.

Nabokov, Peter, and Robert Easton. *Native American Architecture.* New York: Oxford University Press, 1989.

Nash, Gerald, and Richard W. Etulain, eds. *The Twentieth Century West: Historical Interpretations.* Albuquerque: University of New Mexico Press, 1989.

Weber, David J. "The Spanish Legacy in North America and the Historical Imagination." *Western Historical Quarterly* 23 (February 1992): 5–24.

CHAPTER 2. THE IMPORTATION OF ANGLO CULTURE, 1850–1900

Bowie, Patricia Carr. "The Cultural History of Los Angeles, 1850–1967: From Rural Backwash to World Center." Ph.D. diss., University of Southern California, 1980.

Chávez, John. *The Lost Land: The Chicano Image of the Southwest.* Albuquerque: University of New Mexico Press, 1984.

Gallegly, Joseph S. *Footlights on the Border: The Galveston and Houston Stage before 1900.* The Hague: Mouton and Company, 1962.

Gerdts, William H. *Art across America: Two Centuries of Regional Painting.* New York: Abbeville Press, 1990.

Kanellos, Nicolás, ed. *Mexican American Theatre: Then and Now.* Houston: Arte Publico Press, 1984.

———. *A History of Hispanic Theatre in the United States: Origins to 1940.* Austin: University of Texas Press, 1991.

Kaplan, Sam Hall. *LA Lost and Found: An Architectural History of Los Angeles.* New York: Crown Publishers, 1987.

Larsen, Lawrence H. *The Urban West at the End of the Frontier.* Lawrence: Regents Press of Kansas, 1978.

Lummis, Charles F. *The Land of Poco Tiempo.* New York: Charles Scribner's Sons. 1893.

———. *Mesa, Cañon, and Pueblo.* New York: Century Company, 1925.

McDonald, William L. *Dallas Rediscovered: A Photographic Chronicle of Urban Expansion, 1870–1925* Dallas: Dallas Historical Society, 1978.

Meinig, D. W. *Imperial Texas: An Interpretive Essay in Cultural Geography.* Austin: University of Texas Press, 1969.

Nash, Gerald D. *The American West in the Twentieth Century: A Short History of an Urban Oasis.* Englewood Cliffs, N.J.: Prentice-Hall, 1973.

Ramírez, Elizabeth C. *Footlights across the Border: A History of Spanish Language Professional Theatre on the Texas Stage, 1875–1935.* New York: Peter Lang, 1990.

Robinson, Willard B. *Texas Public Buildings of the Nineteenth Century.* Austin: University of Texas Press, 1974.

———. *Gone from Texas: Our Lost Architectural Heritage.* College Station: Texas A&M University Press, 1981.

Starr, Kevin. *Inventing the Dream: California through the Progressive Era.* New York: Oxford University Press, 1985.

———. *Material Dreams: Southern California through the 1920s.* New York: Oxford University Press, 1990.

Trenton, Patricia, ed. *Independent Spirits: Women Painters of the American West.* Berkeley: University of California Press, 1995.

Wheeler, Kenneth W. *To Wear a City's Crown: The Beginnings of Urban Growth in Texas, 1836–1865.* Cambridge: Harvard University Press, 1986.

Wilson, Chris. *The Myth of Santa Fe: Creating a Modern Regional Tradition.* Albuquerque: University of New Mexico Press, 1997.

CHAPTER 3. CITIES AND CULTURE, 1900–1920

Abbott, Carl. *The Metropolitan Frontier: Cities in the Modern American West.* Tucson: University of Arizona Press, 1993.

Boutelle, Sara Holmes. *Julia Morgan: Architect.* New York: Abbeville Press, 1988.

Broder, Patricia Janis. *The American West: The Modern Vision.* Boston: Little, Brown, and Company, 1984.

Brown, E. K. *Willa Cather: A Critical Biography.* Lincoln: University of Nebraska Press, 1987.

Bywaters, Jerry. *Seventy-Five Years of Art in Dallas.* Dallas: Dallas Museum of Fine Arts, 1978.

Fink, Augusta. *I-Mary: A Biography of Mary Austin.* Tucson: University of Arizona Press, 1983.

García, Mario T. *Desert Immigrants: The Mexicans of El Paso, 1880–1920.* New Haven: Yale University Press, 1981.

Gibson, Arrell M. *The Santa Fe and Taos Colonies: Age of the Muses, 1900–1942.* Norman: University of Oklahoma Press, 1983.

Grattan, Virginia L. *Mary Coulter: Builder upon the Red Earth.* Flagstaff: Northland Press, 1980.

Greiff, Constance M., ed. *Lost America: From the Mississippi to the Pacific.* Princeton: Pyne Press, 1972.

Henry, Jay C. *Architecture in Texas: 1895–1945.* Austin: University of Texas Press, 1993.

Hogrefe, Jeffrey. *O'Keeffe: The Life of an American Legend*. New York: Bantam Books, 1992.

Hutchinson, W. H. *A Bar Cross Man: The Life and Personal Writings of Eugene Manlove Rhodes*. Norman: University of Oklahoma Press, 1956.

Jordy, William. *American Buildings and Their Architects, Progressive and Academic Ideals at the Turn of the Twentieth Century*. Garden City: Anchor Books, 1976.

Luckingham, Bradford. *Phoenix: The History of a Southwestern Metropolis*. Tucson: University of Arizona Press, 1989.

Pollitzer, Anita. *A Woman on Paper: The Letters and Memoir of a Legendary Friendship*. New York: Simon and Schuster, 1988.

Sheppard, Carl D. *Creator of the Santa Fe Style*. Albuquerque: University of New Mexico Press, 1988.

Sheridan, Thomas E. *Los Tucsonenses: The Mexican Community in Tucson, 1854–1941*. Tucson: University of Arizona Press, 1986.

CHAPTER 4. A REGIONAL CULTURE IS FORMULATED, 1920–1940

Bunting, Bainbridge. *John Gaw Meem: Southwestern Architect*. Albuquerque: University of New Mexico Press, 1983.

Cohen, Judith Singer. *Cowtown Moderne: Art Deco Architecture of Fort Worth, Texas*. College Station: Texas A&M University Press, 1988.

DeLong, Lea Rosson. *Nature's Forms/Nature's Forces: The Art of Alexandre Hogue*. Norman: University of Oklahoma Press, 1984.

Dunn, Dorothy. *American Indian Painting of the Southwest*. Albuquerque: University of New Mexico Press, 1968.

Eldredge, Charles, Julie Schimmel, and William H. Truettner. *Art in New Mexico: Pathways to Taos and Santa Fe, 1900–1945*. Washington, D.C.: Smithsonian Institution Press, 1986.

Gebhard, David S. *Romanza: The California Architecture of Frank Lloyd Wright*. San Francisco: Chronicle Books, 1988.

Gebhard, David S., and Harriette von Bretow. *Los Angeles in the Thirties*. Salt Lake City: Peregrine Smith, 1975.

Hahn, Emily. *Mabel: A Biography of Mabel Dodge Luhan*. Boston: Houghton Mifflin, 1977.

Highwater, Jamake. *Song from the Earth: American Indian Painting*. Boston: New York Graphic Society, 1976.

Luhan, Mabel Dodge. *Edge of the Taos Desert: An Escape to Reality*. New York: Harcourt, Brace, and Co., 1937.

Roussel, Hubert. *The Houston Symphony Orchestra, 1913–1971*. Austin: University of Texas Press, 1972.

Rudnik, Lois Palken. *Mabel Dodge Luhan: New Woman, New Worlds*. Albuquerque: University of New Mexico Press, 1984.

Stewart, Rick. *Lone Star Regionalism: The Dallas Nine and Their Circle*. Austin: Texas Monthly Press and the Dallas Museum of Art, 1985.

Tulsa Art Deco: An Architectural Era. Tulsa: Junior League of Tulsa, 1980.

Whiffen, Marcus, and Carla Breeze. *Pueblo Deco: The Art Deco Architecture of the Southwest*. Albuquerque: University of New Mexico Press, 1984.

CHAPTER 5. NATIONALIZATION OF A REGIONAL CULTURE, 1940–1960

Balassi, William, John F. Crawford, and Annie O. Eysturoy, eds. *This Is about Vision: Interviews with Southwestern Writers*. Albuquerque: University of New Mexico Press, 1990.

DeLong, David Gibson. *The Architecture of Bruce Goff: Buildings and Projects, 1916–1974*. New York: Garland Publishing Co., 1977.

Dillon, David, and Doug Tomlinson. *Dallas Architecture, 1936–1986*. Austin: Texas Monthly Press, 1986.

Gebhard, David, and Robert Winter. *A Guide to Architecture in Los Angeles and Southern California*. Salt Lake City: Peregrine Smith, 1982.

George, Mary Carolyn Hollers. *O'Neil Ford, Architect*. College Station: Texas A&M University Press, 1992.

Grider, Sylvia Ann, and Lou Halsell Rodenberger, eds. *Texas Women Writers: A Tradition of Their Own*. College Station: Texas A&M University Press, 1997.

Jones, Margo. *Theatre-in-the-Round*. New York: Holt, Rinehart, and Winston, 1951.

Krutch, Joseph Wood. *The Desert Year*. New York: William Sloan Associates, 1952.

Malone, Michael P., and Richard W. Etulain. *The American West: A Twentieth Century History*. Lincoln: University of Nebraska Press, 1989.

Metzger, Robert, ed. *My Land Is the Southwest: Peter Hurd Letters and Journals*. College Station: Texas A&M University Press, 1983.

The Prairie's Yield: Forces Shaping Dallas Architecture from 1840–1962. New York: Reinhold Publishing, 1962.

Ragsdale, Kenneth B. *The Year America Discovered Texas: Centennial '36*. College Station: Texas A&M University Press, 1987.

Smith, Elizabeth A. T., ed. *Blueprints for Modern Living: History and Legacy of the Case Study Houses*. Cambridge: MIT Press, 1989.

CHAPTER 6. INSTITUTIONAL CULTURE/CREATING ICONS, 1960–1980

Bernard, Richard M., and Bradley R. Rice. *Sunbelt Cities: Politics and Growth since World War II*. Austin: University of Texas Press, 1984.

Brutvan, Cheryl A., et al. *In Our Time: Houston's Contemporary Arts Museum*. Houston: Contemporary Arts Museum, 1982.

Fox, Stephen. *Houston: Architectural Guide*. Houston: American Institute of Architects/ Houston Chapter, 1990.

Giesburg, Robert I. *Houston Grand Opera: A History*. Houston: Houston Grand Opera, 1981.

González, Nancie L. *The Spanish-Americans of New Mexico*. Albuquerque: University of New Mexico Press, 1969.

Luckingham, Bradford. *The Urban Southwest*. El Paso: Texas Western Press, 1982.

Northcutt, John Orlando. *Symphony: The Story of Los Angeles Philharmonic Orchestra*. Los Angeles: Southern California Symphony Association, 1963.

Speck, Lawrence. *Landmarks of Texas Architecture*. Austin: University of Texas Press, 1986.

Strickland, Rennard. *The Indians in Oklahoma*. Norman: University of Oklahoma Press, 1980.

CHAPTER 7. A RENAISSANCE WITH MANY VOICES, 1960–1980

Broder, Patricia Janis. *Hopi Painting: The World of the Hopi*. New York: E. P. Dutton, 1978.

Cancel Luis R., ed. *The Latin American Spirit: Arts and Artists in the United States, 1920–1970*. New York: Harry N. Abrams, 1988.

Jensen, Joan M., and Darlis A. Miller, eds. *New Mexico Women: Intercultural Perspectives*. Albuquerque: University of New Mexico Press, 1986.

Lee, Joyce Glover. *Rolando Hinojosa and the American Dream*. Denton: University of North Texas Press, 1997.

Perlman, Barbara. *Allan Houser (Ha-o-zous)*. Boston: David Godine, 1987.

Quirarte, Jacinto. *Mexican American Artists*. Austin: University of Texas Press, 1973.

Schubnell, Matthias. *N. Scott Momaday: The Cultural and Literary Background*. Norman: University of Oklahoma Press, 1985.

Smith, Richard Cándida. *Utopia and Dissent: Art, Poetry, and Politics in California*. Berkeley: University of California Press, 1995.

Vélêz-Ibáñez, Carlos. *Border Visions: Mexican Cultures of the Southwest United States*. Tucson: University of Arizona Press, 1996.

Velie, Alan R. *Four American Indian Literary Masters*. Norman: University of Oklahoma Press, 1982.

CHAPTER 8. THE EXPORTATION OF A REGIONAL CULTURE, 1980–1995

Barna, Joel Warren. *The See-Through Years: Creation and Destruction in Texas Architecture and Real Estate, 1981–1991*. Houston: Rice University Press, 1992.

Brady, Steve. *Presence: The Transco Tower*. Houston: Herring Press, 1985.

Jones, David Richard, ed. *New Mexico Plays*. Albuquerque: University of New Mexico Press, 1989.

Luckingham, Bradford. *Minorities in Phoenix: A Profile of Mexican American, Chinese American, and African American Communities*. Tucson: University of Arizona Press, 1994.

McCoy, Esther. *The Second Generation*. Salt Lake City: Peregrine Smith Books, 1984.

Mead, Christopher. *Houses by Bart Prince: An American Architecture for the Continuous Present*. Albuquerque: University of New Mexico Press, 1991.

Saldívar, José David. *Border Matters: Remapping American Cultural Studies*. Berkeley: University of California Press, 1997.

INDEX

Abbey, Edward, 254–55
Abrams, Mrs. W. H., 105
Adams, Charles Francis, 41
Adams, John, 299
Adams, John C., 43
Adler, Pankmar, 46
African Americans, 107, 170, 216–17, 253
Ahmanson, Howard, 223
Akin, Louis, 62, 89
Albright, Harrison, 71
Albuquerque: architecture of, 37, 43, 72, 87, 172, 216, 284–85; music of, 147; theater of, 151. *See also individual cultural organizations*
Albuquerque Civic Symphony, 147
Albuquerque Little Theater, 151
Albuquerque Symphony Orchestra, 228–29
Alexander, John, 247
Allesandro, Victor, 159, 200–201, 202
Alley Theater (Houston), 208–209, 274, 300–301
Ambasz, Emilio, 284
Amon Carter Museum of Art, 234
Anasazi People, 13
Anaya, Rudolfo A., 8, 262–64
Anderson, Clinton, 151
Anderson, Donald, 250
Anderson, Maxwell, 135–36
Anderson, Robert O., 291
Apple, Max, 218, 271
architecture: Albuquerque, 43, 72; Art Deco style, 114–16; Art Modern style, 114; Austin, 40; bungalow style, 72–76; Dallas, 40–41, 70–71; domestic, nineteenth century, 36–38, 41–42; during 1900–20, 67–87; during

1920–40, 114–23; during 1940–60, 172–77; during 1960–80, 215–22; during 1980–95, 277–86, 295–97; El Paso, 38; Fort Worth, 40–41; Galveston, 39; Guthrie, Okla., 47–48; Houston, 40–41, 70–71; International Style, 121–22; Las Vegas, N.Mex., 46–47; Los Angeles, 37–38, 44–46, 72; mission revival style, 76–79; Native American, 14–18; Oklahoma City, 69–70; Phoenix, 43, 72; Pueblo, Colo., 46; Romanesque revival, 44, 47–48; San Antonio, 38–39; San Diego, 42–43, 71–72; Spanish Colonial revival, 79–82; Spanish influence on, 23–26, 36–37; territorial style, 36–37; Tucson, 43, 72; Victorian influences, 36–48; Waco, Tex., 70. *See also names of architects and urban places*
Arensberg, Louise, 197
Arensberg, Walter, 197
Arizona Civic Theater, 211
Arizona Dance Theater, 275
Arizona Opera Company, 300
Arizona Theater Company, 300
Armory Show, 93, 95, 123
Arroyo School (of art), 64
art: of Southwest, 61–66, 87–96, 123–31, 155–59, 161–65, 184–87, 197–98, 246–53
Art Deco, 114–16
Art Moderne, 114–16
Art Museum of South Texas (Corpus Christi), 240
art museums. *See individual museums*
Asah, Spencer, 129–31, 156
Atchison, Topeka and Santa Fe Railway, 37, 42, 43, 44, 62, 78–79, 92, 103

Auchiah, James, 129–31, 156
Austin: architecture of, 172, 282–83; music of, 106; theater of, 54–55
Austin, Mary, 101–102, 130, 132–33, 137, 138, 139–40, 142, 157
Austin, Stephen F., 89
Austin Museum of Art, 294
Ayres, Atlee B., 80, 193–94
Ayres, Robert M., 193–94

Bacon, Francis, 248
Bacone College, 130, 247
Baker, Paul, 207–208, 272, 273–74
Bakos, Jozef, 127
Balada, Leonardo, 231
Ballard, Louis, 212
ballet, 211–12, 275–76, 304
Ballet Arizona, 304
Ballet Dallas, 276
Ballet El Paso, 275
Bandelier, Adolph F. 58
Bandini, Arturo, 74
Barbirolli, John, 200, 227–28
Barera, Orlando, 228
Barnes, Edward Larrabee, 239, 240–41, 290
Barnett, John, 202
Barnsdall, Aline, 116–17, 154, 197
Bass, Anne, 275–76
Bass, Edward, 297
Bass, Lee, 297
Bass, Robert, 297
Bass, Sid Richardson, 275
Batchelder, Ernest A., 95
Bates, David, 247
Baum, Frank, 43–44
Bear, Donald, 165
Becket, Welton, 223
Bedichek, Roy, 269
Beecham, Thomas, 199
Begay, Harrison, 131
Behymer, Lynden Ellsworth, 51–52, 108, 110–11, 149–50, 160
Bel Geddes, Norman, 117
Belin, Harry, 152

Bellamy, Edward, 45–46
Bello, Mrs. A. H., 97
Bellows, Emma, 125
Bellows, George, 123, 125
Benton, Arthur B., 76
Benton, Joseph, 146
Beringhaus, Oscar E., 90–92, 157–58
Bernhardt, Robert, 298
Bertoia, Harry, 185–86
Bess, Forest, 185
Biano, Ochwiay, 135
Biggers, John, 253
Bindley, Sarah Barton Luke, 151
Bing, Rudolph, 204
Bird, Sarah, 304, 306–307
Birkerts, Gunnar, 239, 244–45
Bissell, Eleanor, 153
Bisttram, Emil, 158
Blitz, Julian, 106
Blue Eagle, Acee, 130–31, 156
Blumenschien, Ernest, L., 90–92
Borein, Edward, 95
Borg, Carl Oscar, 95
Botkin, B. A., 142–43
Brace, Charles, 37
Bradbury, Louis, 44–46
Bradbury Building (Los Angeles), 44–46
Bradford, Richard, 266
Bradley, Tom, 290–91
Brammer, Bill, 266
Braun, Maurice, 65, 95–96
Breaux, Zelia N. Page, 107
Brett, Dorothy, 127, 133–35
Broadmoor Art Academy, 66
Brown, Gilmor, 153–54, 161, 273
Brown, Hine Arthur, 145
Brown, John Mason, 11
Brown, Patricia Ann, 209
Brown, Richard Fargo 236–39
Bryce, James, 10, 35
bungalow style, 72–76
Burgee, John, 217–18, 234–35, 240, 279–80
Bynner, Witter, 136–37, 166
Bywaters, Jerry, 162–65

Cabeza de Baca, Fabiola, 264–65
Cain, James M., 183–84
Callas, Maria, 230–31
Calvin, Ross, 5, 141, 178
Cambridge Seven Associates, 292–94
Campbell, Walter S. (Stanley Vestal), 143
Cannon, T. C., 248–49
Capobianco, Tito, 231
Capps, Benjamin, 182, 267
Carpenter, William J., 38
Carpenter Square Theater, 300
Carroll, Vinnette, 301
Carter, Amon G. 234, 239
Carter, Artie Mason, 149–50
Casa Grande (Arizona), 15
Casas, Melesio, 252–53
Case Study Houses (Los Angeles), 177
Cassidy, Gerald, 93
Cather, Douglass, 103
Cather, Willa, 133, 135, 143; in Arizona, 102–105; in Colorado, 104; in New Mexico, 104, 137–39
Caudill, Rowlett Scott, 227
Chaco Canyon (New Mexico), 13
Chafee, Judith, 286
Chandler, Alexander John, 78
Chandler, Dorothy Buffum, 222–23, 302
Chandler, Norman, 222
Chandler, Raymond, 183–84
Chapman, Kenneth, 81, 93
Chase, William Merritt, 63, 65, 94, 96, 124
Chavez, Abraham, 228
Chávez, César, 274
Chávez, Denise, 265, 302
Chilocco Indian School, 130
Chouteau, Yvonne, 212, 275
Cisneros, Henry, 298
Cisneros, Sandra, 9, 265–66
Clark, William Andrews, 108, 148–49
Clarke, Marie Rankin, 149
Clayton, Nicholas J., 39, 85
Clinton, Jane Heard, 107
Clower, Thom, 276
Cobb, Henry, 280

Coburn, D. L., 272
Colcord, Charles, 69
Collier, John, 157
Colorado Springs, 66, 121
Colorado Springs Fine Arts Center, 121
Colson-Walker, Celeste, 301
Comelin, Jean-Paul, 304
Conrad, Charles M., 36
Contemporary Arts Museum (Houston), 244–45, 247
Cook, Abner, 40
Cooper, Madison, 182
Coppini, Pompeo, 79
Cory, Kate T., 89–90
Cotts, Anson B., 226
Coulter, Mary E. J., 78–79, 81
Couse, E. Irving, 90–92
Covarrubias, Miguel, 137
Cram, Goodhue and Ferguson, 79
Crane, Stephen, 35
Cret, Paul, 191
Crichton, Kyle, 168
Crosby, John O'hea, 204–205
Crosby, Mrs. Robert G., 106
Crumbo, Woodrow, 130–31
Cuero, Texas, 41
Cullen, H. R., 199
Cullen, Lillie, 199
Culwell, Ben L., 185

Dahl, George, 185–86
Dale, E. E., 141–42
Dallas: architecture of, 40–41, 70, 173, 280–81; art in, 161–65, 185–86; music in, 105; opera in, 146, 230–31; theater in, 150–51. *See also individual cultural organizations*
Dallas Art Association, 97
Dallas Ballet (Dallas Civic Ballet), 276–304
Dallas Civic Opera, 230–31
Dallas Little Theater, 150–51
Dallas Museum of Art (Dallas Museum of Fine Arts), 163, 191–92, 240–41, 253, 294

Dallas Nine, The, 161–65
Dallas Symphony Orchestra, 105, 201, 230, 296–97
Dallas Theater Center, 206–207, 272, 274, 300–301, 302
Damrosch, Walter, 107
Dasberg, Andrew, 121, 123, 137
Davey, Randall, 127, 158
Davidson, Gordon, 302
Davis, Stuart, 123, 126
Dean, William, 160
de Baca, Ezequiel C., 55
Delk, Edward B., 194–95
Devereaux, George, 75–76
Dewlin, Al, 267
Didion, Joan, 184, 254, 267–68, 304
Dixon, Maynard, 62, 64, 89
Dobie, J. Frank, 113, 144, 164, 196, 269
Dodge, Walter Luther, 84
Dorati, Antal, 201
Dorrance, Roderick, 106
Douglass, John, 162
Dove, Rita, 216
Dow, Alden, 239–40
Dow, Arthur Wesley, 94
Dozier, Otis, 162
Drought, Harry P., 159, 161
du Bois, Guy Péne, 96
Dunn, Dorothy, 130–31, 249
Dunn, John, 161
Dunne, John Gregory, 267
Dunton, Herbert, 91–92
Durrell, Lawrence, 4
Duvall, Fannie Elya, 63
Duveen, Joseph, 98

Eames, Charles, 177
Earl, Mrs. Emily, 108
Eastlake, William, 254, 255–56
Edison, Helen, 273
Edison, Simon, 273
Edminister, Grace Thompson, 147
Ellis, Fremont, 127
Ellison, Ralph, 107
Ellwood, Craig, 177

El Paso: architecture of, 38, 85–87, 114–15; music in, 50, 106, 145–46. See also individual cultural organizations
El Paso Museum of Art, 294
El Paso Symphony Orchestra, 145–46, 228
Entenza, John, 177
Ernst, Max, 184–85, 288
Eschenbach, Christoph, 296
Evans, John, 131
Evans, Max, 267
Exall, Mrs. Henry, 97

Farnham, Ammi, 64–65
Farr, Ellen, 63
Feldman, Jay, 275
Fentress, Curtis, 284
Ferber, Edna, 9, 143, 182–83
Ferguson, Elva Shartel, 143
Fergusson, Erna, 6, 216
Fergusson, Harvey, 216
Fields, Annie Adams, 105
Fisher, Irene, 151
Ford, O'Neil, 174, 218
Ford Foundation, 209–10, 225, 231
Fort Worth: architecture of, 40–41, 70–71, 116, 218–19, 283; art in, 234, 236–38. See also individual cultural organizations
Fort Worth Ballet, 275–76, 297
Fort Worth Opera, 297
Fort Worth Symphony Orchestra, 297
Foucart, Joseph, 47–48
Franzen, Ulrich, 209
Fred Harvey Company, 27, 28, 78–79, 92, 193
Freeman, Frank, 40
Fried, Walter, 105
Fries, Charles Arthur, 65, 95–96
Furman, Laura, 304–306

Galveston, 39, 41
Gamble, David B., 74
Gamble, Mary, 74
Garrett, Pat, 100

Garrett, Pete Ed., 299
Garrott, James H., 220–21
Garson, Greer, 300
Geffen, David, 292
Gehry, Frank, 297
Gentilz, Jean Louis Theodore, 65
geography: impact of, 3–5. *See also*
 topophilia
Georgia O'Keeffe Museum (Santa Fe),
 295
Getty, J. Paul, 241, 243–44
Gilbert, Gertrude, 52
Gilcrease, Thomas, 194, 195–97
Gill, Irving, 82–84, 85, 121
Glackens, William, 92, 96
Glasco, Joseph, 185
"Globe of the Southwest" (Odessa, Tex.),
 274
Gockley, David, 229–30, 299–300
Goetzmann, William, 235
Goff, Bruce, 119–20, 176–77, 284–85, 286
Goff, Lloyd, 162
Goldberger, Paul, 232, 291
Goldsmith, Pauline Washer, 200
Goldwater, Barry, 193
González, Jovita, 265
Goodhue, Bertram Grosvenor, 79–81, 82,
 83, 116, 190
Goodwin, Kemper, 219
Goodwin, Michael, 219
Gorman, R. C. (Rudolph Carl), 249–50
Gottleib, Adolph, 184–85
Grant, Micki, 301
Grant, Ulysses S., 54
Graves, John, 266–67
Graves, Michael, 278, 281–82
Greene, Charles Sumner, 73–76
Greene, Henry Mather, 73–76
Greene, Herb, 177
Green Mask Players, 152
Gregg, Josiah, 35
Grey, Elmer, 80, 98, 153
Grey, Zane, 99–100
Griffith, D. W., 149
Guerra, Fermina, 265

Guion, David, 146
Guthrie, Okla., 47–48

Hahn, Carl, 106
Hall, Adrian, 301
Hall, Carol, 272
Hamburger, Richard, 301
Hamilton, Harley, 107–108
Hammer, Armand, 289–90
Handel, Bea, 207–208
Hardy Holzman Pfeiffer Associates, 291
Harithas, James, 252
Harjo, Joy, 258, 259–60
Harrington, Sybil, 229
Harrington String Quartet, 229
Harris, Harwell, 123
Harris, Roy, 9, 205
Harrison, Guy Fraser, 202
Harrison, William Preston, 98, 128,
Hartley, Marsden, 93, 124–25
Hassam, Childe, 96
Hayes, Rutherford B., 36
Heard, Dwight B., 193
Heard, Maie Bartlett, 152, 193
Heard Museum (Phoenix), 193
Hearon, Shelby, 304–305
Hearst, William Randolph, 77, 198
Hefner, Jack, 272
Heineman, Madeline, 147
Heiner, Eugene T., 41
Henderson, Alice Corbin, 130, 136–37,
 166–67
Henderson, Nola, 142
Henderson, William Penhallow, 81–82,
 136
Hennings, E. Martin, 91–92
Henri, Robert, 81–82, 92, 93, 96, 123
Herbert Walter, 229, 231
Hermann, George, 189
Herrera, Joe, 247
Herrera, Velino, 130–31
Hershey, Mira, 149
Hertzberg, Anna Goodman, 53, 106
Hewett, Edgar L., 81–82, 93, 130
Higgins, Victor, 92, 157–58, 165

Hightower, Rosella, 211–12

Hillerman, Tony, 270–71

Hines, Gerald D., 217–18, 279

Hinojosa, Rolando, 264

Hinton, Susan Eloise, 266

Hispanic Americans: art of, 250–53, 307; decorative arts of, 25–26; literature of, 260–66; music of, 30–31, 106, 109; oral tradition of, 30; sense of place, 7; theater of, 30–31, 56–67, 109–10, 154–55, 274–75; tinsmiths, 29, 157; weavers, 29, 157; wood carvers, 29–30, 157

Hispanophobia, 31

Hobby, Oveta Culp, 199

Hodge, Leslie, 202

Hoffmann, Ernst, 199

Hogan, Linda, 258, 260

Hogg, Ima Jane, 145, 199–200

Hogg, James S., 145

Hogg, William C., 189

Hogue, Alexandre, 162–65

Hohokam People, 14, 15, 20

Hokeah, Jack, 129–31

Holden, Richard, 275

Hollywood Bowl, 149–50

Holmberg, Frederick, 159

Holmes, David, 72

Holmes, Jesse H., 72

Hopkins, Harry, 151

Hopper, Edward, 123, 126

Hord, Donal, 158–59

Horgan, Paul, 5, 136, 180–82, 254

Horton, Alonzo E., 42, 43, 64

Hotel del Coronado (San Diego), 42, 43–44

House, Edward H., 40

House, Mrs. E. H., 55

Houser, Allan, 9, 131, 249

Housh, Mrs. Harvey, 98

Houston: architecture of, 40–41, 70–71, 217–18, 279–80; music in, 50, 145, 229–30; theater in, 54, 152. *See also individual cultural organizations*

Houston Art League, 96–97

Houston Ballet, 274, 296, 299, 304

Houston Grand Opera, 229–30, 296, 299–300

Houston Museum of Fine Arts, 189–90, 232, 245, 253, 288, 294, 307

Houston Symphony Orchestra, 145, 199–200, 227–28, 296

Hoving, Thomas, 196–97

Howe, Oscar, 248

Humphreys, Kalita, 207–208

Humphreys, Mrs. R. W., 207–208

Hunning, Franz, 37

Hunt, Myron, 80, 98

Hunt, Sumner P., 45

Huntington, Arabella, 98

Huntington, Collis P., 98

Huntington, Henry E., 98–99

Huntington Library, Art Collections and Botanical Gardens, The, 97–98, 290

Hurd, Henriette Wyeth, 180, 186–87

Hurd, Peter, 180, 186–87

Huxtable, Ada Louise, 218, 277

Hyechka Club, 107

Indian Arts and Crafts Board, 157

International Style, 232–33

Irish, Mrs. Leiland Atherton, 149

Isozaki, Arata, 238, 290–91, 295–96

Iturbi, José, 228

Jackson, Helen Fiske Hunt, 57–58

Jacobson, Oscar B., 129–31, 156

James, George Wharton, 99

Jeffers, Robinson, 133

Jewel Box Theater, 300

Jimenez, Luis, 250–52

Johansen, John M., 210

Johns, David R., 226

Johnson, Nell, 106

Johnson, Philip, 217–18, 234–35, 239, 240, 278, 279–81, 288, 296, 299

Johnson, Willard "Spud," 136–37, 183

Johnson, William Templeton, 190

Jones, Jesse H., 145

Jones, Margo, 11, 205–209

Jones, Mayde Mack, 210

Jones, Preston, 206, 272, 274
Jones, Richard Lloyd, 118
Jonson, Raymond, 158
J. Paul Getty Museum, 243–44, 280
Judson, William Lees, 64
Jung, Carl, 133, 135, 140

Kabotie, Fred, 130–31, 247–48
Kahn, Louis I., 236–39, 288
Kavanagh, Marian, 64, 95
Keating, Richard, 280
Kelly, Lawrence, 230–31
Kelton, Elmer, 254, 255, 267, 268
Kern, Richard, 62
Kilpatrick, John, 300
Kimbell, Kay, 236–39
Kimbell, Velma Fuller, 236–39
Kimbell Art Museum, 236–39, 247,
    287–88, 294–95
King, Larry, 272
Kino, Father Eusebio, 22–23
Kiowa Artists, The, 128–31
Kirk, Betty, 168
Klauber, Alice, 64–65, 96
Kleberg, Robert, 49
Klemperer, Otto, 149, 203
Koenig, Pierre, 177
Kramer, Arthur L., 146
Kreissig, Hans, 105
Kroll, Leon, 123
Krutch, Joseph Wood, 183

La Compañía de Teatro de
    Alburquerque, 274–75, 302
Lafayette Players, 107, 153
La Forge, Oliver, 137, 140–41
Laguna Beach art colony, 64–65
La Jolla Civic Orchestra, 203
La Jolla Playhouse, 231, 273
Lamy, John Baptist, 137–38
Lanier, Sidney, 50
La Raza, 261–62
Larkin, Moscelyne, 211–12
Las Vegas, N.Mex., 46–47, 55
Law, F. M., 96

Lawrence, D. H., 127, 133–35
Lawrence, Frieda, 133–35
Lawson, Ernest, 96
Layton, Solomon Andrew, 69–70
Lea, Tom, 186–87
Legorreta, Ricardo, 283–84
Leigh, William R., 89
Lester, William, 162
Lewis, Edith, 104
Liedtke, J. Hugh, 217
literature, 57–61, 99–105, 131–44, 177–84,
    253–71, 304–307. See also individual
    authors
Little Theatre Movement, 150–52
Litton, Andrew, 297
Lobit, Elva, 229–30
Long, Haniel, 136–37, 140–41
Loos, Anita, 109
Los Angeles: architecture of, 37–38,
    44–46, 72, 115–16, 116–18, 122–23, 281;
    art life in, 62–64, 197–98, 246–47;
    music in, 49, 52, 107–108, 148–50, 160;
    opera in, 49, 51–52, 110–11; theater in,
    55–56, 110–11, 153–54. See also individual
    cultural organizations
Los Angeles County Museum of Art,
    97–98, 188, 197–98, 204, 242, 286,
    289–90, 291–92
Los Angeles Federal Art Project, 158
Los Angeles Federal Theater Project,
    160–61
Los Angeles Grand Opera Company,
    110–11
Los Angeles Museum of Contemporary
    Art, 287, 290–91
Los Angeles Music Center, 222–24, 297
Los Angeles Philharmonic Orchestra,
    107–108, 148–50, 198–99, 203, 222–24,
    297
Los Angeles Theater Center, 272–73
Los Cincos Pintores, 127
Lovell, Leah, 122
Lovell, Phillip, 122
Lovett, Mrs. Robert S., 96–97
Lowery, Beverly, 304, 305–306

Lubbock Little Theater, 151–52
Lubbock Symphony Orchestra, 202
Luce, Mrs. Edgar A., 231
Ludlow, Conrad, 275
Luhan, Mabel Dodge, 102, 112, 124, 125, 126, 131–35, 136–37, 166
Luhan, Tony, 132–35, 137, 178
Luks, George, 96
Lummis, Charles Fletcher, 62, 76, 81, 85, 88, 89, 100, 101; as preservationist, 59–60; as regional promoter, 58–59, 61; as writer, 58–61
Lundy, Anne, 229
Lungren, Fernand, 62, 88, 95
Lurie, Allison, 282

Ma, Yo Yo, 232
McArthur, Albert Chase, 118
McBride, Henry, 126
McCloskey, Alberta Binford, 63
McCloskey, William Joseph, 63
McClusky, Katherine, 152
McCormick, Ruth Hanna, 151
McDermott, Mrs. Eugene, 191–92
Macdonald-Wright, Stanton, 128, 158
MacDougal, Daniel T., 139
McGlaughlin, William, 228
Mach, Reginald L., 299
McMurtry, Larry, 5, 216, 253, 254, 255, 268–70, 304, 306
McNally, Terrence, 300
McNay, Marion Koogler, 193–94
McNay Art Museum (San Antonio), 193–94
Mahier, Edith, 129
Malraux, André, 187–88
Mandelman, Beatrice, 185
Mann, Thomas, 150
Marcelli, Nino, 148
Marin, John, 123, 125, 133
Marrion, Anne W., 295
Martin, Steve, 300
Martínez, Crescencio, 130
Martinez, Julián, 27
Martinez, María, 27

Masterson, Peter, 272
Mata, Eduardo, 201, 202, 225–26, 296–97
Mathews, John Joseph, 142
Maxwell, Elsa, 230–31
Maxwell, Everett C., 87
Mazria, Edward, 295
Medoff, Mark, 265, 302–303
Meem, John Gaw, 120–22, 151, 157, 174
Megargee, Lon, 156
Mehta, Zubin, 203, 223, 224
Meier, Richard, 289
Mena, María Cristina, 261
Mencken, H. L., 142–43
Menil, Dominique de, 287–89
Menil, John (Jean) de, 287–89
Menil Collection, 287–89
Meredith, Burgess, 274
Mesa Verde (Colorado), 13; architecture of, 16–17; decorative arts of, 16–17
Metcalf, Willard Leroy, 62
Mexican Players, 155
Meyer, Mrs. George K., 97
Michener, James, 294
Michener, Mari, 294
Millar, Gregory, 228
Millard, Alice, 118
Miller, Frank A., 56
Miller, Melissa, 247
Millicent Rogers Museum, 192–93
Modern Art Museum (Fort Worth), 294
Mogollon People, 14, 19
Momaday, N. Scott, 9, 257–58
Moneo, Rafael, 294
Monijo, Manuel Jr., 154
Montezuma Hotel (New Mexico), 43
Moore, Harry Estill, 6
Mopope, Stephen, 129–31, 156
Moran, Thomas, 62, 95
Morgan, Julia, 77
Morosco, Oliver, 110–11
Morris, Majorie, 274
Morris Aubrey Architects, 279–80
Morrison, Fannie E., 273
Mossin, Mrs. John C., 108

Mruk, Walter, 127
Muir, Edla, 77–78
Mumford, Lewis, 233
Mummers Theater (Oklahoma City), 209–10
Munger, Mrs. S. I., 97
Murray, Earl Bernard, 226–27
Museum of Indian Arts and Culture (Santa Fe), 295
music, 48–54, 105–108, 144–50, 159–60, 198–204, 205, 222–29, 296–99. *See also individual composers, musicians, operas, and orchestras*

Nailor, Gerald, 131
Nash, Willard, 127
Nasher, Raymond D., 294–95
Native Americans, 7, 13–15, 20; architecture of, 14–18; art of, 92, 128–31, 157, 247–50; decorative arts of, 20, 26–27; literature of, 257–60; oral traditions of, 118–19. *See also individual artists, authors, and dancers*
Navajo People (Dineh), 13–14; architecture of 15–18; sand painting of, 29; silver smithing of, 26–27; textiles of, 27–29
Nelson, Willie, 9
Nespoli, Uriel, 145
Neutra, Richard, 122–23, 177
Newhouse, Bertram M., 235, 238
New Mexico Federal Art Project, 157
New Mexico Symphony Orchestra, 298–99
Ney, Elisabet, 88–89
Nichols, John, 254, 256–57
Nichols, Perry, 162
Nicoloff, Peter, 203
Norton, W. R., 43
Norton Simon Museum of Art, 241–43

O'Connor, James, 151
O'Connor, Kathryn, 151
O'Doherty, Brian, 232
Odum, Howard, 6

O'Kane, Regina, 63
O'Keeffe, Claudia, 94–95
O'Keeffe, Georgia, 123, 133, 135; in New Mexico, 126–27; significance of place, 4; in Texas, 93–95
Oklahoma!, 168
Oklahoma City: architecture of, 48, 69–70, 115, 116, 172, 220; art in, 156–57; music in, 54, 107, 159; opera in, 48; theater in, 109, 209–10, 300. *See also individual cultural organizations*
Oklahoma City Ballet, 275
Oklahoma City Symphony Orchestra, 159, 202, 297, 298
Oklahoma Federal Art Project, 156
Oklahoma Theater Center, 210, 300
Old Globe Theater (San Diego), 152, 231–32, 273, 301–302
O'Malley, Ysela Provenicio, 253
Onderdonk, Eleanor, 65–66, 97
Onderdonk, Robert Jenkins, 65–66, 88–89, 97
Onderdonk, Robert Julian, 65–66, 88–89
opera, 48–54, 105–108, 146, 159–60, 204, 229–31, 299–300. *See also individual opera companies*
Ortiz, Simon, 258, 259
Osborn, Carolyn, 183
Overholser, Henry, 48, 109

Pach, Walter, 123, 187
Page, Inman E., 107
Panama-California Exposition, 79–81, 96
Papago People, 16, 19, 22–23
Paris, Walter, 66
Parker, Harry, 240–41
Parsons, Sheldon, 127
Pasadena Museum of Modern Art, 242
Pasadena Playhouse, 153–54, 161, 206, 273, 301–302
Payne, Edgar A., 95
Pearl, George Clayton, 220–22
Pei, I. M., 296
Pelli, Cesar, 217, 281

Peña, Tonita, 131, 247
Pereira, William L., 198
Performing Arts Society of Los Angeles, 273
Perry, George Sessions, 143–44
Peters, Susan Ryan, 128–29
Philbrook Art Center (Tulsa), 194–95, 295
Phillips, Bert, 90–92, 158
Phillips, Waite, 194–95
Phoenix, 216; architecture of, 43, 72, 87, 114, 118, 219; music in, 146–47; theater in, 108–109, 152. *See also individual cultural institutions*
Phoenix Art Museum, 156, 239–40
Phoenix Federal Art Center, 156
Phoenix Little Theater, 152, 211
Phoenix Symphony Orchestra, 202, 224–26, 297, 298
Piano, Renzo, 288–89
Pima People, 16, 23
Poland, Reginald, 191
Polelonema, Otis, 130–31, 247–48
Pollitzer, Anita, 93–94
Porter, Katherine Anne, 144
Porter, William Sidney (O. Henry), 57
Portillo, Estela Trambley, 265
Portman, John, 281
Powell, Earl A., 188, 292
Predock, Antoine, 174, 220, 222
Price, Harold C., 175–76
Price, Joe, 175, 286, 292
Priestley, J. B., 173, 212–13
Prince, Bart, 284–85
Pueblo, Colo., 46
Pueblo (Colorado) Opera House, 46
Pueblo People, 14; architecture of 17–18; decorative arts of, 14, 19–20; pottery of, 16–17, 27
Putnam, Amy, 190–91
Putnam, Anne, 190–91
Putnam, Irene, 190–91
Pyle, Ernie, 216

Quillin, Ellen, 197

Rachmaninoff, Sergei, 108
Ramsey, W. R., 115
Rancho Santa Fe, Calif., 77
Randolph, Hugh Jefferson, 282
Rapp, William Morris, 80–82
Rauschenberg, Robert, 247
Reaugh, Frank, 88, 97, 164
Rebeil, Julia, 154
Redgrave, Corin, 301
Redgrave, Lynn, 300–301
Redgrave, Vanessa, 301
Reid, Whitelaw, 43
Reiter, Max, 200
Remington, Frederic, 62, 88
Rescigno, Nicola, 230
Reves, Emery (Emery Revexz), 240–41
Reves, Wendy (Wyn-Nelle Russell), 240–41
Rhodes, Eugene Manlove, 100–101, 143
Ribak, Louis, 185
Rice, Lillian Jenette, 77–78
Rich, Alan, 227–28
Richardson, H. H., 41
Richardson, Sid, 235–36
Richardson Collection (Fort Worth), 235–36
Richter, Conrad, 179–80
Ridout, Margaret, 231
Riggs, Lutah Maria, 77–78
Riggs, Lynn, 113, 136–37, 143, 151, 161, 165–68
Ripley, E. P., 78
Rivera, Tomás, 261
Rodríguez, Anita, 253
Rodríguez, Carmen, 253
Rodríguez, José, 274–75
Rogers, Millicent, 192–93
Rollins, Warren, 92–93
Rose, Guy, 63–64, 95
Rose, Ralph, 159
Rosenbaum, Samuel, 11
Rosenfield, John, 170, 201, 207
Ross, Glynn, 300

Index

Rothwell, Walter Henry, 108, 148–49
Rupe, D. Gordon, Jr., 201
Russell, Charles M., 88

Saarinen, Eero, 245
Saldívar, José David, 307
Salonen, Esa-Pekka, 297
San Antonio: architecture of, 38–39, 79,
    116, 218, 283–84; art in, 65–66, 97;
    Hispanic Theater in, 109–10; music in,
    49–50, 53, 106; theater in, 151–52. *See
    also individual cultural organizations*
San Antonio Art League, 97
San Antonio Little Theater, 151
San Antonio Museum of Art, 292–94
San Antonio Symphony Orchestra,
    200–201, 297–98
San Diego, 33, 231–32; architecture in,
    42–44, 71–72, 79–80, 82–84; art in,
    95–96, 158–59; music in, 52–53, 147–48,
    159–60; theater in, 56, 152. *See also
    individual cultural organizations*
San Diego Ballet, 231
San Diego Museum of Art, 190–91
San Diego Opera, 231
San Diego Symphony Orchestra, 226–27,
    297–98
Sandzen, Birgir, 93
Sani, Atsídí, 26–27
Santa Fe, 80–82, 92–93, 109
Santa Fe art colony, 92–93
Santa Fe Chamber Orchestra, 229
Santa Fe Opera, 204–205, 230, 300
"Santa Fe Style," 80–82
Santee, Ross, 141
San Xavier del Bac (Arizona), 22–23
Scarborough, Dorothy, 143
Schindler, Rudolph, 122–23, 177
Schlumberger, Conrad, 288
Scholder, Fritz, 9, 248
Schuster, Donna, 95
Schuster, Will, 127
Schwarz, David, 297
Scism, Mack, 209–10

Scott, Virginia Steele, 290
Scott Joplin Chamber Orchestra, 229
Seares, Marian, 95
Sergeant, Elizabeth Shepley, 104
Sharp, John Henry, 90
Shawn, Ted, 146, 149
Sheets, Millard, 128
Sheets, Nan, 156–57
Shepard, Benjamin Jesse Frances, 42–43
Sherman, William Tecumseh, 36
Shinn, Charles, H., 35
Silko, Leslie Marmon, 9, 258–59
Simon, Jennifer Jones, 242
Simon, Norton, 241–43, 291
Skibine, George, 276
Skirvin, William B., 69
Sloan, John, 92, 93, 96, 123–24, 130–31,
    133, 157, 163
Smith, George Washington, 80
Smokey, Louise Bou-Ge-Tah, 129
Snyder, Robert W., 190
Society of Fine Arts of Southern
    California, 63–64
Solti, George, 224
Sorey, Hill and Sorey, 172
Sorey, Tom, 172
Sozanski, Edward J., 234
Spanish Colonial Revival, 79–82
Spanish Conquest, 20–26; architecture
    during, 21–25, 36–37; linguistic
    contribution of, 25–26; theater of, 31
Spellman, Coreen Mary, 185
Spreckels, John D., 71–72, 143
Spruce, Everett, 162
Starlight Theater (San Diego), 160
Staub, John, 173
St. Clair, Norman, 64
Stein, Gertrude, 125
Stein, Leo, 125
Sterling, Ross S., 145
Sterne, Maurice, 131
Stevens, Thomas Wood, 152
Stevenson, Ben, 304
Stevenson, Christine Wetherill, 149–50

Stewart, John J., 38
Stickley, Gustav, 76
Stieglitz, Alfred, 95, 124, 126
Stokowski, Leopold, 199–200
Stone, Edward Durrell, 172, 219, 232–33
Strong, Josiah, 35–36
Suárez, Mario, 261
Sullivan, Louis, 46, 85
Surls, James, 247
Symons, George Gardner, 63–64, 95
Szell, George, 224

Takeda, Yoshimi, 228–29
Tallchief, Maria, 212
Tallchief, Marjorie, 212
Tandler, Adolph, 108
Taos Society of Artists, 90–92
Tapahonso, Luci, 258, 260
Taper, Mark, 223
Taylor, Alice Bemis, 121, 188
Taylor, Guy, 224–25
Teatro, Chicano, 274
Teatro, Urbano, 274
Teatro Campesino, 274
Terekhov, Miguel, 212, 275
Terry, Walter, 212
theater, 54–57, 108–11, 150–55, 160–61,
    205–11, 271–74, 300–304. *See also*
    individual theatrical organizations
Thibaud, Wayne, 248
Thomas, Lorenzo, 279
Thomas Gilcrease Institute of American
    History and Art, 195–97, 295
Thompson, Thomas, 266
Thornton, Robert L., 185–86, 201
topophilia, 3–4, 308
Touvenel String Quartet, 229
Trautwein, George, 228
Trost, Gustavus Adolphus, 85
Trost, Henry Charles, 84–87, 114–15
Tsa Toke, Monroe, 129–31
Tsireh, Awa, 130–31
Tuan, Yi-Fu, 4. *See also* topophilia
Tucson, 171, 215; architecture of, 43, 72,
    85, 172, 219–20; Hispanic theater in,

110; music in, 147, 228, 298. *See also*
    individual cultural organizations
Tucson Symphony Orchestra, 147, 228,
    298
Tulsa: architecture of, 70, 115, 118, 119–20,
    172, 220; music in, 107. *See also*
    individual cultural organizations
Tulsa Little Theater, 211
Tumacacori (Arizona), 23
Turner, Eva, 146

Ufer, Walter, 91–92
urbanization, 10, 32–36, 67–69, 113–14,
    169–72, 214–17

Valdez, Luis, 274
Valentiner, William R., 197–98, 233
Vance, Nina, 11, 205–209, 274
Vance, Vivian, 151
van der Rohe, Ludwig Mies, 189–90, 232
Van Dyke, John C., 61
Van Hulse, Camil, 147
Van Soelen, Theodore, 157–58
Vásquez, Carmen Soto, 110
Vasquez, Richard, 262
Vélêz-Ibáñez, Carlos, 262, 307
Venth, Carl, 105
Venturi, Rauch and Scott Brown, 294
Vierra, Carlos, 81, 92–93, 121
Villareal, José Antonio, 262
Voices of Change, 229

Wachtel, Elmer, 63–64, 95
Waco, Tex.: Amicable Insurance Buiding
    in, 71
Waldo, Corinne Abercrombie, 189
Waldo, Mary, 152
Wallenstein, Alfred, 203
Ward, Charles S., 63
Warren, Nina Otero, 157
Waterman, Hazel Wood, 77–78
Waters, Frank, 137, 178–79
Watkins, William Ward, 189
Watson, A. O., 41
Webb, Walter Prescott, 269

Weber, Kem, 122–23
Weber, Max, 70
Wells, William A., 69
Wendt, William, 95
Wentz, Lew, 129
West, Dick, 130–31
West, Nathaniel, 173
West, Rebecca, 187–88
Weyse, O. G., 51
White, Edith, 63
Whittlesey, Charles F., 72, 78
Whittredge, Worthington, 62
Widforss, Gunnar, 156
Wilkins, Christopher, 297–98
Williams, Cecil Brown, 142
Williams, Paul R., 173–74
Wister, Owen, 79, 88, 99
Witte, Alfred G., 97
Witte Memorial Museum, 97

Woodward, Calvin Milton, 73
Works Progress Administration, 151, 152,
    155–56
Worrell, Kathleen, 86
Wright, Frank Lloyd, 75, 82, 84, 85, 87,
    112, 202, 239, 284; California Houses
    designs of, 116–17, 118; Dallas Theater
    Center, 207–208; Price Tower, 175–76;
    Taliesen West, 118–19; Tulsa home
    design of, 118
Wright, Lloyd, 149–50, 174
Wueste, Louisa Heuser, 65
Wyman, George Herbert, 44–46

Yates, Peter, 203–204
Young, Harvey Otis, 66

Zamora, Bernice, 265